CONTENTS

MAP SECTION

WORLD PROBLEMS

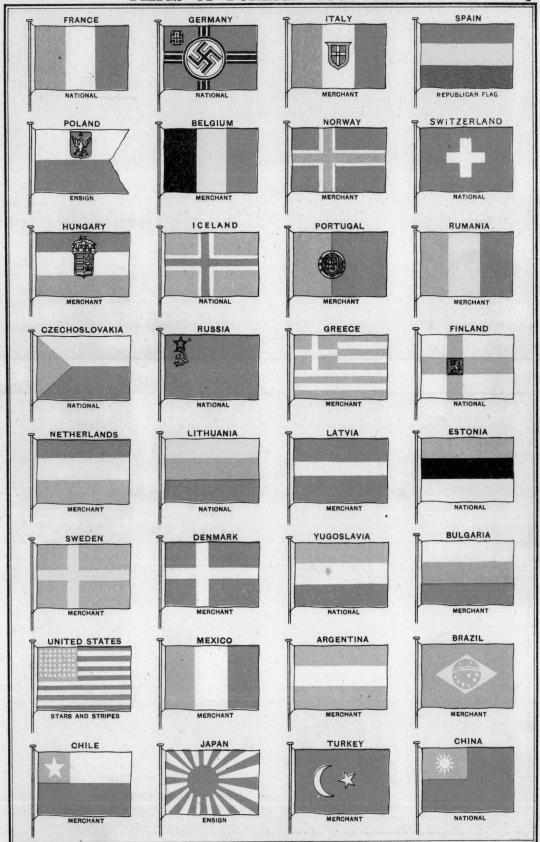

THE WORLD
showing
COLONIAL POWERS and
COMMERCIAL HIGHWAYS

Principal Railways
5 days 1720   Shipping Routes
(Distances in Nautical Miles)
Principal Air Routes (Normal)

UNION JACK	BRITISH ROYAL STANDARD	BRITISH MERCANTILE ENSIGN	DOMINION OF CANADA	COMMONWEALTH OF AUSTRALIA

George Philip & Son, Ltd.

8

EUROPE

Scale 1:20,000,000 (320 miles-1inch)

Statute Miles

Kilometres

Principal Railways

Principal Shipping Routes

Principal Broadcasting Stations

Wireless

Principal Air Mail Routes
(Normal)

George Philip & Son, Ltd.

W. of Greenwich 0 E. of Greenwich

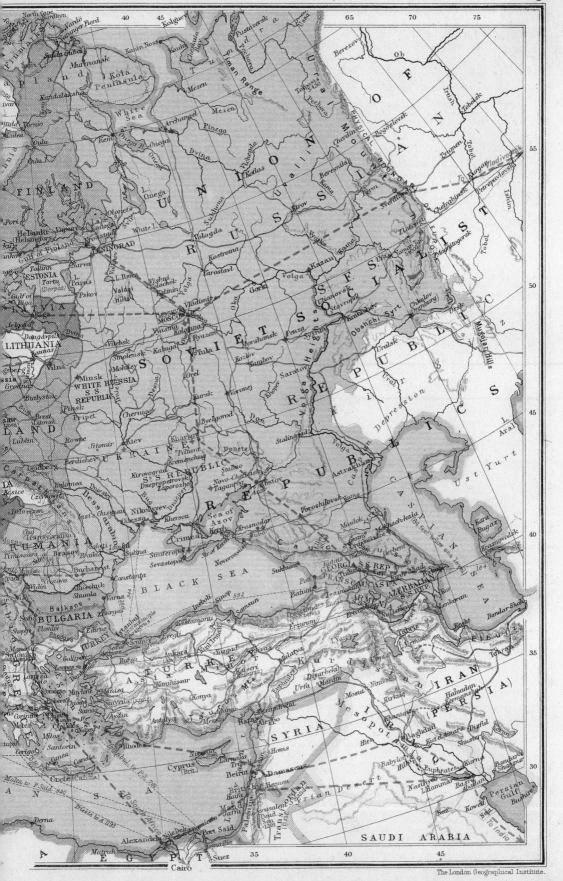

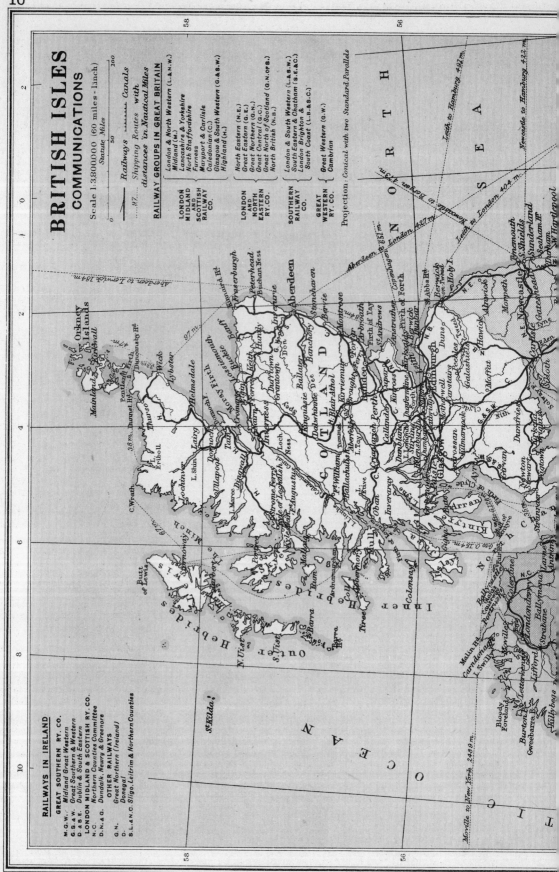

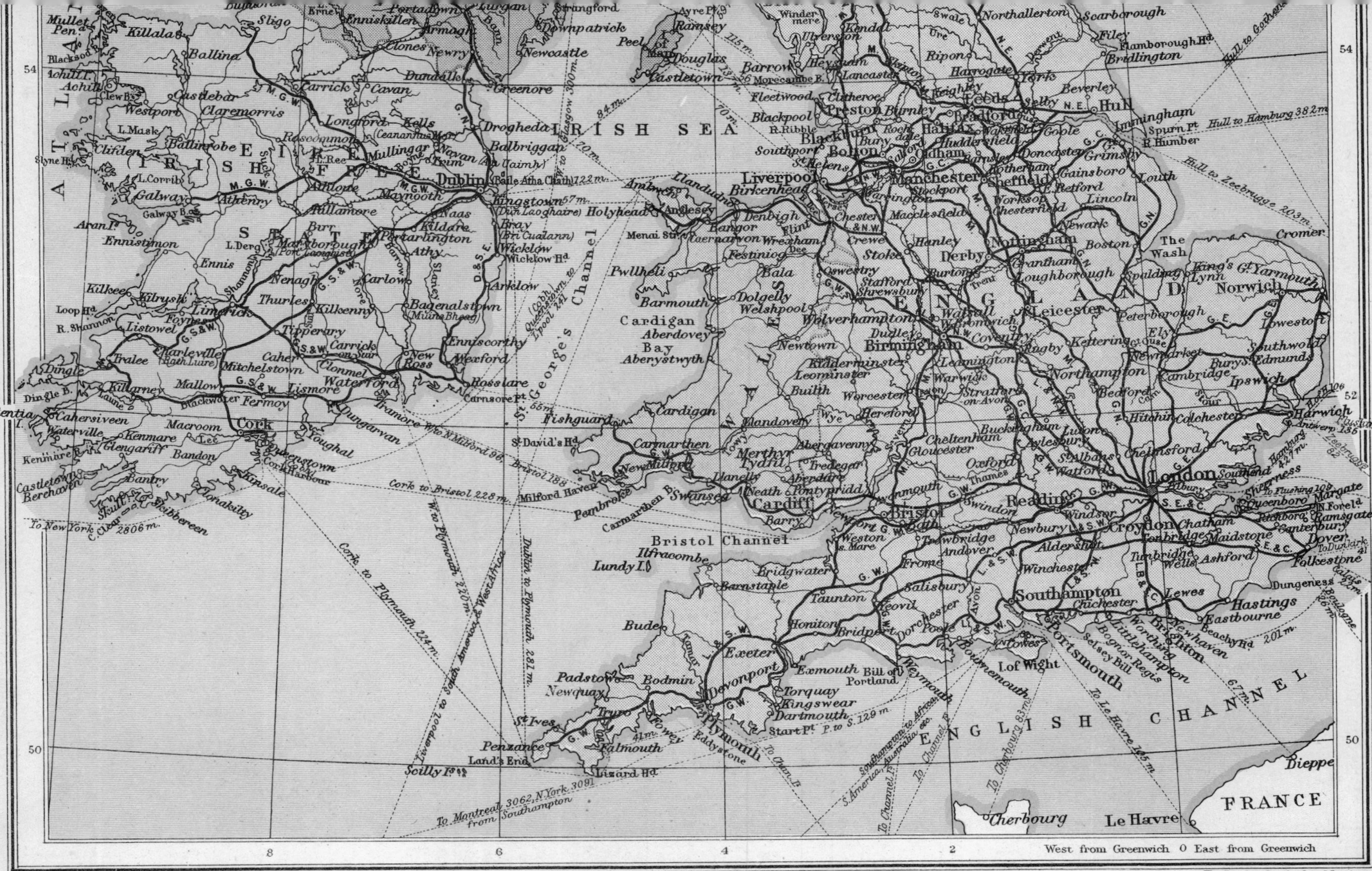

11

ENGLAND

WALES

IRELAND

SCOTLAND

IRISH SEA

ATLANTIC

St. George's Channel

Bristol Channel

ENGLISH CHANNEL

FRANCE

Cherbourg   Le Havre   Dieppe

London

Liverpool   Manchester   Hull

Birmingham   Dublin   Cork

Plymouth   Southampton   Portsmouth   Norwich

Cardigan Bay

Lundy I.   I. of Wight   Scilly Is.   Land's End

West from Greenwich   0   East from Greenwich

The London Geographical Institute.

George Philip & Son, Ld.

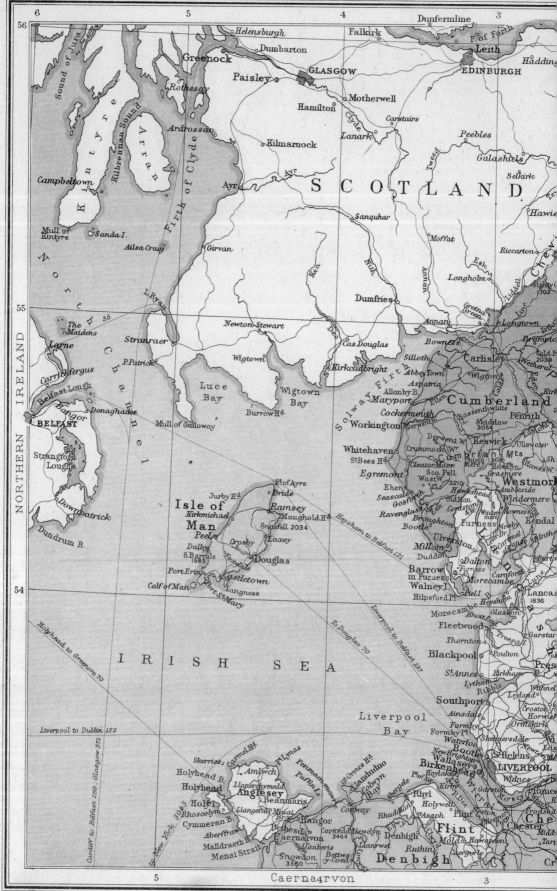

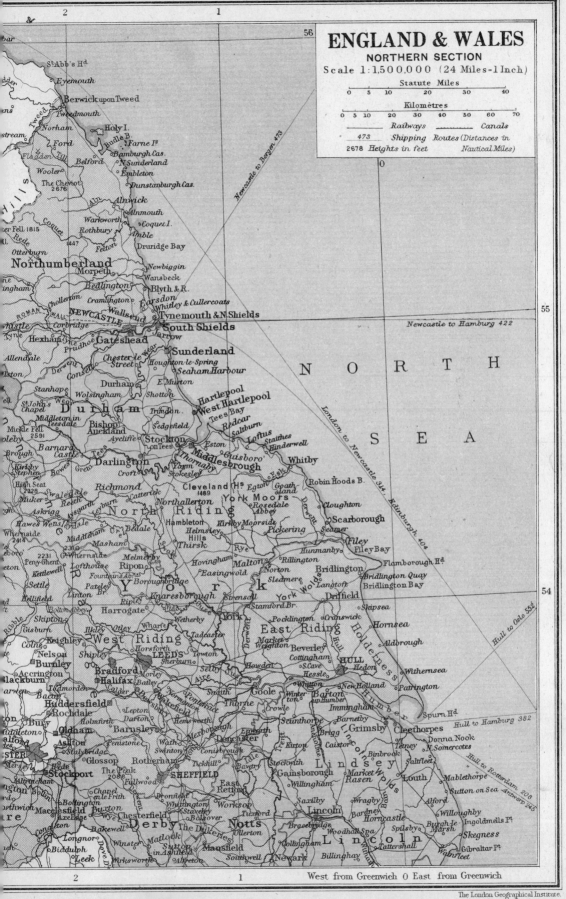

13

ENGLAND & WALES
NORTHERN SECTION
Scale 1:1,500,000 (24 Miles=1 Inch)

Statute Miles

0 5 10   20   30   40

Kilomètres

0 5 10 20 30 40 50 60 70

Railways ———————— Canals
473 Shipping Routes (Distances in
2678 Heights in feet   Nautical Miles)

Newcastle to Bergen 473

Newcastle to Hamburg 422

N O R T H

S E A

London to Newcastle 314

Edinburgh 404

Hull to Oslo 552

Hull to Hamburg 382

Hull to Rotterdam 208
Antwerp 245

St Abb's Hd
Eyemouth
Berwick upon Tweed
Tweedmouth
Norham
Ford
Holy I.
Budle B.
Farne Is.
Bamburgh Cas.
N. Sunderland
Belford
The Cheviot 2676
Wooler
Embleton
Dunstanburgh Cas.
Alnwick
Alnmouth
Warkworth
Coquet I.
Rothbury
Amble
Felton
Druridge Bay
Otterburn
Northumberland
Newbiggin
Morpeth
Wansbeck
Bedlington
Blyth & R.
Cramlington
Earsdon
Whitley & Cullercoats
NEWCASTLE
Wallsend
Tynemouth & N.Shields
Hexham
Corbridge
South Shields
Prudhoe
Gateshead
Jarrow
Allendale
Sunderland
Chester-le-Street
Houghton-le-Spring
Seaham Harbour
Durham
E. Murton
Stanhope
Wolsingham
Shotton
St John's Chapel
Hartlepool
West Hartlepool
Middleton in Teesdale
Bishop Auckland
Sedgefield
Tees Bay
Mickle Fell 2591
Aycliffe
Stockton on Tees
Redcar
Saltburn
Barnard Castle
Loftus
Staithes
Hinderwell
Darlington
Middlesbrough
Thornaby
Eston
Guisboro'
Richmond
Croft
Stokesley
Whitby
Northallerton
Cleveland Hs 1489
Egton
Goathland
Robin Hoods B.
York Moors
Rosedale Abbey
Cloughton
Hambleton
Kirkby Moorside
Scarborough
Helmsley
Pickering
Seamer
Thirsk
Rye
Filey
Filey Bay
Ripon
Hovingham
Malton
Rillington
Hunmanby
Borough bridge
Easingwold
Norton
Bridlington
Flamborough Hd
Knaresborough
Sleamere
Langtoft
Bridlington Quay
Harrogate
Swensall
York
Driffield
Bridlington Bay
Wetherby
Stamford Br.
Skipsea
York
Tadcaster
Pocklington
Cranswick
Hornsea
West Riding
Otley
East Riding
Aldbrough
LEEDS
Market Weighton
Beverley
Bradford
Morley
Cottingham
Halifax
Selby
S. Cave
Hessle
HULL
Huddersfield
Goole
Hedon
Withernsea
Barton upon Humber
New Holland
Patrington
Immingham
Spurn Hd
Barnsley
Doncaster
Grimsby
Cleethorpes
Epworth
Brigg
Tetney
Donna Nook
N. Somercotes
Rotherham
Caistor
Binbrook
Saltfleet
SHEFFIELD
Lindsey
Louth
Mablethorpe
Gainsborough
Market Rasen
Sutton on Sea
Willingham
Wragby
Alford
Chesterfield
Worksop
Saxilby
Bardney
Horncastle
Willoughby
Ingoldmells Pt
Derby
Notts
Lincoln
Woodhall Spa
Spilsby
Burgh le Marsh
Skegness
Mansfield
Southwell
Newark
Lincoln
Tattershall
Gibraltar Pt
Wainfleet

West from Greenwich 0 East from Greenwich

The London Geographical Institute.

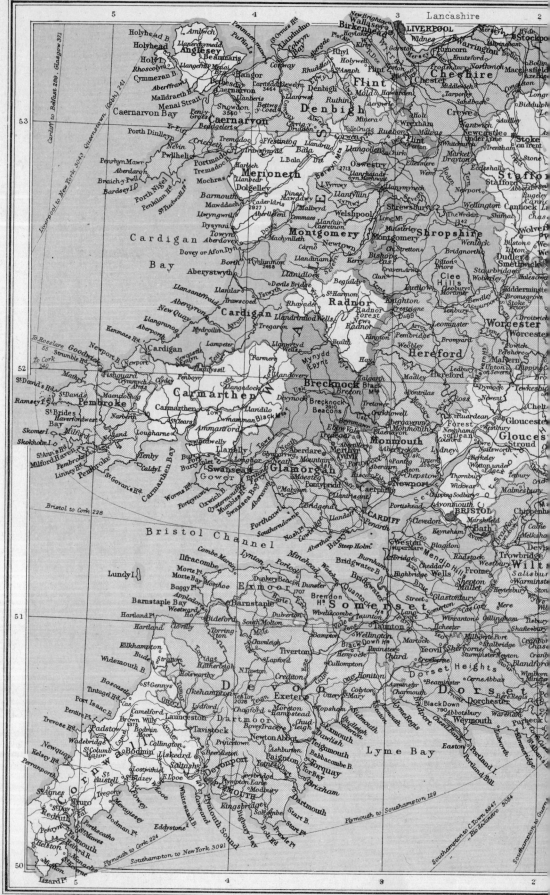

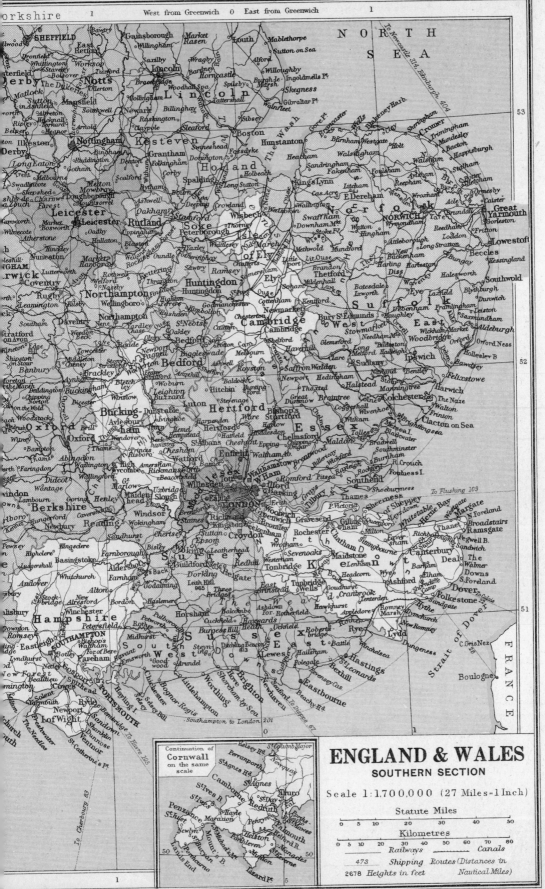

ENGLAND & WALES
SOUTHERN SECTION

Scale 1:1,700,000 (27 Miles=1 Inch)

Statute Miles

Kilometres

Railways ———— Canals

473 Shipping Routes (Distances in Nautical Miles)
2678 Heights in feet

Continuation of Cornwall on the same scale

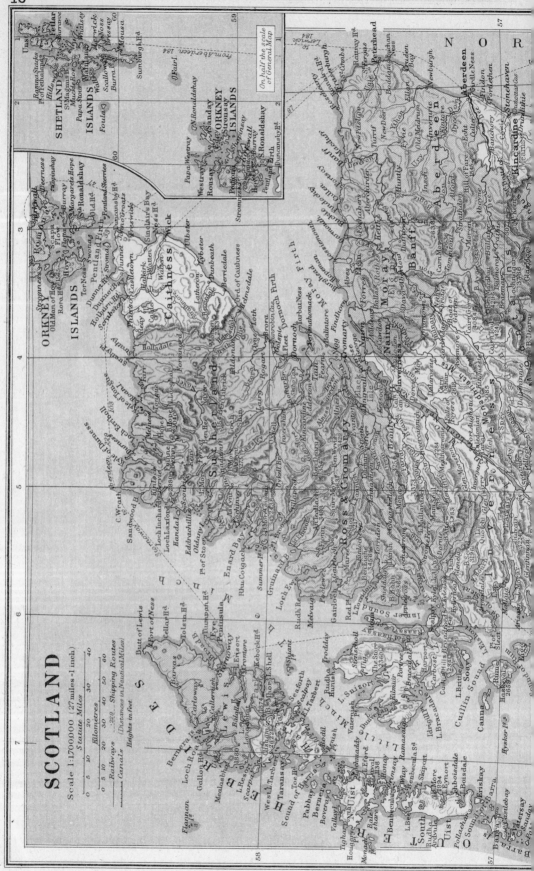

SCOTLAND

Scale 1:1700000 (27 miles=1 inch)

Statute Miles

Kilometres

Railways ..... Shipping Routes

Canals ..... (Distances in Nautical Miles)

Heights in feet

On half the scale
of General Map

SHETLAND
ISLANDS

ORKNEY
ISLANDS

ORKNEY
ISLANDS

Caithness

Sutherland

Ross & Cromarty

Moray

Nairn

Banff

Aberdeen

Kincardine

Inverness

HEBRIDES

OUTER HEBRIDES

Lewis

N O R

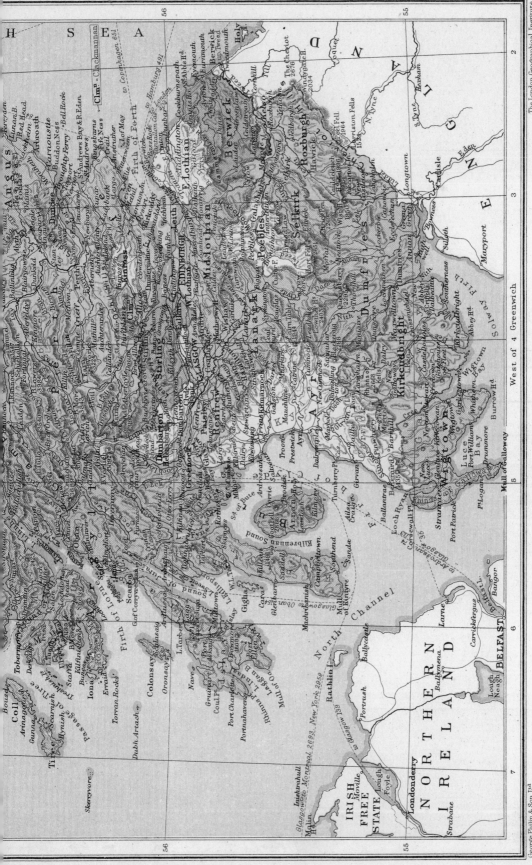

The London Geographical Institute.

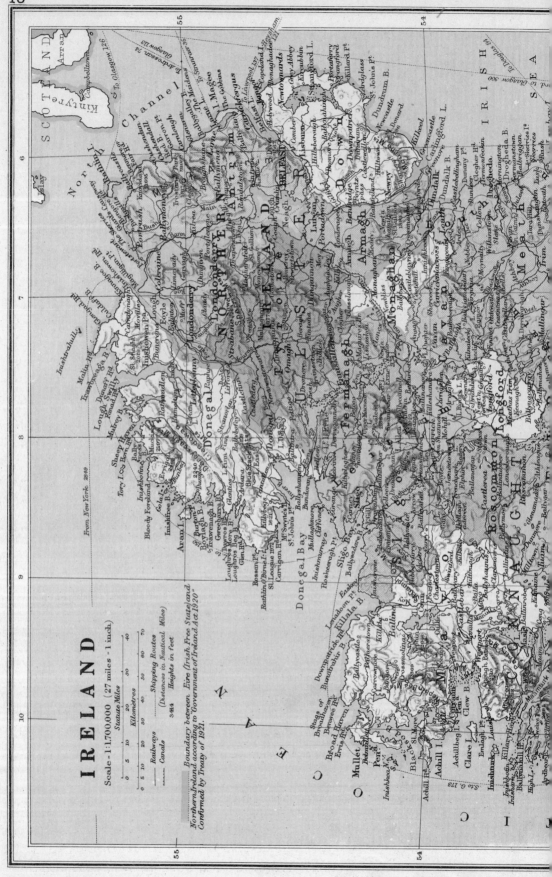

IRELAND

Scale = 1:1,700,000 (27 miles = 1 inch)

Statute Miles

0   10   20   30   40   50   60   70

Kilometres

0 5 10   20   30   40   50   60   70

———— Railways   Shipping Routes
·········· Canals   (Distances in Nautical Miles)
                    3·844 Heights in Feet

Boundary between Eire (Irish Free State) and
Northern Ireland according to Government of Ireland Act 1920"
Confirmed by Treaty of 1921.

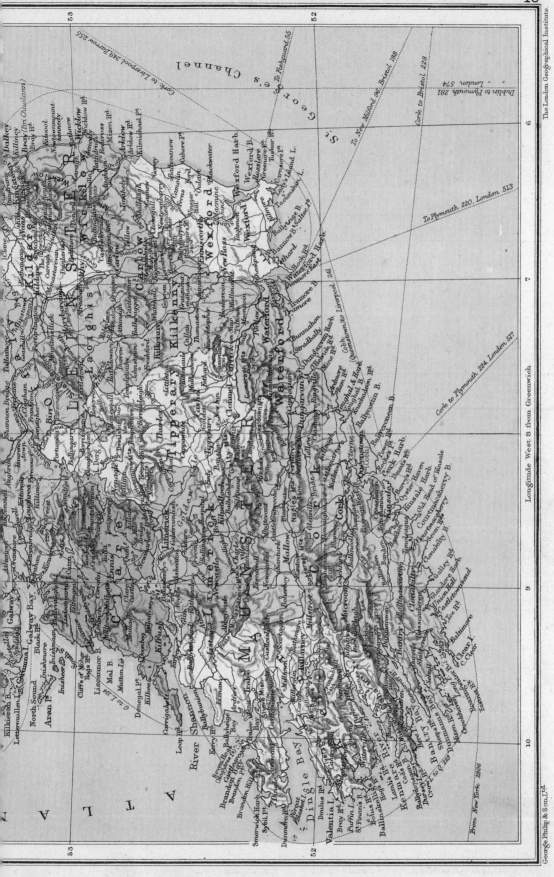

The London Geographical Institute.

St. George's Channel

Cork to Liverpool 249, Barrow 255

To Fishguard 55

To New Milford 96, Bristol 188

Cork to Bristol 228

Dublin to Plymouth 281 , London 574

To Plymouth 220, London 513

To Plymouth 224 London 517

Cork to Plymouth

Cork to Plymouth 224, London 517

Longitude West 8 from Greenwich

From New York 2806

ATLANTIC

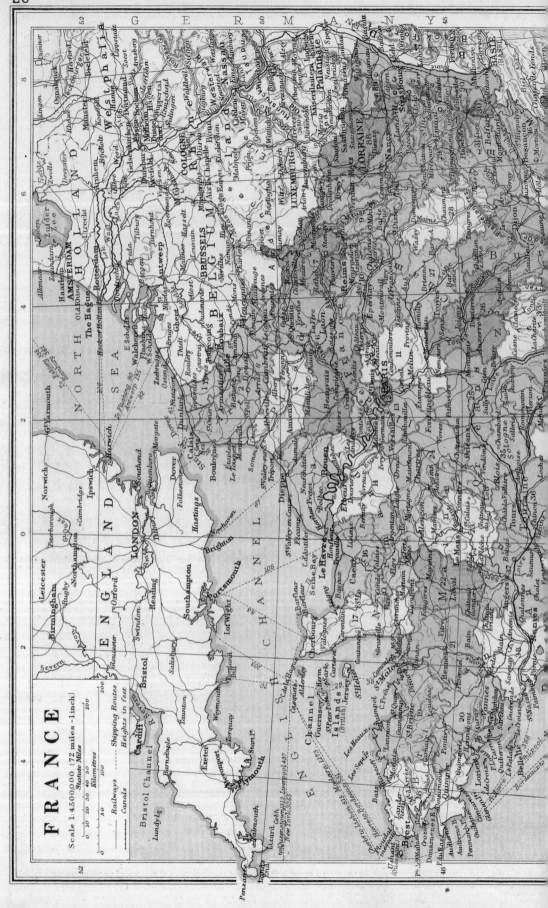

FRANCE

Scale 1:4,500,000 (72 miles =1 inch)

Statute Miles
0 10 20 30 40 50   100   200

Kilometres
0   50   100   200

Railways
Shipping Routes
Canals
Heights in feet

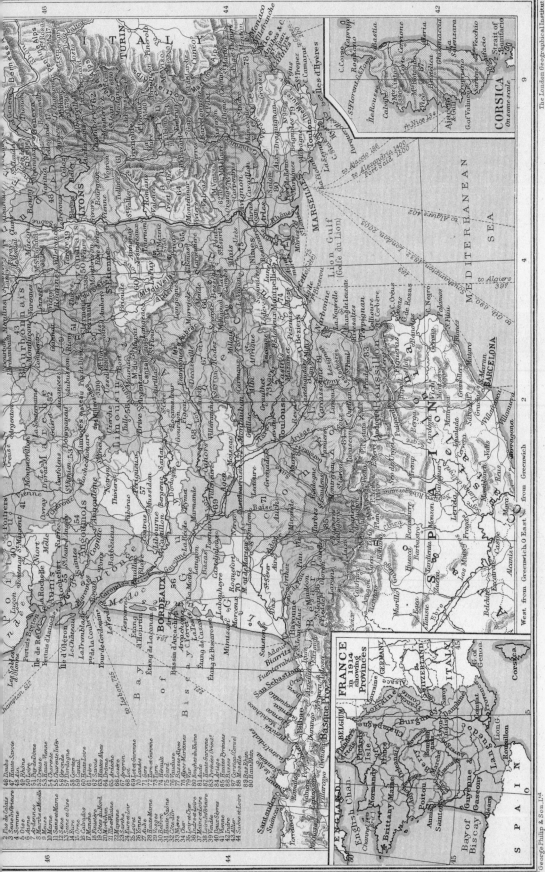

The London Geographical Institute.

CORSICA
On same scale

ITALY
TURIN
CUNEO

MEDITERRANEAN SEA

to Alexandria 1861 1400
to Port Said 1600
to Alexandria 1400
to Algiers 402
to Algiers 397

MARSEILLE
Lion Gulf
(Golfe du Lion)

LYONS

St. ÉTIENNE

Bourbonnais

POITOU

Angoumois

BORDEAUX

Bay of Biscay

BARCELONA

SPAIN

FRANCE
in 1914
showing Provinces

ENGLAND
English Chan.
Channel Is.
Brittany
Normandy
Maine
Poitou
Aunis
Saintonge
Guyenne
Gascony
Béarn
Bay of Biscay

BELGIUM
GERMANY
SWITZERLAND
ITALY
Corsica
G. of Genoa

West from Greenwich 0 East from Greenwich

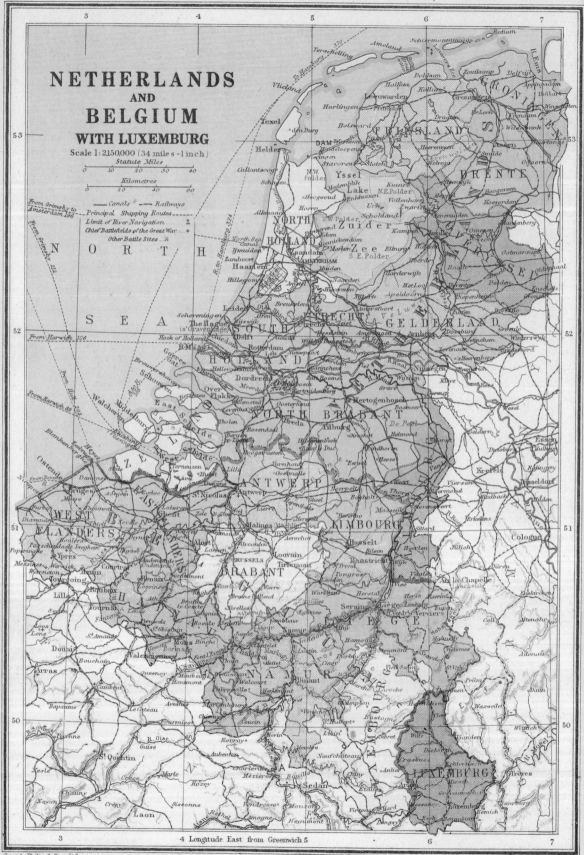

NETHERLANDS
AND
BELGIUM
WITH LUXEMBURG

Scale 1:2150000 (34 miles = 1 inch)

Statute Miles

Kilometres

Canals ---- Railways
Principal Shipping Routes
Limit of River Navigation
Chief Battlefields of the Great War +
Other Battle Sites ✗

Longitude East from Greenwich

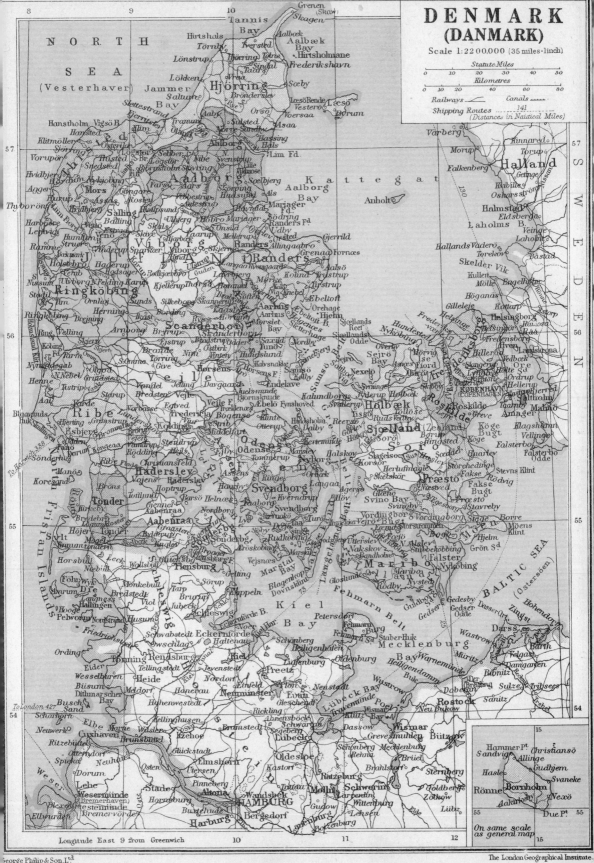

DENMARK
(DANMARK)
Scale 1:2200,000 (35 miles-1inch)
Statute Miles
Kilometres
Railways   Canals
Shipping Routes 141
(Distances in Nautical Miles)

NORTH
SEA
(Vesterhaver)

SWEDEN

Halland

Kattegat

JUTLAND

Aalborg

BALTIC SEA
(Östersöen)

Fünen

Sjælland
(Zealand)

KØBENHAVN
COPENHAGEN

HAMBURG

Mecklenburg

Bornholm

On same scale
as general map

George Philip & Son L.ᵗᵈ   The London Geographical Institute.

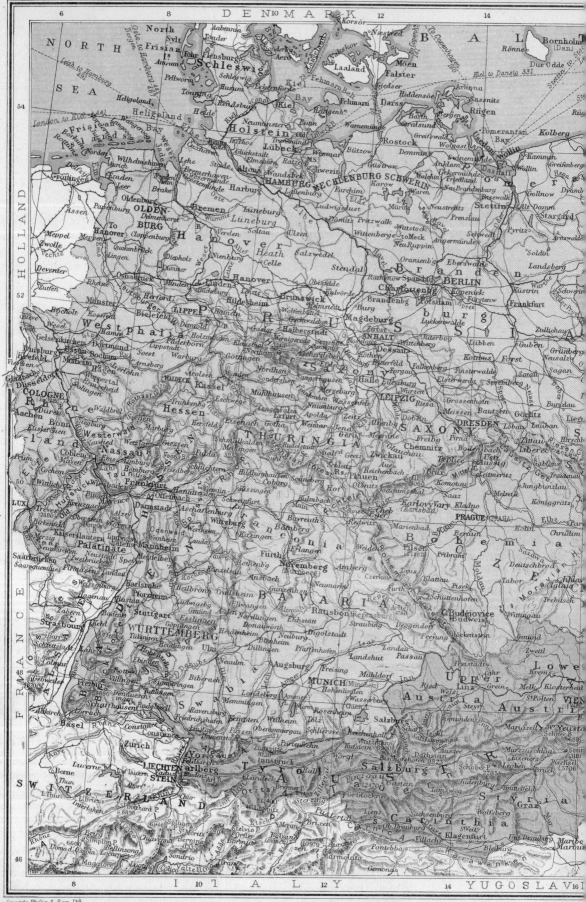

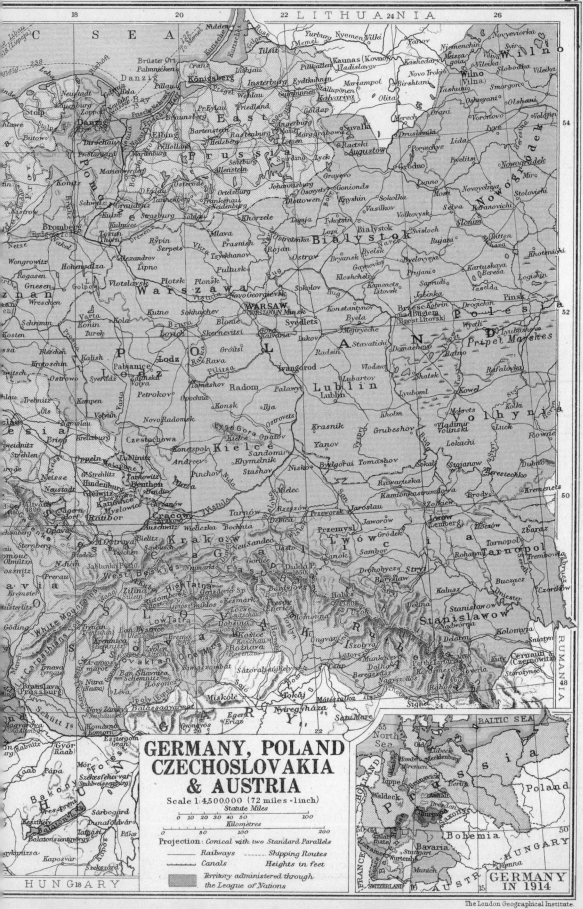

GERMANY, POLAND
CZECHOSLOVAKIA
& AUSTRIA

Scale 1:4,500,000 (72 miles =1inch)

Statute Miles

Projection: Conical with two Standard Parallels

——— Railways ------ Shipping Routes
—•—• Canals .... Heights in feet

Territory administered through
the League of Nations

GERMANY IN 1914

The London Geographical Institute.

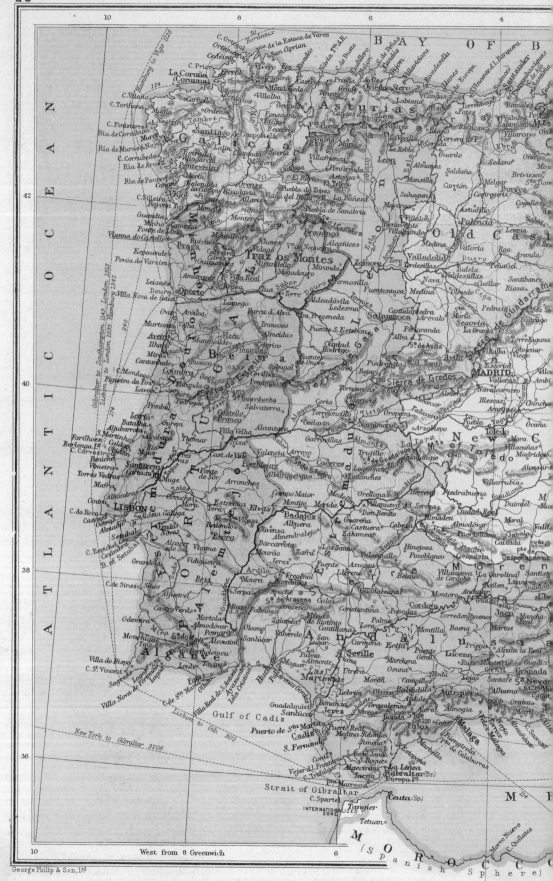

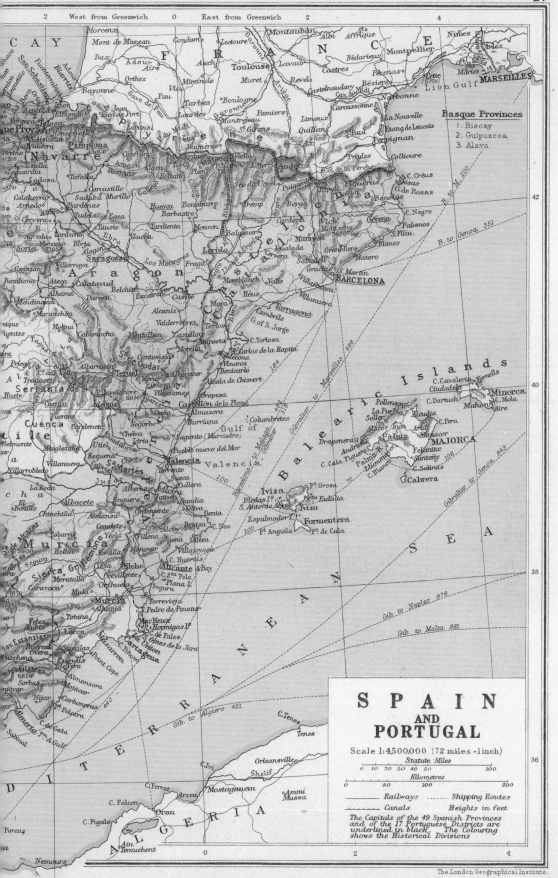

SPAIN
AND
PORTUGAL

Scale 1:4,500,000 (72 miles =1inch)

Statute Miles

Kilometres

Railways · · · · · Shipping Routes
Canals Heights in feet

The Capitals of the 49 Spanish Provinces
and of the 17 Portuguese Districts are
underlined in black. The Colouring
shows the Historical Divisions

Basque Provinces
1. Biscay
2. Guipuzcoa
3. Alava

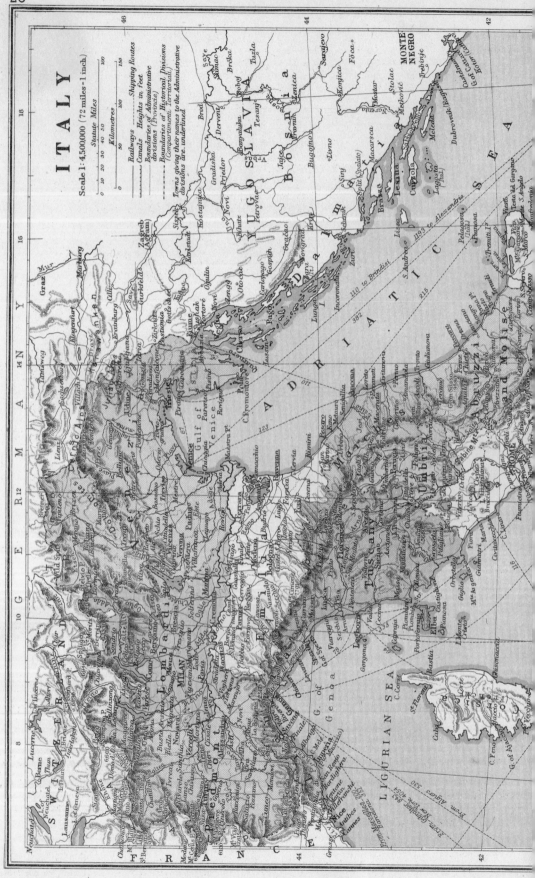

ITALY

Scale 1 : 4500000 (72 miles = 1 inch)

Statute Miles
0   10   20   30   40   50   100   150

Kilometres
0   50   100   150

———— Railways   ······ Shipping Routes
———— Canals   Heights in Feet
———— Boundaries of Administrative
          divisions (Province)
········ Boundaries of Historical Divisions
          (Compartimento, Territorio).
Towns giving their names to the Administrative
divisions are underlined

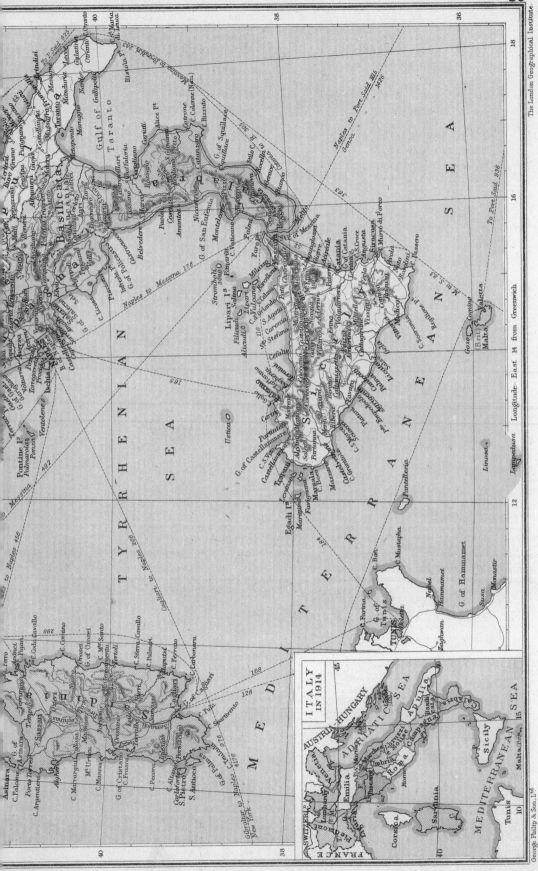

THE
BALKAN
STATES

Scale 1:4 500 000 (72 miles - 1 inch)
Statute Miles
Kilometres

—— Railways
----- Canals

Shipping Routes
(Distances in N.Miles)
Heights in feet

THE
BALKAN STATES
IN 1914

George Philip & Son, L.ʳᵈ

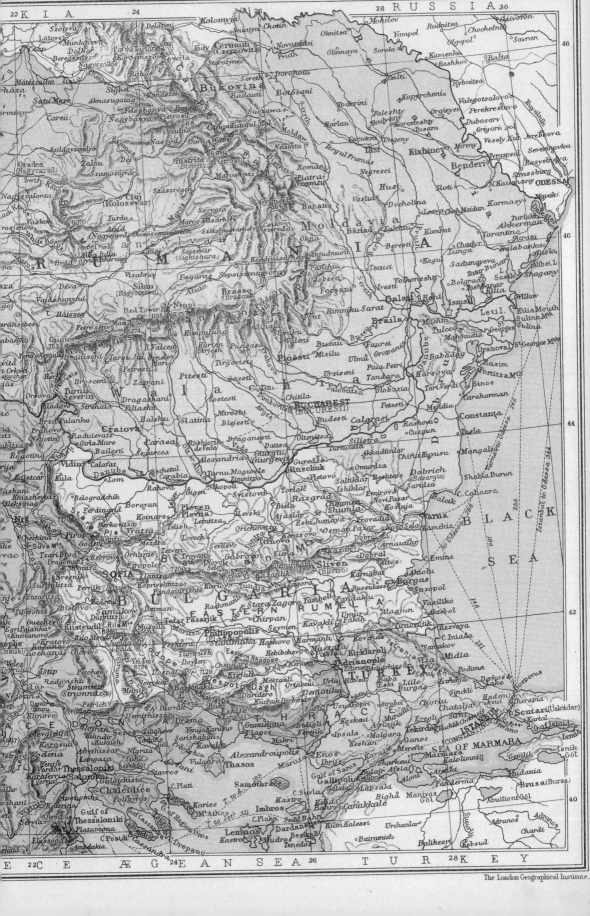

32

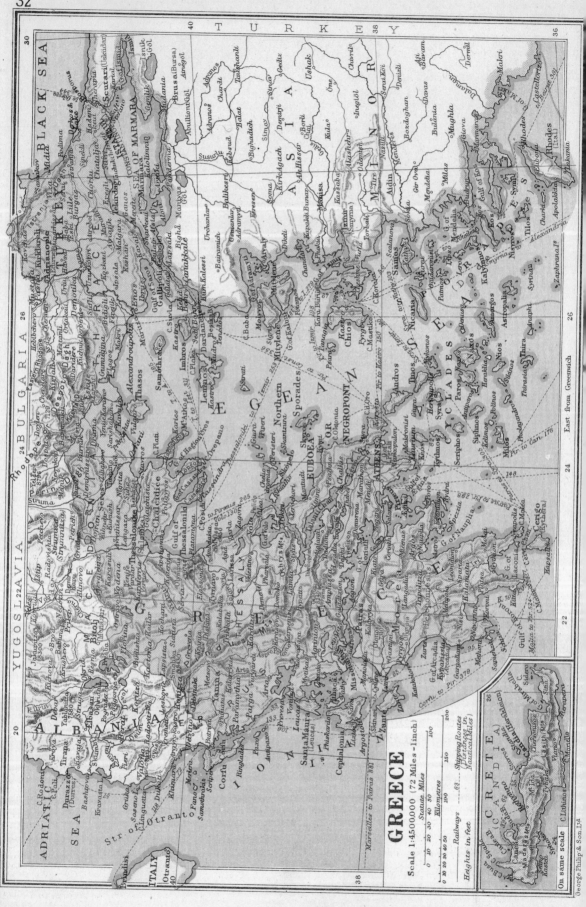

GREECE

Scale 1:4,500,000 (72 Miles=1inch)

Statute Miles

Kilometres

Railways ....
Shipping Routes
(Distances in
Nautical Miles)

Heights in feet

On same scale

George Philip & Son, Ltd.

SWITZERLAND

Scale 1:1,500,000 (24 miles=1 inch)

Statute Miles

Railways ———— Canals ———— Passes =
Limit of River Navigation ↨

Altitudes in Feet

Projection-Conical with
two Standard parallels

Longitude East 8° of Greenwich

The London Geographical Institute.

George Philip & Son, L.ᵈ

I.D.D

SCANDINAVIA AND THE BALTIC LANDS

Scale 1:6,500,000 (105 miles=1inch)

Statute Miles
0   50   100   150   200   250   300
Kilometres
0   50   100   150   200   250   300

Projection: Conical with two Standard Parallels

- - - Railways
—— Canals
—— 65 Shipping Routes [Distances in Nautical Miles]

Territory administered through the League of Nations.

R U S S I A N

F I N L A N D

N O R R L A N D

A T L A N T I C   O C E A N

East from 12 Greenwich

Arctic Circle

The London Geographical Institute

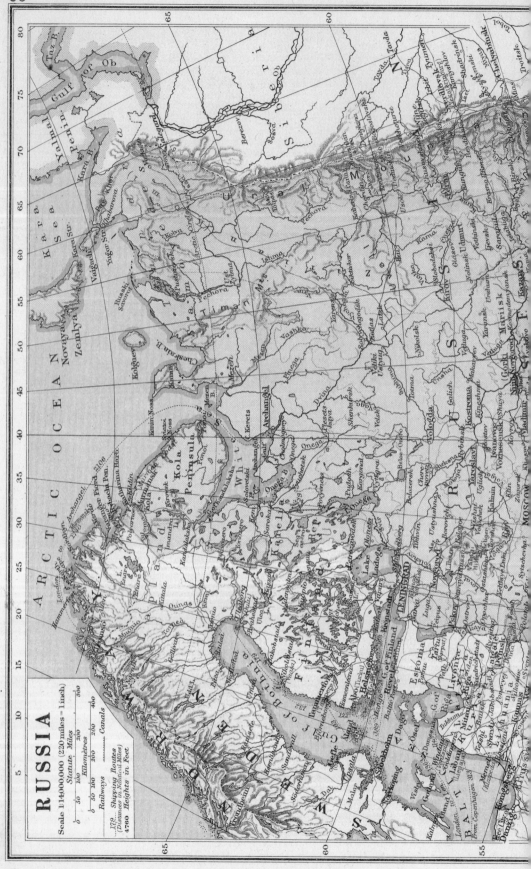

RUSSIA

Scale 1:14,000,000 (220 miles = 1 inch)

Statute Miles

Kilomètres

Railways ———— Canals

179 Shipping Routes
(Distances in Statute Miles)
From Copenhagen 30 miles

4760 Heights in Feet

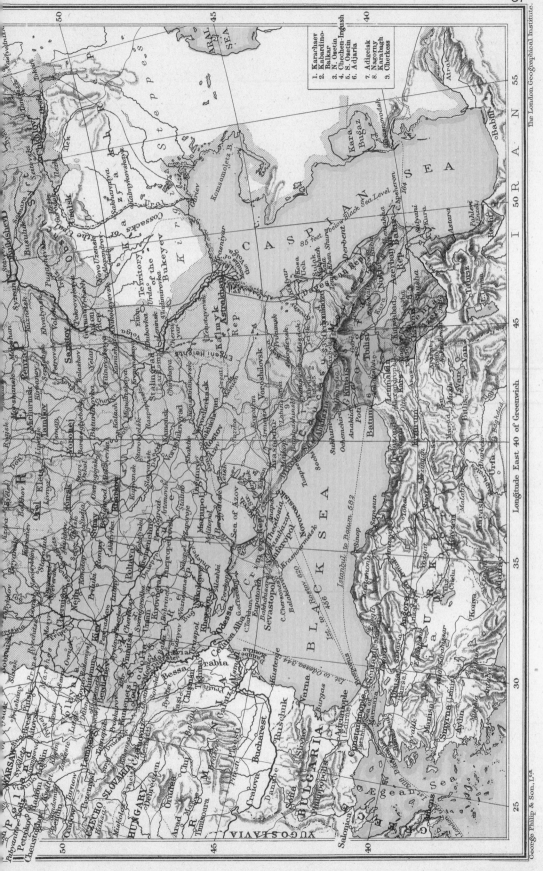

The London Geographical Institute.

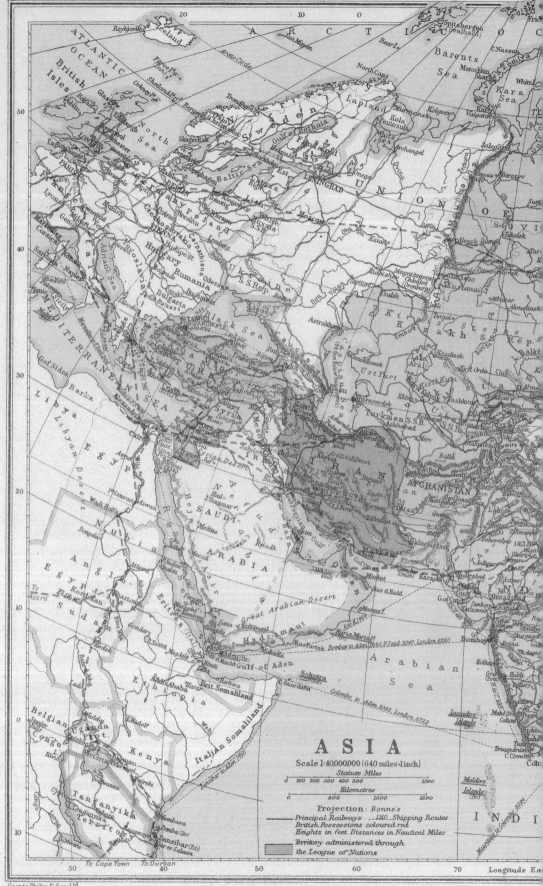

ASIA

Scale 1:40,000,000 (640 miles-1inch)

Statute Miles

Kilometres

Projection: Bonne's

Principal Railways
British Possessions coloured red
Heights in feet Distances in Nautical Miles

Territory administered through
the League of Nations

--- --- Principal Air Mail Routes (Normal) ● Principal Wireless Stations

George Philip & Son, Ltd

The London Geographical Institute.

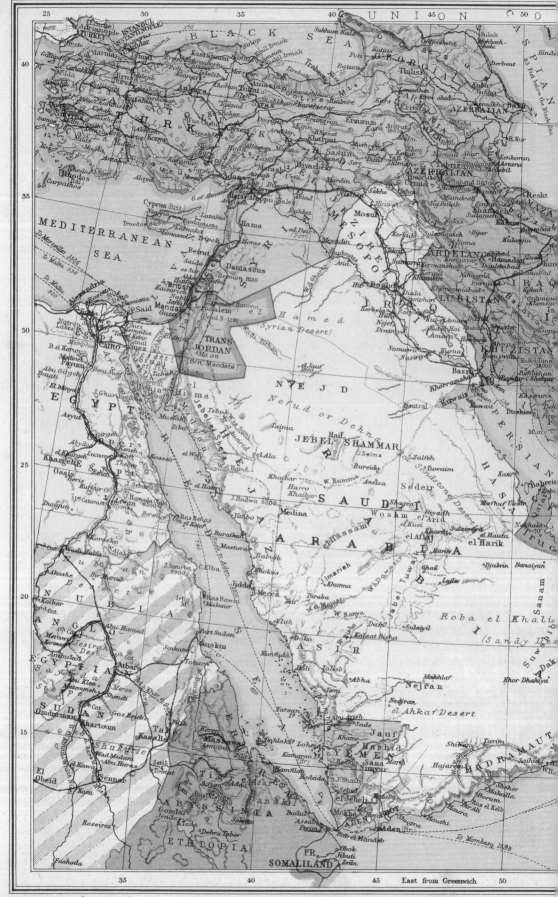

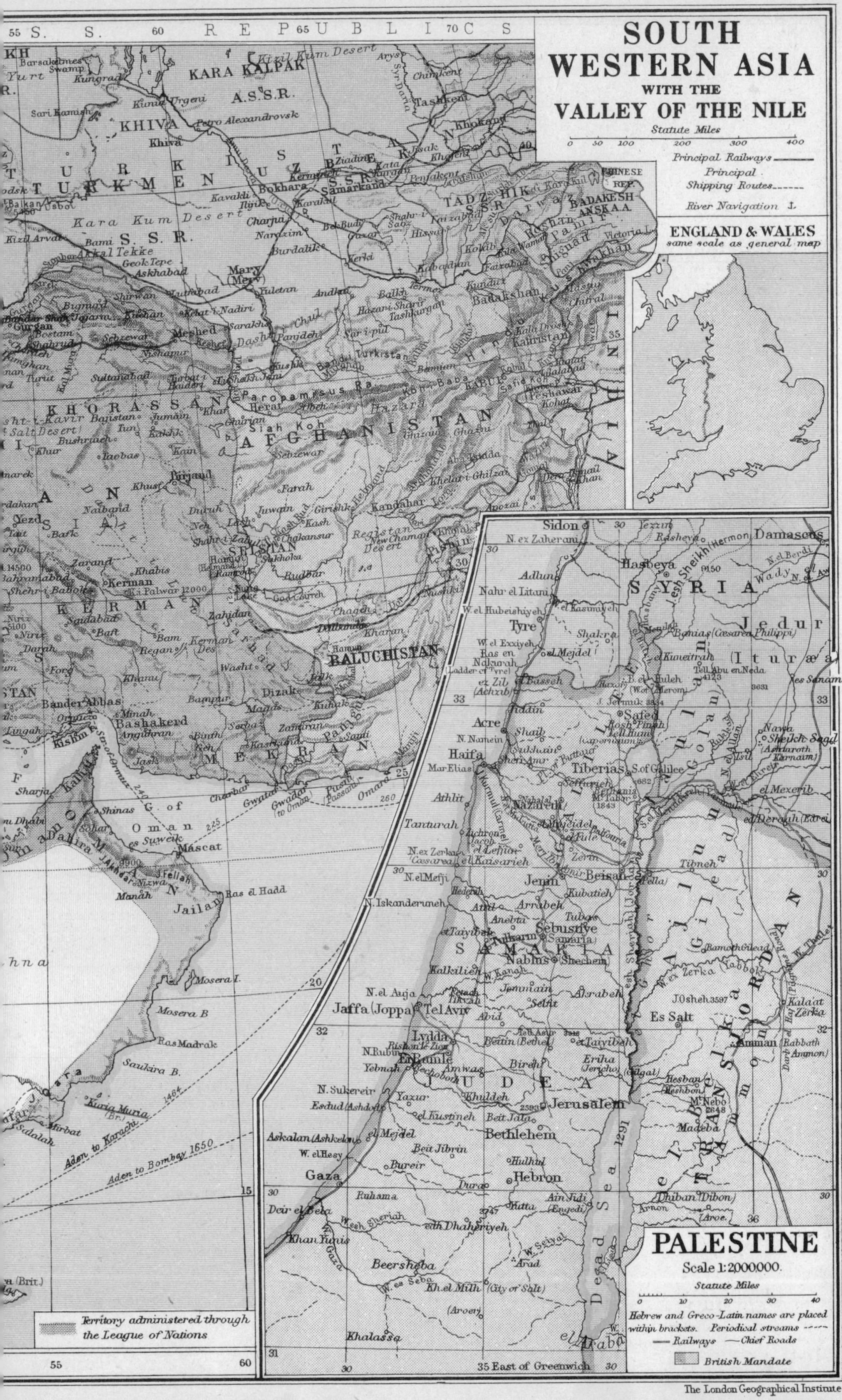
SOUTH
WESTERN ASIA
WITH THE
VALLEY OF THE NILE
Statute Miles
0 50 100 200 300 400
Principal Railways
Principal Shipping Routes
River Navigation
ENGLAND & WALES
same scale as general map
Territory administered through the League of Nations
PALESTINE
Scale 1:2,000,000.
Statute Miles
0 10 20 30 40
Hebrew and Greco-Latin names are placed within brackets.
Periodical streams
Railways
Chief Roads
British Mandate
35 East of Greenwich

The London Geographical Institute.

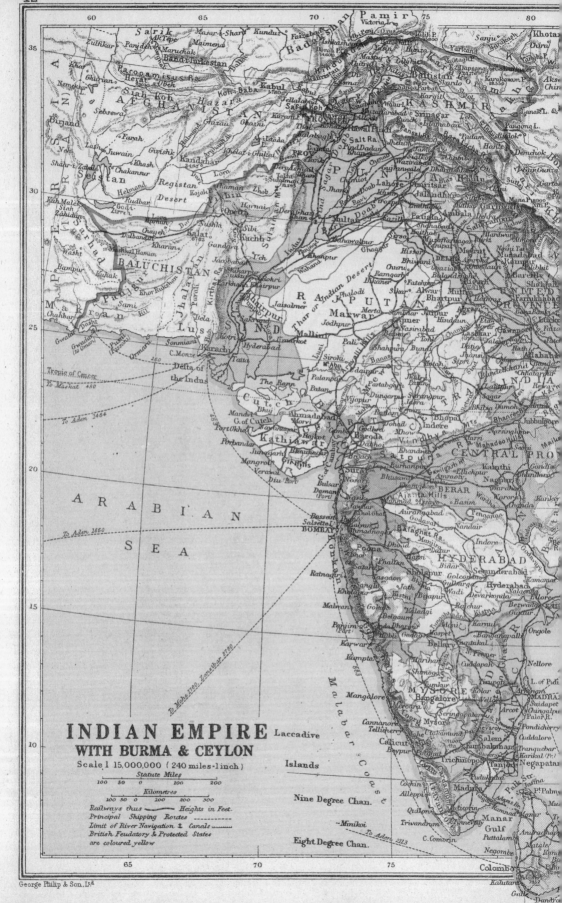

INDIAN EMPIRE Laccadive
WITH BURMA & CEYLON
Scale 1 15,000,000 (240 miles·1inch)

Statute Miles

100 50 0   100   200

Kilometres

100 50 0   200   200   300

Railways thus ━━━ Heights in Feet.
Principal Shipping Routes
Limit of River Navigation ↓ Canals ------
British Feudatory & Protected States
are coloured yellow

Islands

Nine Degree Chan.

Eight Degree Chan.

ARABIAN SEA

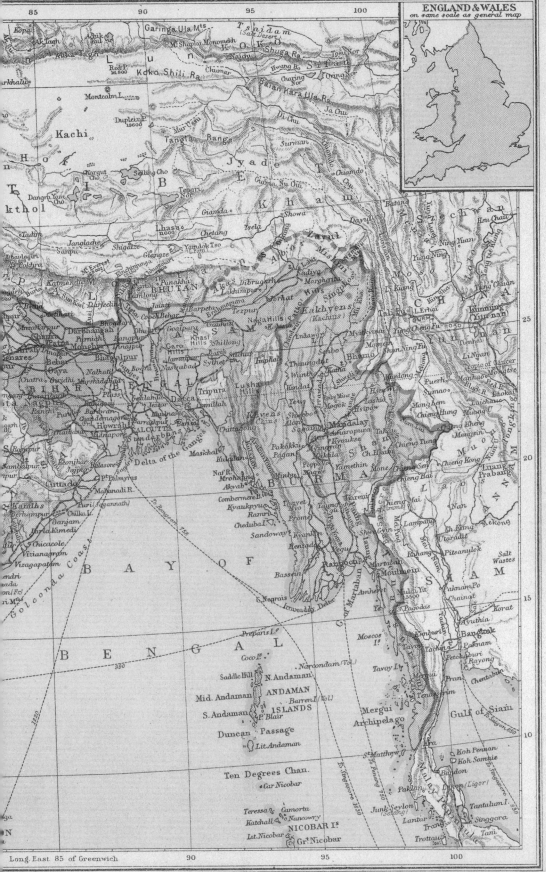

ENGLAND & WALES
on same scale as general map

Long. East 85 of Greenwich

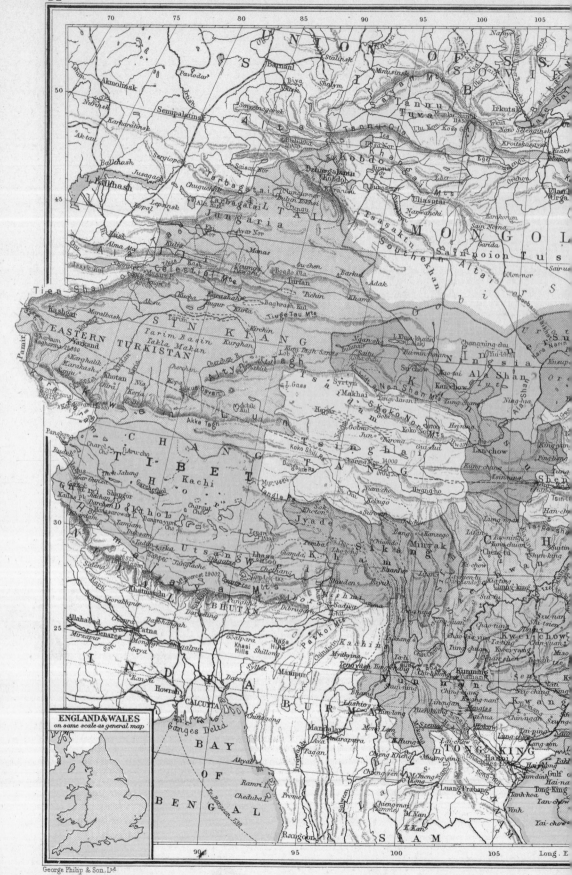

ENGLAND & WALES
on same scale as general map

George Philip & Son, Ltd

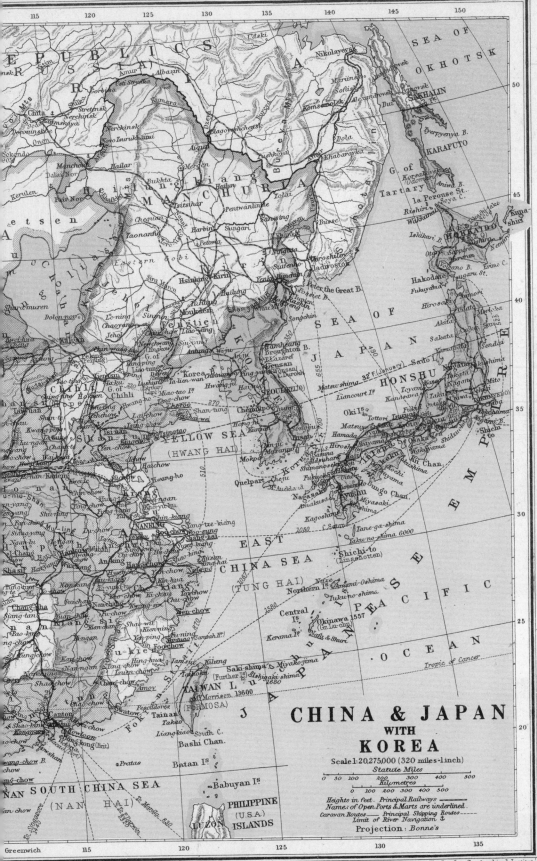

CHINA & JAPAN
WITH
KOREA

Scale 1:20,275,000 (320 miles-1 inch)

Statute Miles

Kilometres

Heights in feet. Principal Railways
Names of Open Ports & Marts are underlined.
Caravan Routes ___ Principal Shipping Routes ____
Limit of River Navigation

Projection: Bonne's

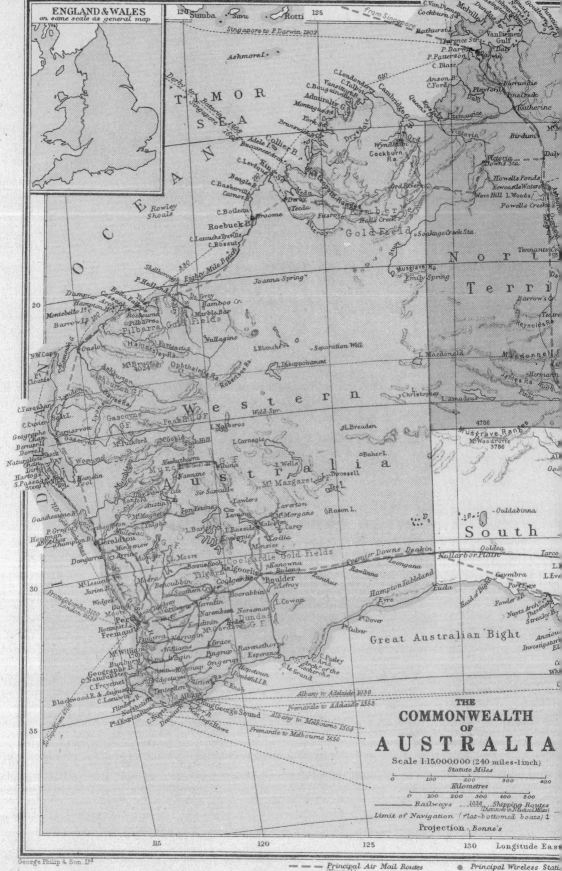

ENGLAND & WALES
on same scale as general map

THE
COMMONWEALTH
OF
AUSTRALIA
Scale 1:15,000,000 (240 miles=1 inch)
Statute Miles

Kilometres

Railways   Shipping Routes
(Distance in Nautical Miles)
Limit of Navigation (flat-bottomed boats)

Projection : Bonne's

George Philip & Son, Ltd

——— Principal Air Mail Routes
(Normal)
● Principal Wireless Station

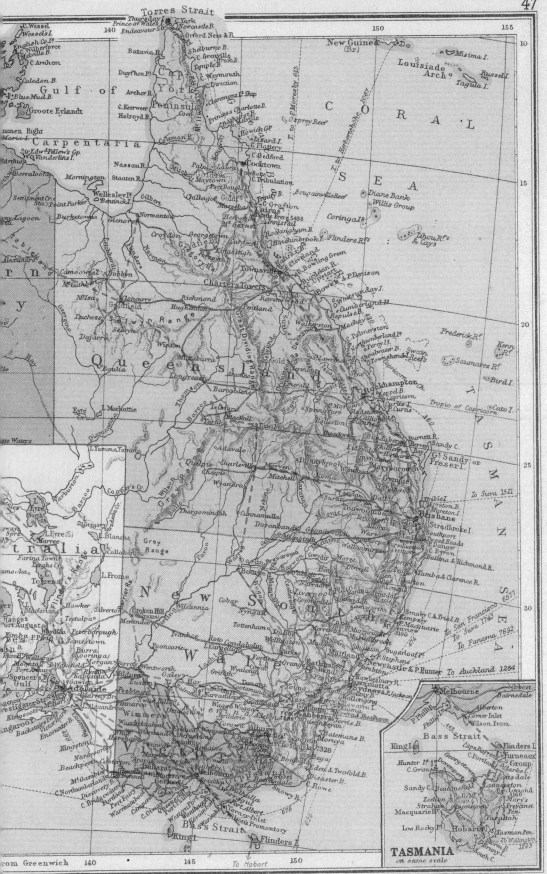

48

George Philip & Son Ltd Copyright

THE
PACIFIC OCEAN

Principal Railways ——————

Principal Shipping Routes
(Distances in Nautical Miles)   1355

- - - - - Principal Air Mail Routes (Normal)

Territory administered thro' the League of Nations

50

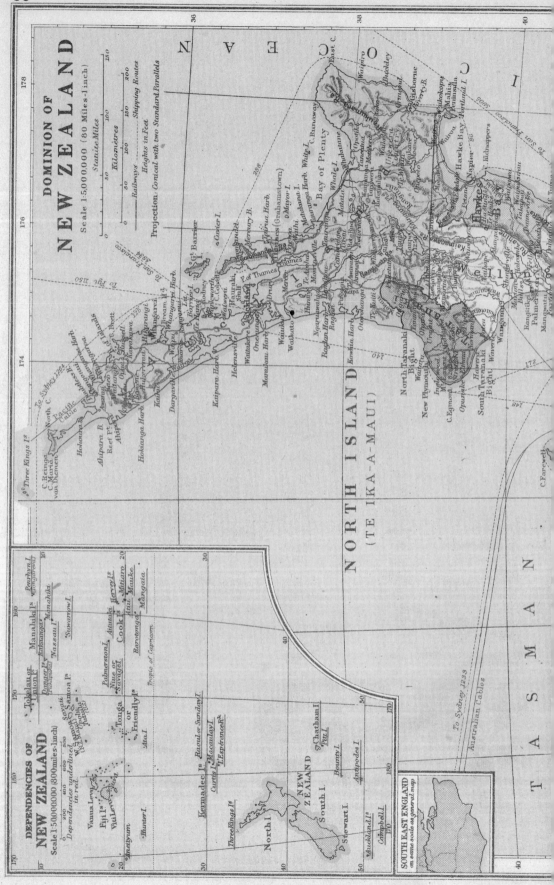

DOMINION OF
NEW ZEALAND

Scale 1:5,000000 (80 Miles=1inch)

Projection: Conical with two Standard Parallels

NORTH ISLAND
(TE IKA-A-MAUI)

DEPENDENCIES OF
NEW ZEALAND

Scale 1:30000000 (800miles=inch)

SOUTH EAST ENGLAND
on same scale as general map

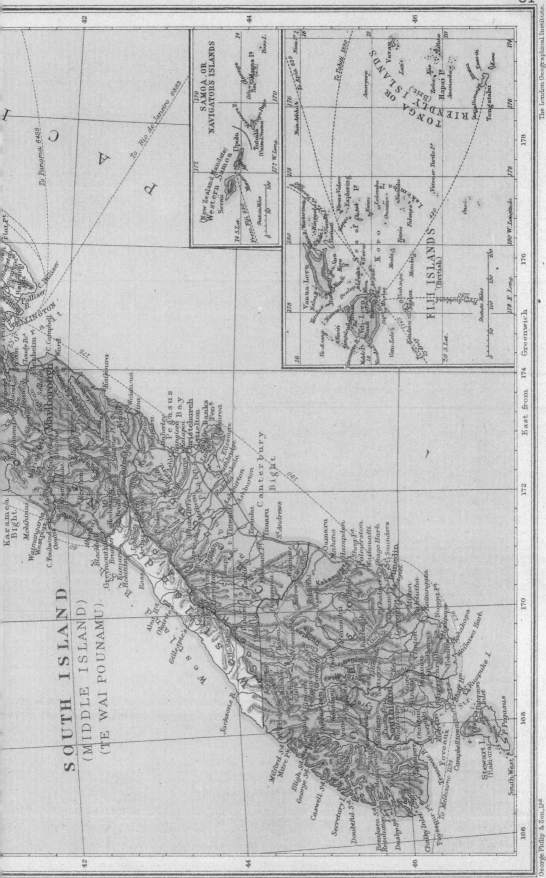

51

SOUTH ISLAND
(MIDDLE ISLAND)
(TE WAI POUNAMU).

SAMOA OR
NAVIGATORS ISLANDS

(New Zealand Mandate)
Western Samoa

TONGA OR FRIENDLY ISLANDS (Brit.)

FIJI ISLANDS
(British)

WELLINGTON

PACIFIC

East from 174   172   170   168   166

Greenwich

The London Geographical Institute.

George Philip & Son, Ltd.

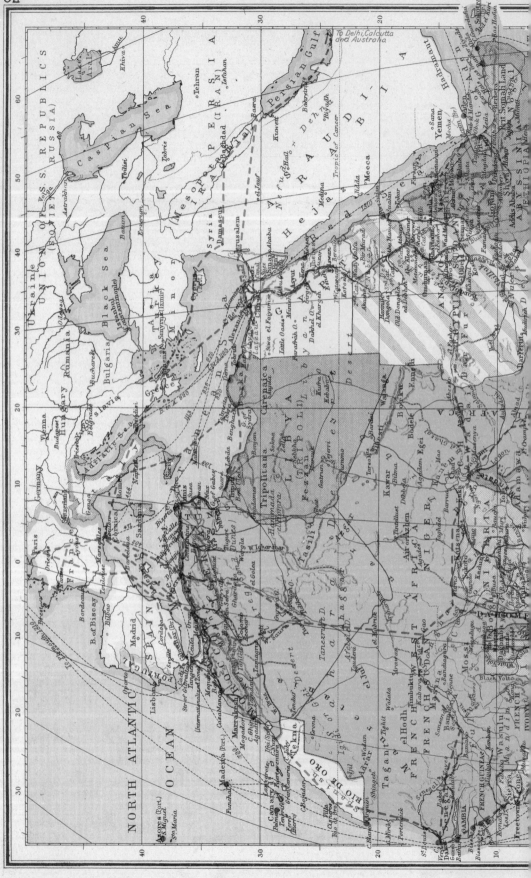

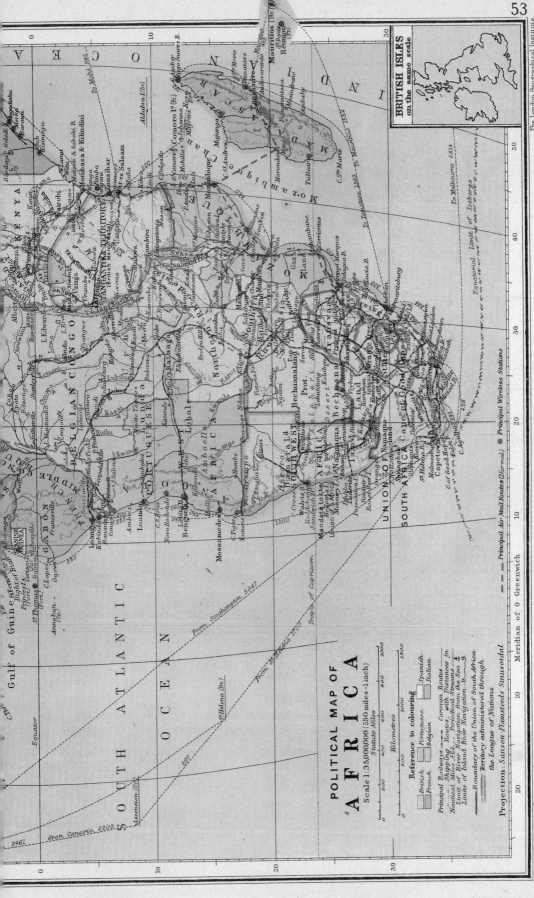

BRITISH ISLES
on the same scale

The London Geographical Institute.

POLITICAL MAP OF
AFRICA
Scale 1:35,000,000 (550 miles=1 inch)

Statute Miles
0   200   400   600   800   1000

Kilometres
0   500   1000   1500

Reference to colouring

British.   Spanish.
French.   Portuguese.   Italian.
                Belgian.

Principal Railways.   Caravan Route
Principal Shipping Routes, with Distances in
   Nautical Miles 485 - Periodical Streams
Limit of River Navigation from the Sea
Limits of Inland River Navigation
Boundary of the Union of South Africa
Territory administered through
   the League of Nations

Projection: Sanson-Flamsteed's Sinusoidal

Principal Air-Mail Routes (Normal).   Principal Wireless Stations

Meridian of 0 Greenwich

George Philip & Son, Ltd.

SOUTH ATLANTIC OCEAN

INDIAN OCEAN

Gulf of Guinea

Equator

Tropic of Capricorn

KENYA

TANGANYIKA TERRITORY
British Mandate

BELGIAN CONGO

FRENCH EQUATORIAL AFRICA

MIDDLE CONGO

GABON

PORTUGUESE WEST AFRICA
(ANGOLA)

SOUTH WEST AFRICA
Mandate to the Union of S. Africa

BECHUANALAND

UNION OF SOUTH AFRICA

Cape of Good Hope

Capetown

MADAGASCAR

Mozambique Channel

Mauritius (Br.)
Réunion (Fr.)

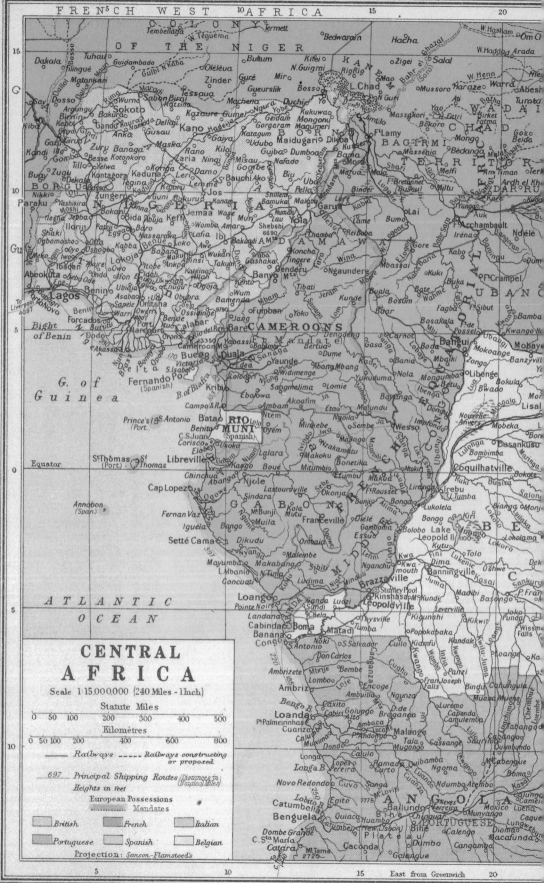

CENTRAL AFRICA

Scale 1:15,000,000 (240 Miles = 1 Inch)

Statute Miles

| | | | | | |
|0|50|100|200|300|400|500|

Kilomètres

|0|50|100|200|400|600|800|

——— Railways ----- Railways constructing
or proposed

697 Principal Shipping Routes (Distances in Nautical Miles)

Heights in feet

European Possessions
Mandates

| British | French | Italian |
| Portuguese | Spanish | Belgian |

Projection: Sanson-Flamsteed's

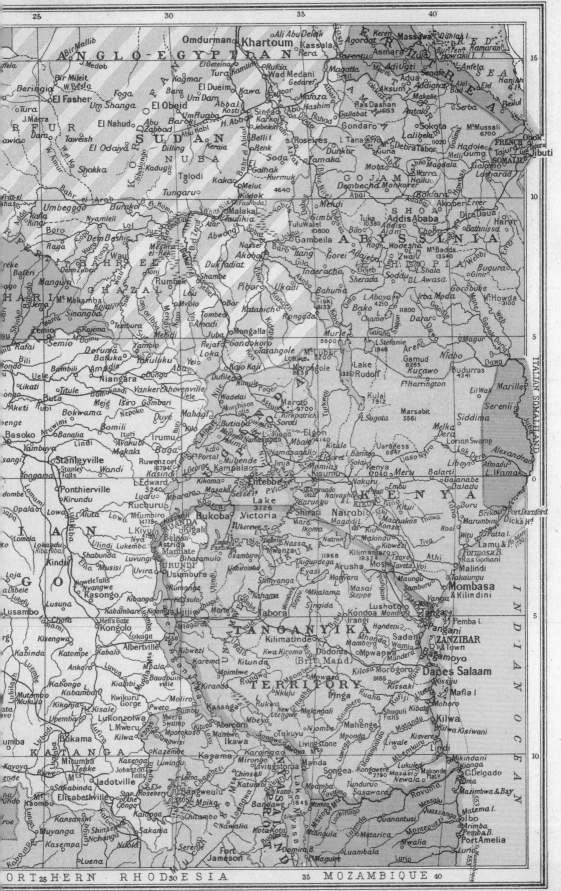

55

ANGLO-EGYPTIAN
Omdurman   Khartoum   Kassala   Massawa
SUDAN
KORDOFAN
NUBA
El Fasher

ABYSSINIA
ETHIOPIA

ITALIAN SOMALILAND

FRENCH
SOMALI.   Jibuti

UGANDA

BAHR EL GHAZAL

Stanleyville

Lake
Victoria
Entebbe

KENYA
Nairobi

Mombasa

Zanzibar

TANGANYIKA
TERRITORY

Dares Salaam

KATANGA

Elisabethville

NORTHERN · RHODESIA   MOZAMBIQUE

The London Geographical Institute.

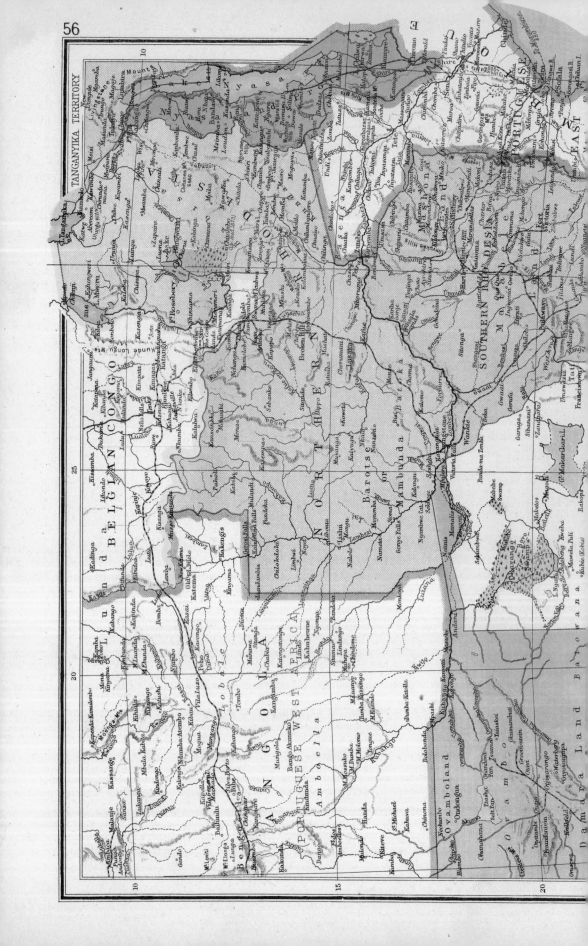

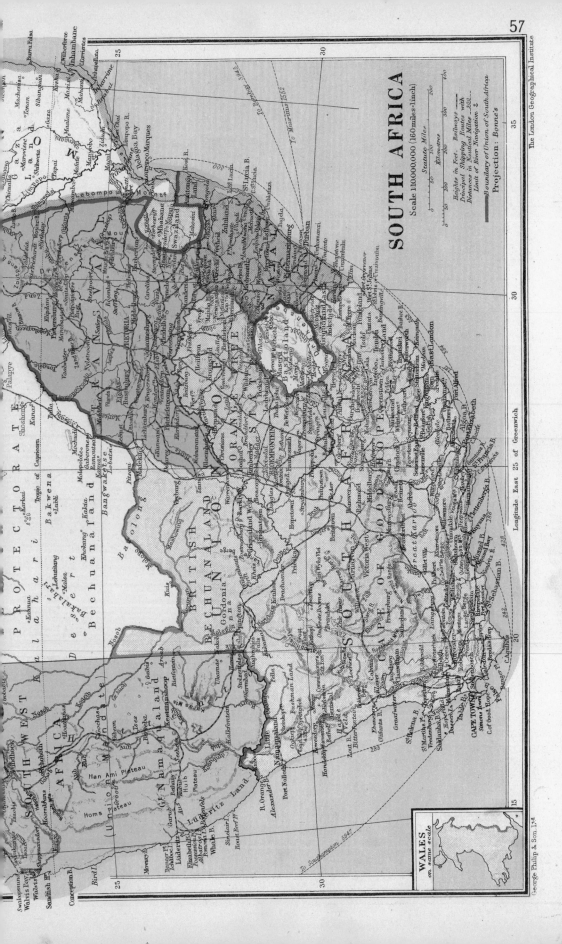

SOUTH AFRICA

Scale 1:10,000,000 (160 miles=1 inch)

Statute Miles

Kilometres

Heights in Feet.   Railways ____
Principal Shipping Routes with
Distances in Nautical Miles _ 300
Limit of River Navigation _ ‡
Boundary of Union of South Africa
Projection: Bonne's

Longitude East 25 of Greenwich

WALES
on same scale

George Philip & Son, L.^{td}

The London Geographical Institute

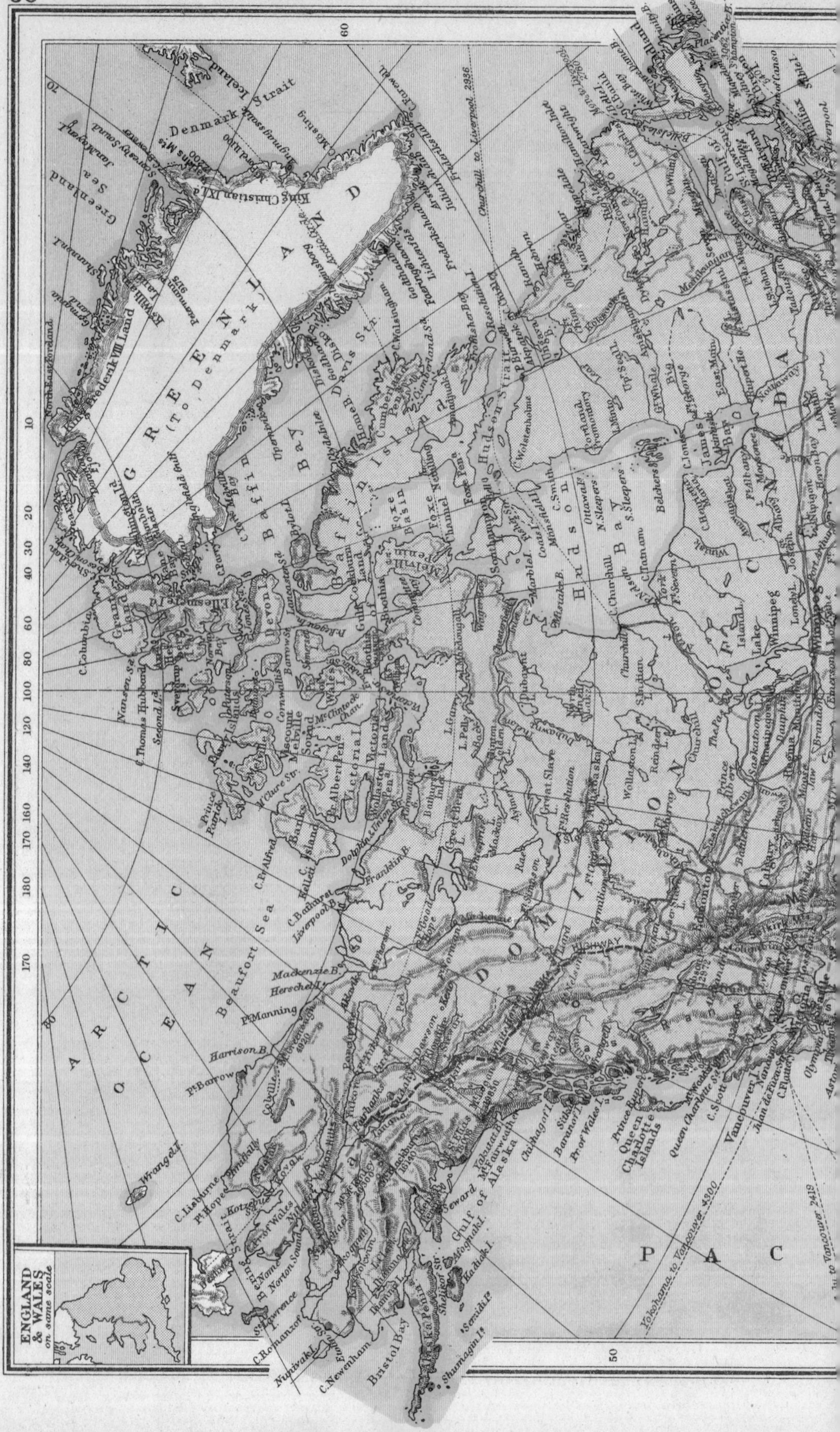

GREENLAND (To Denmark)

Denmark Strait

Iceland

Greenland Sea

Baffin Bay

Davis St.

Hudson Strait

HUDSON BAY

CANADA

DOMINION

ARCTIC OCEAN

Beaufort Sea

Mackenzie B.
Herschel I.
P. Manning

Harrison B.
P. Barrow

Wrangel

C. Lisburne
P. Hope
Kotzebue

Pr. of Wales

Nome
Norton Sound

St. Lawrence
St. Matthew

C. Romanzof
Nunivak I.
C. Newenham
Bristol Bay
Shumagin I.
Kadiak I.

Gulf of Alaska
Seward
Prince Wales I.
Sitka

Queen Charlotte Sd.
Queen Charlotte Islands
Vancouver I.

Winnipeg
Lake Winnipeg

Ellesmere Ld.
C. Columbia

Victoria Land

Banks Land
Prince Patrick Ld.

Melville I.
McClure Str.

Franklin I.

Churchill to Liverpool 2936

Yokohama to Vancouver 4300

P A C I F I C

ENGLAND & WALES
on same scale

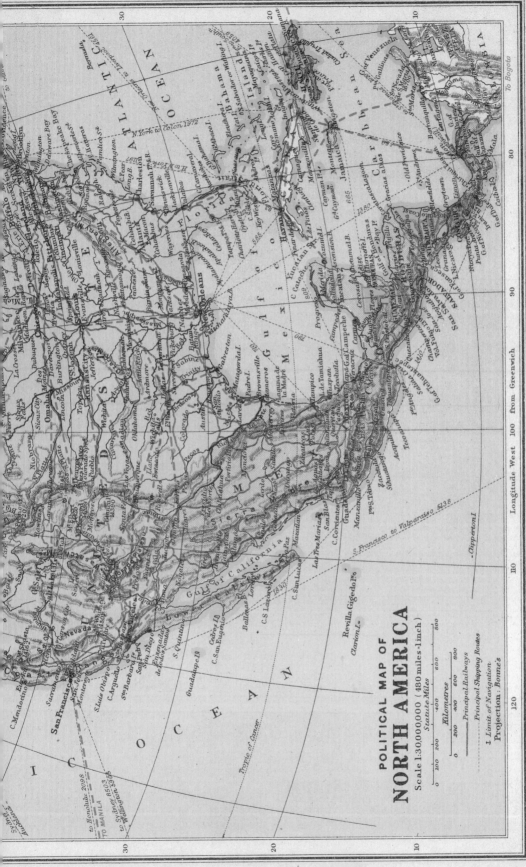

POLITICAL MAP OF
NORTH AMERICA
Scale 1:30,000,000 (480 miles = 1 inch)
Statute Miles
Kilometres

———————— Principal Railways
——————— Principal Shipping Routes
-·-·-·-·- Limit of Navigation
Projection: Bonne's

– – – – Principal Air Mail Routes (Normal)
● Principal Wireless Stations

George Philip & Son, Ltd.

The London Geographical Institute.

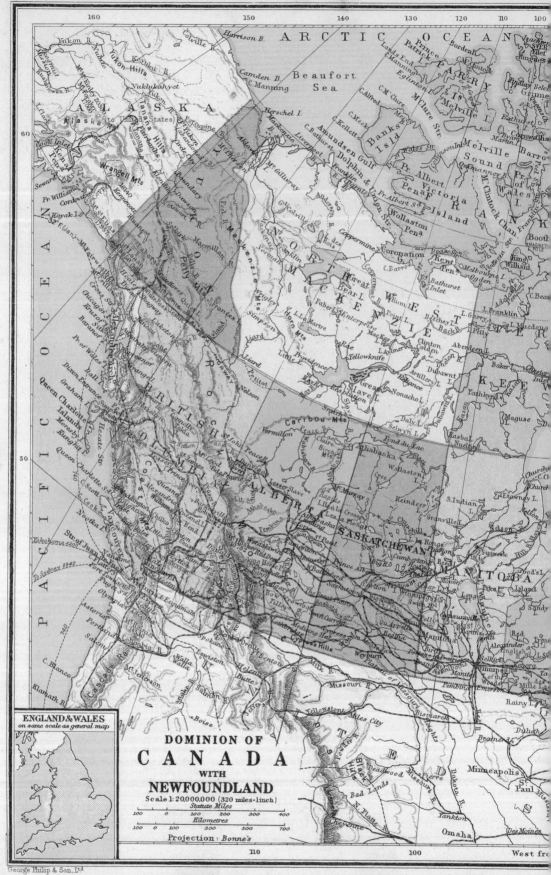

ENGLAND & WALES
on same scale as general map

DOMINION OF
CANADA
WITH
NEWFOUNDLAND
Scale 1:20,000,000 (320 miles=1inch)
Statute Miles
100   0   100   200   300   400
Kilometres
100   0   300   500   700
Projection: Bonne's

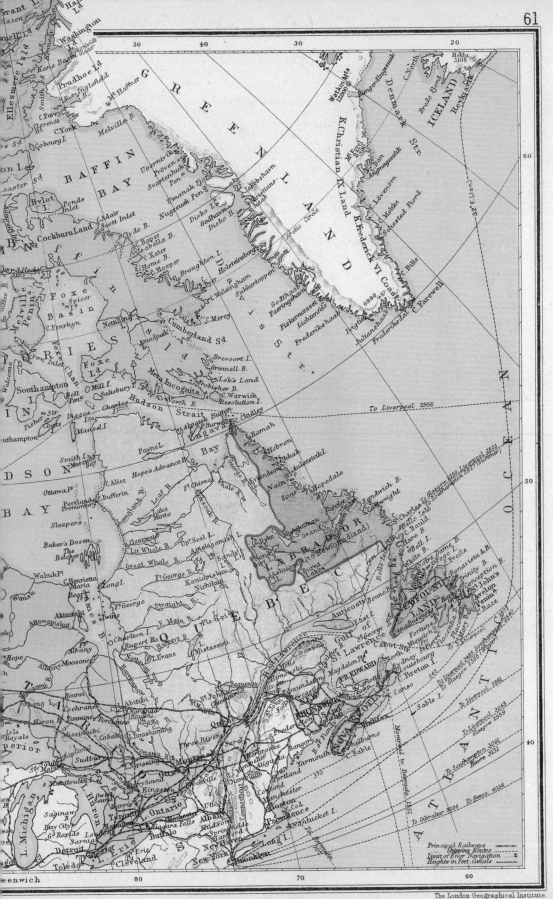

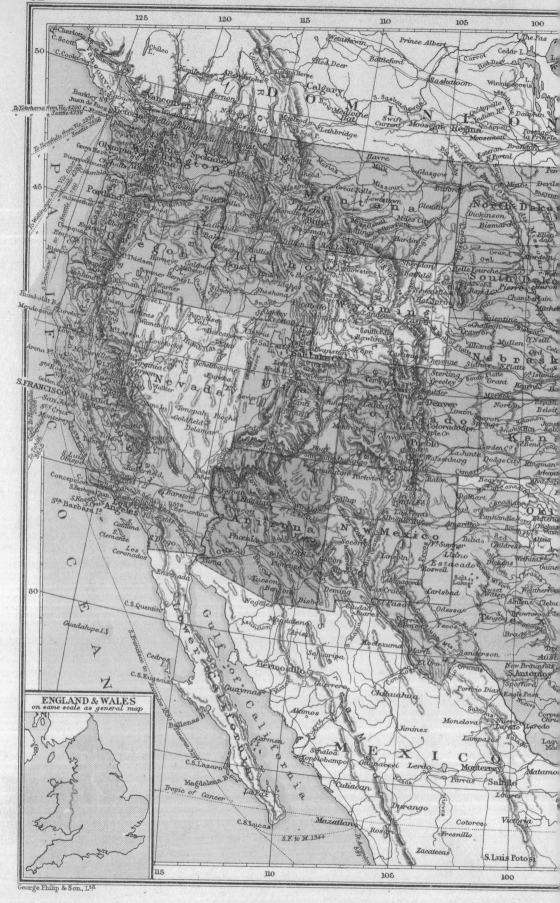

ENGLAND & WALES
on same scale as general map

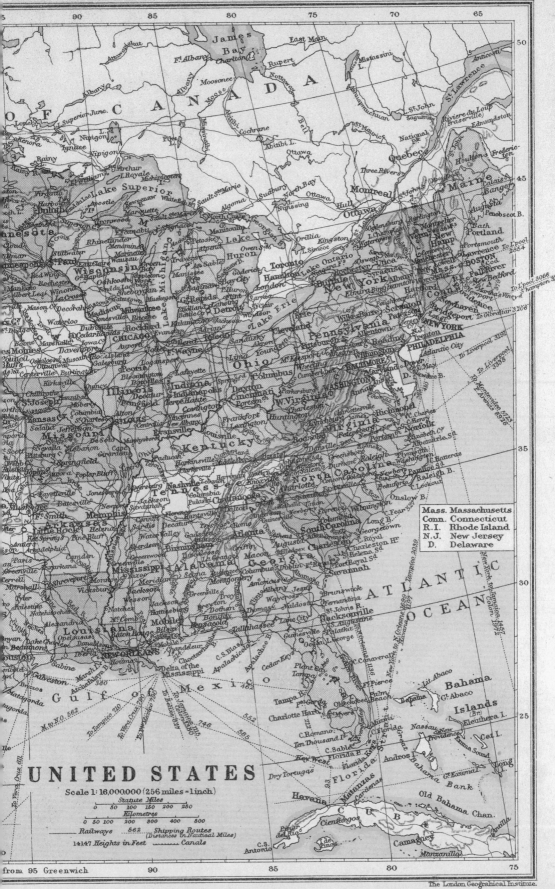

Mass.	Massachusetts
Conn.	Connecticut
R.I.	Rhode Island
N.J.	New Jersey
D.	Delaware

UNITED STATES

Scale 1:16,000,000 (256 miles = 1 inch)

Statute Miles

0 50 100 150 200 250

Kilometres

0 50 100 200 300 400 500

Railways ———— 562 Shipping Routes ————
(Distances in Nautical Miles)

14147 Heights in Feet ———— Canals ————

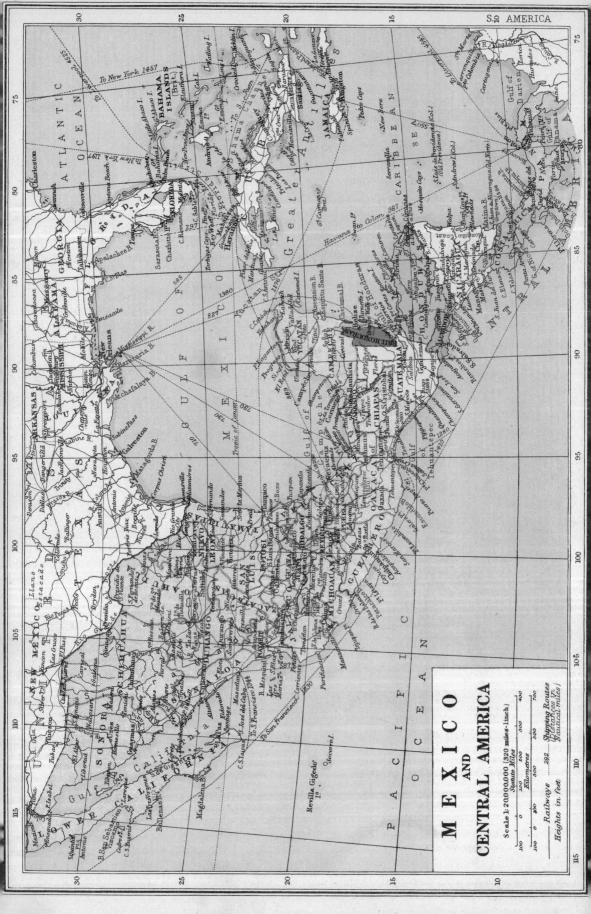

MEXICO
AND
CENTRAL AMERICA

Scale 1:20000000 (320 miles=1 inch)

Railways

Shipping Routes (distances in Nautical miles)

Heights in feet

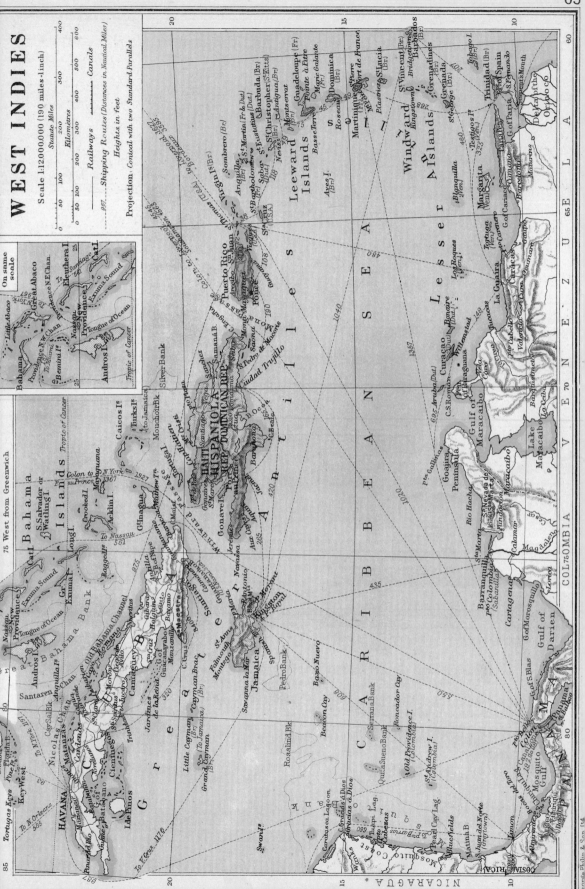

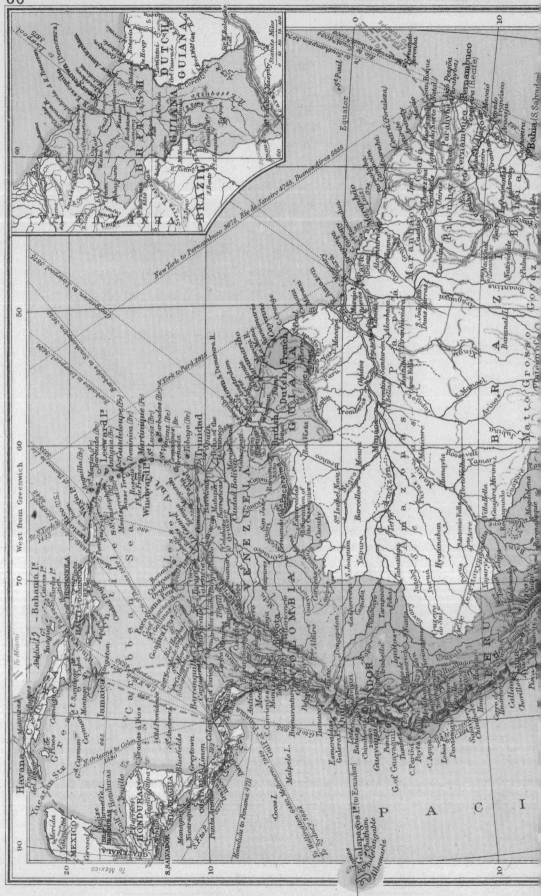

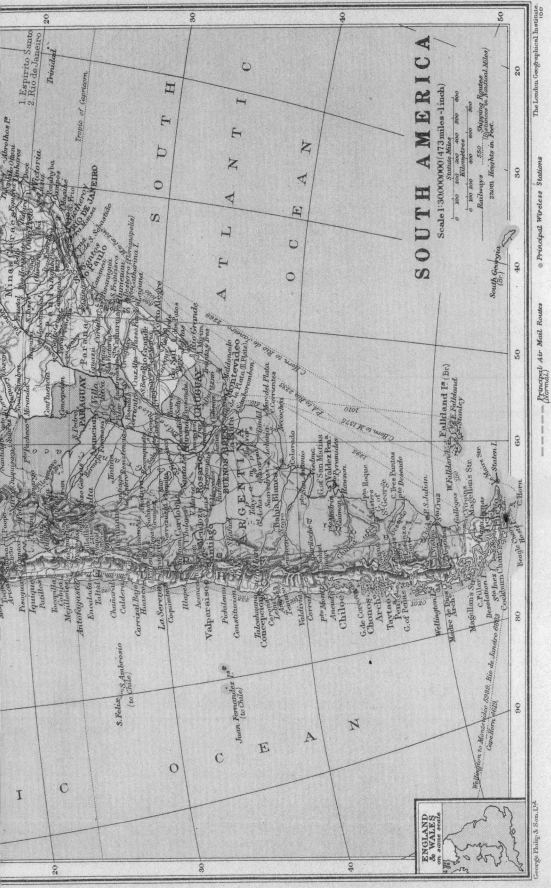

SOUTH AMERICA

Scale 1:30000000 (473 miles=1 inch)

Statute Miles

Kilometres

Railways   Shipping Routes
(Distances in Nautical Miles)

2308m Heights in Feet.

The London Geographical Institute.

- - - - - Principal Air Mail Routes (Normal)   • Principal Wireless Stations

George Philip & Son, Ltd.

ENGLAND & WALES on same scale

1. Espirito Santo
2. Rio de Janeiro

68

THE POLAR REGIONS

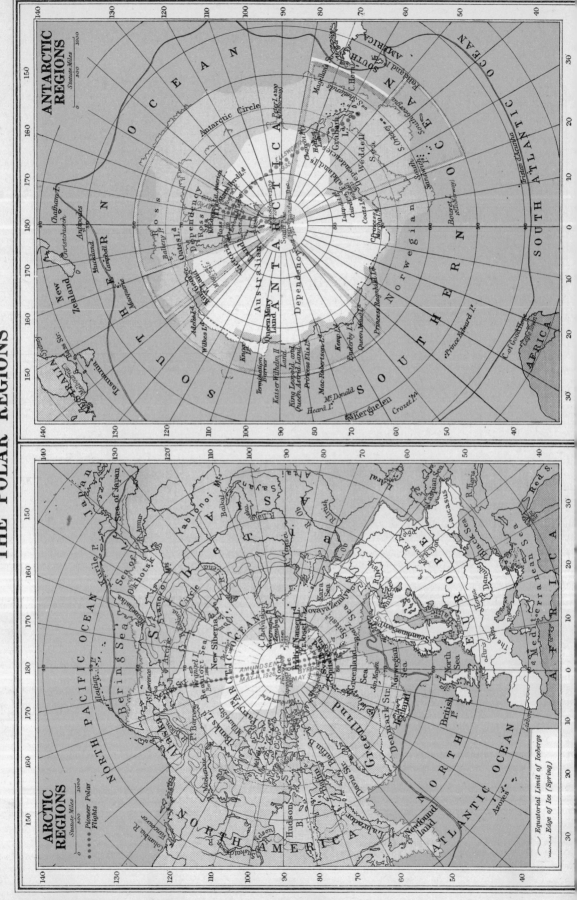

Map 1. WORLD POPULATION.

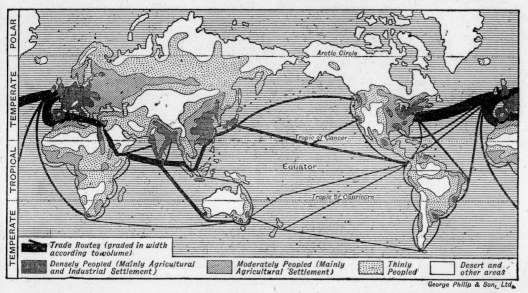

Trade Routes (graded in width according to volume)

Densely Peopled (Mainly Agricultural and Industrial Settlement)

Moderately Peopled (Mainly Agricultural Settlement)

Thinly Peopled

Desert and other areas

George Philip & Son, Ltd.

The difficulties caused by the economic crisis in 1929-31 and the succeeding years led in certain countries to an outcry being raised for "living-space." This outcry was especially vehement in Germany, Italy and Japan, where it was claimed that new outlets must be found for rapidly expanding populations.

In the 19th century the growth of European population did not become a serious problem, for it was met by rapid industrialization and by migration on a large scale. The upheaval caused by the Great War (1914-18), and the economic dislocation that resulted in the years immediately following, made migration again an acute question, but now countries formerly welcoming immigrants framed restrictive laws.

The map above shows the distribution of population throughout the world as well as the principal trade routes. It is seen that the greatest volume of trade is across the North Atlantic between Europe and North America, particularly the United States. Especially in Western Europe and North-East United States is the density of population greatest. Both lie almost entirely within the temperate zone and both climate and soil are very favourable to the growth of vegetation. Thus food production, both plant and animal, is very high. The climate also is stimulating to human endeavour. In addition these regions are richly endowed with minerals. Industrious populations have made these the most highly industrialized and richest regions of the world.

A broad volume of trade passes in normal times from Europe through the Mediterranean and Red Sea to India, Malaya, China and

Japan, and also to Australia and New Zealand. In India, the East Indies, China and Japan are found other regions with a very high density of population. In contrast with Western Europe and North-East United States the teeming millions of these countries enjoy a much lower standard of life. This is largely because industrialization has as yet made comparatively little advance.

Most of the world's area is moderately or even thinly peopled, but it does not follow that an extensive redistribution of population from more crowded areas would bring complete satisfaction. In the less densely populated areas a considerable extent of desert, mountain and plateau exists. There are also forest regions and areas too far north to be capable of supporting a large population. In tropical areas, where the principal colonial empires are situated, the climate is not well suited to white settlement, so that these offer no solution of white population problems.

While some of the newer countries, such as the Dominions and South America, are capable of receiving additional populations, the geographical and economic conditions in areas suggested for settlement will require careful study in order to enable a regulated flow of migration to take place after the war. One other solution of population problems will be development of industrialization in some of the poorer agricultural countries if the necessary mineral resources are to be found, or, as Sir Arthur Salter says, if they can "draw freely upon the resources of the rest of the world." (See page 71.)

MAP 2. UNITED NATION S AND AXIS POWERS.

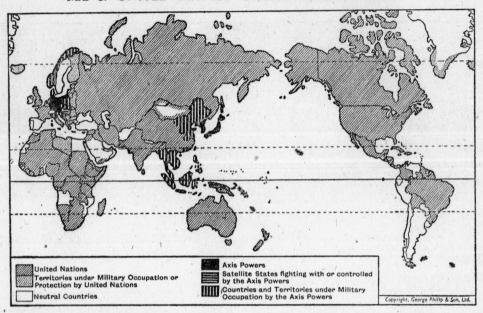

United Nations
Territories under Military Occupation or Protection by United Nations
Neutral Countries

Axis Powers
Satellite States fighting with or controlled by the Axis Powers
Countries and Territories under Military Occupation by the Axis Powers

Copyright, George Philip & Son, Ltd.

The above map illustrates the distribution of territory between the United Nations and the Axis Powers at the close of 1944. Although the war began in September, 1939, Germany had been preparing for it ever since Hitler assumed power in January, 1933 (see page 79). From the first, the war became a World War since the whole of the British Empire was involved. Britain and France were to a large extent shut out from European markets, and for an important share of the raw materials they used had to rely upon the rest of the world. The maintenance of sea communications everywhere was therefore vital for them.

The collapse of France in 1940 brought Italy into the war and left the British Commonwealth to fight alone for a time. Europe lay at the mercy of Germany, who ruthlessly organized its economic resources for her own support. In this changed situation the Mediterranean was in danger of becoming an Axis sea, but throughout Britain retained her hold upon Gibraltar, Malta and the Suez Canal.

Though he had entered into a treaty with the Soviet Union in August, 1939, events proved that Hitler had not abandoned his desire for the Ukraine as German "Lebensraum." Germany attacked the Soviet Union in June, 1941, thus bringing a nation of 180 millions to the side of the United Nations. While actual campaigning was confined to her western territories, the Soviet Union was obliged to take precautions against the threat that the military might of Japan held for her in the east.

Since July, 1937, China has been defending herself against wanton aggression by Japan (see page 104), although war between these nations was not actually declared by China until 1941. This official declaration followed the Japanese attack upon Pearl Harbor on December 7th, 1941, which then brought the United States into the war as one of the United Nations. Germany and Italy both declared war immediately upon the United States, and thus the struggle for world power was set in a new sense, since all the Great Powers of the world were now definitely involved.

The emphasis upon the importance of communications became still more striking, for Japan rapidly over-ran South-east Asia. Both Germany and Japan enjoy the advantage of comparatively short communications, whereas long distances have to be traversed by Britain and the United States to bring supplies to their own forces and to their allies in the various theatres of the war.

The building up of powerful sea and air forces and communications by the United States and Britain has now reached such overwhelming dimensions that the German and Japanese submarines have been virtually chased from the seas. On land and in the air the combined military forces of the United Nations have so battered and compressed German strength in Europe that Germany is now completely surrounded by her enemies. In the Far East the Japanese hold on the western Pacific is gradually receding before American naval and air pressure. Its hold on the Asiatic mainland and the East Indies is stoutly maintained, but its ability to draw supplies from them by sea is curtailed.

Fig. 3. PRODUCTION OF RAW MATERIALS.

COMMODITY The percentage figures in the diagram represent percentage of World production for each country. Figures are mainly pre-war, as reliable figures for war production are not available for all countries	THE "HAVES"							THE "HAVE NOTS"		
	UNITED KINGDOM	UNITED KINGDOM & COLONIES	BRITISH EMPIRE (including Dominions and India)	FRANCE	FRENCH EMPIRE	UNITED STATES	SOVIET UNION	GERMANY	ITALIAN EMPIRE	JAPANESE EMPIRE
COAL	18·6%	18·8%	25%	3·4%	3·4%	34%	9%	17%	·09%	3·3%
OIL (CRUDE)		2%	2·4%	0·29%	0·3%	61·5%	10·5%	0·2%	0·004%	0·2%
IRON ORE (METAL CONTENT)	4%	6·5%	10%	11·5%	13·5%	38%	14%	2·5%	0·6%	0·8%
MANGANESE ORE (METAL CONTENT)			36·5%		1·2%	0·7%	40%	7%	0·04%	1·3%
ALUMINIUM (BAUXITE)		6%	16%	17%	17%	7·8%	6·5%	4·7%		
COPPER ORE (METAL CONTENT)	12·5%	24·5%			0·017%	32·5%	3·8%	1·2%	0·02%	3·1%
RUBBER	48%	48·5%			5·5%					
COTTON		1·8%	13%		1·9%	49%	9·9%		0·05%	0·5%
WOOL	2·7%	3·4%	46·5%	1·4%	3·7%	11·5%	6·8%	1·1%	0·7%	

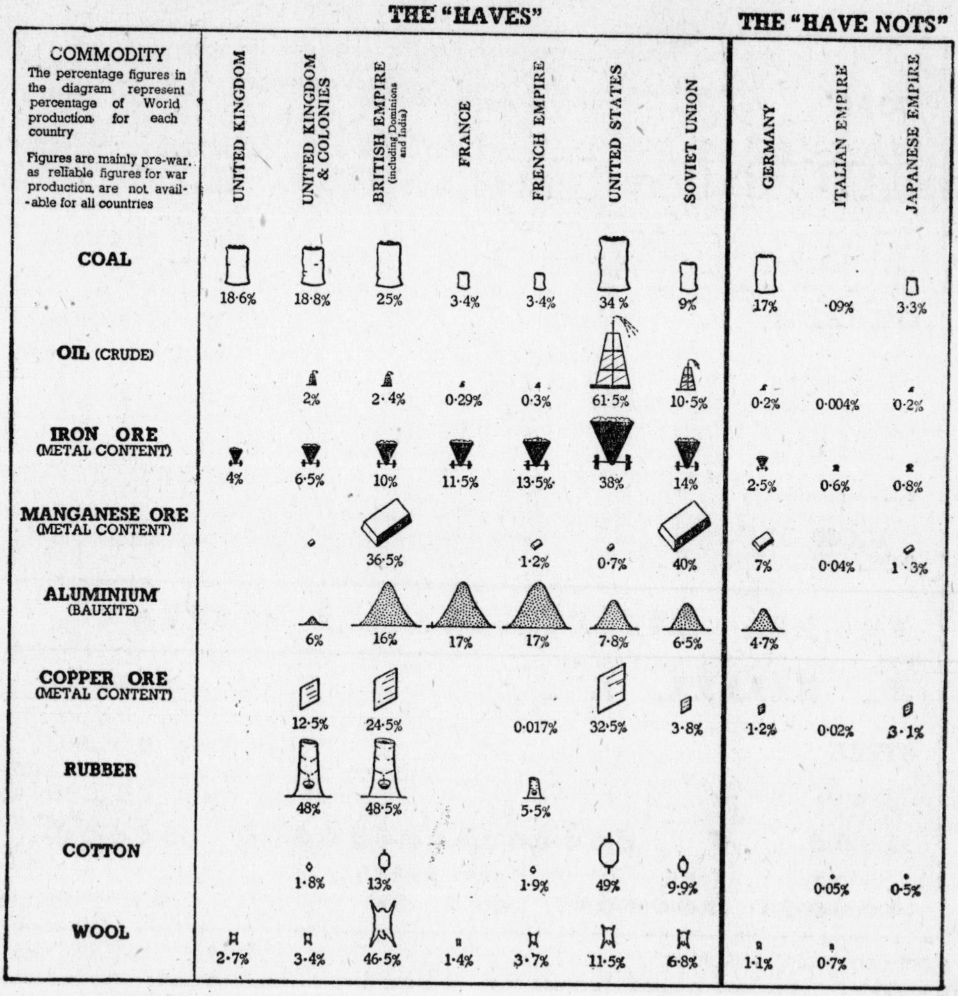

According to Goebbels " The basic materials of modern industrialization are coal, iron, cotton, oil, rubber and copper." The diagram contrasts the production of raw materials by the principal industrial States, among whom Germany, Italy, and the Japanese Empire consider themselves as dissatisfied powers owing to the unequal distribution of raw materials and their own lack of colonies. They are not unmoved by jealousy, for they feel that as Great Powers their national honour and prestige are smirched, without the possession of colonies comparable to those of other great powers and some smaller powers.

In some degree this mal-distribution of raw materials can be considered one of the causes of the present war. The possession of colonies would not in itself, however, solve the problem since, according to the Report of the League Committee of Raw Materials published in 1937, the colonial production of all commercial raw materials at present accounts for no more than 3% of total world production. Even so, in the case of certain products colonial production is of great importance, as, for example, the rubber and tin of British Malaya and the Netherlands Indies.

That there is a raw materials problem was recognized by the fourth point of the Atlantic Charter of August, 1941. This suggests as a solution, " the enjoyment by all States of access, on equal terms, to the trade and to the raw materials of the world, which are needed for their economic prosperity."

It is clear from the diagram that no country is entirely self-sufficient and had it been possible to include a wider range of products and also the principal foodstuffs, the evidence on this point would have been even more convincing.

Fig. 4. UNITED NATIONS AND AXIS POWERS: DISTRIBUTION OF COAL, OIL, IRON-ORE AND STEEL.

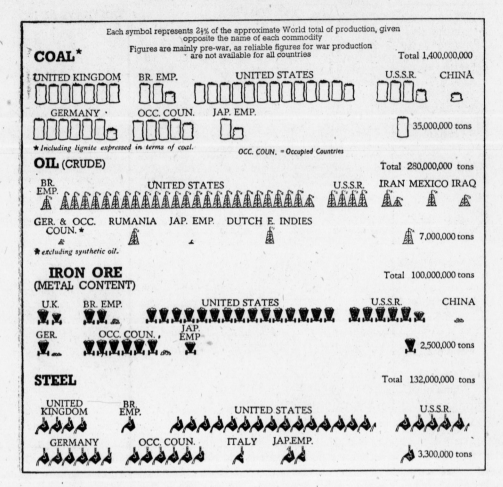

Germany's coal position is good, because she has a surplus for export to Italy and her immediate neighbours; Japan's supplies need to be supplemented from China's resources.

Britain has to import all her oil supplies, though both Burma and Trinidad within the Empire can supply a fraction of her requirements. The United States has a large surplus for export. The Soviet Union has more than sufficient for her own requirements, though her rapid industrialization and her military requirements have reduced the amount available for export. Only small supplies of natural oil are available to Germany, Italy and Japan. Germany, however, has developed very considerably the production of synthetic oil from coal, and is now reputed to produce the greater part of her requirements from this source. Italy has developed a domestic refining industry, but is dependent on other countries for her supplies of crude oil.

As in the case of coal and oil the United Nations have a considerable preponderance of iron-ore. The United Kingdom is dependent upon imports for a considerable proportion of her iron-ore. When the war opened, one of Germany's main problems was to obtain sufficient iron-ore for her requirements, since her domestic sources supplied only one-third. Her conquests in Europe have freed her from this difficulty, because she now controls the Lorraine iron-ore. Japan's deficiency in iron-ore has somewhat hindered the development of her heavy industry. Some supplies have been obtained from Manchuria, but before her attack upon the United States she relied to an appreciable extent upon imports of scrap-iron from that country.

Soviet Russia has suffered from the capture by Germany of virtually the whole of the Ukraine, from which she drew approximately 60% of her supplies both of coal and iron, but her development of newer resources has partially compensated for this.

MAP 5. ATLANTIC OCEAN.

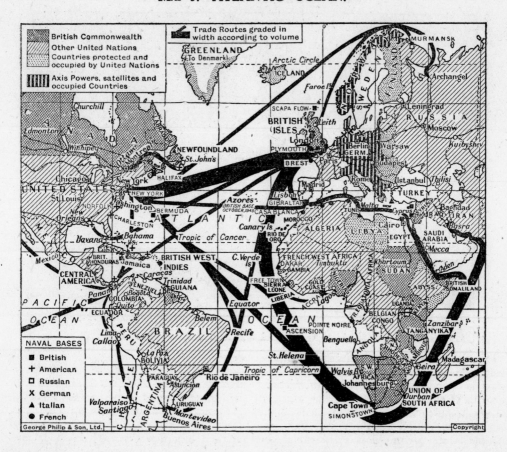

The Atlantic Ocean is the most important of the oceans in regard to the volume of trade carried upon its waters. Of that trade the largest proportion is carried in British ships. Broadly speaking, the four routes of outstanding importance to Britain are :—

1. Across the North Atlantic to Canada and the United States.

2. To Eastern South America.

3. To British possessions in West, South, and East Africa.

4. To the West Indies and the Panama Canal, and beyond to New Zealand and to the Pacific coast of South America.

In view of Britain's vulnerability in regard to food and raw materials, the preservation of the command of the sea in the Atlantic is of pre-eminent importance. For Britain the war has entailed still greater use of the Atlantic, since use of the Mediterranean was denied to her, until the surrender of Italy. Moreover, supplies to Russia have been carried across the Atlantic by the northern route to Murmansk, and by the Cape route to the Persian Gulf.

During the course of the war the attitude of the United States gradually changed, until its active participation became virtually inevitable. In order to strengthen her defensive position, America acquired from Britain certain bases in British possessions on a lease of 99 years. Then she protected Greenland in April, 1941, and in July, 1941, joined Britain in the occupation of Iceland. Patrols of the American Navy and the arming of American merchantmen were established. Steps were also taken by the United States to create joint defence measures with Canada and with other American republics.

Throughout the war German policy concentrated on destroying British and Allied shipping. German success would have reduced Britain's war effort severely through lack of supplies. It would also have prevented vital supplies reaching the Soviet Union. Furthermore it would have made impossible the vast accumulation of American and British forces and supplies in the fortress of Britain, needed for the invasion of Europe.

MAP 6. EUROPE—NATIONALITIES.

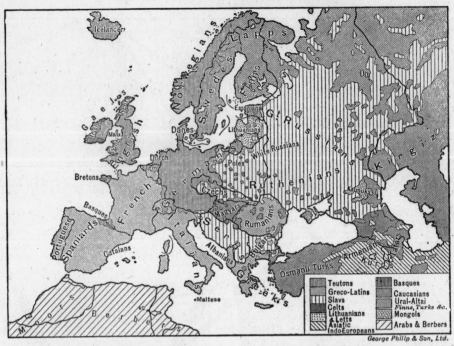

George Philip & Son, Ltd.

The conception of nationality is a comparatively modern one, and although it was established in Britain, France, Spain and Portugal
virtually at the close of the Middle Ages, it
did not come to the rest of Europe until the
19th century. Both Germany and Italy, for
example, were geographical expressions con-
taining a large number of separate sovereign
States. The defeat of the Napoleonic domination of Europe did much to establish the feeling of national consciousness both in Germany
and in Italy, though it was not until 1870 that
the unification of these countries was complete.
Even then many people of German speech
were left outside the German Empire.

The term " race " is often used loosely; as, for
example, the French or German race, when
nationality is meant. This has been especially
so in Germany, where in recent years propaganda has asserted that the German race
derives from the Nordic and Aryan races.
Biologically, however, such a conception is
completely unscientific. In Europe, for
example, the admixture of peoples through
thousands of years has been so great that it is
practically impossible to single out definite
biological racial types.

The conception of Nationality can, however,
be fairly clearly defined, since it covers people
developing under common laws, government,
cultures, traditions and language. One very
powerful sentiment in the growth of the consciousness of nationality has been the desire on
the part of all peoples for freedom from foreign

domination, even though that did not neces-
sarily imply any real degree of freedom within
their own State. Perhaps language is the most
important element of all, and for this reason it
has been adopted as the basis for the map above.
Here, however, owing to the small scale of the
map, it has been necessary to group together
certain linguistic families and in consequence
all the Teutonic peoples, including the English,
Germans and Scandinavians, have been shown
in the same manner despite the fact that each
of these peoples have developed in very
different ways. Similarly the Latin and Slav
groups are shown in the same way.

The boundaries of the newer European
States, as they were after the Treaty of
Versailles at the close of the 1914-18 war,
indicated that an attempt was made to draw
frontiers as far as possible along linguistic lines.
This, however, could not be the sole criterion
in the establishment of frontiers. The pattern
of languages within Europe is extremely complicated, especially in the east and south-east,
because of the earlier waves of migration at
various periods of history. The pattern was
made more confusing also by the settlement of
isolated German colonies throughout these
regions. (See pages 89 and 93.) Furthermore,
consideration had to be paid to factors such as
national economies and strategic conditions;
and it follows that many linguistic minorities
are to be found. The problem of dealing with
minorities and small States constitutes one of
the major European problems after the war.

MAP 7. EUROPE—DENSITY OF POPULATION.

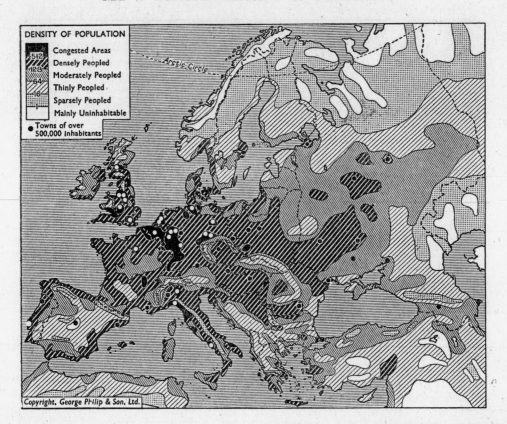

One need only contrast the changes visible before one's eyes in making a journey from London to Manchester, to see how widely density varies—even in a country with such a high average density as our own. Such variations are reproduced on a much larger scale in Europe, and are a response to natural conditions, such as relief, climate, vegetation and soil.

Certain densely populated areas are found in the north-west and are adjacent to, or built upon coalfields, or else related to a port or a metropolitan area. There industry is highly concentrated. Elsewhere man's use of his natural conditions has produced diverse patterns of population density based upon agricultural and pastoral occupations. Less space is required for agricultural than for pastoral life, so density is not in itself a key to the degree of population pressure in any particular area.

Because of population pressure and hard economic conditions, of the desire for greater political and religious freedom, and for many other reasons, people have in the past migrated in large numbers from Europe. Such migration played an important part in relieving the congestion of population, but has not solved the population problem.

The rise of industrialism, particularly in the north-west, led to remarkable increases in population in past decades, but the industrial countries are now showing a different trend. Their populations seem to be definitely declining, for the net reproduction rates have fallen below what is necessary to maintain the present population. This is true of the United Kingdom, Germany, where the fall has to some extent been stemmed, France and Belgium.

On the contrary, in countries where the economy largely depends upon peasant agriculture, as in the Balkans and Portugal, the net rate of reproduction is greater than before. There the increasing population bears very hardly upon the already over-burdened resources of these countries ; for, generally speaking, the standards of life of industrial populations are higher than those of agricultural populations. In the Soviet Union rapid agricultural and industrial expansion are accompanied by a high birth-rate.

As migration is in these days to a large extent closed, it would seem that the best chance of improving the standard of living would be the development of the mineral resources of the poorer countries of Europe and the introduction of industrialization into them. The possibilities of migration should be re-examined.

Map 8. INDUSTRIAL BRITAIN.

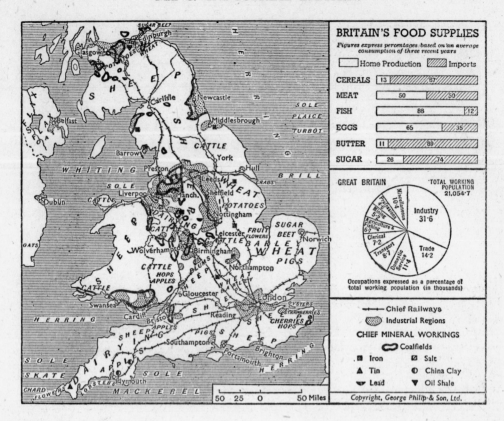

BRITAIN'S FOOD SUPPLIES

Figures express percentages based on an average consumption of three recent years

☐ Home Production   ▨ Imports

	Home Production	Imports
CEREALS	13	87
MEAT	50	50
FISH	88	12
EGGS	65	35
BUTTER	11	89
SUGAR	26	74

GREAT BRITAIN   TOTAL WORKING POPULATION 21,054.7

Industry 31.6
Trade 14.2
Domestic Service 11.4
Transport 8.7
Clerical 7.2
Agriculture & Fishing 6.7
Mining 5.7
Miscellaneous 10.4

Occupations expressed as a percentage of total working population (in thousands)

+—+—+ Chief Railways
⬭ Industrial Regions

CHIEF MINERAL WORKINGS
⬭ Coalfields
▪ Iron   ▨ Salt
▲ Tin   ◎ China Clay
▼ Lead   ▼ Oil Shale

50   25   0   50 Miles

Copyright, George Philip & Son, Ltd.

The permanent unemployment that existed in Britain between the two wars is indicative of the need for some re-adjustment in the industrial fabric of the country. The very high degree of industrialization, technical skill, and wide specialization in an enormous range of manufactured products of every kind, produced in Britain, is based primarily upon resources of coal and iron ore. Britain was first in the industrial field, so that it was not until the later years of the 19th century and the 20th century that the other leading industrial nations, the United States, Germany and France in particular, entered into competition with Britain. Prior to this time, British manufactured products, in particular machinery, textiles, pottery, and other goods, had been exported throughout the world.

In regard to exports, up to at least the year 1900, the intensive development of industry brought with it considerable increases of population and a continual migration from the countryside to the towns. In 1811, the agricultural population of the country represented 34% of the whole. By 1861 it had been reduced to 10% of the whole and to-day, as the diagram above shows, it is still smaller.

Throughout the whole period, except for certain short spells due to external causes, agriculture may be said to have been developing under difficulties, in spite of the progress that was made. More and more arable land gave way to pasture, since it was difficult for home-grown corn to compete in price with that grown on the wide acres of the new lands in America. This dependence on overseas supplies of food that can be produced here, as well as tropical foods and products, is illustrated by the diagram above; and in order to overcome our difficulties a large amount of pasture land has had to be turned over to arable during the war and neglected land has been brought back into cultivation.

The disproportionate number of our population engaged in industry, trade, transport and mining, as compared with the number employed in agriculture, is a problem not of the war but of long standing. As compared with the occupational distribution of other leading industrial countries it indicates a lack of balance requiring re-adjustment, if a healthy condition of the population is to arise after the war.

MAP 9. INDUSTRIAL GERMANY.

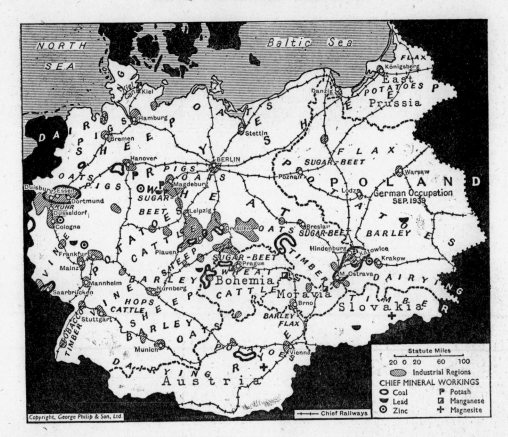

Germany, like Britain, owes her industrial development to her coal and iron, although she also possesses resources of potash, magnesite (from Austria), manganese (from Czechoslovakia), zinc and lead, with a little oil and some copper. Germany developed late, and only entered strongly into the industrial field after the establishment of the German Empire in 1870. She had a large population engaged in an intensive pursuit of agriculture. Though her land and climate are in the main less favourable to agriculture than those of France, by the application of scientific methods and the extensive use of fertilizers, particularly potash, of which she has the most extensive resources in the world, and of nitrates derived from her lignite deposits, she has succeeded in raising the yield of her crops to such a high degree that she has virtually made herself self-sufficient in temperate products. She still needs to import maize, vegetable oils, rubber and cotton.

Her acquisition in 1870 of the Lorraine iron-ore fields, although of low-grade quality, helped very materially in the establishment of her heavy industry, upon which she based armaments. The loss of these after the 1914-18 War made her more dependent upon foreign supplies, especially those from Sweden. The Allied blockade during that war led her to an intensive development of her lignite deposits. Her extensive chemical industry is based upon her potash and coal and that also contributed to the development of her armed forces. She had to rely upon imports for such metals as tin, nickel, aluminium, chromium and other steel hardening products. In addition to the heavy and chemical industries, she developed particularly electrical industries and shipping.

In spite of losses of territory and population after the 1914-18 War and the industrial collapse due to inflation, she succeeded in making a spectacular recovery and raising herself once more to the position of the third exporting nation of the world. Her industrial development has been aided by her splendid system of railway and canal communications, and also by a clever, hard-working, industrious population given to easy regimentation in the cause of developing the greatness of the Fatherland.

MAP 10. GERMANY'S LOST TERRITORIES AFTER VERSAILLES.

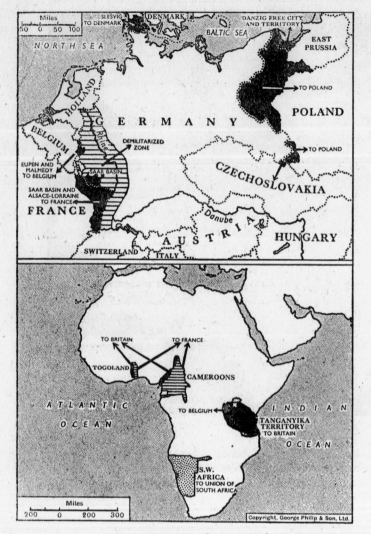

Poland. It was largely populated by Poles, but contained some German elements, largely the result of an active policy of colonization during the nineteenth century. The establishment of what became the Polish Corridor, between Germany and East Prussia, was a perpetual thorn, and its removal became the ostensible cause of Germany's attack upon Poland at the opening of the war. Of the area ceded to Poland the most serious loss industrially was that of the larger part of the Upper Silesian coalfield, whereby a single economic unit was divided between two countries.

The most serious loss of overseas possessions was in Africa. Germany entered late into the field of colonial activity, but made good use of her opportunities once she became convinced that a Colonial Empire was one of the marks of a Great Power.

Tanganyika territory came under British administration as a Mandate, except for a small area administered with the Belgian Congo. Also administered by the British were parts of Togoland and the Cameroons, the former being administered with the Gold Coast and the latter with Nigeria. The remaining portions of Togoland and the Cameroons were transferred to French administration under Mandate, except for a portion of the Cameroons filched by Germany from France after the Agadir Crisis of 1911, which became wholly French. The remaining German African possession, South-West Africa, was transferred to the Union of South Africa as a mandated territory. All of Germany's island possessions in the Pacific were also transferred under Mandate, partly to Britain, partly to Australia, and New Zealand, and partly to Japan.

As the result of the Great War of 1914-18, Germany lost large territories in Europe and the whole of her overseas possessions. Alsace-Lorraine, stripped from France after the Franco-German War, 1870, was returned. Besides the iron-ore deposits (see page 77) this area also possessed useful potash deposits. The Saar Basin with its coal mines was handed over to France until 1935 as compensation for the destruction of the coalfields of North-East France. Small areas were also ceded to Belgium and Denmark. In the latter case it was some compensation for the territory lost after the Schleswig-Holstein War of 1864.

Danzig, a former Hanseatic Port, became a Free City with certain trading rights allowed to Poland. A large part of the territory seized by Prussia in the three Polish Partitions of the 18th century was ceded to the resurrected

Until Hitler came to power these losses were grudgingly accepted, but the loss of the colonial empire always rankled.

MAP 11. GERMAN GAINS UNDER HITLER BEFORE THE WAR.

In the German people Hitler found a ready instrument for the plans made and proclaimed to the world in his book " Mein Kampf." His aim of world conquest was concealed from all at first, since he said he sought no more than to restore German self-respect, and Germany to what he considered her rightful place among the great nations of the world. Hence he claimed that the " inequalities " of the Versailles Treaty should be swept away. As his power increased, a succession of measures was taken which achieved his objective.

French administration of the Saar Basin under the League of Nations ended in March, 1935, when after a plebiscite it returned to Germany. In October of the same year Germany withdrew from the Disarmament Conference and also from the League of Nations, thus giving full warning that she was embarking upon rearmament. Next year, in March, German troops marched into Cologne and immediately began the fortification of the whole of the Rhineland, demilitarized under the Treaty of Versailles. In November, 1936, without consultation with the Allied Powers concerned, Hitler swept away the international control of navigation established

at Versailles for the Rivers Rhine, Elbe, Oder, and Danube, and later, in January, 1937, the International Commission of Control governing the Kiel Canal was abolished.

Having thus unilaterally rid Germany of the above arrangements made by the Versailles Treaty, new aims were proclaimed setting forth the desirability of including all Germans under the Reich, expressed in the words " Ein Volk, ein Reich, ein Führer." Hitler borrowed from the Allies the principle of self-determination as a justification for his proposals to unite all Germans. Despite the failure of an earlier attempt at incorporation and the fact that he had announced more than once that he recognized the independence of Austria, German troops occupied the country in March, 1938, and it became merely a German province. In two stages, October, 1938, and March, 1939, Hitler completely destroyed Czechoslovakia (see page 88). By this time the world realized that the German Reich, greater than ever before, was bent upon aggression and world conquest, and that the policy of appeasement pursued by Allied statesmen had failed, though it had served Hitler's aims admirably for the time being.

MAP 12. THE AXIS POWERS—SEPTEMBER, 1939.

power in the autumn of 1922, having taken advantage of the aftermath of war and the social and economic difficulties under which Italy was then labouring.

Externally he set Italy's face towards expansion, and always claimed that revision of territorial boundaries must come before disarmament; but peaceful adjustments of boundaries in Libya and Italian Somaliland did not satisfy Italian aims (see page 91). In October, 1934, she deliberately set about territorial expansion and establishing a greater Italian Empire in Africa. While the League condemned Italian aggression against Abyssinia and pursued a half-hearted policy of economic sanctions, the failure to apply oil sanctions meant that her aggression could not be stopped. The rapid conquest of Abyssinia meant that even such sanctions as were applied had little effect, and by 1936 they were abandoned.

Thoroughly disillusioned with Britain and France, Italy was now ripe for a reversal of policy and the partner she sought seemed to be available in Hitlerite Germany. At first she believed she was strong enough to use Germany, but it soon became evident that Hitler and not Mussolini was the dominant partner. The alliance with Germany began in October, 1936, and was completed eventually in July, 1939; but their aims were not identical in all spheres, for both wished to tie Austria to themselves. While Mussolini's legions on the Austrian frontier deterred a weak Germany when Dollfuss was murdered in July, 1934, eventually Hitler felt strong enough to take Austria without even consulting Mussolini.

Both Germany and Italy conspired in Spain and helped General Franco to overthrow the Spanish Government during the Civil War of 1936-38. The reluctance of the democracies to embark upon active intervention in the Spanish struggle was interpreted by both Hitler and Mussolini as weakness or effeteness. Their determination to fulfil their aims by taking what they required was strengthened, and in consequence a solid block of territory and armed power was established across Central Europe, in spite of the fact that their interests and designs in some areas, such as the Balkans, conflicted.

Throughout the years immediately succeeding the Peace Treaties of 1919 and 1920, there was a unity of aim on the part of the Allied Powers, Britain, France and Italy, in keeping Germany militarily weak. The chaos brought by the war seriously affected Germany and it had to be recognized, though unwillingly, that a Germany economically weak brought economic stresses and strains for themselves as well. Although their purpose was the same, the three Powers differed in regard to the methods that should be adopted in achieving it.

On the whole, Britain desired to bring Germany back into the community of nations and felt that, by giving her as much equality as possible, she would better succeed in keeping her from the pursuit of war. France, on the other hand, felt that this was a misreading of German character and policy, and that she could only join with Britain in this respect if Britain and other Powers were prepared to guarantee French security. For her, security came before disarmament, whereas many in Britain felt that security could only come after disarmament.

Both Britain and France had received additional territory, partly in the shape of Mandates, and thus could be said to have made territorial gains from the war. Italy, on the other hand, received only slight territorial compensation for her efforts, and was made dissatisfied because she was denied additional territory in Dalmatia and in Turkey, under the clauses of the secret Treaty of London. Italy, therefore, had a grievance which was continually magnified by Mussolini. He had come to

MAP 13. GERMAN EXPANSION AFTER ONE YEAR OF WAR—
SEPTEMBER, 1940.

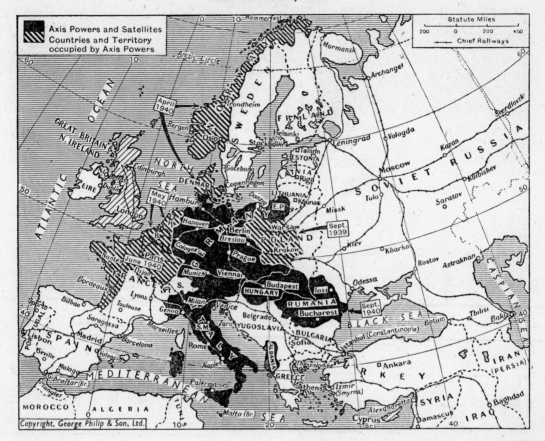

The German attack upon Poland on the 1st September, 1939, brought both France and Britain into the war on the 3rd September. Germany enjoyed a central position, was completely organized, and in the space of a fortnight overwhelmed Poland. Russia then advanced into Poland and together Germany and Russia partitioned that unhappy country. Thus Germany was left free to wage the war only on one front, in the West.

Italy adopted an attitude of non-belligerency. The rest of Europe remained uneasy and neutral in a northern group and a Balkan group, but each lacked sufficient cohesion to act in concert. The "Oslo Group," consisting of the four Scandinavian countries of Norway, Denmark, Sweden and Finland, and the Netherlands, Belgium and Switzerland, all pursued a steady policy of strict neutrality, in the hope that they would avoid being drawn into the war. In April, 1940, Germany invaded Denmark and Norway. In spite of Allied landings in Norway and some naval successes, lack of air support and German ability to increase their reinforce-

ments, rapidly brought about a complete Allied withdrawal early in June.

During the winter months there was practically no engagement of the troops of the opposing sides in the West. On May 10th, Germany struck at the Dutch and Belgian forces and within just over a fortnight both had capitulated. A German thrust at Sedan divided the main body of the British and Belgian and some French forces from the remainder of the French forces, and the Germans captured the Channel ports. To avoid annihilation British and French troops were withdrawn from Dunkirk. Having turned the Maginot Line, the whole strength of the German Army was then thrown against the remaining French armies, which collapsed. On the 21st June, 1940, France sought an armistice. A few days before, Italy invaded France and also imposed an armistice.

Thus, Britain was left to wage the war alone, while Germany now virtually dominated the whole of the continent, for there remained no longer any first-class Power, except Russia, to resist her.

MAP 14. GERMAN EXPANSION AFTER TWO YEARS OF WAR— SEPTEMBER, 1941.

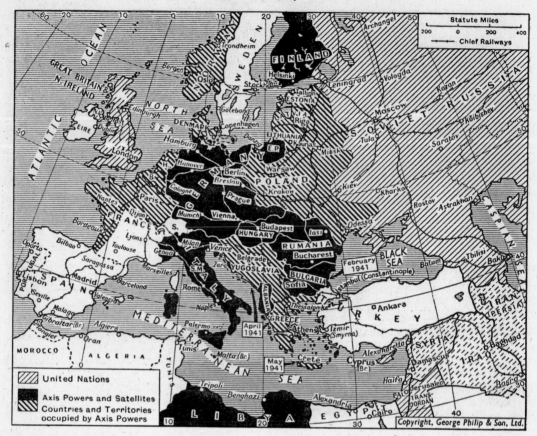

After the German failure in the Battle of Britain, during August, September and October, 1940, the German daylight bombing attacks gave place to night attacks upon London and other important industrial towns and ports in Britain. Apart from this, German arms remained comparatively quiet through the winter months and the advancement of German aims was pressed forward by diplomatic means with the threat of armed force in the background. Germany had succeeded in bringing both Hungary and Rumania into line with Axis aims and was virtually in control of the economic policy of both countries. She left to Italy the task of overwhelming Greece from Albania, but the Italian thrusts failed, and but for German intervention in April, 1941, the Greeks would have driven the Italians from Albania.

Bulgaria granted facilities for military occupation of the country by Germany in February, 1941. Thus German forces were placed in strategic positions surrounding Yugoslavia, whose only contact with the outside world was on her southern frontier with Greece. Yugoslav sentiment resisted German diplomatic pressure, and in April Germany struck, and within a few days overwhelmed the Yugoslav armies. A further month of active compaigning enabled the Germans to compel the Greek armies to capitulate and the British supporting them to evacuate the country. Some of these British troops occupied Crete, but that, too, was overwhelmed by German parachute and air-borne troops in the last days of May.

Thus Germany secured a powerful position in relation to Turkey and the Middle East and also to the campaign being waged in Libya. Here the British advance to Benghazi from December, 1940, to February, 1941, was succeeded by a British withdrawal to the frontier of Egypt in April, 1941, before powerful German armoured reinforcements.

By her Spring campaigns Germany succeeded in safeguarding her right flank for an attack upon Soviet Russia in June, 1941. In spite of swift progress, the end of the second year of war left Germany still engaged in deadly combat with the might of Soviet Russia.

MAP 15. GERMAN EXPANSION AFTER THREE YEARS OF WAR— SEPTEMBER, 1942

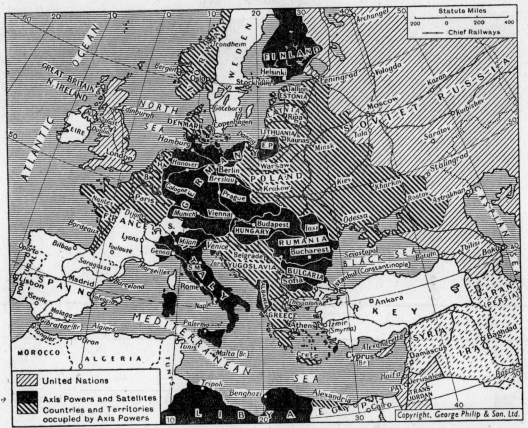

The whole of the third year of the war is dominated by the titanic struggle between Germany and Soviet Russia. The Russian aim throughout was to preserve her armies intact even if it meant yielding territory. On the other hand, the Germans endeavoured to split the Red armies somewhere and to roll them up on Moscow, Leningrad and the Ukraine. Despite enormous gains of territory, including the Ukraine, Russia's richest industrial and agricultural region, the Germans failed to capture Moscow and Leningrad.

By a counter-offensive in December, 1941, the Russians were able to regain substantial territory and to thrust the German armies back from Moscow. They had so dangerously approached this city in October that Hitler felt free to announce its capture and the imminent break-up of the Russian armies. When the Germans mounted their summer offensive of 1942, having failed to break through at Voronezh, they concentrated on the remnants of the Ukraine still in Russian hands and also thrust towards the Caucasus to gain the Baku oilfields. At the end of the third year the Battle for Stalingrad was joined.

The long lull in the fighting in Libya from the end of April, 1941, was broken when the British offensive in November, 1941, swept forward across Cyrenaica during the next two months, capturing Benghazi, and reached El Agheila at the beginning of January, 1942. There, however, British successes ended and before the end of the month the German General, Rommel, had mounted a counter-offensive which compelled the British to evacuate their gains and to retreat upon a defensive zone in the neighbourhood of Gazala. Here they remained until the end of May, when a German attack succeeded in compelling them to retreat still further, and regained Tobruk on June 20th, 1942. The Germans pursued the British until they reached the El Alamein gap between the coast and the Qattara Depression. Here the British stand succeeded in halting Rommel's advance and so prevented Egypt and the Suez Canal from falling into German hands.

During the whole of the year British bombing raids on Germany and German-occupied countries continued.

MAP 16. GERMAN WITHDRAWAL AFTER FOUR YEARS OF WAR—SEPTEMBER, 1943.

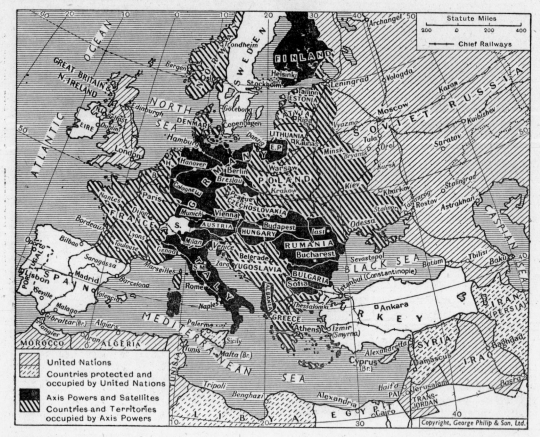

The situation in September, 1942, was critical for the United Nations both on the Egyptian and the Russian fronts. The Germans felt the Suez Canal to be theirs for the plucking, while in the Caucasus the oil of Baku beckoned them on ; but by Christmas it was clear that they had overreached themselves.

The British victory of El Alamein was followed by the expulsion of German and Italian forces from Egypt and Libya. In February, 1943, the Desert Army joined up with Allied forces in Tunisia. A vast amphibious expeditionary force had successfully landed in Algeria and Morocco in November, 1942. Both countries were quickly occupied by the forces of the United Nations. This achievement brought French West Africa to the Allied side, thus making French North and West Africa a solid Allied block, and denying to the Germans the use of Dakar. Germany retaliated by occupying the rest of France and by seizing Tunisia, the final surrender of which to Allied forces came only in May, 1943.

The Allied invasion of Sicily in July, 1943, led to the fall of Mussolini and later to the unconditional surrender of Italy on September 3rd, 1943. The rapid German military occupation of Italy prevented the United Nations from reaping the full benefit of their operations and so bringing about a complete collapse of the whole country. By August, 1943, German resistance in Sicily ceased and Allied landings were effected in southern Italy.

The Russian winter offensive of 1942-43 made several notable gains. It relieved Stalingrad, cleared the territory between the Don and the Donets, and recaptured Kharkov only to lose it in March, 1943. Furthermore it expelled the Germans from the Caucasus and in the north eliminated the Vyazma-Rzhev salient and restored communications between Leningrad and Moscow. In the summer of 1943 the Germans mounted a short-lived offensive to break down the Kursk salient. This was held and for the first time succeeded by a Russian summer-autumn offensive to overthrow the bastions of Bryansk, Orel, Kharkov, Stalino and Taganrog, with a general drive to the south-east towards the Dnieper.

MAP 17. GERMAN WEAKENING AFTER FIVE YEARS OF WAR—SEPTEMBER, 1944.

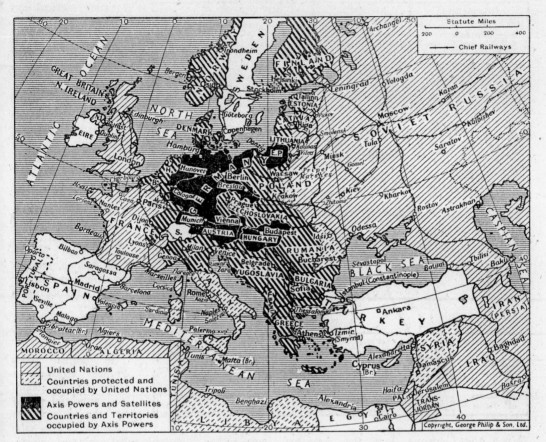

At the end of the fifth year of the war German domination was shrinking. In the Balkans the blows of the Red Army had induced Rumania and Bulgaria to seek armistice terms. The Red Army also compelled Finland to negotiate an armistice. Peninsular Italy was almost entirely cleared of German forces and France also was almost freed by the mighty blows of the Allied forces.

The outstanding event of 1944 was the successful opening of the Second Front in Normandy on June 6th. This had been preceded by terrific air blows on the Luftwaffe, on German communications in Germany, the Low Countries and France, thus making the concentration of German reinforcements at the critical point difficult. German munition and oil industries were pulverized. The immediate Allied aims were the establishment of a beachhead and the capture of a port, Cherbourg. By the middle of August the Battle of Normandy was won and American forces swept into Brittany and down to the Loire in a turning movement, which captured Paris and pushed on towards the frontier. British forces crossed the Seine and advanced to Belgium. Meanwhile an Allied force landed in the south of France and advanced up the Rhône valley to link up with the northern Allied armies.

On the eastern front the initiative rested with the Russians from 1943 onwards and they exploited their superior strength to bleed the Germans white. One by one they sapped German strong points and disrupted their lateral communications. In the north they cleared the Leningrad province and struck into the Baltic States. In the centre they thrust the Germans back to the Pripet Marshes and freed eastern Poland to Warsaw. In the south the Ukraine and Crimea were cleared, the Germans were pinned against the Carpathians and Rumania was invaded and the oil-fields captured.

The Allied front in Italy contained many German divisions, but the mountainous nature of the country made campaigning very severe, in spite of complete Allied air superiority. Brilliant victories freed Naples and Rome and secured air-fields from which to strike at Germany and the Balkans.

MAP 18. INDUSTRIAL FRANCE—SHOWING ARMISTICE TERMS.

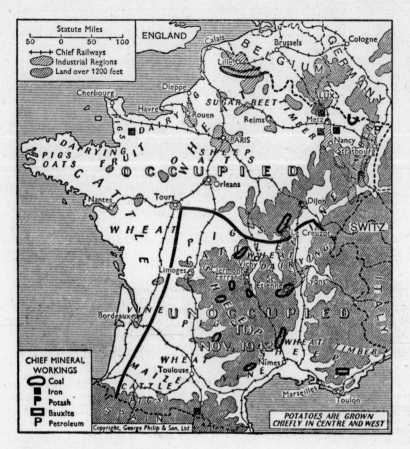

plants. Alsace is both a rich agricultural district and also a large centre of cotton manufactures, and the source of French potash supplies. In addition, Paris, with its diversified industries, is occupied; as are the Schneider armament works at Le Creuzot, together with minor industrial areas and all the Atlantic ports. The principal network of railways and canals, particularly valuable in North-East France, remains in German hands. Vichy France was originally left the port of Marseilles and the naval base of Toulon.

In normal times France enjoyed a well-balanced economy, indicated partly by the occupations diagram. This she owes to her favourable relief, soils and climate, and to her rich and varied resources.

Her main problem in the past has been to secure herself from the attentions of her stronger neighbour, Germany, who is richer both in material resources, political power, and population. The measures taken between the two wars have been shown to be ineffective. For long the population of France has remained virtually stationary. Unemployment has been practically non-existent; and, in fact, prior to the war, there was considerable immigration from other European countries.

When the Germans drew the Armistice line separating Occupied from Unoccupied France in June, 1940, they did so with a very careful eye on the material advantages that would accrue to themselves as well as to strategic necessities. The shaded area on the map shows the whole of the upland and mountainous parts of France. This shows that virtually all of this territory was left in Unoccupied France. East of the Rhône, it consists of the high barrier of the Alps and its foothills; and, west of the Rhône, of the Central Plateau of France. Both these regions have poor soil and sparse population, and the marginal lands and rich Rhône valley with the Mediterranean coast do not produce sufficient food to enable the population to live without drawing upon supplies from Occupied territory, the distribution of which was governed primarily in German interests. In November, 1942, Germany occupied the whole of France.

Germany controls the rich coalfields of North-East France with its woollen, cotton, engineering and chemical industries, the iron-ore of Lorraine, the richest source of supply in Europe, together with its pig-iron and steel

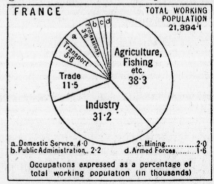

MAP 19. FRENCH COLONIAL EMPIRE.

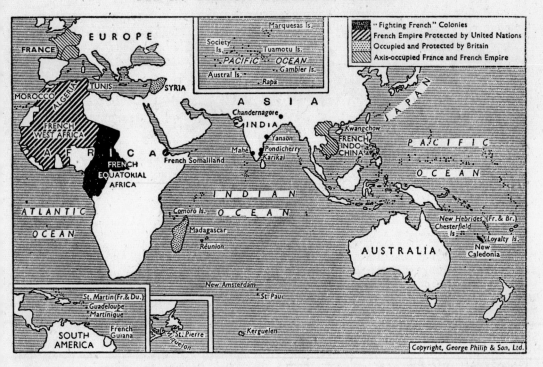

The French Colonial Empire is second in extent only to that of Britain. It contains an area of 4,600,000 square miles, and a population of 65,000,000. The greater part of the Empire is to be found in Africa, where it includes the Mediterranean colonies of Algeria, Tunis and Morocco, the various colonies grouped together as French West Africa, the colonies of French Equatorial Africa, and Madagascar and its dependencies. In Asia it includes French Indo-China, isolated settlements in India, and the mandated territory of Syria. There are in addition the islands of St. Pierre and Miquelon, off the coast of Newfoundland ; Martinique and Guadaloupe in the West Indies ; French Guiana in South America; New Caledonia and its dependencies; the New Hebrides, administered jointly with Britain, and numerous French establishments widely scattered over the Eastern Pacific.

The Empire is inhabited by peoples of very different standards of culture and civilization, as, for example, the Arabs and Berbers of North Africa, the Negroes of West Africa, Indo-China. Moreover, it is endowed by the Annamese and other peoples of French nature with varying soils, climates, products and mineral resources. In spite of this variety of peoples and conditions, French administration was informed throughout by a single purpose. It was designed to assimilate each part of the Empire and its people to French ideals and civilization as rapidly as possible.

Quite apart from any difficulties that have been raised by the demands of local peoples, French possession of its vast Empire has not been undisturbed by other foreign powers. France, being early in the field, forestalled Germany and Italy to a large extent. After the 1914-18 War, France shared with Britain the former German colonies in West Africa. In the 19th century there were difficulties with Britain, particularly in Egypt and the Sudan, where French territorial ambitions were thwarted. France shares control of the Suez Canal with Britain. Her relations with Germany and Spain in regard to Morocco brought trouble ; and only strong support by Britain at the time of the Agadir Crisis in 1911 prevented the outbreak of war. Latterly tension has been aroused because of Germany's demand for the return of her former colonies, and because Italy has re-asserted her claims over Tunis, where the foreign population is almost equally divided between French and Italians. In Indo-China she seemed, not long ago, to be free from external trouble, but the Japanese policy of expansion to the south led Japan to occupy Indo-China upon the collapse of France against Germany. The mandated territory of Syria has brought special problems of its own, unavoidable because the Arab population there have never been content with French administration.

Map 20.   CZECHOSLOVAKIA.

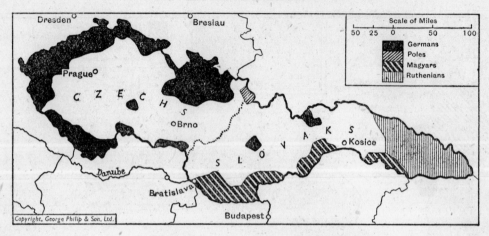

The new State of Czechoslovakia was created in 1919, after the disruption of the former Austro-Hungarian Empire. It consisted of the basin of Bohemia and Moravia, and part of Austrian Silesia and Slovakia. It was a curious combination of lands, possessing elements both of strength and of weakness. The Bohemian basin in the west, the real home of the Czech peoples, was the most advanced part of the new country, both politically and economically. On the other hand, the eastern portion, consisting of Slovakia and Ruthenia on the southern slopes of the Carpathian highlands, with plains and foothills in the south, was much more primitive and difficult.

The name of the new State was derived from the two Slav groups who formed the majority of the population, namely, the Czechs and the Slovaks, whose languages have strong affinities. A large minority of the population, 35%, were neither Czechs nor Slovaks. These minority groups consisted of rather more than 3,000,000 Germans, of 750,000 Magyars, of 500,000 Ruthenians and

about 75,000 Poles. The policy of the new Czech State was to seek Allies among Powers who were interested in maintaining the Versailles settlements, namely, France, Yugoslavia and Rumania.

Hitler's accession to power in Germany immediately meant that the position of Czechoslovakia was more precarious. Employing his usual tactics, Hitler stirred up disaffection among the German minority. During the summer months of 1938 all attempts at reconciliation failed. At Munich the Czechs were deserted by their Allies, the French, and by Britain ; and in consequence Hitler was able to compel the surrender of the Sudeten lands. Both Hungary and Poland immediately took advantage of Czech weakness to secure territory for themselves. During the winter Hitler sowed further disaffection between the Czechs and Slovaks and in March, 1939, occupied Prague and the whole country. He proclaimed a Protectorate of Bohemia and Moravia within the Reich and also a Protectorate of Slovakia, nominally independent but garrisoned by German troops.

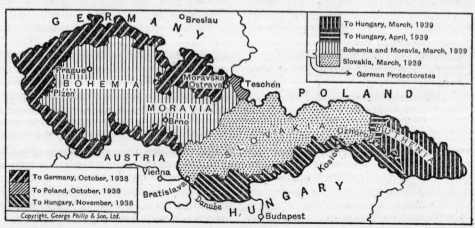

MAP 21. POLAND.

Poland was resurrected by the Peace Conference at Versailles after having experienced more than a century as a subject people. The three portions of the new Polish State were taken from the former German, Austro-Hungarian and Russian Empires. The Treaty-makers at Versailles had intended that the eastern boundary of Poland should be what is known as the Curzon Line. This, however, did not satisfy Polish aspirations, and, taking advantage of the disintegration in Russia owing to the Russian Revolution of 1917, the Poles seized a block of territory in the east. Though this territory was inhabited by many Polish-speaking peoples, the majority of its inhabitants were White Russians and Ukrainians. In 1923 the seizure from Lithuania of Vilna, the former Lithuanian capital, led to continual friction with Lithuania.

The new Polish State was given an outlet on the Baltic Sea, and certain rights for trade in Danzig, a preponderantly German city. Danzig itself was cut off from Germany, and a Free City and Territory was created under the supervision of the League of Nations. The strip of territory known as the Polish Corridor, dividing Western from Eastern Prussia, remained a bone of contention throughout the period between the two wars. The division of the Silesian coalfield between Poland and Germany also created difficulties. Thus external as well as internal problems beset the development of the new State.

When, in September, 1939, Hitler invaded Poland and overwhelmed it, the country was again partitioned between Germany and Soviet Russia. The new partition followed roughly the Curzon Line, although certain predominantly Polish-speaking districts about Bialystok were included in the Russian portion. In the main, however, it incorporated the White Russian and Ukrainian-speaking territories and passed to Lithuania the Vilna district.

Since Russia was brought into the war, more friendly relations between Poland and Russia have been established than existed previously. A working arrangement has been established whereby the Partition of Poland between Germany and Russia has become void, but so far no definitive arrangements have been made between Russia and Poland as to what shall constitute the eastern boundary of Poland when the country comes to be resurrected. It is scarcely to be expected, however, that Russia will be content that the White Russians and Ukrainians shall again pass under Polish administration. Another problem of great difficulty will be that of finding a suitable outlet on the Baltic Sea for Poland, since the Germans have annexed the Corridor territory. They have ruthlessly removed the Polish population from this area and resettled it with German peasants.

MAP 22. MEDITERRANEAN SEA.

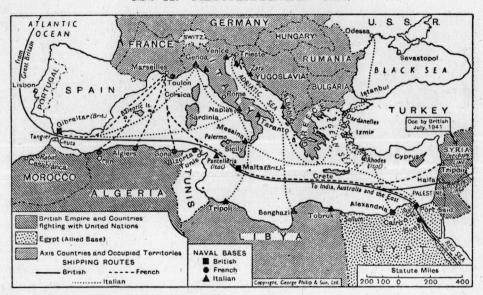

Apart from the smaller Powers, the Mediterranean Sea is of interest to three major Powers—Britain, France and Italy. Britain controls two exits of the Sea—Gibraltar and the Suez Canal, and occupies the mid-way naval fortress of Malta. Her fleet has the task of protecting one of the most important of Britain's trade routes as well as her interests in Cyprus, Palestine and Transjordan.

France has an overwhelming interest in the western Mediterranean, although she has also been strongly concerned in the eastern Mediterranean through Syria and her interest in the Suez Canal. While France remained in the war the combined British and French fleets were in a position to dominate the whole sea and to keep Italy non-belligerent. Italy's entrance into the war altered the whole balance of power in the Mediterranean Sea, for what remained of the French Fleet after the bombardment of Oran stayed neutral in French naval bases and at Alexandria. When Germany occupied " Vichy " France in November, 1942, the Toulon fleet was scuttled.

Italy's geographical position in the centre of the Mediterranean, from which she could threaten both British and French interests, possessed elements of power and vulnerability. Its power was shown especially in the difficulties of conveying supplies to British forces in Malta from either end of the Mediterranean. Because of its vulnerability, Britain's command of the exits has crippled her trade with the outside world. Her inability either to supply or send reinforcements to her forces in Italian East Africa made its conquest in the end inevitable.

Malta, the central key base of Britain, has withstood the most intensive air bombardment of any fortress throughout the war, and has remained inviolate. The German conquest of South-east Europe and Crete, the German advance from Libya almost to the confines of Alexandria, together with the neutrality of French North Africa, rendered the maintenance of British naval power hazardous. All shipping was subject to bombing from bases north and south of the channel between Crete and Libya in its journey between Alexandria and Malta. Apart from necessary convoys, the military situation meant that Britain must convey all reinforcements and supplies to the Near and Middle East round the Cape and up through the Red Sea, a very considerable handicap as compared with the much shorter route through the Mediterranean. The weaknesses of the British position have been overcome by driving the Axis from Egypt and Libya. Now that French Africa has been jointly occupied by American and British forces, together with France, Italy and Greece, the whole Mediterranean has been re-opened to the navies of the United Nations.

The third exit from the Mediterranean Sea through the Dardanelles to the Black Sea is controlled by Turkey. This control prevented the use of Italian warships against the Russians on the Black Sea before their surrender to the Allies in September, 1943. For long in the past, Britain and France upheld the tottering Ottoman Empire, that the Turks might retain control of the Dardanelles to prevent its falling into the hands of any other Great Power, such as Russia or Germany.

MAP 23. ITALY AND THE ITALIAN EMPIRE.

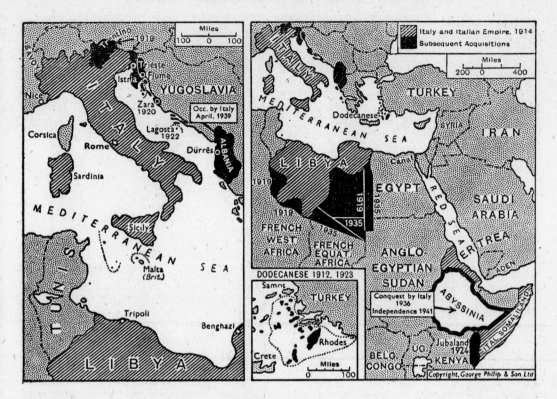

The unification of Italy as a single State only came about in the second half of the 19th century after centuries of division. Italy's growing pains had barely been overcome when the war of 1914-18 arrived. Forsaking the Triple Alliance, she threw in her lot with the Allies, but was dissatisfied with the rewards she gained when the treaties came to be made. She received new territory in the Trentino, in the Austrian Tyrol, and also in Istria, which gave her the naval base of Trieste, but was denied the coveted Dalmatian coast. The Italian seizure of Fiume was recognized by Yugoslavia in 1924.

The necessity for unification in Italy meant that she lagged behind other European powers in seizing colonies in the Partition of Africa.

An attempt to occupy Abyssinia in 1896 was repelled, though she was able to obtain coastal territories in Eritrea and Somaliland in 1889 and 1890. Her ambitions in Tunis were forestalled by the French in 1881, but later she obtained some compensation in Tripoli, now known as Libya, after the Italo-Turkish War of 1911-12, and also in the Dodecanese Islands in the Eastern Ægean. Possession of these islands was confirmed by the Peace Treaties. Now Libya has been conquered by the British. Its future, however, remains to be determined. If restored to Italy, guarantees against the kind of misrule that halved its population before the war will be required.

Mussolini's advent to power in 1922 brought with it a whipping-up of nationalist sentiment in Italy, and an ambition to restore to that country something of the greatness of the Roman Empire. The solid material foundations for supporting such an empire did not exist, for apart from mercury, sulphur, bauxite, zinc and lead, Italy was almost entirely lacking in the minerals, especially coal, petroleum and iron, which are so necessary as the basis of a modern industrial State. Furthermore, she was almost entirely without cotton, wool, vegetable oils, rubber and fertilizers. In spite of these handicaps, she made good use of her hydro-electric power, and developed her industries and agriculture as far as possible.

Attempts were made by Britain and France, in adjusting the frontiers of Libya and Jubaland, to offset Italian disappointments, but these failed. Bent upon expansion, Italy rapidly conquered Abyssinia in 1935-36. Later, in April, 1939, taking a leaf out of Hitler's book, she seized Albania. (See page 80.)

The boastfully proclaimed Italian East African Empire proved of short-lived duration after Italy entered the war. (See page 109.)

MAP 24. BALKAN STATES UP TO THE PEACE TREATIES OF 1919-1923.

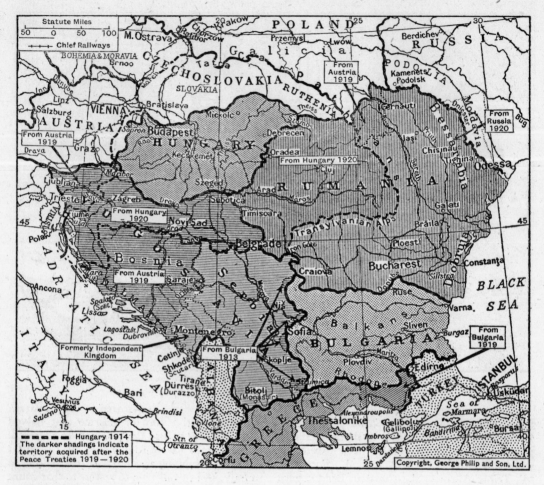

The Balkan States occupy South-East Europe and include Rumania, Yugoslavia, Bulgaria, Albania, Greece and Turkey-in-Europe. Strictly speaking, Hungary belongs to Central Europe ; but, since it occupies a position in the Middle Danube Plain and also on account of its traditions, the fate of Hungary is bound up with the fate of the Balkan States.

After the 1914-18 War the territory of the former Austro-Hungarian Empire broke into fragments. In its defeat the former subject peoples saw their opportunity to express their nationalism and their independence. The States which fought on the side of the Allies, namely, Rumania and Serbia, sought occasion to increase their territory by adding to it the lands occupied by their kinsmen in the now defunct empire. On the other hand, Bulgaria and Hungary, defeated States, lost territories by the Peace Treaties, and felt grievances against their neighbours which prevented them from co-operating in any schemes designed to give some degree of unity to the Balkans. The boundary fixed between Greece and European Turkey by the Treaty of Sèvres proved unacceptable. It was readjusted by the Treaty of Lausanne in favour of Turkey, which thus recovered the Maritza as its western boundary.

The countries of the Little Entente, Czechoslovakia, Rumania and Yugoslavia, were determined to retain their frontiers under the Versailles settlements. In this they were supported by France, which needed their help against a resurgent Germany. On the other hand, Italy, herself dissatisfied, established amicable relations with Hungary, also bent upon revision. Owing to her seizure of Fiume and her intrigues, particularly with the Croats, Italy's relations with Yugoslavia were never very cordial.

The poverty of the large peasant population made the Balkan States dependent upon industrial countries for manufactured goods. Both Germany and Italy strove to make the Balkans economically dependent upon themselves.

MAP 25. LINGUAL DIVISIONS OF THE BALKANS.

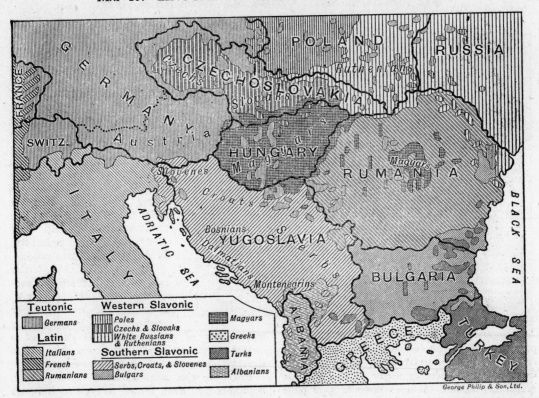

George Philip & Son, Ltd.

In spite of its small scale and generalization the map shows that the peoples of the Balkans are greatly intermingled. (See also page 76.) The growth of the spirit of nationalism during the 19th century influenced the manner in which the boundaries laid down in the various Treaties of Versailles were drawn. The principle of self-determination was accepted as governing the selection of the boundaries. The map above shows the boundaries as they were laid down, but it is clear that in all cases this principle was not rigidly followed. For example, numbers of Magyars dwell outside the boundaries of Hungary in Czechoslovakia, Yugoslavia and Rumania, quite apart from the considerable block of Magyars residing in Transylvania.

In all of these Balkan States considerable minority populations are found. In Rumania there were Germans, Magyars, Ruthenians, Russians, Bulgarians and Turks. Altogether, approximately 25% of the population of Rumania consisted of minority peoples. Yugoslavia also has both German and Magyar minorities within its boundaries together with a considerable Albanian minority and Macedonians in the south-east. The Macedonians dwell on the boundaries of Yugoslavia, Greece and Bulgaria, and in many ways have stronger affinities with Bulgaria than with either Greece or Yugoslavia. A revolutionary and terrorist organization working from Bulgarian headquarters has long disturbed the peace of Macedonia, and has at all times made it difficult for Yugoslavia and Bulgaria to maintain amicable relations. Bulgaria's principal minority consists of more than 500,000 Turks. When the Peace Treaty boundaries were laid down there were considerable minorities of Turks in Greece and of Greeks in Turkey, particularly in the neighbourhood of Smyrna and Constantinople. But these two countries were able to arrive at an exchange of populations by friendly arrangements.

In the light of the experience gained in Greece and Turkey it seems that a hope of creating more homogeneous States in the future might be fostered by a friendly exchange of populations. This would need to be carried out under close international supervision to prevent injustices towards individuals, for it is a method that should be operated humanely, and not in the ruthless manner in which the Germans have moved peoples from occupied countries like pawns on a chessboard.

In all these Balkan countries Minority Treaties were arranged, which were to operate under the supervision of the League of Nations. The treaties were designed to secure to the minorities the free exercise of their own tongue and religion, and the free development of their own traditions and culture.

Map 26. HUNGARY: GAINS SINCE MUNICH, 1938.
RUMANIA: LOSSES IN THE WAR.

Dacia, the cradle of their nation. Except for a large block of Szeklers, akin to the Magyars, the majority of the inhabitants were Rumanians, but a fringe of Magyar-speaking peoples had been included within Rumania after the Peace Treaties, largely for economic reasons. The cities occupied by these peoples depended to a considerable degree for their existence upon the valleys of the Transylvanian upland and their Rumanian peasantry. By the Vienna "Arbitration" of August 30th, 1940, Hitler awarded Northern Transylvania to Hungary. Although the new frontier satisfied to some extent the major part of the Magyar aspirations, it is obvious that a careful eye was cast upon strategic considerations when drawing it.

Prior to the settlement in Transylvania, Rumania had been forced to cede to Bulgaria the Southern Dobruja, largely occupied by Bulgarians. This settlement disposed of a long-standing issue between Rumania and Bulgaria, since the former had succeeded in acquiring the territory in question after the defeat of Bulgaria in the Second Balkan War in 1913.

With the collapse of Yugoslavia, Hungary secured further gains. She annexed—with Germany's consent—a strip of territory between the Danube and the Tiza. In addition, she was successful in obtaining a smaller strip in the north-east of Yugoslavia, where Magyars form a minority of the population.

Hungary's foreign policy throughout the period between the two wars was directed to revision of her boundaries, in order to bring within her frontiers as many of the Magyar minorities outside them as possible (see page 93). In consequence she gravitated towards Germany in her foreign policy. This alignment was reinforced by the commercial ties between the two countries, which were rapidly strengthened after the Nazis came to power.

After the Munich Conference she put forward claims of her own against Czechoslovakia, and was successful in obtaining a strip of Magyar-speaking territory along her northern frontier. Later, when Germany occupied Prague, Hungary secured Ruthenia, not inhabited by Magyars (see page 93).

After Germany had virtually occupied Rumania and the latter had, after remonstrance, been forced to cede Bessarabia and Northern Bukovina to Soviet Russia, Hungary thought the time opportune to advance her claims against Rumania in regard to Transylvania, formerly part of the old Magyar Kingdom. It had close ties with the Magyars, and members of the Magyar aristocracy had large landed estates there. But Transylvania was regarded affectionately by the Rumanians, since they looked upon it as the old Roman province of

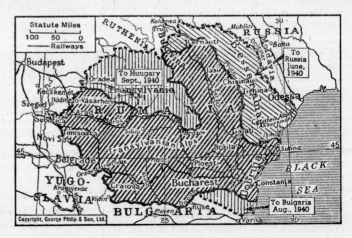

MAP 27. YUGOSLAVIA: LOSSES IN THE WAR.
BULGARIA: GAINS FROM THE WAR.

Boundary of Yugoslavia Sept. 1939
Territory annexed from Yugoslavia
Nominally "Independent" States under Axis Military Occupation
Areas occupied by Italy
Areas occupied by Bulgaria

Copyright, George Philip & Son, Ltd.

Apart from difficulties caused by various minorities within the new State of Yugoslavia (see pages 92, 93), even the South Slavs, the Serbs, Croats and Slovenes found it hard to adjust themselves to their union. This is not surprising, for their past traditions, history, culture and religions were entirely different.

The Croats and Slovenes had for long been under the Austro-Hungarian Monarchy. The Serbs themselves were divided, some of them having struggled to independence against the Ottoman Empire, while others had exchanged subservience to the Ottoman Empire for dependence upon the Austro-Hungarian Empire. Religious differences also tended to keep these peoples apart. Most of the Serbs belonged to the Greek Orthodox Church, although many, particularly in Bosnia and Hercegovina, had become Moslems. The Slovenes and Croats were members of the Roman Catholic Church.

The Serbs, who were in the ascendency, wanted to create a strong centralized State. This desire was not echoed by the Croats or the Slovenes, who, while not wishing to break away from Yugoslavia, preferred a federal union with autonomy for themselves. Eventually, in 1938, the Croats were successful in obtaining an autonomous State.

German propaganda took every opportunity of widening the differences existing among the Yugoslavs, and the division of the country after its overthrow shows clearly the German desire to create ruptures so wide that mutual suspicions on the part of the various peoples would militate against recreating the union after the war. The whole country is under German and Italian military occupation, though a strip of the hinterland behind the Adriatic Coast has been left entirely in Italian occupation.

Almost half the area of the so-called independent Serbia in the south has been occupied by Bulgarian troops, while virtually the whole of Serb Macedonia and the Vardar province has been annexed by Bulgaria. From Greece, she has annexed Eastern Macedonia and Western Thrace, except for a narrow strip along the boundary of Turkey, which has been left in Greek occupation. The whole country of Greece is occupied by German and Italian troops, but the port of Salonika (Thessalonike) is entirely in German hands.

A strip of territory east of the Albanian boundary has been incorporated in Albania.

Bulgaria Sept. 1939
Territories Annexed

Copyright, George Philip & Son, Ltd.

MAP 28. RUSSIAN GAINS IN THE WEST.

Statute Miles
50   0   50   100

Copyright, George Philip & Son, Ltd.

Western Boundary of Russian Empire, 1914.

Western Boundary of Soviet Russia August, 1939.

ence, though she did not accept the transfer of Bessarabia. When Germany re-armed, resuming her place as a Great Power, and revealing her intention of proceeding to enlarge her self-styled " Lebensraum " by aggression, the Soviet Union felt that something more than small independent States was necessary as a barrier in the West. But the centuries-old antipathy between the Poles and the Russians, based upon differences of culture and religion, could not be overcome.

After the German invasion and overthrow of Poland, Russia seized Eastern Poland for herself. Almost immediately approaches were made to Finland to cede territory in the neighbourhood of Viipuri to Russia and to grant facilities for the establishment of a naval base at Hangö. These were rejected, and a short war ensued, lasting from December, 1939, to March, 1940. Military exhaustion compelled the Finns to accept the Soviet demands, to cede territory along the Karelian Isthmus and also further north, and to agree to the establishment of a Soviet naval base at the entrance to the Gulf of Finland.

The German overthrow of France and Western Europe made it obvious to the Soviet Union that Hitler would turn East, in spite of the treaty between the two countries negotiated in August, 1939. Not being ready to attack Russia in 1940, Hitler had to consent to Russian annexations of Estonia, Latvia and Lithuania. He arranged for the German Balts to emigrate from these countries and to be resettled in Germany. In June, 1940, when it was obvious that Germany was strengthening her position in Rumania to such an extent that Rumania would be unlikely to remain independent, Russia had forced the latter to cede Bessarabia and Northern Bukovina.

In regaining this wide strip of territory in the west, Russia had almost succeeded in re-establishing her western boundary of 1914. Strategically she had prepared a cushion to take the first impact of any German attack upon Russia. This came in June, 1941, and Finland joined Germany to regain her lost territories.

One of the problems for the treaty-makers will be to decide the future of these regions. As the tendency to-day seems to be clearly in the direction of a few large World States, it is difficult to foresee the small Baltic States regaining their independence. Moreover, since the area of Poland, seized by Russia, was mainly occupied by White Russians and Ukrainians it is perhaps not unlikely that most of the area may belong to the Soviet Union.

After the Russian Revolution Germany occupied the Baltic States and White Russia ; and she took over most of the Ukraine after the Treaty of Brest-Litovsk, March, 1918. Though this treaty was annulled by the Peace Conference, the desire of many of the peoples in the German-occupied area for independence gained recognition. In consequence three Baltic States—Estonia, Latvia and Lithuania— were created. Poland became independent, and later seized a strip of territory in the east from Russia (see page 89), while Rumania seized Bessarabia. The Allied Powers felt that a cordon of small independent States would be a useful barrier in preventing the spread of Communism, then militantly expansionist, further westwards from Russia.

During the years following the Peace Treaties, Soviet Russia was prepared to be on friendly terms with these small independent States, and fully recognized their independ-

MAP 29. UNION OF SOVIET SOCIALIST REPUBLICS.

The Russian Empire never took full advantage of the rich resources, agricultural and industrial, which it possessed. Though shorn of some territory, the Union of Soviet Socialist Republics resolved to discover the full extent of its resources and to exploit them as rapidly as possible. Great strides in modernization, both of agriculture and industry, have brought the country at a bound, as it were, from the backwardness of the eighteenth century to the progress and advancement of the twentieth.

It was realized by Lenin and other leaders that this was necessary, both in the interests of the people as a whole and also to ensure the strength of the State and the stability of the new Socialist society. Agriculture has been mechanized to a very large extent. Large-scale agriculture, including both State and collective farms, has superseded the small peasant farms, which replaced the estates of the former landowners after the Revolution. The enormous extent of this change can be measured by the statement that nearly nineteen million peasant households were combined to form 250,000 collective farms.

Communications by rail, road, river, canal, sea and air have all been improved. Many new projects have been developed and the newer industrial areas linked to older centres. Large-scale electrification, to provide power for the development of both heavy and light industry, has been instituted. Education,

DISTRIBUTION OF INDUSTRIAL STRENGTH
(Percentage of total Production)

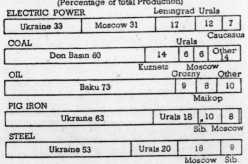

ELECTRIC POWER			Leningrad	Urals	
Ukraine 33	Moscow 31		17	12	7
					Caucasus
COAL				Urals	
Don Basin 60			14	6	6	Other 14
		Kuznetz	Moscow Grozny		
OIL					Other
Baku 73			9	8	10
			Maikop		
PIG IRON					
Ukraine 63			Urals 18	10	8
			Sib. Moscow		
STEEL					
Ukraine 53			Urals 20	18	9
			Moscow	Sib.	

particularly technical education, has been intensified in order to change an illiterate peasantry into highly trained and efficient technical workers.

In developing the country the Soviet Union has paid particular attention to the resources of Siberia, and to advancing industry in formerly backward areas, where both the necessary raw materials and power were to be found. New industrial centres in the Urals and in the Kuznetsk Basin have grown up to supplement those in the Leningrad, Moscow and Ukraine industrial districts. The foresight shown in this development, in spite of some mistakes and harshness in carrying it through, has been abundantly justified by the magnificent resistance of the Russian armies and people to the German onslaught. Moreover, this policy is creating a much better balanced economy throughout the vast territory of the Union and has been greatly to the advantage of agriculture and industry.

MAP 30. UNION OF SOVIET SOCIALIST REPUBLICS : NATIONALITIES.

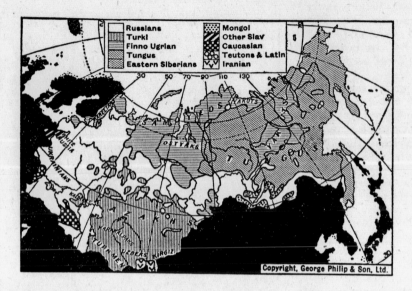

The above map, though much simplified, shows that there are many nationalities within the Union of Soviet Socialist Republics. The majority of the people are undoubtedly Great Russians, especially in European Russia and in a band of settlement stretching right across to the Pacific coast. In European Russia both the Ukrainians and the White Russians, speaking languages akin to Great Russian, form substantial minorities. Of the two the Ukrainians, numbering more than 30,000,000, have a stronger individuality, based upon a different culture and religion, and upon dreams of independence.

Each of the small Baltic States has its own language. In the Caucasus there is a mixture of different peoples, each with its own language, culture and tradition. East of the Caspian, in Turkistan and in Siberia, dwell many nationalities, mostly branches of the great and widely dispersed race of Mongolic peoples. Throughout the Soviet Union there are many Jews, who were persecuted under the Empire and debarred from agriculture. A Jewish State has been established at Birobijan in the Far East.

Under the Russian Empire the Russians were the dominant people, and the development of other nationalities was hindered and actively discouraged. A reversal of this policy has taken place under the Soviet Union. Schools have been introduced throughout the country, where the different peoples must be taught in their own languages, and active steps have been instituted to encourage the development of the culture of all these peoples—their literature, drama, and music.

Politically, these nationalities have been organized into States with varying degrees of autonomy. Large minority populations, such as the Ukrainians and White Russians, belong to constituent Republics of the Soviet Union. Less numerous nationalities have been given a degree of autonomy either as Autonomous Soviet Socialist Republics or merely as Autonomous Regions. Both in their States and in their local government institutions and work, the nationalities within the Soviet Union have been taught to feel that the Union is their State in which they have an equal part to play with the Russians themselves. It is worth noting that Stalin is a Georgian and not a Russian.

Finally, the interests of the nationalities are further safeguarded under the 1936 Constitution by the creation of a second chamber, a Soviet of Nationalities. In this chamber equal representation for the various nationalities is the rule, irrespective of the total number of each nationality. Thus the Russian Soviet Federal Socialist Republic, the largest of the constituent republics, has no more representatives than one of the smaller constituent republics, such as Georgia. Union republics send 25 representatives, autonomous republics 11, autonomous regions 5 and national areas a single representative.

The Soviet of Nationalities and the Soviet of the Union, the first chamber, together form the Supreme Soviet of the Union, which is the highest organ of government. The first chamber is elected on a population basis, one deputy representing an electorate of 300,000 citizens, who have attained the age of 18.

MAP 31. NEAR AND MIDDLE EAST.

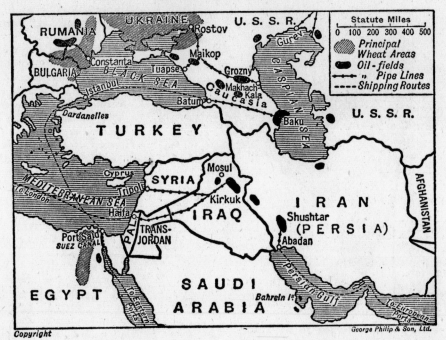

The Near and Middle East have throughout history formed one of the key regions of the world. They have always been a meeting place for commerce, and the control of the Dardanelles and of Suez has determined history. In modern times the decline of the Ottoman Empire brought about a great increase in the interest of the Great Powers—Britain, Russia, France and Germany, in this part of the world.

Britain was fearful for the safety of the Suez Canal and her Indian Empire (see page 109). Russia wanted control of the Dardanelles for entry to the Mediterranean. France has been interested from the time of Napoleon, who said: " Really to ruin England we must make ourselves masters of Egypt." Germany pursued her policy of " Drang nach Osten." In 1916 a German publicist wrote, " The War comes from the East; the War is waged for the East; the War will be decided in the East." If this was true then, it is likely to be as true to-day. Next to Britain, this region is of vital interest to the United Nations, both for strategic reasons and for its oil resources.

Another factor of importance is that Mohammedanism is the religion of the inhabitants of the region. Apart from Turks and Persians, the inhabitants of Syria, Iraq, Palestine, Transjordan, Egypt and Saudi Arabia are largely Arab. During the present century, Arab Nationalism has developed considerably, and use was made of it by Britain in bringing about the collapse of the Ottoman

Empire in the 1914-1918 War. As a result a number of Arab States (excepting Arabia itself) were created, at first as mandated territories to Britain and France. It was understood that as soon as possible these States should become entirely independent. Iraq received her independence in 1922, which was cemented by a treaty with Britain in 1930, giving her the right to retain certain troops and aerodromes there. Syria was mandated to France, but her independence was later recognized.

Palestine and Transjordan still remain mandated territories. Because of the establishment of the Jewish National Home in Palestine and the enormous migration of Jews which has taken place between the two wars, and because of the fear of the Arabs that they would be swamped, great difficulty has been experienced by Britain in trying to arrive at a settlement of this problem which will secure justice for the competing claims of both Arabs and Jews.

British military action prevented these countries from becoming Axis satellites, and joint British and Russian co-operation in occupying Persia stopped similar German threats to Allied security. This occupation secured the backdoor of Turkey. It prevented her from being open to a threat from Germany from both sides, and enabled British and American supplies through the Persian Gulf to reach the Middle East front and Russia.

MAP 32. INDIA : POPULATION.

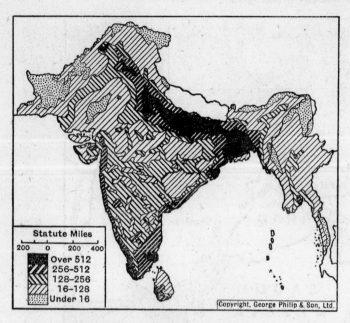

Statute Miles

200   0   200   400

Over 512
256–512
128–256
16–128
Under 16

Copyright, George Philip & Son, Ltd.

powerful impetus to industrial expansion, particularly iron and steel.

Since British rule was established, the country has had the advantage of secure d e f e n c e f r o m external enemies both by sea and land. Since the Indian Mutiny it has also enjoyed a long period of internal peace and considerable moderation of the strife of creeds and races, though riots occur from time to time. Moreover, justice is a d m i n i s t e r e d equitably according to a body of law. This system replaces the arbitrary decisions of the despots of earlier days. Western education has been introduced, but its effect has not really spread beyond the more fortunate, since 90% of the total population still remain illiterate. English has become the common medium of communication among the educated classes. Among material benefits have been the introduction of an efficient system of railway communication—a considerable extent being State-owned, and also the development of vast irrigation projects, which has done much to reduce the periodic famines previously experienced in India.

While accepting the material benefits of western civilization, there has been a general movement towards nationalism. This has taken the form of asserting the supremacy of Indian civilization and Indian qualities of thought over western civilization. Nationalists have demanded Dominion status and, in some quarters, actual independence. As the result of the Cripps Mission, both of these have been promised by the British Government after the war.

India is frequently referred to as a sub-continent and is in fact as large as Europe if Russia is excluded. It embraces the massive mountain ranges of the north-west and north-east, the Indo-Gangetic plain and the peninsula of the Deccan plateau. The critical factor in its climate is the coming of the south-west monsoon and the amount of rainfall it brings. In some regions it is especially liable to variation—this has sometimes brought famine to millions. This danger has been met by irrigation by tanks and in modern times by vast works supplying life-giving water through canals, thousands of miles in total length, to areas covering many thousands of square miles.

India's population of nearly 400,000,000 is about one-sixth of that of the whole world and about three-quarters of that of the British Empire. More than two-thirds of the population are employed in agriculture, either as ryots cultivating their own land, or as tenants cultivating the land of zamindars or large proprietors, but the standard of life generally is very low. Taxation is largely based on land revenue. In recent years there has, been an improvement in the standard of agriculture, particularly in regard to better strains of crops and the breeding of cattle.

Domestic industry, which was highly developed in India, has suffered from the competition of cheaper imported goods and from the introduction of western factory methods. Especially in textiles the home-spun product has not been able to compete with the factory product. The war, however, has given a

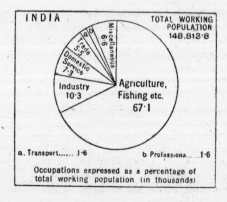

INDIA

TOTAL WORKING POPULATION 148.813·8

Miscellaneous 6·6
Trade 5·3
Domestic Service 7·3
Industry 10·3

Agriculture, Fishing etc. 67·1

a. Transport...... 1·6   b Professions......1·6

Occupations expressed as a percentage of total working population (in thousands)

MAP 33. INDIA : RELIGIONS AND GOVERNMENT.

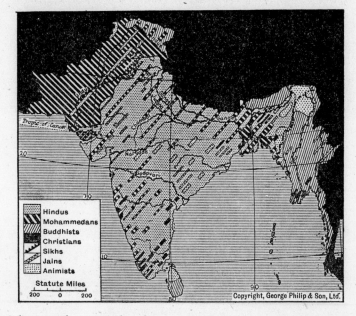

Hindus
Mohammedans
Buddhists
Christians
Sikhs
Jains
Animists

Statute Miles
200   0   200

Copyright, George Philip & Son, Ltd.

While British rule has steadily worked towards an ever greater participation of Indians in the government of the country, differences of race, language and creed have made the realization of democracy more than usually difficult. More than twice as many different languages are spoken than in Europe; many having different alphabets.

Difference of religion has exercised a more profound influence upon the development of India than have differences of race and language. The two main religions are Hinduism and Mohammedanism. Hinduism is both a religion and a social system, since all Hindus are born into one of more than 200 different castes, of high and low grade. Outside the castes are 50,000,000 outcasts or untouchables—more than the total population of the British Isles. While many Hindus, led by Gandhi and others, are desirous of improving their lot, their representatives feel that their interests must be safeguarded if British rule gives place to Indian rule. Hindus venerate the family and the village rather than the individual.

On the other hand, Mohammedanism attaches far more importance to the individual dignity of man. For many centuries Mohammedan rulers have governed Hindu subjects, and the rivalries between the two religions have frequently led to disorder. The Mohammedans represent about 80,000,000 as compared with the 240,000,000 of Hindus. If Indian government were established Mohammedans fear Hindu domination. In consequence the Moslem League has advanced a demand for Pakistan, which is, that the regions of India where the Moslems are in the majority, especially the Punjab, should be allowed to become independent.

Other religions represent but 6% of the population, but since this 6% is approximately 25,000,000 people the importance of safeguarding their minority interest can be well understood.

An attempt at a solution of the problem presented by Indian complexities resulted in the passing of the India Act of 1935, which looked forward to the establishment of the federation of the Provinces and States into a single union, to the development of Indian authority at the centre, and also of local autonomous government.

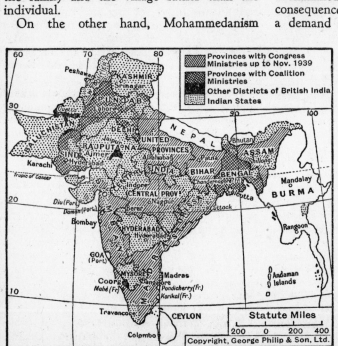

Provinces with Congress Ministries up to Nov. 1939
Provinces with Coalition Ministries
Other Districts of British India
Indian States

Statute Miles
200   0   200   400
Copyright, George Philip & Son, Ltd.

MAP 34.　EAST INDIES : ECONOMIC.

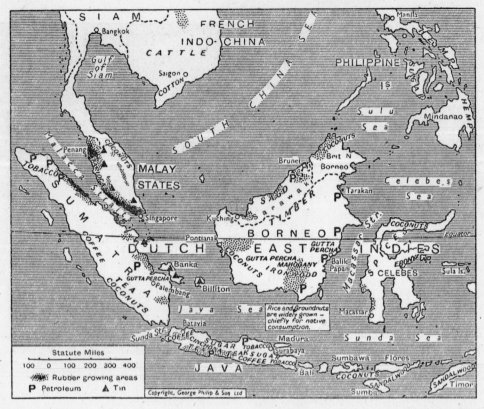

Broadly speaking, the East Indies consist of Burma, Thailand (or Siam), French Indo-China, Malaya, Netherlands Indies, and the Philippine Islands. Of these only Thailand (or Siam) is independent, but, even so, it has not been free from the influence of the Great Powers.

Nominally, the Commonwealth of the Philippines is also independent, though complete independence would not normally have been reached, under the Tydings-McDuffie Act, until 1946. Even then the United States would retain an interest in certain places, such as the naval base at Manila, and would be strongly interested economically. All other areas are colonies of European Powers and are among the richest, economically, since in Malaya and the Netherlands Indies are produced the larger part of the world's supplies of both rubber and tin. The Netherlands Indies is also important for oil, tea, sugar, copra and quinine, the exports of the latter product going almost entirely to the United States.

Burma is important for oil and teak, and all the Indies are important for their rice. Burma, Siam, and French Indo-China in particular, have an export for surplus, especially useful to countries such as China and Japan.

Speaking in April, 1940, Mr. Cordell Hull, the American Secretary of State, said that " Intervention in the domestic affairs of the Netherlands Indies, or any alteration in their *status quo* by other than peaceful processes would be prejudicial to the cause of stability, peace and security, not only in the region of the Netherlands Indies, but in the entire Pacific area."

What was said of the Netherlands Indies applies with equal force to the remaining countries of the East Indies, so that if Japanese occupation became permanent the balance of power in the Far East and the Pacific would be completely changed. (See page 105.)

Even the temporary occupation of the Japanese cannot be without permanent effect. Unquestionably within recent years the native peoples dwelling in these countries have felt a quickening of nationalist feeling. That the white man, hitherto regarded as unassailable, should have been driven, even temporarily, from these countries will permanently disturb the prestige he had hitherto enjoyed. A much greater share in the government of these regions will have to be given to the natives, and the gradual readjustment of relations between the Powers and the native inhabitants will require most careful handling.

MAP 35. CHINA : ECONOMIC.

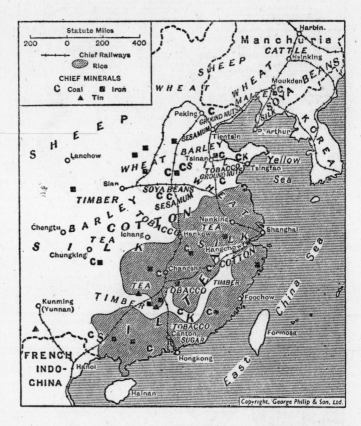

Chinese civilization rests upon the family (including the dead as well as the living) and upon the village rather than upon a political society. As Professor Tawney has written, " Even to-day many Chinese think in centuries, where the West thinks in decades."

But while the family was the basis of the social system there still remained a general division into classes, consisting of nobility and bureaucracy, artisans and craftsmen, merchants and farmers, with soldiers as the lowest grade of all. The impact of the West burst very strongly upon China in the 19th century, when Western Powers — Britain, France, Germany, Russia, and the United States —sought trading advantages for themselves. They succeeded in obtaining spheres of influence, trading rights, and rights of extra-territoriality, that is, the right of trying offences in their own courts instead of in Chinese courts, and other privileges. In the closing years of the 19th century Japan also joined the Western Powers in exploiting the weaknesses of Chinese government.

A revolutionary movement, led by Dr. Sun Yat Sen, overthrew the Manchu dynasty in 1911, but resulted in division and anarchy for decades. This division has been less marked since the Japanese attacks upon China in 1931 and later in 1937. These have brought about a tremendous growth in the desire for political unity among the Chinese. The Three Principles of Dr. Sun Yat Sen, adopted by the Kuomintang in 1924, are informing the whole of the revolutionary movement in China.

These are (1) nationalism : the growth of a strong Chinese patriotism and expulsion of the foreign political interest ; (2) democracy : based on the direct participation and control of the government by the people ; (3) livelihood : that is, the improvement of working conditions for everyone with the guarantee of food, clothing, dwelling and transport.

The abandonment of extra-territoriality has resulted from the Treaties with Great Britain and the United States signed in January, 1943. The revolutionary movement in the last few years has brought about a real Chinese renaissance. Vast schemes for the improvement of education and the abolition of illiteracy have been initiated and are making steady progress so that the Chinese peasant and artisan will be able to serve the nation.

The rapid growth of Chinese industrial co-operatives has had a marked effect upon the development of industrialization and has exercised a predominating influence in bringing relief to the 60,000,000 refugees who have fled from territory in Japanese occupation. Furthermore, the emancipation of women is making vast strides under the leadership of Madame Chiang Kai-Shek and other modern women leaders.

The production of cotton and silk is extensive and is the basis of a prosperous and growing textile industry. Large resources of coal, iron and other metals hold rich promise of a great industrial future for China. There exist also a ready-made market and an enormous labour force in its industrious population of 400,000,000. But communications must be greatly expanded, and political stability established, before China realizes her full potentialities.

Map 36. GROWTH OF THE JAPANESE EMPIRE.

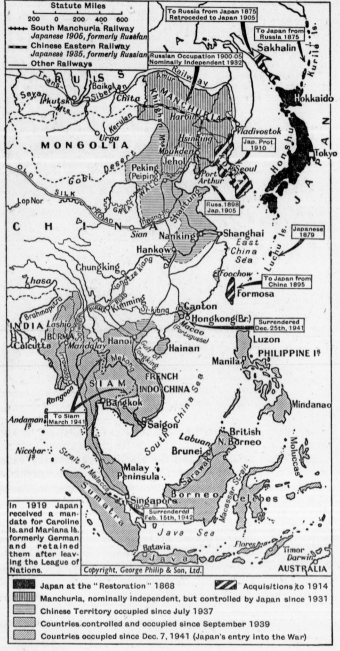

Statute Miles

200   0   200   400   600

++++ South Manchuria Railway
        Japanese 1905, formerly Russian
▬▬▬ Chinese Eastern Railway
        Japanese 1935, formerly Russian
▬▬▬ Other Railways

To Russia from Japan 1875
Retroceded to Japan 1905

To Japan from Russia 1875

Sakhalin

Russian Occupation 1900-05
Nominally Independent 1932

In 1919 Japan received a mandate for Caroline Is. and Mariana Is. formerly German and retained them after leaving the League of Nations.

Copyright, George Philip & Son, Ltd.

■ Japan at the "Restoration" 1868   ▨ Acquisitions to 1914
▥ Manchuria, nominally independent, but controlled by Japan since 1931
▤ Chinese Territory occupied since July 1937
▦ Countries controlled and occupied since September 1939
▧ Countries occupied since Dec. 7, 1941 (Japan's entry into the War)

tries, but engineering has been stimulated owing to the desire to rank as the greatest military Power in the Far East. Japan is a small country, and only one-fifth of her area is cultivable, so that pressure of population has tended towards a very low living standard, even though industrialization has eased the burden.

Her determination to dominate China and Eastern Asia is of fairly long standing. These aims, stated most clearly in the Tanaka Memorial of 1927, have been steadily pursued, especially in China, since the first Sino-Japanese War of 1894-5. The disruption of China and the pre-occupation of the Great Powers in the World War led Japan to present the Twenty-One Demands upon the China of 1915. Only with reluctance was she induced to abandon most of these after the war ended, and to withdraw from Shantung.

Within recent years the same policy of domination has been pursued. Manchuria was occupied in 1931, when other Great Powers were considering measures to meet the economic depression of that year. In 1932 a puppet State, called Manchukuo by Japan, was created. What Japan describes as " The China Incident " began in July, 1937, and has continued ever since with the attempt to occupy the whole of China. Only after the unprovoked attack of the Japanese upon Pearl Harbor on December 7th, 1941, did China find allies in the United States and Britain.

The growth of modern Japan dates from the Restoration of 1868, which resulted in the abolition of the feudal system. Since that date the population has more than doubled. Owing to the adoption by the Japanese of intensive westernization, particularly in regard to commercial life, there have grown up considerable industries, a large merchant marine and also a large navy. Overseas markets have been rapidly developed. The textile industry has been the most important of the indus-

The Japanese desire for domination is based on a spiritual feeling that destiny calls them to fulfil a high purpose of leading firstly in the Far East and then, indeed, throughout the world. This belief is reinforced by a desire for a huge closed market in the Far East and Southern Pacific as an outlet for her industrial products, and as a source of the raw materials necessary to a modern industrial State, in many of which she is herself deficient.

MAP 37. PACIFIC OCEAN.

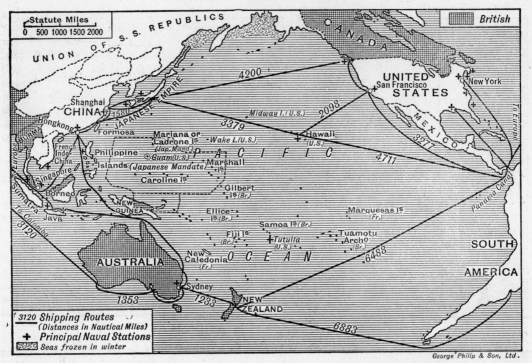

George Philip & Son, Ltd.

The Pacific Ocean is greater in area than the whole of the land masses of the world put together. This vast extent, and the enormous distances between ports on the western and eastern shores of the Pacific, or between the north and south, govern the maintenance of naval power upon its broad waters. That naval power could only be exercised by Britain and the United States through the acquisition of bases, especially in the central and western Pacific, where Japan was strongest through the advantage of being based on the homeland. The interests of European Powers, America and Japan, both in China and the countries of South-East Asia, have made them tremendously concerned about the balance of power in the Pacific. Japan constantly pushed southwards into the Pacific to acquire new sea and air bases.

Quite apart from her interests in maintaining the open-door policy in China, the United States must always be Pacific-minded owing to her possession of a Pacific coast. After the Spanish-American War of 1898 she acquired Hawaii and established in Pearl Harbor a first-class naval base. Later she acquired the Panama Canal Zone and constructed the Panama Canal, mainly to provide a short route to the Pacific for her Atlantic-based fleet. American defence primarily depends upon the triangle Pearl Harbor-Puget Sound-Panama.

The third great Power interested in the Pacific is Britain, whose interests lie mainly in the South-West and South Pacific, Malaya, Australia, New Zealand, and various Pacific islands. Between the two World Wars Britain established a first-class sea and air base at Singapore, which was conquered from the land by the Japanese.

The interests of Britain, America, and Japan meet and clash in the vicinity of the Philippines. It is interesting to consider the Four Power Naval Treaty of Washington in 1922, more especially the clause under which Britain and America agreed not to strengthen fortifications in the Pacific, except for certain specified zones.

As Professor Toynbee has observed, " the result was to make the defensive position of Japan absolutely impregnable by sea, and thus not only to safeguard herself against any attack or invasion, but to assure one of the chief objects of her policy—which was the uninterrupted security of her communications in wartime with her continental possessions and with China. On the other hand, Hongkong and the Philippines were left at the Japanese navy's mercy, so that in a war with the British Commonwealth or the United States Japan was now certain to gain the valuable advantage of the first success." Written in 1923, this was a striking forecast of the outcome of events at the close of 1941 and the beginning of 1942.

MAP 38. AUSTRALIA : ECONOMIC.

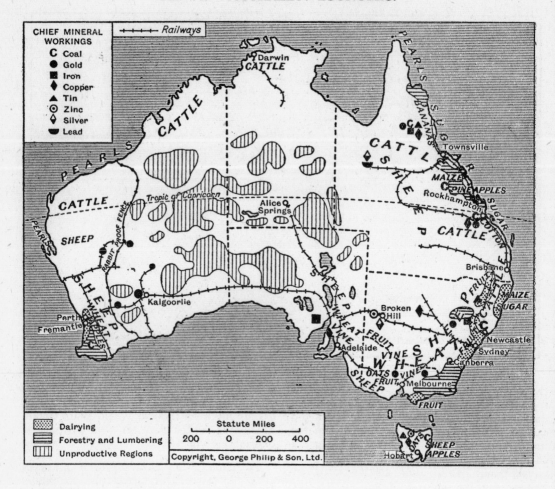

Australia is situated rather on the edge of the habitable world, so that its contacts with Britain and Western Europe and with the United States are distant. The Commonwealth was proclaimed in 1901, when the six States formed a Federation.

Australia depends very largely upon its agricultural and pastoral industries, being the largest producer of wool in the world, exporting considerable quantities of wool and pastoral products. Mining also is important, particularly for coal, gold, lead, zinc, silver, copper and tin. Since the 1914-1918 War, Australian manufacturing capacity has grown considerably, particularly in the development of iron and steel manufactures. Many of these have expanded behind a strong tariff fence. During the war Australia has been in a much stronger position to undertake the manufacture of many kinds of armaments and aircraft. The most densely inhabited portions of the continent are the Eastern and South-Eastern regions extending from Rockhampton to Adelaide, and the S.W. corner in the neighbourhood of Perth and Coolgardie. There is a tropical region in the north, extending from Broome to Rockhampton where white settlement is much more difficult and uncomfortable on account of the hot, muggy climate. In this region 90% of the settlement clings to the coastal margins of Northern Queensland. Many of the aborigines live in this area, approximately 50% being nomadic.

There remain the central desert areas, mainly with a rainfall of less than ten inches in the year, where the population is extremely scanty. The future of both this and the tropical region presents a serious problem to the Australians, particularly that of tropical Australia, since although the region is not specially suited to the white man, the Australians strongly desire to preserve their policy of White Australia. Another problem requiring solution is the excessive urbanizing of the population, since almost 50% dwell in the six capital cities.

MAP 39. NEW ZEALAND : ECONOMIC.

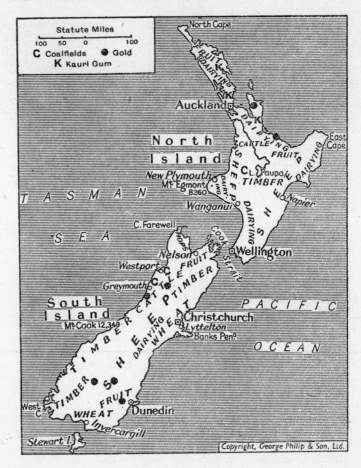

New Zealand is even more remote and isolated from the world than Australia, from which it is more than 1,000 miles distant. It lies at the antipodes of Southern Spain, and, like the British Isles, consists of two large islands, North and South Island, and several small islands. The opening of the Panama Canal brought it nearer to Britain. Under the Treaty of Versailles, 1919, the former German territory of Samoa became a mandated territory under New Zealand. In its immediate vicinity is the American naval base in the Samoan islands.

Discovered in 1642 by the Dutchman, Tasman, North Island was first settled by British missionaries in 1814. New Zealand was annexed to Britain in 1840, and the colony became a dominion in 1907.

The islands are rugged and mountainous. The mountains of North Island are volcanic and possess wonderful hot springs. Those of South Island bear the name of Southern Alps, owing to their resemblance to the snow-capped peaks of Switzerland.

Like Australia, New Zealand is mainly agricultural and pastoral in character, though it possesses more numerous forests. The pastoral industry and the export of wool, mutton, butter and cheese, have been the mainstay of the country. Its prosperity owes a great deal to the invention of refrigerating machinery, enabling its products to be carried to Britain and other extremities of the world.

Possession of mountains and abundant rainfall has led to intensive development of hydroelectric power. Minerals, particularly coal and gold, have been developed, but are less rich than those of Australia. Kauri gum, the fossilized gum of the giant kauri pine and " New Zealand flax," fruit and wheat, are other valuable products. The developed industries rest to a large extent upon the character of the primary produce of the islands. While, therefore, New Zealand has been able to produce small arms and similar munitions, her industry is insufficiently endowed for the pro-

duction of heavy armaments.

The main population is British in character and intensely British in sentiment, but there is a strong minority of native Maori inhabitants. This race, with a fine physique and mentality, enjoys equal rights and opportunities with the British. They number about 80,000 and, unlike the Australian aborigines, are increasing. They dwell mainly in the North Island. Apart from the Maoris, New Zealand is concerned with the maintenance of a white population by the encouragement of white immigration, especially British, and the exclusion of Asiatics.

New Zealand is interested also in the island of Nauru, a British mandated territory administered by Australia, from which she obtains large quantities of phosphates, valuable as fertilizers for her agriculture. As a Pacific country she shares with Australia a vital interest in British international policy in that ocean, and especially in the Far East. Both countries contributed towards the establishment of the naval base of Singapore.

MAP 40. INDIAN OCEAN.

The Indian Ocean is the vast oceanic connecting link between the Atlantic and the Pacific, stretching from Africa in the west to the East Indies and Western Australia in the east. Open in the south to the waters of the Southern Ocean it is enclosed in the north by the land mass of Asia, with the massive peninsula of India jutting out towards the Equator. Across its broad waters a constant stream of traffic passes from the Far Eastern countries, Australia and New Zealand, and from India, through the Red Sea, towards the Mediterranean and Western Europe. In the south traffic passes from Cape Town to Australia and New Zealand, and between India and the eastern coast of Africa. Communications across this ocean are therefore of vital importance, and they have assumed still greater significance during the course of the war owing to the great difficulties of the Mediterranean route and the consequent need to transport both men and materials round the Cape to the Middle East, India and Australia.

In this ocean the United Nations are concerned to prevent Japanese control from spreading further west than the eastern shores of the Bay of Bengal and eventually to free these shores from that control. Apart from captured Singapore, no first-class British naval base has been established in the Indian Ocean, though a number of good bases exist. In order to safeguard the interests of the United Nations, after the weakness of France in regard to Indo-China, it was necessary to occupy the French naval base of Diego Suarez, and the whole island of Madagascar, in 1942.

On all landward sides of the ocean are found territories of the British Empire. They occupy approximately two-thirds of the land area of the Empire and in them dwell about four-fifths of its population. One important characteristic, which all these countries share in common, is their great dependence for foreign trade upon Britain, in some cases amounting to more than 50%. These facts have a very important bearing on one of the most significant organisations created during the course of the war.

Because of the need to reduce long distance voyages and thus to conserve shipping, an Eastern Group Council was set up at Delhi in October, 1940, after the collapse of France. Representatives from all members of the British Empire east and south of Suez, and including Palestine, were present. The main purpose of this Council was to develop as far as possible the component parts of the Empire into a single economic unit for the production and exchange of war supplies of all kinds, covering munitions, aircraft, shipping, equipment, clothing, oil and food. The intensive development of industrial facilities, particularly in South Africa, India and Australia, has assisted in keeping theatres of war in the Middle East and Australia supplied from their own resources as far as possible, and in consequence has relieved British and American production from supplying what the Group itself could provide.

Until they were overrun by Japan the contribution of British colonies in the Far East was most valuable. Malaya exported rubber and tin. Quite useful also were the rubber and petroleum exported from Brunei, British North Borneo and Sarawak (see also page 102).

To her impressive contribution of steel and manganese India has added the production of armoured cars, field guns and light guns of all kinds, shells and small arms ammunition, and even aeroplanes. Moreover, she has built many small ships. Her exports include jute, cotton, timber, hides, and coal for the Royal Navy. Ceylon exports tea, rubber, copra, coir, coconut oil and graphite. Burma's rice, as well as her petroleum and teak, are most valuable.

East African resources include copper, cobalt and vanadium from Northern Rhodesia. Among agricultural products these countries produce cotton, sisal, flax, oilseeds, tea and coffee, while Mauritius exports sugar. (For South Africa, Australia and New Zealand see pages 112, 106 and 107.)

MAP 41. THE RED SEA GATEWAY in 1939.

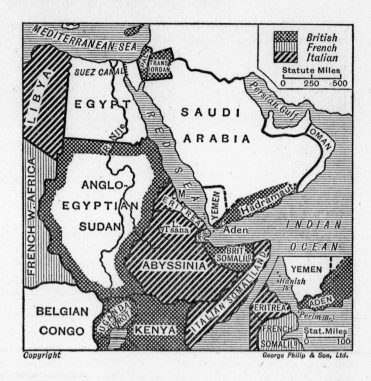

Natural exits from the Indian Ocean in the north-west do not exist, in spite of the narrow arms of the Persian Gulf and the Red Sea, but where nature has failed to provide an exit, one has been constructed by man in the Suez Canal, connecting the Red Sea across the narrow Suez Isthmus with the Mediterranean. This Canal, with which the name of Ferdinand de Lesseps will always be associated, was formally opened in 1869. Britain acquired her stake in it by the purchase of the financial interest of the Khedive of Egypt in 1875.

The narrow neck of land, joining Asia and Africa, has from time immemorial been one of the key points in world history. Its control has been vital, as was recognized by Napoleon (see page 99). In all British negotiations with Egypt after Egyptian independence was recognized in 1922, difficulty in arriving at a settlement turned on certain issues, which Britain felt it was necessary to reserve absolutely. Among these issues was the control of the Suez Canal, essential for the preservation of Empire communications and also for the defence of Egypt itself in the west and of Palestine in the east.

Mussolini's invasion of Abyssinia brought home to the Egyptians the strategic importance of control of the Canal being in friendly hands and also their own inability to defend it in case of necessity. The Anglo-Egyptian Treaty of 1936 provided for Britain maintaining an Air Force and troops in the Canal zone. British Forces were withdrawn from Cairo and were to be withdrawn from Alexandria after a period of eight years. The Egyptians undertook the construction of a number of strategic roads to permit rapid mobilization, when necessary. The treaty has produced friendly understanding and co-operation with Egypt. It has enabled the British to withstand Axis penetration into Egypt itself and also into neighbouring Arabic countries. During the present war the defence of the Suez Canal has been regarded by Britain as second only in importance to defence of Britain herself.

The narrow exit at the southern end of the Red Sea, at the Straits of Bab el Mandeb, is controlled by Britain's possession of the naval station of Aden. Before the war, particularly since the conquest of Abyssinia in 1935-6, the Italians had endeavoured to erect fortified bases of their own to neutralize British power. By International Convention the waters of the Suez Canal are free to all nations both in peace and war. While we respected it during the Italo-Abyssinian War, Italy found, when she joined in the war against Britain, that her sea power was insufficient to enable her to capture either of the exits of the Red Sea. As a result she was deprived of its use, and in the end her East African Empire melted away for lack of reinforcements, both of men and materials. This merely confirmed the sober and reflective judgment of some German experts who, writing in 1938, concluded that, " so long as Italy has no weapon to conquer England's dominating position at the exits of that sea, so long will the existence of the Italian Empire depend on England's love of peace or readiness for war."

Throughout, Britain has been careful to maintain friendly relations with Saudi Arabia and other smaller Arab states established along the eastern shores of the Red Sea. The importance of this cannot be over-emphasized, for German agents, both before and after the war began, have sought in their own interests to enlist Arab nationalism against Britain.

MAP 42.   AFRICA : POPULATION.
AFRICA : POLITICAL DIVISIONS IN 1914.

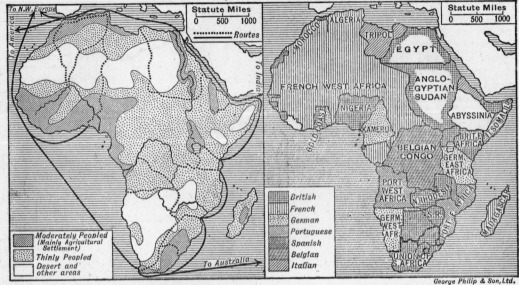

George Philip & Son, Ltd.

The total population of Africa is approximately 150,000,000. Nowhere, except in the narrow Nile Valley and a few isolated areas on the Guinea Coast and South Africa, are there dense populations, and even these are not comparable with areas of dense population elsewhere in the world. The main concentrations of moderate density are to be found in the Guinea Lands, the Great Lakes Region of the African Plateau, the coast belt of Eastern and South Africa, the Plateau of Abyssinia, and along the fringe of the Barbary Coast. The vast desert of the Sahara, virtually as great in extent as Europe itself, and the Kalahari Desert of South Africa, are unpopulated except for isolated nomadic tribes and settlements.

The native peoples of this vast continent may be classified into negroid and non-negroid. Broadly speaking, in the Nile Valley and along the Barbary Coast the inhabitants are of Semitic and Hamitic stock, though much of it is mixed. In a general way the southern edge of the Sahara region marks the northern boundary of negroid Africa.

The backwardness of the peoples of the Dark Continent laid them open to conquest and subjection, once the era of European expansion had begun. Long before this, Arab seamen and traders had trickled through the Red Sea and down the eastern shores of Africa, where they established small communities which still remain. The real scramble for the partition of the whole of Africa commenced in the latter part of the nineteenth century, when European Great Powers

succeeded in partitioning the whole Continent.

As a result of the Great War of 1914-18 the German Colonies were allocated to Britain and France, and a small part to Belgium under the Mandate System. Administration is in the nature of a trusteeship, and trade is open to all members of the League of Nations on equal terms.

The idea of trusteeship has also been generally accepted in the British Colonies; the interests of the native being considered paramount, although practice has not always been as idealistic as theory. The results of European penetration of the continent have been both good and bad. Agriculture, through the introduction of European scientific technique, has greatly benefited and inter-tribal warfare, which had such disastrous effects upon the African population, has disappeared. Communications have also been vastly improved. On the other hand, native society has suffered from the expropriation of its lands by European settlers. The customs of native societies and their tribal organization have been too little studied by administrators. As a result native standards have grown weak without being replaced by western standards.

The whole future of colonies and of the native peoples dwelling in them has been subjected to enlightened criticism within recent years. The feeling has unquestionably grown that native advancement through education, the development of health regulations, and the abandonment of economic exploitation, should be a concern not only of Colonial Powers but also of the whole world.

Map 43. NORTH AFRICA : COMMUNICATIONS.

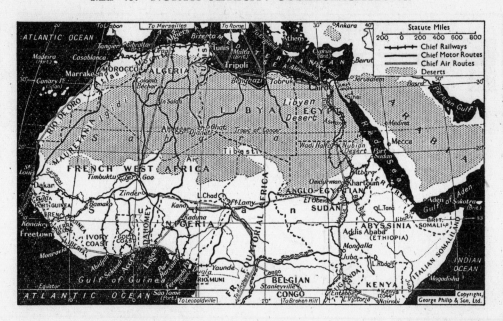

The extent of North Africa, that is, approximately, Africa lying north of the Equator, is considerably greater than the whole of Europe, though its population is not much more than one-tenth of that of Europe. The most striking physical feature is the Sahara Desert, which separates the Mediterranean fringe of the Barbary States from the savanna lands and equatorial forests of Guinea. The greater part of this vast expanse is French territory. Libya is Italian, Egypt and Abyssinia are independent and Anglo-Egyptian Sudan is a condominium.

The climate and vegetation, agricultural and pastoral products of the countries north and south of the Sahara are entirely different in character. In the north they are Mediterranean, and from Algeria, Tunis, and Morocco, France has derived cereals, olive oil, alfa or esparto grass, tobacco and wool, besides valuable minerals such as iron-ore and phosphates. From Guinea both British and French tropical products, such as palm oil, ground nuts, cocoa, bananas, coffee and hardwoods and some cotton are derived, while some gold, manganese, tin and coal are mined.

The main problem for French Africa has been the improvement of communications, since both in the Mediterranean colonies and in the disjointed colonies of French West Africa, railway communications are lateral, with spurs running south and north towards the Sahara. Prior to the outbreak of the war the French had been engaged for many years in the pacification of the savage desert tribes.

Their aim, in the words of Marshal Lyautey, " is a constructive one, bringing order, peace, and progress into what was previously anarchy, disaster, stagnation, and barbarism."

The traditional method of communication across the desert is by caravan. The invention of the internal combustion engine has resulted in quicker communications across the Sahara. Routes have been established to link up Algeria and French Sudan with the easterly route running from Bamako to the Belgian Congo. The project of a Trans-Saharan railway has been discussed for many years and it is said that progress in its construction has been made by the Germans since the overthrow of France. But the occupation of French North and West Africa by the forces of the United Nations has delayed it once more.

Air communication has been established, linking up France and Belgium with Algeria, the Belgian Congo and Madagascar, while a more westerly and more important route hugs the Atlantic coast between Casablanca and Dakar. Dakar's great importance lies in its being the starting point for the shortest route to South America.

The events of the war cannot help but have serious effects upon the influence of France and Italy in their colonies and also upon the aspirations of the native peoples. For some time nationalism among the tribes has been growing in North Africa, but it is doubtful whether the unifying factor of Mohammedanism will be strong enough to counteract separatist tendencies.

MAP 44. UNION OF SOUTH AFRICA.

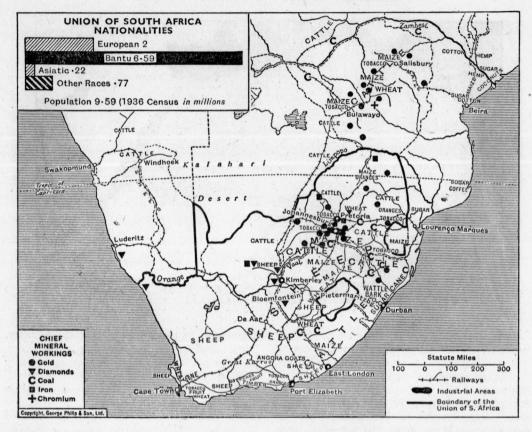

The Union of South Africa came into being in 1910, nearly ten years after the close of the Boer War. The Boer War was the culmination of struggles between the British and Dutch peoples who had earlier settled in this area. The social and cultural background of each of these peoples was very different, and each has shown itself determined to maintain its independence and way of life. The Dutch, or Afrikanders, as they have come to be called, are primarily farmers, but have always been intensely interested in politics. The discovery of gold in the Transvaal was for them of doubtful value. They greatly feared some of its results, especially the influx of new settlers, both British and Jew. While the desire for commercial gain was the strongest influence leading to the development of the gold fields, more far-sighted statesmen realized that such wealth could be used for the wider development of the whole of South Africa.

In contrast to the Afrikanders, many of the British are city dwellers, either in mining towns on the Rand and elsewhere or in the seaports. British preponderance is mainly in the provinces of the Cape of Good Hope and Natal, while Afrikander preponderance is very largely in the provinces of Transvaal and Orange Free State. The difficulties of adjustment between the British and Afrikander are small, as compared with those between black and white.

The white population totals about 2,000,000, whereas there are about 6,500,000 Bantus, 750,000 Cape mixed population and 250,000 Indians in Natal. The difficulties have been aggravated by the more liberal legislation as regards black and mixed population passed in Cape Colony before the Union, as compared with the views of the Afrikanders and the Boer Republics. The aim of the white man has been to preserve his standard of life and to maintain his superiority in spite of his inferior numbers. In consequence the native franchise has been severely restricted, and the area where blacks could own land has been strictly limited. Furthermore, types of jobs that could be undertaken by blacks have been carefully defined, and kept very largely in the category of labouring jobs.

Mining is the chief industry and, because of the nature of the climate pastoral farming is more important than pure agriculture.

MAP 45. CANADA: ECONOMIC.

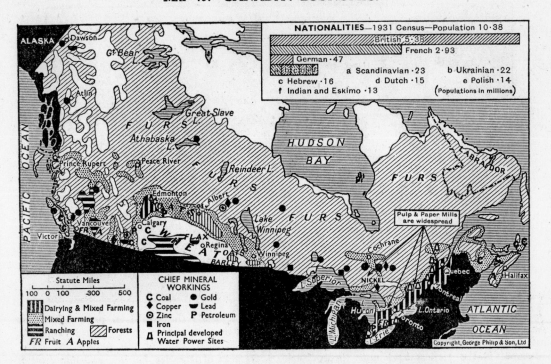

The Dominion of Canada is rather larger than the United States of America, but since it lies in high latitudes much of its territory is largely unproductive. Almost the entire population dwells in a fringe of territory north of the United States border. Geography has therefore led to the Canadian outlook upon life being deeply influenced by the United States of America. In spite of this, the national spirit of Canadians is very strong and firmly attached to the British Commonwealth of Nations. The necessities of defence during the war have led to the establishment of a Joint Defence Board, serving both countries, in August, 1940.

Canada was first settled by the French, who after the Peace of Paris, 1763, became part of the British Empire. These French Canadians dwell mainly in Quebec, but in recent years have spread into other provinces. Their language, culture, and religion have always been guaranteed. As a type they have preserved a remarkable degree of racial continuity, which has been fostered by their hereditary traditions and Catholic education. The most fecund of all Canadian peoples, their proportion to other nationalities in Canada has gradually increased, so that in time there is a possibility that they may outnumber the English Canadians. The persistency of the French Canadians in preserving their type has at times led to difficulties between the two principal nationalities in Canada, as, for example, their different attitude towards conscription during the present war. The English have tended to assimilate other nationalities, who have immigrated to the continent, to their own particular type and way of life.

Canadian economy has a very broad basis, resting upon agriculture, forests, mining and manufacture. In spite of a comparatively small population of rather more than 10,000,000 inhabitants, owing to rapid and intensive development, Canada has become one of the greatest exporting countries in the world. Her primary products, especially wheat and flour, bacon, cheese, timber, pulp and paper, and base metals have been of great value to Britain during the course of the present war. In every direction her economy between the two wars has greatly improved. At one time, primarily an agricultural and mining community, the exigencies of the 1914-18 War led to the development of manufactures on a considerably increased scale. This development was fostered between the two wars by substantial tariff walls, and during the present war the range of Canadian manufactures has increased enormously. Though neither the coal nor oil resources of the Dominion are considerable, when viewed on the world scale, Canada is fortunate in the possession of large hydro-electric power.

MAP 46. THE UNITED STATES: ECONOMIC.

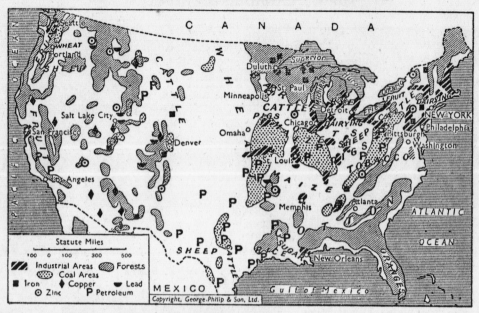

The United States, with an area rather smaller than that of Europe and a population of 130,000,000, about a quarter of that of Europe, is the richest and most prosperous economic unit in the whole world. In such an enormous area there is considerable diversity of relief and of climate and therefore of agricultural production. The population of the country is also diverse, and problems arising from it are complicated by the strong negro element, which is greatest in the south-east.

Ever since the Union was formed, sectional interests of different parts of the country strongly asserted themselves, so that frequently advance has been due to compromise between the various sections. The issue of the secession of any State, strongly at variance with the policy pursued by the Federal Government, was settled by the outcome of the Civil War. The elements making for unity have proved stronger than those making for sectionalism. In the political sphere the strongest of these elements has proved to be the Constitution. Although written, it has proved elastic under the successive interpretations of the Supreme Court. Thus a strong nationalism has developed. While this has fostered the growth of communications of all kinds, it has itself been strengthened by their development. The communication system of the United States is perhaps the most highly developed of any comparable region in the world.

So richly endowed is the United States with natural resources that, in regard to many of them, it leads the world in production. Its agriculture is very strong and supports approximately 25% of the population. The possession of iron ore, copper, and many other base metals in abundance, together with the possession of fuels such as coal, oil, natural gas, and water power, also in abundance, has formed the basis of an extensive manufacturing industry. The north-east is the richest manufacturing area and exports machinery, steel, textiles and manufactures of every kind, but agriculture is much less important.

In contrast the south-east possesses a large poverty-stricken agricultural population of white tenant farmers and negroes. Its staple products are cotton, tobacco, lumber, coal and oil, but in recent years heavy industry and textile manufacturing have increased. The Middle States possess a well-balanced economy, depending upon a rich agriculture and diversified manufactures. The Great Plains, and the mountain area beyond, depend primarily upon agricultural and pastoral products and much mining, though here agriculture in many areas is complicated by the problem of severe land erosion, and the necessity for irrigation.

In the north-west Pacific region lumbering and fishing are leading industries. Wheat and apples are also important. In California, oil and gold are the most important minerals. Agriculture concentrates on production of citrus fruits, winter vegetables, and grapes. This region is the home of the film industry and is also important for the manufacture of aircraft.

MAP 47. CARIBBEAN SEA AND PANAMA CANAL.

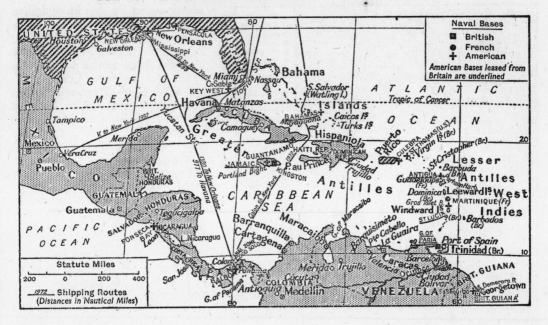

The geographical position of the United States in relation to the Gulf of Mexico and the Caribbean Sea made it inevitable that she should be interested both in the Latin American countries and in the West Indian Islands. Her interests are both economic and strategic, and ever since the construction of the Panama Canal the strategic interests have tended to become of paramount importance. Commercially the saving of distance, approximately 6,000 miles, between the Atlantic and the Pacific, and of time by using the Canal, is considerable. Valuable as this is, the most significant reason for building it is that it provided a quick passage for the American navy from the Atlantic to the Pacific.

American direct participation in the affairs of the Caribbean States and islands was greatest during the period of so-called " Dollar Diplomacy," when American trade interests were being furthered by State influence as far as possible. The returns from heavy capital investment in the area suffered from the lack of stable government in many of these small States. This led to American intervention, and to garrisoning by American marines on numerous occasions for varying lengths of time.

The nominal independence of Cuba was secured after the Spanish-American War of 1898, but the passage of the Platt Amendment made the island practically an American protectorate. This Amendment was only repealed in 1934, but American influence is still strong. The Panama Zone through which the Panama

Canal is cut became American territory, and American influence secured the independence of Cuba and Panama. Nicaragua, Haiti and the Dominican Republic were occupied for long periods of time and all became virtually American protectorates. After the 1914-18 War, the temper of America became less imperialist and more isolationist. By degrees this led to the feeling that the abandonment of intervention would produce better relations between the United States and these small Republics and—more important still—would improve the relations between the United States and the various States of South America, which have always regarded the immense power of their northern partner somewhat jealously. President Franklin D. Roosevelt introduced the " Good Neighbour " policy, which has put Pan-Americanism on a much sounder basis than it previously enjoyed.

Owing to its strategic importance, the United States, besides fortifying the Panama Canal Zone, had established a number of naval and air bases in this region. After the collapse of France the number of these was increased when Britain agreed to lease to America certain sites for the construction of naval and air bases in the West Indies and British Guiana, and in Newfoundland and Bermuda for a period of 99 years, in return for receiving fifty American destroyers. Action was taken to prevent both French and Dutch possessions falling into the hands of the Nazis. Bases have also been guaranteed to the United States by treaties with both Cuba and Nicaragua.

MAP 48. SOUTH AMERICA : ECONOMIC.

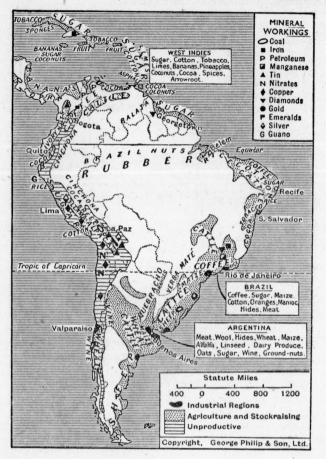

The various American Indian tribes of South America were first conquered and settled by the Spanish conquistadores and the Portuguese in the 16th century. Many Spaniards were also missionaries, but the Portuguese were settlers.

Independence from Spain and Portugal was achieved by South America in the early 19th century. British support of the revolutionary movement, and the powerful exercise of her sea power, prevented the forces of European reaction from intervening in favour of Spain and Portugal in the continent. At this time, too, the Monroe Doctrine was issued with a view to preserving Latin America from intervention by any European power. Independence did not of itself bring democratic self-government and freedom. Much bloodshed, internecine wars, political and social experiment have contributed to the settlement of the boundaries and institutions of the various Republics as known to-day.

Immigration has been an important factor in the settlement of the country, and to the Spanish and Portuguese newcomers were added, especially, blocks of Italian and German colonists. The more numerous Italians favoured Argentina and Brazil, while Germans have settled in southern Brazil and southern Chile, planting solid German communities in the areas settled. Under Nazi influence, these have become centres of disruption. This century has seen the settlement of Japanese communities in Brazil and Peru.

Types of population and their social conditions vary greatly in different parts of the continent. In Argentina and Uruguay the pure white population constitutes 90% of the whole, while in Brazil and Chile it constitutes about one-third. In the other Republics it sinks to 10% or lower. In them the Indian and mestizo (mixed Indian and European) constitute the main elements. Their standard of life is low, and presents a vital problem for the future. In Brazil and Colombia the negro and mulatto element is considerable. It is significant that the population pattern of the various States corresponds closely with their prosperity.

The greatest centres of population have grown up near the sea, about La Plata estuary, Rio de Janeiro, Valparaiso and Santiago, and Lima. Elsewhere population has concentrated mainly in the agricultural areas both temperate and tropical. In the cattle lands it is less dense, and extremely sparse in the Amazonian forests, owing to unfavourable climate, and in the semi-desert regions of Patagonia.

Besides immigration, much capital, especially British and American, for the development of railways and trade has contributed to the growth of the continent and the opening of markets in Europe and the United States for foodstuffs and industrial raw materials. In return for these, manufactures were largely imported. The influence of the stringent conditions of trade in the thirties, and now the war, have naturally led to a movement for economic nationalism in Argentina, Brazil and Chile. These countries are developing textile and other manufactures in spite of the almost entire absence of coal. Though Brazil possesses enormous deposits of iron-ore the establishment of large-scale heavy industry will prove difficult. Strenuous efforts are now being made to develop plantation rubber in Brazil.

INDEX

MAP			
49	**Apsley**, Tasmania	42 20 S	147 7 E
29	**Apulia, Dept.**, Italy	41 0 N	17 0 E
28	**Aquila**, Italy	42 21 N	13 21 E
40	**Arabian Des.**, Egypt	27 30 N	32 0 E
38	**Arabian Sea**, Asia	20 0 N	65 0 E
40	**Arabkir**, Turkey	38 51 N	38 30 E
66	**Aracajú**, Brazil	11 0 S	37 0 W
66	**Aracaty**, Brazil	4 40 S	37 30 W
26	**Aracena**, Spain	37 53 N	6 33 W
31	**Arad**, Rumania	46 12 N	21 20 E
40	**Aradan**, Iran	35 15 N	52 29 E
27	**Aragon, old prov.**, Sp.	41 30 N	1 0 W
66	**Araguayá, R.**, Brazil	8 0 S	49 30 W
38	**Aral, L.**, U.S.S.R.	43 30 N	59 30 E
47	**Aramac**, Queensland	23 0 S	145 17 E
29	**Aranci**, Sardinia	41 2 N	9 38 E
26	**Aranda**, Spain	41 40 N	3 40 W
26	**Aranjuez**, Spain	40 1 N	3 38 W
25	**Aranyosmarot**, Czechoslovakia	48 25 N	18 25 E
48	**Ararat**, Victoria	37 10 S	142 30 E
40	**Ararat, Mt.**, Turkey	39 50 N	44 15 E
35	**Arboga**, Sweden	59 30 N	15 50 E
33	**Arbon**, Switzerland	47 33 N	9 26 E
35	**Arbra**, Sweden	61 27 N	16 28 E
17	**Arbroath**, Scotland	56 34 N	2 35 W
20	**Arc**, France	47 28 N	5 25 E
21	**Arcachon**, France	44 39 N	1 12 W
32	**Arcadia.** *See* **Kgharissia**		
32	**Arcadia, G. of**, Greece	37 22 N	21 40 E
36	**Archangel**, U.S.S.R.	64 38 N	40 36 E
26	**Arcos**, Spain	36 48 N	5 46 W
42	**Arcot**, India	12 54 N	79 16 E
68	**Arctic Ocean**, North Pole Regions		
26	**Ardales**, Spain	36 52 N	4 50 W
41	**Ardakan**, Iran	32 25 N	54 0 E
40	**Ardebil**, Iran	38 12 N	48 30 E
21	**Ardèche, dept.**, France	44 38 N	4 52 E
18	**Ardee**, Eire	53 52 N	6 33 W
20	**Ardennes, dept.**, Fr.	49 33 N	3 37 E
22	**Ardennes Mts.**, Belg.	50 0 N	5 30 E
19	**Ardfert**, Eire	52 0 N	9 47 W
18	**Ardglass**, N. Ireland	54 16 N	5 37 W
17	**Ardgour**, Scotland	56 44 N	5 15 W
40	**Ardistan**, Iran	33 29 N	52 21 E
17	**Ardlui**, Scotland	56 18 N	4 43 W
17	**Ardlussa**, Scotland	56 2 N	5 46 W
19	**Ardmore**, Eire	51 57 N	7 44 W
62	**Ardmore**, U.S.A.	51 57 N	7 44 W
19	**Ardnacrusha**, Eire	52 42 N	8 38 W
19	**Ardrahan**, Eire	53 9 N	8 49 W
17	**Ardrishaig**, Scotland	56 1 N	5 26 W
17	**Ardrossan**, Scotland	55 39 N	4 48 W
48	**Ardrossan**, S. Aust.	34 24 S	137 52 E
34	**Åre**, Sweden	64 25 N	13 10 E
65	**Arecibo**, Pto. Rico	18 29 N	66 46 W
26	**Arenas**, Spain	40 15 N	5 5 W
35	**Arendal**, Norway	58 28 N	8 51 E
35	**Arensburg**, Estonia	58 10 N	22 29 E
67	**Arequipa**, Peru	16 10 S	71 25 W
21	**Ares**, France	44 48 N	1 7 W
26	**Arevalo**, Spain	41 4 N	4 44 W
28	**Arezzo**, Italy	43 28 N	11 52 E
28	**Argenta**, Italy	44 37 N	11 50 E
20	**Argentan**, France	48 44 N	0 3 W
21	**Argentat**, France	45 7 N	1 57 E
67	**Argentina, St.**, S. Am.	35 0 S	65 0 W
21	**Argenton**, France	46 33 N	1 30 E
40	**Arghana**, Turkey	38 18 N	39 57 E
32	**Argos**, Greece	37 38 N	22 43 E
32	**Argostoli**, Greece	38 9 N	20 30 E
52	**Arguin**, Fr. W. Africa	20 48 N	16 26 W
17	**Argyll, Co.**, Scotland	56 0 N	5 55 W
30	**Argyokastro**, Albania	40 7 N	20 10 E
29	**Ariano**, Italy	41 11 N	15 6 E
67	**Arica**, Chile	18 15 S	70 10 W
21	**Ariège, dept.**, France	42 54 N	1 25 E
18	**Arigna**, Eire	54 5 N	8 7 W
17	**Arinagour**, Scotland	56 37 N	6 31 W
16	**Arisaig**, Scotland	56 55 N	5 50 W
62	**Arizona, St.**, U.S.A.	35 0 N	112 0 W
34	**Arjeplog**, Sweden	66 0 N	18 3 E
62	**Arkansas City**, U.S.A.	37 3 N	97 2 W
62	**Arkansas R.**, U.S.A.	34 30 N	92 10 W
63	**Arkansas, St.**, U.S.A.	34 30 N	92 30 W
19	**Arklow**, Eire	52 47 N	6 10 W
21	**Arles**, France	43 41 N	4 39 E
33	**Arlesheim**, Switz.	47 30 N	7 35 E
22	**Arlon**, Belgium	49 40 N	5 47 E
16	**Armadale**, Inverness, Sc.	57 4 N	5 53 W
17	**Armadale**, W. Lothn., Sc.	55 54 N	3 42 W
18	**Armagh, & Co.**, N. Ire.	54 22 N	6 35 W
37	**Armavir**, U.S.S.R.	45 2 N	41 2 E
37	**Armenia, rep.**, U.S.S.R.	40 0 N	41 0 E
20	**Armentieres**, France	50 41 N	2 53 E
49	**Armidale**, N.S.W.	30 19 S	151 36 E
31	**Arnautlar**, Bulgaria	42 55 N	27 45 E
23	**Arnborg**, Denmark	56 2 N	8 58 E
27	**Arnedo**, Spain	42 12 N	2 3 W
22	**Arnhem**, Netherlands	51 58 N	5 54 E
28	**Arno, R.**, Italy	43 40 N	10 16 E
15	**Arnold**, England	53 1 N	1 7 W
24	**Arnsberg**, Germany	51 22 N	8 5 E
24	**Arnswalde**, Germany	53 9 N	15 24 E
26	**Aroche**, Spain	37 57 N	7 0 W
33	**Arosa**, Switzerland	46 46 N	9 39 E
26	**Aróuca**, Portugal	40 55 N	8 20 W
43	**Arrah**, India	25 30 N	84 44 E
20	**Arras**, France	50 16 N	2 48 E
17	**Arrochar**, Scotland	56 13 N	4 42 W
26	**Arronches**, Portugal	39 2 N	7 20 W
26	**Arroyo**, Spain	39 26 N	6 38 W
36	**Arsamas**, U.S.S.R.	55 29 N	43 58 E
32	**Arta**, Greece	39 8 N	21 0 E
32	**Artaki**, Turkey	40 27 N	27 48 E
37	**Artemovsk**, U.S.S.R.	48 27 N	37 40 E
33	**Arth**, Switzerland	47 4 N	8 32 E
51	**Arthur's P.**, N. Zea.	42 57 S	171 19 E
20	**Artois, old prov.**, Fr.	50 20 N	2 20 E
15	**Arun, R.**, England	50 55 N	0 35 W
15	**Arundel**, England	50 51 N	0 34 W
55	**Arusha**, Tanganyika	3 22 S	36 42 E
34	**Arvidsjaur**, Sweden	65 35 N	19 5 E
35	**Arvika**, Sweden	59 38 N	12 35 E
6	**Ascension I.**, At. Oc.	7 55 S	14 20 W
24	**Aschaffenburg**, Ger.	49 58 N	9 6 E
24	**Aschersleben**, Ger.	51 45 N	11 28 E
28	**Asciano**, Italy	43 12 N	11 34 E
28	**Ascoli**, Italy	42 52 N	13 35 E
34	**Åsele**, Sweden	64 10 N	16 40 E
52	**Ashanti, dist.**, G. Cst.	7 15 N	1 20 W
14	**Ashbourne**, England	53 1 N	1 44 W
14	**Ashburton**, England	50 31 N	3 46 W
51	**Ashburton**, N. Zealand	43 53 S	171 45 E
46	**Ashburton, R. & Gf.**, W. Australia	22 0 S	115 3 E
15	**Ashby de la Zouch**, England	52 45 N	1 27 W
41	**Ashdod.** *See* **Esdod**		
63	**Asheville**, U.S.A.	35 35 N	82 32 W
15	**Ashford**, England	51 9 N	0 52 E
41	**Ashkelon.** *See* **Askalan**		
62	**Ashland**, U.S.A.	46 32 N	90 55 W
41	**Ashraf**, Iran	36 40 N	53 24 E
13	**Ashton-under-Lyne**, England	53 30 N	2 7 W
15	**Ashwell (Hert.)**, Eng.	52 3 N	0 8 W
15	**Ashwell (Rut.)**, Eng.	52 44 N	0 44 W
40	**Asia Minor**, Asia	39 0 N	31 0 E
40	**Asir, Dist.**, Arabia	19 30 N	42 30 E
41	**Askalan**, Palestine	31 40 N	34 33 E
35	**Askersund**, Sweden	59 0 N	15 0 E
41	**Askhabad**, U.S.S.R.	37 58 N	58 25 E
13	**Askrigg**, England	54 19 N	2 3 W
42	**Asmar**, India	35 3 N	71 30 E
55	**Asmara**, Eritrea	25 30 N	38 40 E
12	**Aspatria**, England	54 46 N	3 22 W
40	**Assab**, Eritrea	13 1 N	42 45 E
43	**Assam, prov.**, India	25 0 N	93 30 E
42	**Assaye**, India	20 13 N	76 0 E
22	**Assen**, Netherlands	53 0 N	6 34 E
23	**Assens**, Denmark	55 16 N	9 55 E
53	**Assinie**, Ivory Coast	5 8 N	3 17 W
28	**Assisi**, Italy	43 4 N	12 38 E
32	**Astako**, Greece	38 34 N	21 6 E
37	**Astara**, Iran	38 22 N	48 59 E
41	**Asterabad**, Iran	36 50 N	54 28 E
28	**Asti**, Italy	44 54 N	8 12 E
15	**Aston Manor**, Eng.	52 30 N	1 54 W
26	**Astorga**, Spain	42 30 N	6 6 W
62	**Astoria**, U.S.A.	46 7 N	123 48 W
37	**Astrakhan**, U.S.S.R.	46 13 N	48 0 E
55	**Astrida**, Belg. Congo	2 30 S	29 40 E
32	**Astros**, Greece	37 23 N	22 44 E
26	**Astudillo**, Spain	42 12 N	4 20 W
26	**Asturias, old prov.**, Spain	43 10 N	6 0 W
67	**Asuncion**, Paraguay	25 15 S	57 35 W
40	**Aswan**, Egypt	24 6 N	32 51 E
40	**Asyut**, Egypt	27 12 N	31 2 E
67	**Atacama Des.**, Chile	25 0 S	70 20 W
32	**Atalanti**, Greece	38 39 N	23 3 E
40	**Atbara**, A.-E. Sudan	17 20 N	34 30 E
38	**Atbasar**, U.S.S.R.	52 5 N	68 10 E
63	**Atchison**, U.S.A.	39 33 N	95 10 W
27	**Ateca**, Spain	41 21 N	1 48 W
22	**Ath**, Belgium	50 39 N	3 47 E
60	**Athabaska, L.**, Can.	59 10 N	110 0 W
60	**Athabaska Landing**, Canada	54 44 N	113 5 W
60	**Athabaska, R.**, Can.	58 0 N	111 19 W
18	**Athboy**, Eire	53 38 N	6 55 W
19	**Athenry**, Eire	53 18 N	8 45 W
32	**Athens**, Greece	37 59 N	23 47 E
63	**Athens**, U.S.A.	33 50 N	83 15 W
15	**Atherstone**, England	52 35 N	1 32 W
18	**Athleague**, Eire	53 34 N	8 17 W
41	**Athlit**, Palestine	32 38 N	34 54 E
16-17	**Atholl**, Scotland	56 48 N	3 40 W
32	**Athos, Mt.**, Greece	40 10 N	24 25 E
19	**Athy**, Eire	52 59 N	6 59 W
63	**Atlanta**, U.S.A.	33 45 N	84 20 W
63	**Atlantic City**, U.S.A.	39 26 N	74 30 W
6	**Atlantic Ocean**	0 0	30 0 W
52	**Atlas Mts.**, Africa	31 40 N	6 20 W
15	**Attleborough**, England	52 32 N	1 0 E
42	**Attock**, India	33 55 N	72 20 E
21	**Aubagne**, France	43 18 N	5 36 E
20	**Aube, dept. & R.**, Fr.	48 18 N	4 20 E
21	**Aubenas**, France	44 36 N	4 23 E
20	**Aubigny**, France	47 28 N	2 26 E
21	**Aubin**, France	44 30 N	2 14 E
33	**Aubonne**, Switzerland	46 28 N	6 22 E
21	**Aubusson**, France	45 56 N	2 9 E
21	**Auch**, France	43 39 N	0 34 E
17	**Auchterarder**, Scot.	56 18 N	3 42 W
17	**Auchtermuchty**, Scot.	56 18 N	3 13 W
50	**Auckland**, N. Zealand	36 54 S	174 46 E
50	**Auckland Is.** Inset 50	32 S	166 13 E
50	**Auckland, prov.**, N.Z.	37 0 S	175 0 E
21	**Aude, dept. & R.**, Fr.	43 10 N	2 40 E
22	**Audenaarde**, Belgium	50 51 N	3 37 E
20	**Audierne**, France	48 2 N	4 35 W
14	**Audley**, England	53 4 N	2 22 W
18	**Augher**, N. Ireland	54 26 N	7 7 W
18	**Aughnacloy**, N. Ire.	54 25 N	6 59 W
19	**Aughrim**, Eire	52 52 N	6 20 W
24	**Augsburg**, Germany	48 23 N	10 55 E
57	**Augsburg**, U. of S. Af.	32 9 S	18 54 E
29	**Augusta**, Sicily	37 12 N	15 15 E
46	**Augusta**, W. Australia	34 15 S	115 15 E
63	**Augusta**, Ga., U.S.A.	33 26 N	81 57 W
63	**Augusta**, Maine, U.S.A.	44 20 N	69 56 W
52	**Aujila**, Libya	29 0 N	21 0 E
16	**Auldearn**, Scotland	57 35 N	3 48 W
20	**Aumale**, France	49 47 N	1 43 E
42	**Aurangabad**, India	19 53 N	75 21 E
20	**Auray**, France	47 29 N	3 0 W
35	**Aurdal**, Norway	60 52 N	9 30 E
24	**Aurich**, Germany	53 29 N	7 29 E
21	**Aurillac**, France	44 56 N	2 27 E
35	**Aurland**, Norway	60 54 N	7 15 E
28	**Auronzo**, Italy	46 35 N	12 30 E
63	**Aurora**, Ill., U.S.A.	41 45 N	88 20 W
63	**Aurora**, Mo., U.S.A.	36 59 N	93 45 W
57	**Aus**, S. W. Africa	26 39 S	16 10 E
25	**Auschwitz**, Poland	50 1 N	19 15 E
24	**Aussee**, Aust., Ger.	47 36 N	13 47 E
24	**Aussig.** *See* **Usli**		
35	**Aust-Agder, Co.**, Nor.	58 30 N	8 10 E
46	**Austin**, W. Australia	27 35 S	117 50 E
62	**Austin**, U.S.A.	43 43 N	92 55 W
49	**Australian Alps**, Aust.	36 30 S	148 15 E
68	**Australian Dependency**, Antarctica	60 S to 90 S	45 E to 160 E
24	**Austria, st.**, Germany	48 0 N	14 0 E
35	**Auts**, Latvia	56 28 N	22 55 E
20	**Autun**, France	46 57 N	4 21 E
21	**Auvergne, old prov.**, France	45 40 N	3 0 E
20	**Auxerre**, France	47 48 N	3 35 E
20	**Auxonne**, France	47 12 N	5 26 E
21	**Auzances**, France	46 2 N	2 30 E
43	**Ava**, Burma	21 57 N	95 55 E
20	**Avallon**, France	47 30 N	3 52 E
14	**Avebury**, England	51 26 N	1 50 W
26	**Aveiro**, Portugal	40 36 N	8 40 W
29	**Avellino**, Italy	40 59 N	14 46 E
33	**Avenches**, Switz.	46 52 N	7 2 E
29	**Aversa**, Italy	40 59 N	14 12 E
20	**Avesnes**, France	50 8 N	3 55 E
21	**Aveyron, dept.**, Fr.	44 26 N	2 40 E
21	**Aveyron, R.**, France	44 20 N	2 20 E
28	**Avezzano**, Italy	42 2 N	13 22 E
16	**Aviemore**, Scotland	57 12 N	3 49 W
29	**Avigliano**, Italy	40 47 N	15 42 E
21	**Avignon**, France	43 56 N	4 50 E
26	**Avila**, Spain	40 38 N	4 40 W
26	**Aviles**, Spain	43 32 N	5 56 W
30	**Avlonia.** *See* **Valona**		
29	**Avola**, Sicily	36 53 N	15 9 E
15	**Avon, R.** (Glouc.), Eng.	51 15 N	1 48 W
14	**Avon, R.** (Som.), Eng...		
14	**Avonmouth**, England	51 30 N	2 41 W
20	**Avranches**, France	48 42 N	1 22 W
32	**Avrethissar**, Greece	40 55 N	22 28 E
50	**Awanui**, N. Zealand	35 2 S	173 18 E
17	**Awe, Loch**, Scotland	56 15 N	5 15 W
14	**Awre**, England	51 52 N	2 15 W
21	**Ax**, France	42 46 N	1 52 E
14	**Axbridge**, England	51 18 N	2 49 W
22	**Axel**, Netherlands	51 17 N	3 54 E
53	**Axim**, Gold Coast	4 52 N	2 15 W
14	**Axminster**, England	50 49 N	3 0 W
14	**Axmouth**, England	50 43 N	3 3 W
20	**Ay**, France	49 5 N	4 2 E
66	**Ayacucho**, Peru	12 50 S	74 10 W
26	**Ayamonte**, Spain	37 13 N	6 55 W
13	**Aycliffe**, England	54 36 N	1 34 W
15	**Aylesbury**, England	51 49 N	0 49 W
15	**Aylsham**, England	52 48 N	1 15 E
15	**Aynho**, England	52 0 N	1 15 W
17	**Ayr, tn., R. & Co.**, Scotland	55 28 N	4 37 W
56	**Ayrshire**, S. Rhod.	17 12 S	30 20 E
13	**Aysgarth**, England	54 18 N	1 59 W
17	**Ayton**, Scotland	55 51 W	2 7 W
43	**Ayuthia**, Siam	14 25 N	100 30 E
43	**Azamgarh**, India	26 0 N	83 20 E
40	**Azerbaijan, prov.**, Iran	37 0 N	48 0 E
37	**Azerbaijan, rep.**, U.S.S.R.	40 30 N	48 0 E
6	**Azores Is.**, At. Oc.	37 30 N	26 0 W
37	**Azov**, U.S.S.R.	47 0 N	39 23 E

MAP			
37	Azov, S. of, U.S.S.R.	46 0N	36 30E
27	Azpeitia, Spain	43 10N	2 18W
26	Azuaga, Spain	38 17N	5 42W
33	Baar, Switzerland	47 13N	8 31E
22	Baar le Duc, Neth.	51 27N	4 56E
31	Babadag, Rumania	44 54N	28 52E
34	Babinsk, U.S.S.R.	67 31N	31 36E
40	Babul, Iran	36 32N	52 30E
31	Bacua, Rumania	46 10N	27 35E
20	Baccarat, France	48 28N	6 46E
15	Bacton, England	52 50N	1 27E
13	Bacup, England	53 42N	2 13W
26	Badajoz, Spain	38 51N	6 56W
24	Baden, Aust., Germany	48 1N	16 12E
24	Baden, & St., Germany	48 56N	8 15E
33	Baden, Switzerland	47 28N	8 17E
16	Badenoch, Scotland	57 0N	4 5W
42	Badulla, Ceylon	7 2N	81 5E
61	Baffin B., Canada	73 0N	67 0W
61	Baffin I., Canada	68 0N	71 0W
55	Bagamoyo, Tanganyika	13 42N	10 50E
67	Bagé, Brazil	31 10S	54 0W
40	Baghdad, Iraq	33 18N	44 30E
29	Bagheria, Sicily	38 4N	13 30E
19	Ba naistown, Eire	52 42N	6 58W
21	Bagneres de Bigorre, France	43 5N	0 35E
21	Bagnères de Luchon, France	42 48N	0 39E
65	Bahama, Bahama Is.	26 40N	79 0W
65	Bahama Is., W. Indies	24 0N	75 0W
42	Bahawalpur, India	28 55N	71 30E
66	Bahia, Brazil	10 40S	36 27W
66	Bahia, Ecuador	0 40S	78 40W
67	Bahia Blanca, Arg.	38 30S	62 20W
55	Bahr el Ghazal, R., A.-E. Sudan	9 0N	29 40E
55	Bahr el Jebel, R., A.-E.Sudan	6 0N	32 0E
42	Bahrach, India	27 32N	81 42E
41	Bahramabad, Iran	30 27N	55 58E
40	Bahrein Is., Arabia	26 0N	50 35E
40	Baiburt, Turkey	40 17N	40 10E
44	Baikal L., U.S.S.R.	53 0N	107 0E
44	Baikal Mts., U.S.S.R.	53 30N	106 0E
19	Baile Atha Cliath. *See* Dublin		
26	Bailen, Spain	38 5N	3 45W
31	Bailesti, Rumania	44 2N	23 21E
18	Bailieborough, Eire	53 55N	6 59W
54	Bailundo, Angola	12 10S	15 52E
20	Bain, France	47 54N	1 48W
32	Biaramich, Turkey	39 48N	26 40E
47	Bairnsdale, Victoria	37 50S	147 39E
30	Baja, Hungary	46 13N	13 59E
41	Bajistan, Iran	34 32N	58 16E
62	Baker, U.S.A.	44 46N	117 51W
62	Bakerfield, U.S.A.	35 26N	118 58W
13	Bakewell, England	53 12N	1 41W
37	Bakhchisarai, U.S.S.R.	44 47N	33 56E
30	Bakony Forest, Hung.	47 20N	18 0E
37	Baku, U.S.S.R.	40 22N	49 46E
54	Bakura, Nigeria	12 41N	5 52E
14	Bala, & L., Wales	52 55N	3 36W
31	Balabanka, Rumania	45 55N	30 15E
42	Balaghat Ra., India	18 30N	76 0E
27	Balaguer, Spain	41 57N	0 50E
37	Balaklava, U.S.S.R.	44 34N	33 32E
16	Balallan, Scotland	58 6N	6 36W
37	Balashov, U.S.S.R.	51 32N	43 0E
43	Balasore, India	21 31N	86 58E
30	Balassagyarmat, Hungary	48 4N	19 10E
32	Balat, Turkey	39 32N	28 38E
30	Balaton, L., Hungary	46 48N	17 40E
30	Balatonszentgyörgy, Hungary	46 42N	17 18E
65	Balboa, Panama Canal	9 10W	79 55W
18	Balbriggan, Eire	53 37N	6 12W
31	Balcik, Rumania	43 24N	28 10E
51	Balclutha, N. Z.	46 12S	169 47E
15	Balcombe, England	51 4N	0 9W
15	Baldock, England	51 59N	0 12W
27	Balearic Is., Spain	40 0N	3 0E
41	Balfouria, Palestine	32 38N	35 20E
32	Balikesri, Turkey	39 39N	27 55E
16	Balintore, Scotland	57 45N	3 55W
31	Balkan Mts., Bulgaria	43 0N	25 0E
38	Balkash, L., U.S.S.R.	46 0N	75 0E
41	Balkh, Afghanistan	36 46N	67 5E
18	Balla, Eire	53 48N	9 8W
46	Balla Balla, W. Austral.	20 43S	117 45E
17	Ballachulish, Scotland	56 41N	5 7W
18	Ballaghadereen, Eire	53 54N	8 35W
17	Ballantrae, Scotland	55 6N	5 0W
48	Ballarat, Victoria	31 32S	143 50E
16	Ballater, Scotland	57 2N	3 2W
68	Balleny Is., Antarctica	67 0S	163 0E
23	Ballerup, Denmark	55 44N	12 23E
18	Ballina (Mayo), Eire	54 7N	9 10W
19	Ballina (Tipp.), Eire	52 49N	8 26W
47	Ballina, N.S.W.	28 50S	153 34E
18	Ballinamore, Eire	54 3N	7 48W
19	Ballinascarthy, Eire	51 40N	8 52W
19	Ballinasloe, Eire	53 20N	8 13W
19	Ballincollig, Eire	51 53N	8 37W
19	Ballineen, Eire	51 44N	8 58W
19	Ballingarry, Eire	52 23N	8 52W
17	Ballinluig, Scotland	56 39N	3 38W
18	Ballinrobe, Eire	53 38N	9 14W
18	Ballintra, Eire	54 35N	8 8W
18	Ballintubber, Eire	53 43N	8 25W
19	Ballitore, Eire	53 2N	6 49W
17	Balloch, Scotland	56 0N	4 35W
18	Ballybay, Eire	54 8N	6 53W
18	Ballybofey, Eire	54 48N	7 47W
19	Ballybunion, Eire	52 30N	9 40W
18	Ballycastle, Eire	54 17N	9 23W
18	Ballycastle, N. Ireland	55 12N	6 15W
18	Ballyclare, N. Ireland	54 46N	6 0W
18	Ballyconnell, Eire	54 7N	7 36W
18	Ballyhaunis, Eire	53 47N	8 47W
19	Ballylongford, Eire	52 33N	9 28W
18	Ballymena, N. Ireland	54 52N	6 16W
18	Ballymoney, N. Ireland	55 5N	6 30W
18	Ballymote, Eire	54 6N	8 31W
19	Ballymurphy, Eire	52 34N	6 52W
18	Ballynacarrgy, Eire	53 35N	7 33W
18	Ballynahinch, N. Ire.	54 24N	5 54W
19	Ballyragget, Eire	52 47N	7 20W
18	Ballysadare, Eire	54 12N	8 31W
18	Ballyshannon, Eire	54 30N	8 12W
18	Ballyvary, Eire	53 54N	9 9W
16	Balmoral, Scotland	57 2N	3 13W
47	Balranald, N.S.W.	34 35S	143 31E
31	Balshu, Rumania	44 21N	24 6E
33	Balsthal, Switzerland	47 22N	7 47E
37	Balta, U.S.S.R.	47 59N	29 30E
31	Balti, Rumania	47 48N	28 0E
35	Baltic Port. *See* Paldiski		
8	Baltic Sea, Europe	56 0N	25 0E
19	Baltimore, Eire	51 29N	9 22W
63	Baltimore, U.S.A.	39 23N	76 35W
19	Baltinglass, Eire	52 57N	6 42W
42	Baluchistan, prov., India	25 to 30N	61 to 70E
41	Bam, Iran	29 4N	58 20E
52	Bamako, Fr. W. Africa	12 35N	7 53W
24	Bamberg, Germany	49 54	10 50E
41	Bamian, Afghanistan	34 55N	68 0E
14	Bampton, England	50 59N	3 29W
15	Bampton, England	51 45N	1 33W
41	Bampur, Iran	27 19N	60 15E
40	Banaiyan, Arabia	23 15N	51 30E
19	Banagher, Eire	53 11N	8 0W
54	Banana, Belgian Congo	1 0S	12 10E
30	Banat, dist., Yugoslavia	45 40N	21 0E
16	Banavie, Scotland	56 51N	5 5W
18	Banbridge, N. Ireland	54 22N	6 17W
15	Banbury, England	52 4N	1 20W
16	Banchory, Scotland	57 3N	2 30W
42	Banda, India	25 24N	80 25E
41	Bandar Abbas, Iran	27 15N	56 19E
40	Bandar - i - Shahpur, Iran	30 10N	48 40E
52	Bandar Ziyada, Br. Somaliland	11 20N	48 50E
55	Bandawe, Nyasaland	11 55S	34 11E
23	Bandholm, Denmark	54 51N	11 28E
19	Bandon, Eire	51 44N	8 43W
43	Bandon, Siam	9 0N	99 20E
60	Banff, Canada	51 10N	115 38W
16	Banff & Co, Scotland	57 40N	2 32W
42	Bangalore, India	12 59N	77 38E
43	Bangkok, Siam	13 45N	100 30E
18	Bangor, Eire	54 9N	9 45W
18	Bangor, N. Ireland	54 40N	5 40W
63	Bangor, U.S.A.	44 46N	68 45W
12	Bangor, Wales	53 14N	4 7W
54	Bangui, Fr. Eq. Af.	4 22N	18 25E
55	Bangweulu, L., N.Rhod.	11 0S	30 0E
41	Banias, Syria	33 12N	35 42E
30	Banjaluka, Yugoslavia	44 50N	17 13E
39	Banjermassin, Borneo	3 30S	114 13E
60	Banks I., Canada	53 30N	130 10W
42	Bannu, India	33 0N	70 35E
17	Bannockburn, Scotland	56 5N	3 56W
25	Banska Bystrice, Czechoslovakia	48 32N	19 10E
25	Banska Sliavnica, Czechoslovakia	48 28N	18 58E
19	Banteer, Eire	52 7N	8 55W
19	Bantry, Eire	51 40N	9 27W
54	Banzyville, Bel: Congo	4 0N	21 20E
37	Bar, U.S.S.R.	49 10N	27 34E
42	Bara Banki, India	26 56N	81 13E
47	Baradine, N.S.W.	30 54S	149 1E
65	Barahona, S. Domingo	18 5N	71 10W
27	Barahona, Spain	41 20N	2 38W
25	Baranovichi, Poland	53 8N	26 0E
53	Barawa, It. Somaliland	1 20N	44 0E
65	Barbados, I., West Ind.	13 10N	59 30W
27	Barbastro, Spain	42 2N	0 6E
57	Barberton, U. of S. Af.	25 50S	31 6E
21	Barbezieux, France	45 28N	0 11W
65	Barbuda, Leeward Is.	17 33N	61 45W
47	Barcaldine, Queensland	23 30S	145 17E
26	Barcarrota, Spain	38 32N	6 53W
29	Barcellona, Sicily	38 9N	15 13E
66	Barcellos, Brazil	1 10S	62 50W
27	Barcelona, Spain	41 22N	2 10E
66	Barcelona, Venezuela	10 0N	64 55W
21	Barcelonnette, France	44 22N	6 38E
30	Barcs, Hungary	45 59N	17 29E
52	Bardai, Fr. W. Africa	21 0N	17 10E
27	Bardenas, Spain	42 10N	1 41W
53	Bardera, It. Somaliland	2 20N	42 20E
13	Bardney, England	53 13N	0 18W
43	Bardwan, India	23 10N	88 0E
25	Bardyjor, Cz. slov.	49 18N	21 19E
54	Bare, Cameroons	5 0N	10 0E
42	Bareilly, India	28 20N	79 30E
47	Barellan, N.S.W.	34 12S	146 32E
20	Barfleur, France	49 41N	1 16W
40	Barfrush. *See* Babul		
45	Bargusinsk, U.S S.R.	53 40N	109 30E
15	Barham, England	51 12N	1 10E
29	Bari, Italy	41 8N	16 52E
67	Bariloche, Argentina	41 8S	71 18W
43	Barisal, India	22 41N	90 24E
60	Barkerville, Canada	53 3N	121 25W
15	Barking, England	51 33N	0 5E
57	Barkly East, U. of S. Africa	31 0S	27 37E
57	Barkly West, U. of S. Africa	28 31S	24 32E
47	Barkly Tableland, N. Territory, Australia	19 10S	138 30E
44	Barkul, Sinkiang	43 40N	93 0E
31	Bârlad, Rumania	46 16N	27 37E
20	Bar-le-Duc, France	48 46N	5 11E
29	Barletta, Italy	41 17N	16 20E
14	Barmouth, Wales	52 43N	4 3W
13	Barnard Castle, Eng.	54 33N	1 53W
44	Barnaul, U.S.S.R.	53 25N	83 0E
15	Barnet, England	51 39N	0 12W
13	Barnetby, England	53 34N	0 23W
13	Barnsley, England	52 33N	1 29W
14	Barnstaple, England	51 5N	4 2W
54	Baro, Nigeria	8 38N	6 20E
42	Baroda, India	22 0N	73 14E
44	Barong, China	35 10N	97 20E
43	Barpeta, India	26 20N	91 5E
66	Barquisimeto, Venez.	9 55N	69 10W
66	Barra Mansa, Brazil	22 30S	44 5W
47	Barraba, N.S.W.	30 19S	150 18E
43	Barrackpur, India	22 45N	88 30E
66	Barrancas, Venezuela	8 25N	62 35W
26	Barrancos, Portugal	38 9N	6 57W
66	Barranquilla, Colombia	11 1N	74 52W
17	Barrhead, Scotland	55 48N	4 25W
17	Barrhill, Scotland	55 6N	4 46W
61	Barrie, Canada	44 23N	79 45W
60	Barrow, C., Canada	68 0N	111 30W
12	Barrow in Furness, Eng.	54 7N	3 13W
14	Barry, Wales	51 24N	3 17W
42	Barsi, India	18 10N	75 50E
62	Barstow, U.S.A.	34 55N	116 45W
20	Bar-sur-Aube, France	48 16N	4 44E
20	Bar sur Seine, France	48 7N	4 22E
24	Bartenstein, Germany	54 14N	20 52E
24	Barth, Germany	54 20N	12 42E
66	Bartica, Brit. Guiana	6 15N	58 40W
13	Barton-upon-Humber, Eng.	53 41N	0 27W
35	Bärum, Norway	59 50N	10 30E
16	Barvas, Scotland	58 22N	6 31W
20	Bas Rhin, dept., France	48 50N	7 30E
37	Bashkir, rep., U.S.S.R.	54 0N	57 0E
31	Bashmakli, Bulgaria	41 33N	24 39E
29	Basilicata, Dept., Italy	40 30N	16 0E
42	Basim, India	20 10N	76 10E
15	Basingstoke, England	51 15N	1 5W
33	Basle, & Canton, Switzerland	47 33N	7 34E
55	Basoko, Belgian Congo	1 18N	23 40E
27	Basque Provinces, Sp.	43 0N	2 40W
40	Basra, Iraq	30 34N	47 50E
47	Bass Strait, Australia	39 28S	146 0E
28	Bassano, Italy	45 48N	11 43E
65	Basse Terre, Guadeloupe I.	16 2N	61 45W
43	Bassein, Burma	17 45N	94 53E
42	Bassein, India	19 25N	72 52E
12	Bassenthwaite, L., Eng.	54 40N	3 14W
21	Basses-Alpes, dept., France	44 0N	6 6E
21	Basses Pyrénées, dept., France	43 11N	0 45W
35	Båstad, Sweden	56 30N	12 45E
21	Bastelica, Corsica	42 1N	9 5E
21	Bastia, Corsica	44 41N	9 28E
22	Bastogne, Belgium	50 0N	5 42E
57	Basutoland, South Af.	29 30S	28 0E
26	Batalha, Portugal	39 40N	8 53W
37	Batalpashinsk, U.S.S.R.	44 16N	42 3E
44	Batang (Baanfu), China	30 0N	99 30E
39	Batangas, Philippines	14 0N	121 10E
30	Bátaszék, Hungary	46 14N	18 41E
39	Batavia, Java	6 10S	106 50E
47	Bateman, N.S.W.	35 46S	150 8E
63	Batesville, U.S.A.	35 45N	91 43W

MAP
14 **Bath**, England 51 23N 2 20W
63 **Bath**, U.S.A. 43 23N 69 25W
17 **Bathgate**, Scotland 55 54N 3 38W
58 **Bathurst**, Canada 47 37N 64 43W
52 **Bathurst**, Gambia 13 23N 16 38W
49 **Bathurst**, N.S.W. 33 28S 149 31E
57 **Bathurst**, U. of S. Africa 33 33S 26 50E
13 **Batley**, England 53 43N 1 38W
42 **Batticaloa**, Ceylon 7 44N 81 42E
15 **Battle**, England 50 55N 0 29E
37 **Batum**, U.S.S.R. 41 37N 41 33E
66 **Baturité**, Brazil 4 20S 39 0W
20 **Batz**, France 48 45N 4 0W
54 **Bauchi**, Nigeria 10 18N 9 50E
20 **Baugé**, France 47 32N 0 10W
35 **Bausk**, Latvia 56 27N 24 11E
24 **Bautzen**, Germany 51 12N 14 26E
24 **Bavaria, St.**, Germany 47 24 to 50 30N 9 0 to 14 0E
15 **Bawdsey**, England 52 1N 1 25E
13 **Bawtry**, England 53 26N 1 1W
63 **Bay City**, U.S.A. 43 33N 83 50W
20 **Bayeux**, France 49 18N 0 45W
20 **Bayonne**, France 43 28N 1 28W
24 **Bayreuth**, Germany 49 57N 11 34E
27 **Baza**, Spain 37 15N 2 45W
31 **Bazargic.** *See* **Dobrich**
21 **Bazas**, France 44 28N 0 12W
48 **Beachport**, S. Australia 37 30S 139 59E
15 **Beachy Hd.**, England 50 44N 0 15E
15 **Beaconsfield**, England 51 36N 0 39W
49 **Beaconsfield**, Tasmania 41 11S 146 48E
57 **Beaconsfield**, U. of S. Africa 28 55S 24 40E
51 **Bealey**, New Zealand 43 18S 171 36E
14 **Beaminster**, England 50 48N 2 44W
21 **Bearn, old prov.**, France 43 14N 0 50W
33 **Beatenberg**, Switz. 46 42N 7 47E
63 **Beatrice**, U.S.A. 40 22N 96 43W
17 **Beattock**, Scotland 55 18N 3 27W
21 **Beaucaire**, France 43 50N 4 38E
49 **Beaudesert**, Queensland 27 59S 153 2E
63 **Beaufort**, U.S.A. 34 49N 76 36W
48 **Beaufort**, Victoria 37 27S 143 23E
57 **Beaufort W.**, U. of S. Africa 32 23S 22 35E
15 **Beaulieu**, England 50 50N 1 27W
16 **Beauly**, Scotland 57 29N 4 28W
12 **Beaumaris**, Wales 56 16N 4 5W
22 **Beaumont**, Belgium 50 14N 4 14E
63 **Beaumont**, U.S.A. 30 2N 94 0W
20 **Beaune**, France 47 1N 4 51E
20 **Beauvais**, France 49 28N 2 6E
62 **Beaver**, U.S.A. 36 50N 100 40W
42 **Beawar**, India 26 2N 74 21E
15 **Beccles**, England 52 27N 1 33E
57 **Bechuanaland Prot.**, Africa 24 0S 22 0E
15 **Beckenham**, England 51 24N 0 2W
13 **Bedale**, England 54 17N 1 36W
21 **Bédarieux**, France 43 37N 3 9E
14 **Beddgelert**, Wales 53 2N 4 6W
57 **Bedford**, U. of S. Africa 32 44S 26 10E
15 **Bedford & Co.**, Eng. 52 9N 0 28W
13 **Bedlington**, England 55 7N 1 38W
48 **Beech Forest**, Victoria 38 39S 143 32E
49 **Beechworth**, Victoria 36 20S 146 42E
14 **Beer Alston**, England 50 29N 4 12W
41 **Beersheba**, Palestine 31 17N 34 54E
49 **Bega**, N.S.W. 36 11S 149 48E
14 **Beguildy**, Wales 52 25N 3 12W
34 **Beieren**, Norway 67 0N 15 48E
55 **Beilul**, Eritrea 13 10N 42 24E
26 **Beira, prov.**, Portugal 40 30N 8 0W
40 **Beirut**, Syria 33 54N 35 32E
41 **Beisan**, Palestine 32 31N 35 36E
41 **Beit Jala**, Palestine 31 55N 35 12E
41 **Beit Jibrin**, Palestine 31 8N 34 52E
57 **Beitbridge**, S. Rhodesia 22 15S 30 12E
17 **Beith**, Scotland 55 45N 4 37W
41 **Beitin**, Palestine 31 55N 35 15E
26 **Beja**, Portugal 38 2N 7 53W
26 **Bejar**, Spain 40 21N 5 45W
30 **Békéscsaba**, Hungary 46 41N 21 9E
42 **Bela**, India 26 17N 66 17E
31 **Bela Crkva**, Yugoslavia 44 55N 21 28E
61 **Belcher Is.**, Canada 56 30N 80 10W
18 **Belcoo**, N. Ireland 54 18N 7 52W
66 **Belem**, Brazil 1 10S 48 15W
18 **Belfast**, N. Ireland 54 37N 5 55W
13 **Belford**, England 55 36N 1 49W
20 **Belfort, dept.**, France 47 39N 6 52E
24 **Belgard**, Germany 54 0N 16 0E
42 **Belgaum**, India 15 55N 74 33E
54 **Belgian Congo, Col.**, Central Africa 5 to 12S 12 to 31E
8 **Belgium, Kingdom**, Europe 50 31N 4 0E
30 **Belgrade**, Yugoslavia 44 50N 20 31E
51 **Belgrove**, New Zealand 41 29S 172 56E
64 **Belize**, Brit. Honduras 17 30N 88 12W
28 **Bellagio**, Italy 45 46N 9 19E
33 **Bellano**, Italy 46 3N 9 18E
42 **Bellary**, India 15 16N 76 55E
19 **Bellaugh**, Eire 52 26N 7 59W

MAP
20 **Belle Ile**, France 47 15N 3 20W
61 **Belle I.**, Newfoundland 51 50N 55 10W
18 **Belleek**, N. Ireland 54 29N 8 5W
21 **Bellegarde**, France 47 59N 2 27E
49 **Bellerive**, Tasmania 42 47S 147 27E
21 **Belley**, France 45 47N 5 43E
13 **Bellingham**, England 55 10N 2 15W
62 **Bellingham**, U.S.A. 48 45N 122 25W
33 **Bellinzona**, Switzerland 46 12N 9 2E
67 **Bello Horizonte**, Brazil 19 50S 44 25W
28 **Belluno**, Italy 46 8N 12 17E
28 **Belmez**, Spain 38 15N 5 15W
67 **Belmonte**, Brazil 16 5S 39 0W
27 **Belmonte**, Spain 39 35N 2 43W
18 **Belmullet**, Eire 54 13N 10 0W
31 **Belogradchik**, Bulg. 43 35N 22 41E
62 **Beloit**, U.S.A. 39 26N 98 7W
33 **Belp**, Switzerland 46 53N 7 30E
15 **Belper**, England 53 2N 1 29W
48 **Beltana**, S. Australia 30 51S 138 22E
18 **Belturbet**, Eire 54 6N 7 27W
29 **Belvedere**, Italy 39 40N 15 50E
15 **Bembridge**, England 50 42N 1 5W
17 **Ben Cruachan**, Scot. 56 25N 5 5W
16 **Ben Dearg**, Scotland 56 53N 3 50W
17 **Ben Lawers**, Scotland 53 33N 4 13W
47 **Ben Lomond**, N.S.W. 30 0S 151 44E
17 **Ben Lomond**, Scot. 56 11N 4 37W
49 **Ben Lomond**, Tas. 41 37S 147 40E
16 **Ben Macdhui**, Scot. 57 3N 3 38W
17 **Ben More**, Scotland 56 26N 6 5W
16 **Ben More Assynt**, Scot. 58 8N 4 47W
17 **Ben Nevis**, Scotland 56 48N 4 58W
49 **Benalla**, Victoria 36 31S 145 59E
43 **Benares**, India 25 18N 83 2E
26 **Benavente**, Spain 42 1N 5 43W
39 **Bencoolen**, Sumatra 3 50S 102 5E
46 **Bencubbin**, W. Aust. 31 0S 117 50E
31 **Benderi**, Rumania 46 52N 29 21E
49 **Bendigo**, Victoria 36 45S 144 19E
25 **Bendin**, Poland 50 20N 19 10E
49 **Bendock**, Victoria 37 20S 149 0E
29 **Benevento**, Italy 41 7N 40 47E
43 **Bengal, prov.**, India 24 15N 89 45E
39 **Bengal, B. of**, Asia 18 0N 91 0E
52 **Benghazi**, Libya 32 0N 20 0E
54 **Benguella**, Angola 12 35S 13 25E
40 **Beni Suef**, Egypt 29 2N 31 5E
54 **Benin**, Nigeria 6 30N 5 30E
62 **Benson**, U.S.A. 31 59N 110 19W
15 **Bentley**, England 51 59N 1 7E
24 **Bentschen**, Poland 52 14N 15 55E
54 **Benue, R.**, Nigeria 7 46N 8 30E
30 **Beograd.** *See* **Belgrade**
18 **Beragh**, N. Ireland 54 33N 7 10W
30 **Berane**, Yugoslavia 42 50N 19 50E
30 **Berat**, Albania 40 44N 19 59E
24 **Beraun**, Cz.-slov. 49 58N 14 6E
52 **Berbera**, Br. Som. 10 15N 44 50E
66 **Berbice, R.**, Br. Guiana 5 40N 57 40W
37 **Berdichev**, U.S.S.R. 49 55N 28 30E
37 **Berdyansk**, U.S.S.R. 46 45N 36 46E
14 **Bere Regis**, England 50 46N 2 13W
57 **Berea**, Basutoland 29 16S 27 40E
25 **Beregszász**, Cz.-slov. 48 14N 22 41E
15 **Berehaven**, Eire 51 40N 9 55W
40 **Berenice**, Egypt 23 56N 35 24E
25 **Berestechko**, Poland 50 20N 25 6E
31 **Beresti**, Rumania 46 5N 27 54E
36 **Berezov**, U.S.S.R. 64 5N 65 0E
27 **Berga**, Spain 42 5N 1 50E
28 **Bergamo**, Italy 45 42N 9 40E
23 **Bergedorf**, Germany 53 30N 10 13E
33 **Bergen**, Norway 60 25N 5 20E
22 **Bergen op-Zoom**, Neth. 51 29N 4 17E
21 **Bergerac**, France 44 51N 0 29E
35 **Bergsjö**, Sweden 61 58N 17 6E
33 **Bergün**, Switzerland 46 38N 9 44E
43 **Berhampur**, India 19 18N 84 50E
6 **Bering Sea**, Pacific Oc. 56 0N 174 0E
6 **Bering Str.**, N. Amer. 66 0N 170 0W
40 **Beris**, Egypt 24 39N 30 34E
26 **Berja**, Spain 36 55N 2 58W
14 **Berkeley**, England 51 42N 2 25W
15 **Berkhampstead**, Eng. 51 45N 0 35W
31 **Berkovitza**, Bulgaria 43 15N 23 8E
15 **Berkshire, Co.**, Eng. 51 26N 1 0W
34 **Berlevaåg**, Norway 70 42N 29 10E
24 **Berlin**, Germany 52 34N 13 20E
27 **Bermeo**, Spain 43 26N 2 48W
6 **Bermuda I.**, At. Ocean 32 15N 64 50W
20 **Bernay**, France 50 16N 1 44E
24 **Bernburg**, Germany 51 46N 11 45E
33 **Berne, and Canton**, Switzerland 46 58N 7 28E
33 **Bernese Oberland**, Switzerland 46 25N 7 30E
16 **Berriedale**, Scotland 58 11N 2 29W
49 **Berrigan**, N.S.W. 35 39S 145 50E
49 **Berry**, N.S.W. 34 47S 150 41E
57 **Berseba**, S. W. Africa 25 55S 17 41E
16 **Bervie**, Scotland 56 51N 2 27W
17 **Berwick, Co.**, Scotland 55 55N 2 30W
13 **Berwick upon Tweed**, England 55 48N 2 04W

MAP
14 **Berwyn Mts.**, Wales 52 52N 3 34W
20 **Besançon**, France 47 16N 6 1E
31 **Bessarabia, dist.**, Rum. 47 0N 28 30E
21 **Bessèges**, France 44 17N 4 5E
26 **Betanzos**, Spain 43 18N 8 11W
41 **Bethania**, Palestine 31 47N 35 17E
57 **Bethanie**, U. of S. Af. 29 32S 26 1E
57 **Bethany**, S.W. Af. 26 30S 16 52E
41 **Bethel.** *See* **Beitin**
57 **Bethel**, U. of S. Africa 30 25S 29 1E
12 **Bethesda**, Wales 53 12N 4 0W
41 **Bethlehem**, Palestine 31 42N 35 12E
57 **Bethlehem**, U. of S. Af. 28 5S 28 30E
57 **Bethulie**, U. of S. Af. 30 31S 25 59E
20 **Bethune**, France 50 32N 2 40E
22 **Bettemburg**, Luxem. 49 31N 6 5E
43 **Bettia**, India 26 45N 84 37E
12 **Bettws-y-Coed**, Wales 53 5N 3 48W
25 **Beuthen**, Germany 50 22N 19 0E
13 **Beverley**, England 53 51N 0 27W
22 **Beverloo**, Belgium 51 5N 5 13E
33 **Bex**, Switzerland 46 15N 7 0E
14 **Bewdley**, England 52 23N 2 19W
15 **Bexhill**, England 50 50N 0 28E
29 **Beziers**, France 43 21N 3 14E
42 **Bezwadi**, India 16 33N 80 36E
43 **Bhagalpur**, India 25 12N 87 5E
43 **Bhamo**, Burma 24 15N 97 12E
42 **Bhartpur**, India 27 11N 77 35E
42 **Bhaunagar**, India 21 47N 72 14E
42 **Bhilsa**, India 23 32N 77 50E
42 **Bhiwani**, India 28 45N 76 13E
42 **Bhopal**, India 23 15N 77 28E
42 **Bhor**, India 18 5N 74 0E
42 **Bhuj**, India 23 18N 69 43E
42 **Bhusawal**, India 21 0N 75 15E
43 **Bhutan, St.**, Asia 27 30N 91 0E
25 **Bialystok**, Poland 53 6N 23 18E
29 **Bianco**, Italy 38 8N 16 9E
21 **Biarritz**, France 43 27N 1 36W
33 **Biasca**, Switzerland 46 22N 9 58E
24 **Biberach**, Germany 48 8N 9 48E
15 **Bicester**, England 51 54N 1 9W
54 **Bida**, Nigeria 9 5N 4 49E
42 **Bidar**, India 17 55N 77 34E
13 **Biddulph**, England 53 8N 2 8W
14 **Bideford**, England 51 1N 4 13W
32 **Bidigli**, Greece 41 2N 26 19E
33 **Biel**, Switzerland 47 8N 71 4E
31 **Biela**, Bulgaria 43 25N 25 46E
24 **Bielefeld**, Germany 52 2N 8 30E
25 **Bielitz**, Poland 49 50N 19 1E
28 **Biella**, Italy 45 32N 8 6E
30 **Bielopolye**, Y.-slavia 43 1N 19 42E
31 **Bielovo**, Bulgaria 43 26N 22 45E
62 **Big Horn Mts.**, U.S.A. 44 30N 107 30W
17 **Biggar**, Scotland 55 37N 3 31W
15 **Biggleswade**, Eng. 52 6N 0 15W
32 **Bigha**, Turkey 40 15N 27 18E
32 **Bighadich**, Turkey 39 28N 28 10E
30 **Bihač**, Yugoslavia 44 51N 15 56E
43 **Bihar, & Prov.**, India 25 11N 85 32E
54 **Bihé**, Angola 12 40S 16 58E
42 **Bijapur**, India 16 53N 75 50E
42 **Bikamer**, India 28 2N 73 22E
42 **Bilaspur**, India 22 0N 82 15E
27 **Bilbao**, Spain 44 17N 2 55W
15 **Bildeston**, England 52 6N 0 55E
40 **Bilejik**, Turkey 40 10N 29 58E
30 **Bilek**, Yugoslavia 42 54N 18 25E
15 **Billericay**, England 51 37N 0 25E
13 **Billinghay**, England 53 5N 0 16W
62 **Billings**, U.S.A. 45 47N 108 40W
22 **Bilsen**, Belgium 50 53N 5 31E
14 **Bilston**, England 52 33N 2 3W
13 **Binbrook**, England 53 27N 0 10W
22 **Binche**, Belgium 50 24N 4 10E
34 **Bindal**, Norway 65 5N 12 40E
24 **Bingen**, Germany 49 58N 7 57E
56 **Bingerville**, Fr. W. Af. 5 20N 3 52W
15 **Bingham**, England 52 57N 0 37W
63 **Binghampton**, U.S.A. 42 7N 75 50W
48 **Birdsville**, N. Terr. 25 50S 139 20E
46 **Birdum**, N. Terr. 15 30S 133 0E
41 **Bireh**, Palestine 31 50N 35 12E
40 **Birejik**, Turkey 37 3N 38 0E
41 **Birjand**, Iran 32 57N 59 8E
24 **Birkenfeld**, Germany 49 40N 7 8E
12 **Birkenhead**, England 53 23N 3 2W
15 **Birmingham**, Eng. 52 29N 1 52W
63 **Birmingham**, U.S.A. 33 30N 86 54W
17 **Birnam**, Scotland 56 33N 3 13W
24 **Birnbaum**, Poland 52 33N 15 55E
19 **Birr**, Eire 53 6N 7 55W
35 **Birshtani**, Lithuania 54 35N 23 55E
36 **Birsk**, U.S.S.R. 55 25N 55 30E
57 **Birthday**, U. of S. Af. 23 23S 30 48E
60 **Birtle**, Canada 51 0N 101 30W
8 **Biscay, B. of**, At. Oc. 45 50N 2 10W
29 **Bisceglie**, Italy 41 15N 16 29E
33 **Bischofszell**, Switz. 47 31N 9 13E
13 **Bishop Auckland**, Eng. 54 40N 1 40W
14 **Bishops Castle**, Eng. 53 30N 3 0W
15 **Bishop's Stortford**, England 51 52N 0 10E

MAP	Place	Lat.	Long.
15	**Bishop's Waltham,** England	50 58N	1 12W
52	**Biskra,** Algeria	34 55N	5 36E
15	**Bisley,** England	51 45N	2 8W
62	**Bismarck,** U.S.A.	46 38N	100 47W
52	**Bismarckburg,** Togo	8 10N	0 40E
52	**Bissago Is.,** W. Af.	11 30N	16 20W
52	**Bissao,** W. Africa	11 50N	15 40W
31	**Bîstrita,** Rumania	47 9N	30 31E
31	**Bistritz.** See **Bistrita**		
31	**Bistritza, R.,** Rum.	47 0N	26 0E
40	**Bitlis,** Turkey	28 39N	42 0E
31	**Bitolj,** Yugoslavia	41 2N	21 20E
29	**Bitonto,** Italy	41 8N	16 42E
24	**Bitterfeld,** Germany	51 38N	12 18E
57	**Bitterfontein,** U. of S. Africa	30 26S	19 3E
29	**Bivona,** Sicily	37 38N	13 22E
52	**Bizerta,** Tunis	37 30N	10 0E
30	**Bjelovar,** Yugoslavia	45 58N	16 51E
35	**Bjorkö,** Finland	60 20N	28 45E
34	**Björna,** Sweden	63 35N	18 40E
35	**Björneborg.** See **Pori**		
34	**Björnör,** Norway	64 12N	10 16E
23	**Björnsholm,** Denmark	56 53N	9 12E
34	**Bjurholm,** Sweden	63 55N	19 10E
62	**Black Cañon,** U.S.A.	35 50N	115 0W
24	**Black Forest,** Germany	48 20N	8 10E
9	**Black Sea,** Europe	43 0N	35 0E
47	**Blackall,** Queensland	42 24S	171 23E
51	**Blackball,** N.Z.	42 24S	171 23E
13	**Blackburn,** England	53 45N	2 29W
12	**Blackpool,** England	53 49N	3 3W
19	**Blackrock,** Eire	53 18N	6 11W
14	**Blaenavon,** England	51 45N	3 4W
14	**Blagdon,** England	51 19N	2 42W
45	**Blagoveshchensk,** U.S.SR.	50 25N	127 30E
20	**Blain,** France	47 28N	1 46W
17	**Blair Atholl,** Scotland	56 46N	3 50W
17	**Blairgowrie,** Scotland	56 36N	3 20W
31	**Blaj,** Rumania	46 10N	24 0E
21	**Blanc, Mt.,** France	45 50N	6 53E
62	**Blanca Pk.,** U.S.A.	37 30N	105 30W
14	**Blandford,** England	50 52N	2 8W
27	**Blanes,** Spain	41 40N	2 50E
22	**Blankenberghe,** Bel.	51 18N	3 7E
56	**Blantyre,** Nyasaland	15 46S	35 7E
17	**Blantyre,** Scotland	55 47N	4 6W
19	**Blarney,** Eire	51 56N	8 35W
15	**Blaston,** England	52 28N	0 46W
21	**Blaye,** France	45 8N	0 40W
49	**Blayney,** N.S.W.	33 30S	149 13E
24	**Bleiburg,** Austria, Ger.	46 38N	14 51E
31	**Blejesti,** Rumania	44 19N	25 27E
35	**Blekinge, Co.,** Sweden	56 20N	15 10E
24	**Blenheim,** Germany	48 40N	10 40E
51	**Blenheim,** N.Z.	41 29S	173 59E
19	**Blessington,** Eire	53 11N	6 32W
15	**Bletchley,** England	52 0N	0 45W
23	**Blexen,** Germany	53 32N	8 16E
48	**Bligh,** S. Australia	33 50S	136 35E
57	**Bloemfontein,** S. Afr.	29 9S	26 13E
57	**Bloemhof,** U. of S. Af.	27 40S	25 37E
20	**Blois,** France	47 36N	1 19E
25	**Blonie,** Poland	52 12N	29 39E
18	**Bloody Foreland,** Eire	55 8N	8 18W
63	**Bloomington,** U.S.A.	40 30N	89 5W
24	**Bludenz,** Austria, Ger.	47 10N	9 50E
49	**Blue Mts.,** N.S.W.	33 40S	150 25E
62	**Blue Mts.,** U.S.A.	45 0N	117 15W
55	**Blue Nile, R.,** Africa	10 0N	37 0E
18	**Blue Stack Mts.,** Eire	54 46N	8 5W
65	**Bluefields,** Nicaragua	11 59N	83 46W
51	**Bluff.** See **Campbelltown**		
62	**Bluff,** U.S.A.	37 19N	109 32W
51	**Bluff Harb.,** N.Z.	46 33S	168 10E
67	**Blumenau,** Brazil	27 0S	49 0W
48	**Blyth,** S. Australia	33 50S	138 35E
13	**Blyth, & R.,** England	55 8N	1 30W
15	**Blythburgh,** England	52 20N	1 35E
57	**Blythswood,** U. of S. A.	32 7S	28 0E
66	**Boa Vista,** Brazil	8 50S	39 50W
16	**Boat of Garten,** Scot.	57 15N	3 45W
28	**Bobbio,** Italy	44 49N	9 25E
37	**Bobrinets,** U.S.S.R.	48 2N	32 2E
37	**Bobruisk,** U.S.S.R.	53 8N	29 13E
64	**Bocas del Toro,** Pan.	9 30N	82 22W
25	**Bochnia,** Poland	49 59N	20 38E
22	**Bocholt,** Belgium	51 12N	2 35E
24	**Bocholt,** Germany	51 52N	6 37E
24	**Bochum,** Germany	51 28N	7 17E
35	**Boda,** Sweden	57 45N	10 17E
16	**Boddam,** Scotland	47 27N	1 47W
34	**Boden,** Sweden	65 50N	22 0E
14	**Bodmin,** England	50 29N	4 43W
34	**Bodö,** Norway	67 15N	14 25E
57	**Bogenfels,** S.W. Africa	27 20S	15 20E
23	**Bogense,** Denmark	55 34N	10 7E
49	**Boggabri,** N.S.W.	30 39S	150 0E
15	**Bognor Regis,** Eng.	50 47N	0 40W
23	**Bogö,** Denmark	54 56N	12 3E
66	**Bogota,** Colombia	4 30N	74 30W
43	**Bogra,** India	24 50N	89 30E
24	**Bohemia, Prov.,** Czech.	50 0N	14 0E
24	**Bohemian Forest,** Cz.	49 20N	13 5E
62	**Boise,** U.S.A.	43 43N	116 13W
23	**Boizenburg,** Germany	53 22N	10 43E
41	**Bokhara,** U.S.S.R.	39 45N	64 35E
57	**Bokkeveld,** U. of S. Af.	30 40S	19 0E
57	**Boksburg,** U. of S. Af.	26 17S	28 15E
31	**Bolgrad,** Rumania	45 42N	28 39E
67	**Bolivar,** Argentina	36 0S	61 15W
67	**Bolivia, St.,** S. America	17 0S	64 0W
37	**Bolkhov,** U.S.S.R.	53 28N	35 28E
33	**Bolligen,** Switzerland	46 59N	7 30E
13	**Bollington,** England	53 18N	2 7W
35	**Bollnäs,** Sweden	61 20N	16 40E
49	**Bollon,** Queensland	28 0S	147 25E
28	**Bologna,** Italy	44 29N	11 21E
39	**Bolsheryetsk,** U.S.S.R.	53 0N	156 20E
13	**Bolsover,** England	53 13N	1 0W
27	**Boltana,** Spain	42 28N	0 4E
13	**Bolton,** England	53 35N	2 28W
13	**Bolton Abbey,** Eng.	53 59N	1 54W
28	**Bolzano,** Italy	46 31N	11 21E
54	**Boma,** Belgian Congo	5 48S	13 12E
49	**Bombala,** N.S.W.	36 58S	149 12E
42	**Bombay & Prov.,** Ind.	19 0N	72 55E
52	**Bona,** Algeria	37 0N	7 50E
26	**Bonanza,** Spain	36 48N	6 20W
16	**Bonar Bri.,** Scotland	57 53N	4 20W
61	**Bonavista,** Newf.	48 40N	53 30W
17	**Bonawe,** Scotland	56 27N	5 12W
17	**Bo'ness,** Scotland	56 1N	3 36W
21	**Bonifacio,** Corsica	41 22N	9 11E
39	**Bonin Is.,** Japan	27 40N	142 10E
24	**Bonn,** Germany	50 43N	7 4E
21	**Bonneville,** France	46 4N	6 25E
54	**Bonny,** Nigeria	4 30N	7 23E
17	**Bonnyrigg,** Scotland	55 52N	3 6W
63	**Boone,** U.S.A.	42 2N	93 55W
46	**Boorabbin,** W. Aust.	31 15S	120 28E
48	**Boorthanna,** S. Aust.	28 40S	135 55E
12	**Bootle (Cumb.),** Eng.	54 17N	3 22W
12	**Bootle (Lancs.),** Eng.	53 27N	2 59W
35	**Boras,** Sweden	57 45N	13 30E
21	**Bordeaux,** France	44 50N	0 31W
48	**Border Town,** S. Aust.	36 17S	140 45E
28	**Bordighera,** Italy	43 49N	7 40E
15	**Bordon,** England	51 8N	0 51W
35	**Borga.** See **Porvoo**		
35	**Borgholm,** Sweden	56 50N	16 50E
28	**Borgo St. Domino,** It.	44 54N	10 1E
28	**Borgo S. Lorenzo,** It.	43 59N	11 29E
37	**Borisoglyebsk,** U.S.S.R.	51 26N	42 0E
37	**Borisov,** U.S.S.R.	54 12N	28 28E
27	**Borja,** Spain	41 50N	1 31W
22	**Borkulo,** Netherlands	52 7N	6 32E
24	**Borkum I.,** Germany	53 36N	6 40E
35	**Borlänge,** Sweden	62 25N	15 20E
28	**Bormio,** Italy	46 28N	10 22E
39	**Borneo I.,** Dut. E. Ind.	1 0N	115 0E
23	**Bornholm I.,** Denmark Inset	55 5N	15 0E
13	**Boroughbridge,** Eng.	54 6N	1 24W
36	**Borovich,** U.S.S.R.	28 27N	33 47E
15	**Borris,** Eire	52 36N	6 55W
14	**Borth,** Wales	52 29N	4 3W
23	**Borup Ringsted,** Den.	55 30N	11 58E
25	**Boryslaw,** Poland	49 19N	23 22E
29	**Bosa,** Sardinia	40 19N	8 29E
14	**Boscastle,** England	50 42N	4 40W
57	**Boshof,** U. of S. Africa	28 30S	25 12E
30	**Bosnia, dist.,** Y.-Slav.	44 0N	17 0E
32	**Bosporus,** Turkey	41 5N	29 5E
15	**Boston,** England	52 59N	0 1W
63	**Boston,** U.S.A.	42 25N	71 5W
49	**Botany B.,** N.S.W.	34 0S	151 12E
15	**Botesdale,** England	52 20N	1 1E
57	**Bothaville,** U. of S. Afr.	27 22S	26 40E
34	**Bothnia, G. of,** Europe	63 23N	20 40E
48	**Bothwell,** Tasmania	42 15S	147 1E
15	**Botley,** England	50 55N	1 17W
31	**Botosani,** Rumania	47 45N	26 39E
21	**Bouches-du Rhône, dept.,** France	43 34N	5 13E
33	**Boudry,** Switzerland	46 57N	6 51E
52	**Bougie,** Algeria	36 45N	5 0E
62	**Boulder,** U.S.A.	40 2N	105 22W
46	**Boulder,** W. Australia	31 47S	121 30E
20	**Boulogne,** France	50 43N	1 38E
20	**Boulogne,** France	50 43N	1 38E
21	**Boulogne,** France	43 18N	0 19E
60	**Boundary,** Canada	64 40N	141 0W
50	**Bounty I.,** N.Z. Inset	47 40S	178 40E
21	**Bourbon Lancy,** France	46 37N	3 47E
21	**Bourbon l'Archambault,** France	46 36N	3 3E
21	**Bourbonnais, old prov.,** France	46 26N	3 0E
21	**Bourg,** France	46 14N	5 15E
21	**Bourganeuf,** France	45 57N	1 44E
20	**Bourges,** France	47 5N	2 21E
20	**Bourgneuf,** France	47 2N	1 58W
21	**Bourgoin,** France	45 36N	5 17E
15	**Bourn,** England	52 47N	0 23W
14	**Bournemouth,** Eng.	50 44N	1 52W
49	**Bourke,** N.S.W.	30 5S	145 55E
22	**Bourtange,** Netherlands	53 1N	7 12E
68	**Bouvet I.,** S. Ocean	54 0S	4 0W
14	**Bovey Tracey,** Eng.	50 36N	4 40W
29	**Bovino,** Italy	41 12N	15 20E
47	**Bowen,** Queensland	20 0S	148 16E
13	**Bowes,** England	54 32N	2 1W
57	**Bowesdorp,** U. of S. Af.	30 7S	17 55E
17	**Bowmore,** Scotland	55 45N	6 16W
12	**Bowness,** England	54 57N	3 12W
49	**Bowral,** N.S.W.	34 29S	150 22E
18	**Boyle,** Eire	53 59N	8 19W
62	**Bozeman,** U.S.A.	45 37N	110 58W
28	**Bra,** Italy	44 42N	7 51E
22	**Brabant, prov.,** Belg.	50 40N	4 30E
16	**Bracadale,** Scotland	57 22N	6 23W
13	**Bracebridge,** England	52 14N	0 33W
34	**Bräcke,** Sweden	62 45N	16 30E
15	**Brackley,** England	52 2N	1 9W
31	**Brád,** Rumania	46 8N	22 48E
13	**Bradford,** England	53 48N	1 45W
14	**Bradford-on-Avon,** England	51 21N	2 13W
15	**Bradwell,** England	51 44N	0 55E
62	**Brady,** U.S.A.	31 9N	99 18W
16	**Braemar,** Scotland	57 1N	3 24W
16	**Braes of Angus,** Scot.	56 52N	3 0W
26	**Braga,** Portugal	41 35N	8 30W
66	**Bragança,** Brazil	0 55S	47 10W
26	**Bragança,** Portugal	41 50N	6 50W
34	**Brahestad.** See **Raahe**		
23	**Brahlstorf,** Germany	53 43N	11 43E
43	**Brahmaputra, R.,** Ind.	26 40N	93 30E
49	**Braidwood,** N.S.W.	35 29S	149 48E
31	**Braila,** Rumania	45 19N	27 59E
22	**Braine l Alleud,** Belg	50 40N	4 21E
22	**Braine le Comte,** Belg.	50 36N	4 9E
15	**Braintree,** England	51 53N	0 33E
24	**Brake,** Germany	53 20N	8 25E
12	**Brampton,** England	54 57N	2 43W
15	**Brancaster,** Eng.	52 48N	0 39E
66	**Branco, R.,** Brazil	1 0N	61 0W
23	**Brande,** Denmark	55 58N	9 8E
24	**Brandenburg, & Prov.,** Germany	52 24N	12 34E
57	**Brandfort,** U. of S. Af.	28 35S	26 30E
60	**Brandon,** Canada	49 50N	99 58W
15	**Brandon,** England	52 26N	0 38E
57	**Brandvlei,** U. of S. Af.	30 30S	20 30E
31	**Brasov.** See **Brasso**	45 38N	25 34E
54	**Brass,** Nigeria	4 15N	6 10E
31	**Brasso,** Rumania	45 40N	25 39E
25	**Bratislava,** Cz.-slov.	48 10N	17 6E
25	**Braunsberg,** Germany	54 22N	19 50E
19	**Bray,** Eire	53 13N	6 6W
66	**Brazil, St.,** S. Am.	0 30S	35 75W
54	**Brazzaville,** Fr. Eq. Af.	4 18S	15 15E
30	**Brčko,** Yugoslavia	44 53N	18 47E
17	**Breadalbane,** Scot.	56 30N	4 0W
17	**Brechin,** Scotland	56 44N	2 40W
14	**Brecknock, Co.,** Wales	52 0N	3 30W
14	**Brecon,** Wales	51 57N	3 23W
22	**Breda,** Netherlands	51 36N	4 47E
57	**Bredasdorp,** U. of S. Africa	34 25S	20 6E
23	**Bredebro,** Denmark	55 4N	8 50E
24	**Bremen,** Germany	53 6N	8 46E
24	**Bremerhaven,** Ger.	53 32N	8 32E
57	**Bremersdorp,** Swazi.	26 33S	31 29E
28	**Brenner P.,** Italy	47 0N	11 20E
15	**Brentford,** England	51 29N	0 19W
15	**Brentwood,** England	51 37N	0 11E
28	**Brescia,** Italy	45 36N	10 12E
25	**Breslau,** Germany	51 8N	17 0E
31	**Bresnik,** Bulgaria	42 45N	22 54E
20	**Brest,** France	48 26N	4 30W
25	Brest **Litovsk.** See **Brzesc nad Bugiem**		
35	**Brevik,** Norway	59 10N	9 40E
25	**Brezno,** Czechoslovakia	48 50N	19 40E
21	**Briancon,** France	44 53N	6 38E
20	**Briare,** France	47 39N	2 48E
19	**Bri Chualann** See **Bray**		
14	**Bridgend,** Wales	51 30N	3 34W
63	**Bridgeport,** U.S.A.	41 14N	73 20W
65	**Bridgetown,** Barbados	13 0N	60 0W
46	**Bridgetown,** W. Austl.	33 58S	116 7E
14	**Bridgnorth,** England	52 32N	2 25W
14	**Bridgwater,** England	51 7N	3 0W
13	**Bridlington,** England	54 5N	0 12W
13	**Bridlington Quay,** England	54 5N	0 12W
14	**Bridport,** England	50 44N	2 45W
25	**Brieg, Germany**	50 54N	17 26E
33	**Brieg,** Switzerland	46 19N	8 0E
20	**Brienne,** France	48 24N	4 32E
33	**Brienz,** Switzerland	46 46N	8 1E
20	**Briey,** France	49 17N	5 56E
13	**Brigg,** England	53 34N	0 29W
15	**Brightlingsea,** Eng.	51 49N	1 2E
15	**Brighton,** England	50 49N	0 9W
49	**Brighton,** Victoria	37 55S	145 0E
21	**Brignoles,** France	43 24N	6 3E
27	**Brihuega,** Spain	40 44N	2 52W
15	**Brill,** England	51 49N	1 3W
29	**Brindisi,** Italy	40 39N	17 54E

MAP
21 Brioude, France .....45 16N 3 23 E
47 Brisbane, Queensland..27 30 s 153 0 E
14 Bristol, England 51 27N 2 33w
62 Bristol, U.S.A. 36 35N 82 17w
14 Bristol Channel, Eng. 51 20N 3 30w
57 British Bechuanaland,
　　U. of S. Africa ....27 0N 23 0 E
60 British Columbia,
　　prov., Canada 50 to 60N 115 to 135w
66 British Guiana, Col.,
　　S. America 4 0N 59 0w
64 British Honduras,
　　Cent. America 17 0N 88 45w
39 British North Borneo,
　　East Indies .... 5 0N 118 0 E
52 British Somaliland,
　　Prot., Africa .... 9 30N 46 30 E
14 Briton Ferry, Wales...51 38N 3 49w
57 Britstown, U. of S. Afr.30 35 s 23 31 E
20 Brittany, old prov., Fr.48 0N 2 40w
26 Briviesca, Spain 42 35N 3 20w
28 Brixen, Italy ....46 45N 11 40 E
14 Brixham, England 50 24N 3 30w
25 Brno. See Brünn
42 Broach, India 58 15N 6 15w
17 Broad Law, Scotland ..55 30N 3 20w
16 Broadford, Scotland ..57 14N 5 53w
15 Broadstairs, England 51 21N 1 26 E
14 Broadway, England ..42 5N 1 57w
61 Brockville, Canada ...44 37N 75 46w
30 Brod, Yugoslavia ....45 8N 18 0 E
17 Brodick, Scotland 55 35N 5 8w
25 Brody, Poland ....50 5N 25 7 E
47 Broken Hill, N.S.W. .31 58 s 141 29 E
56 Broken Hill, N. Rhod. 14 19 s 28 40 E
25 Bromberg. See Bydgoszcz
15 Bromley, England .....51 25N 0 1 E
15 Bromsgrove, England 52 20N 2 4w
14 Bromyard, England ..52 11N 2 29w
34 Brönnöysund, Norway 65 29N 12 20 E
23 Bröns, Denmark ......55 12N 8 45 E
46 Broome, W. Australia .18 0 s 122 15 E
16 Brora, Scotland 58 0N 3 50w
31 Brosceni, Rumania ..44 48N 22 55 E
13 Brough, England 54 32N 2 20w
12 Broughton, England .54 17N 3 12w
16 Broughton, Scotland ..55 37N 3 25w
17 Broughty Ferry, Scot..56 29N 2 52w
14 Brown Willy, England.50 30N 4 40w
62 Brownsville, U.S.A. ..25 58N 97 30w
62 Brownwood, U.S.A. ..31 42N 98 47w
46 Bruce, Mt., W. Austrl. 22 29 s 118 28 E
24 Bruck, Austria Ger. ..47 26N 15 19 E
22 Bruges, Belgium ......51 13N 3 12 E
33 Brugg, Switzerland ..47 29N 8 11 E
41 Brundall, England ...52 37N 1 26 E
39 Brunei, Brit. prot.,
　　Borneo .... 4 55 114 55 E
25 Brünn, Czechoslovakia 46 11N 16 38 E
33 Brunnen, Switzerland ..47 0N 8 36 E
51 Brunner, New Zealand 42 29 s 171 21 E
23 Brunsbüttel, Germany 53 53N 9 7 E
24 Brunswick, Germany ..52 15N 10 30 E
63 Brunswick U.S.A. ..31 13N 81 30w
32 Brusa, See Bursa
22 Brussels, Belgium.....50 51N 4 21 E
24 Brux, Czechoslovakia .50 22N 13 40 E
37 Bryansk, Poland ......52 48N 22 50 E
37 Bryansk, U.S.S.R. ..53 20N 34 20 E
14 Brynmawr, Wales ...51 48N 3 7w
23 Bryrup, Denmark ...56 2N 9 31 E
31 Brza Palanka, Yugo. .44 26N 22 30 E
25 Brzesc nad Bugiem,
　　Poland..............52 10N 23 40 E
51 Bua, Fiji Is. ....Inset16 40 s 178 35 E
66 Bucaramanga, Col. ... 7 20N 73 20w
31 Bucharest, Rumania ..44 25N 26 5 E
17 Buchlyvie, Scotland ..56 6N 4 17w
16 Buckie, Scotland 57 40N 2 58w
15 Buckingham & Co.,
　　England 52 1N 1 0w
50 Buckley, New Zealand 38 22 s 178 20 E
31 Bucuresti. See Bucharest
25 Buczacz, Poland ......49 5N 25 24 E
30 Budapest, Hungary ..47 29N 19 5 E
14 Bude, England 50 49N 4 33w
31 Budesti, Rumania ....44 14N 26 28 E
14 Budleigh Salterton,
　　England 50 38N 3 18w
28 Budrio, Italy ....44 36N 11 33 E
32 Budrun, Turkey ....37 1N 27 30 E
54 Buea, Nigeria .... 4 12N 9 0 E
67 Buenaventura, Col. .. 4 5N 77 0w
67 Buenos Aires, Argen. 34 40 s 58 30w
62 Buffalo, U.S.A. 44 30N 106 50w
62 Buffalo, U.S.A. 42 55N 78 58w
29 Buffaloria, Italy ......39 45 16 26 E
37 Bug R., Poland ....52 38N 21 35 E
37 Bug R., U.S.S.R. 47 20N 31 30w
14 Builth, Wales 52 9N 3 24w
41 Bujnurd, Iran ....37 22N 57 12 E
54 Bukama, Belgian Con. 9 10 s 25 50 E
55 Bukoba, Tanganyika . 1 10 s 37 50 E
31 Bukovina, dist., Rum. 47 53N 25 30 E

MAP
54 Bukuru, Nigeria ..... 9 46N 8 53 E
33 Bülach, Switzerland ..47 31N 8 35 E
32 Bulair, Turkey. See Gelibolu
32 Bulania, Turkey ....37 26N 28 40 E
56 Bulawayo, S. Rhod. ..20 13 s 28 41 E
40 Buldur, Turkey ....37 42N 30 8 E
9 Bulgaria, King., Eur. .42 30N 25 0 E
40 Bullar, Br. Somali.....10 15N 44 0 E
33 Bulle, Switzerland ....46 37N 7 3 E
50 Bulls, New Zealand ..40 9 s 175 21 E
46 Bulong, W. Australia .30 45 s 121 50 E
42 Bulsar, India ....20 36N 72 59 E
39 Bulun, U.S.S.R. ....70 50N 124 0 E
57 Bulwer, U. of S. Africa 29 49 s 29 46 E
46 Bunbury, W. Austl. ...33 16 s 115 41 E
19 Bunclody. See Newtownbarry
18 Buncrana, Eire 55 8N 7 27w
47 Bundaberg, Queens. ..24 50 s 152 22 E
14 Bundelkhand, India ..24 30N 79 30 E
18 Bundoran, Eire 54 29N 8 17w
17 Bunessan, Scotland ..56 18N 6 12w
15 Bungay, England .....52 27N 1 25 E
15 Buntingdorf, England 51 57N 0 2w
57 Buntingville, U. of S.
　　Africa ....31 38 s 28 54 E
24 Bunzlau, Germany ....51 16N 15 36 E
40 Buraikah, Arabia .....23 30N 38 40 E
40 Bureida, Arabia ....26 30N 44 0 E
31 Bureir, Palestine .....31 35N 34 35 E
33 Buren, Switzerland ...47 8N 7 20 E
15 Burford, England .....51 49N 1 28 E
24 Burg, Germany ....54 27N 11 13 E
31 Burgas, Bulgaria .....42 30N 27 29 E
33 Burgdorf, Switzerland 47 3N 7 35 E
57 Burgersdorp, U. of S.
　　Africa ....31 5 s 26 15 E
15 Burgess Hill, England.50 58N 0 8w
13 Burgh-le-Marsh, Eng. 53 10N 0 15 E
13 Burghead, Scotland ...57 43N 3 28w
26 Burgos, Spain 42 42N 3 40w
21 Burgundy, old prov.,
　　France ....46 50N 4 40 E
42 Burhanpur, India .....21 20N 76 20 E
47 Burketown, Queens. ..17 48 s 139 35 E
63 Burlington, U.S.A. ...40 47N 91 10w
63 Burlington, Vt., U.S.A.44 29N 73 13w
43 Burma, St., Asia......21 0N 96 0 E
15 Burnham, England ....51 37N 0 49 E
15 Burnham Westgate,
　　England 52 57N 0 44w
47 Burnie, Tasmania ....41 2 s 145 52 E
13 Burnley England 53 47N 2 15w
17 Burnmouth, Scotland .55 51N 2 5w
47 Burns, N.S.W. ....32 5 s 141 0 E
17 Burntisland, Scotland 56 4N 3 13w
48 Burra. See Kooringa
16 Burravoe, Scotland....60 30N 1 2w
47 Burren Junc., N.S.W. 30 2 s 148 58 E
27 Burriana, Spain 39 52N 0 5w
49 Burrinjuck & Res.,
　　N.S.W. ....35 0 s 148 31 E
46 Burrundie, N. Territory13 33 s 131 55 E
14 Burry Port, Wales 51 39N 4 16w
32 Bursa, Turkey ....40 8N 29 10 E
12 Burton, England 53 15N 3 2w
15 Burton on Trent, Eng. 52 48N 1 38w
14 Burujird, Iran ....33 56N 48 47 E
13 Bury, England 53 27N 0 7w
15 Bury St. Edmunds,
　　England ....52 15N 0 43 E
40 Bushire, Iran ....29 0N 50 45 E
18 Bushmills, N. Ireland .55 13N 6 31w
35 Buskerud, Co., Nor. ..60 20N 8 20 E
46 Busselton, W. Austl. ..33 31 s 115 21 E
28 Busto Arsizio, Italy...45 40N 8 40 E
37 Busuluk, U.S.S.R. ....52 50N 52 3 E
23 Büsum, Germany .....54 8N 8 52 E
17 Bute, Co., & Kyles of,
　　Scotland 55 50N 5 5w
55 Butiaba, Uganda ..... 1 44N 31 30 E
23 Bütow, Germany .....54 11N 17 29 E
62 Butte, U.S.A. 46 0N 112 30w
57 Butterworth, U. of S.
　　Africa ....32 23 s 28 12 E
24 Butzow, Germany ....53 52N 11 58 E
13 Buxton, England 53 15N 1 54w
31 Buzau, Rumania .....45 8N 26 54 E
56 Bwana M'Kubwa, N.
　　Rhodesia ....12 57 s 28 50 E
25 Bydgoszcz, Poland ...53 8N 18 0 E
25 Byela, Poland ....52 3N 23 3 E
35 Byelaya, U.S.S.R. ....58 15N 27 5 E
37 Byelaya Tserkov,
　　U.S.S.R. ....49 50N 30 4 E
37 Byelgorod, U.S.S.R. ..50 34N 36 29 E
25 Byelitsi, Poland ......53 40N 25 20 E
25 Byelovyeja, Poland ..52 41N 23 52 E
25 Byelsk, Poland ....52 47N 23 11 E
34 Bygdeå, Sweden .....64 2N 20 59 E
35 Bygland, Norway .....58 50N 7 50 E
37 Bykhov, U.S.S.R. ....53 30N 30 17 E
23 Byllderup, Denmark ..54 57N 9 8 E
47 Byron, B. & C., N.S.W.30 50 s 153 35 E
15 Bytham, England 52 45N 0 29w

MAP
26 Cabeza, Spain.........38 42N 5 14w
54 Cabinda, Belgian Congo 6 08 s 24 20 E
61 Cabot Str., N. America 47 0N 59 0w
29 Caccamo, Sicily ....37 54N 13 36 E
67 Cacequy, Brazil ....30 0 s 54 30w
26 Caceres, Spain 39 5N 6 21w
67 Cachinal, Chile ....24 40 s 69 30w
66 Cachoeira, Brazil .....12 40 s 39 0w
54 Caconda, Angola .....13 45 s 15 20 E
54 Cabiri, Angola .... 9 0 s 13 30 E
14 Cader Idris, Mt.,Wales 52 43N 3 55w
26 Cadiz, Spain 36 30N 6 20w
14 Caerleon, England ...51 37N 2 57w
20 Caen, France 49 13N 0 21w
12 Caergwrle, Wales 53 7N 3 04w
12 Caernarvon, & Co.,
　　Wales 53 8N 4 15w
14 Caerphilly, Wales ...51 35N 3 13w
41 Caesarea. See El Kaisarieh
41 Caesarea Philippi. See Banias
28 Cagli, Italy ....43 36N 12 39 E
29 Cagliari, Sardinia ....39 15N 9 08 E
19 Caha Mts., Eire.......51 47N 9 40w
52 Caherconlish, Eire ...52 36N 8 29w
19 Cahir, Eire 52 22N 7 55w
19 Cahirciveen, Eire 51 57N 10 14w
19 Cahore Pt., Eire 52 35N 6 12w
21 Cahors, France ....44 26N 1 25 E
65 Caibarien, Cuba 22 28N 79 32w
65 Caicos Is., Jamaica ..21 50N 72 0w
65 Caimanera, Cuba 20 0N 75 10w
68 Caird Coast, Antarctica 75 0 s 28 0w
47 Cairns, Queensland ..16 58 s 145 44 E
40 Cairo, Egypt ....30 1N 31 13 E
63 Cairo, U.S.A. 37 1N 89 11w
13 Caister, England ......52 38N 1 43 E
13 Caistor, England 53 30N 0 18w
16 Caithness, Co., Scot. .58 25N 3 25w
66 Cajamarca, Peru ..... 7 0 s 79 30w
26 Cala, Spain 37 57N 6 21w
57 Cala, U. of S. Africa ..31 31 s 27 41 E
54 Calabar, Nigeria ..... 4 57N 8 20 E
66 Calabozo, Venezuela . 8 40N 67 30w
29 Calabria, dept., Italy .39 0N 16 30 E
31 Calafat, Rumania ....43 49N 23 0 E
27 Calahorra, Spain 42 18N 1 59w
20 Calais, France ....50 58N 1 50 E
63 Calais, U.S.A. 45 9N 67 14w
66 Calamar, Colombia ...10 19N 74 49w
39 Calamianes I., Philip-
　　pines ....12 0N 120 0 E
27 Calamocha, Spain 40 51N 1 15w
31 Calarasi, Rumania ...44 12N 17 22 E
27 Calatayud, Spain.....41 22N 1 38w
43 Calcutta, India.......22 32N 88 30 E
26 Caldas, Portugal 39 22N 9 10w
13 Calder R., England...53 42N 1 43w
67 Caldera, Chile ....27 0 s 70 50w
62 Caldwell, U.S.A. 43 43N 116 40w
14 Caldy I., Wales 51 38N 4 40w
57 Caledon, U. of S. Af. .29 30N 27 0 E
57 Caledon R., U. of S. Af. 30 0 s 26 50 E
66 Caledonia, Brit. Guiana 7 40N 58 25w
16 Caledonian Canal,
　　Scotland 57 0N 5 0w
12 Calf of Man, I. of Man.54 3N 4 40w
60 Calgary, Canada 51 0N 114 2w
66 Cali, Colombia 3 30N 76 50w
42 Calicut, India.........11 15N 75 45 E
64 California, G. of, Mexico 28 0N 112 0w
62 California, St., U.S.A.
　　32 to 40 0N, 115 0 to 124 0w
57 Calitzdorp, U. of S. Af. 33 31 s 21 41 E
19 Callan, Eire 52 33N 7 23w
17 Callander, Scotland ..56 14N 4 12w
66 Callao, Peru ....12 2 s 77 10w
16 Callernish, Scotland..58 12N 6 44w
14 Callington, England...50 30N 4 18w
47 Calliope, Queensland .24 4 s 151 6 E
14 Caine, England 51 26N 1 59w
47 Caloundra, Queensland 26 35 s 153 10 E
29 Caltagirone, Sicily ...37 14N 14 31 E
29 Caltanissetta, Sicily ..37 29N 14 1 E
20 Calvados, dept.,France 49 3N 0 12w
21 Calvi, Corsica ....42 34N 8 43 E
57 Calvinia, U. of S.Africa 31 30 s 19 45 E
26 Calzada, Spain 38 39N 3 49w
15 Cam, R., England ....52 10N 0 05 E
65 Camagüey, Cuba 21 22N 77 59w
67 Camana, Peru ....16 20 s 72 30w
67 Camargo, Bolivia .....20 50 s 64 40w
64 Camargo, Mexico 26 19N 98 58w
42 Cambay, India........22 22N 72 38 E
42 Cambay, G. of, India..22 0N 72 0 E
39 Cambodia, st., Fr.
　　Indo-China ....12 0N 105 0 E
15 Camborne, England
　　Inset 50 13N 5 18w
20 Cambrai, France......50 10N 3 16 E
15 Cambridge, & Co.,
　　England ....53 13N 0 07 E
50 Cambridge, New
　　Zealand ....37 52 s 175 29 E
27 Cambrils, Spain ......41 5N 1 4 E
17 Cambuslang, Scotland.55 49N 4 10w

MAP
47 Camden, N.S.W. .....34 5 s 150 37 E
63 Camden, U.S.A........33 30N 92 50w
14 Camelford, England..50 37N 4 41w
28 Camerino, Italy ....43 11N 13 1 E
54 Cameroon Mt., Camer-
oons .... 4 30N 9 45 E
54 Cameroons, Fr. Mand.
Africa .... 5 30N 13 0 E
66 Cametá, Brazil........ 2 25 s 49 40w
26 Caminha, Portugal ...41 49N 8 50w
66 Camocim, Brazil...... 2 58 s 40 51w
19 Camolin, Eire 52 37N 6 26w
47 Camooweal, Queens-
land ....19 58 s 138 13 E
29 Campagna, Italy.....40 40N 15 7 E
29 Campagna, dept., It...41 0N 14 0 E
68 Campbell I., Southern
Oc. ....52 37 s 168 50 E
49 Campbelltown, N.S.W.34 4 s 150 37 E
47 Campbell Town,
Tasmania ....41 51 s 147 30 E
51 Campbelltown, N.Z. ..44 35 s 168 19 E
17 Campbeltown, Scot. ..55 26N 5 36w
64 Campêche, Mexico ...19 50N 90 32w
64 Campêche, G. of, Mex. 20 0N 93 0w
47 Camperdown, Victoria 38 12 s 143 10 E
26 Campillos, Spain....37 3N 4 50w
67 Campinas, Brazil....22 50 s 47 0w
67 Campo Maior, Portugal 38 58N 7 9w
28 Campobasso, Italy...41 33N 14 41 E
67 Campos, Brazil......22 0 s 41 30w
31 Campulungul Mol.,
Rumania ....47 31N 25 33 E
58 Canada, Dom. of,
N. Amer. 42 0 to 70 0N, 60 0 to
140 0w
62 Canadian R., U.S.A...35 59N 101 0w
32 Canakkale, Turkey....40 5N 26 30 E
67 Cananéa, Brazil.....25 0 s 48 0w
52 Canary Is., N. Atlan. O. 28 30N 16 0w
17 Canberra, Fed. Terr. ..35 15 s 149 10 E
20 Cancale, France......48 41N 1 51w
26 Candás, Spain 43 45N 5 47w
32 Candià, Crete Inset 35 15N 25 0 E
32 Canea, Crete Inset 35 32N 24 1 E
27 Canfranc, Spain......42 42N 0 30w
26 Cangas, Spain 43 23N 5 12w
26 Cangas de Tineo,
Spain 43 10N 6 32w
29 Canicatti, Sicily....37 21N 13 48 E
27 Canjáyar, Spain......37 1N 2 42w
42 Cannanore, India ...11 53N 75 23 E
21 Cannes, France .....43 32N 6 59 E
14 Cannock, England....52 43N 62 1w
14 Cannock Chase, Eng. .52 45N 2 0w
33 Canobbio, Italy ....46 4N 8 40 E
17 Canonbie, Scotland...55 5N 0 55w
29 Canosa, Italy ....41 13N 16 3 E
28 Canossa, Italy .....44 37N 10 31 E
21 Cantabrian Mts.,Spain 43 5N 4 30w
21 Cantal, dept., France ..45 13N 2 45 E
26 Cantalapiedra, Spain ..41 7N 5 14w
27 Cantavieja, Spain 40 32N 0 23w
26 Cantanhede, Portugal .40 20N 8 37w
15 Canterbury, England .51 17N 1 05 E
51 Canterbury, prov.,
N. Z. ....43 40 s 171 20 E
51 Canterbury Plains,
N.Z. ....43 50 s 171 30 E
51 Canterbury Bight,
N.Z. ....44 20 s 172 0 E
26 Cantillana, Spain 37 36N 5 50w
45 Canton, China......23 15N 113 20 E
48 Cantoni, Pac. Oc. .. 3 0s 171 30w
61 Cap Haitien, Haiti....19 42N 72 22w
61 Cape Breton I., Can. .46 30N 60 45w
63 Cape Girardeau,U.S.A.37 12N 89 40w
57 Cape of Good Hope,
prov., U. of S. Africa
31 48 s, 18 0 to 30 0 E
57 Cape Town, U. of S.
Africa ....33 58 s 18 26 E
6 Cape Verde Is., At. O. .15 0N 23 0w
47 Cape York Pen.,
Queensland ....14 0 s 143 0 E
41 Capernaum. See Tell Hum
41 Capodistria, Italy....45 33N 13 45 E
28 Caporetto, Italy .....46 14N 13 34 E
19 Cappoquin, Eire 52 9N 7 51w
28 Capri, I., Italy ...40 31N 14 12 E
28 Caprino, Italy ....45 38N 10 50 E
29 Capua, Italy .....41 6N 14 18 E
31 Carabia, Rumania ...43 47N 24 29 E
31 Caracal, Rumania ...44 8N 24 21 E
66 Caracas, Colombia 1 40N 69 0w
26 Caracas, Venezuela...31 N 66 59w
31 Caraharman, Rum. ...44 28N 28 45 E
27 Caravaca, Spain 38 6N 1 53w
66 Caravellas, Brazil ...17 35 s 39 25w
26 Carballo, Spain 43 10N 8 46w
27 Carboneras, Spain ...36 55N 1 55w
16 Carbost, Scotland ...57 18N 6 22w
21 Carcassonne, France ..43 11N 2 21 E
27 Carcastillo, Spain ...42 20N 1 25w
47 Carcour, N.S.W......33 40 s 149 0 E

MAP
42 Cardamom Hills, India 10 0N 77 10 E
65 Cardenas, Cuba......23 0N 81 15w
27 Cardenete, Spain 39 46N 1 35w
14 Cardiff, Wales 51 28N 3 10w
14 Cardigan, & Co., Wales 52 5N 4 39w
14 Cardigan Bay, Wales..52 20N 4 40w
27 Cardona, Spain ......41 55N 1 41 E
47 Cardwell, Queensland .18 0 s 145 30 E
31 Careii, Rumania .....47 42N 22 30 E
20 Carentan, France 49 18N 1 14w
49 Cargelligo, N.S.W. ...33 18 s 146 22 E
20 Carhaix, France 48 17N 3 34w
21 Cariati, Italy ....39 30N 16 58 E
65 Caribbean Sea,
Central America 15 0N 72 0w
60 Caribou Mts., Canada .53 30N 121 0w
66 Carinhanha, Brazil....14 0 s 43 50w
29 Carini, Sicily ....38 8N 13 11 E
24 Carinthia, Prov.,
Austria, Germany ....46 50N 14 0 E
18 Carlingford, Eire 54 2N 6 12w
18 Carlingford, L., N. Ire..54 2N 6 12w
14 Carlisle, England 54 54N 2 55w
29 Carloforte, Sardinia ..39 16N 8 19 E
27 Carlos de la Rapita,
Spain ....40 42N 0 50 E
19 Carlow, & Co., Eire ..52 50N 6 55w
16 Carloway, Scotland...58 17N 6 46w
62 Carlsbad, U.S.A......32 27N 104 12w
19 Carlton, Canada 52 52N 106 31w
17 Carluke, Scotland ...55 44N 3 51w
14 Carmarthen, & Co.,
Wales 51 51N 4 18w
14 Carmarthen B., Wales.51 42N 4 30w
21 Carmaux, France ....44 3N 2 8 E
41 Carmel Mt. See Kurmul J.
64 Carmen, Mexico 18 40N 91 50w
26 Carmona, Spain 37 27N 5 43w
20 Carnac, France .....47 36N 79 0 E
46 Carnarvon, W. Aust. ..24 52 s 114 0 E
57 Carnarvon, U. of S. Af. 31 2 s 22 10 E
18 Carndonagh, Eire.....55 15N 7 15w
12 Carnedd Llewelyn,
Wales 53 12N 3 57w
46 Carnegie, L., W. Aust. 26 10 s 122 30 E
12 Carnforth, England ..54 7N 2 45w
24 Carnic Alps, Austria,
Germany ....46 40N 12 55 E
30 Carniola, dist., Y.-slav.45 55N 14 30 E
18 Carnlough, N. Ireland 55 0N 6 0w
14 Carno, Wales 52 33N 3 32w
54 Carnot, Fr. Eq. Africa .5 01N 16 2 E
17 Carnoustie, Scotland ..56 31N 2 43w
17 Carnwath, Scotland ...55 42N 3 37w
66 Carolina, Brazil...... 6 45 s 47 45w
57 Carolina, U. of S. Af...26 8 s 30 12 E
7 Caroline Is., Pacific Oc.10 0 s 150 0w
29 Caronia, Sicily......38 1N 14 28 E
33 Carouge, Switzerland .46 11N 6 8 E
31 Carpathians, Mts.,
Balkans ....49 0N 19 0 E
47 Carpentaria, G. of,
Australia ....15 30 s 139 0 E
21 Carpentras, France ...43 3N 5 3 E
19 Carrantuohill, Mt.,
Eire 52 0N 9 45w
28 Carrara, Italy ....44 5N 10 7 E
16 Carrbridge, Scotland..57 17N 3 49w
17 Carrick, Scotland 55 13N 4 37w
18 Carrick-on-Shannon,
Eire 53 57N 8 05w
19 Carrick-on-Suir, Eire .52 21N 7 25w
18 Carrickfergus, N. Ire-
land 54 43N 5 49w
18 Carrickmacross, Eire 53 58N 6 43w
47 Carrieton, S. Australia .32 27 s 138 32 E
26 Carrión, Spain.......42 25N 4 38w
67 Carrizal Bajo, Chile...28 0 s 71 10w
64 Carrizal, Mexico 30 30N 106 35w
47 Carroll, N.S.W.......31 0 s 150 25 E
62 Carson City, U.S.A....39 13N 119 47w
62 Carson Sink, U.S.A....39 45N 118 14w
17 Carsphairn, Scotland..55 13N 4 14w
17 Carstairs, Scotland ...55 42N 3 41w
66 Cartagena, Colombia .10 30N 75 31w
27 Cartagena, Spain 37 37N 0 57w
64 Cartago, Costa Rica .. 9 57N 84 0w
26 Cartaxo, Portugal 39 10N 8 48w
13 Carter Fell, England ..55 22N 2 28w
20 Carteret, France 49 22N 1 48w
51 Carterton, N.Z. ......40 59 s 175 31 E
12 Cartmel, England 54 13N 2 58w
61 Cartwright, Labrador .53 40N 57 0w
52 Casablanca, Morocco ..33 30N 8 0w
28 Casale, Italy ....45 10N 8 26 E
28 Casalmaggiore, Italy .49 59N 10 27 E
47 Cascade Range, U.S.A.45 0N 121 30w
26 Cascaes, Portugal 38 40N 9 6w
28 Caserta, Italy ....41 4N 14 20 E
19 Cashel, Eire 53 31N 7 54w
47 Casino, N.S.W.......28 50 s 153 1 E
27 Caspe, Spain 41 15N 0 1w
62 Casper, U.S.A........42 53N 106 25w
38 Caspian Sea, U.S.S.R..43 0N 51 0 E
20 Casquets, Channel Is..49 47N 2 20w

MAP
32 Cassandra, Greece ....39 59N 23 26 E
29 Cassano, Italy ....39 48N 16 19 E
24 Cassel (Kassel) Ger....51 18N 9 25 E
28 Cassino, Italy.........41 30N 13 48 E
66 Cassiquiare, Bif. of the,
Venezuela 2 30N 65 0w
28 Castel di Sangio, Italy 41 46N 14 8 E
28 Castel San Pietro, Italy44 23N 11 32 E
29 Castelbuono, Sicily ...37 56N 14 5 E
21 Casteljaloux, France ..
29 Castellammare, Italy .40 41N 14 27 E
29 Castellaneta, Italy ....40 40N 17 · 6 E
26 Castello Branco,
Portugal 39 50N 7 33w
26 Castello de Vide, Port. 39 26N 7 25w
27 Castellon, prov., Spain 41 40N 1 20 E
27 Castellón de la Plana,
Spain 39 58N 0 1w
32 Castellorizo I. (It.),
Turkey ....36 15N 29 45 E
27 Castellote, Spain 40 50N 0 12w
21 Castelnaudary, France 43 18N 1 57 E
30 Castelnuovo, Y.-slav. .42 30N 18 33 E
21 Castelsarrasin, France 44 2N 1 7 E
29 Castelvetrano, Sicily ..37 42N 12 46 E
47 Casterton, Victoria ...37 33 s 141 27 E
28 Castiglione, Italy .....42 45N 10 50 E
21 Castillon, France......44 51N 0 3w
21 Castle Acre, England..52 43N 0 41 E
14 Castle Cary, England..51 5N 2 30w
17 Castle Douglas, Scot. .54 57N 3 56w
18 Castlebar, Eire 53 52N 9 18w
16 Castlebay, Scotland ..56 18N 7 29w
18 Castlebellingham,
Eire 53 54N 6 23w
18 Castleblaney, Eire 54 7N 6 45w
19 Castlecomer, Eire.....52 48N 7 14w
18 Castlederg, N. Ireland.54 43N 7 35w
18 Castlefinn, Eire.......54 48N 7 35w
18 Castlegregory, Eire ..52 16N 10 2w
18 Castleisland, Eire.....52 14N 9 28w
52 Castlemaine, Eire.....52 10N 9 37w
47 Castlemaine, Victoria .37 4 s 144 14 E
19 Castlemartyr, Eire....51 54N 8 4w
19 Castlerea, Eire.......53 47N 8 29w
19 Castletown, Eire......52 58N 7 30w
12 Castletown, I. of Man .54 5N 4 40w
16 Castletown, Scotland .58 36N 3 22w
18 Castlewellan, N. Ire-
land 54 15N 5 57w
21 Castres, France ......43 36N 2 16 E
26 Castro Urdiales, Spain 43 25N 3 18w
26 Castrocucco, Italy ....39 56N 15 46 E
26 Castropol, Spain 43 40N 7 3w
29 Castroreale, Sicily ....38 5N 15 10 E
29 Castrovillari, Italy ....39 51N 16 12 E
26 Castuera, Spain 38 44N 5 32w
67 Catalão, Brazil.......17 50 s 48 25w
27 Catalonia. See Castellon
67 Catamarca, Argentina 28 20 s 66 0w
29 Catania, Sicily ....37 29N 15 6 E
29 Catanzaro, Italy .....38 57N 16 38 E
57 Cathcart, U. of S. Af..32 22 s 27 15 E
57 Cathkin Pk., S. Africa .29 0 s 29 15 E
64 Catorce, Mexico 23 36N 101 0w
17 Catrine, Scotland.....55 31N 4 19w
30 Cattaro. See Kotor
13 Catterick, England ...54 23N 1 38w
54 Catumbella, Angola ..12 30 s 13 24 E
66 Cauca R., Colombia .. 8 0N 76 0w
37 Caucasus Mts.,
U.S.S.R...........43 0N 45 0 E
20 Caudebec, France ....49 17N 1 3 E
27 Caudete, Spain.......38 45N 0 58w
21 Cavaillon, France ....43 50N 5 2 E
18 Cavan & Co., Eire ...53 59N 7 22w
15 Caversham, England .51 58N 0 58w
26 Cavez, Portugal 41 40N 7 55w
26 Castro Verde, Portugal 37 42N 8 05w
16 Cawdor, Scotland 57 32N 3 56w
42 Cawnpore, India .....26 24N 80 24 E
14 Cawsand, England ...50 19N 4 11w
66 Caxios, Brazil....... 5 10 s 43 35w
15 Caxton, England 52 14N 0 05w
66 Cayenne, Fr. Guiana . 4 49N 52 18w
26 Cazorla, Spain 37 54N 2 59w
18 Ceannanus Mor, Eire .53 44N 6 53w
66 Ceará, and St., Brazil .3 50 s 38 40w
39 Cebu I., Philippines ..10 30N 124 0 E
28 Cecina, Italy.........43 19N 10 30 E
26 Ceclavin, Spain 39 53N 6 45w
62 Cedar, U.S.A.........39 25N 110 31w
63 Cedar Keys, U.S.A. ..29 0N 83 5w
63 Cedar Rapids, U.S.A. .41 55N 91 38w
26 Cedéira, Spain 43 35N 8 3w
29 Cefalu, Sicily........38 1N 14 1 E
28 Celano, Italy ....42 7N 13 32 E
19 Celbridge, Eire 53 20N 6 34w
39 Celebes, I., Dutch
East Indies .... 2 0 s 120 30 E
39 Celebes Sea, Dutch E.
Indies .... 3 20N 122 0 E
30 Celje, Yugoslavia ....46 15N 15 15 E
24 Celle, Germany........52 40N 10 9 E

MAP
26 Celorico, Portugal.....40 37N 7 28w
14 Cemmaes, Wales......53 25N 4 26w
21 Cenis, Mt., France....45 15N 6 54 E
63 Centerville, U.S.A...40 45N 92 58w
28 Cento, Italy..........44 43N 11 10 E
64 Central America 7 0 to 18 30N, 77 0 to 94 30w
62 Central City, U.S.A...39 49N 105 30w
42 Central India Agency, India............24 0N 76 0E
42 Central Provinces & Berar, prov., India...21 50N 80 0E
63 Centralia, U.S.A......38 30N 89 20w
39 Ceram I., Dutch E. Indies............3 0s 129 30E
57 Ceres, U. of S. Africa.33 25s 19 16 E
21 Céret, France.........42 29N 2 45 E
29 Cerignola, Italy......41 18N 15 57 E
31 Cernauti, Rumania....48 18N 25 56 E
31 Cerne Abbas, England.50 48N 2 27w
29 Cerreto, Italy.........41 20N 14 33 E
14 Cerrig-y-Druidon, Wales...........53 1N 3 34w
66 Cerro de Pasco, Peru .10 50s 76 0w
27 Cervera, Spain.......42 1N 1 57w
28 Cervia, Italy.........44 18N 12 21 E
21 Cervione, Corsica....42 20N 9 32 E
28 Cesena, Italy.........44 7N 12 18 E
24 Ceské Budejovice (Budweis), Czechoslovakia .48 59N 14 30 E
47 Cessnock, N.S.W....32 52s 151 18 E
25 Cetinje, Yugoslavia...42 25N 18 58 E
21 Cette, France........42 23N 3 41 E
21 Ceuta, Africa........35 50N 5 15w
28 Ceva, Italy..........44 25N 8 2 E
21 Cevennes, mts., France 44 30N 4 0 E
42 Ceylon, Br. cr. col., Asia.............7 30N 81 0 E
26 Cezimbra, Portugal ...38 27N 9 5w
66 Chachapoyas, Peru... 6 20s 77 22w
54 Chad, L., Africa......14 0N 14 0 E
54 Chad Terr., Fr. Equatorial Africa.........12 0N 19 50 E
62 Chadron, U.S.A......42 49N 103 0w
31 Chadyr Lunga, Rum...46 3N 28 51 E
42 Chageh, India........29 20N 64 43 E
14 Chagford, England....50 41N 3 50w
7 Chagos Is., Indian Oc.. 6 0s 72 0 E
45 Chahar, prov., China..42 30N 115 0 E
43 Chaibasa, India.......22 30N 85 50 E
43 Chainat, Siam........15 15N 100 10 E
41 Chakansur, Afghanistan............31 15N 62 8 E
44 Chaklik, Sinkiang....39 5N 88 3 E
67 Chala, Peru..........16 0s 74 0w
32 Chalcidice dist., Greece.............40 25N 23 20 E
32 Chalkis, Greece......38 26N 23 40 E
20 Challans, France......46 52N 1 52w
21 Challis, U.S.A........44 23N 114 5w
21 Chalon sur Saône, Fr. 46 48N 4 52 E
20 Chalonnes, France....47 22N 0 45w
20 Châlons sur Marne, France............48 59N 4 23 E
42 Chaman, India........30 55N 66 28 E
42 Chamba, India........32 35N 76 0 E
64 Ceiba, Honduras......15 45N 86 50w
42 Chambal R., India....25 40N 76 20 E
62 Chamberlain, U.S.A...43 49N 99 9w
21 Chambéry, France....45 43N 5 55 E
55 Chambezi R., N. Rhod.10 10s 31 49 E
20 Chambord, France....47 37N 1 32 E
21 Chamonix, France....45 55N 6 51 E
20 Champagne, old prov., France............48 50N 4 30 E
64 Champerico, Guatemala 14 25N 91 51w
33 Champery, Switzerland 46 11N 6 55 E
63 Champlain, L., U.S.A..44 30N 73 30w
22 Champlon, Belgium...50 7N 5 30 E
64 Champoton, Mexico...19 20N 90 47w
64 Chañaral, Chile.......26 0s 70 30w
42 Chanda, India........19 57N 79 28 E
42 Chandarli, Turkey....38 58N 26 58 E
42 Chandausi, India.....28 23N 78 50 E
43 Chandernagore, India.22 50N 88 28 E
45 Chang-chow, China...24 30N 117 30 E
45 Chang-sha, China.....28 30N 112 40 E
45 Chang-te, China......29 0N 111 25 E
39 Changtu, Manchuria..42 51N 123 59 E
31 Channel Is., Brit. Isles.49 30N 2 40w
26 Chantada, Spain......42 36N 7 46w
45 Chao-chow, China....23 55N 116 30 E
44 Chao-kia-ying, China .27 0N 103 0 E
44 Chao-tung, China.....27 30N 103 55 E
45 Chaoyang, Manchuria..41 42N 120 26 E
64 Chapala, L., Mexico...20 15N 103 0 E
13 Chapel en le Frith, England.............53 20N 1 56w
43 Chapra, India........25 45N 84 47 E
41 Charbar, Iran.........25 15N 60 42 E
68 Charcot Land, Antarctica...........70 0s 78 0w
14 Chard, England 50 53N 2 57w
41 Chardeh, Iran........36 40N 54 20 E
32 Chardi, Turkey.......39 38N 29 10 E

MAP
21 Charente, dept., Fr....45 50N 0 15 E
21 Charente, R., France..46 0N 0 15 E
41 Charjui, U.S.S.R......39 5N 63 20 E
21 Charente Inférieure, dept., France........45 57N 0 40w
22 Charleroi, Belgium...50 28N 4 28 E
63 Charleston, S. Carolina, U.S.A.........32 50N 80 0w
63 Charleston, W. Virginia, U.S.A.........38 25N 81 5w
18 Charlestown, Eire 53 57N 8 48w
57 Charlestown, U. of S. Africa.............27 25s 29 55 E
19 Charleville, Eire 52 22N 8 41w
20 Charleville, France....49 47N 4 43 E
47 Charleville, Queensland ....26 28s 146 13 E
63 Charlotte, U.S.A......35 15N 80 50w
47 Charlotte Water, N. Territory.........25 56s 134 54 E
35 Charlottenberg, Sweden...........59 55N 12 20 E
24 Charlottenburg, Ger..52 32N 13 15 E
63 Charlottesville, U.S.A.38 0N 77 35w
61 Charlottetown, Can...46 19N 63 10w
47 Charlton, Victoria....36 17s 143 20 E
14 Charmouth, England..50 45N 2 52w
56 Charter, S. Rhodesia..18 33s 81 8 E
47 Charters Towers, Queensland..........20 1s 146 8 E
20 Chartres, France......48 28N 1 29 E
32 Chatalja, Turkey......41 8N 28 30 E
33 Chateau d'Oex, Switz..46 28N 7 07 E
20 Chateau du Loir, France.............47 42N 0 25 E
20 Château Gontier, Fr ..47 50N 0 43w
20 Château la Vallière, France.............47 33N 0 29 E
20 Château Thierry, France..............49 4N 3 25 E
20 Châteaubriant, France 47 43N 1 24w
20 Châteaudun, France..48 3N 1 19 E
21 Châteauroux, France..46 47N 1 41 E
33 Châtel St. Denis, Switz.46 32N 6 54 E
22 Châtelet, Belgium.....50 24N 4 30 E
21 Châtellerault, France..46 48N 0 32 E
15 Chatham, England....51 23N 0 32 E
68 Chatham, I., Southern Oc...............43 50s 176 30w
20 Châtillon, Italy........45 48N 7 35 E
20 Châtillon sur Seine, France............47 52N 4 34 E
43 Chatra, India.........24 15N 84 55 E
63 Chattanooga, U.S.A...35 3N 85 7w
15 Chatteris, England ...52 29N 0 3 E
20 Chaumont, France....48 8N 5 7 E
20 Chauny, France......49 38N 3 14 E
26 Chaves, Portugal.....41 45N 7 30w
24 Cheb., Czechoslovakia..50 7N 12 22 E
31 Chechelnik, U.S.S.R...48 13N 29 20 E
37 Chechen-Ingush, rep., U.S.S.R...........43 10N 46 2 E
31 Chechina, Yugoslavia..43 10N 21 55 E
14 Cheddar, England.....51 16N 2 45w
19 Cheekpoint, Eire......52 16N 7 0w
49 Cheepie, Queensland..26 40s 144 59 E
45 Chefoo, China........37 30N 122 0 E
45 Cheguan, Manchuria..46 35N 123 10 E
62 Chehalis, U.S.A.......46 40N 123 5w
45 Che-ju, Japan........33 29N 126 34 E
45 Che-kiang, prov., China 29 0N 120 0 E
32 Cheliodromia, Greece .39 10N 23 50 E
15 Chelmsford, England..51 42N 0 28 E
14 Cheltenham, England.51 53N 2 05w
27 Chelva, Spain........39 34N 0 59w
36 Chelyabinsk, U.S.S.R..55 26N 61 28 E
39 Chelyuskin, C., U.S.S.R.............77 50N 103 0 E
24 Chemnitz, Germany..50 52N 12 50 E
45 Chemulpo, Korea....37 10N 126 55 E
42 Chenab, R., India....30 45N 71 45 E
33 Chêne, Switzerland...46 12N 6 12 E
44 Cheng-tu, China......31 0N 104 10 E
43 Chentabun, Siam.....12 35N 101 45 E
31 Chepelare, Bulgaria..41 43N 24 42 E
14 Chepstow, England...51 38N 2 40w
20 Cher, dept., France...47 0N 2 30 E
20 Cher, R., France.....47 0N 2 15 E
20 Cherbourg, France....49 38N 1 38w
44 Cherchen, Sinkiang...38 5N 85 30 E
36 Cherdin, U.S.S.R......60 31N 56 28 E
39 Cheremkovo, U.S.S.R. 53 20N 103 0 E
36 Cherpovetz, U.S.S.R..59 14N 37 58 E
37 Cherkasy, U.S.S.R....49 27N 32 0 E
37 Cherkess, prov., U.S.S.R...........44 27N 41 40 E
37 Chernigov, U.S.S.R...51 30N 31 12 E
32 Chersonisos, Crete Inset 35 19N 25 24 E
15 Chertsey, England....51 24N 0 31w
15 Cherwell, R., England.51 57N 1 19w
63 Chesapeake B., U.S.A. 38 0N 76 0w
15 Chesham, England ...51 42N 0 36w
12 Cheshire, Co., England 53 15N 2 30w
32 Cheshme, Turkey.....38 19N 26 20 E

MAP
15 Cheshunt, England....51 43N 0 1w
14 Chesil Bank, England .50 33N 2 33w
12 Chester, England.....53 12N 2 54w
13 Chester-le-street, Eng.54 52N 1 34w
13 Chesterfield, England .53 14N 1 25w
15 Chesterton, England ..52 14N 0 9 E
44 Chethang, Tibet......29 0N 92 0 E
13 Cheviot, The, England.55 30N 2 10w
12 Cheviot Hills, Eng....55 20N 2 35w
62 Cheyenne, U.S.A.....41 7N 104 51w
42 Chhatarpur, India....24 55N 79 40 E
44 Chiamdo, China......31 10N 97 45 E
64 Chiapas, St., Mexico..16 30N 92 30w
28 Chiavari, Italy........44 18N 9 21 E
28 Chiavenna, Italy......46 19N 9 27 E
45 Chiba, Japan.........35 43N 140 13 E
43 Chicacole, India......18 15N 84 0 E
63 Chicago, U.S.A.......41 50N 87 45w
15 Chichester, England...50 51N 0 47w
45 Chi-chow, China......38 22N 115 28 E
61 Chicoutimi, Canada ..48 32N 70 50w
43 Chieng Hkam, Burma.20 45N 93 0 E
43 Chieng Kang, Siam...17 56N 101 40 E
43 Chieng Mai, Siam....19 0N 99 0 E
43 Chieng Sen, Siam....20 18N 100 8 E
43 Chieng Tung, Burma..21 15N 99 40 E
28 Chieri, Italy..........45 1N 7 49 E
28 Chieti, Italy..........42 22N 14 12 E
31 Chifut Kuyusu, Rum..43 50N 28 8 E
45 Chihli, prov., China...39 40N 116 40 E
45 Chihli, G. of, China...38 30N 18 30 E
64 Chihuahua, Mexico ..28 32N 106 5w
64 Chihuahua, St., Mexico 26 0 to 31 48N 104 0 to 108 40w
42 Chilas, India.........35 25N 74 10 E
47 Childers, Queensland .25 9s 152 17 E
62 Childress, U.S.A.......34 26N 100 15w
67 Chile, St., S. America 17 30 to 55 0s 71 15w
47 Chillagoe, Queensland .17 20s 144 29 E
67 Chillan, Chile........36 30s 72 15w
63 Chillicotte, U.S.A.....39 50N 93 35w
33 Chillon, Switzerland..46 25N 6 55 E
67 Chiloé, I., Chile......42 40s 74 0w
64 Chilpancingo, Mexico .17 31N 99 12w
47 Chiltern, Victoria.....36 10s 146 30 E
15 Chiltern Hills, England 51 40N 0 54w
56 Chilwa, L., Nyasaland .15 5s 35 50 E
22 Chimay, Belgium.....50 3N 4 17 E
66 Chimborazo, Vol., Ecuador............1 15s 81 0w
66 Chimbote, Peru......9 0s 78 30w
42 Chimiot, India........31 45N 73 10 E
41 Chimkent, U.S.S.R....42 15N 69 30 E
45 China, rep., Asia...... 18 0N to 48 0N 74 0 E to 135 0 E
64 Chinandego, Nicaragua 12 30N 87 0w
47 Chinchilla, Queensland 26 42s 150 42 E
27 Chinchilla, Spain.....38 56N 1 35w
26 Chinchon, Spain......40 8N 3 25w
45 Chin-chow, Manchuria.41 0N 121 0 E
42 Chingalput, India.....12 45N 80 0 E
45 Ching-ting, China.....37 40N 114 45 E
42 Chini, India..........31 30N 78 15 E
45 Chin-ju, Korea.......35 10N 128 0 E
45 Chin-kiang, China....32 20N 119 45 E
45 Chinnampo, Korea...38 50N 125 20 E
44 Chin-ngan, China.....23 30N 106 25 E
20 Chinon, France.......47 12N 0 15 E
56 Chinsali, N. Rhodesia .10 39s 32 2 E
45 Chin-wangtao, Manch. 40 0N 119 55 E
22 Chiny, Belgium......49 44N 5 20 E
44 Chin-yuan, China.....32 45N 114 10 E
28 Chioggia, Italy.......45 17N 12 25 E
32 Chios I., Greece......38 20N 26 0 E
14 Chippenham, England.51 27N 2 5w
14 Chipping Campden, England...........52 3N 1 47w
15 Chipping Norton, England...........51 57N 1 33w
15 Chipping Ongar, Eng. 51 42N 0 15 E
14 Chipping Sodbury, England...........51 32N 2 21w
67 Chiquita, Mar., Argentina...........31 0s 61 30w
44 Chira, Sinkiang......36 54N 80 45 E
64 Chiriqui Lagoon, Panama...........9 15N 82 15w
64 Chiriqui, Vol., Panama 8 45N 82 15w
14 Chirk, Wales.........52 57N 3. 4w
56 Chiromo, Nyasaland..16 30s 35 10 E
31 Chirpan, Bulgaria....42 13N 25 20 E
37 Chirskaya, U.S.S.R....48 20N 42 54 E
36 Chistopol, U.S.S.R....55 18N 50 28 E
56 Chita, U.S.S.R........52 0N 113 50 E
56 Chitambo, N. Rhod...12 25s 30 28 E
31 Chitila, Rumania.....44 32N 26 0 E
42 Chitral, India........35 47N 71 40 E
31 Chitila, Rumania.....44 32N 26 0 E
42 Chitral, India........35 47N 71 40 E
43 Chittagong, India ....22 25N 91 58 E
28 Chiusi, Italy.........43 0N 11 57 E
27 Chiva, Spain.........39 28N 0 41w
28 Chivasso, Italy.......45 14N 7 52 E
32 Chivril, Turkey.......38 15N 29 42 E

MAP

37 Chkalov, U.S.S.R.....51 48N 55 10 E
13 Chollerton, England..55 4N 2 8w
36 Cholmogory, U.S.S.R..41 32N 64 49 E
67 Chonos Arch., Chile ..45 0s 74 0w
66 Chorillos, Peru 12 10s 76 50w
12 Chorley, England 53 39N 2 38w
32 Chorlu, Turkey .....41 10N 27 48 E
40 Chorum, Turkey ....40 40N 43 54 E
25 Chorzow, Poland .....50 18N 19 0 E
45 Chosen. See Korea
43 Chota Nagpur, div., India ....23 10N 84 0 E
31 Chotin, Rumania .....48 15N 26 28 E
31 Choumen, Bulgaria ...43 20N 26 52 E
15 Christchurch, England 50 44N 1 47w
51 Christchurch, N.Z....43 31s 172 37 E
57 Christiana, U. of S. Af. 27 58s 25 10 E
35 Christiana. See Oslo
23 Christiansfeld, Denmark ....55 22N 9 29 E
61 Christianshaab, Greenland 69 0N 51 0w
6 Christmas I., Pacific Oc. 2 0N 157 20w
24 Chrudim, Cz.-slov...49 58N 15 55 E
25 Chrzanów, Poland 50 8N 19 23w
44 Chu-ching, China ....25 30N 103 45 E
45 Chu-chow, China .....29 0N 118 50 E
14 Chudleigh, England ..50 37N 3 36w
44 Chuguchak, Sinkiang .46 50N 83 0 E
43 Chumbi, India.......27 30N 89 0 E
45 Chung-ju, Korea .....37 10N 127 40 E
44 Chung-king, China ...29 35N 106 38 E
67 Chuquisaca. See Sucre, Bolivia
33 Chur, Switzerland ....46 52N 9 33 E
14 Church Stretton, Eng. 52 33N 2 49w
60 Churchill, Canada 58 45N 94 0w
61 Churchill, C., Canada .58 55N 93 7w
60 Churchill, Harb., Can. 58 40N 94 0w
60 Churchill, R., Canada .57 8N 96 30w
42 Churu, India........28 19N 75 1 E
45 Chusan, China ....30 10N 122 5 E
36 Chuvash, rep., U.S.S.R.55 30N 47 30 E
36 Ciego de Avilo, Cuba..21 50N 78 49w
65 Cienfuegos, Cuba 22 12N 80 32w
27 Cieza, Spain 38 15N 1 25w
27 Cifuentes, Spain 40 46N 2 35w
63 Cincinnati, U.S.A....39 3N 84 30w
22 Ciney, Belgium......50 18N 5 5 E
21 Cinto, Mte, Corsica ..42 30N 8 50 E
26 Cintra, Portugal.....38 46N 9 25w
60 Circle City, Alaska ..65 35N 144 0w
52 Cirenaica, dist., Libya.32 0N 22 0 E
14 Cirencester, England ..51 43N 1 58w
28 Citta della Pieve, Italy 42 58N 12 0 E
28 Cittadella, Italy......45 39N 11 44 E
29 Cittanova, Italy......38 22N 6 3 E
41 City of Salt. See Tell el Milh
66 Ciudad Bolivar, Venezuela 8 7N 63 52w
64 Ciudad Juarez, Mex. .31 33N 107 45w
26 Ciudad Real, Spain...38 58N 3 55w
26 Ciudad Rodrigo, Spain 40 35N 6 30w
65 Ciudad Trujillo, Dominican Rep. 18 55N 70 30w
27 Ciudadela, Minorca I. .29 59N 3 52 E
64 Ciudadvieja, Nicaragua 13 30N 85 50w
28 Civita Castellana, Italy 42 17N 12 25 E
28 Civitanova, Italy......43 18N 13 20 E
28 Civitavecchia, Italy ..42 7N 11 48 E
21 Civray, France ....46 9N 0 17 E
17 Clackmannan, & Co., Scotland 56 6N 3 44w
15 Clacton, England ....51 47N 1 10 E
17 Cladich, Scotland 56 22N 5 4w
20 Clamecy, France .....47 28N 3 30 E
57 Clanwilliam, U. of S. Africa ....32 8s 18 52 E
19 Clara Eire 53 21N 7 37w
47 Claraville, N. Territory 23 23s 134 45 E
15 Clare, England........52 5N 0 35 E
47 Clare, S. Australia ...33 48s 138 36 E
19 Clare, Co., Eire 52 36 to 53 10N 8 30 to 9 50w
19 Clarecastle, Eire......52 48N 8 58w
18 Claremorris, Eire.....53 44N 9 0w
19 Clarenbridge, Eire ...53 13N 8 55w
47 Clarencetown, N.S.W. 32 35s 151 44 E
33 Clarens, Switzerland ..46 26N 6 54 E
57 Clarkebury, U of S. Africa ....31 46s 28 20 E
63 Clarksville, U.S.A. ..36 30N 87 23w
19 Clashmore, Eire 52 1N 7 48w
15 Claypole, England....53 3N 0 45w
19 Clear, C., Eire 51 25N 9 30w
12 Cleator Moor, England 54 32N 3 30w
12 Cleethorpes, England..53 35N 0 2w
14 Cleobury Mortimer, England 52 23N 2 29w
22 Clerf, Luxemburg ....50 4N 6 3 E
47 Clermont, Queensland .22 49s 147 38 E
21 Clermont Ferrand, France............45 46N 3 4 E
14 Clevedon, England ...51 26N 2 52w
47 Cleveland, Queensland 27 30s 153 20 E

MAP

63 Cleveland, New York, U.S.A. 43 17N 75 54w
63 Cleveland, Ohio, U.S.A. 41 30N 81 30w
13 Cleveland Hills, Eng. 54 25N 1 10w
18 Clew B., Eire 53 50N 9 45w
18 Cley, England ....52 57N 1 3 E
18 Clifden, Eire........53 29N 10 1w
47 Clifton, Queensland...27 53s 151 50 E
63 Clifton, U.S.A. 33 10N 109 5w
60 Clinton, Canada 51 5N 121 38w
51 Clinton, New Zealand..46 12s 169 23 E
60 Clinton Colden, L., Canada 64 0N 108 30w
13 Clitheroe, England ..53 53N 2 23w
19 Clogheen, Eire.......52 16N 8 0w
18 Clogher, N. Ireland...54 24N 7 10w
19 Clonakilty, Eire......51 37N 8 54w
47 Cloncurry, Queensland.20 40s 140 28 E
19 Clonegall, Eire.......52 42N 6 39w
18 Clones, Eire 54 11N 7 15w
19 Clonmel, Eire 52 21N 7 43w
19 Clontarf, Eire........53 22N 6 12w
24 Cloppenburg, Germany 52 50N 8 3 E
13 Cloughton, England ..54 20N 0 26w
14 Clova, Scotland 56 51N 3 6w
14 Clovelly, England 51 0N 4 24w
19 Cloyne, Eire 51 52N 8 8w
31 Cluj, Rumania ......46 47N 23 40 E
14 Clun, England 52 26N 3 1w
20 Cluny, France ....46 28N 4 42 E
33 Clusone, Italy ....45 54N 9 57 E
14 Clwydd, R., Wales ...53 10N 3 20w
51 Clyde, New Zealand ..45 12s 169 22 E
17 Clyde, R., Scotland ..55 52N 4 35w
17 Clyde Bank, Scotland..55 55N 4 24w
17 Clyde, Firth of, Scot. .55 25N 4 55w
14 Clydey, Wales 51 55N 4 34w
16 Clyne, Scotland 58 2N 3 57w
21 Coachford, Eire......51 54N 8 47w
64 Coahuila, St., Mexico..27 0N 102 0w
13 Coalburn, Scotland....55 35N 3 54w
63 Coalgate, U.S.A. 34 29N 96 11w
58 Coast Ra., Canada....52 0N 126 0w
47 Coast Ra. N.S.W. ....36 0s 149 30 E
62 Coast Ra., U.S.A. ...44 40N 123 0w
17 Coatbridge, Scotland .55 52N 4 1w
68 Coats Ld., Antarctica..73 0s 82 30w
64 Coatzacoalcos, Mexico.18 7N 94 35w
61 Cobalt, Canada 47 25N 79 50w
64 Coban, Guatemala ...15 30N 90 22w
47 Cobar, N.S.W. ....31 25s 145 50 E
47 Cobargo, N.S.W. .....36 26s 149 50 E
19 Cobh, Eire...........51 51N 8 17w
66 Cobija, Brazil........11 2s 68 45w
67 Cobija, Chile........22 30s 70 25w
24 Coblence, Germany ..50 20N 7 35 E
24 Coburg, Germany ....50 18N 11 0 E
43 Cocanada, India......17 0N 82 15 E
66 Cochabamba, Bolivia..17 10s 66 30w
24 Cochem, Germany....50 10N 7 10 E
42 Cochin, & st., India ..9 55N 76 18 E
39 Cochin China, st., Fr Indo-China......10 0N 107 0 E
17 Cockburnspath, Scot. .55 57N 2 22w
47 Cockburn, S. Australia.32 3s 140 57 E
61 Cochrane, Canada 49 2N 81 50w
12 Cockermouth, England 54 40N 3 22w
7 Cocos Is., Indian Oc. ..12 0s 98 0 E
28 Codogno, Italy ....45 10N 9 44 E
47 Coff's Harb., N.S.W. .30 30s 153 0 E
15 Coggeshall, England ..51 52N 0 40 E
21 Cognac, France 45 42N 0 18w
26 Cogollos, Spain 42 12N 3 41w
26 Coimbra, Portugal ...40 13N 8 27w
26 Coin, Spain 36 41N 4 44w
33 Coire. See Chur
28 Col di Tenda, Italy ..44 12N 7 40 E
47 Colac, Victoria ......38 19s 143 38 E
15 Colchester, England ..51 53N 0 53 E
12 Cold Fell, England ...54 53N 2 40w
17 Coldstream, Scotland .53 40N 2 15w
17 Coleford, England 51 48N 2 36w
57 Colenso, U. of S. Africa 28 45s 29 50 E
18 Coleraine, N. Ireland .55 8N 6 40w
57 Colenso, U. of S. Africa 28 5s 29 50 E
18 Coleraine, N Ireland ..55 8N 6 40w
47 Coleraine, Victoria ...37 33s 141 44 E
57 Colesberg, U. of S. Afr..30 46s 25 3 E
15 Coleshill, England ...52 30N 1 42w
28 Colico, Italy ....46 9N 9 26 E
64 Colima, and st., Mex..19 12N 103 45w
64 Colima, Vol. de, Mex..19 30N 103 45w
17 Coll, I., Scotland 56 38N 6 30w
49 Collarenebri East, N.S.W. ....29 35s 148 35 E
46 Collie, W. Australia ...33 21s 116 15 E
13 Collingham, England ..53 5N 1 25w
50 Collingwood, N. Zeal. .40 41s 172 42 E
15 Collioure, France .....42 32N 3 5 E
18 Collooney, Eire 54 11N 8 30w
18 Colmar, France ......48 7N 7 20 E
21 Colmars, France ......44 10N 6 40 E
26 Colmenar Viejo, Spain 40 39N 3 46w
13 Colne, England.......53 52N 2 10w

MAP

24 Cologne, Germany.....50 56N 7 0 E
52 Colomb Bechar, Alg...31 36N 2 15w
66 Colombia, st., S. Amer. 3 45N 73 0w
42 Colombo, Ceylon .....6 58N 79 58 E
64 Colon, Panama Canal Zone 9 28N 79 51w
67 Colonia, Uruguay 34 15s 57 50w
17 Colonsay, I., Scotland .56 3N 6 12w
62 Colorado Plat., U.S.A..35 0N 111 30w
62 Colorado, R., N. Amer..32 0N 115 7w
67 Colorado, R., Argentina 39 0s 64 0w
62 Colorado Springs, U.S.A. 38 50N 104 50w
62 Colorado, st., U.S.A. .37 41N 106 0w
63 Columbia (Mo.), U.S.A.39 0N 92 20w
63 Columbia (Pa.), U.S.A. 40 20N 76 23w
63 Columbia (S.C.) U.S.A. 33 58N 81 0w
62 Columbia, R., U.S.A. .46 10N 123 0w
63 Columbus, Ga., U.S.A. 32 30N 84 57w
62 Columbus, Ind., U.S.A.39 15N 85 20w
63 Columbus, Ohio, U.S.A.39 57N 83 0w
12 Colwyn, Wales.......53 17N 3 41w
12 Colwyn B., Wales 53 17N 3 42w
14 Colyton, England.....50 45N 3 5w
28 Comacchio, Italy .....44 40N 12 20 E
64 Comyagua, Honduras .14 30N 87 32w
18 Comber, N. Ireland ...54 33N 5 45w
19 Comeragh Mts., Eire..52 18N 7 40w
43 Comillah, India.......23 27N 91 20 E
29 Comiso, Sicily ....36 59N 14 33 E
64 Comitan, Mexico......16 14N 92 14w
20 Commentry, France...46 18N 2 45 E
20 Commercy, France....48 46N 5 36 E
28 Como, & L., Italy ....45 47N 9 9 E
42 Comorin, C., India ...8 0N 77 35 E
53 Comoro Is., Ind. Oc. ..12 0s 44 0 E
57 Compass Bg., U. of S Africa ....31 44s 24 33 E
20 Compiègne, France ...49 6N 2 53 E
17 Comrie, Scotland 56 23N 3 58w
20 Concarneau, France ..47 53N 3 56w
67 Concepcion, Argentina.32 20s 61 57w
67 Concepcion, Chile 36 40s 72 50w
66 Concepcion, Colombia .0 20N 75 10w
64 Concepcion, Mexico ..24 40N 101 20w
67 Concepcion, Paraguay.23 20s 57 30w
67 Concord (N.C.), U.S.A.35 27N 80 33w
63 Concord (N.H.), U.S.A.43 8N 71 35w
67 Concordia, Argentina .31 15s 58 0w
47 Condamine, Queensland 26 59s 150 15 E
20 Condé, France 48 51N 0 31w
47 Condobolin, N.S.W. ..33 2s 147 13 E
21 Condom, France .....43 58N 0 22 E
21 Congolens, France ....46 1N 0 40 E
13 Congleton, England ..53 10N 2 13w
54 Congo, R., C. Africa ..2 0N 21 0 E
13 Conil, Spain 36 19N 6 8w
13 Conisbrough, England.53 28N 1 14w
12 Coniston, & Water, England 54 23N 3 4w
18 Conn, L., Eire........54 4N 9 15w
18 Connaught, Prov., Eire 53 45N 9 15w
63 Connecticut, st., U.S.A. 41 45N 73 0w
17 Connel, Scotland 56 27N 5 22w
60 Connelly, Canada 55 58N 127 0w
12 Connemara, dist., Eire 53 28N 9 45w
21 Connerré, France .....48 5N 0 29 E
26 Conquista, Spain 38 28N 4 30w
13 Consett, England 54 50N 1 50w
33 Constance, & L. of, Europe ....47 30N 9 25 E
31 Constanta, Rumania ..44 12N 28 41 E
26 Constantina, Spain ...37 52N 5 38w
52 Constantine, Algeria...36 30N 6 30 E
32 Constantinople. See Istanbul
67 Constitucion, Chile ...35 25s 72 25w
29 Conversano, Italy ....41 0N 17 7 E
12 Conway, Wales 53 17N 3 50w
12 Conway, R., Wales ...53 13N 3 50w
43 Cooch Behar, India ...26 18N 89 35 E
50 Cook Is........Inset 8 0 to 23 0s, 156 0 to 170 0w
51 Cook Mt., New Zealand 43 36s 170 7 E
51 Cook Str., New Zealand 41 20s 174 30 E
51 Cookstown, N. Ireland.54 39N 6 45w
47 Cooktown, Queensland.15 22s 145 15 E
47 Coolabah, N.S.W. ....31 1s 146 44 E
47 Coolah, N.S.W. ......31 48s 149 44 E
18 Coolaney, Eire 54 11N 8 36w
47 Coolgardie, W. Aust...30 55s 121 13 E
47 Cooma, N.S.W. ......36 17s 149 6 E
47 Coonabarabran, N.S.W. ....31 17s 149 15 E
47 Coonalpyn, S. Aust. ..35 42s 139 52 E
47 Coonamble, N.S.W. ..30 58s 148 24 E
47 Coondambo, S. Aust...31 2s 135 52 E
47 Coonoor, India.......11 20N 76 50 E
47 Cooper's Creek, S. Australia ......28 35s 138 0 E
42 Coorg, prov., India ...12 20N 74 40 E
47 Cootamundra, N.S.W..34 37s 148 2 E
48 Cootanoorina, S. Aust. 28 15s 135 30 E
18 Cootehill, Eire 54 4N 7 5w
47 Cooyar, Queensland ..26 58s 151 48 E

MAP
23 **Copenhagen.** *See* **Kobenhavn**
67 **Copiapo**, Chile ....27 15 s 70 15w
60 **Coppermine**, Canada .47 5N 84 44w
13 **Coquet I.**, England 55 20N 1 32w
13 **Coquet, R.**, England ...55 17N 1 43w
54 **Coquilhatville**, Belgian Congo ....0 0 18 18 E
67 **Coquimbo**, Chile ......30 1 s 71 20w
7 **Coral Sea**, Pacific Oc...10 20 s 160 0 E
29 **Corato**, Italy ....41 12N 16 23 E
20 **Corbeil**, France ....48 37N 2 26 E
13 **Corbridge**, England ...54 59N 20 1w
15 **Corby**, England 52 50N 0 30w
67 **Cordoba**, Argentina ...31 10 s 64 25w
60 **Cordova**, Alaska 54 47N 132 22w
26 **Cordova**, Spain 37 52N 4 48w
14 **Corfe Castle**, England .50 40N 2 3w
26 **Coria**, Spain 40 0N 6 32w
29 **Corigliano**, Italy 39 38N 16 32E
32 **Corinth**, Greece 37 58N 23 0E
63 **Corinth**, U.S.A. 34 57N 88 36w
32 **Corinth, Canal**, Greece 37 56N 22 56 E
32 **Corinth, G. of**, Greece .38 10N 22 40 E
64 **Corinto**, Nicaragua ...12 29N 87 0w
19 **Cork, & Co.**, Eire 52 54N 8 28w
29 **Corleone**, Sicily ......37 48N 13 18 E
29 **Corleto**, Italy ....40 25N 16 2 E
17 **Cornhill**, Scotland.....57 37N 2 43w
14 **Cornwall**, England 50 51N, 4 12 to 5 42w
60 **Cornwallis I.**, Canada .75 0N 95 0w
66 **Coro**, Venezuela 11 21N 69 42w
67 **Corocoro**, Bolivia 16 50N 68 30w
50 **Coromandel**, N.Z......36 46 s 175 31 E
42 **Coromandel Coast**, India ....13 26N 80 21 E
60 **Coronation G.**, Canada 68 0N 112 0w
67 **Coronel**, Chile 37 1s 73 0w
66 **Coronie**, Dutch Guiana 5 52N 56 20w
47 **Corowa**, N.S.W.........35 59 s 146 53 E
64 **Corozal**, Brit. Honduras18 32N 88 26w
62 **Corpus Christi**, U.S.A. 27 50N 97 32w
67 **Corral**, Chile..........40 0s 73 35w
27 **Correggio**, Italy ......44 48N 10 48 E
21 **Corrèze, dept.**, France.45 16N 1 55 E
18 **Corrib., L.**, Eire.......53 25N 9 15w
17 **Corrie**, Scotland.......55 39N 5 8w
67 **Corrientes**, Argentina .27 40 s 58 30w
19 **Corrofin**, Eire 52 57N 9 4w
47 **Corryong**, Victoria ....36 10 s 147 45 E
21 **Corse.** *See* **Corsica**
21 **Corsica I., dept.**, France...............42 11N 9 10 E
12 **Corte**, Corsica.........42 18N 9 9 E
28 **Cortona**, Italy ....43 19N 12 0 E
26 **Coruche Mora**, Port. .38 57N 8 30w
67 **Corumba**, Brazil 19 0s 57 40w
26 **Corunna.** *See* **La Coruña**
47 **Corunna**, S. Australia..33 45 s 135 45 E
26 **Corvera de Pisuerga**, Spain 42 52N 4 33w
14 **Corwen**, Wales.........52 58N 3 22w
29 **Cosenza**, Italy ....39 20N 16 17 E
20 **Cosne**, France..........47 25N 2 55 E
46 **Cossack**, W. Australia .20 45 s 117 15 E
33 **Cossonay**, Switzerland 46 37N 6 30 E
64 **Costa Rica, st.**, C. America 10 0N 84 0w
31 **Costesti**, Rumania.....44 38N 24 54 E
20 **Côte-d'Or, dept.**, France...............47 10N 4 50 E
220 **Côtes du Nord**, dept., France.........48 23N 2 47w
66 **Cotopaxi, vol.**, Ecuador 0 40 s 78 45w
29 **Cotrone**, Italy ....39 4N 17 8 E
14 **Cotswold Hills**, Eng...51 50N 2 0w
15 **Cottenham**, England ..52 17N 0 7 E
13 **Cottingham**, England .53 47N 0 25w
20 **Coulommiers**, France .48 49N 3 5 E
63 **Council Bluffs**, U.S.A..41 15N 95 58w
17 **Coupar Angus**, Scot. .56 33N 3 16w
33 **Courtelary**, Switz. ....47 11N 7 4 E
19 **Courtmacsherry**, Eire.51 37N 8 43w
22 **Courtrai**, Belgium......50 49N 3 15 E
20 **Coutances**, France 49 3N 1 27w
21 **Coutras**, France 45 3N 0 7w
22 **Couvin**, Belgium ....50 3N 4 30 E
15 **Coventry**, England 52 25N 1 30w
26 **Covilhã**, Portugal 40 17N 7 32w
63 **Covington**, U.S.A......39 0N 84 35w
14 **Cowbridge**, Wales......51 28N 3 25w
17 **Cowdenbeath**, Scotland56 7N 3 20w
47 **Cowell**, S. Australia ..33 40 s 137 0 E
15 **Cowes**, England 50 45N 1 18w
47 **Cowra**, N.S.W. ....33 48 s 148 41 E
67 **Coxim**, Brazil 18 15s 55 0w
25 **Cracow**, Poland ....50 5N 19 59 E
47 **Cradle Mt.**, Tasmania .41 40 s 145 55 E
57 **Cradock**, U. of S. Af. ..32 10 s 25 36 E
17 **Crail**, Scotland........56 16N 2 38w
24 **Crailsheim**, Germany..49 8N 10 5 E
31 **Craiova**, Rumania......44 20N 23 49 E
13 **Cramlington**, England 55 5N 1 35w
14 **Cranborne**, England ..50 55N 1 55w
15 **Cranbrook**, England ..51 6N 0 33 E

MAP
13 **Cranswick**, England...53 57N 0 25w
25 **Cranz**, Germany.......54 57N 20 35 E
66 **Cratheús**, Brazil 6 0s 40 48w
16 **Crathie**, Scotland......57 3N 3 12w
66 **Crato**, Brazil 7 0s 39 45w
19 **Craughwell**, Eire 53 14N 8 44w
14 **Craven Arms**, England 52 28N 2 50w
17 **Crawford**, Scotland....55 28N 3 39w
62 **Crawford**, U.S.A. 42 41N 103 25w
20 **Crécy**, France..........48 52N 2 54 E
14 **Crediton**, England.....50 47N 3 40w
17 **Creetown**, Scotland....54 54N 4 22w
20 **Creil**, France..........49 15N 2 28 E
28 **Cremona**, Italy ....45 7N 10 1 E
62 **Crescent City**, U.S.A. .41 42N 124 12w
47 **Cressy**, Victoria ....38 1s 143 42 E
21 **Crest**, France ....44 33N 5 2 E
32 **Crete (Candia)** Inset 35 15N 25 0 E
21 **Creuse**, dept., France..46 8N 2 6 E
21 **Creuse, R.**, France ....46 40N 1 5 E
27 **Crevillente**, Spain.....38 15N 0 45w
12 **Crewe**, England 53 5N 2 28w
14 **Crewkerne**, England ..50 53N 2 48w
17 **Crianlarich**, Scotland..56 24N 4 36w
14 **Criccieth**, Wales 52 55N 4 8w
14 **Crickhowell**, Wales ...51 51N 3 8w
14 **Cricklade**, England....51 39N 1 51w
17 **Crieff**, Scotland 56 17N 3 43w
37 **Crimea, rep.**, U.S.S.R..45 15N 34 30 E
17 **Crinan, & Canal**, Scot. 56 6N 5 32w
30 **Croatia-Slavonia**, dist., Yugoslavia......45 30N 18 0 E
57 **Crocodile R., U. of S.** Africa ....25 20 s 27 34 E
33 **Crodo**, Italy ....46 12N 8 20 E
13 **Croft**, England 54 28N 1 35w
16 **Cromarty**, Scotland ...57 41N 4 2w
16 **Cromarty Firth**, Scot..57 40N 4 30w
15 **Cromer**, England .....52 56N 1 18 E
16 **Cromore**, Scotland 58 6N 6 23w
51 **Cromwell**, N.Z. ....45 2s 169 12 E
19 **Crookhaven**, Eire 51 27N 9 44w
63 **Crookston**, U.S.A......47 50N 96 40w
49 **Crookwell**, N.S.W. ....34 28 s 149 28 E
19 **Croom**, Eire 52 31N 8 43w
22 **Crosbus**, Luxemburg ..49 45N 5 59 E
12 **Crosby**, I. of Man 54 11N 4 32w
12 **Cross Fell**, England ...54 43N 2 27w
19 **Crosshaven**, Eire 51 47N 8 18w
17 **Crossmichael**, Scot....54 59N 3 58w
12 **Crossmolina**, Eire 54 6N 9 20w
18 **Croston**, England 53 38N 2 38w
15 **Crouch, R.**, England...51 37N 1 0 E
47 **Crowes**, Victoria ......38 42 s 143 19 E
60 **Crowfoot**, Canada 50 55N 112 30w
15 **Crowland**, England....52 42N 0 10w
13 **Crowle**, England 53 37N 0 50w
68 **Crown Princess Martha Ld.**, Antarctic 71 0s 10 0w
47 **Crows Nest**, Queensland ....27 17 s 154 2 E
15 **Croydon**, England 51 22N 0 6w
47 **Croydon**, Queensland ..18 11 s 142 22 E
68 **Crozet Is.**, Southern Oc.47 0s 51 0 E
20 **Crozon**, France 48 16N 4 28w
64 **Cruces**, Mexico 29 30N 107 25w
16 **Cruden Bay**, Scotland .57 24N 1 52w
18 **Crumlin**, N. Ireland ..54 38N 6 13w
12 **Crummock Water**, Eng...................54 34N 3 19w
19 **Crusheen**, Eire.........52 57N 8 54w
67 **Cruz Alta**, Brazil......28 30 s 53 30w
66 **Cruzeiro do Sul**, Brazil 7 0s 71 50w
14 **Crymmych Arms**, Wales................51 58N 4 39w
47 **Crystal Brook**, S. Australia ....33 20 s 138 15 E
25 **Csap**, Czechoslovakia ..48 25N 22 12 E
31 **Csikszereda**, Rumania.46 24N 25 50 E
40 **Ctesiphon**, Iraq........35 7N 44 37 E
54 **Cuanza, R.**, Angola ... 9 20 s 13 10 E
65 **Cuba, I.**, W. Indies 20 33N 75 85w
15 **Cuckfield**, England ...51 0N 0 9w
66 **Cucuhy**, Venezuela 1 30N 66 55w
66 **Cucuta**, Colombia 8 0N 72 45w
58 **Cudahay**, Alaska 54 30N 140 32w
42 **Cuddalore**, India......11 45N 79 45 E
42 **Cuddapah**, India ......14 29N 78 50 E
26 **Cudillero**, Spain 43 34N 6 9w
46 **Cue**, W. Australia ....27 25 s 117 58 E
26 **Cuéllar**, Spain 41 22N 4 18w
66 **Cuenca**, Ecuador ..... 2 55 s 79 15w
27 **Cuenca**, Spain 40 5N 2 7w
27 **Cuevas de Vera**, Spain 37 13N 1 56w
49 **Culcairn**, N.S.W.......35 42 s 147 5 E
22 **Culenborg**, Netherlands51 58N 5 12 E
64 **Culiacan**, Mexico 24 50N 107 30w
16 **Cullen**, Scotland 57 41N 2 50w
27 **Cullera**, Spain 39 0N 0 13w
16 **Culloden**, Scotland ...57 30N 4 0w
14 **Cullompton**, England..50 52N 3 23w
33 **Cully**, Switzerland ....40 29N 6 41 E
31 **Culoz**, France ....45 52N 5 50 E
16 **Culter**, Scotland 55 36N 3 32w
51 **Culverden**, N.Z........42 45 s 172 52 E

MAP
66 **Cumana**, Venezuela ...10 25N 64 25w
63 **Cumberland**, U.S.A. ..39 45N 78 45w
12 **Cumberland Co.**, Eng. 54 45N 3 5w
60 **Cumberland House**, Canada 53 57N 102 20w
12 **Cambrian Mts.**, Eng. .54 32N 3 5w
17 **Cumnock**, Scotland....55 28N 4 14w
66 **Cunani**, Brazil 2 55N 50 55w
28 **Cuneo**, Italy ....44 24N 7 31 E
47 **Cunnamulla**, Queensland ....28 6s 145 37 E
17 **Cupar**, Scotland.......56 19N 3 0w
31 **Cuprija**, Yugoslavia ...43 56N 21 25 E
66 **Cura**, Venezuela....... 6 46N 61 36w
65 **Curaçao I.**, W. Indies..12 15N 69 0w
67 **Curico**, Chile..........34 50 s 71 10w
67 **Curitiba**, Brazil ....25 30 s 49 20w
47 **Currathool**, N.S.W. ...34 27 s 145 27 E
18 **Curry**, Eire 54 0N 8 46w
30 **Curzöla I.**, Yugoslavia..42 55N 17 0E
18 **Cushendall**, N. Ireland 55 5N 6 4w
18 **Cushendun**, N. Ireland 55 8N 6 3w
21 **Cusset**, France........46 6N 3 28 E
42 **Cutch**, India ....23 20N 69 30 E
42 **Cutch, G. of**, India ....22 35N 69 0 E
43 **Cuttack**, India ....20 24N 85 50 E
24 **Cuxhaven**, Germany...53 52N 8 41 E
66 **Cuyaba**, Brazil 15 0s 56 0w
66 **Cuzco**, Peru ....13 30 s 72 0w
31 **Cuzgun**, Rumania ....44 7N 27 49 E
14 **Cwmamman**, Wales...51 49N 3 53w
32 **Cyclades**, Greece .....37 0N 25 0 E
32 **Cyllene**, Greece ....37 55N 21 8 E
60 **Cypress**, Canada 49 42N 109 39w
60 **Cypress Hills**, Canada.49 30N 110 0w
40 **Cyprus I.**, Medit. Sea .35 0N 33 0 E
8 **Czechoslovakia, rep.**, Europe 48 to 51 0N, 12 to 24 E
30 **Czegled**, Hungary ....47 10N 19 50 E
31 **Czernowitz.** *See* **Cernauti**
25 **Czestochowa**, Poland .50 49N 19 3 E
25 **Czortków**, Poland.....49 1N 25 47 E

43 **Dacca**, India ....23 46N 90 30 E
32 **Dadion**, Greece........38 38N 22 40 E
37 **Dagestan, rep.**, U.S.S.R...............42 0N 47 30 E
35 **Dagö I.**, Estonia.......58 50N 22 40 E
52 **Dahomey, Col.**, Fr. W. Africa .... 8 30N 2 20 E
26 **Daimiel**, Spain 39 4N 3 35w
45 **Dairen**, Manchuria ....39 0N 121 35 E
31 **Daitsa**, Rumania .....44 1N 26 1 E
47 **Dajarra**, Queensland ..21 36 s 140 30 E
52 **Dakar**, Fr. W. Africa .14 40N 17 28w
52 **Dakhla Oasis**, Egypt. .25 20N 29 20 E
16 **Dalarossie**, Scotland .57 18N 4 3w
42 **Dalbandin**, India......28 57N 64 30 E
17 **Dalbeattie**, Scotland ..54 56N 3 50w
23 **Dalby**, Denmark .....55 31N 10 37 E
12 **Dalby**, I. of Man 54 10N 4 43w
49 **Dalby**, Queensland.....27 14 s 151 18 E
47 **Dalgety**, N.S.W. .....36 30 s 148 51 E
62 **Dalhart**, U.S.A. 35 59N 102 30w
47 **Dalhousie**, S. Australia 26 20 s 135 30 E
27 **Dalias**, Spain 36 51N 2 58w
30 **Dálj**, Yugoslavia .....45 30N 19 0 E
17 **Dalkeith**, Scotland ...55 53N 3 4w
18 **Dalkey**, Eire 53 16N 6 7w
16 **Dallas**, Scotland.......57 33N 3 28w
63 **Dallas**, U.S.A. 32 50N 96 50w
17 **Dalmally**, Scotland ...56 24N 4 59w
30 **Dalmatia, dist.**, Y.-slav. 43 50N 16 10 E
17 **Dalmellington**, Scot. ..55 19N 4 24w
16 **Dalnaspidal**, Scotland .56 50N 4 13w
45 **Dalny.** *See* **Dairen**
17 **Dalry**, Scotland 55 43N 4 43w
17 **Dalrymple**, Scotland ..55 24N 4 35w
63 **Dalton**, U.S.A. 34 45N 84 55w
12 **Dalton in Furness**, England 54 10N 3 12w
43 **Daltonganj**, India ....24 5N 83 52 E
16 **Dalwhinnie**, Scotland .56 56N 4 14w
46 **Daly Waters**, N. Terr. .16 10 s 133 35 E
66 **Dam**, Dutch Guiana ... 4 50N 55 15w
42 **Daman**, India..........20 25N 72 57 E
56 **Damara Land, dist.**, S. W. Africa ....21 0s 17 0 E
41 **Damascus**, Syria .....33 30N 36 20 E
23 **Damgarten**, Germany .54 15N 12 29 E
40 **Damietta**, Egypt .....31 22N 31 46 E
22 **Damme**, Belgium ......51 16N 3 17 E
50 **Danger Is.**, Inset
30 **Danilovgrad**, Y.Slav. ..43 35N 19 16 E
35 **Dannemora**, Sweden ..60 10N 17 50 E
50 **Dannevirke**, N.Z. .....40 11 s 176 6 E
31 **Danube R.**, Balkans ...45 0N 20 0 E
63 **Danville**, U.S.A. 36 35N 79 29w
25 **Danzig**, Europe .....54 20N 18 40 E
55 **Dar es Salaam**, Tang. 6 50 s 39 40 E
43 **Darbhangah**, India....26 11N 86 0 E
32 **Dardanelles**, Turkey .40 0N 26 10 E
55 **Darfur, Prov.**, Anglo-Egyptian Sudan ......13 0N 24 40 E
50 **Dargaville**, N.Z. ......35 53 s 173 53 E

MAP

49 Dargo, Victoria ....37 30s 147 10 E
31 Daridere, Bulgaria ...41 23N 25 6 E
43 Darjeeling, India ....27 3N 88 18 E
33 Darligen, Switzerland
46 Darling Ra., W. Austl. 32 30s 116 5 E
49 Darling, R., Australia .31 0s 144 15 E
13 Darlington, England ..54 32N 1 32w
24 Darmstadt, Germany .49 54N 8 38 E
27 Daroca, Spain 41 8N 1 25w
14 Dartmoor, England ..50 35N 4 0w
14 Dartmouth, England .50 21N 3 35w
13 Darton, England 53 35N 1 32w
17 Darvel, Scotland 55 37N 4 17w
13 Darwen, England 53 45N 2 28w
46 Darwin, N. Territory .53 50N 14 20 E
23 Darum, Denmark
41 Dasht-i-Kavir, Iran ..34 40N 55 0 E
41 Dasht-i-Lut, Iran ....31 30N 58 0 E
23 Dassow, Germany ....53 54N 11 58 E
42 Datia, India ....25 37N 78 38 E
35 Daugavpils, See Dvinsk
40 Dauletabad, Iran ....34 18N 48 40 E
21 Dauphiné, old prov.,
France ....45 0N 5 30 E
16 Dava, Scotland 57 27N 3 38w
32 Davas, Turkey ....37 30N 28 52 E
63 Davenport, U.S.A. ...41 30N 90 33w
15 Daventry, England ..56 16N 1 10w
23 Davgaard, Denmark ..55 44N 9 42 E
64 David, Panama 8 32N 82 30w
61 Davis Str., Canada ...67 0N 58 0w
33 Davos, Val., Switz. ..46 49N 9 50 E
33 Davos Platz, Switz. ..46 48N 9 50 E
14 Dawlish, England 50 35N 3 28w
60 Dawson, Canada 64 8N 139 20 0w
21 Dax, France 43 42N 1 3w
46 Day Dawn, W. Austl. .27 29s 117 56 E
48 Daylesford, Victoria .37 20s 114 9 E
63 Dayton, U.S.A. 39 42N 84 12w
57 De Aar, U. of S. Africa.30 35s 24 5 E
41 Dead Sea, Asia ......31 30N 35 30 E
62 Deadwood, U.S.A. ...44 25N 103 45w
46 Deakin, W. Austl. ...30 52s 129 0 E
15 Deal, England........51 13N 1 23 E
14 Dean, For. of, England 51 47N 2 33w
30 Debar, Yugoslavia ....
15 Debenham, England...52 14N 1 10 E
25 Debica, Poland.......50 4N 21 15 E
55 Debra Tabor, Abys. ..11 50N 38 5 E
31 Debrecen, Hungary ..47 33N 21 40 E
63 Decatur, U.S.A. 34 34N 87 8w
21 Decazeville, France ..44 34N 2 16 E
42 Deccan, dist., India ...14 0N 77 0 E
63 Decorah, U.S.A. 43 11N 91 49w
15 Deddington, England .51 59N 1 20w
36 Dediuchin, U.S.S.R. ..59 36N 56 34 E
56 Dedza, Nyasaland
12 Dee, R., England 53 17N 3 8w
17 Dee, R., Scotland 57 3N 2 35w
57 Deepwalls, U. of S. Afr.33 53s 23 7 E
49 Deepwater, N.S.W. ...29 30s 151 50 E
16 Deerness, Scotland ..58 57N 2 45w
24 Degerfors, Sweden ...64 15N 19 45 E
24 Deggendorf, Germany 48 50N 12 58 E
41 Dehbid, Iran ....30 35N 53 20 E
42 Dehra, India ....30 19N 78 4 E
40 Dehrud, Iran ....36 8N 59 6 E
41 Deir el Bela, Pal. ...31 25N 34 25 E
31 Déj, Rumania ....47 10N 23 52 E
62 Delamar, U.S.A. 37 29N 114 49w
57 Delarey, U. of S. Africa 26 45s 25 30 E
63 Delaware B., U.S.A. ..39 0N 75 0w
63 Delaware, St., U.S.A. 39 0N 75 30w
22 Delden, Netherlands ..52 15N 6 44 E
26 De Leek, Netherlands .
25 Delatyn, Poland......48 32N 24 39 E
33 Delémont, Switzerland 47 24N 7 20 E
22 Delfshaven, Neth. ...51 55N 4 25 E
22 Delft, Netherlands ...52 0N 4 20 E
22 Delfzijl, Netherlands .53 20N 6 55 E
42 Delhi, & prov., India .28 35N 77 18 E
52 Dellys, Algeria ......36 55N 3 45 E
24 Delmenhorst, Germany 53 2N 8 55 E
49 Deloraine, Tasmania .41 30s 147 0 E
32 Delphi, Greece ......38 45N 22 34 E
35 Delsbo, Sweden .....61 46N 16 36 E
32 Delvinaki, Greece ....39 57N 20 30 E
32 Delvino, Albania .....39 57N 20 9 E
40 Demavend, Mt., Iran .36 0N 52 6 E
66 Demerara R., Brit.
Guiana 5 40N 58 30w
32 Demerle, Greece .....39 20N 22 18 E
62 Deming, U.S.A. 32 15N 107 50w
32 Demirhissar, Greece ..41 13N 23 28 E
32 Demirji, Turkey .....39 3N 28 45 E
24 Demmin, Germany ...53 55N 13 0 E
32 Demotika, Greece ....41 20N 26 34 E
21 Denain, France ......50 20N 2 35 E
12 Denbigh, Wales 53 11N 3 26w
12 Denbigh, Co., Wales ..53 10N 3 30w
22 Den Burg, Netherlands 53 3N 4 48 E
22 Dendermonde, Belgium 51 2N 4 6 E
27 Denia, Spain ....38 50N 0 6 E
49 Deniliquin, N.S.W. ...35 30s 144 58 E
63 Denison, U.S.A. 33 45N 96 35w

MAP

32 Denizli, Turkey ......37 46N 29 8 E
49 Denman, N.S.W. .....32 25s 150 42 E
46 Denmark, W. Australia 35 1s 117 30 E
8 Denmark, King., Eur. 56 0N 10 0 E
61 Denmark Str., Green. .66 0N 29 0w
62 Denver, U.S.A........39 43N 104 59w
15 Denton, England 52 48N 0 42w
42 Dera Ghazi Khan, Ind.30 5N 70 46 E
42 Dera Ismail, Khan, Ind.31 52N 70 52 E
37 Derbent, U.S.S.R. ....42 5N 48 8 E
49 Derby, Tasmania .....41 8s 147 50 E
46 Derby, W. Australia ..17 23s 123 40 E
15 Derby, & Co., England 52 56N 1 28w
19 Derg, L., Eire 52 58N 8 17w
32 Dermil, Turkey ......37 2N 29 35 E
52 Derna, Libya ....32 40N 22 10 E
19 Derryveagh Mts., Eire 55 0N 8 5w
17 Dervaig, Scotland 56 36N 6 10w
30 Dervent, Yugoslavia ..45 0N 17 58 E
12 Derwent R. (Cumb.),
Eng. 54 40N 3 26w
13 Derwent R. (Durham),
England 54 50N 2 0w
13 Derwent R. (Yorks),
England 54 20N 0 32w
13 Derwent Water, Eng. .54 35N 3 10w
63 Des Moines, U.S.A. ..41 33N 93 35w
24 De Soto, U.S.A. 38 7N 90 30w
24 Dessau, Germany ....51 50N 12 16 E
67 Desterro, Brazil 27 30s 48 30w
24 Detmold, Germany ...51 56N 8 50 E
63 Detroit, U.S.A........42 20N 83 5w
35 Deutschbrod, Czech. ..49 39N 15 34 E
25 Deutsch Krone, Ger. ..53 17N 16 26 E
21 Deux-Sèvres, dept.,
France 46 43N 0 20w
31 Déva, Rumania ......45 52N 25 58 E
31 Deva, Spain 43 15N 2 20w
42 Devarkonda, India ...16 42N 78 58 E
14 Deventer, Netherlands .52 14N 6 9 E
14 Devils Bridge, Wales .53 0N 4 7w
62 Devils Lake, U.S.A. ..48 0N 99 0w
14 Devizes, England.....51 21N 1 58w
14 Devon, Co., England .51 0N 3 30w
61 Devon, I., Canada 75 0N 86 0w
14 Devonport, England ..50 23N 4 11w
14 Devonport, Tasmania .41 9s 146 21 E
14 Devynock, Wales 51 52N 3 35w
57 De Wets Dorp, U. of S.
Africa ....29 30s 26 18 E
13 Dewsbury, England ..53 42N 1 37w
42 Deynze, Belgium .....50 58N 3 32 E
42 Dharmsala, India ....32 15N 75 20 E
42 Dharwar India ....15 29N 75 5 E
41 Dhiban, Transjordan .31 31N 35 44 E
42 Dhond, India ....17 35N 74 55 E
43 Dhubri, India ....26 0N 90 0 E
41 Diala, Iraq ....33 20N 44 25 E
67 Diamantina, Brazil...18 20s 43 31w
47 Diamantina, R.,Queens.24 0s 141 10 E
42 Dibrugarh, India .....27 29N 95 0 E
62 Dickens, U.S.A. 33 30N 100 40w
62 Dickinson, U.S.A. ...46 80N 102 30w
31 Dicsöszentmárton,
Rumania ....46 20N 24 18 E
15 Didcot, England......51 37N 1 15w
21 Die, France ....44 50N 5 38 E
22 Diedenhofen, France .49 23N 6 12 E
22 Diekirch, Luxemburg .49 53N 6 11 E
22 Diepholz, Germany ...47 37N 10 11 E
20 Dieppe, France.......49 56N 1 4 E
22 Diest, Belgium ....50 58N 5 5 E
20 Dieuze, France.......48 50N 6 40 E
21 Digne, France........44 4N 6 13 E
20 Dijon, France........47 19N 5 4 E
32 Dikeli Turkey ....39 3N 26 55 E
54 Dikoa, Nigeria ....12 0N 13 58 E
24 Dillingen, Germany ..48 34N 10 28 E
62 Dillon, U.S.A. ....45 13N 112 38 E
40 Dilman, Iran ....38 5N 44 45 E
54 Dilolo, Belgian Congo .10 28s 22 23 E
42 Dinajpur, India ......25 30N 88 50 E
43 Dinapur, India ......25 38N 85 5 E
21 Dinan, France 48 28N 2 4w
22 Dinant, Belgium .....50 18N 4 58 E
21 Dinard, France 48 38N 2 6w
30 Dinaric Alps, Y.-slav. .44 0N 16 40 E
14 Dinas Mawddwy,
Wales 52 43N 3 41w
39 Dindings, Malay Pen...4 19N 100 37 E
15 Dingle, & Bay, Eire ..52 8N 10 16w
16 Dingwall, Scotland ...57 36N 4 26w
49 Dir, India ....35 14N 71 47 E
49 Dirranbandi, Queens..28 29s 148 26 E
46 Disappointment, L.,
W. Australia ....46 30N 123 0 E
32 Diskata, Greece ......39 52N 21 48 E
13 Diss, England ....52 22N 1 6 E
33 Dissentis, Switzerland .46 44N 8 54 E
42 Ditton Priors, Eng. ..52 30N 2 34w
42 Diu, I., India ....20 43N 70 48 E
40 Divinaje, Iraq ....32 5N 44 55 E
42 Dixmude, Belgium ...51 2N 2 52 E
40 Diyarbekr, Turkey ...37 50N 39 51 E
41 Dizak, Iran ....27 30N 62 15 E

MAP

40 Dizful, Iran ....32 26N 48 29 E
40 Djabrin, Arabia ......23 2N 49 0 E
25 Djottowen, Poland ...53 28N 21 53 E
37 Dnepropetrovsk,
U.S.S.R. ....48 20N 35 0 E
37 Dnieper, R., U.S.S.R. .48 0N 33 0 E
37 Dniester, R., U.S.S.R. .46 15N 33 0 E
47 Dobbyn, Queensland ..19 50s 140 0 E
14 Döbeln, Germany ....51 7N 13 7 E
23 Deberan, Germany ...54 6N 11 53 E
30 Doboj, Yugoslavia ...44 55N 18 5 E
31 Dobral, Bulgaria .....42 47N 26 55 E
31 Dobrich, Rumania ...43 33N 29 49 E
31 Dobruja, dist., Ruman. 44 40N 28 30 E
25 Dobsina, Cz.slov. ....48 49N 20 22 E
17 Dochart, Scotland ...56 24N 4 36w
31 Docholina, Rumania ..43 33N 27 50 E
32 Dodecanese. See Sporades
62 Dodge City, U.S.A. ..37 47N 100 0w
55 Dodoma, Tanganyika .6 11s 35 45 E
22 Doetinchem, Neth. ..51 58N 6 17 E
42 Dohad, India ....22 28N 74 5 E
32 Dojran, Greece ......41 10N 22 44 E
22 Dokkum, Netherlands .53 20N 6 0 E
20 Dôle, France ....47 7N 5 31 E
14 Dolgelley, Wales 52 45N 3 53w
25 Dolha, Czechoslovakia .48 21N 23 15 E
25 Dolina, Poland ......49 0N 24 0 E
53 Dolo, It. Somaliland ..4 15N 42 0 E
28 Dolomites, Mts., Italy.46 30N 11 40 E
17 Dolphinton, Scotland .55 42N 3 25w
25 Domachevo, Poland ..51 45N 21 32 E
35 Dombas, Norway .....62 7N 9 5 E
20 Domfront, France 48 36N 0 40w
65 Dominica, I. 15 30N 61 5w
65 Dominican Rep. 18 55N 70 30w
56 Domira B , Nyasaland .13 37s 34 25 E
24 Dömitz, Germany ....53 10N 11 15 E
28 Domo d'Ossola, Italy.46 8N 8 17 E
32 Domoko, Greece .....39 8N 29 19 E
20 Domrémy, France ....48 28N 5 52 E
32 Domvrena, Greece ...38 17N 23 0 E
26 Don Benito, Spain ...38 52N 5 50w
13 Don, R. (Yorks), Eng. 53 27N 1 43w
16 Don, R., Scotland ...57 16N 2 25w
37 Don R., U.S.S.R. ....50 0N 40 0 E
18 Donaghadee, N.Ireland 54 39N 5 33w
63 Donald, Canada 51 28N 117 12w
63 Donaldsonville, U.S.A.30 5N 90 55w
20 Donard, Eire 53 2N 6 37w
24 Donaueschingen, Ger. .47 58N 8 30 E
24 Donauwörth, Germany 48 45N 10 44 E
13 Doncaster, England ..53 31N 1 8w
18 Donegal & Co., Eire ..54 54N 8 0w
18 Donegal B., Eire 54 33N 8 26w
37 Donets, U.S.S.R. .....48 30N 39 20 E
18 Dongaloa, Fiji Is. Inset 17 20s 117 30 E
46 Dongarra, W. Austl. .29 14s 115 0 E
32 Dongola, Anglo E. Sud.19 0N 30 5 E
15 Donington, England ..52 54N 0 12w
47 Donnybrook, Queens..26 5s 147 52 E
19 Donoughmore, Eire ..52 0N 8 45w
14 Dorchester, England ..50 43N 2 25w
21 Dordogne, dept., Fr. ..45 5N 0 40 E
21 Dordogne, R., France .45 15N 0 40 E
22 Dordrecht, Netherlands.51 49N 4 40 E
57 Dordrecht, U. of S. Afr.31 23s 27 7 E
21 Dore, Mt., France ....45 32N 2 52 E
16 Dores, Scotland ......57 23N 4 20 E
15 Dorking, England 51 14N 0 20w
16 Dornie, Scotland 57 17N 5 30w
16 Dornoch, Scotland ...57 53N 4 1w
16 Dornoch Firth, Scot. .57 53N 8 50w
31 Dorohoiu, Rumania ..47 59N 26 23 E
35 Dorpat, Estonia ......58 20N 26 45 E
14 Dorset, Co., England .50 30N 2 30w
14 Dorset Heights, Eng...50 50N 2 40w
24 Dortmund, Germany .51 32N 7 26 E
23 Dorum, Germany ....53 43N 8 34 E
31 Dospat, Bulgaria .....40 38N 24 10 E
63 Dothan, U.S.A. 31 13N 85 23w
21 Douai, France........50 21N 3 6 E
20 Douarnenez, France ..48 8N 4 15w
20 Doubs, dept., France .47 10N 6 32 E
20 Doubs, R., France ...47 20N 6 20 E
12 Douglas, I. of Man ...54 9N 4 29w
17 Douglas, Scotland ...55 33N 3 50w
57 Douglas, U. of S.Africa 29 7s 23 50 E
17 Doune, Scotland 56 11N 4 3w
26 Douro R., Portugal ..41 15N 6 40w
15 Dover, England ......51 7N 1 19 E
63 Dover, U.S.A. 40 0N 76 57w
15 Dover, Str. of, Eng. ..50 50N 1 20 E
14 Dovey, R., Wales 52 33N 4 5w
31 Dovlen, Bulgaria .....41 46N 24 26 E
14 Dovre Fjell, Norway ..62 25N 9 40 E
35 Dovre Snehetta, Mt.,
Norway ....62 20N 9 0 E
56 Dowa, Nyasaland ....13 40s 33 55 E
18 Down, Co., N. Ireland 54 20N 5 40w
15 Downham Market, Eng.52 37N 0 23 E
18 Downpatrick, N. Ire. .24 20N 5 44w
15 Downs, North, Eng. ..51 13N 0 30 E
15 Downs, South, Eng. ..50 55N 0 30w
15 Downton, England 51 0N 1 44w

MAP

61 Ellesmere I., Canada .79 30N 80 0w
12 Ellesmere Port, Eng. .53 20N 2 50w
6 Ellice Is., Pacific Oc.
     5 to 11 s 176 to 180 E
42 Ellichpur, India ...21 20N 77 33 E
16 Ellon, Scotland.......57 22N 2 5w
42 Ellore, India ....16 48N 81 8 E
24 Ellwangen, Germany 49 0N 10 8 E
23 Ellwurden, Germany..53 38N 8 26 E
33 Elm, Switzerland ....46 55N 9 10 E
63 Elmira, U.S.A. 42 5N 76 58w
24 Elmshorn, Germany...53 43N 9 40 E
18 Elphin, Eire 53 51N 8 12w
57 Elsburg, U. of S. Africa.26 20s 28 10 E
  Elsterwerda, Ger. ....51 30N 13 28 E
50 Eltham, N.Z. ....39 36s 174 16 E
26 Elvas, Portugal 38 50N 7 14w
35 Elverum, Norway ...60 55N 11 30 E
15 Ely, England ....52 24N 0 16 E
62 Ely, U.S.A. 39 20N 114 58w
15 Ely, I. of, Co., Eng. 52 to 52N 0 to 0 E
13 Embleton, England....55 31N 1 38w
21 Embrun, France .....44 33N 6 29 E
24 Emden, Germany .....53 24N 7 12 E
47 Emerald, Queensland .23 32s 148 17 E
60 Emerson, Canada ...49 1N 97 10w
28 Emilia, Dept., Italy ..44 35N 10 40 E
31 Emirova, Bulgaria ....43 30N 27 35 E
35 Emmaboda, Sweden .56 35N 15 0 E
47 Emmaville, N.S.W. ..29 27s 151 33 E
57 Empandhleni,
  U. of S. Africa .....28 38s 31 8 E
62 Empire City, U.S.A. .43 32N 124 5w
28 Empoli, Italy ....43 42N 10 58 E
63 Emporia, U.S.A. 38 26N 96 14w
24 Ems, Germany ....50 20N 7 45 E
24 Ems, R., Germany ...53 20N 7 0 E
15 Emsworth, England ..50 51N 0 56w
46 Emungalan, N. Terr. .14 32s 132 28 E
35 Enånger, Sweden ...61 29N 17 7 E
67 Encalada, Chile 24 30s 70 50w
67 Encarnacion, Para. ..21 30N 102 20w
48 Enderbury I., Pac. Oc. 3 0s 171 10w
68 Enderby L., Antarc...67 0s 50 0 E
15 Enfield, England 51 40N 0 5w
33 Engadin, Val., Switz. .46 47N 10 20 E
41 Engedi. See Ain Jidi
33 Engleberg, Switz......46 49N 8 25 E
33 Engelburg, Switz. ....47 26N 9 20 E
22 Enghien, Belgium .....50 42N 4 2 E
11 England, British Is.
     50 to 56N 2 E to 6w
8 English Chan., Europe 50 0N 2 0w
27 Enguera, Spain 39 0N 0 42w
62 Enid, U.S.A. 36 30N 98 0w
56 Enkeldoorn, S. Rhod. .18 50s 30 50 E
22 Enkhuizen, Netherlands 52 42N 5 18 E
29 Enna, Sicily ....37 33N 14 23 E
19 Ennis, Eire 52 51N 8 59w
63 Ennis, U.S.A. 32 24N 96 50w
19 Enniscorthy, Eire 52 29N 6 35w
18 Enniskillen, N. Ireland 54 20N 7 39w
19 Ennistymon, Eire 52 57N 9 17w
32 Enos, Turkey ....40 41N 26 7 E
22 Enschede, Netherlands 52 12N 6 55 E
64 Ensenada, Mexico ...31 59N 116 45w
55 Entebbe, Uganda ... 0 4N 32 26 E
60 Enterprise, Canada ..44 20N 76 41w
26 Entrambaságuas, Sp. .43 22N 3 45w
21 Entraygues, France ..44 38N 2 38 E
26 Entre Minho e Douro,
  prov., Portugal 41 30N 8 20w
67 Entre Rios, Brazil ..22 0s 43 25w
67 Entre Rios, terr.,
  Argentina 30 0s 58 0w
54 Enugu, Nigeria.......6 35N 7 30 E
37 Enzeli. See Pahlevi
54 Epe, Nigeria.........6 40N 3 58 E
20 Epernay, France .....49 2N 3 56 E
20 Épinal, France ......48 11N 6 30 E
32 Epirus, dist., Greece .39 30N 20 30 E
15 Epping, England .....51 42N 0 6 E
15 Epsom, England 51 20N 0 17w
56 Epukiro, S.W. Africa .21 25s 19 0 E
13 Epworth, England ...53 32N 0 48w
41 Er Ramle, Palestine .31 55N 31 53 E
68 Erebus, Mt., Antarc. .77 30s 166 0 E
40 Eregli, Turkey ......37 37N 34 5 E
24 Erfurt, Germany .....51 0N 11 0 E
16-17 Ericht Loch, Scot. .56 50N 4 25w
63 Erie, U.S.A. 40 25N 80 0w
61 Erie, L., N. America ..42 10N 80 50w
41 Eriha, Palestine .....31 51N 35 27 E
15 Erith, England ......51 23N 0 12 E
52 Eritrea, Africa ....15 0N 39 0 E
37 Erivan, U.S.S.R. ....40 10N 44 31 E
33 Erlach, Switzerland ...47 2N 7 5 E
24 Erlangen, Ger. ......49 35N 11 2 E
30 Erlau. See Eger
57 Ermelo, U. of S. Africa 26 31s 30 2 E
18 Erne, Lower L., N. Ire.54 30N 7 50w
18 Erne, Upper L., N. Ire.54 10N 7 30w
47 Eromanga, Queens. ..26 39s 143 12 E
18 Errigal, Mt., Eire ...55 3N 8 7w
40 Eringyan, Turkey ...39 33N 39 51 E

40 Erzerum, Turkey.....39 57N 41 27 E
41 Es Salt, Transjordan..32 01N 35 44 E
41 Es Sanamein, Syria ..33 10N 36 12 E
23 Esbjerg, Denmark....55 28N 8 30 E
63 Escanabu, U.S.A. 45 45N 87 10w
27 Escatron, Spain 41 18N 0 19w
22 Esch, Luxemburg ....49 33N 1 59 E
24 Eschwege, Germany ..51 10N 10 4 E
41 Esdud, Palestine .....31 45N 34 40 E
41 Esh Sheikh, Jebel,
  Syria ....33 26N 35 50 E
57 Eshowe, U. of S. Africa 28 55s 31 30 E
47 Esk, Queensland......27 15s 152 20 E
12 Esk, R., Cumb., Eng. ..55 10N 3 1w
13 Esk, R., York., Eng. ..54 30N 0 38w
17 Esk, R., Scotland 55 11N 3 2w
50 Eskdale, New Zealand .39 20s 176 50 E
31 Eski Jumaya, Bul. ...46 16N 26 37 E
32 Eskije, Greece ......41 9N 24 56 E
35 Eskilstuna, Sweden ..59 25N 16 30 E
40 Eskishehr, Turkey ...39 40N 30 27 E
66 Esmeraldas, Ecuador . 0 50N 79 30w
66 Esmeraldas, Venezuela 3 10N 66 3w
40 Esneh, Egypt ....25 18N 32 30 E
46 Esperance, W. Austl. .33 47s 121 50 E
26 Espinosa, Spain 43 5N 3 33w
67 Espirito Santo, st.,
  Brazil 20 0s 41 0w
26 Espozende, Port......41 30N 8 48w
60 Esquimalt, Canada ..48 29N 123 22w
30 Esseg. See Osijek
24 Essen, Germany......51 26N 6 45 E
66 Essequibo, R.,
  Brit. Guiana 7 0N 58 0w
15 Essex, co., England
     51 to 52N 0 to 1 E
25 Essling, Aus. Ger. ...48 13N 16 36 E
24 Esslingen, Germany ..48 46N 9 17 E
33 Estavayer, Switz. ....46 50N 6 50 E
28 Este, Italy ....45 18N 11 40 E
27 Estella, Spain 42 42N 2 2w
26 Estepona, Spain 36 27N 5 10w
27 Esterri, Spain ......42 37N 1 8 E
63 Estherville, U.S.A. ..43 25N 94 50w
15 Eston, England 54 34N 1 7w
35 Estonia, rep., Europe
     57 to 59N 22 to 28 E
26 Estrada, Spain 42 38N 8 32w
26 Estremadura, prov.,
  Portugal 39 0N 6 10w
26 Estremadura, old
  prov., Spain 38 to 40N 8 to 9 30w
26 Estremoz, Portugal ..38 52N 8 58 E
30 Esztergom, Hungary .47 47N 18 44 E
41 Et Taiyibeh, Palestine .31 58N 35 20 E
40 Et Tih, Jebel &
  Desert, Egypt ......30 0N 33 40 E
58 Etah, Greenland 78 20N 72 42w
22 Etalle, Belgium .....49 40N 5 36 E
20 Étampes, France ....48 24N 2 7 E
20 Étaples, France .....50 33N 1 41 E
41 Etawah, India ....26 45N 79 8 E
60 Etawney, L., Canada .58 0N 97 0w
52 Ethiopia. See Abyssinia
17 Etive, Loch, Scotland .56 28N 5 10w
29 Etna, Mt., Sicily ....37 44N 15 0 E
15 Eton, England 51 30N 0 37w
56 Etosha Pan, S.W. Afr. .18 45s 16 45 E
17 Ettrick, Scotland 55 25N 3 12w
20 Eu, France ....50 2N 1 25 E
32 Euboea I., Greece ...22 30N 24 0 E
46 Eucla, W. Australia ..31 45s 128 55 E
37 Eugene, U.S.A. 44 1N 123 1w
37 Eupatoria, U.S.S.R. ..45 13N 33 16 E
22 Eupen, Belgium .....50 38N 6 3 E
40 Euphrates, R.,
  S. W. Asia ....34 30N 41 30 E
20 Eure, dept., France....48 56N 0 58 E
20 Eure-et-Loir, dept.,
  France 48 20N 1 25w
62 Eureka, Cal., U.S.A. .40 50N 124 12w
62 Eureka, Nev., U.S.A. .39 30N 115 58w
47 Eurelia, S. Austral. ..32 32s 138 31 E
47 Euston, N.S.W. .....34 31s 142 45 E
24 Eutin, Germany .....54 9N 10 37 E
47 Evandale, Tasmania .41 27s 147 20 E
63 Evanston, Ill., U.S.A. 42 0N 87 47w
63 Evanston, Wy., U.S.A..41 12N 111 0w
63 Evansville, U.S.A. ...37 0N 87 3w
16 Evanton, Scotland ...57 40N 4 19w
43 Everest, Mt., Asia...28 0N 87 0 E
63 Everett, U.S.A. 47 55N 122 7w
14 Evesham, England ..52 5N 1 56w
26 Évora, Portugal 38 34N 7 55w
20 Évreux, France .....49 2N 1 7 E
16 Ewe, Loch, Scotland .57 53N 5 40w
14 Exe, R., England 51 5N 3 32w
14 Exeter, England 50 44N 3 32w
14 Exmoor, England 51 9N 3 45w
14 Exmouth, England ...50 37N 3 23w
51 Exploring Is., Fiji Is.
       Inset 17 0s 179 0w
55 Eyasi, L., Tanganyika. 3 40s 35 0 E

25 Eydtkuhnen, Germany.54 32N 22 50 E
15 Eye, England ....52 19N 1 9 E
17 Eyemouth, Scotland ..55 52N 2 5w
21 Eymet, France ......44 41N 0 23 E
46 Eyre, W. Australia ...32 20s 126 30 E
  Eyre, L., S. Australia .28 30s 137 15 E
  Eyre, L. Sth., S. Austra.29 15s 137 30 E
19 Eyrecourt, Eire 53 13N 8 8w
47 Eyre's Pen., S. Austral.33 30s 136 0 E
41 Ez Zib, Palestine ....33 3N 35 8 E

23 Faaborg, Denmark ..55 6N 10 15 E
28 Fabriano, Italy ......43 20N 12 52 E
31 Faenza, Italy ....44 18N 11 52 E
61 Faeringehavn, Green. .63 40N 51 20w
31 Fagaras, Rumania ...45 46N 24 54 E
12 Faido, Switzerland ...46 58N 8 48 E
16 Fair, L., Scotland ...59 30N 1 40w
63 Fairbanks, Alaska ..64 59N 148 10w
51 Fairlie, New Zealand .44 4s 170 52 E
60 Fairweather, Mt.,
  Alaska 59 0N 137 58w
41 Faizabad, Afghanistan 37 5N 70 35 E
41 Faizabad, India ......26 40N 82 10 E
15 Fakenham, England ..52 51N 0 51 E
23 Fakse, Denmark ....55 15N 12 12 E
20 Falaise, France 48 53N 0 12w
31 Falchiu, Rumania ...46 18N 28 12 E
31 Faleshty, Rumania ..47 30N 27 17 E
24 Falkenberg, Ger......53 28N 16 0 E
35 Falkenberg, Sweden .56 55N 12 25 E
17 Falkirk, Scotland ...56 0N 3 47w
17 Falkland, Scotland ..56 15N 30 13w
67 Falkland Is., S. Am. .51 0s 57 0w
68 Falkland Is., depend.
  Antarctica 51 0s 57 0w
35 Falköping, Sweden ..58 10N 13 40 E
63 Fall River, U.S.A. ...41 45N 71 0w
14 Falmouth, England ..50 10N 5 5w
65 Falmouth, Jamaica ..50 10N 5 5w
57 False B., U. of S. Afr. .34 15s 18 45 E
35 Falsterbo, Sweden ..55 20N 12 50 E
35 Falun, Sweden ......60 35N 33 59 E
49 Famagusta, Cyprus ..35 3N 33 59 E
6 Fanning I., Pacific Oc. 3 50N 159 21w
28 Fano, Italy ....43 52N 12 59 E
23 Fanö I., Denmark ...55 25N 8 25 E
40 Fao, Iraq ....29 55N 48 33 E
52 Farafrah, O., Egypt ..26 48N 28 30 E
41 Farah, Afghanistan ..32 25N 62 8 E
15 Fareham, England ...50 52N 1 10w
62 Fargo, U.S.A. 46 51N 96 55w
47 Farina, S. Australia .30 0s 138 15 E
15 Faringdon, England ..51 40N 1 35w
15 Farmers, Wales......52 5N 3 58w
62 Farmington, U.S.A. ..42 30N 78 29w
17 Farnborough, England 51 17N 0 45w
13 Farne Is., England ...55 39N 1 36w
15 Farnham, England ...51 13N 0 48w
26 Faro, Portugal 37 2N 7 55w
8 Faroe Is., Atlantic Oc. .62 0N 7 0w
16 Farr, Scotland 58 32N 4 12w
42 Farrukhabad, India ..27 20N 79 38 E
40 Fars, Prov., Iran....30 0N 53 0 E
23 Farsö, Denmark .....56 47N 9 20 E
35 Farsund, Norway ...58 0N 6 40 E
29 Fasano, Italy ....40 52N 17 11 E
55 Fashoda, A. E. Sudan .9 54N 32 7 E
42 Fatehpur, Raj., India..28 0N 75 3 E
42 Fatehpur, U. Prov.,
  India ....25 52N 80 50 E
34 Fatmomakke, Sweden 65 0N 15 10 E
31 Faurei, Rumania .....45 5N 27 16 E
57 Fauresmith, U. of S.
  Africa ....29 45s 25 17 E
29 Favara, Sicily ....37 19N 13 30 E
15 Faversham, England .51 19N 0 54 E
63 Faxina, Brazil ....55 16N 12 9 E
63 Fayetteville, Ark.,
  U.S.A. 36 3N 94 15w
63 Fayetteville, N. Car.,
  U.S.A. 35 1N 78 50w
40 Fayum, Egypt ....29 25N 30 45 E
42 Fazilka, India ....30 25N 74 4 E
51 Fearn, Scotland 57 47N 40 0w
51 Featherston, N.Z. ...41 5s 175 19 E
20 Fécamp, France .....49 46N 0 24 E
40 Federal Terr., Austl. .35 30s 148 45 E
39 Federated Malay
  States, Asia .... 4 0N 104 0 E
56 Feira, N. Rhodesia ..15 35s 30 20 E
27 Felanitx, Majorca I. .39 27N 3 10 E
24 Feldkirch, Aust. Ger. .47 16N 9 40 E
15 Felixstowe, England .51 58N 1 22 E
31 Felsöbánya, Rumania .47 40N 23 43 E
13 Felton, England 55 18N 1 43w
28 Feltre, Italy ....46 1N 11 54 E
45 Fengtien, prov., Man. .41 30N 124 0 E
19 Fenit, Eire 52 17N 9 53w
15 Fenny Stratford, Eng..52 0N 0 43w
15 Fens, The, England ..52 45N 0 2 E
31 Ferdinand, Bulgaria .43 23N 23 14 E
32 Ferejik, Greece .....40 55N 26 12 E
28 Ferentino, Italy......41 40N 13 11 E
63 Fergus Falls, U.S.A. .46 16N 96 3w

MAP
29 Ferla, Sicily ....37 8N 14 55 E
18 Fermanagh, co.,
    N. Ireland............54 20N 7 35w
28 Fermo, Italy ....43 10N 13 40 E
26 Fermosilla, Spain ...41 19N 6 25w
19 Fermoy, Eire 52 8N 8 18w
66 Fernando Noronha, I.,
    Brazil ....3 30N 8 45 E
54 Fernando Po, I., G.
    of Guinea ....3 30N 8 45 E
47 Fernmouth, N.S.W. ..30 30 s 153 0 E
28 Ferrara, Italy ....44 50N 11 38 E
26 Ferrol, Spain 43 30N 8 15w
17 Ferryden, Scotland ..56 42N 2 25w
31 Fetesti, Rumania .....44 23N 27 50 E
19 Fethard, Eire 52 27N 7 42w
16 Fettercairn, Scotland .56 58N 2 15w
21 Feurs, France ....45 44N 4 14 E
14 Ffestiniog, Wales 52 58N 3 55w
53 Fianarantsoa, Madag. .21 15 s 47 0 E
57 Ficksburg, U. of S. Afr.28 50 s 27 58 E
30 Fieri, Albania ....40 42N 19 36 E
28 Fiesole, Italy ....43 50N 11 19 E
56 Fife. See Isoka
17 Fife, Co., Scotland ...56 15N 3 0w
17 Fife Ness, Scotland ..56 17N 2 35w
21 Figeac, France ......44 36N 2 1 E
15 Figig, Morocco 32 10N 1 15w
26 Figueira da Foz, Port..40 8N 8 52w
27 Figueros, Spain ......42 17N 3 0 E
15 Fiji Is., Pac. Oc. Inset 17 20 s 179 0 E
56 Filabusi, S. Rhodesia .20 30 s 29 20 E
31 Filey, England 54 13N 0 16w
31 Filiashu, Rumania ...44 33N 23 32 E
28 Finale, Italy ....44 50N 11 19 E
16 Findhorn, Scotland ..57 40N 3 36w
16 Findhorn, R., Scotland 77 30N 105 0w
16 Findochty, Scotland ..57 42N 2 54w
16 Findon, Scotland 57 4N 2 6w
15 Finedon, England 52 22N 0 40w
20 Finistère, dept., France 48 20N 4 5w
20 Finisterre, C., Spain ...42 40N 9 17w
9 Finland, rep., Europe .65 0N 26 0w
35 Finland, G. of, Europe .59 50N 25 0 E
34 Finmark, co., Norway 69 50N 25 30 E
24 Finsterwalde, Germany 51 40N 13 40 E
11 Fintona, N. Ireland ...54 30N 7 20w
42 Firozpur, India......27 47N 76 59 E
40 Firuzabad, Iran......28 47N 52 28 E
14 Fishguard, Wales 51 59N 4 58w
61 Fiskernoesset, Green. .62 45N 50 40w
28 Fiume, Italy ....45 21N 14 26 E
28 Fiumicino, Italy .....41 47N 12 16 E
28 Fjellbacka, Sweden ..58 36N 11 18 E
62 Flagstaff, U.S.A. 35 15N 111 42w
13 Flamborough Hd.,
    England 54 8N 0 5w
33 Flawyl, Switzerland ..47 25N 9 10 E
12 Fleetwood, England ..53 56N 3 1w
35 Flekkefiord, Norway ..58 20N 6 40 E
24 Flensburg, Germany .54 43N 9 30 E
20 Flers, France 48 45N 0 34w
46 Flinders, S. Australia .32 50 s 134 15 E
47 Flinders Range, S. Aus.31 30 s 138 20 E
60 Flinflon, Canada 55 0N 101 45w
12 Flint, & Co., England .53 15N 3 8w
63 Flint, U.S.A. 42 58N 83 40w
11 Flodden, England 55 37N 2 7w
28 Florence, Italy ....43 46N 11 17 E
63 Florence, Ala., U.S.A. .34 52N 87 47w
63 Florence, Ariz., U.S.A.33 0N 111 22w
63 Florence, S.C., U.S.A. .34 10N 79 45w
64 Flores, Guatemala ...16 53N 89 59w
39 Flores I., Dut. E. Ind. ..8 30 s 121 0 E
66 Florianopolis, Brazil ..27 30 s 48 30w
63 Florida, St., U.S.A. ...28 0N 82 0w
63 Florida, C., U.S.A. ...25 45N 80 15w
22 Flushing, Netherlands .51 27N 3 35 E
16 Fochabers, Scotland ..57 37N 3 5w
31 Focsani, Rumania ....45 42N 27 5 E
28 Foggia, Italy ....41 26N 15 33 E
28 Foligno, Italy........42 58N 12 40 E
15 Folkestone, England .51 5N 1 11 E
15 Folkingham, England .52 53N 0 24w
28 Follonica, Italy ......42 56N 10 43 E
63 Fond du Lac, U.S.A...43 48N 88 30w
26 Fonsagrada, Spain ...43 7N 7 5w
64 Fonseca, G. of, Salv. .13 0N 87 54w
26 Fontainebleau, France.48 23N 2 42 E
21 Fontenay, France 46 35N 0 56w
21 Fontevrault, France ..47 11N 0 3 E
45 Foo-chow, China .....26 0N 119 20 E
54 Forcados, Nigeria ....5 26N 5 26 E
19 Ford, Eire 52 31N 0 17w
13 Ford, England 55 38N 2 5w
17 Ford, Scotland 56 11N 5 26w
15 Fordingbridge, Eng. .50 55N 1 46w
61 Forel, Mt., Greenland .66 70N 37 0w
15 Foreland, N., England 51 23N 1 27 E
15 Foreland, S., England .51 10N 1 24 E
17 Forfar, Scotland 56 39N 2 53w
28 Forli, Italy ....44 13N 12 1 E
12 Formby, England 53 34N 3 6w
27 Formentera, I., Spain .38 40N 1 30 E
67 Formosa, Argentina ..26 10 s 58 10w

MAP
66 Formosa, Brazil .....15 25 s 47 15w
45 Formosa, I. See Taiwan I.
28 Fornova, Italy ....44 40N 10 10 E
16 Forres, Scotland 57 37N 3 36w
16 Forsinard, Scotland .58 21N 3 54w
24 Forst, Germany ......51 45N 14 38 E
16 Fort Augustus, Scot. .57 59N 4 42w
57 Fort Beaufort, U. of S.
    Africa ....32 50 s 26 38 E
58 Fort Chipewyan, Can. 58 51N 110 57w
65 Fort de France,
    Martinique I. 14 36N 61 2w
63 Fort Dodge, U.S.A. ..42 27N 97 7w
16 Fort George, Scotland 57 35N 4 5w
58 Fort Good Hope,
    Canada 66 30N 129 0w
56 Fort Hill, Nyasaland...9 41 s 33 17 E
61 Fort Hope, Canada ...51 20N 87 32w
56 Fort Jameson, N.
    Rhodesia ....13 30 s 31 45 E
56 Fort Johnston, Nyasa. 14 25 s 13 35 E
54 Fort Lamy, Fr. Equa.
    Africa ....12 10N 15 5 E
55 Fort Maguire, Nyasa. 4 35N 35 10 E
55 Fort Portal, Uganda .. 0 40N 30 15 E
56 Fort Rosebery, N.
    Rhodesia ....10 30 s 28 50 E
61 Fort Severn, Canada ..56 0N 87 50w
54 Fort Sibut, Fr. Equa.
    Africa ....5 46N 19 6 E
62 Fort Sumner, U.S.A. .34 26N 104 15w
63 Fort Wayne, U.S.A. ..41 0N 85 2w
61 Fort William, Canada .48 26N 89 15w
17 Fort William, Scotland 56 48N 5 6w
62 Fort Worth, U.S.A. ...32 45N 97 20w
60 Fort Yukon, Alaska ..66 35N 145 3w
66 Fortaleza, Brazil 5 0s 40 0w
46 Fortescue, W. Austl. ..21 0 s 116 0 E
17 Forth Bridge, Scotland 56 1N 3 23w
17 Forth, Firth of, Scot. ..56 5N 2 55w
17 Forth, R., Scotland ...56 8N 4 10w
17 Fortingal, Scotland ...56 36N 4 3w
16 Fortrose, Scotland ...57 35N 4 10w
28 Fossano, Italy ....44 34N 7 41 E
15 Fossdyke, England ...52 53N 0 3w
15 Fotheringhay, England 52 32N 0 27w
15 Fougères, France 48 21N 1 12w
15 Foulness I., England ..51 36N 0 53 E
15 Foulsham, England ...52 48N 1 2 E
13 Fountains Abbey,
    England 54 6N 1 35w
20 Fourchambault, Fr. ...47 0N 3 7 E
20 Fourmies, France ....50 1N 4 2 E
17 Foveaux, str., N.Z. ...46 30 s 168 0 E
55 Foweira, Uganda .....2 9N 32 20 E
12 Fowey, England 50 21N 4 48w
12 Foxdale, I. of Man 54 10N 4 40w
61 Foxe Chan., Canada ..65 0N 80 0w
13 Foxford, Eire 53 59N 9 7w
50 Foxton, New Zealand .40 27 s 175 16 E
18 Foyle, L., N. Ireland .55 8N 7 5w
19 Foynes, Eire 52 37N 9 7w
27 Foz, Spain 43 32N 7 20w
27 Fraga, Spain ....41 35N 0 20 E
29 Framlingham, Eng. ...52 14N 1 18 E
29 Francavilla, Italy ....40 37N 17 35 E
8 France, rep., Europe
    43 to 51N 4 to 8 E
54 Franceville, Fr. Equa.
    Africa ....1 38 s 13 32 E
56 Francistown, Bech. ...21 7 s 27 33 E
22 Francker, Netherlands 53 12N 5 32 E
25 Frankenau, Germany .51 5N 8 57 E
24 Frankenburg, Ger. ....51 5N 8 48 E
24 Frankenhausen, Ger. .51 22N 11 5 E
19 Frankford, Eire 53 11N 7 45w
57 Frankfort, U. of S.
    Africa ....27 15 s 28 42 E
63 Frankfort, U.S.A. 38 14N 84 50w
24 Frankfurt on Main,
    Germany ....50 7N 8 40 E
24 Frankfurt on Oder,
    Germany ....52 20N 14 34 E
60 Franklin, terr., Can. ..67 30N 90 0w
30 Franz Joseph Can.,
    Yugoslavia ....45 30N 19 32 E
56 Franzfontein, S. W.
    Africa ....26 6 s 15 15 E
28 Frascati, Italy ....41 49N 12 40 E
47 Fraser I. See Gt. Sandy I.
61 Fraser, R., Canada ...53 30N 121 0w
57 Fraserburg, U. of S.
    Africa ....31 58 s 21 30 E
16 Fraserburgh, Scot. ...57 41N 2 0w
33 Frauenfeld, Switz. ....47 34N 8 54 E
67 Fray Bentos, Uruguay 33 15 s 58 10w
23 Fredensburg, Denmark 55 59N 12 27 E
23 Fredericia, Denmark .55 35N 9 48 E
61 Fredericton, Canada ..45 57N 66 43w
61 Frederiksdal, Green. ..59 58N 44 15w
61 Frederikshaab, Green..62 0N 49 10w
23 Frederikshavn, Den. ..57 28N 10 33 E
23 Frederiksvoerk, Den. .55 58N 12 1 E
35 Fredrikshamn. See Hamina
35 Fredrikstad, Norway .59 10N 10 55w

MAP
52 Freetown, Sierra Leone 8 30N 13 12w
26 Fregenal, Spain 38 12N 6 36w
24 Fregenal, Spain 38 12N 6 36w
24 Freiberg, Germany ..50 55N 13 21 E
24 Freiburg, Germany ...48 0N 7 49 E
24 Freising, Germany ...48 25N 11 44 E
24 Freistadt, Aust., Ger. .48 33N 14 29 E
21 Frejus, France ....45 10N 6 40 E
46 Fremantle, W. Austl. .32 1 s 115 47 E
63 Fremont, U.S.A. 41 23N 96 30w
54 French Equatorial
    Africa, Col. 20 to 5 s 10 to 25 E
66 French Guiana, Col.,
    S. America 4 0N 52 40w
52 French Guinea, Fr. W.
    Africa 11 0N 11 30w
39 French Indo-China,
    Asia 10 to 25N 100 to 109 E
52 French Ivory Coast,
    W. Africa 5 to 7 30N 3 to 7 30w
52 French Sudan, Fr. W.
    Africa 15 0N 5 0w
55 French Somaliland,
    col., Africa ....12 0N 42 30 E
52 French West Africa,
    col., Africa 5 to 25N 15 to 20 E
19 Freshford, Eire 52 44N 7 25w
13 Freshwater, England .50 42N 1 30w
64 Fresnillo, Mexico 23 6N 102 58w
62 Fresno, U.S.A. 36 42N 119 42w
16 Freswick, Scotland ..58 35N 3 5w
24 Freyung, Germany ...48 48N 13 33 E
33 Fribourg, & Canton,
    Switzerland ....46 48N 7 8 E
38 Fridtjof Nansen Ld.,
    Arctic Oc. ....82 0N 60 0 E
24 Friedberg, Germany ..50 22N 8 45 E
25 Friedland, Germany ..53 38N 13 28 E
24 Friedrichshafen, Ger. .47 40N 9 28 E
24 Friedrichstadt, Ger. ..54 23N 9 7 E
51 Friendly Is., See Tonga Is.
22 Friesland, prov., Neth. 53 2N 5 50 E
15 Frinton, England......51 49N 1 15 E
67 Frio, C., Brazil ....23 0 s 42 0w
17 Friockheim, Scotland..56 40N 2 40w
25 Frisches Haff, Ger.....54 25N 19 40 E
24 Frisian Is., N. Germany 54 50N 8 20 E
15 Fritton, England ......52 32N 1 39 E
61 Frobisher B., Canada..63 0N 67 0w
13 Frodsham, England ..53 17N 2 45w
14 Frome, England 51 14N 2 18w
35 Fron, Norway ....61 32N 9 55 E
64 Frontera, Mexico 18 31N 92 44w
28 Frosinone, Italy 41 38N 92 44w
33 Frutigen, Switzerland .46 35N 7 43 E
45 Fu-chow, China ......39 30N 121 30 E
26 Fuengirola, Spain 36 33N 4 35w
26 Fuente, Spain 38 17N 6 17w
26 Fuenterrabia, Spain ..43 21N 1 8w
27 Fuentes, Spain 39 52N 1 59w
26 Fuentes de Onoro, Sp. 40 35N 6 50w
27 Fuentesauca, Spain ..41 15N 5 30w
64 Fuerte, Mexico 26 30N 108 38w
45 Fuerte, R., Mexico ...26 30N 109 38w
45 Fuji Yama, Mt., Jap. .35 26N 138 45 E
45 Fukien, prov., China ..33 0N 118 0 E
45 Fukuoka, Japan ......33 32N 130 26 E
45 Fukushima, Japan ....37 41N 140 30 E
45 Fukuyama, Japan.....41 37N 140 5 E
24 Fulda, Germany .....50 34N 9 40 E
13 Fullwood, England ...53 22N 1 33w
52 Funchal, Madeira 32 45N 17 0w
61 Fundy, B. of, Canada .45 0N 66 0w
30 Funfkirchen. See Pécs
45 Fu-ning, China ....26 45N 120 0 E
33 Furka, P., Switzerland .46 35N 8 40 E
17 Furnace, Scotland 56 10N 5 10w
22 Furnes, Belgium ......51 4N 2 39 E
12 Furness Ab., England .54 8N 3 13w
12 Furness, dist., Eng. ..54 18N 3 7w
24 Fürth, Germany ......49 32N 11 0 E
24 Fürstenwalde, Ger. ...52 22N 14 4 E
35 Furusund, Sweden ....57 40N 19 0 E
61 Fury & Hecla Str.,
    Canada 70 0N 84 0w
45 Fusan, Korea ....35 15N 129 10 E
24 Fussen, Germany ....47 37N 10 40 E
17 Fyne, Loch, Scotland .56 9N 5 10w
16 Fyvie, Scotland 57 26N 2 24w
52 Gabes, Tunis ....34 0N 10 0 E
24 Gablons, Czech........50 42N 15 10 E
54 Gabon, terr., Fr. Eq.
    Africa ....0 15N 9 20 E
31 Gabrovo, Bulgaria ....42 50N 25 25 E
31 Gadag, India ....15 25N 75 42 E
63 Gadsden, U.S.A. 34 0N 86 0w
31 Gaesti, Rumania .....44 44N 25 20 E
29 Gaeta, Italy ....41 13N 13 32 E
21 Gaillac, France ......43 34N 1 53 E
67 Gaiman, Argentina ..43 25 s 65 55w
62 Gainesville, U.S.A. ...33 35N 97 10w
13 Gainsborough, Eng. ..53 23N 0 46w
47 Gairdner L., S. Aust...31 30 s 136 0 E
16 Gairloch, Scotland ...57 43N 5 45w

MAP
32 Galadixion, Greece....38 21N 22 23E
66 Galapagos Is., Ecuador 0 30s 90 30w
17 Galashiels, Scotland...55 37N 2 48w
32 Galata, Turkey........40 22N 26 37E
32 Galatchista, Greece 40 32N 23 19E
31 Galati, Rumania 45 28N 28 2E
29 Galatina, Italy.........40 12N 18 6E
35 Galdhopig, mt., Nor...61 45N 8 40E
63 Galena, U.S.A.........37 1N 94 40w
63 Galesburg, U.S.A......40 57N 90 20w
25 Galicia, dist., Poland..49 40N 22 20E
26 Galicia, old prov.,
  Spain..............42 45N 8 0w
41 Galilee, Sea of, Pal...32 45N 35 38E
43 Galle, Ceylon 6 5N 80 10E
67 Gallegos, Argentina ...51 40s 69 25w
32 Gallipoli, Italy........40 2N 18 0E
32 Gallipoli, Turkey......40 25N 26 35E
34 Gällivare, Sweden.....67 5N 20 40E
17 Galloway, Scotland...54 58N 4 20w
62 Gallup, U.S.A. 35 30N 108 45w
19 Galty Mts., Eire......52 22N 8 10w
63 Galveston, U.S.A......29 17N 94 50w
19 Galway, & Co., Eire .53 17N 9 4w
52 Gambaga, Gold Coast .10 33N 0 25w
55 Gambeila, Abyssinia .. 8 16N 34 35E
44 Gambia, Col., W.Africa13 30N 16 0w
   Gamla Karleby. See Kokkola
34 Gamvik, Norway.....70 58N 28 15E
42 Gandava, India 28 32N 67 32E
27 Gandia, Spain........38 58N 0 12w
43 Ganges, R., India....25 40N 81 50E
43 Gangi, Sicily.........37 50N 14 11E
43 Ganjam, India 19 27N 85 8E
21 Gannat, France.......46 6N 3 12E
52 Gao, Fr. W. Africa....16 15N 0 15E
21 Gap, France 44 33N 6 5E
28 Garda, L., Italy 45 45N 10 45E
62 Garden City, U.S.A...37 48N 100 52w
17 Garelochhead, Scot...56 5N 4 49E
21 Gargaliani, Greece 37 4N 21 40E
44 Gar Gunza, Tibet 32 10N 80 0E
42 Garhwal, dist., India..30 48N 78 30E
44 Garida, Mongolia....46 0N 102 0E
17 Garliestown, Scotland.54 47N 4 25w
16 Garmouth, Scotland...57 40N 3 6w
43 Garo Hills, India....25 30N 90 30E
21 Garonne, R., France...44 45N 0 30w
26 Garrovillas, Spain ...39 44N 6 31w
12 Garstang, England...53 54N 2 47w
17 Garston, England...53 21N 2 55w
17 Gartness, Scotland....56 3N 4 25w
44 Gartok, Tibet 31 45N 80 30E
54 Garua, Cameroons...... 9 20N 13 23E
67 Garub, S. W. Africa ..26 30s 15 50E
18 Garvagh, N. Ireland...54 59N 6 42w
21 Gascony, old prov.,
  France...........43 40N 0 20E
24 Gastein, Austria, Ger.
17 Gatehouse of Fleet,
  Scotland.........54 53N 4 10w
13 Gateshead, England ..54 58N 1 36w
56 Gatooma, S. Rhodesia .18 12s 30 0E
52 Gatrun, Libya 25 0N 15 0E
35 Gatschina, U.S.S.R. ..59 33N 30 6E
31 Gauhati, India.......26 4N 91 54E
35 Gaula, Norway......61 16N 5 45E
35 Gävle, Sweden 60 50N 17 20E
34 Gävleborg, co., Sweden61 30N 16 0E
34 Gavrilova, U.S.S.R. ..69 10N 35 40E
47 Gawler, S. Australia...34 7s 138 12E
47 Gawler Ranges,
  S. Australia 32 30s 136 0E
43 Gaya, India..........24 45N 85 5E
47 Gayndah, Queensland .25 38s 151 36E
41 Gaza, Palestine.......31 30N 34 30E
25 Gdynia, Poland 54 28N 18 20E
19 Geashill, Eire........53 14N 7 21w
20 Gebweiler, France ...47 54N 7 10E
55 Gedaref, A. E. Sudan ..14 2N 35 24E
47 Geelong, Victoria 38 11s 144 20E
24 Geestemünde, Ger.....53 30N 8 34E
43 Gela, Sicily...........37 6N 14 15E
22 Gelderland, prov.,
  Neth...............52 5N 6 0E
32 Gelibolu. See Gallipoli 40 25N 26 35E
24 Gelsenkirchen, Ger....51 32N 7 8E
32 Gemlik, Turkey......40 29N 29 9E
22 Gembloux, Belgium ..50 34N 4 40E
33 Gemmi P., Switz. 46 25N 7 32E
28 Gemona, Italy........46 16N 13 10E
22 Genemuiden, Neth....52 36N 6 3E
67 General Acha,
  Argentina 37 0s 64 50E
33 Geneva, and L. of,
  Switzerland........46 12N 6 9E
57 Genisdai, U. of S.Africa30 31s 18 0E
28 Genoa, Italy 44 24N 9 0E
45 Gensan, Korea........39 0N 127 35E
57 George, U. of S. Africa 33 58s 22 30E
47 George Town, S.
  Australia...........33 25s 138 30E
66 Georgetown, Brit.
  Guiana.............. 6 46N 58 8w

MAP
47 Georgetown, Queens. .18 20s 143 40E
47 Georgetown, Tasmania 41 0s 146 55E
63 Georgetown, U.S.A. ..33 20N 78 18w
37 Georgia, rep., U.S.S.R. 41 0N 45 0E
63 Georgia, St., U.S.A. ..32 45N 83 0w
37 Georgievsk, U.S.S.R...44 28N 43 28E
24 Gera, Germany.......50 55N 12 6E
29 Gerace, Italy.........38 13N 16 15E
46 Geraldton, W. Aust...28 44s 114 37E
20 Gerardmer, France ...48 5N 6 52E
8 Germany, fed. rep.
  Europe 49 0N 14 0E
24 Germünden, Germany .49 54N 7 28E
29 Gerona, Spain 41 57N 2 46E
21 Gers, dept., France...43 46N 32E
33 Gersau, Switzerland ...47 0N 8 30E
22 Gertruidenberg, Neth. 51 42N 4 51E
52 Geryville, Algeria 33 40N 1 0E
52 Ghadames, Libya 30 0N 9 0E
52 Ghat, Libya 25 0N 10 15E
42 Ghats, Eastern, mts.,
  India.............15 0N 79 0E
42 Ghats, Western, mts.,
  India.............15 30N 74 30E
42 Ghaziabad, India 28 40N 77 35E
41 Ghazni, Afghanistan ..33 37N 68 25E
22 Gheel, Belgium 51 11N 4 59E
22 Ghent, Belgium 51 4N 3 43E
41 Ghurian, Afghanistan .34 27N 61 28E
57 Giants Castle Mt.,
  U. of S. Africa 29 30s 29 30E
18 Giants' Causeway, N.I. 55 14N 6 31w
29 Giarre, Sicily 37 45N 15 11E
57 Gibeon, S.W. Africa ...25 7s 17 50E
26 Gibraltar, Spain (Br.) .36 10N 5 22w
21 Gien, France........47 42N 2 37E
24 Giessen, Germany.....50 36N 8 40E
17 Gifford, Scotland....55 54N 2 46w
31 Gigen, Bulgaria 43 39N 44 29E
26 Gijon, Spain 43 32N 5 40w
6 Gilbert Is., Pacific Oc. 1 0s 176 0E
34 Gildeskaal, Norway ..66 57N 14 10E
41 Gilgal, Palestine 31 52N 35 30E
47 Gilgandra, N.S.W....31 41s 148 11E
42 Gilghit, India.......35 50N 74 15E
23 Gilleleje, Denmark 56 8N 12 20E
51 Gillespie's, N. Zealand.43 25s 169 51E
15 Gillingham, Kent,
  England 51 24N 0 33w
14 Gillingham, Dorset,
  England 51 3N 2 15w
39 Gilolo I. See Halmahera Is.
33 Gimel, Switzerland ...46 31N 6 15E
46 Gingin, W. Australia ..31 19s 115 55E
26 Ginzo, Spain 42 3N 7 45w
29 Gioia, Italy..........40 49N 16 54E
32 Giova, Turkey........37 6N 28 21E
47 Gippsland, region,
  Victoria...........37 30s 147 0E
31 Giren, Bulgaria 42 12N 25 1E
40 Girgeh, Egypt 26 18N 31 53E
43 Giridhi, India........24 5N 86 30E
47 Girilambone, N.S.W...31 14s 146 59E
21 Gironde, and dept.,
  France...........45 25N 0 50w
31 Girurgevo. See Giurgiu
17 Girvan, Scotland....55 14N 4 51w
50 Gisborne, N. Zealand..38 41s 178 1E
31 Gisburn, England ...53 56N 2 17w
39 Gishiginsk, U.S.S.R....62 0N 160 2E
21 Gisors, France.......49 19N 1 45E
28 Giulianova, Italy 42 47N 13 55E
31 Giurgiu, Rumania....43 51N 25 57E
28 Giveno, Italy 45 3N 7 22E
21 Givors, France........45 35N 4 47E
35 Gjovik, Norway......60 50N 10 35E
24 Gladbach, Germany ..51 33N 6 27E
47 Gladstone, N.S.W....23 4s 152 58E
47 Gladstone, Queensland.23 47s 151 18E
47 Gladstone, S. Australia 33 16s 138 20E
47 Gladstone, Tasmania .40 58s 148 0E
17 Glamis, Scotland.....56 37N 3 0w
14 Glamorgan Co., Wales 51 35N 3 25w
33 Glarus, Switzerland ...47 4N 9 4E
33 Glarus, Canton,
  Switzerland........46 59N 9 5E
17 Glasgow, Scotland ...55 52N 4 15w
62 Glasgow, U.S.A......48 11N 106 40w
19 Glasslough, Eire 54 18N 6 59w
12 Glasson, England 54 0N 2 52s
19 Glastonbury, England 51 9N 2 43w
25 Glatz, Germany 50 27N 16 40E
24 Glauchau, Germany ..50 50N 12 34E
25 Gleiwitz, Germany ...50 20N 18 40E
15 Glemsford, England...52 7N 0 39E
47 Glen Innes, N.S.W...29 41s 151 42E
16 Glen More, Scotland ..57 10N 4 40w
18 Glenamaddy, Eire 53 38N 8 34w
18 Glenarm, N. Ireland...54 58N 5 57w
17 Glenbarr, Scotland....55 34N 5 41w
62 Glendive, U.S.A. 47 9N 104 41w
47 Glenelg, S. Australia ..34 58s 138 30E
16 Glenelg, Scotland 57 13N 5 37w
16 Glenfinnan, Scotland ..56 53N 5 26w
19 Glengarriff, Eire......51 49N 9 33w

MAP
17 Glenluce, Scotland 54 53N 4 48w
60 Glenora, Canada 57 50N 131 30w
47 Glenorchy, Victoria ..36 52s 142 40E
47 Glenore, Queensland...17 50s 141 10E
18 Glenties, Eire........54 48N 8 18w
19 Glenville, Eire 52 3N 8 26w
23 Gleschendorf, Ger....54 3N 10 38E
24 Glogau, Germany 51 38N 16 8E
35 Glommen, R., Norway .60 30N 11 50E
13 Glossop, England 53 27N 1 56w
47 Gloucester, N.S.W....32 1s 115 57E
14 Gloucester, & Co.,Eng. 51 52N 2 14w
24 Glückstadt, Germany .53 47N 9 25E
37 Glukhov, U.S.S.R....51 46N 33 56E
14 Glyncorrwg, Wales ...51 41N 3 35w
24 Gmünd, Germany 48 50N 9 48E
24 Gmunden, Austria, Ger. 47 56N 13 48E
25 Gnesen, Poland 52 34N 17 38E
42 Goa, Port. terr., India.15 27N 74 2E
43 Goalanda, India 23 45N 89 45E
43 Goalpara, India......26 3N 90 40E
13 Goathland, England...54 25N 0 44w
57 Gobabis, S.W. Africa ..22 25s 19 2E
44 Gobi Des., Mongolia ..43 30N 105 0E
24 Goch, Germany 51 40N 6 8E
57 Gochas, S.W. Africa ..24 50s 18 45E
15 Godalming, England ..51 10N 0 37w
42 Godavari, R., India...18 50N 80 0E
61 Godhavn, Greenland ..69 22N 53 30w
42 Godhra, India 22 48N 73 40E
25 Göding, Czechoslovakia 48 50N 17 6E
15 Godmanchester, Eng..52 18N 0 12w
30 Gödöllő, Hungary 47 38N 19 21E
61 Godthaab, Greenland .64 15N 51 10w
42 Godwin Austen, mt.
  Asia 36 0N 77 0E
55 Gojam, dist., Abyss....10 14N 37 20E
42 Gokak, India 16 11N 74 52E
35 Gol, Norway 60 44N 8 55E
42 Golconda, India......17 27N 78 23E
52 Gold Coast, col.,
  W. Africa 5 40N 1 20w
25 Goldap, Germany 54 18N 22 18E
23 Goldberg, Germany ..52 36N 12 6E
19 Golden, Eire.........52 31N 7 59w
19 Golden Vale, Eire ...52 33N 8 17w
62 Goldfield, U.S.A......37 35N 117 15w
35 Goldingen, Latvia 56 56N 21 59E
63 Goldsboro, U.S.A....35 20N 77 58w
24 Gollnow, Germany ...53 35N 14 50E
16 Golspie, Scotland 57 59N 3 58w
55 Gombari, Bel.Congo .. 2 52N 28 55E
37 Gomel, U.S.S.R.......52 25N 31 3E
55 Gonaives, Haiti 19 29N 72 35w
42 Gonda, India 27 10N 82 5E
55 Gondar, Abyssinia.....12 36N 37 30E
55 Gondokoro, A.E.Sudan 4 54N 31 40E
28 Gonzago, Italy........44 58N 10 50E
57 Good Hope, C. of,
  Union of S. Africa ..34 24s 18 29E
14 Goodwick, Wales 53 0N 5 0w
15 Goodwood, England...50 42N 0 53w
13 Goole, England 53 42N 0 53w
47 Goolwa, S. Australia...35 30s 138 55E
47 Goombalie, N.S.W....30 0s 145 20E
47 Goondiwindi,
  Queensland........28 32s 150 22E
24 Göppingen, Germany..48 44N 9 38E
25 Gora Kalvaria, Poland 51 59N 21 10E
43 Gorakhpur, India....26 42N 83 30E
51 Gore, New Zealand ...46 4s 168 53E
39 Gorelovsk, U.S.S.R....67 1N 85 15E
19 Goresbridge, Eire....52 37N 7 0w
19 Gorey, Eire..........52 40N 6 17w
15 Goring, England 51 32N 1 8w
28 Gorizia, Italy........45 56N 13 38E
26 Gorki, U.S.S.R.......56 18N 44 0E
15 Gorleston, England ...52 35N 1 42E
25 Gorlice, Poland 49 15N 21 14E
24 Görlitz, Germany 51 30N 15 0E
47 Gormanston, Tasman..42 0s 145 35E
18 Gormanstown, Eire ..53 38N 6 14w
27 Gormaz, Spain.......41 32N 3 3w
47 Goroke, Victoria 36 42s 141 29E
19 Gort, Eire 53 4N 8 50w
33 Göschenen, Switzerland46 41N 8 35E
49 Gosford, N.S.W.......33 28s 151 18E
13 Gosforth, England ...54 25N 3 26w
24 Goslar, Germany.....51 54N 10 15E
30 Gospić, Yugoslavia ...44 38N 15 21E
15 Gosport, England 50 48N 1 8w
33 Gossau, Switzerland ..47 25N 9 15E
30 Gostivar, Yugoslavia .41 48N 20 54E
35 Göteborg. See Gothenburg
35 Göteborg & Bohus, co.,
  Sweden 58 30N 11 30E
24 Gotha, Germany 50 59N 10 40E
15 Gotham, England 52 52N 1 12w
35 Gothenburg, Sweden ..57 40N 12 0E
35 Gotland, co., Sweden .58 10N 15 0E
35 Gotland, I., Sweden ...57 30N 19 20E
24 Göttingen, Germany ..51 35N 9 57E
30 Gottschee, Yugoslavia .45 41N 14 50E
22 Gouda, Netherlands ..52 0N 4 42E
15 Goudhurst, England...51 7N 0 28E

MAP			
47	**Goulburn**, N.S.W.	34 46 S	149 42 E
47	**Goulburn R.**, Victoria	36 8 S	145 0 E
21	**Gourdon**, France	44 45 N	1 23 E
17	**Gourock**, Scotland	55 58 N	4 50 W
14	**Gower**, Wales	51 38 N	4 5 W
67	**Goya**, Argentina	29 20 S	59 10 W
67	**Goyaz**, Brazil	16 20 S	49 55 W
66	**Goyaz, st.**, Brazil	13 50 N	48 20 W
29	**Goza I.**, Medit. Sea	36 2 N	14 17 E
57	**Graaf Reinet**, U. of S. Africa	32 15 S	24 35 E
57	**Graafwater**, U. of S. Af.	32 3 S	18 35 E
27	**Gracia**, Spain	41 25 N	2 7 E
64	**Gracias á Dios**, Nic.	14 55 N	83 20 W
28	**Gradisca**, Italy	45 54 N	13 36 E
26	**Grado**, Spain	43 24 N	6 5 W
47	**Grafton**, N.S.W.	29 43 S	152 57 E
68	**Graham Land**, Antarctica	67 0 S	64 0 W
57	**Grahamstown**, U. of S. Africa	37 8 S	175 33 E
22	**Grammont**, Belgium	50 47 N	3 52 E
16-17	**Grampian Mts.**, Scotland	56 55 N	4 0 W
47	**Grampians, mts.**, Victoria	37 10 S	142 30 E
30	**Gran.** *See* **Esztergom**		
67	**Gran Chaco, Terr.**, S. America	25 0 S	61 0 W
64	**Granada**, Nicaragua	11 58 N	85 58 W
26	**Granada**, Spain	37 10 N	3 35 W
18	**Granard**, Eire	53 47 N	7 30 W
53	**Grand Bassam**, Fr. W. Africa	5 12 N	3 42 W
65	**Grand Cayman Is.**, Jamaica	19 15 N	81 20 W
61	**Grand Falls**, Newf.	47 0 N	67 54 W
62	**Grand Forks**, U.S.A.	47 56 N	97 3 W
62	**Grand Island**, U.S.A.	41 0 N	98 0 W
62	**Grand Junction**, U.S.A.	39 6 N	108 41 W
61	**Grand L.**, Labrador	54 0 N	63 0 W
52	**Grand Lahu**, Fr. W. Af.	5 0 N	5 0 W
63	**Grand Rapids**, U.S.A.	44 15 N	89 47 W
26	**Grandas**, Spain	43 13 N	6 56 W
26	**Grandola**, Portugal	38 10 N	8 35 W
18	**Grange**, Eire	54 24 N	8 31 W
12	**Grange**, England	54 12 N	2 56 W
16	**Grange**, Scotland	57 32 N	2 57 W
17	**Grangemouth**, Scot.	56 0 N	3 44 W
62	**Grangeville**, U.S.A.	45 58 N	116 4 W
35	**Granna**, Sweden	58 0 N	14 25 E
27	**Granollers**, Spain	41 38 N	2 19 E
33	**Granson**, Switzerland	46 48 N	6 38 E
62	**Grant**, U.S.A.	40 51 N	101 45 W
61	**Grant Land**, Canada	82 0 N	80 0 W
15	**Grantham**, England	52 56 N	0 39 W
16	**Grantown**, Scotland	57 20 N	3 36 W
17	**Grants Ho.**, Scotland	55 53 N	2 19 W
62	**Grants Pass**, U.S.A.	42 26 N	123 21 W
20	**Granville**, France	48 50 N	1 35 W
57	**Graskop**, U. of S. Af.	25 0 S	31 0 E
12	**Grasmere**, England	54 28 N	3 0 W
21	**Grasse**, France	43 39 N	6 55 E
25	**Graudenz**, Poland	53 28 N	18 46 E
21	**Graulhet**, France	43 45 N	1 58 E
22	**Grave**, Netherlands	51 46 N	5 44 E
33	**Gravedona**, Italy	46 9 N	9 17 E
20	**Gravelines**, France	50 59 N	2 8 E
15	**Gravesend**, England	51 27 N	0 22 E
29	**Gravina**, Italy	40 52 N	16 27 E
15	**Grays**, England	51 29 N	0 19 E
24	**Graz**, Austria, Germany	47 4 N	15 26 E
46	**Gt. Australian Bight**, Australia	33 30 S	128 0 E
50	**Great Barrier I.**, N.Z.	36 12 S	175 27 E
60	**Great Bear L.**, Canada	66 0 N	120 0 W
23	**Great Belt**, Denmark	55 30 N	11 0 E
62	**Great Bend**, U.S.A.	38 25 N	98 45 W
47	**Great Dividing Ra.**, Queensland	23 0 S	146 0 E
15	**Great Dunmow**, Eng.	51 52 N	0 22 E
65	**Great Exhuma I.**, Bahama Is.	23 30 N	76 0 W
57	**Great Namaqualand**, S.W. Africa	26 15 S	18 0 E
28	**Great St. Bernard P.**, Italy	45 53 N	7 15 E
41	**Great Salt Des.** *See* **Dasht-i-Kavir**		
62	**Great Salt L.**, U.S.A.	41 0 N	112 30 W
60	**Great Slave L.**, Canada	62 0 N	114 0 W
25	**Great Strehlitz**, Ger.	50 34 N	18 15 E
13	**Gt. Whernside**, Eng.	54 12 N	2 0 W
15	**Great Yarmouth**, Eng.	52 36 N	1 43 E
65	**Greater Antilles**, W. Indies	20 0 N	75 0 W
9	**Greece, King.**, Europe.	41 to 36 N	20 to 26 E
62	**Greeley**, U.S.A.	40 23 N	104 4 W
63	**Green Bay**, U.S.A.	44 30 N	88 0 W
58	**Greenland**, Arctic Oc.	60 to 80 N	20 to 70 W
68	**Greenland Sea**, Arctic Ocean	75 0 N	10 0 W
17	**Greenlaw**, Scotland	55 43 N	2 27 W
17	**Greenock**, Scotland	55 57 N	4 45 W
18	**Greenore**, Eire	54 2 N	6 8 W
63	**Greensboro**, U.S.A.	36 0 N	80 0 W
63	**Greenville, Ala.**, U.S.A.	31 49 N	86 35 W
63	**Greenville, Miss.**, U.S.A.	33 7 N	95 55 W
63	**Greenville, S.C.** U.S.A.	34 52 N	82 13 W
63	**Greenville, Texas**, U.S.A.	33 25 N	91 0 W
15	**Greenwich**, England	51 29 N	0 0
24	**Greifenberg**, Germany	53 54 N	15 10 E
33	**Greifensee**, Switz.	47 22 N	8 41 E
62	**Great Falls**, U.S.A.	47 29 N	111 15 W
57	**Great Fish, R.** U. of S. Africa	33 0 S	26 15 E
65	**Great Inagua I.**, Bahama Is.	21 0 N	73 30 W
57	**Great Karroo**, U. of S. Africa	32 40 S	23 0 E
33	**Great Laufenburg**, Switzerland	47 34 N	8 3 E
56	**Great Makarikari L.**, Bechuanaland	20 45 S	26 0 E
15	**Great Marlow**, Eng.	51 34 N	0 47 W
24	**Greifswald**, Germany	54 6 N	13 20 E
24	**Grein**, Austria, Ger.	48 15 N	14 50 E
24	**Greiz**, Germany	50 40 N	12 10 E
23	**Grenaa**, Denmark	56 25 N	10 55 E
65	**Grenada I.**, Windward Islands	12 5 N	61 45 W
21	**Grenade**, France	43 45 N	1 15 E
65	**Grenadines**, Windward Is.	12 45 N	61 15 W
47	**Grenfell**, N.S.W.	33 52 S	148 10 E
21	**Grenoble**, France	45 11 N	5 46 E
17	**Gretna Green**, Scot.	55 0 N	3 3 W
22	**Grevenmacher**, Luxem.	49 41 N	6 26 E
23	**Grevesmuhlen**, Ger.	53 52 N	11 12 E
18	**Grey Abbey**, N. Ireland	54 32 N	5 34 W
47	**Grey Ra.**, Queensland	28 0 N	143 0 E
47	**Grey Town**, S. Austl.	37 40 S	140 5 E
57	**Greylingstadt**, U. of S. Africa	26 53 S	28 47 E
51	**Greymouth**, N.Z.	42 28 S	171 12 E
51	**Greytown**, N.Z.	41 2 S	175 25 E
57	**Greytown**, U. of S. Af.	25 5 S	30 37 E
64	**Greytown**, Nicaragua	10 59 N	83 50 W
63	**Griffin**, U.S.A.	33 15 N	84 13 W
34	**Grigoriev**, U.S.S.R.	63 46 N	31 6 E
31	**Grigoriopol**, Russia	47 10 N	29 20 E
33	**Grimmialp**, Switz.	46 32 N	7 30 E
13	**Grimsby**, England	53 34 N	0 4 W
33	**Grimsel P.**, Switz.	46 40 N	8 25 E
35	**Grimstad**, Norway	58 22 N	8 25 E
23	**Grimstrup**, Denmark	55 33 N	8 39 E
33	**Grindelwald**, Switz.	46 38 N	8 3 E
23	**Grindsted**, Denmark	55 46 N	8 57 E
57	**Griqualand E.**, U. of S. Africa	30 30 S	29 0 E
57	**Griqualand West.**, U. of S. Africa	28 45 S	23 30 E
57	**Griquatown**, U. of S. Africa	28 53 S	23 15 E
20	**Gris Nez, C.**, France	50 52 N	1 36 E
33	**Grisons, Canton**, Switzerland	46 40 N	9 35 E
25	**Grodek**, Poland	49 48 N	23 58 E
25	**Grodno**, Poland	53 41 N	23 53 E
23	**Grön Sd.**, Denmark	54 53 N	12 10 E
22	**Gronau**, Netherlands	52 12 N	7 1 E
22	**Groningen, & prov.**, Netherlands	53 10 N	6 50 E
56	**Grootfontein**, S.W. Af.	25 1 S	16 35 E
37	**Grosny**, U.S.S.R.	43 27 N	45 39 E
24	**Grossenhain**, Germany	51 20 N	13 30 E
28	**Grosseto**, Italy	42 44 N	11 7 E
25	**Grubeshov**, Poland	50 50 N	23 52 E
29	**Grumo**, Italy	41 1 N	16 42 E
24	**Grünberg**, Germany	51 46 N	15 30 E
33	**Gruyères**, Switz.	46 35 N	7 5 E
26	**Guadix**, Spain	37 57 N	3 10 W
66	**Guacipati**, Venezuela	7 15 N	61 50 W
64	**Guadalajara**, Mexico	21 0 N	102 30 W
27	**Guadalajara**, Spain	40 38 N	3 10 W
26	**Guadalcanal**, Spain	38 6 N	5 50 W
48	**Guadalcanal**, Pac. Oc.	9 55 S	160 0 E
26	**Guadalquivir. R.**, Sp.	38 0 N	4 0 W
26	**Guadalupe**, Spain	39 28 N	5 14 W
65	**Guadeloupe I.**, W. Ind.	16 12 N	61 30 W
26	**Guadiana, R.**, Portugal	39 5 N	3 50 W
66	**Guajara Mirim**, Brazil	11 0 S	65 0 W
7	**Guam I.**, Pacific Oc.	13 0 N	144 45 E
64	**Guanajuato, & st.**, Mexico	21 0 N	100 42 W
26	**Guándia**, Spain	41 52 N	8 52 W
66	**Guanare**, Venezuela	8 40 N	69 35 W
65	**Guane**, Cuba	22 2 N	83 40 W
65	**Guantanamo**, Cuba	20 12 N	75 15 W
66	**Guapore, R.**, S. Amer.	13 30 S	63 0 W
26	**Guarda**, Portugal	40 32 N	7 20 W
52	**Guardafui, C.**, It. Somaliland	11 50 N	51 20 E
26	**Guardo**, Spain	42 48 N	4 52 W
26	**Guareña**, Spain	38 51 N	6 2 W
28	**Guastalla**, Italy	44 47 N	10 39 E
64	**Guatemala, & st.**, Cent. America	14 41 N	90 35 W
66	**Guaviare, R.**, Colombia	2 30 N	71 0 W
65	**Guayama**, Pt. Rico	18 0 N	66 5 W
66	**Guayaquil**, Ecuador	2 15 S	79 55 W
64	**Guaymas**, Mexico	27 58 N	111 2 W
28	**Gubbio**, Italy	43 21 N	13 32 E
24	**Guben**, Germany	51 57 N	14 44 E
23	**Gudhjem, Bornholm**, Denmark	55 12 N	14 57 E
23	**Gudow**, Germany	53 33 N	10 43 E
35	**Gudvangen**, Norway	60 50 N	6 46 E
31	**Guéchev**, Yugoslavia	42 12 N	22 20 E
20	**Guérande**, France	47 19 N	2 28 W
21	**Guéret**, France	46 11 N	1 52 E
27	**Guernica**, Spain	43 20 N	2 45 W
20	**Guernsey, I**, Channel I.	49 28 N	2 35 W
64	**Guerrero, st.**, Mexico	17 51 N	99 18 E
33	**Guggisberg**, Switz.	46 47 N	7 18 W
15	**Guildford**, England	51 14 N	0 34 W
54	**Guinea, terr.**, W. Afr.	8 30 N	0 0
53	**Guinea, G. of**, Africa	2 0 N	0 0
65	**Guines**, Cuba	22 48 N	82 3 W
20	**Guingamp**, France	48 34 N	3 9 W
65	**Guines**, Cuba	22 48 N	82 3 W
20	**Guingamp**, France	48 34 N	3 9 W
13	**Guisboro'**, England	54 32 N	1 3 W
20	**Guise**, France	49 54 N	3 39 E
42	**Gujranwala**, India	32 12 N	74 12 E
42	**Gulbarga**, India	17 22 N	76 50 E
35	**Gulen**, Norway	60 56 N	5 15 E
47	**Gulgong**, N.S.W.	32 22 S	149 30 E
40	**Gulpaigan**, Iran	33 21 N	50 17 E
25	**Gumbinnen**, Germany	54 35 N	22 12 E
32	**Gumuljina**, Greece	41 7 N	25 27 E
40	**Gumushkhane**, Turkey	40 29 N	39 28 E
47	**Gunbar**, N.S.W.	34 5 S	145 25 E
47	**Gundagai**, N.S.W.	35 1 S	148 5 E
47	**Gunnedah**, N.S.W.	30 59 S	150 15 E
47	**Gunning**, N.S.W.	34 45 S	149 0 E
42	**Guntakal**, India	15 8 N	77 25 E
42	**Guntur**, India	16 25 N	80 27 E
24	**Gunzenhausen**, Ger.	49 7 N	10 47 E
40	**Gurgan.** *See* **Asterabad**		
37	**Guriev**, U.S.S.R.	47 4 N	51 47 E
54	**Gusau**, Nigeria	12 0 N	6 30 E
30	**Gusinye**, Yugoslavia	42 34 N	19 49 E
24	**Güstrow**, Germany	53 48 N	12 10 E
63	**Guthrie**, U.S.A.	35 52 N	97 25 W
31	**Guvedze**, Bulgaria	43 54 N	26 28 E
21	**Guyenne, old prov.**, France	44 40 N	1 0 E
42	**Gwadar**, India	25 8 N	62 19 E
42	**Gwalior**, India	26 16 N	78 13 E
42	**Gwalior, st.**, India	26 25 N	78 0 E
56	**Gwanda**, S. Rhodesia	21 0 S	29 20 E
42	**Gwatar**, India	25 41 N	61 28 E
56	**Gwelo**, S. Rhodesia	19 24 S	30 5 E
44	**Gyang-tse**, Tibet	28 50 N	89 30 E
47	**Gympie**, Queensland	26 13 S	152 42 E
30	**Gyoma**, Hungary	46 54 N	20 54 E
30	**Gyöngyös**, Hungary	47 8 N	20 12 E
30	**Györ**, Hungary	47 41 N	17 40 E
60	**Gypsumville**, Canada	52 0 N	98 20 W
32	**Gythion**, Greece	36 43 N	22 37 E
30	**Gyula**, Hungary	46 40 N	21 20 E
35	**Hå**, Norway	58 35 N	5 40 E
35	**Haapsalu**, Estonia	58 55 N	23 32 E
22	**Haarlem**, Netherlands	52 21 N	4 39 E
23	**Haaler**, Denmark	55 21 N	12 13 E
33	**Habsburg**, Switz.	47 27 N	8 12 E
19	**Hacketstown**, Eire	52 52 N	6 34 W
17	**Haddington**, Scotland	55 57 N	2 47 W
32	**Hademkeui**, Turkey	41 6 N	28 40 E
23	**Haderup**, Denmark	56 25 N	9 0 E
15	**Hadleigh**, England	52 3 N	0 57 E
40	**Hadramaut, dist.**, Arabia	16 0 N	50 0 E
23	**Hadsund**, Denmark	56 44 N	10 7 E
24	**Hagen**, Germany	51 20 N	7 28 E
20	**Hagenau**, France	48 49 N	7 47 E
45	**Hagi**, Japan	34 25 N	131 22 E
22	**Hague, The**, Neth.	52 5 N	4 18 E
45	**Haichow**, China	34 44 N	119 30 E
41	**Haifa**, Palestine	32 44 N	35 1 E
45	**Hai-ju**, Korea	38 0 N	126 0 E
40	**Hail**, Arabia	27 35 N	42 30 E
45	**Hailar**, Manchuria	49 17 N	119 45 E
15	**Hailsham**, England	50 52 N	0 16 E
45	**Hailun**, Manchuria	47 17 N	127 10 E
45	**Hailung**, Manchuria	42 40 N	125 43 E
45	**Hainan, I.**, China	19 30 N	110 0 E
22	**Hainaut, prov.**, Belg.	50 30 N	4 0 E
44	**Hai-phong**, Fr. Indo-China	20 50 N	106 30 E
65	**Haiti Republic**, Hispaniola	17 35 to 20 N	68 15 to 74 30 W
40	**Hajarein**, Arabia	15 20 N	48 20 E
31	**Hajduböszörmény**, Hungary	47 40 N	21 32 E
45	**Hakata**, Japan	33 36 N	130 25 E
45	**Hakodate**, Japan	41 50 N	140 36 E

MAP
24 **Halberstadt**, Germany 51 55N 11 3E
50 **Halcombe**, N. Zealand 40 10S 175 30E
35 **Halden**, Norway 59 8N 11 25E
40 **Haleb.** *See* **Aleppo**
14 **Halesowen**, England 52 27N 2 3W
15 **Halesworth**, England 52 20N 1 30E
40 **Hali**, Arabia 18 55N 41 36E
61 **Halifax**, Canada 44 38N 63 33W
13 **Halifax**, England 43 0N 1 52W
16 **Halkirk**, Scotland 58 31N 3 29W
24 **Hall**, Austria, Germany 47 19N 11 32E
35 **Halland, co.**, Sweden 57 0N 12 35E
15 **Hallaton**, England 52 33N 0 50W
24 **Halle**, Germany 51 30N 12 0E
23 **Hallingen I.**, Germany 54 35N 8 35E
63 **Hallock**, U.S.A. 48 49N 96 54W
46 **Hall's Creek**, W. Aust. 18 15S 127 55E
22 **Hallum**, Netherlands 53 18N 5 48E
39 **Halmahera I.**, Dutch E. Indies 1 0N 128 0E
35 **Halmstad**, Sweden 56 40N 12 45E
23 **Hals**, Denmark 57 0N 10 19E
34 **Halsa**, Norway 63 8N 8 15E
15 **Halstead**, England 51 57N 0 38E
23 **Haltenau**, Germany 54 24N 10 8E
13 **Haltwhistle**, England 54 59N 2 27W
40 **Hama**, Syria 35 13N 36 40E
45 **Hamada**, Japan 35 13N 132 12E
40 **Hamadan**, Iran 34 50N 48 18E
35 **Hamar**, Norway 60 50N 11 5E
42 **Hambantota**, Ceylon 6 8N 81 5E
13 **Hambleton Hills**, Eng. 54 15N 1 15W
24 **Hamburg**, Germany 53 34N 10 2E
24 **Hamburg, and St.**, Ger. 53 34N 10 2E
35 **Hämeenlinne**, Finland 61 0N 24 30E
24 **Hameln**, Germany 56 6N 9 20E
45 **Hamheung**, Korea 39 58N 127 40E
17 **Hamilton**, Scotland 55 47N 4 2W
47 **Hamilton**, Victoria 37 45S 142 1E
50 **Hamilton**, New Zealand 37 48S 175 18E
61 **Hamilton**, Canada 43 16N 79 54W
62 **Hamilton**, U.S.A. 46 14N 114 10W
35 **Hamina**, Finland 60 30N 27 20E
47 **Hamley Br.**, S. Austrl. 34 18S 138 10E
24 **Hamm**, Germany 51 40N 7 46E
23 **Hammel**, Denmark 56 15N 9 50E
34 **Hammerdal**, Sweden 63 35N 15 15E
34 **Hammerfest**, Norway 70 40N 23 40E
47 **Hammond**, S. Austl. 32 30S 138 25E
22 **Hamoir**, Belgium 50 26N 5 31E
51 **Hampden**, N. Zealand 45 20S 170 50E
15 **Hampshire, co.**, Eng. 51 9N 1 14W
46 **Hampton Tableland**, W. Australia 31 30S 128 0E
24 **Hanau**, Germany 50 7N 8 56E
44 **Han-chung**, China 33 0N 107 5E
55 **Handeni**, Tanganyika 5 22S 38 2E
35 **Hanebo**, Sweden 61 15N 16 35E
23 **Hanerau**, Germany 54 7N 9 28E
45 **Hang-chow**, China 30 10N 120 5E
35 **Hango.** *See* **Kanko**
57 **Hankey**, U. of S. Africa 33 47S 24 55E
35 **Hanko**, Finland 59 50N 23 3E
45 **Hankow**, China 30 50N 114 15E
63 **Hannibal**, U.S.A. 39 40N 91 24W
39 **Hanoi**, Fr. Indo-China 21 0N 105 45E
24 **Hanover**, Germany 52 23N 9 53E
57 **Hanover**, U. of S. Afr. 31 5S 24 28E
24 **Hanover, prov.**, Ger. 52 20N 9 40E
23 **Hansted**, Denmark 57 6N 8 37E
23 **Hanstholm**, Denmark 57 7N 8 36E
45 **Han-yang**, China 30 35N 114 5E
51 **Hapai Is.**, Tonga Is. Inset 20 0S 117 30W
34 **Haparanda**, Sweden 65 45N 24 5E
15 **Happisburgh**, England 52 50N 1 32E
55 **Harar**, Abyssinia 9 19N 42 18E
45 **Harbin**, Manchuria 45 50N 126 30E
61 **Harbour Grace**, Newf. 47 40N 53 35W
24 **Harburg**, Germany 53 28N 10 0E
35 **Hardanger Fiord**, Nor. 60 0N 6 0E
35 **Hardanger Fjell**, mts., Norway 60 20N 7 20E
22 **Hardenberg**, Neth. 52 34N 6 37E
22 **Harderwijk**, Neth. 52 20N 5 39E
62 **Hardin**, U.S.A. 45 35N 107 25W
57 **Harding**, U. of S. Africa 30 36S 29 53E
42 **Hardwar**, India 29 58N 78 16E
20 **Harfleur**, France 49 31N 0 13E
35 **Harg**, Sweden 60 12N 18 27E
42 **Harihar**, India 14 31N 75 52E
31 **Harlau**, Rumania 47 22N 27 1E
14 **Harlech**, Wales 52 51N 4 6W
15 **Harleston**, England 52 23N 1 18E
22 **Harlingen**, Netherlands 53 10N 5 26E
15 **Harlow**, England 51 47N 0 8E
31 **Harmanli**, Bulgaria 41 55N 25 58E
42 **Harnai**, India 30 8N 68 0E
62 **Harney**, U.S.A. 43 39N 118 50W
15 **Harpenden**, England 51 50N 0 23W
63 **Harriman**, U.S.A. 35 57N 84 34W
16 **Harris, (with Lewis)**, Scotland 57 52N 6 50W
63 **Harrisburg**, U.S.A. 40 20N 76 58W
57 **Harrismith**, U. of S. Africa 32 56S 117 50E
13 **Harrogate**, England 53 59N 1 33W
15 **Harrow**, England 51 34N 0 20W
47 **Harrow**, Victoria 37 7S 141 33E
31 **Hârsova**, Rumania 44 41N 27 59E
17 **Hart Fell, Mt.**, Scot. 55 23N 3 24W
63 **Hartford**, U.S.A. 41 15N 72 47W
14 **Hartland**, England 50 59N 4 27W
13 **Hartlepool**, England 54 42N 1 10W
56 **Hartley**, S. Rhodesia 18 5S 30 12E
15 **Harwich**, England 51 56N 1 17E
24 **Harz, Mts.**, Ger. 51 40N 10 40E
40 **Hasa, dist.**, Arabia 27 0N 48 30E
41 **Hasbeiya**, Syria 33 20N 35 45E
35 **Hasenpot**, Latvia 56 45N 21 32E
31 **Haskovo**, Bulgaria 41 55N 25 34E
23 **Hasle**, Bornholm, Den. 55 12N 14 42E
15 **Haslemere**, England 51 5N 0 42W
23 **Haslev**, Denmark 55 18N 11 56E
22 **Hasselt**, Belgium 50 56N 5 20E
23 **Hassing**, Denmark 57 5N 10 14E
15 **Hastings**, England 50 51N 0 34E
50 **Hastings**, New Zealand 39 39S 176 50E
62 **Hastings**, U.S.A. 40 30N 98 30W
34 **Hasvik**, Norway 70 30N 22 0E
15 **Hatfield**, England 51 46N 0 12E
14 **Hatherleigh**, England 50 49N 4 5W
42 **Hathras**, India 27 30N 78 8E
31 **Hátszeg**, Rumania 45 37N 22 57E
47 **Hattah**, Victoria 34 45S 142 18E
22 **Hattem**, Netherlands 52 28N 6 4E
63 **Hatteras, C.**, U.S.A. 35 15N 75 30W
63 **Hattiesburg**, U.S.A. 31 19N 89 18W
30 **Hatvan**, Hungary 47 40N 19 44E
35 **Haugesund**, Norway 59 25N 5 20E
15 **Haughley**, England 52 14N 0 58E
40 **Hauran Jebel,**, Syria 32 10N 37 30E
35 **Hausjarvi**, Finland 60 50N 21 52E
20 **Haut Rhin, dept.**, Fr. 47 50N 7 0E
21 **Haute Garonne, dept.**, France 43 25N 1 18E
21 **Haute-Loire, dept.**, Fr. 45 8N 3 48E
20 **Haute-Marne, dept.**, France 48 3N 5 20E
20 **Haute-Saône, dept.**, France 47 44N 6 24E
21 **Haute Savoie, dept.**, France 46 2N 6 27E
21 **Haute-Vienne, dept.**, Fr. 45 54N 1 15E
21 **Hautes Alpes, dept.**, France 44 43N 6 27E
21 **Hautes Pyrénées, dept.**, France 43 5N 0 12E
65 **Havana**, Cuba 23 0N 82 30W
15 **Havant**, England 50 51N 1 0W
51 **Havelock**, New Zealand 41 15S 173 45E
14 **Haverfordwest**, Wales 51 47N 4 58W
15 **Haverhill**, England 52 5N 0 27E
23 **Havndal**, Denmark 56 39N 10 11E
62 **Havre**, U.S.A. 48 31N 109 50W
32 **Havsa**, Turkey 41 31N 26 50E
6 **Hawaii Is.**, Pacific Oc. 19 to 22N 155 to 160E
12 **Hawarden**, Wales 53 11N 2 3W
50 **Hawera**, New Zealand 39 37S 174 18E
13 **Hawes**, England 54 18N 2 11W
12 **Hawes Water**, Eng. 54 32N 2 48W
17 **Hawick**, Scotland 55 26N 2 46W
40 **Hawizeh**, Iran 31 20N 47 40E
50 **Hawke B.**, N. Zealand 39 20S 177 30E
47 **Hawker**, S. Australia 31 52S 138 28E
50 **Hawkes Bay, prov.**, New Zealand 39 40S 176 40E
15 **Hawkhurst**, England 51 3N 0 30E
12 **Hawkshead**, England 54 24N 3 0W
47 **Hay**, N.S.W. 34 29S 144 48E
14 Hay, Wales 52 5N 3 6W
60 **Hay River**, Canada 60 30N 116 30W
15 **Hayle**, England Inset 50 11N 5 24W
15 **Hayling I.**, England 50 48N 0 58W
15 **Haywards Heath**, England 51 1N 0 9W
43 **Hazaribagh**, India 23 58N 85 25E
60 **Hazelton**, Canada 40 58N 75 59W
15 **Heacham**, England 52 56N 0 31E
15 **Headcorn**, England 51 10N 0 37E
60 **Healey**, Alaska 59 30N 135 30W
15 **Heanor**, England 53 1N 1 20W
18 **Headford**, Eire 51 10N 0 37E
61 **Hearst**, Canada 49 40N 83 30W
68 **Hearst Land**, Antarc. 70 5S 70 0W
31 **Hebibchevo**, Bulgaria 41 50N 26 6E
61 **Hebron**, Labrador 58 10N 62 40W
41 **Hebron**, Palestine 31 32N 35 8E
35 **Hede**, Sweden 62 25N 13 40E
35 **Hedemora**, Sweden 60 20N 16 0E
41 **Hederah**, Palestine 32 25N 34 57E
15 **Hedingham**, England 51 59N 0 37E
35 **Hedmark, co.**, Nor. 61 0N 12 0E
13 **Hedon**, England 53 44N 0 11W
22 **Heerenveen**, Neth. 52 58N 5 56E
22 **Heerde**, Netherlands 52 23N 6 2W
22 **Heerlen**, Netherlands 50 54N 5 57E
22 **Heeze**, Netherlands 51 23N 5 35E
24 **Heide**, Germany 54 12N 9 5E
24 **Heidelberg**, Germany 48 41N 10 8E
57 **Heidelberg**, U. of S. Africa 26 32S 28 24E
24 **Heidenheim**, Germany 48 41N 10 8E
34 **Heikura**, Finland 69 28N 25 56E
57 **Heilbron**, U. of S. Afr. 27 22S 28 25E
24 **Heilbronn**, Germany 49 8N 9 10E
23 **Heiligendamm**, Ger. 54 8N 11 49E
25 **Heilsberg**, Germany 54 9N 20 40E
45 **Heilung-kiang, dist.**, Manchuria 48 0N 117 to 130E
35 **Heinola**, Finland 61 16N 26 12E
40 **Hejaz, dist.**, Arabia 23 0N 40 0E
23 **Hejls**, Denmark 55 23N 9 35E
8 **Hekla, Mt.**, Iceland 63 0N 19 0W
22 **Helder**, Netherlands 52 58N 4 45E
62 **Helena**, U.S.A. 46 37N 112 1W
63 **Helena**, U.S.A. 34 32N 90 33W
17 **Helensburgh**, Scotland 56 1N 4 43W
50 **Helensville**, N.Z. 36 42S 174 29E
23 **Helgenoes**, Denmark 56 8N 10 29E
24 **Heligoland, I.**, Ger. 54 5N 7 55E
23 **Hellerup**, Denmark 55 42N 12 36E
13 **Hellifield**, England 54 0N 2 13W
27 **Hellin**, Spain 38 30N 1 40W
41 **Helmand, L.**, *See* **Hamun, L.**
41 **Helmand, R.**, Afghan. 30 10N 62 30E
22 **Helmond**, Netherlands 51 30N 5 41E
16 **Helmsdale**, Scotland 58 7N 3 38W
13 **Helmsley**, England 54 15N 11 0E
24 **Helmstedt**, Germany 52 16N 11 0E
23 **Helnoes**, Denmark 55 8N 10 1E
35 **Helsingborg**, Sweden 56 0N 12 45E
23 **Helsinge**, Denmark 56 2N 12 11E
35 **Helsingfors.** *See* **Helsinki**
23 **Helsingör**, Denmark 56 2N 12 32E
35 **Helsinki**, Finland 60 13N 24 58E
14 **Helston**, England 50 57N 5 16W
12 **Helvellyn**, England 54 32N 3 3W
57 **Helvetia**, U. of S. Africa 25 36S 30 24E
15 **Hemel Hempstead**, England 51 45N 0 29W
35 **Hemse**, Sweden 57 15N 18 20E
14 **Hemyock**, England 50 55N 3 13W
33 **Henau**, Switzerland 47 27N 9 7E
45 **Heng-chow**, China 27 0N 111 55E
15 **Henley**, England 51 33N 0 55W
23 **Henne**, Denmark 55 44N 8 16E
20 **Hennebont**, France 47 48N 3 16W
43 **Henzada**, Burma 17 25N 95 35E
41 **Herat**, Afghanistan 34 21N 62 7E
21 **Hérault, dept.**, France 43 35N 3 35E
47 **Herberton**, Queensland 17 20S 145 12E
14 **Hereford, & co.**, Eng. 52 3N 2 41W
22 **Herenthals**, Belgium 51 12N 4 50E
24 **Herford**, Germany 52 8N 8 20E
33 **Herisau**, Switzerland 47 23N 9 17E
23 **Herlufmagle**, Den. 55 19N 11 44E
20 **Herm, I.**, Channel Is. 49 29N 2 27W
46 **Hermannsburg**, Northern Territory 24 0S 132 55E
47 **Hermidale**, N.S.W. 31 30S 146 45E
51 **Hermitage**, N.Z. 43 44S 170 13E
41 **Hermon, Mt.**, *See* **Esh Sheikh**
64 **Hermosillo**, Mexico 22 23N 110 58W
32 **Hermupolis**, Greece 37 25N 24 58E
15 **Herne Bay**, England 51 22N 1 13E
23 **Herning**, Denmark 56 8N 9 0E
34 **Hernösand**, Sweden 62 35N 18 0E
26 **Herrera**, Spain 39 10N 5 5W
35 **Herrijunga**, Sweden 58 3N 13 5E
57 **Herschel**, U. of S. Afr. 30 37S 27 14E
24 **Hersfeld**, Germany 50 52N 9 40E
22 **Hersselt**, Belgium 51 3N 4 52E
22 **Herstal**, Belgium 50 41N 5 38E
15 **Hertford & Co.**, Eng. 51 48N 0 5W
22 **Herve**, Belgium 50 38N 5 47E
50 **Hervey Is.**, Pac. O. Inset 19 30S 159 0E
30 **Herzegovina, dist.**, Yugoslavia 43 20N 18 0E
33 **Herzogenbuchsee**, Switzerland 47 11N 7 41E
41 **Hesban**, Transjordan 31 50N 35 45E
41 **Heshbon.** *See* **Hesban**
24 **Hessen, St.**, Germany 50 20N 8 50E
24 **Hessen-Nassau, prov.**, Germany 51 0N 9 0E
35 **Hessleholm**, Sweden 56 10N 13 50E
13 **Hessle**, England 53 44N 0 26W
22 **Het Loo**, Netherlands 52 15N 5 58E
13 **Hexham**, England 54 25N 21 25E
13 **Heysham**, England 54 2N 2 54W
22 **Heyst**, Belgium 51 5N 4 43E
14 **Heytesbury**, England 51 12N 2 5W
47 **Heywood**, Victoria 38 5S 141 40E
66 **Hicanay**, Bolivia 15 0S 68 0W
64 **Hidalgo & St.**, Mexico 26 10N 104 49W
32 **Hierapetra**, Crete Inset 35 1N 25 41E
13 **High Seat**, England 54 23N 2 15W
25 **High Tatra Mts.**, Czechoslovakia 49 20N 20 0W
15 **High Wycombe**, Eng. 51 38N 0 45W
15 **Higham Ferrers**, Eng. 53 19N 0 36W

MAP
14 **Highbridge**, England .51 13N 2 57W
15 **Highclere**, England ..51 19N 1 20W
15 **Highworth**, England ..51 37N 1 43W
50 **Hikurangi**, N.Z. .....35 36 s 174 18 E
24 **Hildburghausen**, Ger. 50 25N 10 43 E
24 **Hildesheim**, Germany .50 18N 6 39 E
47 **Hill End**, N.S.W. .....33 0 s 149 30 E
40 **Hilla**, Iraq ....32 15N 44 35 E
22 **Hillegom**, Netherlands.52 17N 4 35 E
23 **Hilleröd**, Denmark ....55 56N 12 18 E
47 **Hillgrove**, N.S.W. ....30 31 s 151 54 E
63 **Hillsboro**, U.S.A. 38 57N 75 53W
18 **Hillsborough**, N. Ire...54 28N 6 5W
17 **Hillside**, Scotland 56 44N 2 28W
47 **Hillston**, N.S.W. ......33 28 s 145 51 E
16 **Hillswick**, Scotland ..60 28N 1 32W
18 **Hilltown**, N. Ireland ..54 12N 6 9W
22 **Hilvarenbeek**, Neth. .51 29N 5 11 E
22 **Hilversum**, Neth. ....52 13N 5 10 E
43 **Himalayas**, Asia .....38 0N 80 30 E
15 **Hinckley**, England ....52 33N 1 22 E
42 **Hindaun**, India ....26 40N 76 5 E
22 **Hindeloopen**, Neth. ...52 58N 5 26 E
25 **Hindenburg**, Germany.50 20N 18 50 E
13 **Hinderwell**, England ..54 32N 18 45W
41 **Hindu Kush, Mts.**,
Asia ....36 0N 71 0 E
15 **Hingham**, England ...52 34N 0 59 E
26 **Hinojosa**, Spain 38 30N 5 11W
45 **Hirosaki**, Japan .....40 28N 140 32 E
45 **Hiroshima**, Japan ....40 28N 140 32 E
24 **Hirschberg**, Germany .50 55N 15 48 E
65 **Hispaniola, I.**, West
Indies 17 35 to 20N 68 15 to 74 30W
42 **Hissar**, India ....29 14N 75 44 E
40 **Hit**, Iraq ....33 32N 42 51 E
15 **Hitchin**, England 51 57N 0 18W
13 **Hjarboek**, Denmark ...56 32N 9 21 E
23 **Hjelm**, Denmark ......54 56N 12 15 E
23 **Hjerting**, Denmark ....55 33N 8 23 E
35 **Hjo**, Sweden ....58 20N 14 20 E
47 **Hobart**, Tasmania ....42 49 s 147 17 E
23 **Hobro**, Denmark .....56 39N 9 50 E
33 **Hochdorf**, Switzerland 47 10N 8 17 E
15 **Hoddesdon**, England...51 45N 0 1W
40 **Hodeida**, Arabia .....14 40N 42 57 E
30 **Hódmezö-Vásárhely**,
Hungary ....46 27N 20 21 E
23 **Hodsager**, Denmark ..56 20N 8 53 E
24 **Hof**, Germany ....50 20N 11 54 E
40 **Hofhuf**, Arabia ......25 18N 49 36 E
57 **Hofmeyr**, U. of S. Afr. 23 3 s 29 35 E
15 **Hog's Back**, England..51 14N 0 40W
23 **Hohendorf**, Germany .54 26N 13 0 E
24 **Hohenlinden**, Ger. ...48 10N 12 0 E
25 **Hohensalza**, Poland ..52 48N 18 20 E
23 **Hohenwestedt**, Ger. ..54 6N 9 40 E
50 **Hohoura**, New Zealand 34 45 s 173 5 E
45 **Hoiryeng**, Korea .....42 0N 129 0 E
45 **Hokien**, China ....38 35N 116 0 E
51 **Hokitika**, N. Zealand ..42 42 s 171 1 E
45 **Hokkaido I.**, Japan ...43 30N 142 30 E
15 **Holbeach**, England ...52 49N 0 1 E
23 **Holboek**, Denmark ....55 43N 11 46 E
13 **Holderness**, England 53 50N 0 10W
65 **Holguin**, Cuba 20 53N 76 28W
15 **Holland, Co.**, England 52 50N 0 6W
8 **Holland, King.**, Europe52 0N 5 0 E
63 **Holland**, U.S.A. 42 48N 86 7W
13 **Holmfirth**, England ...53 35N 1 48W
35 **Holmsbo**, Norway.....59 35N 10 30 E
23 **Holstebro**, Denmark...56 22N 8 39 E
14 **Holsworthy**, England..50 48N 4 20W
15 **Holt**, England ....52 56N 1 6 E
14 **Holt**, Wales 53 5N 2 54W
34 **Holtaalen**, Norway ...62 55N 11 15 E
12 **Holy I.**, England 55 42N 1 48W
12 **Holy I.**, Wales 53 18N 4 38W
12 **Holyhead**, Wales 53 20N 4 37W
12 **Holywell**, Wales 53 17N 3 13W
18 **Holywood**, Eire 54 38N 5 51W
24 **Holzminden**, Germany.51 48N 9 26 E
24 **Homburg**, Germany ..50 15N 8 38 E
25 **Homonna**, Cz.-slovakia.48 57N 21 52 E
40 **Homs**, Syria ....34 40N 36 42 E
45 **Ho-nan**, China ....34 50N 113 0 E
45 **Honan, prov.**, China 34 30N 113 0 E
65 **Honduras, Rep.**,
C. America .. 13 to 17N 83 to 89W
35 **Hönefoss**, Norway.....60 10N 10 10 E
20 **Honfleur**, France .....49 30N 0 13 E
45 **Hong-ju**, Korea ......36 35N 127 0 E
45 **Hong-Kong, I.**, China .22 20N 113 55 E
14 **Honiton**, England 50 48N 3 12W
35 **Honkajoki**, Finland ...62 0N 22 20 E
6 **Honolulu**, Hawaii Is. ..21 25N 157 55W
45 **Honshu I.**, Japan ... 34 41N 131 140 E
22 **Hoogeveen**, Neth. ....52 43N 6 28 E
43 **Hooghly, R.**, India ...21 45N 88 10 E
22 **Hoogstraeten**, Belgium 51 26N 4 46 E
22 **Hoogwoud**, Nether. ...52 43N 4 56 E
22 **Hook of Holland**,
Netherlands ....51 57N 4 6 E
60 **Hooker, Mt.**, Canada ..52 20N 119 0W
47 **Hookina**, S. Austl.....31 45 s 138 20 E

MAP
57 **Hoopstad**, U. of S. Afr. 28 0 s 26 18 E
22 **Hoorn**, Netherlands ...52 39N 5 4 E
61 **Hopedale**, Labrador ...55 35N 50 30W
57 **Hopefield**, U. of S. Af. 33 10 s 18 20 E
45 **Hopei, prov.** *See* **Chihli**
57 **Hopetown**, U. of S. Af. 29 36 s 24 6 E
47 **Hopetoun**, Victoria ...35 43 s 142 19 E
46 **Hopetoun**, W. Australia33 58 s 120 2 E
63 **Hopkinsville**, U.S.A. ..36 55N 87 30W
23 **Hoptrup**, Denmark ...55 11N 9 28 E
35 **Hordaland, Co.**, Nor. .61 0N 6 50 E
23 **Hordum**, Denmark ...56 52N 8 32 E
33 **Horgen**, Switzerland ..47 16N 8 35 E
67 **Horn, C.**, Chile......... 60 8 s 67 0W
60 **Horn Mts.**,Canada ...63 0N 121 0W
13 **Horncastle**, England ..53 13N 0 6W
35 **Hornidal**, Norway ....61 55N 6 40 E
23 **Hörning**, Denmark ...56 9N 10 2 E
34 **Hornavan, L.**, Sweden 66 15N 17 40 E
23 **Horneburg**, Germany..53 31N 9 35 E
13 **Hornsea**, England 53 55N 0 11W
35 **Hornsland**, Sweden ..61 70W 17 30 E
23 **Horsbüll**, Germany ...54 52N 8 40 E
23 **Horsens**, Denmark ...54 52N 8 40 E
13 **Horsforth**, England ..53 50N 1 38W
15 **Horsham**, England....51 3N 0 19W
48 **Horsham**, Victoria ....36 40 s 142 12 E
22 **Horst**, Netherlands ...51 28N 6 2 E
35 **Horten**, Norway.......59 30N 10 23 E
12 **Horwich**, England .....53 56 N 2 34W
42 **Hospet**, India ....15 16N 76 26 E
19 **Hospital**, Eire 52 28N 8 26W
51 **Hot Springs**, N.Z. ...42 30 s 172 45 E
63 **Hot Springs**, U.S.A....34 30N 93 6W
62 **Hot Springs**, U.S.A....43 0N 103 12W
13 **Houghton-le-Spring**,
England 54 51N 1 26W
63 **Houlton**, U.S.A. 46 5N 67 53W
63 **Houston**, U.S.A. 29 49N 95 20W
23 **Höv**, Denmark ....55 9N 10 55 E
15 **Hove**, England 50 50N 0 12W
13 **Hovingham**, England ..54 10N 0 58W
47 **Howard**, Queensland ..25 16 s 152 33 E
13 **Howden**, England 53 44N 0 52W
47 **Howe, C.**, N.S.W. ...37 32 s 149 58 E
43 **Howrah**, India ....22 37N 88 17 E
19 **Howth**, Eire 52 23N 6 4W
12 **Hoylake**, England 53 23N 30 11W
42 **Hsen Wi**, Burma .....23 20N 97 57 E
44 **Hsing-ngan**, China ...32 40N 109 5 E
44 **Hsi-ning**, China ......37 0N 101 40 E
45 **Hsinking**, Manchuria 44 0N 125 0 E
43 **Hsipaw**, Burma ....22 40N 97 25 E
66 **Huacho**, Peru ....11 10 s 77 30W
64 **Huajuapan**, Mexico ...17 50N 97 55W
54 **Huambo**, Angola .....13 0 s 17 0 E
66 **Huanuco**, Peru .... 9 40 s 76 15W
66 **Huaraz**, Peru .... 9 30 s 77 25W
66 **Huascan, Mt.**, Peru ... 9 0 s 77 40W
67 **Huasco**, Chile ....28 30 s 71 20W
42 **Hubli**, India ....15 25N 75 15 E
45 **Hu-chau**, China .....30 55N 120 0 E
15 **Hucknall Torkard**,
England 53 3N 1 12W
13 **Huddersfield**, Eng. ...53 39N 1 47W
35 **Hudiksvall**, Sweden ...61 45N 17 0 E
61 **Hudson B.**, Canada ...41 40N 74 0W
61 **Hudson Str.**, Canada .63 0N 73 0W
39 **Hué**, Fr. Indo-China ...16 30N 107 35 E
26 **Huelva**, Spain 37 16N 6 55W
27 **Huércal Overa**, Spain .37 22N 2 2W
27 **Huesca**, Spain 42 8N 0 25W
27 **Huéscar**, Spain 37 47N 2 31W
27 **Huete**, Spain 40 8N 2 42W
47 **Hughenden**, Queens. ..20 50 s 143 40 E
53 **Huilla**, Port. W. Africa.15 0 s 14 0 E
22 **Huissen**, Netherlands .51 56N 5 57 E
50 **Hukerenui**, N. Zealand .35 30 s 174 15 E
41 **Hulhul**, Palestine ....31 35N 35 8 E
13 **Hull**, England 53 45N 0 20W
13 **Hull, R.**, England 53 50N 0 23W
22 **Hulst**, Netherlands ...51 17N 4 5 E
57 **Humansdorp**, U. of South
Africa ....34 2 s 24 45 E
66 **Humayta**, Brazil .... 7 40 s 63 10s
13 **Humber, R.**, England 53 42N 0 33W
58 **Humboldt Glacier**,
Greenland 79 30N 63 0W
62 **Humboldt, R.**, U.S.A. .40 40N 117 0W
49 **Hume Reservoir**, Vic. 36 0 s 147 20 E
45 **Hu-nan, prov.**, China .
25 to 30N 109 to 113 E
45 **Hunchun**, Manchuria ..43 0N 130 30 E
23 **Hundslund**, Denmark..55 56N 10 3 E
30 **Hungary, King.**, Eur. .46 48N 16 23 E
15 **Hungerford**, England..51 25N 1 31W
49 **Hungerford**, Queens. ..29 0 s 144 38 E
13 **Hunmanby**, England ..54 11N 0 20W
24 **Hunsrück Taunus**,
Mts., Germany ....50 0N 7 20 E
15 **Hunstanton**, England .52 58N 0 31 E
47 **Hunter, Is.**, Tasmania .40 20 s 144 50 E
50 **Hunterville**, N.Z. ....39 57 s 175 36 E
15 **Huntingdon & Co.**,
England 52 21N 0 11W

MAP
63 **Huntington**, U.S.A. ..38 24N 82 30W
51 **Huntly**, New Zealand ..37 33 s 175 10 E
16 **Huntly**, Scotland 57 27N 2 47W
63 **Huntsville**, U.S.A. ...30 40N 95 24W
42 **Hunza**, India ....36 22N 74 35 E
45 **Hupeh, prov.**, China 31 0N 112 0 E
62 **Huron**, U.S.A. 44 30N 98 17W
61 **Huron, L.**, N. America 44 30N 98 17W
23 **Hurup**, Denmark .....56 45N 8 26 E
31 **Husi**, Rumania ....46 45N 28 11 E
24 **Husum**, Germany .....54 30N 9 3 E
62 **Hutchinson**, U.S.A. ...38 1N 98 0W
51 **Hutt**, New Zealand ...41 10 s 175 5 E
33 **Huttwyl**, Switzerland ..47 7N 7 50 E
22 **Huy**, Belgium ....50 32N 5 15 E
22 **Huysse**, Belgium .....50 53N 3 36 E
23 **Hvalpsund**, Denmark .56 42N 9 12 E
23 **Hvidbjerg**, Denmark .56 50N 8 20 E
45 **Hwangchow**, China ..30 40N 115 0 E
45 **Hwang Hai**, *See*
Yellow Sea 34 to 37N 119 to 126 E
45 **Hwang-ho, R.**, China .38 0N 119 0 E
45 **Hwai-king**, China ....35 0N 113 0 E
45 **Hwei-chow**, China ...28 0N 114 30 E
13 **Hyde**, England 53 27N 2 5W
51 **Hyde**, New Zealand ...45 19 s 170 16 E
46 **Hyden**, W. Australia ..32 30 s 118 58 E
42 **Hyderabad**, India .....25 25N 68 22 E
42 **Hyderabad**, India .....17 16N 78 28 E
42 **Hyderabad, st.**, India
15 to 20N 74 to 81 E
21 **Hyères**, France ....43 6N 6 7 E
17 **Hynish**, Scotland 56 27N 6 53W
34 **Hyrnsalmi**, Finland ..64 40N 29 15 E
15 **Hythe**, England ....51 5N 1 5 E
35 **Hyvinkää**, Finland ....60 40N 25 0 E

54 **Ibadan**, Nigeria .... 7 22N 3 54 E
54 **Ibi**, Nigeria .... 8 10N 9 45 E
55 **Ibo, & I.**, Mozambique.12 15 s 0 41 E
32 **Ibrije**, Turkey........40 35N 26 33 E
66 **Ica**, Peru ....14 0 s 75 30W
8 **Iceland, Kingdom**, Eur. 65 0N 18 0W
45 **I-Chang**, China ....31 0N 111 15 E
45 **Ichow**, China ....35 5N 118 30 E
32 **Ida, Mt.**, Crete Inset 35 15N 24 47 E
62 **Idaho, st.**, U.S.A. 45 30N 114 0W
62 **Idaho Falls**, U.S.A....43 30N 112 5W
13 **Idle, R.**, England 53 27N 0 54W
28 **Idria**, Italy ....46 0N 14 0 E
45 **Idsuhara**, Japan ......34 12N 129 12 E
52 **Ifni (Sp. Col.)**, Africa..29 30N 10 0W
39 **Igarka**, U.S.S.R. ....68 0N 87 0 E
24 **Iglau.** *See* **Jihlava**
29 **Iglesias**, Sardinia......39 20N 8 28 E
52 **Igli**, Algeria ....29 45 s 1 40 E
27 **Igualada**, Spain.......41 35N 1 38 E
66 **Iguatú**, Brazil........ 6 0 s 39 57W
31 **Ihtiman**, Bulgaria ....42 23N 23 47 E
36 **Ijevsk**, U.S.S.R. ....56 50N 53 1 E
22 **Ijmuiden**, Netherlands.52 27N 4 36 E
22 **Ijsselstein**, Neth......52 2N 5 4 E
35 **Ikaalinen**, Finland ....61 45N 23 5 E
56 **Ikawa**, N. Rhodesia.... 8 30 s 32 30 E
14 **Ilchester**, England 51 0N 2 40W
20 **Ile de France, old**
prov., France.........49 10N 2 45 E
21 **Ile de Ré**, France.....46 13N 1 30W
21 **Iles d'Hyères**, France .43 0N 6 25 E
21 **Ile d'Oléron**, France ..45 55N 1 20W
21 **Ile Rousse**, Corsica ...42 38N 8 55 E
37 **Ilezk**, U.S.S.R. ....51 12N 54 59 E
37 **Ilezki Gorodok**,
U.S.S.R. ....51 29N 53 29 E
15 **Ilford**, England ....51 34N 0 5 E
14 **Ilfracombe**, England ..51 13N 4 7 E
26 **Ilhavo**, Portugal.......40 34N 8 40W
66 **Ilhéos**, Brazil ....14 48 s 39 2W
36 **Iliisk**, U.S.S.R...........43 57N 77 11W
41 **Ilijik**, U.S.S.R. ....39 30N 63 0 E
39 **Ilimsk**, U.S.S.R. ......56 20N 104 10 E
34 **Ilinsalmi**, Finland.....63 38N 27 30 E
15 **Ilkeston**, England 52 59N 1 19W
13 **Ilkley**, England 53 55N 1 49W
67 **Illapel**, Chile..........31 30 s 71 10W
20 **Ille-et-Vilaine, dept.**,
France 48 4N 1 40W
26 **Illescas**, Spain 40 7N 3 51W
63 **Illinois, st.**, U.S.A. 40 0N 93 0W
14 **Ilminster**, England.....50 56N 2 53W
39 **Iloilo**, Philippines......10 50N 122 30 E
54 **Ilorin**, Nigeria .... 8 30N 4 30 E
32 **Imbros, I.**, Turkey .....40 10N 25 50 E
58 **Imitkilly**, Alaska.......69 0N 165 30W
24 **Immenstadt**, Germany 47 34N 10 13 E
13 **Immingham**, England.53 38N 0 12W
28 **Imola**, Italy ....44 20N 11 41 E
28 **Imperia**, Italy ....43 55N 8 0 E
43 **Imphal**, India.........24 45N 94 0 E
51 **Inangahua**, N. Zealand.41 50 s 171 59 E
27 **Inca**, Majorca I. ......39 43N 2 56 E
16 **Inchnadamff**, Scotland 58 9N 4 58W
34 **Indals**, Sweden........63 11N 15 30 E
42 **Indian Des.**, India ....27 30N 71 0 E

MAP

38 **Indian Emp.**, Asia 8 0N to 37 0N 61 0E to 101 0E
7 **Indian Ocean**, Asia 10 0S 75 0E
63 **Indiana, st.**, U.S.A. 39 50N 86 0W
63 **Indianapolis**, U.S.A. 39 45N 86 17W
42 **Indore**, India 22 44N 75 52E
21 **Indre, dept.**, France 46 45N 1 30E
20 **Indre-et-Loire, dept.**, France 47 12N 0 45E
42 **Indus, R.**, India 28 40N 70 15E
57 **Indwe**, U. of S. Africa 31 30S 27 25E
13 **Ingleboro'**, England 54 12N 2 22W
13 **Ingleton**, England 54 9N 2 29W
50 **Inglewood**, N.Z. 39 10S 174 12E
47 **Inglewood**, Queensland 28 27S 151 8E
47 **Inglewood**, Victoria 36 32S 143 48E
24 **Ingolstadt**, Germany 48 46N 11 25E
47 **Injune**, Queensland 25 58S 148 33E
45 **Inland Sea**, Japan 34 30N 133 30E
44 **Inner Mongolia, div.**, China 37 0 to 46 0N 97 0 to 122 0E
17 **Innerleithen**, Scotland 55 37N 3 3W
47 **Innisfail**, Queensland 17 38S 146 0E
19 **Innishannon**, Eire 51 46N 8 40W
24 **Innsbrück**, Austria, Germany 47 17N 11 24E
16 **Insch**, Scotland 57 21N 2 37W
35 **Insjön**, Sweden 60 35N 15 2E
25 **Insterburg**, Germany 54 38N 21 50E
33 **Interlaken**, Switzerland 46 41N 7 50E
17 **Inveraray**, Scotland 56 14N 5 5W
16 **Invercannich**, Scotland 57 21N 4 45W
51 **Invercargill**, N.Z. 46 23S 168 21E
47 **Inverell**, N.S.W. 29 45S 151 3E
16 **Invergarry**, Scotland 57 4N 4 47W
16 **Invergordon**, Scotland 57 40N 4 10W
17 **Inverkeithing**, Scot. 56 3N 3 24W
16 **Inverness, & Co.**, Scot. 57 29N 4 13W
16 **Invershin**, Scotland 57 56N 4 23W
16 **Inverurie**, Scotland 57 17N 2 22W
56 **Inyati**, S. Rhodesia 19 33S 29 0E
17 **Iona, I.**, Scotland 56 18N 6 24W
32 **Ionian Is.**, Greece 38 40N 20 40E
63 **Iowa, City and st.**, U.S.A. 41 30N 93 0W
30 **Ipek**, Yugoslavia 42 39N 20 17E
63 **Iowa, R.**, U.S.A. 42 10N 93 0W
15 **Ipswich**, England 52 4N 1 10E
47 **Ipswich**, Queensland 27 38S 152 38E
66 **Ipu**, Brazil 4 30S 40 50W
67 **Iquique**, Chile 20 25S 70 10W
66 **Iquitos**, Peru 3 40S 73 25W
41 **Iran, King.**, Asia 25 0 to 39 50N 44 18 to 63 30E
40 **Iraq, King.**, Asia 29 0N to 37 0N 39 30E to 47 50E
36 **Irbit**, U.S.S.R. 57 43N 62 59E
11 **Irish Sea**, Brit. Isles 53 0N 5 0W
44 **Irkutsk**, U.S.S.R. 52 10N 104 15E
31 **Iron Gate**, Rumania 44 42N 22 30E
47 **Iron Knob**, S. Austl. 32 42S 137 8E
43 **Irrawaddy, R.**, Burma 23 0N 96 0E
12 **Irthing, R.**, England 55 0N 2 35W
38 **Irtish, R.**, U.S.S.R. 51 0N 78 30E
27 **Irun**, Spain 43 19N 1 41W
17 **Irvine**, Scotland 55 37N 4 39W
18 **Irvinestown**, N. Ireland 54 28N 7 38W
20 **Is**, France 47 28N 5 6E
57 **Isandhlwana**, U. of S. Africa 28 20S 30 38E
24 **Ischl**, Austria, Ger. 47 44N 13 37E
22 **Iseghem**, Belgium 50 55N 3 12E
28 **Iseo**, Italy 45 40N 10 3E
21 **Isère, dept.**, France 45 17N 5 45E
40 **Isfahan**, Iran 32 44N 51 36E
31 **Ishiklar**, Bulgaria 43 30N 26 45E
20 **Isigny**, France 49 20N 1 8W
29 **Isili**, Sardinia 39 44N 9 1E
40 **Iskenderon**, Turkey 36 40N 36 12E
42 **Islamabad**, India 33 45N 75 12E
17 **Islay, I.**, Scotland 55 45N 6 15W
15 **Isle of Ely, co.**, Eng 52 30N 0 20E
61 **Isle Royale**, Canada 47 50N 88 15W
31 **Ismail**, Rumania 45 21N 28 49E
41 **Ismailia**, Egypt 30 36N 32 56E
32 **Ismid**, Turkey 40 42N 28 57E
32 **Istanbul**, Turkey 41 1N 28 58E
31 **Ištip**, Yugoslavia 41 40N 22 8E
32 **Istraiya**, Turkey 41 25N 28 10E
67 **Itabira**, Brazil 19 30S 43 15W
66 **Itaituba**, Brazil 4 20S 56 0W
67 **Itajuba**, Brazil 22 15S 45 40W
52-53 **Italian Somaliland** 0 12S 42 51E
8 **Italy, King.**, Europe 37 0 to 47 0N 7 0 to 18 0E
67 **Itapura**, Brazil 20 15S 51 25W
42 **Itarsi**, India 22 35N 76 50E
67 **Itatiaya, Mt.**, Brazil 22 55S 44 40W
24 **Itzehoe**, Germany 53 55N 9 31E
25 **Ivangorod**, Poland 51 33N 21 50E
47 **Ivanhoe**, N.S.W. 32 49S 144 18E
30 **Ivanitza**, Yugoslavia 43 32N 20 12E
36 **Ivanovo Voznesensk, U.S.S.R.** 57 3N 40 58E

MAP

31 **Ivesti**, Rumania 45 40N 27 30E
61 **Ivigtut**, Greenland 68 50N 47 0W
15 **Ivinghoe**, England 51 50N 0 38W
27 **Iviza**, Spain 38 55N 1 30E
27 **Iviza I.**, Spain 39 0N 130 0E
52 **Ivory Coast**, Fr. W. Africa 6 0N 5 0W
28 **Ivrea**, Italy 45 29N 7 50E
20 **Ivry**, France 48 50N 2 23E
14 **Ivybridge**, England 50 24N 3 55W
25 **Ivye**, Poland 53 56N 25 50E
57 **Ixopo**, U. of S. Africa 30 10S 30 6E
15 **Ixworth**, England 52 18N 0 52E
32 **Izmir**, Turkey 38 25N 27 9E

35 **Jaakkima**, Finland 61 35N 30 18E
25 **Jabinka**, Poland 52 14N 24 7E
30 **Jablanitza**, Yugoslavia 42 50N 20 19E
25 **Jablunka P.**, Czech. 49 30N 18 45E
27 **Jaca**, Spain 42 35N 0 30W
51 **Jackson**, New Zealand 42 46S 171 31E
63 **Jackson, Ala.**, U.S.A. 31 30N 87 55W
63 **Jackson, Mich.**, U.S.A. 42 15N 84 30W
63 **Jackson, Miss.**, U.S.A. 32 17N 90 13W
63 **Jackson, Tenn.**, U.S.A. 35 35N 88 57W
63 **Jacksonville**, U.S.A. 39 33N 89 30W
65 **Jacmel**, Haiti 18 18N 52 40W
42 **Jacobabad**, India 28 17N 68 29E
57 **Jacobsdal**, U. of S. Afr. 25 38S 24 3E
27 **Jadraque**, Spain 40 57N 2 55W
26 **Jaen**, Spain 37 49N 3 46W
41 **Jaffa**, Palestine 32 5N 34 22E
42 **Jaffna**, Ceylon 9 37N 79 57E
43 **Jagannath.** *See* **Puri.**
42 **Jagdalpur**, India 19 0N 82 0E
25 **Jagerndorf**, Czech. 50 6N 17 43E
57 **Jagersfontein**, U. of S. Africa 29 45S 25 29E
41 **Jahrum**, Iran 28 30N 53 27E
43 **Jainti**, India 26 43N 89 37E
43 **Jaipur, and st.**, India 26 58N 75 47E
42 **Jaisalmer**, India 34 27N 70 28E
64 **Jalisco, st.**, Mexico 20 30N 103 30W
61 **Jakobshavn**, Greenland 69 15N 51 0W
35 **Jakobstadt**, Latvia 56 30N 25 50E
30 **Jakova**, Yugoslavia 42 25N 20 26E
41 **Jalalabad**, Afghanistan 34 24N 70 26E
64 **Jalapa**, Mexico 17 41N 92 50W
42 **Jalandhar**, India 31 30N 75 40E
42 **Jalaun**, India 26 10N 79 30E
64 **Jalisco, St.**, Mexico 20 30N 103 30W
41 **Jalk**, Iran 27 50N 62 45E
65 **Jamaica, I.**, W. Indies 18 15N 77 30W
43 **Jamalpur**, India 24 55N 90 1E
61 **James B.**, Canada 54 0N 80 30W
47 **Jamestown**, S. Austl. 33 8S 138 8E
35 **Jamma**, Estonia 58 2N 22 6E
42 **Jammu and Kashmir, st.** 32 46N 74 50E
35 **Jämsa**, Finland 61 58N 22 15E
34 **Jämtland, co.**, Sweden 62 50N 14 10E
6 **Jan Mayen I.**, Arc. Oc. 70 40N 8 0W
57 **Jansenville**, U. of S. Af. 32 55S 24 41E
42 **Jaora**, India 23 45N 75 5E
45 **Japan, king.**, Asia 30 0 to 43 0N 125 0 to 142 0E
45 **Japan, Sea of**, Asia 39 0N 134 0E
25 **Jaroslau**, Poland 50 1N 22 42E
13 **Jarrow**, England 54 58N 1 30W
41 **Jask**, Iran 25 46N 57 50E
25 **Jaslo**, Poland 49 45N 21 26E
25 **Jastrow**, Germany 53 25N 16 50E
30 **Jászoerény**, Hungary 47 30N 19 55E
42 **Jath**, India 17 3N 75 15E
27 **Jativa**, Spain 39 0N 0 30W
27 **Jativa**, Spain 39 0N 0 30W
66 **Jatoba**, Brazil 9 0S 38 25W
42 **Jaunpur**, India 25 46N 82 46E
39 **Java, I.**, Dut. E. Indies 7 30S 110 0E
42 **Jawhar**, India 19 52N 73 21E
25 **Jaworow**, Poland 49 55N 23 21E
54 **Jebba**, Nigeria 9 5N 4 48E
17 **Jedburgh**, Scotland 55 29N 2 34W
63 **Jefferson**, U.S.A. 38 37N 92 16W
45 **Jehol**, Manchuria 40 59N 117 55E
45 **Jehol, prov.**, Manch. 42 0N 120 0E
35 **Jelgava.** *See* **Mitau**
54 **Jemaa**, Nigeria 9 29N 8 18E
22 **Jemappes**, Belgium 50 27N 3 53E
41 **Jemmain**, Palestine 32 8N 35 10E
24 **Jena**, Germany 50 58N 11 38E
41 **Jenin**, Palestine 32 27N 35 20E
31 **Jerebkova**, Russia 47 8N 30 23E
65 **Jerémie**, Haiti 18 35N 74 10W
26 **Jerez**, Spain 36 40N 6 10W
35 **Jerfsö**, Sweden 61 42N 16 10E
41 **Jericho.** *See* **Eriha**
47 **Jerilderie**, N.S.W. 35 20S 145 46E
34 **Jerpen**, Sweden 63 25N 13 32E
63 **Jersey City**, U.S.A. 40 50N 74 10W
20 **Jersey, I.**, Channel Is. 49 13N 2 10W
41 **Jerusalem**, Palestine 31 48N 35 12E
28 **Jesi**, Italy 43 31N 13 12E
43 **Jessor**, India 23 6N 89 17E
23 **Jevenstedt**, Germany 54 15N 9 41E

MAP

42 **Jhalawan, dist.**, India 27 30N 6 30E
42 **Jhalra Patan**, India 24 40N 75 10E
42 **Jhang**, India 31 16N 72 22E
42 **Jhansi**, India 25 25N 78 36E
42 **Jhelum**, India 33 0N 73 5E
44 **Jiachan**, Tibet 31 33N 81 30E
55 **Jibuti**, Fr. Somaliland 11 34N 43 10E
40 **Jidda**, Arabia 21 38N 39 17E
41 **Jiddin**, Palestine 33 0N 35 14E
24 **Jihlava**, Czechoslov. 49 23N 15 35E
27 **Jijona**, Spain 38 32N 0 25W
26 **Jimena**, Spain 36 26N 5 25W
55 **Jinja**, Uganda 0 28N 33 12E
66 **Jirardot**, Colombia 4 25N 75 0W
41 **Jisak**, U.S.S.R. 40 18N 67 55E
66 **João Pessoa**, Brazil 7 12S 35 0W
66 **Joazeiro**, Brazi 9 25S 40 30W 9 20S 40 31W
24 **Jochimsthal**, Czechosl. 50 21N 12 58E
42 **Jodhpur**, India 26 20N 73 5E
34 **Joensuu**, Finland 65 25N 30 0E
57 **Johannesburg**, U. of S. Africa 26 15S 28 5E
25 **Johannisburg**, Ger. 53 38N 21 48E
16 **John o' Groats**, Scot. 58 38N 3 2W
17 **Johnshaven**, Scotland 56 47N 2 21W
48 **Johnston, I.**, Pac. Oc. 17 0N 162 25W
17 **Johnstone**, Scotland 55 50N 4 30W
63 **Johnstown**, U.S.A. 40 23N 78 55W
20 **Joigny**, France 47 59N 3 23E
39 **Jokjokarta**, Java 7 57S 110 20E
34 **Jokkmokk**, Sweden 66 35N 18 55E
63 **Joliet**, U.S.A. 41 38N 88 8W
63 **Jonesboro**, U.S.A. 35 53N 90 35W
66 **Jonestown**, Br. Guiana 6 35N 58 5W
35 **Jönköping, & Co.**, Sweden 57 50N 14 10E
63 **Joplin**, U.S.A. 37 6N 94 32E
41 **Joppa.** *See* **Jaffa**
41 **Jordan, R.** *See* **Esh Sheriah.**
43 **Jorhat**, India 26 46N 94 16E
34 **Jörn**, Sweden 65 5N 20 10E
24 **Josefstadt**, Czechoslav. 50 21N 15 54E
67 **Juan Fernandez Is.**, Chili 33 50S 80 0W
55 **Juba**, A.-E. Sudan 4 45N 31 32E
55 **Juba, R.**, It. Somaliland 1 0N 42 30E
42 **Jubbulpore**, India 23 20N 80 0E
41 **Judea, dist.**, Palestine 31 40N 34 55E
24 **Judenburg**, Austria, Germany 47 10N 14 41E
67 **Jujuy**, Argentina 24 0S 65 30W
34 **Jukkasjärvi**, Sweden 67 52N 20 50E
40 **Julfa**, Iran 38 58N 45 32E
66 **Juliaca**, Peru 16 45S 70 25W
28 **Julian Alps**, Italy 46 20N 13 40E
61 **Julianehaab**, Greenland 60 40N 45 35W
41 **Jumain**, Iran 34 30N 58 50E
22 **Jumet**, Belgium 50 24N 4 25E
27 **Jumilla**, Spain 38 30N 1 18W
42 **Jumna, R.**, India 26 0N 80 0E
43 **Junagarh**, India 19 52N 82 59E
42 **Junagarh**, India 21 22N 70 30E
62 **Junction City**, U.S.A. 39 2N 96 51W
60 **Juneau**, Alaska 58 8N 134 0W
47 **Junee**, N.S.W. 34 52S 147 32E
24 **Jungbunzlau**, Czech. 50 27N 14 53E
33 **Jungfrau, Mt.**, Switz. 46 31N 7 56E
67 **Junin**, Argentina 34 30S 61 0W
34 **Juopperi**, Finland 66 56N 33 15E
21 **Jura, dept.**, France 46 33N 5 48E
17 **Jura, I.**, Scotland 56 0N 5 50W
21 **Jura Mts.**, France 47 0N 6 40E 47 10N 7 0E
17 **Jura, Sd. of**, Scotland 56 0N 5 45W
66 **Juruá, R.**, Brazil 5 30S 67 30W
44 **Jusagach**, U.S.S.R. 46 50N 79 30E
20 **Jussey**, France 49 48N 5 55E
33 **Jussy**, Switzerland 46 14N 6 16E
24 **Jüterbog**, Germany 51 59N 13 4E
64 **Jutigalpa**, Honduras 14 42N 85 49E
34 **Juuka**, Finland 63 15N 28 30E
41 **Juwain**, Afghanistan 31 49N 61 35E
34 **Jyväskylä**, Finland 62 15N 25 55E

55 **Kabalo**, Belgian Congo 6 2S 26 56E
55 **Kalambare**, Belg. Congo 4 39S 28 0E
37 **Kabardino-Balkar, rep.**, U.S.S.R. 43 30N 43 23E
54 **Kabba**, Nigeria 7 55N 6 4E
55 **Kabinda**, Angola 6 8S 24 21E
41 **Kabul**, Afghanistan 34 33N 69 10E
30 **Kachanik**, Yugoslavia 42 17N 21 15E
48 **Kadina**, S. Australia 33 55S 137 33E
54 **Kaduna**, Nigeria 10 27N 7 25E
50 **Kaeo**, New Zealand 35 5S 173 48E
56 **Kafue**, N. Rhodesia 15 48S 28 0E
55 **Kafue, R.**, N. Rhodesia 15 48S 26 45E
45 **Kagoshima**, Japan 31 37N 130 29E
31 **Kagul**, Rumania 45 54N 28 13E
36 **Kai**, U.S.S.R. 59 50N 53 20E
51 **Kaiapoi**, New Zealand 43 22S 172 40E
45 **Kaifeng**, China 34 50N 114 35E
50 **Kaihu**, New Zealand 35 46S 173 43E
44 **Kai-hua**, China 23 30N 104 5E

MAP
51 **Kaikoura,** New Zealand 42 26 S 173 40 E
32 **Kailar,** Greece ....40 32N 21 43 E
38 **Kainsk,** U.S.S.R. ......50 55N 78 10 E
50 **Kaipara Harb.,** N.Z. .36 25 S 174 14 E
45 **Kaiping,** China........39 41N 118 16 E
52 **Kairwan,** Tunis ....35 31N 10 0 E
68 **Kaiser Wilhelm II. Ld.,**
Antarctica ....65 0 S 99 0 E
24 **Kaiserslautern,** Ger. ..49 30N 7 45 E
33 **Kaiserstuhl,** Switz. ...47 35N 8 25 E
51 **Kaitangata,** N.Z. .....46 15 S 169 54 E
42 **Kaithal,** India ....29 48N 76 26 E
34 **Kajaana,** Finland......64 12N 27 45 E
34 **Kajaani.** *See* **Kajaana**
57 **Kakamas,** U. of S. Afr. 28 50 S 20 35 E
41 **Kakhk,** Iran ....34 12N 58 38 E
35 **Kakisalmi,** Finland ...61 2N 30 10 E
41 **Kala Drosh,** India.....35 38N 71 50 E
40 **Kalaat Bisha,** Arabia..20 0N 43 30 E
41 **Kala'at Zerka,** Transv. 32 8N 36 11 E
42 **Kalabagh,** India .....32 58N 71 36 E
32 **Kalabaka,** Greece ....39 41N 21 39 E
37 **Kalach,** U.S.S.R. .....50 20N 40 59 E
42 **Kaladgi,** India ....16 13N 75 53 E
57 **Kalahari Desert, Afr.** 23 20 S 21 0 E
34 **Kalajoki,** Finland ....64 20N 24 0 E
32 **Kalamata,** Greece ....32 2N 22 7 E
63 **Kalamazoo,** U.S.A. ...42 17N 85 40W
32 **Kalarrytae,** Greece ...39 34N 21 7 E
42 **Kalat,** India ....29 12N 66 40 E
32 **Kalavryta,** Greece ....38 1N 22 8 E
45 **Kalgan,** China ....40 50N 115 0 E
46 **Kalgoorlie,** W. Austl. .30 40 S 121 30 E
36 **Kalinin,** U.S.S.R.......56 52N 35 40 E
25 **Kalish,** Poland ....51 54N 18 7 E
62 **Kalispell,** U.S.A. 48 11N 114 19W
42 **Kalka,** India ....30 40N 75 55 E
30 **Kalkandelen,** Yugosl...42 1N 21 1 E
56 **Kalkfeld,** S.W. Africa ..20 45 S 16 25 E
57 **Kalkfontein,** S. W. Afr. 27 51 S 18 36 E
41 **Kalkilieh,** Palestine....32 12N 34 57 E
35 **Kalmar, & co.** Sweden 56 40N 16 20 E
37 **Kalmyk, rep.,**
U.S.S.R. ....46 30N 45 30 E
30 **Kalocsa,** Hungary ....46 34N 19 0 E
56 **Kalomo,** N. Rhodesia..17 8 S 26 28 E
42 **Kalpi,** India ....26 8W 79 47 E
37 **Kaluga,** U.S.S.R. .....54 34N 36 12 E
23 **Kalundborg,** Denmark.55 42N 11 6 E
25 **Kalusz,** Poland........49 1N 24 21 E
42 **Kalutara,** Ceylon ..... 6 30N 79 59 E
35 **Kalvariya,** Lithuania ..54 26N 23 10 E
24 **Kalvörde,** Germany ..52 25N 11 19 E
42 **Kalyan,** India ....19 14N 73 10 E
32 **Kalymnos, Tn. & I.,**
Aegean Sea ....37 0N 27 0 E
42 **Kamamat,** India ......17 20N 80 10 E
55 **Kamaran, I.,** Red Sea .15 25N 42 35 E
39 **Kamchatka Pen.,**
U.S.S.R. ....56 0N 158 0 E
25 **Kamenets Litovsk,**
Poland ....52 25N 23 50 E
37 **Kamenets Podolia,**
U.S.S.R. ....48 41N 26 32 E
31 **Kamenka,** Russia .....48 1N 28 40 E
37 **Kamensk,** U.S.S.R.....48 18N 40 4 E
25 **Kamionkastrumilowa,**
Poland ....50 8N 24 20 E
37 **Kamishin,** U.S.S.R. ...50 6N 45 26 E
60 **Kamloops,** Canada ...50 39N 119 20W
24 **Kammin,** Germany ...53 58N 14 47 E
55 **Kampala,** Uganda ... 0 20N 32 34 E
22 **Kampen,** Netherlands..52 33N 5 55 E
42 **Kamthi,** India ....21 20N 79 10 E
36 **Kamyshlov,** U.S.S.R. .56 49N 62 34 E
46 **Kanasawa,** Japan ....36 45N 136 52 E
43 **Kanburi,** Siam ....14 1N 99 30 E
45 **Kan-chow,** China ....39 0N 100 40 E
41 **Kandahar,** Afghanistan 31 42N 65 47 E
36 **Kandalaksha,** U.S.S.R. 67 12N 32 28 E
33 **Kandersteg,** Switz. ...46 29N 7 40 E
42 **Kandy,** Ceylon .... 7 20N 80 33 E
48 **Kangaroo, I.,** S. Austl..35 45 S 137 0 E
40 **Kangavar,** Iran ......34 28N 47 54 E
61 **Kangerdlugssuak,**
Greenland 68 14N 30 0W
52 **Kankan,** Fr. W. Africa 10 22N 9 12W
42 **Kanker,** India ....20 18N 81 32 E
54 **Kano,** Nigeria ....12 0N 8 31 E
46 **Kanowna,** W. Austl. ..30 31 S 124 41 E
62 **Kansas, st.,** U.S.A. ...38 0N 98 0W
63 **Kansas City,** U.S.A. ..39 0N 94 30W
44 **Kan-su, prov.,** China .37 0N 103 0 E
19 **Kanturk,** Eire 52 10N 8 55W
30 **Kanye,** Yugoslavia.....43 10N 19 45 E
44 **Kanzego,** China ......32 0N 100 15 E
44 **Kao-tai,** China ....39 10N 100 15 E
32 **Kapakli Bunar,** Turkey 48 49N 27 48 E
30 **Kaposvár,** Hungary ...46 25N 17 47 E
23 **Kappeln,** Germany....54 38N 9 56 E
32 **Kapsali,** Greece ....36 5N 23 0 E
47 **Kapunda,** .S Austl. ...34 18 S 138 24 E
41 **Kara Kum, Des.,**
U.S.S.R. ....39 20N 60 0 E
36 **Kara Sea,** U.S.S.R. ...72 0N 63 0 E

MAP
37 **Karachaev, prov.,**
U.S.S.R. ....43 50N 41 38 E
37 **Karachev,** U.S.S.R.....53 12N 34 57 E
42 **Karachi,** India ....24 52N 67 0 E
32 **Karaferria,** Greece ....40 33N 22 17 E
45 **Karafuto I.,** Japan ....48 0N 142 30 E
44 **Karakash,** Sinkiang ...38 0N 79 30 E
41 **Karakul,** U.S.S.R. ....39 30N 63 44 E
42 **Karakoram, Ra.,** Ind. 36 0N 76 0 E
44 **Karakorum,** Mongolia 47 23N 102 28 E
52 **Karam,** Br. Somaliland 10 40N 45 10 E
40 **Karaman,** Turkey ....37 9N 33 20 E
31 **Karánsebes,** Rumania .45 28N 22 19 E
40 **Karapunar,** Turkey ...38 42N 31 21 E
42 **Karashahr,** Sinkiang ..42 0N 87 0 E
37 **Karasubazar,** U.S.S.R. 45 5N 34 2 E
32 **Karasuli,** Greece ......40 58N 22 41 E
30 **Karczag,** Hungary ....47 20N 21 0 E
32 **Karditza,** Greece .....39 12N 21 53 E
35 **Karelia, rep.,** U.S.S.R..64 10N 32 30 E
55 **Karema,** Tanganyika .. 6 51 S 30 26 E
43 **Karenni, st.,** Burma ..19 15N 97 30 E
34 **Karesuando,** Sweden ..68 20N 22 30 E
38 **Kargan,** U.S.S.R. ....56 0N 66 0 E
44 **Karghalik,** Sinkiang ..38 20N 77 30 E
42 **Kargil,** India ....34 30N 75 5 E
57 **Karibib,** S. W. Africa .22 0 S 15 47 E
32 **Karies,** Greece ....40 14N 24 20 E
42 **Karikal,** India ....11 0N 79 50 E
45 **Karimskaya,** U.S.S.R. 51 40N 115 0 E
44 **Karkaralinsk,** U.S.S.R.49 30N 75 37 E
30 **Karlovac,** Yugoslavia .45 32N 15 35 E
31 **Karlovo,** Bulgaria .....42 39N 24 48 E
24 **Karlovy Vary,** Czecho..50 13N 12 50 E
24 **Karlsbad.** *See* **Karlovy Vary**
35 **Karlsborg,** Sweden ...58 35N 14 25 E
35 **Karlshamn,** Sweden ...56 10N 14 54 E
35 **Karlskrona,** Sweden ...56 10N 15 40 E
24 **Karlsruhe,** Germany...49 3N 8 20 E
35 **Karlstad,** Sweden ....59 25N 13 25 E
30 **Karlstadt.** *See* **Karlovac**
31 **Karmasy,** Rumania ...46 25N 30 0 E
31 **Karnobat,** Bulgaria ...42 40N 27 0 E
42 **Karnul,** India.........15 50N 78 0 E
56 **Karonga,** Nyasaland .. 9 58 S 33 50 E
24 **Karow,** Germany ....53 32N 12 15 E
32 **Karpenisi,** Greece ....38 55N 21 46 E
57 **Karree Berge, mts.,**
U. of S. Africa ....30 45 S 22 0 E
40 **Kars,** Turkey ....40 34N 43 3 E
34 **Karsamaki,** Finland...64 0N 25 40 E
32 **Kartal,** Turkey ....40 53N 29 10 E
25 **Kartuskaya Beresa,**
Poland ....52 38N 25 0 E
23 **Karup,** Denmark .....56 19N 9 10 E
32 **Karvosara,** Greece ....38 50N 20 59 E
42 **Karwar,** India ....14 15N 74 25 E
32 **Karysto,** Greece .....38 1N 24 29 E
54 **Kasai, R.,** Belg. Congo. 7 0 S 21 30 E
55 **Kasama,** N. Rhodesia..10 10 S 31 23 E
55 **Kasanga,** Tanganyika .. 7 49 S 30 55 E
55 **Kasempa,** N. Rhodesia 13 24 S 25 40 E
55 **Kasenga,** Belgian Congo 10 32 S 28 39 E
56 **Kasenga,** N. Rhodesia . 9 49 S 37 53 E
41 **Kash,** Afghanistan ....31 40N 63 0 E
40 **Kashan,** Iran ....33 58N 51 22 E
35 **Kashedary,** Lithuania .54 50N 24 30 E
44 **Kashgar,** Sinkiang.....39 30N 76 0 E
42 **Kashmir, dist.,** India..34 30N 76 30 E
36 **Kasimov,** U.S.S.R. ....55 0N 41 30 E
34 **Kaskinen,** Finland.....62 20N 21 10 E
34 **Kaskö.** *See* **Kaskinen**
55 **Kasongo,** Bel. Con. ....4 30 S 26 35 E
41 **Kasrkund,** Iran ......26 14N 60 35 E
32 **Kassaba,** Turkey .....38 30N 27 45 E
55 **Kassala,** A.-E. Sudan ..15 26N 36 42 E
40 **Kastamuni,** Turkey ...41 16N 33 59 E
23 **Kastorf,** Germany .....53 45N 10 33 E
32 **Kastoria,** Greece .....40 30N 21 19 E
32 **Kastro, Chios,** Greece .38 22N 26 8 E
32 **Kastro, Lemnos,** Gr. .39 53N 25 10 E
23 **Kastrup,** Denmark ....55 40N 12 38 E
56 **Kasungu,** Nyasaland... 8 30 S 33 10 E
40 **Kasvin,** Iran ....36 19N 49 59 E
32 **Katakolon,** Greece....37 39N 21 20 E
55 **Katanga, dist.,** Belg.
Congo ....10 0 S 26 30 E
55 **Katende,** Bel. Con. ...10 55 S 23 50 E
32 **Katerina,** Greece .....40 18N 22 35 E
43 **Katha,** Burma ....24 12N 96 20 E
42 **Kathiawar, penin,** Ind.21 55N 71 0 E
40 **Katif,** Arabia 26 30N 50 0W
57 **Katkop,** U. of S. Africa.30 7 S 20 5 E
43 **Katmandu,** Nepal ....27 42N 85 20 E
42 **Katni,** India ....22 40N 80 25 E
47 **Katoomba,** N.S.W. ...33 42 S 150 15 E
25 **Katowice,** Poland .....50 17N 19 3 E
17 **Katrine, Loch,** Scot. ..56 15N 4 30W
35 **Katrineholm,** Sweden 59 0N 16 10 E
54 **Katsina,** Nigeria ......13 1N 7 30 E
35 **Kattegat,** Denmark ...56 50N 11 30 E
35 **Kaunas.** *See* **Koono**
34 **Kautokeino,** Norway ..69 0N 23 0 E
30 **Kavaja,** Albania ......41 12N 19 33 E
32 **Kavak,** Turkey ....40 35N 26 52 E

MAP
31 **Kavakli,** Bulgaria ....42 5N 26 21 E
32 **Kavala,** Greece ....40 58N 24 27 E
50 **Kawakawa,** N.Z. ......35 22N 174 3 E
52 **Kayes,** Fr. W. Africa...42 22N 11 25W
40 **Kayseri,** Turkey .....38 42N 35 28 E
38 **Kazak, rep.,** U.S.S.R. ..48 0N 65 0 E.
38 **Kazalinsk,** U.S.S.R. ...45 40N 62 0 E
31 **Kazan,** Bulgaria ......42 50N 26 29 E
36 **Kazan,** U.S.S.R. ......55 42N 49 6 E
31 **Kazanlik,** Bulgaria ....42 39N 25 38 E
55 **Kazambe,** N. Rhodesia 9 49 S 28 52 E
40 **Kazerun,** Iran ....29 38N 51 40 E
18 **Keady,** N. Ireland 54 15N 6 42W
62 **Kearney,** U.S.A. 40 35N 99 9W
30 **Kecskemet,** Hungary .46 58N 19 42 E
18 **Keenagh,** Eire 53 38N 7 49W
57 **Keetmanshoop,** S. W.
Africa ....26 30 S 18 3 E
60 **Keewatin, dist.,** Can. .65 0N 95 0W
54 **Keffi,** Nigeria .... 8 50N 7 45 E
35 **Kegel,** Estonia ....59 18N 24 25 E
39 **Kei Is.,** Dut. E. Indies . 5 30 S 132 0 E
35 **Keidani,** Lithuania ....55 17N 23 59 E
13 **Keighley,** England ...53 52N 1 54W
45 **Keijo.** *See* **Seoul**
16 **Keith,** Scotland........57 33N 2 57 E
47 **Keith,** S. Australia ....35 3 S 140 20 E
44 **Kekugo,** China ....34 0N 97 0 E
39 **Kelantan,** Malay Pen. . 6 0N 102 20 E
41 **Kelat-i-Nadiri,** Iran...37 2N 59 53 E
32 **Kelid Bahr,** Turkey ...40 9N 26 22 E
32 **Kelimos,** Greece ......37 0N 24 30 E
23 **Kellinghusen,** Germany53 58N 9 45 E
18 **Kells,** Eire 53 44N 6 53W
41 **Kelso,** New Zealand ..44 54 S 169 15 E
17 **Kelso,** Scotland 55 37N 2 25W
36 **Kem,** U.S.S.R. ....64 58N 34 30 E
34 **Kemass Osersk,**
U.S.S.R. ....64 28N 21 12 E
34 **Kemi,** Finland ....65 41N 24 42 E
34 **Kemi, R.,** Finland ....66 5N 25 0 E
34 **Kemijärvi,** Finland ...66 40N 27 35 E
68 **Kemp Ld.,** Antarctica 67 0 S 60 0 E
25 **Kempen,** Poland .....51 18N 18 0 E
47 **Kempsey,** N.S.W. .....31 5 S 152 50 E
24 **Kempten,** Germany ..47 45N 10 18 E
12 **Kendal,** England 54 20N 2 45W
40 **Keneh,** Egypt ....26 10N 32 44 E
44 **Keng Hung,** China ....22 0N 100 50 E
57 **Kenhart,** U. of S. Afr. .29 22 S 20 30 E
15 **Kenilworth,** England .52 22N 1 35W
19 **Kenmare,** Eire 51 53N 9 34W
17 **Kenmore,** Scotland ...56 35N 4 0W
15 **Kennet, R.,** England ..51 25N 1 23W
60 **Kenora,** Canada 49 40N 94 30W
15 **Kent, Co.,** England ...51 15N 0 45 E
12 **Kent, R.,** England 54 20N 2 45W
15 **Kentford,** England ...52 16N 0 31 E
63 **Kentucky, St.,** U.S.A...38 0N 84 0W
55 **Kenya, Col. & Prot.,**
E. Africa 5 0N to 5 0 S 35 to 41 E
55 **Kenya, Mt.,** Kenya ... 0 10 S 37 28 E
43 **Keonjhar,** India ....21 36N 85 42 E
47 **Kerang,** Victoria .....35 40 S 143 55 E
31 **Kerasovo,** Bulgaria ...43 6N 25 58 E
32 **Kerasovo,** Greece .....39 1N 21 36 E
40 **Kerbela,** Iraq ....32 30N 44 12 E
37 **Kerch,** U.S.S.R. ....45 21N 36 14 E
55 **Keren,** Eritrea ....15 45N 38 28 E
32 **Keresen,** Turkey .....39 24N 27 45 E
68 **Kerguelen I.,** S. Ocean.48 30 S 69 40 E
44 **Keria,** Sinkiang ......36 47N 81 40 E
40 **Kerind,** Iran ....34 0N 46 15 E
41 **Kerki,** U.S.S.R. ......37 50N 65 7 E
34 **Kerkkala,** Finland ....66 20N 30 0 E
40 **Kerkuk,** Iraq. ....35 20N 44 22 E
40 **Kermadec Is.,** Inset 30 0 S 178 0W
41 **Kerman,** Iran ....30 17N 57 0 E
41 **Kerman, prov.,** Iran ...30 21N 57 5 E
40 **Kermanshah,** Iran ....34 15N 47 2 E
19 **Kerry, Co.,** Eire 52 0N 10 0W
14 **Kerry,** Wales 52 30N 3 12W
23 **Kerteminde,** Denmark55 27N 10 40 E
32 **Keshan,** Turkey ....40 52N 26 39 E
44 **Kes-hoi.** *See* **Hanoi**
25 **Késmark,** Cz-slovakia .49 8N 20 28 E
15 **Kessingland,** England 52 25N 1 42 E
16 **Kessock,** Scotland . . .57 31N 4 14W
15 **Kesteven, co.,** England 52 55N 0 33W
12 **Keswick,** England 54 36N 3 9W
30 **Keszthely,** Hungary ...46 48N 17 15 E
15 **Kettering,** England ...52 25N 0 43W
13 **Kettlewell,** England ...54 9N 2 3W
34 **Keuruu,** Finland .....62 18N 24 48 E
35 **Kexholm.** *See* **Kakisalmi**
63 **Key West,** U.S.A. 24 30N 81 30W
14 **Keynsham,** England ..51 25N 2 28W
36 **Khabarova,** U.S.S.R. ..69 38N 60 20 E
45 **Khabarovka,** U.S.S.R. 48 30N 135 10 E
39 **Khabarovsk,** U.S.S.R. 48 40N 135 5 E
41 **Khabis,** Iran ....30 26N 57 42 E
41 **Khaf,** Iran ....34 41N 59 56 E
40 **Khaibar,** Arabia ......25 55N 40 0 E
42 **Khairpur, & st.,** India 27 23N 68 45 E
41 **Khalassa,** Palestine....31 3N 34 40 E

MAP			
42	**Khamgaon,** India	20 40N	75 35E
44	**Khami,** Sinkiang	42 45N	93 35E
40	**Khamr,** Arabia	16 59N	44 0E
40	**Khamseh,** Iran	36 20W	48 30E
44	**Khan Tengri, mt.,** Sinkiang	42 0N	80 0E
41	**Khan Yunis,** Palestine	31 20N	32 20E
42	**Khandwa,** India	21 13N	76 24E
40	**Khanikin,** Iraq	34 17N	45 19E
41	**Khanu,** Iran	27 58N	57 31E
42	**Kharan,** India	28 42N	65 25E
44	**Khardam,** Tibet	30 20N	81 20E
40	**Kharfa,** Arabia	24 12N	46 13E
40	**Khargeh Oasis,** Egypt	25 20N	30 40E
37	**Kharkov,** U.S.S.R.	49 59N	36 12E
40	**Kharput,** Turkey	38 40W	39 16E
55	**Khartoum,** A.-E. Sud.	15 37N	32 30E
43	**Khasi Hills,** India	25 30N	92 0E
39	**Khatansk,** U.S.S.R.	71 40N	102 0E
57	**Kheis,** U. of S. Africa	20 50S	22 2E
41	**Khelat-i-Ghilzai,** Afghan.	32 10N	66 56E
37	**Kherson,** U.S.S.R.	46 42N	32 32E
34	**Khibinogorsk,** U.S.S.R.	67 30N	33 0E
30	**Khimara,** Albania	40 7N	19 45E
45	**Khingan Mts.,** Manch.	45 0N	120 0E
41	**Khiva,** U.S.S.R.	41 15N	60 50E
40	**Khoi,** Iran	38 28N	45 2E
41	**Khojent,** U.S.S.R.	40 15N	69 35E
41	**Khokand,** U.S.S.R.	40 42N	71 0E
42	**Kholapur,** India	20 56N	77 34E
25	**Kholm,** Poland	51 7N	23 28E
40	**Khoramshah,** Iraq	30 32N	48 11E
41	**Khorassan, prov.,** Iran	35 0N	58 40E
40	**Khoremmabad,** Iran	33 30N	48 10E
25	**Khorzele,** Poland	53 14N	20 58E
40	**Khosat,** Turkey	39 8N	39 30E
44	**Khotan,** Sinkiang	37 0N	79 55E
25	**Khotenichi,** Poland	52 40N	26 18E
41	**Khuldeh,** Palestine	31 45N	34 55E
43	**Khulna,** India	22 50N	89 45E
41	**Khur,** Iran	33 55N	54 55E
40	**Khuzistan, prov.,** Iran	31 30N	49 30E
37	**Khvalynsk,** U.S.S.R.	52 30N	48 0E
42	**Khyber Pass,** India	34 6N	71 5E
25	**Khymelnik,** Poland	50 38N	20 46E
44	**Kiakhta,** U.S.S.R.	50 20N	106 30E
47	**Kiama,** N.S.W.	34 40S	150 50E
47	**Kiandra,** N.S.W.	35 32S	148 32E
40	**Kiangri,** Turkey	40 40N	33 40E
45	**Kiangsi, prov.,** China	27 40N	115 0E
45	**Kiangsu, prov.,** China	33 0N	119 0E
45	**Kiaochow,** China	36 20N	120 15E
44	**Kia-ting,** China	29 40N	104 0E
32	**Kiato,** Greece	38 1N	22 46E
55	**Kibwezi,** Kenya	2 25S	38 0E
55	**Kibwezi,** Tanganyika	6 32S	29 57E
39	**Kichiginsk,** U.S.S.R.	59 50N	164 0E
30	**Kichova,** Yugoslavia	41 42N	20 59E
60	**Kicking Horse Pass,** Canada	51 30N	115 0W
14	**Kidderminster,** Eng.	52 24N	2 13W
14	**Kidwelly,** Wales	51 45N	4 18W
24	**Kiel,** Germany	54 20N	10 10E
24	**Kiel Canal,** Germany	54 15N	9 38E
25	**Kielce, co.,** Poland	50 51N	20 43E
35	**Kielkona,** Estonia	58 22N	22 5E
45	**Kien-ning,** China	27 13N	118 27E
37	**Kiev,** U.S.S.R.	50 26N	30 31E
55	**Kigoma,** Tanganyika	4 53S	29 40E
45	**Kü Chan.,** Japan	34 0N	134 50E
30	**Kijva,** Yugoslavia	42 33N	20 44E
55	**Kikoma,** Uganda	0 5S	31 30E
19	**Kilbeggan,** Eire	53 22N	7 30W
17	**Kilbirnie,** Scotland	55 46N	4 41W
17	**Kilbrennan Sd.,** Scot.	55 35N	5 25W
17	**Kilchoan,** Scotland	56 42N	6 7W
19	**Kilchreest,** Eire	53 10N	8 40W
19	**Kilcock,** Eire	53 24N	6 40W
19	**Kilconnell,** Eire	53 21N	8 24W
19	**Kilcool,** Eire	53 7N	6 4W
47	**Kilcoy,** Queensland	26 50S	152 32E
19	**Kilcullen,** Eire	53 8N	6 45W
19	**Kildare, & co.,** Eire	53 10N	6 55W
16	**Kildonan,** Scotland	58 10N	3 50W
19	**Kilfenora,** Eire	52 55N	9 13W
19	**Kilfinane,** Eire	52 22N	8 29W
17	**Kilfinichen,** Scotland	56 23N	6 4W
17	**Kilfinon,** Scotland	55 57N	5 19W
19	**Kilgarvan,** Eire	51 54N	9 26W
53	**Kilimane,** Mozambique	18 0S	37 0E
55	**Kilimanjaro, Mt.,** E. Africa	3 4S	37 21E
55	**Kilimatinde,** Tang. Terr.	5 51S	35 0E
55	**Kilindini,** Kenya	4 4S	39 40E
32	**Kilindir,** Greece	41 10N	22 45E
19	**Kilkee,** Eire	52 41N	9 39W
18	**Kilkeel,** N. Ireland	54 4N	6 0W
19	**Kilkelly,** Eire	53 53N	8 51W
19	**Kilkenny, & co.,** Eire	52 39N	7 15W
14	**Kilkhampton,** England	50 52N	4 28W
47	**Kilkivan,** Queensland	26 0S	152 12E
19	**Killadysert,** Eire	52 41N	9 7W
18	**Killala,** Eire	54 13N	9 14W
19	**Killaloe,** Eire	52 48N	8 27W
47	**Killarney,** Queensland	28 23S	152 14E
19	**Killarney, & Lakes of,** Eire	52 4N	9 30W
19	**Killeagh,** Eire	51 57N	8 0W
17	**Killean,** Scotland	55 39N	5 40W
19	**Killenaule,** Eire	53 54N	7 40W
17	**Killiecrankie,** Scotland	56 44N	3 47W
19	**Killimor,** Eire	53 10N	8 17W
17	**Killin,** Scotland	56 28N	4 19W
19	**Killiney,** Eire	53 15N	6 7W
19	**Killorglin,** Eire	52 6N	9 47W
18	**Killybegs,** Eire	54 38N	8 27W
18	**Killylea,** N. Ireland	54 21N	6 47W
19	**Kilmacthomas,** Eire	52 13N	7 25W
18	**Kilmaine,** Eire	53 35N	9 7W
19	**Kilmallock,** Eire	52 24N	8 36W
17	**Kilmarnock,** Scotland	55 37N	4 37W
17	**Kilmelfort,** Scotland	56 16N	5 29W
19	**Kilmore,** Eire	52 12N	6 33W
47	**Kilmore,** Victoria	37 17N	144 58E
17	**Kilmory,** Scotland	55 55N	5 40W
16	**Kilmuir,** Scotland	57 26N	6 34W
18	**Kilnaleck,** Eire	53 52N	7 19W
17	**Kilninver,** Scotland	56 20N	5 30W
55	**Kilosa,** Tang. Terr.	6 49S	37 0E
18	**Kilrea,** N. Ireland	54 57N	6 33W
19	**Kilrush,** Eire	52 38N	9 30W
15	**Kilsby,** England	52 19N	1 11W
17	**Kilsyth,** Scotland	55 49N	4 4W
18	**Kiltimagh,** Eire	53 50N	9 0W
19	**Kiltormer,** Eire	10 14N	8 16W
19	**Kiltyclogher,** Eire	54 21N	8 2W
45	**Kilung,** Taiwan	25 5N	121 50E
55	**Kilwa,** Belgian Congo	9 18S	28 14E
55	**Kilwa,** Tanganyika Terr.	8 30S	38 30E
55	**Kilwa Kisiwani,** Tanganyika Territory	8 55S	39 36E
17	**Kilwinning,** Scotland	55 40N	4 42W
47	**Kimba,** S. Australia	33 0S	136 30E
57	**Kimberley,** U. of S. Afr.	28 45S	24 45E
15	**Kimbolton,** England	52 19N	0 25W
14	**Kimmeridge,** England	50 37N	2 7W
31	**Kimpulung,** Rumania	45 16N	25 5E
16	**Kincardine, & co.,** Scotland	56 4N	3 42W
43	**Kindat,** Burma	23 44N	94 29E
55	**Kindu,** Belgian Congo	2 55S	25 58E
36	**Kineshma,** U.S.S.R.	56 50N	42 20E
15	**Kineton,** England	52 10N	1 30W
61	**King Christian IX Ld.,** Greenland	67 30N	38 0W
68	**King Edward VII Ld.,** Antarctica	77 0S	150 0W
61	**King Frederick VI Coast,** Greenland	63 0N	43 0W
58	**King Frederick VIII Land,** Greenland	79 0N	26 0W
68	**King George V Ld.,** Antarctica	70 0S	140 0E
68	**King Leopold Ld.,** Antarctica	66 0S	85 0E
60	**King William I.,** Can.	69 0N	108 0W
58	**King William Ld.,** Greenland	75 15N	25 0W
57	**King Williams Town,** U. of S. Africa	32 55S	27 28E
47	**Kingaroy,** Queensland	26 30S	151 50E
45	**King-chow,** China	37 33N	116 13E
62	**Kingman,** U.S.A.	35 12N	114 2W
62	**Kingnan,** U.S.A.	35 10N	114 0W
47	**Kingoonya,** S. Austl.	31 58S	135 24E
15	**Kings Lynn,** England	52 56N	0 25E
17	**Kingsbarns,** Scotland	56 18N	2 40W
14	**Kingsbridge,** England	50 17N	3 47W
15	**Kingsclere,** England	51 19N	1 14W
47	**Kingscote,** S. Austral.	35 40S	137 40E
18	**Kingscourt,** Eire	53 54N	6 48W
61	**Kingston,** Canada	44 17N	76 32W
15	**Kingston,** England	51 25N	0 18W
65	**Kingston,** Jamaica	18 0N	76 52W
51	**Kingston,** New Zealand	45 20S	168 48E
47	**Kingston,** S. Australia	36 50S	139 50E
19	**Kingstown,** Eire	53 17N	6 9W
65	**Kingstown,** W. Indies	13 10N	61 12W
14	**Kington,** England	52 12N	3 0W
16	**Kingussie,** Scotland	57 5N	4 3W
44	**King-yang,** China	36 0N	107 40E
44	**King-yuan,** China	24 35N	108 5E
45	**Kin-hua,** China	29 8N	119 34E
51	**Kinloch,** New Zealand	45 20S	168 25E
17	**Kinloch,** Scotland	57 1N	6 17W
16	**Kinloch Bervie,** Scot.	58 27N	5 3W
17	**Kinloch Rannoch,** Scotland	57 42N	4 11W
16	**Kinlochewe,** Scotland	57 36N	5 17W
18	**Kinnegad,** Eire	53 28N	7 6W
17	**Kinross, & co.,** Scot.	56 12N	3 25W
19	**Kinsale,** Eire	51 42N	8 32W
54	**Kinshasha,** Belg. Congo	4 22S	15 20E
16	**Kintore,** Scotland	57 14N	2 21W
17	**Kintyre, & Mull of,** Scotland	55 35N	3 35W
19	**Kinvarra,** Eire	53 8N	8 57W
55	**Kioga, L.,** Uganda	1 30N	30 0E
18	**Kircubbin,** N. Ireland	54 29N	5 32W
39	**Kirensk,** U.S.S.R.	57 30N	108 0E
38	**Kirghiz rep.,** U.S.S.R.	41 0N	75 0E
37	**Kirghiz Steppes,** U.S.S.R.	49 30N	54 0E
45	**Kirin,** Manchuria	43 50N	126 40E
31	**Kirjali,** Bulgaria	41 38N	25 24E
32	**Kirk Agach,** Turkey	35 9N	27 42E
12	**Kirkby Lonsdale,** Eng.	54 14N	2 36W
13	**Kirkby Moorside,** Eng.	54 16N	0 56W
13	**Kirkby Stephen,** Eng.	54 27N	2 23W
17	**Kirkcaldy,** Scotland	57 7N	3 9W
17	**Kirkcowan,** Scotland	54 55N	4 35W
17	**Kirkcudbright & Co.,** Scotland	54 50N	4 3W
23	**Kirkeby,** Denmark	55 6N	8 33E
12	**Kirkham,** England	54 46N	2 52W
17	**Kirkintilloch,** Scotland	55 57N	4 8W
32	**Kirklareli,** Turkey	42 15N	27 30E
12	**Kirkmichael,** I. of Man	54 17N	4 35W
17	**Kirkmichael,** Scotland	55 21N	4 36W
12	**Kirkoswald,** England	54 46N	2 42W
17	**Kirkmichael,** Scotland	55 21N	4 36W
12	**Kirkoswald,** England	54 46N	2 42W
63	**Kirksville,** U.S.A.	40 12N	92 37W
16	**Kirkwall,** Orkney Is.	58 59N	2 57W
36	**Kirov,** U.S.S.R.	58 40N	49 33E
37	**Kirovabad,** U.S.S.R.	40 38N	46 26E
37	**Kirovograd,** U.S.S.R.	48 30N	32 8E
36	**Kirovsk,** U.S.S.R.	67 45N	33 35E
17	**Kirriemuir,** Scotland	56 41N	3 0W
37	**Kirsanov,** U.S.S.R.	52 42N	42 33E
40	**Kirsheher,** Turkey	39 3N	34 20r
13	**Kirton,** England	53 28N	0 36W
34	**Kiruna,** Sweden	67 50N	20 20E
55	**Kisengwa,** Belgian C.	5 59S	25 56E
40	**Kishin,** Arabia	15 30N	51 40E
31	**Kishinev,** Rumania	47 4N	28 41E
48	**Kiskal,** N. Amer.	52 0N	77 30E
30	**Kiskunfélegyháza,** Hungary	46 41N	19 50E
30	**Kiskunhalas,** Hungary	46 27N	19 32E
30	**Kiskunmajsa,** Hung.	46 30N	19 48E
37	**Kislyar,** U.S.S.R.	43 53N	46 41E
24	**Kissingen,** Germany	50 16N	10 0E
30	**Kisújszállas,** Hungary	47 14N	20 49E
55	**Kisumu,** Kenya	0 7S	34 46E
55	**Kisvere,** Tang. Terr.	9 26S	39 34E
55	**Kitale,** Kenya	1 0N	35 0E
32	**Kitta,** Greece	36 48N	22 25E
34	**Kittilä,** Finland	67 34N	25 0E
55	**Kitui,** Kenya	1 5S	37 50E
55	**Kitunda,** Tan. Terr.	8 25S	38 46E
24	**Kitzingen,** Germany	49 44N	10 10E
45	**Kiu-kiang,** China	29 44N	116 8E
45	**Kiung-chow,** China	32 35N	111 10E
45	**Kiushu, I.,** Japan	33 30N	131 0E
55	**Kivu, L.,** Belgian Congo	2 0S	29 5E
51	**Kiwi,** New Zealand	41 45S	172 40E
41	**Kizil Arvat,** U.S.S.R.	39 0N	56 15E
23	**Kjellerup,** Denmark	56 17N	9 32E
57	**Klaarstroom,** U. of S. Africa	33 18S	22 32E
24	**Kladno,** Czechoslovakia	50 10N	14 7E
31	**Kladovo,** Yugoslavia	44 38N	22 33E
24	**Klagenfurt,** Austria, Germany	46 37N	14 19E
35	**Klaipeda.** *See* **Memel.**		
24	**Klattau,** Czechoslovakia	49 23N	13 19E
24	**Klausthal,** Germany	51 48N	10 20E
57	**Klaver,** U. of S. Africa	31 40S	18 40E
57	**Klerksdorp,** U. of S. Africa	26 55S	26 40E
25	**Kleshcheli,** Poland	52 48N	23 20E
24	**Kleve,** Germany	51 48N	6 8E
36	**Klin,** U.S.S.R.	56 26N	36 34E
30	**Klina,** Yugoslavia	42 48N	20 44E
33	**Klingnau,** Switzerland	47 35N	8 15E
31	**Klinovo,** Yugoslavia	41 15N	21 55E
23	**Klinte,** Denmark	55 34N	10 13E
57	**Klipdam,** U. of S. Afr.	23 45S	29 31E
23	**Klitmöller,** Denmark	57 3N	8 31E
60	**Klondike, dist.,** Alaska	60 40N	138 0W
24	**Klosterneuburg,** Austria, Germany	48 19N	16 21E
33	**Klosters,** Switzerland	46 53N	9 54E
23	**Klütz,** Germany	53 58N	11 9E
17	**Knapdale,** Scotland	55 53N	5 32W
13	**Knaresborough,** Eng.	54 0N	1 27W
34	**Kniashaia,** U.S.S.R.	66 52N	32 30E
31	**Kniazhevatz,** Yugosl.	43 33N	22 17E
14	**Knighton,** Wales	52 21N	3 2W
19	**Knights Town,** Eire	51 56N	10 17W
24	**Knittelfeld** Austria, Germany	47 13N	14 49E
19	**Knockmealdown Mts.,** Eire	52 15N	7 57W
19	**Knocktopher,** Eire	52 29N	7 14W
12	**Knott End,** England	53 55N	3 0W
15	**Knowle,** England	52 24N	1 45W
68	**Knox Land,** Antarctica	65 0S	105 0E
63	**Knoxville,** U.S.A.	35 59N	84 0W
13	**Knutsford,** England	53 18N	2 22W
25	**Knyshin,** Poland	53 20N	22 52W
57	**Knysna,** U. of S. Africa	34 0S	23 5E

MAP			
44	Kobdo, Mongolia	48 5N	91 35E
45	Kobe. See Hiogo.		
37	Kobelyaki, U.S.S.R.	49 9N	34 4E
23	Kobenhavn, Denmark	53 43N	12 38E
25	Kobrin, Poland	52 14N	24 24E
31	Kochana, Yugoslavia	41 55N	22 50E
49	Kodiak I., N. Amer.	57 30N	153 20W
55	Kodok, A.-E. Sudan	9 54N	32 7E
24	Koesfeld, Germany	51 58N	7 10E
22	Koevorden, Netherlands	52 40N	6 44E
57	Koffiefontein, U. of S. Africa	29 20S	25 1E
45	Kofu, Japan	35 30N	139 0E
42	Kohat, India	33 38N	71 28E
43	Kohima, India	25 40N	94 5E
31	Koinare, Bulgaria	43 20N	24 10E
46	Kojanup, W. Australia	34 45S	117 15E
35	Kokemäen, Finland	61 20N	22 10E
34	Kokkola, Finland	63 50N	23 10E
44	Koko Nor, China	37N	100E
57	Kokstad, U. of S. Afr.	30 32S	29 30E
25	Kola, Poland	52 11N	18 38E
36	Kola & Pen., U.S.S.R.	69 0N	33 0E
41	Kolab, U.S.S.R.	37 50N	69 48E
42	Kolar, India	13 8N	78 10E
30	Kolashin, Yugoslavia	42 52N	19 34E
24	Kolberg, Germany	54 10N	15 35E
23	Kolby, Denmark	55 48N	10 33E
23	Kolding, Denmark	55 30N	9 30E
24	Kolin, Czechoslovakia	50 1N	15 10E
23	Kolind, Denmark	56 22N	10 34E
25	Kolki, Poland	51 5N	25 42E
22	Kollum, Netherlands	53 16N	16 8E
24	Köln. See Cologne.		
36	Kolomna, U.S.S.R.	55 5N	38 38E
25	Kolomyja, Poland	48 45N	25 5E
31	Kolozsvar. See Cluj.		
25	Komárno, Czechoslov.	47 45N	18 3E
36	Komi rep., U.S.S.R.	59 70N	46 66E
24	Komotau, Czechoslov.	50 29N	13 30E
29	Kompakovo, U.S.S.R.	54 0N	156 0E
31	Komrat, Rumania	46 18N	28 41E
52	Konakri, Fr. W. Africa	9 30N	13 46W
46	Kondinin, W. Austl.	32 25S	118 8E
55	Kondoa Irangi, Tang. T.	4 55S	35 58E
25	Konetspol, Poland	50 48N	19 42E
45	Kongmun, China	22 45N	113 0E
55	Kongolo, Belgian Congo	5 20N	27 0E
35	Kongsberg, Norway	59 40N	9 30E
35	Kongsvinger, Norway	60 50N	12 4E
24	Königgrätz, Czechoslov.	50 14N	15 15E
25	Königsberg, Germany	54 42N	20 32E
25	Konin, Poland	52 10N	18 16E
25	Konitz, Poland	53 40N	17 38E
32	Konitza, Greece	40 5N	28 46E
30	Konjica, Yugoslavia	43 43N	18 0E
25	Konsk, Poland	51 12N	20 24E
39	Konstantinov, U.S.S.R.	64 35N	169 0E
37	Konstantinovsk, U.S.S.R.	47 33N	41 0E
25	Konstantynov, Poland	52 15N	23 0E
40	Konya, Turkey	37 50N	32 30E
46	Kookynie, W. Austl.	29 25S	121 25E
47	Koondrook, N.S.W.	25 38S	144 7E
47	Koonenberry, N.S.W.	30 25S	142 15E
47	Kooringa, S. Australia	33 37S	138 54E
47	Koorowatha, N.S.W.	34 1S	148 31E
38	Kopal, U.S.S.R.	45 20N	79 0E
24	Köpenick, Germany	52 28N	13 32E
35	Köping, Sweden	59 30N	16 0E
35	Koppang, Norway	61 32N	11 0E
35	Kopparberg, Co., Sweden	59 55N	15 0E
30	Koprivnica, Yugoslavia	46 12N	16 49E
31	Koprivshtitza, Bulg.	42 39N	24 21E
31	Köprülü, Yugoslavia	41 40W	21 49E
43	Korat, Siam	14 58N	102 6E
55	Kordofan, A.-E. Sudan	13 30W	30 0E
45	Korea, Japan	36 30N	127 0E
45	Korea B., Korea	39 0N	124 0E
45	Korea Str., Korea	34 15N	129 30E
30	Koritza, Albania	40 38N	20 48E
31	Koroneshty, Rumania	47 21N	28 2E
47	Korong Vale, Victoria	36 25N	143 38E
32	Koroni, Greece	36 49N	21 58E
40	Korosko, Egypt	22 19N	32 19E
25	Körösmezö (Jasina) Czechoslovakia	48 15N	24 20E
45	Korsakovsk, Japan	46 42N	142 47E
23	Korsör, Denmark	55 19N	11 8E
47	Korumburra, Victoria	38 25S	145 49E
32	Kos Tn. and I., Aegean Sea	36 53N	27 20E
47	Kosciusko Mt., N.S.W.	36 20S	148 10E
25	Košice, Czechoslovakia	48 41N	21 19E
24	Köslin, Germany	54 10N	16 10E
36	Kosmodemyansk, U.S.S.R.	56 24N	46 28E
40	Kosseir, Egypt	26 8N	34 18E
30	Kostajnica, Yugoslavia	45 18N	16 32E
25	Kosten, Poland	52 5N	16 35E
55	Kosti, A.-E. Sudan	13 11N	32 38E
36	Kostroma, U.S.S.R.	57 48N	40 56E
55	Kota Kota, Nyasaland	12 56S	34 15E
39	Kota Raja, Dut. E. Ind.	5 30S	95 15E
42	Kotah, India	25 14N	75 59E
24	Köthen, Germany	51 46N	11 59E
35	Kotka, Finland	60 28N	27 2E
36	Kotlas, U.S.S.R.	61 9N	46 35E
30	Kotor, Yugoslavia	42 23N	18 46E
42	Kotri, India	25 22N	68 22E
24	Kottbus, Germany	51 45N	14 20E
35	Kouvola, Finland	60 55N	26 42E
32	Kovchas, Turkey	41 58N	27 12E
34	Kovda, U.S.S.R.	66 45N	32 30E
35	Kovno, Lithuania	54 52N	23 55E
36	Kovrov, U.S.S.R.	56 26N	41 15E
25	Kowel, Poland	51 13N	24 41E
45	Kowloon, China	22 30N	114 0E
32	Kozhani, Greece	40 20N	21 48E
32	Kozkeui, Turkey	41 0N	26 38E
31	Kozluja, Bulgaria	43 19N	27 30E
43	Kra, & Isth. of, Siam	10 25N	98 46E
35	Kragero, Norway	58 55N	9 20E
30	Kragujevac, Yugoslavia	44 1N	20 52E
30	Krainburg, Yugoslavia	46 15N	14 25E
25	Krakow. See Cracow		
30	Kralyevo, Yugoslavia	48 40N	20 40E
32	Krania, Greece	39 52N	21 18E
32	Kranidion, Greece	37 20N	23 10E
35	Kraslavka, Latvia	55 50N	27 10E
25	Krasnik, Poland	50 55N	22 12E
37	Krasniyar, U.S.S.R.	46 26N	48 27E
36	Krasno Ufimsk, U.S.S.R.	56 39N	57 35E
37	Krasnoarmeisk, U.S.S.R.	44 25N	34 10E
37	Krasnodar, U.S.S.R.	45 2N	38 56E
39	Krasnoe, U.S.S.R.	67 20N	121 0E
41	Krasnovodsk, U.S.S.R.	43 0N	53 0E
39	Krasnoyarsk, U.S.S.R.	56 8N	93 0E
24	Krefeld, Germany	51 20N	6 34E
37	Kremenchug, U.S.S.R.	49 11N	33 26E
25	Kremenets, Poland	50 5N	25 43E
37	Kremenskaya, U.S.S.R.	49 20N	43 20E
25	Kremnica, Cz.-slov.	48 40N	18 52E
24	Krems, Aus., Germany	48 25N	15 36E
25	Kremsier, Cz.-slov.	49 18N	17 20E
35	Kreutsburg, Latvia	56 32N	26 0E
24	Kreuz, Germany	52 53N	16 2E
25	Kreuzburg, Germany	51 0N	18 14E
33	Kreuzlingen, Switz.	47 38N	9 11E
24	Kreuznach, Germany	49 51N	7 52E
54	Kribi, Cameroons	2 55N	9 58E
33	Kriens, Switzerland	47 2N	8 17E
30	Krin, Yugoslavia	44 2N	16 11E
35	Kristiansand, Norway	58 0N	7 55E
35	Kristianstad, & co., Sweden	56 5N	14 10E
34	Kristiansund, Norway	63 10N	7 45E
34	Kristiina, Finland	62 17N	21 28E
35	Kristinehamn, Sweden	59 20N	14 10E
30	Križevci, Yugoslavia	46 1N	16 18E
44	Kroitskasavsk, U.S.S.R.	50 30N	106 10E
37	Krolevets, U.S.S.R.	51 30N	33 15E
35	Kronoberg, co., Swed.	56 45N	14 20E
35	Kronoborg, Finland	61 20N	30 0E
35	Kronstadt, U.S.S.R.	60 0N	29 45E
57	Kroonstad, U. of S. Afr.	27 46S	27 23E
25	Krotoschin, Poland	51 41N	17 20E
30	Kroya, Albania	41 35N	19 47E
57	Krugersdorp, U. of S. Africa	26 10S	27 47E
30	Krusevac, Yugoslavia	43 30N	21 20E
30	Krusha, Yugoslavia	42 19N	20 40E
30	Krushevo, Yugoslavia	41 21N	21 19E
57	Kub, S. W. Africa	24 26S	17 50E
37	Kuba, U.S.S.R.	41 22N	48 28E
41	Kubatieh, Palestine	32 23N	35 16E
25	Kubin, Czechoslovakia	49 13N	19 19E
44	Kucha, Sinkiang	41 30N	83 40E
41	Kuchan, Iran	37 0N	58 0E
39	Kuching, Borneo	1 35N	110 25E
32	Kuchuk Chekmeje, Turkey	41 0N	28 59E
52	Kufra Oasis, Libya	25 30N	23 0E
24	Kufstein, Aus., Ger.	47 35N	12 11E
34	Kuhmoniemi, Finland	64 10N	29 50E
37	Kuibishev, U.S.S.R.	53 14N	50 4E
22	Kuinre, Netherlands	52 47N	5 52E
34	Kuivaniemi, Finland	65 30N	25 18E
32	Kukush, Greece	40 59N	22 58E
31	Kula, Bulgaria	43 50N	22 32E
32	Kula, Turkey	38 34N	28 35E
43	Kuladan, Burma	21 4N	93 0E
40	Kulanjin, Iran	35 45N	49 30E
44	Kulja, Sinkiang	43 40N	81 0E
25	Kulm, Poland	53 20N	18 30E
33	Kulm, Switzerland	47 18N	8 6E
24	Kulmbach, Germany	50 8N	11 28E
25	Kulm Sea, Poland	53 10N	18 40E
40	Kum, Iran	34 38N	50 56E
32	Kum Kalessi, Turkey	40 0N	26 12E
45	Kumamoto, Japan	32 48N	130 53E
31	Kumanovo, Yugoslavia	42 8N	21 42E
51	Kumara, New Zealand	42 39S	171 10E
52	Kumasi, Gold Coast	6 50N	2 16W
42	Kumbakonam, India	11 0N	79 25E
40	Kumishah, Iran	32 1N	51 50E
42	Kumpta, India	14 26N	74 27E
39	Kumursk, U.S.S.R.	51 20N	127 20E
41	Kunar, Afghanistan	34 36N	70 48E
35	Kunda, Estonia	59 28N	23 34E
41	Kunduz, Afghanistan	36 50N	69 0E
40	Kunfuda, Arabia	19 12N	41 5E
44	Kung-chang, China	35 0N	104 35E
41	Kungrad, U.S.S.R.	42 58N	58 50E
35	Kungsbacka, Sweden	57 28N	12 5E
36	Kungur, U.S.S.R.	57 27N	56 51E
43	Kunlong, Burma	23 23N	98 40E
44	Kunming, China	25 3N	102 40E
24	Kunzelsau, Germany	49 17N	9 42E
34	Kuolajärvi, Finland	66 44N	29 20E
34	Kuopio, Finland	62 58N	27 38E
37	Kupyansk, U.S.S.R.	49 40N	37 31E
40	Kurdistan, dist., Asia	38 0N	42 0E
35	Kuressaar. See Arensburg		
41	Kuria Muria, Is., Arab.	17 43N	56 10E
34	Kurikka, Finland	62 53N	22 0E
39	Kurile, Is., Japan	47 0N	152 0E
44	Kurla, Sinkiang	41 35N	86 30E
35	Kurland, dist., Latvia	56 30N	24 0E
55	Kurmuk, A.-E. Sudan	10 30N	34 7E
40	Kurna, Iraq	25 45N	32 39E
51	Kurow, New Zealand	44 44S	170 28E
35	Kurshani, Lithuania	56 2N	22 57E
30	Kurshumlie, Y.-slavia	43 8N	21 18E
37	Kursk, U.S.S.R.	51 47N	36 33E
31	Kurtea Arjesh, Rum.	45 8N	24 45E
45	Kushiro, Japan	43 0N	144 6E
41	Kushk, U.S.S.R.	35 25N	62 23E
33	Küsnacht, Switzerland	47 18N	8 34E
44	Kusnetsk, U.S.S.R.	54 0N	87 0E
33	Küssnacht, Switzerland	47 5N	8 26E
38	Kustanai, U.S.S.R.	52 58N	64 0E
31	Küstendil, Bulgaria	42 15N	22 41E
24	Küstrin, Germany	52 34N	14 38E
40	Kutahia, Turkey	39 28N	30 1E
37	Kutais, U.S.S.R.	42 15N	42 33E
40	Kut el Hai, Iraq	32 15N	46 0E
40	Kut-el-Amara, Iraq	32 40N	46 0E
25	Kutno, Poland	52 13N	19 21E
25	Kuty, Poland	48 18N	25 9E
34	Kuusamo, Finland	65 5N	29 5E
40	Kuwait, & st., Arabia	29 30N	48 2E
37	Kuznetsk, U.S.S.R.	53 10N	46 31E
34	Kvalöy Kistrand, Nor.	70 25N	25 30E
23	Kverndrup, Denmark	55 10N	10 31E
34	Kvikjokk, Sweden	66 58N	17 48E
45	Kwang-chow, China	32 15N	115 10E
44	Kwang-nan, China	24 10N	105 0E
45	Kwang-ping, China	37 0N	115 0E
44	Kwangsi, prov., China	24 0N	109 0E
45	Kwang-sin, China	28 20N	118 0E
45	Kwang-tung, prov., China	21 0N	112 0E
44	Kweichow, China	31 0N	110 44E
44	Kwei-chow, prov., Ch.	30 58N	111 0E
45	Kwei-hwa Cheng, Ch.	41 0N	111 40E
44	Kwei-lin, China	25 0N	110 0E
45	Kwei-te, China	34 30N	116 0E
44	Kwei-yang, China	26 30N	107 45E
44	Kwen Lun, Mts., Sink.	36 0N	80 0E
43	Kyankin, Burma	18 19N	95 17E
43	Kyaukpyu, Burma	19 20N	93 38E
43	Kyaukse, Burma	21 35N	96 6E
16	Kyleakin, Scotland	57 16N	54 4W
16	Kylerhea, Scotland	57 14N	5 40W
17	Kyles of Bute, Scot.	55 55N	5 10W
32	Kymi, Greece	38 38N	24 10E
49	Kyneton, Victoria	37 15S	144 28E
47	Kyogle, N.S.W.	28 31S	153 0E
45	Kyoto, Japan	34 57N	135 56E
32	Kyparissia, Greece	37 14N	21 40E
34	Kyro, Finland	68 46N	27 50E
35	Kyrola, Finland	60 37N	29 30E
36	Kyshtymski, U.S.S.R.	55 39N	60 35E
32	Kythera. See Cerigo I.		
26	La Bañeza, Spain	42 15N	5 56W
28	La Bochetta, P., Italy	44 30N	8 40E
52	La Calle, Algeria	36 50N	7 50E
26	La Carolina, Spain	38 17N	3 36W
65	La Ceiba, Venezuela	9 28N	70 48W
33	La Chaux des Fonds, Switzerland	47 5N	6 50E
66	La Chorrera, Colombia	0 40S	73 0W
21	La Ciotat, France	43 12N	5 38E
26	La Coruña, Spain	43 20N	8 25W
63	La Crosse, U.S.A.	42 47N	91 6W
20	La Fère, France	49 39N	3 24E
26	La Fregeneda, Spain	41 0N	6 53W
21	La Grande Combe, Fr.	44 14N	4 2E
62	La Grande, U.S.A.	45 17N	117 58W
63	La Grange, U.S.A.	33 0N	85 1W
66	La Guaira, Venezuela	10 43N	66 59W
62	La Junta, U.S.A.	38 0N	103 27W
26	La Linea, Spain	36 10N	5 24W
66	La Mana, Fr. Guiana	5 50N	53 55W
21	La Mothe, France	44 36N	1 0W
21	La Nouvelle, France	43 0N	3 1E
26	La Palma, Spain	37 22N	6 37W
67	La Paz, Bolivia	16 10S	68 15W
64	La Paz, Mexico	24 8N	110 23W

MAP			
45	**La Perouse Sd.**, Japan	45 40N	142 0E
67	**La Plata**, Argentina	34 55S	58 0W
31	**La Pont**, Rumania	45 25N	26 20E
27	**La Puebla**, Majorca I.	39 50N	3 4E
26	**La Puebla**, Spain	39 50N	4 21W
67	**La Quiaca**, Argentina	22 15S	65 50W
21	**La Réole**, France	44 36N	0 3W
26	**La Robla**, Spain	42 50N	5 40W
21	**La Roche sur Yon**, Fr.	46 40N	1 28W
21	**La Rochelle**, France	46 11N	1 11W
27	**La Roda**, Spain	38 12N	2 11W
33	**La Sarraz**, Switz.	46 40N	6 32E
67	**La Serena**, Chile	29 50S	71 20W
21	**La Seyne**, France	43 4N	5 53E
21	**La Solenzara**, Corsica	41 52N	9 25E
64	**La Union**, Salvador	13 8N	87 52W
27	**La Union**, Spain	37 37N	0 52W
23	**Laasby**, Denmark	56 10N	9 48E
64	**Laboah**, Mexico	21 20N	87 30W
25	**Labiau**, Germany	54 52N	21 8E
37	**Labinskaya**, U.S.S.R.	44 40N	40 45E
21	**Labouheyre**, France	44 12N	0 53W
61	**Labrador**, Newf.	56 0N	61 0W
39	**Labuan I.**, Br.N.Borneo	5 20N	115 15E
21	**Lacaune**, France	43 42N	2 40E
38	**Laccadive Is.**, India	11 0N	73 0E
47	**Lachlan, R.**, N.S.W.	33 45S	144 50E
42	**Ladakh, dist.**, India	34 0N	77 15E
57	**Ladismith**, U. of S. Af.	33 32S	21 20E
36	**Ladoga, L.**, U.S.S.R.	61 0N	31 30E
7	**Ladrone Is.**, Pacific Oc.	17 0N	145 50E
57	**Lady Grey**, U. of S. Af.	30 52S	27 24E
17	**Ladybank**, Scotland	56 17N	3 7W
57	**Ladybrand**, U. of S. Af.	29 10S	27 31E
57	**Ladysmith**, U. of S. Af.	28 33S	29 40E
22	**Laeken**, Belgium	50 53N	4 21E
63	**Lafayette**, U.S.A.	40 24N	86 58W
54	**Lafia**, Nigeria	8 30N	8 30E
18	**Lagan, R.**, N. Ireland	55 43N	6 15W
26	**Lagoa**, Portugal	37 7N	8 29W
17	**Lagg**, Scotland	55 57N	5 50W
52	**Laghuat**, Algeria	33 48N	2 53E
29	**Lagonegro**, Italy	40 10N	15 47E
54	**Lagos**, Nigeria	6 27N	3 25E
26	**Lagos**, Portugal	37 5N	8 40W
28	**Lagosta, I.**, Italy	42 47N	16 52E
27	**Laguardia**, Spain	42 32N	2 35W
67	**Laguna**, Brazil	28 15S	48 40W
35	**Laholm**, Sweden	56 30N	13 0E
42	**Lahore**, India	31 31N	74 22E
24	**Lahr**, Germany	48 22N	7 50E
35	**Lahti**, Finland	61 3N	25 42E
54	**Lai**, Fr. Eq. Africa	9 12N	16 18E
30	**Laibach**, Yugoslavia	46 2N	14 33E
45	**Lai-chow**, China	37 5N	119 55E
20	**Laigle**, France	48 46N	0 38E
30	**Laikovatz**, Yugoslavia	44 24N	20 10E
40	**Laila**, Arabia	22 21N	47 0E
57	**Laings Nek**, U. of S. Africa	27 33S	30 0E
57	**Laingsburg**, U. of S. Africa	33 8S	20 56E
16	**Lairg**, Scotland	58 2N	4 24W
63	**Lake Charles**, U.S.A.	30 15N	93 10W
63	**Lake City**, U.S.A.	30 12N	82 37W
46	**Lake Grace**, W. Aust.	33 10S	118 30E
60	**Lake Louise**, Canada	51 20N	116 10W
51	**Lakemba Is.**, Fiji Is Inset	19 0S	179 0W
60	**Laketon**, Canada	58 40N	130 5W
43	**Lakhimpur**, India	27 12N	94 0E
43	**Lakon**, Siam	17 30N	99 30E
42	**Lalitpur**, India	24 30N	78 30E
18	**Lambay I.**, Eire	53 30N	6 0W
66	**Lambayeque**, Peru	6 40S	79 55E
15	**Lambourn**, England	51 31N	1 31W
54	**Lame**, Fr. Eq. Africa	9 12N	14 38E
32	**Lamia**, Greece	38 55N	22 29E
26	**Lamego**, Portugal	41 6N	7 52W
17	**Lamlash**, Scotland	55 32N	5 8W
17	**Lammermuir Hills**, Scotland	55 52N	2 40W
29	**Lampedusa I.**, Medit. Sea	36 32N	12 30E
14	**Lampeter**, Wales	52 7N	4 4W
55	**Lamu**, Kenya	2 20S	40 40E
17	**Lanark**, Scotland	55 44N	3 47W
17	**Lanark, co.**, Scotland	55 41N	3 47W
12	**Lancashire, co.**, Eng.	54 40N	2 30W
12	**Lancaster**, England	54 3N	2 48W
61	**Lancaster Sd.**, Canada	45 8N	74 31W
44	**Lan-chow**, China	36 0N	103 30E
28	**Lanciano**, Italy	42 17N	14 22E
54	**Landana**, Belg. Congo	5 18S	12 6E
24	**Landau**, Germany	49 12N	8 7E
24	**Landeck**, Aust., Ger.	47 8N	10 37E
22	**Landen**, Belgium	50 46N	5 4E
62	**Lander**, U.S.A.	42 52N	108 40W
20	**Landerneau**, France	48 27N	4 16W
21	**Landes, dept.**, France	44 2N	0 50W
15	**Land's End**, Eng. Inset	50 4N	4 42W
24	**Landsberg**, Germany	52 42N	15 12E
24	**Landsberg**, Germany	48 4N	10 55E
24	**Landshut**, Germany	48 34N	12 10E
35	**Landskrona**, Sweden	55 55N	12 55E
18	**Lanesborough**, Eire	53 41N	7 59W
23	**Langaa**, Denmark	55 12N	10 43E
23	**Langaa**, Denmark	56 23N	9 59E
32	**Langadia**, Greece	37 41N	22 2E
32	**Langaza**, Greece	40 46N	23 8E
57	**Lange Berge**, U. of S. Africa	28 30S	22 30E
21	**Langeac**, France	45 6N	3 30E
23	**Langeland, I.**, Den.	55 0N	10 50E
23	**Langeland Belt.**, Den.	55 0N	11 0E
24	**Langensalza**, Germany	51 7N	10 38E
33	**Langenthal**, Switzerland	47 13N	7 47E
35	**Langesund**, Norway	58 58N	9 40E
17	**Langholm**, Scotland	55 9N	3 2W
33	**Langnau**, Switzerland	46 56N	7 46E
21	**Langon**, France	44 33N	0 15W
21	**Langogne**, France	44 33N	3 52E
14	**Langport**, England	51 3N	2 49W
20	**Langres**, France	47 52N	5 21E
44	**Lang-son**, China	21 55N	106 40E
13	**Langtoft**, England	54 5N	0 26W
21	**Languedoc**, France	43 50N	3 40E
20	**Lannion**, France	48 44N	3 27W
63	**Lansing**, U.S.A.	42 45N	84 30W
52	**Lanzarote I.**, Can. Is.	29 0N	13 40W
28	**Lanzo**, Italy	33 18N	7 38E
39	**Laoag**, Philippine Is.	18 5N	120 35E
19	**Laoighis**, Eire	52 58N	7 25W
39	**Laokai**, Fr. Indo-China	22 30N	103 52E
20	**Laon**, France	49 33N	3 37E
14	**Lapford**, England	50 52N	3 49W
25	**Lapi**, Poland	53 0N	22 40E
34	**Lapinlahti**, Finland	63 25N	27 38E
34	**Lapland, terr.**, Scand.	68 0N	26 0E
34	**Lappajärva**, Finland	63 20N	23 38E
34	**Lappi**, Finland	64 31N	25 4E
34	**Lappo**, Finland	62 59N	23 0E
32	**Lapsaki**, Turkey	40 20N	26 44E
32	**Lapsista**, Greece	40 18N	21 28E
41	**Lar**, Iran	27 34N	54 18E
19	**Laragh**, Eire	53 1N	6 18W
62	**Laramie**, U.S.A.	41 15N	105 43E
62	**Laredo**, U.S.A.	27 40N	99 30W
17	**Largo**, Scotland	56 13N	2 55W
17	**Largs**, Scotland	55 48N	4 51W
28	**Larino**, Italy	41 50N	14 57E
32	**Larissa**, Greece	39 39N	22 28E
17	**Larkhall**, Scotland	55 45N	3 59W
40	**Larnaka**, Cyprus	34 58N	33 40E
18	**Larne**, N. Ireland	54 52N	5 50W
22	**Laroche**, Belgium	50 10N	5 33E
23	**Larrenlin**, Germany	53 34N	10 53E
21	**Laruns**, France	42 59N	0 26W
35	**Larvik**, Norway	59 10N	10 0E
62	**Las Cruces**, U.S.A.	32 53N	106 50W
52	**Las Gori**, Br. Somal.	11 5N	48 5E
64	**Las Tres Marias, Is.**, Mexico	21 30N	106 30W
62	**Las Vegas**, U.S.A.	35 37N	105 12W
41	**Lasgird**, Iran	35 28N	53 1E
41	**Lash**, Afghanistan	31 48N	61 31E
43	**Lashio**, Burma	22 57N	97 47E
42	**Lashkar**, India	26 10N	78 13E
66	**Latacunga**, Ecuador	1 0S	79 45W
40	**Latakia**, Syria	35 31N	35 50E
35	**Latgale, dist.**, Latvia	56 30N	27 30E
16	**Latheron**, Scotland	58 17N	3 31W
28	**Latium, dept.**, Italy	42 2N	12 30E
47	**Latrobe**, Tasmania	40 22N	79 20W
42	**Latur**, India	18 20N	75 35E
35	**Latvia, rep.**, Europe	59 0N	26 0E
24	**Lauban**, Germany	51 8N	15 15E
24	**Lauda**, Germany	49 35N	9 40E
17	**Lauder**, Scotland	55 43N	2 46W
24	**Lauenburg**, Germany	53 25N	10 42E
25	**Lauenburg, Pom.**, Ger.	52 25N	10 42E
33	**Laufen**, Switzerland	47 27N	7 29E
14	**Launceston**, England	50 38N	4 21W
47	**Launceston**, Tasmania	41 20S	147 2E
33	**Laupen**, Switzerland	46 54N	7 15E
47	**Laura**, Queensland	15 45S	144 30E
48	**Laura**, S. Australia	33 3S	138 25E
35	**Laurdal**, Norway	59 29N	8 20E
16	**Laurencekirk**, Scot.	56 50N	2 27W
19	**Laurencetown**, Eire	53 12N	8 15W
29	**Lauria**, Italy	40 5N	15 51E
32	**Laurium**, Greece	37 40N	24 2E
33	**Lausanne**, Switz.	46 32N	6 37E
24	**Lausitz Geb.**, Cz.-slov.	50 40N	15 0E
33	**Lauterbrunnen**, Switz.	46 35N	7 53E
28	**Laveno**, Italy	45 56N	8 41E
20	**Laval**, France	48 46N	69 5W
21	**Lavaur**, France	43 42N	1 48E
46	**Laverton**, W. Australia	28 37S	122 28E
26	**Lavos**, Portugal	40 5N	8 50W
23	**Lavrbjerg**, Denmark	56 23N	9 54E
51	**Lawrence**, N. Zealand	45 55S	169 41E
63	**Lawrence, Kan.**, U.S.A.	39 0N	95 14W
63	**Lawrence, Mass.**, U.S.A.	42 48N	71 5W
34	**Laxelv**, Norway	69 55N	24 59E
12	**Laxey**, I. of Man	54 13N	4 24W
15	**Laxfield**, England	52 18N	1 22E
21	**Le Blanc**, France	46 38N	1 4E
33	**Le Brassus**, Switz.	46 36N	6 12E
20	**Le Cateau**, France	50 7N	3 17E
21	**Le Chateau**, France	45 52N	1 15W
21	**Le Creuzot**, France	46 48N	4 23E
20	**Le Croisic**, France	40 17N	2 32W
21	**Le Dorat**, France	46 13N	1 4E
20	**Le Havre**, France	49 30N	0 7E
33	**Le Locle**, Switzerland	47 3N	6 43E
67	**Le Maire Str.**, Argen.	54 40S	65 0W
20	**Le Mans**, France	48 1N	0 9E
20	**Le Palais**, France	47 20N	3 10W
21	**Le Puy**, France	45 1N	3 50E
20	**Le Touquet**, France	50 32N	1 35E
21	**Le Verdon**, France	45 33N	1 3W
62	**Lead**, U.S.A.	44 29N	104 10W
17	**Leadburn**, Scotland	55 47N	3 12W
17	**Leadhills**, Scotland	55 25N	3 45W
62	**Leadville**, U.S.A.	39 17N	106 23W
15	**Leamington**, England	52 17N	1 32W
15	**Leatherhead**, England	51 18N	0 20W
63	**Leavenworth**, U.S.A.	39 23N	95 59W
25	**Leba**, Germany	54 46N	17 40E
63	**Lebanon, Tenn.**, U.S.A.	36 8N	86 45W
69	**Lebanon**, U.S.A.	37 26N	92 32W
40	**Lebanon, mts.**, Syria	34 0N	26 30E
52	**Lebda**, Libya	32 30N	14 30E
34	**Lebesby**, Norway	70 30N	27 0E
26	**Lebrija**, Spain	36 55N	6 5W
67	**Lebu**, Chile	37 30S	73 50W
29	**Lecce**, Italy	40 22N	18 7E
28	**Lecco**, Italy	45 52N	9 29E
14	**Lechlade**, England	51 42N	1 42W
23	**Leck**, Germany	54 42N	8 59E
21	**Lectoure**, France	43 56N	0 37E
14	**Ledbury**, England	52 3N	2 25W
26	**Ledesma**, Spain	41 5N	5 59W
19	**Lee, R.**, Eire	51 50N	9 17W
13	**Leeds**, England	53 48N	1 33W
13	**Leek**, England	53 7N	2 3W
24	**Leer**, Germany	55 15N	7 25E
22	**Leeuwarden**, Neth.	53 12N	5 49E
46	**Leeuwin, C.**, W. Austl.	34 16S	115 12E
65	**Leeward Is.**, W. Indies	16 30N	63 30W
28	**Leghorn**, Italy	43 33N	10 20E
28	**Legnago, Verona**, Italy	45 13N	11 10E
28	**Legnano, Lombardy,** Italy	45 38N	8 58E
24	**Lehe**, Germany	53 35N	8 35E
62	**Lehi**, U.S.A.	40 25N	111 55W
24	**Lehrte**, Germany	52 21N	10 0E
23	**Lehsen**, Germany	53 28N	11 2E
57	**Lehutitang**, Bechuanaland	23 25S	22 0E
45	**Lei-chow**, China	20 55N	110 0E
15	**Leicester, & Co.**, Eng.	52 39N	1 8W
22	**Leiden**, Netherlands	52 9N	4 29E
12	**Leigh**, England	53 29N	2 32W
19	**Leighlinbridge**, Eire	52 44N	6 58W
15	**Leighton Buzzard,** England	51 55N	0 40W
19	**Leinster, mt.**, Eire	52 28N	6 45W
19	**Leinster, prov.,** Ireland	53 0N	7 0W
24	**Leipzig**, Germany	51 20N	12 20E
26	**Leiria**, Portugal	39 45N	8 52W
15	**Leiston**, England	52 13N	1 33E
17	**Leith**, Scotland	55 58N	3 10W
15	**Leith Hill**, England	51 11N	0 24W
24	**Leitmeritz**, Cz.-slov.	50 32N	14 14E
18	**Leitrim, & Co.**, Eire	54 0N	8 4W
18	**Leix, co.**, Eire. *See* Laoighis		
19	**Leixlip**, Eire	53 22N	6 30W
26	**Leixoes**, Portugal	41 10N	8 42W
34	**Leka**, Norway	65 5N	11 20E
35	**Leksand**, Sweden	60 42N	15 2E
57	**Leliefontein**, U. of S. Africa	30 18S	18 8E
25	**Lemberg.** *See* Lwow		
32	**Lemnos I.**, Greece	39 59N	25 10E
23	**Lemvig**, Denmark	56 34N	8 18E
26	**Lena**, Spain	43 10N	5 52W
39	**Lena, R.**, U.S.S.R.	65 0N	12 0E
15	**Lenham**, England	51 14N	0 44E
37	**Leninakan**, U.S.S.R.	40 40N	43 50E
36	**Leningrad**, U.S.S.R.	60 0N	30 20E
37	**Leninsk**, U.S.S.R.	39 2N	63 0E
33	**Lenk**, Switzerland	46 28N	7 26E
17	**Lennox Hills**, Scotland	56 4N	4 10W
17	**Lennoxtown**, Scotland	55 58N	4 12W
20	**Lens**, France	50 26N	2 52E
29	**Lentini**, Sicily	37 18N	15 0E
34	**Lenura**, Finland	64 24N	30 0E
33	**Lenzburg**, Switzerland	47 24N	8 9E
14	**Leominster**, England	52 14N	2 42W
64	**Leon**, Mexico	21 1N	101 45W
64	**Leon**, Nicaragua	12 26N	86 45W
26	**Léon, prov.**, Spain	42 0N	6 0W
26	**Léon**, Spain	42 38N	5 32W
32	**Leonidion**, Greece	37 10N	22 53E
46	**Leonora**, W. Australia	28 50S	121 28E
54	**Leopold II L.**, Belgian Congo	2 0S	18 25E
66	**Leopoldina**, Brazil	21 25S	42 50W
54	**Leopoldville**, Belgian Congo	4 22S	15 20E
31	**Leova**, Rumania	46 29N	28 11E
32	**Lepanto**, Greece	28 21N	21 50E

MAP
33 **Lepontine Alps**, Switz. 46 25N 9 0E
44 **Lepsinsk**, U.S.S.R. 45 35N 80 20E
13 **Lepton**, England 53 42N 1 40E
27 **Lequeitio**, Spain 43 23N 2 29W
29 **Lercara**, Sicily 37 45N 13 30E
54 **Lere**, Fr. Equat. Africa 9 40N 14 17E
27 **Lerida**, Spain 41 38N 0 40E
26 **Lerma**, Spain 42 3N 3 48W
16 **Lerwick**, Scotland 60 10N 1 10W
20 **Les Andelys**, France 49 6N 1 38E
21 **Les Sables d'Olonne**, France 40 29N 1 48W
33 **Les Verrières**, Switz. 46 55N 6 27E
30 **Lesina, I.**, Yugoslavia 43 11N 16 40E
31 **Leskovac**, Yugoslavia 43 0N 21 58E
31 **Leskovic**, Albania 40 18N 20 40E
17 **Leslie**, Scotland 57 18N 2 40W
21 **Lesparre**, France 45 19N 0 57W
65 **Lesser Antilles**, W. Ind. 13 0N 64 0W
60 **Lesser Slave L.**, Can. 55 27N 115 30W
22 **Lessines**, Belgium 50 44N 3 50E
60 **Lethbridge**, Canada 49 44N 112 41W
31 **Letnitza**, Bulgaria 43 18N 25 0E
32 **Leucas**, Greece 38 40N 20 40E
32 **Leucas.** *See* **Santa Maura**
18 **Letterkenny**, Eire 54 47N 7 45W
17 **Leuchars**, Scotland 56 22N 2 53W
33 **Leuk**, Switzerland 46 19N 7 37E
33 **Leukerbad**, Switzerland 46 23N 7 37E
22 **Leuze**, Belgium 50 36N 3 37E
25 **Léva**, Czechoslovakia 48 12N 18 37E
32 **Levadia**, Greece 38 27N 22 52E
34 **Levanger**, Norway 63 45N 11 20E
40 **Levant**, E. Medit. Sea 33 0N 34 0E
28 **Levanto**, Italy 44 11N 9 34E
17 **Leven**, Scotland 56 12N 3 0W
17 **Leven, Loch**, Scotland 56 12N 3 23W
46 **Levêque, C.**, W. Austl. 16 20S 122 54E
50 **Levin**, N. Zealand 40 36S 175 16E
61 **Levis**, Canada 46 40N 71 15W
31 **Levski**, Bulgaria 43 21N 25 10E
51 **Levuka**, Fiji Is. Inset 17 30S 178 50E
15 **Lewes**, England 50 52N 0 1E
16 **Lewis, I.**, Scotland 58 10N 6 40W
62 **Lewiston**, U.S.A. 45 58N 117 0W
63 **Lexington**, U.S.A. 38 3N 84 35W
13 **Leyburn**, England 54 19N 1 49W
47 **Leyburn**, Queensland 28 0S 151 40E
57 **Leydsdorp**, U. of S. Africa 24 1S 30 29E
12 **Leyland**, England 53 41N 2 42W
15 **Leysdown**, England 51 24N 0 55E
39 **Leyte I.**, Philippine Is. 11 0N 125 0E
21 **Lézignan**, France 43 12N 2 46E
44 **Lhasa**, Tibet 29 50N 91 10E
44 **Lho-jong**, China 30 50N 96 30E
39 **Liakhov Is.**, U.S.S.R. 73 30N 143 0E
56 **Lailui**, N. Rhodesia 20 15S 23 3E
45 **Liang-kiao**, Taiwan 22 5N 120 55E
45 **Liao-tung, G. of**, China 39 30N 121 0E
45 **Liao-yang**, Manchuria 61 0N 123 30W
60 **Liard**, Canada 61 0N 123 30W
35 **Libau**, Latvia 56 32N 21 1E
54 **Libenge**, Belgian Congo 3 30N 18 38E
24 **Liberec**, Cz.-slov. 50 42N 15 7E
52 **Liberia**, Africa 6 20N 9 30W
64 **Libertad**, Mexico 29 55N 112 40W
22 **Libin**, Belgium 49 59N 5 15E
21 **Libourne**, France 44 56N 0 15W
54 **Libreville**, Fr. Eq. Af. 0 25N 9 28E
52 **Libya, col.**, Africa 23 to 0 33N 9 to 25E
52 **Libyan Desert**, Africa 26 3N 25 0E
29 **Licata**, Sicily 37 7N 13 55E
14 **Lichfield**, England 52 40N 1 50W
57 **Lichtenburg**, U. of S. Africa 26 10S 26 10E
33 **Lichtensteig**, Switz. 47 18N 9 6E
25 **Lida**, Poland 53 53N 25 18E
35 **Lidköping**, Sweden 58 30N 13 10E
24 **Liechtenstein, princ.**, Europe 47 10N 9 35E
22 **Liège, & prov.**, Belgium 50 39N 5 34E
24 **Liegnitz**, Germany 51 12N 16 12E
24 **Lienz**, Aust. Germany 46 50N 12 46E
35 **Liepaja.** *See* **Libau**
22 **Lierre**, Belgium 51 9N 4 34E
33 **Liesthal**, Switzerland 47 29N 7 43E
44 **Lifan**, China 32 0N 104 0E
19 **Liffey, R.**, Eire 53 10N 6 25W
18 **Lifford**, Eire 54 50N 7 40W
28 **Liguria, dept.**, Italy 44 0N 8 0E
28 **Ligurian Sea**, Italy 43 0N 8 30E
23 **Liim Fd.**, Denmark 57 0N 9 20E
20 **Lille**, France 50 37N 3 4E
35 **Lillehammer**, Norway 61 10N 10 25E
35 **Lillesand**, Norway 58 15N 8 20E
35 **Lillherrdal**, Sweden 61 55N 14 0E
22 **Lillo**, Belgium 51 19N 4 17E
60 **Lillooet**, Canada 50 43N 121 59W
23 **Lim Fd.**, Denmark 56 50N 8 30E
66 **Lima**, Peru 12 15S 76 50W
63 **Lima**, U.S.A. 40 42N 84 5W
40 **Limassol**, Cyprus 34 32N 33 5E
18 **Limavady**, N. Ireland 55 3N 6 57W

MAP
22 **Limbourg, prov.**, Belg. 51 0N 5 30E
24 **Limburg**, Germany 50 22N 8 4E
22 **Limburg, prov.**, Neth. 51 10N 6 0E
44 **Lim-chow**, China 21 50N 109 20E
19 **Limerick, & co.**, Eire 52 40N 8 44W
32 **Limni**, Greece 38 45N 23 22E
21 **Limoges**, France 45 49N 1 16E
62 **Limon**, U.S.A. 39 15N 103 41W
64 **Limon**, Costa Rica 10 0N 83 10W
21 **Limousin, old prov.**, France 45 23N 2 0E
21 **Limoux**, France 43 3N 2 13E
57 **Limpopo R.**, Africa 23 0S 32 15E
64 **Linares**, Mexico 25 8N 99 17W
26 **Linares**, Spain 38 9N 3 39W
13 **Lincoln, & co.**, England 53 15N 0 32W
51 **Lincoln**, N. Zealand 43 38S 173 29E
62 **Lincoln**, U.S.A. 40 51N 96 46W
63 **Lincoln**, U.S.A. 44 2N 71 48W
13 **Lincoln Wolds**, Eng. 53 26N 0 14W
24 **Lindau**, Germany 48 40N 12 40E
24 **Linden**, Germany 52 22N 9 42E
47 **Lindesay Mt.**, Queens. 28 10S 152 0E
35 **Lindesnes, C.**, Norway 58 0N 7 0E
55 **Lindi**, Tanganyika Terr. 10 0S 39 41E
57 **Lindley**, U. of S. Africa 27 55S 28 30E
13 **Lindsey**, England 53 25N 0 15W
41 **Lingah**, Iran 32 20N 51 0E
39 **Lingayen**, Philippine Is. 16 0N 120 20E
24 **Lingen**, Germany 52 32N 7 22E
67 **Linhares**, Brazil 19 10S 60 0W
35 **Linköping**, Sweden 58 30N 15 40E
17 **Linlithgow** Scotland 55 58N 3 37W
44 **Lin-nganio**, China 23 50N 103 0E
17 **Linnhe L.** Scotland 55 46N 5 10W
45 **Linsehotten I.** *See* **Shichi-to**
13 **Linton**, England 54 4N 2 1W
24 **Linz**, Aust., Germany 48 17N 14 18E
21 **Lion G.**, France 43 0N 4 30E
29 **Lipari Is.**, Italy 38 30N 14 40E
37 **Lipetsk**, U.S.S.R. 52 42N 39 32W
44 **Li-ping**, China 26 25N 109 0E
25 **Lipno**, Poland 52 48N 19 13E
31 **Lippa**, Rumania 46 9N 21 40E
24 **Lippe, st.**, Germany 52 0N 9 0E
24 **Lippstadt**, Germany 51 40N 8 20E
25 **Liptoszentmiklos**, Czechoslovakia 49 5N 18 40E
27 **Liria**, Spain 39 37N 35W
26 **Lisbon**, Portugal 39 32N 9 10W
18 **Lisburn**, N. Ireland 54 31N 6 3W
58 **Lisburne C.**, Alaska 69 30N 166 30W
19 **Liscannor**, Eire 52 57N 9 24W
19 **Liscarroll**, Eire 52 16N 8 49W
19 **Lisdoonvarna**, Eire 53 2N 9 17W
20 **Lisieux**, France 49 11N 0 12E
14 **Liskeard**, England 50 28N 4 27W
19 **Lismore**, Eire 52 8N 7 56W
49 **Lismore**, N.S.W. 28 42S 153 19E
47 **Lismore**, Victoria 37 52S 143 21E
18 **Lisnaskea**, N. Ireland 54 15N 7 27W
25 **Lissa**, Poland 51 50N 16 32E
30 **Lissa I.**, Yugoslavia 43 0N 16 10E
19 **Listowel**, Eire 52 27N 9 30W
34 **Lit**, Sweden 63 20N 14 50E
44 **Litang**, China 30 0N 100 35E
15 **Litcham**, England 52 45N 0 48E
47 **Lithgow**, N.S.W. 33 29N 150 10E
35 **Lithuania, rep.**, Europe 55 0N 25 0E
65 **Little Abaco**, Bahama Is. 26 50N 77 45W
23 **Little Belt**, Denmark 55 10N 9 50E
65 **Little Cayman I.**, Jamaica 19 32N 80 2W
57 **Little Namaqualand**, U. of S. Africa 29 0S 17 30E
63 **Little Rock**, U.S.A. 34 45N 92 20W
21 **Little St. Bernard Pass**, France 45 43N 6 55E
15 **Littlehampton**, Eng. 50 48N 0 32W
15 **Littleport**, England 52 28N 0 18E
19 **Littleton**, Eire 52 39N 7 44W
28 **Littoria**, Italy 41 27N 12 58E
30 **Liubovya**, Yugoslavia 44 11N 19 22E
44 **Liuchow**, China 24 10N 109 0E
35 **Livenhof**, Latvia 56 18N 26 12E
12 **Liverpool**, England 53 24N 2 59W
47 **Liverpool Plains**, N.S.W. 31 12S 149 45E
47 **Liverpool**, N.S.W. 33 55S 150 54E
47 **Liverpool Ra.**, N.S.W. 31 30S 151 0E
64 **Livingston**, Guatemala 15 50N 89 0W
55 **Livingstone Mts.**, Tanganyika Territory 9 50S 34 35E
56 **Livingstone**, Rhodesia 17 56S 25 40E
62 **Livingston**, U.S.A. 43 37N 110 33W
55 **Livingstonia**, Nyasaland Protectorate 10 35S 34 7E
30 **Livno**, Yugoslavia 43 50N 17 2E
37 **Livny**, U.S.S.R. 52 30N 37 33E
35 **Livonia, dist.**, Latvia 57 30N 26 0E
19 **Lixnaw**, Eire 52 24N 9 36W
32 **Lixuri**, Greece 38 11N 20 27E
14 **Lizard Pt.**, England 49 57N 5 13E
35 **Ljusdal**, Sweden 61 45N 16 5E

MAP
14 **Llanbedr**, Wales 52 49N 4 6W
12 **Llanberis**, Wales 53 2N 4 5W
14 **Llandaff**, Wales 51 29N 3 12W
14 **Llandilo**, Wales 51 53N 3 59W
14 **Llandrillo**, Wales 52 55N 3 26W
14 **Llandrindod Wells**, Wales 52 14N 3 22W
12 **Llandudno**, Wales 53 20N 3 50W
14 **Llandyssil**, Wales 52 3N 4 22W
14 **Llanelly**, Wales 51 41N 4 9W
12 **Llanerchymedd**, Wales 53 20N 4 22W
26 **Llanes**, Spain 43 72N 4 50W
14 **Llanfair Caereinon**, Wales 52 39N 3 20W
14 **Llanfyllin**, Wales 52 45N 3 18W
14 **Llangadock**, Wales 51 57N 3 53W
12 **Llangefni**, Wales 53 16N 4 18W
14 **Llagnollen**, Wales 52 58N 3 10W
14 **Llangranog**, Wales 52 10N 4 27W
14 **Llanidloes**, Wales 52 27N 3 32W
14 **Llanilar**, Wales 52 21N 4 1W
14 **Llandovery**, Wales 52 0N 3 45W
62 **Llano Estacado**, U.S.A. 33 45N 103 0W
66 **Llanos**, S. America 6 30N 69 30W
14 **Llawrhaidr-yn Morhnant**, Wales 52 49N 3 17W
12 **Llanrwst**, Wales 53 9N 3 48W
14 **Llansantffraid**, Wales 52 16N 4 10W
14 **Llantrisant**, Wales 51 32N 3 21W
14 **Llanwyrtyd Wells**, Wales 52 7N 3 38W
14 **Llanymynech**, Wales 52 47N 36 0W
26 **Llerena**, Spain 38 15N 6 1W
60 **Lloydminster**, Canada 53 18N 110 2W
30 **Llubljana.** *See* **Laibach**
67 **Llullaillaco Mt.**, Chile 24 30S 67 30W
27 **Llummayor**, Spain 39 28N 2 55E
14 **Llwyngwril**, Wales 52 40N 4 5W
54 **Loanda**, Angola 8 48S 13 10E
54 **Loango** Fr. Eq. Africa 4 45S 11 55E
55 **Loangwa, R.**, N. Rhod. 12 35S 33 30E
17 **Loanhead**, Scotland 55 52N 3 9W
24 **Löbaü**, Germany 51 5N 14 40E
67 **Loberia**, Argentina 38 10S 58 50W
44 **Lob Nor**, Sinkiang 39 30N 90 0E
66 **Lobos Is.**, Peru 7 0S 81 0W
33 **Locarno**, Switzerland 46 12N 8 47E
16 **Lochaber**, Scotland 56 58N 5 0W
16 **Lochaline**, Scotland 56 32N 5 46W
16 **Lochboisdale**, Scot. 57 9N 7 18W
17 **Lochbuy**, Scotland 56 21N 5 54W
16 **Lochcarron**, Scotland 57 24N 5 30W
17 **Lochdonhead**, Scotland 56 27N 5 40W
17 **Lochearnhead**, Scotland 56 23N 4 17W
20 **Loches**, France 47 8N 0 59E
17 **Lochgilphead**, Scot. 56 3N 5 24W
17 **Lochgoilhead**, Scot 56 11N 4 5W
16 **Lochinver**, Scotland 58 9N 5 13W
17 **Lochmaben**, Scotland 55 8N 3 26W
16 **Lochmaddy**, Scotland 57 36N 7 10W
17 **Lockerbie**, Scotland 55 7N 3 21W
49 **Lockhart**, N.S.W. 35 11S 146 14E
25 **Locse**, Czechoslovakia 49 0N 20 39E
21 **Lodève**, France 43 43N 3 18E
28 **Lodi**, Italy 45 19N 9 32E
26 **Lodosa**, Spain 42 15N 2 8W
25 **Lodz**, Poland 51 44N 19 27E
57 **Loeriesfontein**, U. of S. Africa 30 57S 19 25E
34 **Löfänger**, Sweden 64 20N 21 27E
34 **Lofoten Is.**, Norway 68 10 12 0E
35 **Lofthammar**, Sweden 57 50N 16 50E
13 **Loftus**, England 54 34N 0 54W
48 **Lofty Mt.**, S. Austl. 34 57S 138 45E
60 **Logan, mt.**, Canada 60 30N 139 30W
62 **Logan**, U.S.A. 41 43N 111 50W
63 **Logansport**, U.S.A. 40 50N 86 26W
25 **Logishin**, Poland 52 19N 26 0E
27 **Logroño**, Spain 42 27N 2 30W
26 **Logrosan**, Spain 39 18N 5 30W
23 **Lögstör**, Denmark 56 58N 9 17E
23 **Lögstör Bredning**, Denmark 56 58N 9 5E
23 **Lögumkloster**, Den. 55 3N 8 57E
40 **Loheia**, Arabia 15 50N 42 30E
34 **Loimolu**, Finland 62 0N 31 45E
21 **Loire, dept.**, France 47 20N 1 45W
20 **Loire, R.**, France 47 44N 0 45E
20 **Loire Inférieure, dept.**, France 47 20N 1 42W
20 **Loiret, dept.**, France 47 52N 2 20E
20 **Loir-et-Cher, dept.**, Fr. 47 33N 1 25E
66 **Loja**, Ecuador 4 10N 79 15W
26 **Loja**, Spain 37 10N 4 10W
25 **Lokachi**, Poland 50 45N 24 42E
22 **Lokeren**, Belgium 51 7N 4 0E
23 **Lökken**, Denmark 57 23N 9 45E
34 **Lökken**, Norway 63 10N 9 45E
54 **Lokojo**, Nigeria 7 47N 6 42E
31 **Lom**, Bulgaria 43 51N 23 13E
65 **Loma Tima**, Dominican Rep. 18 40N 70 30W
55 **Lomani. R.**, Belg. Con. 1 30S 24 30E
33 **Lombard Alps**, Italy 45 58N 9 50E
28 **Lombardia, dept.**, It. 45 35N 9 45E

MAP

39 Lombok I., Dut.E.Ind. .8 40s 116 0 E
52 Lome, Fr. W. Africa.... 6 7N 1 15 E
54 Lomie, Cameroons..... 3 20N 14 5 E
25 Lomja, Poland.........53 10N 22 4 E
17 Lomond, Loch, Scot. ..56 5N 4 35W
42 Londa, India.........15 30N 74 30 E
61 London, Canada.......43 0N 81 17W
15 London, &co.,England 51 30N 0 5W
18 Londonderry,&Co.,N.I.55 0N 7 21W
15 Long Eaton, England..52 54N 1 16W
65 Long I., Bahama Is. ..23 15N 75 12W
63 Long I., U.S.A.......40 50N 73 0W
17 Long, Loch, Scotland ..56 8N 4 49W
15 Long Melford, England52 5N 0 43 E
61 Long Ra., Newfound. ..50 0N 57 0W
15 Long Stratton, Eng...52 30N 1 13 E
15 Long Sutton, England .52 48N 0 7 E
47 Longford, Tasmania ..41 32s 147 1 E
18 Longford, & Co., Eire.53 44N 7 49W
17 Longforgan, Scotland..56 28N 3 8W
13 Longnor, England....53 10N 1 54W
47 Longreach, Queensland 23 17N 144 17 E
12 Longridge, England ..53 49N 2 37W
62 Long's Pk., U.S.A....40 15N 106 0W
17 Longtown, England ...55 2N 2 55W
17 Longtown, Scotland ..55 2N 2 55W
45 Lo-ning, Manchuria ..42 10N 118 20 E
21 Lons le Saunier, Fr. ..46 40N 5 33W
23 Lönstrup, Denmark ..57 28N 9 47 E
63 Lookout, C., U.S.A. ..34 30N 76 25 E
46 Loongana, W. Austl. ..30 40s 127 5 E
19 Loop Hd., Eire.......52 34N 9 56W
39 Lopatka I., U.S.S.R. ..51 0N 157 0 E
26 Lora, Spain.........37 38N 5 36W
27 Lorca, Spain.........37 39N 1 41W
28 Loreto, Italy.........43 26N 13 36 E
64 Loreto, Mexico.......26 2N 111 25W
66 Lorica, Colombia.... 9 18N 75 48W
20 Lorient, France.......47 44N 3 24W
17 Lorne, Firth of, Scot. .56 15N 5 50W
17 Lorne, Scotland.......56 30N 5 15W
47 Lorne, Victoria.......38 32s 143 58 E
24 Lörrach, Germany....47 38N 7 40 E
21 Lorraine, dist., France 48 40N 6 0 E
62 Los Angeles, U.S.A...34 1N 118 20W
21 Los I., Fr. W. Africa .. 9 30N 13 50W
66 Los Roques, Venezuela 10 30N 67 0W
65 Los Roques I., W. Ind. 11 50N 66 45W
26 Los Santos, Spain....38 29N 6 21W
25 Losoncz, Cz.-slov.....48 20N 19 42 E
17 Lossiemouth, Scotland 57 43N 3 16W
14 Lostwithiel, England ..50 25N 4 39W
21 Lot, dept., France ....44 34N 1 33 E
21 Lot, R., France.......44 25N 0 25 E
21 Lot-et-Garonne, dept.,
   France..............44 18N 0 28 E
16 Loth, Scotland.......58 4N 3 44W
33 Lothian, Scotland....55 49N 3 10W
33 Lottigna, Switzerland..46 28N 8 56 E
20 Lötzen, Germany....54 2N 21 48 E
20 Loudéac, France....48 11N 2 45 E
23 Loudun, France......47 1N 0 5 E
14 Loughor, Wales.....51 40N 4 5W
15 Loughborough, Eng. ..52 47N 1 12W
14 Lougharne, Wales...51 37N 4 28W
19 Loughrea, Eire......53 13N 8 35W
18 Loughros More B.,
   Eire...............54 48N 8 33W
57 Louis Trichardt,
   U. of S. Africa.....23 10s 30 0 E
63 Louisbourg, Canada ..45 53N 60 1W
18 Louisburgh, &Co.,Eire 53 46N 9 48W
7 Louisiade Arch.,Pac.Oc.11 0s 153 30 E
63 Louisiana, st., U.S.A. .30 0N 91 0W
63 Louisville, U.S.A....38 15N 85 45W
26 Loulé, Portugal.....37 7N 7 59W
55 Lourenço Marques,
   Mozambique........26 0s 32 40 E
18 Louth, & Co., Eire ...53 57N 6 33W
17 Louth, England......53 22N 0 1W
47 Louth, N.S.W........30 30s 145 0 E
22 Louvain, Belgium ...50 33N 4 41 E
31 Lovech, Bulgaria ....43 6N 24 44 E
62 Lovelocks, U.S.A.....40 10N 118 25W
13 Lovere, Italy........45 49N 10 7 E
25 Lovich, Poland.......52 5N 19 55 E
35 Lovisa, Finland.....60 30N 26 20 E
6 Low Arch., Pacific Oc..17 0s 144 0W
25 Low Tatra Mts.,
   Czechoslovakia......48 54N 19 30 E
63 Lowell, U.S.A.......42 30N 71 30 E
64 Lower California Terr.,
   Mexico.............28 0N 114 0W
39 Lower Tunguska R.,
   U.S.S.R...........64 0N 96 0 E
33 Lowerz, Switzerland..47 2N 8 35 E
15 Lowestoft, England...52 29N 1 45 E
17 Lowther Hills, Scot...55 22N 3 47W
48 Loyalty Is., Pac. Oc...21 20s 167 30 E
21 Lozère, dept., France.44 24N 3 30 E
30 Loznitza,Yugoslavia ..40 30N 19 14 E
55 Lualaba, R., Belg. Con. 8 0s 28 0 E
44 Luang Prabang,
   Fr. Indo-China.......19 50N 101 50 E

MAP

55 Luapula, R., Africa.... 7 30s 28 0 E
25 Lubartov, Poland .....51 28N 22 41 E
24 Lübben, Germany ....51 56N 13 45 E
24 Lübeck, & B., Germany53 52N 10 40 E
24 Lüben, Germany .....51 23N 16 12 E
25 Lublin, & Co., Poland .51 13N 22 34 E
25 Lublinitz, Poland ....50 40N 18 42 E
37 Lubny, U.S.S.R.......50 2N 32 58 E
23 Lübz, Germany......53 28N 12 3 E
28 Lucca, Italy.........43 50N 10 30 E
17 Luce B., Scotland....55 45N 4 50W
26 Lucena, Spain.......37 25N 4 29W
28 Lucera, Italy........41 31N 15 20 E
45 Lu-chow, China.......29 0N 105 5 E
45 Lu-chu Is., Japan ....26 30N 127 30 E
25 Lucindale, S. Australia 37 0s 140 20 E
25 Luck, Poland........50 45N 25 20 E
24 Luckenwalde, Ger.....52 7N 13 6 E
42 Lucknow, India......26 47N 80 59 E
21 Luçon, France.......46 27N 1 10W
57 Lüderitz, S. W. Africa..27 30s 16 0 E
15 Ludgershall, England .51 15N 1 35W
14 Ludlow, England......52 22N 2 42W
24 Ludwigsburg, Ger.....48 56N 9 12 E
24 Ludwigshafen, Ger. ..49 30N 8 22 E
24 Ludwigslust, Germany 53 19N 11 30 E
36 Luga, U.S.S.R.......58 45N 29 51 E
33 Lugano, Switzerland ..46 1N 8 57 E
53 Lugh, Abyssinia .... 3 50N 42 35 E
19 Lugnaquilla, Mt., Eire 52 58N 6 28W
28 Lugo, Italy.........44 24N 11 55 E
26 Lugo, Spain........43 28N 7 33W
68 Luitpold Land,
   Antarctica..........78 0s 30 0W
54 Lukoleia, Belg. Congo.. 1 0s 17 8 E
25 Lukov, Poland ....51 56N 22 24 E
55 Lukuga, R., Belg. Con.. 5 50s 27 30 E
32 Lüle Burgas, Turkey ..41 25N 27 27 E
34 Luleå, Sweden.......65 35N 22 20 E
54 Lulua, R., Belg. Congo . 7 0s 22 30 E
54 Luluabourg, Belg. Con. 5 52s 22 28 E
14 Lulworth, England....50 38N 2 10W
51 Lumsden, New Zealand 45 42s 168 25 E
35 Lund, Sweden........55 40N 13 15 E
56 Lundi, S. Rhodesia ..20 45s 30 40 E
25 Lundenburg, Cz.-slov. .48 43N 16 52 E
23 Lunderskov, Denmark .55 28N 9 18 E
11 Lundy, I., England ...51 11N 4 40W
12 Lune, R., England 54 35N 2 12W
24 Lüneburg, Germany ..53 13N 10 23 E
24 Lüneburg Heath, Ger..53 0N 10 0 E
21 Lunel, France........43 41N 4 8 E
21 Luneville, France....48 34N 6 31 E
45 Lu-ngan, China.......31 50N 116 30 E
44 Lung-chow, China ....22 20N 103 0 E
44 Lung-ngan, China....32 35N 104 45 E
25 Lunno, Poland.......53 28N 24 16 E
20 Lure, France........47 41N 6 30 E
18 Lurgan, N. Ireland ...54 27N 6 20W
55 Lurio, Mozambique ..13 27s 40 30 E
40 Luristan, prov., Iran ..33 45N 48 0 E
30 Lurja, Albania......41 52N 20 10 E
56 Lusaka, N. Rhodesia ..15 30s 28 0 E
54 Lusambo, Belg. Congo. 5 0s 23 22 E
43 Lushai Hills, India...23 30N 93 0 E
55 Lushoto, Tang. Terr. .. 4 55s 38 0 E
45 Lushun, Japan.......38 40N 121 10 E
18 Lusk, Eire..........53 32N 6 11W
28 Lussin, I., Italy......44 35N 14 22 E
22 Lustin, Belgium ....50 23N 4 54 E
41 Lutfabad, U.S.S.R....37 30N 59 30 E
15 Luton, England......51 52N 0 26W
32 Lutra, Greece.......37 50N 21 10 E
33 Lutry, Switzerland....46 30N 6 42 E
15 Lutterworth, England .52 27N 1 11W
22 Luxembourg, prov.,
   Belgium............49 37N 6 7 E
22 Luxembourg, & grand
   duchy, Europe.....49 47N 6 0 E
40 Luxor, Egypt........25 41N 32 39 E
33 Luzern, & Can., Canton,
   Switzerland.........47 0N 8 16 E
33 Luzerne (L. of 4
   Cantons), Switzerland.47 0N 8 03 E
39 Luzon I., Philippine Is..16 30N 121 30 E
25 Lwow, Poland.......49 50N 24 1 E
21 Luz, France.........42 52N 0 0
16 Lybster, Scotland....58 18N 3 16W
34 Lycksele, Sweden ....64 35N 18 30 E
15 Lydd, England.......50 56N 0 56 E
41 Lydda, Palestine ....31 57N 34 56 E
57 Lydenburg, U.of S.Afr. 25 7s 30 30 E
14 Lydford, England....51 5N 2 36W
14 Lydney, England.....51 44N 2 30W
51 Lyell, New Zealand ..41 46s 172 4 E
51 Lyell Mt., New Zealand 45 16s 167 35 E
14 Lyme B., England....50 36N 3 0W
14 Lyme Regis, England .50 44N 2 55W
15 Lymington, England ..50 45N 1 32W
63 Lynchburg, U.S.A....37 28N 79 10W
15 Lyndhurst, England ..50 54N 1 34W
47 Lyndhurst, S. Austral..30 17s 138 18 E
23 Lyngby, Denmark....55 48N 12 32 E
14 Lynton, England.....51 13N 3 50W
23 Lyö, Denmark........55 4N 10 8 E

MAP

21 Lyonnais, old prov.,
   France..............45 46N 4 20 E
21 Lyons, France........45 44N 4 51 E
47 Lyrup, S. Australia ...34 16s 140 42 E
35 Lys, R., Belgium ....50 55N 3 25 E
35 Lysekil, Sweden.....58 15N 11 25 E
36 Lyskovo, U.S.S.R.....56 0N 45 0 E
12 Lytham, England....53 44N 2 57W
51 Lyttelton, N. Zealand ..43 35s 172 42 E
60 Lytton, Canada......50 7N 121 23W
25 Lyubashevo, Poland ..51 47N 25 33 E
25 Lyuboml, Poland....51 12N 24 4 E

18 Maam, Eire.........53 30N 9 35W
40 Ma'an, Transjordan ..30 12N 35 40 E
34 Maan Selka Mts., Fin. 68 30N 24 0 E
35 Maarianhamina, Fin. .60 10N 19 50 E
22 Maas, R., Netherlands .50 30N 5 20 E
22 Maaseijk, Belgium ...51 6N 5 46 E
22 Maastricht, Neth. ....50 49N 5 40 E
13 Mablethorpe, Eng. ...53 20N 0 15 E
63 McAlester, U.S.A. ...34 50N 95 40W
60 M'Clintock Ch., Can...72 0N 104 0W
60 M'Clure Str., Canada..75 0N 118 0W
63 McComb, U.S.A......31 17N 90 28W
68 McDonald I., S. Ocean.54 0s 73 0 E
63 McKeesport, U.S.A. ..40 23N 79 46W
60 McKinley Mt., Alaska .63 10N 151 20W
60 McLeod, Canada.....65 0N 123 30W
60 McMurray, Canada ..56 40N 111 27W
60 McPherson, Canada ..67 25N 134 40W
66 Macahé, Brazil......23 30s 42 0W
66 Macáo, Brazil.......50 0s 46 30W
45 Macao, China.......22 25N 113 30 E
66 Macapá, Brazil.......0 15N 51 15W
39 Macassar, E. Indies .. 5 0s 119 20 E
39 Macassar, Str., E. Indies1 0s 118 0 E
50 Macaulay I., Inset 30 15s 178 30 E
33 Maccagno, Italy......46 3N 8 44 E
13 Macclesfield, Eng.....53 16N 2 8W
46 Macdonald, L., Austr. .23 40s 128 30 E
46 Macdonnell Ra., Austr. 23 20s 134 0 E
16 Macduff, Scotland ...57 40N 2 29W
32 Macedonia, dist., Gr. ..41 10N 23 0 E
66 Maceió, Brazil....... 9 30s 35 40W
28 Macerata, Italy......43 18N 13 24 E
47 Macfarlane, L., S.Aust.30 0s 136 12 E
19 Macgillicuddy's
   Reeks, Eire.........52 3N 9 47W
55 Machabos, Kenya .... 1 35s 37 18 E
31 Machin, Rumania ....45 16N 28 12 E
17 Machrihanish, Scot...55 26N 5 43W
14 Machynlleth, Wales ..52 36N 3 51W
47 Macintyre, R., Austl...28 30s 150 15 E
47 Mackay, Queensland ..21 11s 149 17 E
60 Mackenzie, dist., Can. 65 0N 115 0W
60 Mackenzie, B., Canada 69 30N 137 0W
60 Mackenzie Mts., Can. .64 0N 128 0W
60 Mackenzie, R., Canada 67 0N 130 30W
63 Mackinaw, U.S.A. ...45 45N 84 45W
49 Maclean, N.S.W. ....29 29s 153 12 E
57 Maclear, U. of S. Africa31 8s 28 25 E
29 Macomer, Sardinia ...40 18N 8 46 E
21 Macon, France.......46 19N 4 49 E
63 Macon, U.S.A.......32 50N 83 38W
47 Macpherson Ra., Aust. 28 15s 153 0 E
40 Macquarie, Har., Tas. .42 17s 145 15 E
47 Macquarie, Ra.,N.S.W.34 0s 149 13 E
47 Macquarie, R., N.S.W. 32 40s 149 10 E
19 Macroom, Eire.......51 54N 8 57W
47 Macumba, S. Austl. ..27 0s 135 30 E
53 Madagascar I., Africa .20 0s 47 0 E
41 Madeba, Transjordan .31 42N 35 51 E
66 Madeira, R., Brazil ... 6 0s 62 0W
52 Madeira I., N. At. Oc..32 45N 17 0W
64 Madera, Mexico.....29 15N 107 57W
40 Madinet el Fayum,
   Egypt..............29 5N 30 40 E
63 Madison, Ind., U.S.A..38 47N 85 32W
62 Madison, Wis., U.S.A. 43 5N 89 25W
33 Madiswyl, Switzerland.47 9N 7 47 E
14 Madley, England.....52 2N 2 51W
42 Madras, India........13 7N 80 15 E
42 Madras, prov., India .14 45N 79 0 E
42 Madre, L., de la, U.S.A.27 0N 97 30W
67 Madre de Dios Arch.,
   Chile...............50 30s 78 0W
26 Madrid, Spain.......40 25N 3 45W
39 Madura I., E. Indies .. 7 0s 113 30 E
42 Madura, India.......9 50N 78 10 E
14 Maenclochog, Wales .51 55N 4 47W
14 Maesteg, Wales.....51 37N 3 40W
57 Mafeking, U. of S. Afr. 25 55s 25 38 E
57 Mafeteng, Basutoland .29 50s 27 18 E
47 Maffra, Victoria......37 59s 147 0 E
55 Mafia, I., East Africa . 7 50s 39 50 E
26 Mafra, Portugal.....38 57N 9 20W
55 Magadi, L., Kenya .. 1 46s 36 20 E
55 Magas, Iran.........27 10N 61 45 E
55 Magdala, Abyssinia ..11 42N 39 18 E
61 Magdalen Is., Canada .47 30N 61 45W
66 Magdalena, Bolivia ..13 0s 64 0W
64 Magdalena, B., Mexico 24 30N 112 10W
66 Magdalena, R., Col. .. 6 0N 75 0W
24 Magdeburg, Germany .52 8N 11 40 E

MAP
67 Magellan's Str., S. Am. 52 50S 66 0W
28 Magenta, Italy 45 30N 8 52E
34 Mageröy I., Norway 71 10N 26 0E
57 Magersfontein, U. of S. Africa 28 58S 24 45E
33 Maggia, Switzerland 46 15N 8 42E
28 Maggiore, L., Italy 45 50N 8 35E
18 Magherafelt, N. Ire. 54 45N 6 37W
68 Magnetic Pole, Arc. 70 40N 96 5W
68 Magnetic Pole, Antarc. 71 10S 150 45E
37 Magnitogorsk, U.S.S.R. 53 10N 59 0E
18 Maguire's Bri., N.Ire. 54 17N 7 28W
43 Magwe, Burma 20 10N 95 3E
30 Magyarova, Hungary 47 54N 17 20E
55 Mahagi, Belgian Congo 2 14N 31 10E
43 Mahanadi, R., India 20 30N 85 15E
42 Mahé, India 11 40N 75 35E
55 Mahenge, Tanganyika 8 50S 36 45E
51 Maheno, New Zealand 45 11S 170 51E
31 Mahmudia, Rumania 45 5N 29 6E
27 Mahon, Minorca, I.
15 Maidenhead, Eng. 51 32N 0 43W
15 Maidstone, England 51 17N 0 31E
54 Maidugari, Nigeria 11 52N 13 13E
33 Maienfeld, Switzerland 47 1N 9 32E
19 Maigue, R., Eire 52 32N 8 46W
37 Maikop, U.S.S.R. 44 38N 40 4E
24 Main, R., Germany 50 8N 11 10E
20 Maine, old prov., Fr. 48 20N 0 0
63 Maine, st., U.S.A. 46 0N 69 0W
20 Maine-et-Loire, dept., France 47 28N 0 25W
16 Mainland, I., Shetld. Is. 60 20N 1 30W
20 Maintenon, France 48 35N 1 35E
66 Maipures, Colombia 5 30N 68 30W
65 Maisi, C., Cuba 20 10N 74 10W
47 Maitland, N.S.W. 32 48S 151 30E
27 Majorca I., Spain 39 30N 3 0E
57 Majuba Hill, Natal 27 40S 29 45E
53 Majunga, Madagascar 15 50S 46 30E
40 Makalla, Arabia 14 37N 49 18E
55 Makalle, Abyssinia 13 29N 39 42E
36 Makaryev, U.S.S.R. 57 58N 43 45E
37 Makhach Kala, U.S.S.R. 43 0N 47 30E
40 Makhlaf, Arabia 18 40N 46 40E
55 Makindu, Kenya 2 18S 37 36E
57 Maklutsi, Bech. 21 45S 28 0E
30 Makó, Hungary 46 18N 20 33E
56 Makoni, S. Rhodesia 19 41S 31 0E
57 Makosini, Swaziland 27 11S 31 16E
32 Makri, Greece 40 50N 25 46E
32 Makri, Turkey 36 40N 29 17E
32 Makronisi, Greece 37 41N 24 10E
19 Mal B., Eire 52 52N 9 26W
34 Malå, Sweden 65 15N 18 45E
42 Malabar Coast, India 11 0N 75 0E
39 Malacca, Malay Pen. 2 15N 102 15E
27 Maladetta, Mt., Spain 42 40N 0 40E
26 Malaga, Spain 36 43N 4 23W
26 Malahide, Eire 53 27N 6 10W
55 Malakal, A.-E. Sud. 9 33N 31 40E
55 Malangali, Tang. 8 40S 34 48E
54 Malange, Angola 9 32S 16 18E
35 Mälar, L., Sweden 59 30N 17 0E
40 Malatia, Turkey 38 27N 38 27E
39 Malay Pen., Asia 5 0N 101 0E
24 Malchin, Germany 53 45N 12 50E
46 Malcolm, W. Australia 29 0S 121 30E
6 Malden I., Pacific Oc. 4 0S 154 58W
7 Maldive Is., Indian Oc. 5 0N 73 30E
15 Maldon, England 51 44N 0 41E
47 Maldon, Victoria 37 0S 144 5E
67 Maldonado, Uruguay 34 45S 55 0W
35 Målilla, Sweden 57 25N 15 46E
18 Malin Hd., Eire 55 23N 7 23W
55 Malindi, Kenya 3 12S 40 8E
22 Malines, Belgium 51 2N 4 27E
16 Mallaig, Scotland 57 0N 5 48W
19 Mallow, Eire 52 8N 8 38W
14 Mallwyd, Wales 52 42N 3 40W
22 Malmedy, Belgium 50 26N 6 3E
14 Malmesbury, England 51 35N 2 5W
57 Malmesbury, S. Afr. 33 30S 18 45E
47 Malmesbury, Victoria 37 11S 144 22E
35 Malmö, Sweden 55 35N 13 5E
35 Malmöhus, co., Swed. 55 55N 12 45E
33 Maloja P., Switzerland 46 28N 9 47E
14 Malpas, England 53 1N 2 46W
29 Malta, I., Med. Sea 36 0N 14 30E
13 Malton, England 54 8N 0 48W
14 Malvern, England 52 7N 2 19W
14 Malvern Hills, Eng. 52 5N 2 17W
16 Mam Soul, Mt., Scot. 57 17N 5 10W
20 Mamers, France 48 19N 0 21E
66 Mamore, R., S. Amer. 13 0S 65 25W
12 Man, I. of 54 15N 4 30W
27 Manacor, Majorca I. 39 35N 3 15E
64 Managua, Nicaragua 12 7N 86 15W
64 Managua, L., Nica. 12 15N 86 15W
50 Manahiki, Is. Inset 1 0S 1 68W
50 Manakau, N.Z. 40 45S 175 18E
66 Manáos, Brazil 3 0S 60 0W
51 Manapouri, N.Z. 45 34S 167 40E

MAP
42 Manar, Ceylon 9 2N 79 54E
42 Manar G., Ceylon 8 0N 78 30E
44 Manasarowar, L., Tibet 30 45N 81 30E
36 Mancha Real, Spain 37 50N 3 38W
20 Manche, dept., France 49 8N 1 18W
13 Manchester, England 53 29N 2 16W
63 Manchester, U.S.A. 43 2N 71 29W
45 Manchouli, Manchuria 49 35N 118 25E
45 Manchukuo. *See* Manchuria
45 Manchuria, st., Asia 47 30N 127 0E
55 Manda, Tanganyika 10 30S 34 40E
35 Mandal, Norway 58 2N 7 30E
43 Mandalay, Burma 22 3N 96 2E
55 Mandera, Tanganyika 6 14S 38 23E
29 Manduria, Italy 40 25N 17 39E
42 Mandvi, India 22 55N 69 21E
28 Manfredonia, Italy 41 38N 15 58E
50 Mangaia I. Inset 22 0S 158 0E
31 Mangalia, Rumania 43 48N 28 38E
42 Mangalore, India 12 55N 74 52E
49 Mangalore, Queensland 26 45S 146 5E
50 Mangonui, N.Z. 35 0S 173 30E
42 Mangrol, India 21 8N 70 14E
26 Mangualde, Portugal 40 37N 7 50W
56 Mangwe, S. Rhodesia 20 45S 28 30E
43 Manhao, China 23 10N 102 4E
37 Manich, R., U.S.S.R. 46 30N 42 30E
48 Manihiki Is., Pac. Oc. 10 25S 161 0W
39 Manila, Philippines 14 40N 121 0E
49 Manilla, N.S.W. 30 42S 150 42E
43 Manipur, India *See* Imphal
32 Manisa, Turkey 38 36N 27 17E
63 Manistee, U.S.A. 44 10N 86 20W
60 Manitoba, L., Canada 51 0N 98 58W
60 Manitoba, prov., Can. 53 0N 97 0W
60 Manitou, Canada 49 20N 98 30W
32 Maniyas, Göl, Turkey 40 10N 28 0E
66 Manizales, Colombia 5 0N 75 40W
42 Manmad, India 20 15N 74 29E
48 Mannahill, S. Australia 32 58S 149 58E
24 Mannheim, Germany 49 30N 8 26E
18 Mannin, B., Eire 53 27N 10 5W
60 Manning C., Canada 76 0N 123 0W
15 Manningtree, Eng. 51 56N 1 4E
48 Mannum, S. Australia 34 52S 139 18E
23 Manö I., Denmark 55 17N 8 34E
32 Manolada, Greece 38 3N 21 21E
18 Manorhamilton, Eire 54 18N 8 11W
21 Manosque, France 43 50N 5 48E
27 Manresa, Spain 41 48N 1 50E
13 Mansfield, England 53 8N 1 12W
47 Mansfield, Victoria 37 5S 146 5E
26 Mansilla, Spain 42 30N 5 24W
20 Mantes, France 48 59N 1 43E
62 Manti, U.S.A. 39 16N 111 40W
67 Mantiqueira, Sa de, Brazil 22 30S 45 0W
28 Mantua, Italy 45 9N 10 47E
32 Mantudi, Greece 38 45N 23 30E
51 Manua I., Samoa, Inset 14 20S 169 20W
50 Manukau Harb., N.Z. 37 5S 174 45E
18 Manulla, Eire 53 51N 9 11W
26 Manzanares, Spain 39 0N 3 21W
65 Manzanillo, Cuba 20 21N 77 3W
64 Manzanillo, Mexico 19 3N 104 20W
54 Mao, Fr. Equat. Afr. 14 8N 15 20E
67 Mar, Sa. do, Brazil 26 50S 49 10W
67 Mar del Plata, Argen. 37 50S 57 30W
57 Marabastad, Trans. 24 0S 29 20E
66 Maracaibo, Venezuela 10 42N 71 50W
66 Maracaibo, G. of, Ven. 11 30N 71 0W
66 Maracaibo, L., Ven. 9 30N 71 30W
40 Maragha, Iran 37 16N 46 19E
66 Marajo, I., Brazil 1 0S 49 40W
27 Maranchon, Spain 41 2N 2 12W
40 Marand, Iran 38 23N 45 45E
56 Marandellas, S. Rhod. 18 25S 31 20E
66 Maranhão, Brazil 2 0S 44 0W
66 Maranhão, st., Brazil 5 0S 45 0W
47 Maranoa, R., Queens. 27 30S 148 0E
66 Marañon, R., Peru 5 0S 76 0W
40 Marash, Turkey 37 31N 36 59E
32 Marathon, Greece 38 10N 23 57E
15 Marazion, Eng. Inset 50 8N 5 28W
26 Marbella, Spain 36 32N 4 55W
46 Marble Bar, W. Austl. 21 20S 119 30E
24 Marburg, Germany 50 48N 8 48E
15 March, England 52 34N 0 6E
25 March, R., Cz.-slov. 48 30N 17 0E
22 Marche, Belgium 50 14N 5 19E
21 Marche, old prov., Fr. 46 13N 1 40E
26 Marchena, Spain 37 20N 5 25W
28 Marches, dept., Italy 43 40N 13 0E
40 Mardin, Turkey 37 12N 40 38E
47 Mareeba, Queensland 17 7S 145 12E
28 Marengo, Italy 44 52N 8 48E
21 Marennes, France 45 49N 1 7W
62 Marfa, U.S.A. 30 24N 104 5W
14 Margam, Wales 51 35N 3 46W
65 Margarita I., Ven. 10 50N 64 0W
15 Margate, England 51 23N 1 23E
25 Marggrabowa, Ger. 54 5N 22 28E
43 Margherita, India 27 18N 95 42E
50 Maria van Diemen, C., New Zealand 34 30S 172 40E

MAP
23 Mariager, Denmark 56 40N 10 1E
23 Mariager Fd., Den. 56 43N 10 20E
7 Mariana Is., Pac. Oc. 17 0N 145 50E
24 Mariazell, Aus., Ger. 47 50N 15 19E
40 Marib, Arabia 15 30N 45 13E
23 Maribo, Denmark 54 48N 11 32E
30 Maribor, M'bg., Y-Slav. 46 36N 15 40E
68 Marie Byrd Land, Antarctica 82 0S 125 0W
65 Marie Galante I., W. Indies 16 0N 61 15W
22 Mariembourg, Belgium 50 6N 4 32E
24 Marienbad, Cz.-slov. 49 58N 12 41E
35 Marienburg, Latvia 57 24N 27 0E
25 Marienwerder, Ger. 53 45N 18 57E
35 Mariestad, Sweden 58 40N 13 50E
28 Marignano, Italy 45 21N 9 22E
65 Mariguana, Bahama Is. 22 28N 73 0W
39 Mariinsk, U.S.S.R. 56 0N 88 0E
36 Mariisk, rep., U.S.S.R. 56 30N 47 30E
26 Marin, Spain 42 21N 8 42W
63 Marinette, U.S.A. 45 5N 87 38W
21 Maritime Alps, Fr. 44 15N 7 0E
31 Maritza, R., Bulgaria 40 43N 26 0E
37 Mariupol, U.S.S.R. 47 6N 37 27E
35 Markaryd, Sweden 56 28N 14 2E
15 Mkt. Bosworth, Eng. 52 37N 1 24W
15 Market Deeping, Eng. 52 42N 0 19W
14 Market Drayton, Eng. 52 54N 2 29W
15 Market Harboro, Eng. 52 29N 0 56W
13 Market Rasen, Eng. 53 24N 0 20W
13 Market Weighton, England 53 52N 0 41W
15 Marlboro' Dns., Eng. 51 32N 1 46W
15 Marlborough, Eng. 51 26N 1 43W
51 Marlborough, N.Z. 41 50S 173 30E
21 Marmande, France 44 30N 0 9E
32 Marmara I., Turkey 40 38N 27 39E
32 Marmara, Sea of, Tur. 40 40N 28 30E
32 Marmaros, Turkey 36 53N 28 20E
23 Marne, Germany 53 58N 9 2E
20 Marne, dept., France 49 1N 4 10E
20 Marne, R., France 49 0N 3 5E
47 Maroona, Victoria 37 28S 142 51E
31 Maros, R., Rumania 46 7N 22 0E
31 Maroskéviz, Rum. 46 53N 25 25E
31 Maros-Vásárhely 46 23N 24 31E
6 Marquesas Is., Pac. Oc. 9 30S 140 0W
63 Marquette, U.S.A. 46 30N 87 29W
52 Marrakesh, Morocco 31 30N 7 50W
29 Marsala, Sicily 37 49N 12 25E
47 Marsden, N.S.W. 33 43S 147 32E
21 Marseilles, France 43 18N 5 25E
63 Marsh, I., U.S.A. 29 30N 91 50W
63 Marshall, U.S.A. 32 31N 94 24W
7 Marshall Is., Pac. Oc. 9 0N 171 0E
63 Marshalltown, U.S.A. 41 58N 92 53W
14 Marshfield, England 51 28N 2 19W
23 Marslev, Denmark 55 23N 10 28E
23 Marstal, Denmark 54 51N 10 31E
23 Marstal B., Denmark 54 50N 10 32E
35 Marstrand, Sweden 57 55N 11 35E
43 Martaban, Burma 16 33N 97 35E
43 Martaban, G. of, Bur. 15 30N 96 30E
63 Martha's Vineyard I., U.S.A. 41 25N 71 40W
21 Martigues, France 43 24N 5 3E
33 Martigny, Switzerland 46 7N 7 5E
65 Martinique, Wind. Is. 14 35N 61 0W
14 Martock, England 50 59N 2 45W
26 Martos, Spain 37 44N 3 59W
66 Maruca, R., Brit. Gui. 7 55N 58 40W
42 Maruchak, Afghan. 35 40N 63 18E
29 Maruggio, Italy 40 18N 17 33E
21 Marvejols, France 44 33N 3 18E
42 Marwar, dist., India 27 0N 72 30E
47 Maryboro', Victoria 37 3S 143 44E
19 Maryborough, Eire 53 2N 7 19W
47 Maryborough, Queens. 25 28S 152 40E
63 Maryland, st., U.S.A. 30 30N 77 0W
14 Maryport, England 54 43N 3 30W
62 Marysville, U.S.A. 39 5N 121 38W
55 Masai Steppe, Tang. 4 20S 37 0E
45 Masanpo, Korea 35 0N 128 30E
55 Masasi, Tanganyika 11 0S 38 42E
39 Masbate, Philippines 12 0N 123 30E
41 Mascat, Arabia 23 36N 58 40E
57 Maseru, Basutoland 29 17S 28 35E
13 Masham, England 54 14N 1 40W
56 Mashona Ld., S.Rhod. 17 10S 31 30E
55 Masindi, Uganda 1 40N 31 45E
18 Mask, L., Eire 53 36N 9 20W
63 Mason, U.S.A. 43 5N 93 15W
28 Massa, Italy 44 1N 10 10E
63 Massachusetts, U.S.A. 42 0N 72 0W
29 Massafra, Italy 40 35N 17 6E
55 Massawa, Eritrea 15 30N 39 30E
51 Masterton, N.Z. 40 52N 175 40E
42 Mastuj, India 36 15N 72 40E
40 Mastura, Arabia 23 0N 39 0E
42 Masulipatam, India 16 17N 81 17E
56 Matabele Ld., S. Rhod. 20 0S 30 0E
54 Matadi, Belgian Congo 5 45S 13 45E
64 Matagalpa, Nicaragua 13 10N 85 38W
63 Matagorda, U.S.A. 28 15N 96 0W

MAP

42 Matale, Ceylon .... 7 30N 80 35 E
65 Matamóros, Mexico ...25 50N 97 32w
39 Matan, Borneo .... 2 0s 110 0 E
64 Matanzas, Cuba 23 0N 81 40w
32 Matapan, C., Greece ..36 23N 22 30 E
27 Matara, Spain ....41 34N 2 27 E
50 Matata, New Zealand .37 54s 176 46 E
57 Matatiele, U. of S. Afr..30 23s 29 53 E
51 Mataura, New Zealand.46 12s 168 51 E
29 Matera, Italy ....40 40N 16 39 E
35 Matfors, Sweden .....62 17N 17 0 E
14 Mathry, Wales 51 57N 5 5w
64 Matina, B., Nicaragua .11 5N 83 40w
13 Matlock, England 53 8N 1 33w
56 Matope, Nyasaland ...15 30s 35 0 E
52 Matruh, Egypt ....31 0N 27 35 E
57 Matseng, Basutoland .29 36s 27 38 E
45 Matsu-shima, Japan ..37 15N 130 45 E
45 Matsuyama, Japan ...33 47s 132 57 E
45 Matsuye, Japan ....35 25N 133 2 E
33 Matterhorn, Switz.....45 58N 7 39 E
66 Matto Grosso, Brazil .15 0s 59 56w
66 Matto Grosso, plat.,
　 Brazil ....14 25 s 53 40w
66 Matto Grosso, st.,
　 Brazil ....13 45 s 56 0w
66 Maturin, Venezuela .. 9 25N 63 0w
42 Mau, India ....25 15N 79 15 E
20 Maubeuge, France ...50 18N 3 57 E
17 Mauchline, Scotland ..55 32N 4 22w
47 Maude, N.S.W. ....34 30s 144 20 E
51 Mauleon, France ......42 58N 0 33 E
42 Mauretania. dist., Fr.
　 W. Africa 25 0N 10 0w
53 Mauritius, I., Ind. Oc. 20 10s 57 25 E
17 Maxwelltown, Scot. ..55 4N 3 38w
65 Mayaguana, Bahama Is.22 28N 73 0w
17 Mayaguez, Pto. Rico ..18 10N 67 15w
17 Maybole, Scotland ...55 22N 4 40w
24 Mayen, Germany .....50 20N 7 10 E
24 Mayence, Germany ...50 0N 18 15 E
21 Mayenne, France......48 24N 0 45w
20 Mayenne, dept., Fr. ..48 19N 0 40w
19 Maynooth, Eire 53 23N 6 35w
18 Mayo, Eire 53 46N 9 6w
18 Mayo, Co., Eire 53 55N 9 20w
52 Mayorga, Spain 42 10N 5 15w
47 Maytown, Queensland .16 0s 144 20 E
54 Mayumba, Fr. W. Afr. 3 20s 10 40 E
8 Mazagan, Morocco ...33 10N 8 30w
21 Mazamet, France .....43 29N 2 22 E
40 Mazanderan, Iran ....36 30N 52 0 E
27 Mazarron, Spain 37 38N 1 20w
32 Mazatlan, Mexico.....23 8N 106 22w
29 Mazazra, Sicily........37 40N 12 33 E
55 Mbabane, Swaziland ..26 15s 33 15 E
55 Mbale, Uganda ...... 0 1N 34 0 E
47 Mbeya, Tanganyika . 8 55s 33 10 E
47 Meandarra,Queensland 27 18s 149 42 E
18 Meath, Co., Eire 53 38N 6 35w
18 Meathas Trim, Eire ...53 42N 7 37w
21 Meaux, France ....48 58N 2 52 E
40 Mecca, Arabia ....21 30N 40 17 E
23 Mecklenburg, Germany53 15N 11 25 E
23 Mecklenburg, B., Ger. 54 20N 11 45 E
24 Mecklenburg
　 Schwerin, St., Ger. ..53 50N 11 26 E
22 Mechlin. See Malines
39 Medan, Dut. E. Ind ... 3 35N 98 30 E
17 Medea, Algeria ....37 0N 3 0 E
66 Medellin, Colombia . 6 25N 75 50w
22 Medellin, Spain 38 55N 5 57w
22 Medemblik, Neth. ....52 46N 5 8 E
64 Medicine Hat, Canada .50 0N 110 30w
40 Medina, Arabia ....24 25N 40 0 E
26 Medina, Spain 41 19N 4 53w
3 Mediterranean Sea, ..35 0N 20 0 E
15 Medway, R., England 51 25N 0 33 E
24 Meekatharra, W.Aust. 26 30s 118 0 E
24 Meerane, Germany ...50 52N 12 25 E
42 Meerut, India.........29 1N 77 48 E
32 Megara, Greece ......37 59N 23 21 E
20 Mehun, France........47 9N 2 13 E
43 Meiktila, Burma ......20 57N 95 50 E
33 Meilen, Switzerland ..47 17N 8 39 E
24 Meiningen, Germany ..50 37N 10 22 E
33 Meiringen, Switzerland 46 43N 8 10 E
24 Meissen, Germany ....51 10N 13 25 E
31 Mejidia, Rumania ....44 18N 28 18 E
67 Mejillones, Chile 23 10s 70 30w
25 Mejiryeche, Poland ..52 1N 22 45 E
43 Mekong, R., Siam ....21 0N 100 30 E
41 Mekran, Region, Iran 25 30N 61 0 E
15 Melbourn, Cam., Eng. 52 5N 0 1 E
15 Melbourne, England ..52 21N 1 27w
47 Melbourne, Victoria .37 50N 144 58 E
24 Meldorf, Germany....54 7N 9 5 E
29 Melfi, Italy ....41 1N 15 40 E
52 Melgar, Spain 42 26N 4 12w
52 Melilla, Algeria 35 20N 3 0w
29 Melito, Italy ....37 58N 15 47 E
37 Melitopol, U.S.S.R. ..46 46N 35 15 E

24 Melk, Austria, Germany48 16N 15 20 E
14 Melksham, England ..51 22N 2 6w
21 Melle, France 46 13N 0 8w
23 Mellerup, Denmark ..56 32N 10 12 E
33 Mellingen, Switzerland 47 25N 8 15 E
13 Melmerby, England ..54 6N 1 54w
57 Melmoth, U. of S. Afr..28 35s 31 25 E
16 Melness, Scotland 58 31N 4 26w
31 Melnik, Bulgaria ......41 30N 23 22 E
24 Melnik, Czechoslovakia 50 23N 14 26 E
17 Melrose, Scotland 56 36N 2 43w
15 Melton Mowbray, Eng.52 47N 0 54w
20 Melun, France ....44f32N 2 40 E
16 Melvaig, Scotland 57 59N 5 48w
61 Melville B., Greenland 75 30N 58 0w
60 Melville I., Canada ...75 30N 111 0w
46 Melville I., N. Territory11 30s 131 0 E
61 Melville, Pen., Can. ...68 0N 84 0w
60 Melville Sd., Canada ..74 0N 105 0w
22 Membre, Belgium .....49 52N 4 54 E
35 Memel, Lithuania .....55 42N 21 10 E
24 Memmingen, Germany 47 58N 10 10 E
52 Memphis, Egypt ......29 50N 31 10 E
63 Memphis, U.S.A. 35 9N 90 0w
26 Mena, N. Rhodesia ...12 47s 26 14 E
39 Menado, Dut. E. Indies 1 30N 124 50 E
33 Menaggio, Italy ....46 2N 9 14 E
12 Menai Bri., Wales 53 13N 4 10w
12 Menai Str., Wales 53 7N 4 22w
21 Mende, France ....44 31N 3 31 E
32 Mendelia, Turkey .....37 28N 27 40 E
32 Menderes, R., Turkey .37 55N 28 30 E
14 Mendip Hills, England 51 18N 2 45w
62 Mendocino, C., U.S.A..40 30N 124 25w
47 Mendooran, N.S.W. ..31 50s 149 5 E
67 Mendoza, Argentina ..32 4s 68 50w
29 Menfi, Sicily ....37 39N 12 58 E
44 Mengtsz, China ....23 35N 103 15 E
32 Menidi, Greece ....38 5N 23 45 E
22 Menin, Belgium ....50 48N 3 7 E
47 Meninndee, N.S.W. ...32 22s 142 54 E
63 Menominee, U.S.A. ...45 12N 87 35w
39 Mentawei Is., E. Indies 2 0s 99 30 E
21 Menton, France ....43 48N 7 31 E
46 Menzies, W. Australia .29 40s 121 5 E
22 Meppel, Netherlands ..52 42N 6 10 E
24 Meppen, Germany.....52 40N 7 20 E
52 Mequeniz, Morocco ...33 50N 5 30w
34 Meråker, Norway .....63 25N 11 40 E
28 Merano, Italy ....46 41N 11 12 E
47 Merbein, Victoria ....34 10s 142 0 E
42 Mercara, India ....12 30N 75 40 E
62 Merced, U.S.A. 37 18N 120 29w
50 Mercer, New Zealand .37 18s 175 5 E
14 Mere, England 51 6N 2 15w
45 Mergen, Manchuria ...49 0N 125 0 E
43 Mergui, Burma ....12 25N 98 40 E
43 Mergui Arch., Burma .12 30N 96 30 E
64 Merida, Mexico 8 28N 71 1w
26 Merida, Spain 38 52N 6 22w
66 Merida, Venezuela . 8 16N 71 5w
66 Merida, Sa. de, Ven... 9 0N 70 0w
63 Meridian, U.S.A.......32 21N 88 42w
14 Merioneth, Co., Wales.52 48N 3 50w
53 Merka, It. Somaliland . 1 40N 44 50 E
22 Merlemont, Belgium ..50 11N 4 37 E
40 Meroe, A.-E.-Sudan ...17 0N 34 0 E
17 Merrick, Mt., Scotland 55 7N 4 30w
46 Merridin, W. Australia 31 30s 118 30 E
47 Merriwa, N.S.W. ......32 9s 150 18 E
22 Mersch, Luxemburg ..49 44N 6 6 E
24 Merseburg, Germany..51 20N 12 0 E
12 Mersey, R., England..53 19N 2 53w
40 Mersifun, Turkey .....40 55N 35 35 E
40 Mersin, Turkey ....36 44N 34 19 E
14 Merthyr Tydvil, Wales 51 45N 3 21w
26 Mertola, Portugal 37 40N 7 40w
55 Meru, Kenya ....49 15N 2 7 E
41 Merv, U.S.S.R. ....37 30N 61 55 E
41 Meshed, Iran ....36 10N 59 34 E
55 Meshra-el-Rek,Sudan. 8 23N 29 18 E
33 Mesocco, Switz.......46 23N 9 13 E
40 Mesopotamia. See Iraq
22 Messancy, Belgium....49 36N 5 48 E
29 Messina, Sicily........38 11N 12 32 E
57 Messina, U. of S. Af. ..22 16s 29 59 E
29 Messina, str. of, Italy 38 0N 15 40 s
22 Messines, Belgium ....50 46N 2 55 E
31 Mestanli, Bulgaria ....41 32N 25 26 E
28 Mestre, Italy ....45 33N 12 18 E
66 Meta, R., Colombia . 5 40N 71 0w
61 Meta Incognita, Can...63 0N 68 0w
29 Metaponto, Italy......40 25N 16 48 E
40 Mettemmeh, A.-E. Sud. 16 50N 33 40 E
17 Methil, Scotland 56 10N 3 2w
32 Methoni, Greece ......36 50N 21 43 E
51 Methven, N.Z. ....43 48N 171 40 E
17 Methven, Scotland 56 25N 3 35w
13 Methwold, England ...52 32N 0 34 E
61 Metis, Canada 48 41N 68 8w
30 Metkovic, Yugoslavia..43 5N 17 40 E
32 Metsovo, Greece .....39 45N 21 12 E
20 Metz, France ....49 8N 6 10 E
20 Meurthe et Moselle,
　 dept., France.........48 40N 6 30 E

20 Meuse, dept., France ..49 0N 5 25 E
20 Meuse, R., France ....49 52N 4 41 E
14 Mevagissey, England ..50 17N 4 47w
13 Mexborough, Eng. 53 29N 1 17w
64 Mexcala, R., Mexico ..18 29N 101 30w
64 Mexico, Mexico 19 25N 99 17w
59 Mexico, rep., N. Amer. 20 0N 100 0w
64 Mexico St., Mexico ...19 30N 99 45w
63 Mexico, G. of, N. Amer.25 0N 93 0w
31 Mezdra, Bulgaria .....43 8N 23 42 E
21 Meze, France ....43 30N 3 35 E
36 Mezen, U.S.S.R. ......65 56N 44 28 E
36 Mezen R., U.S.S.R. ...65 0N 46 45 E
20 Mézieres, France......49 44N 4 43 E
30 Mezötur, Hungary ....47 0N 20 41 E
55 Mfumbiro, mt.,
　 Belgian Congo 1 30s 29 30
42 Mhow, India..........22 15N 76 30 E
63 Miami, U.S.A. 25 45N 80 15w
40 Miandoab, Iran.......37 0N 46 0 E
40 Mianeh, Iran ....37 22N 47 51 E
32 Micenae, Greece......37 45N 22 45 E
61 Michigan, L., N. Amer..44 0N 87 0w
63 Michigan, st., U.S.A. ..45 0N 85 0w
64 Michoacán, st., Mex. ..19 0N 102 0w
37 Michurinsk, U.S.S.R. ..53 2N 40 21 E
13 Mickle Fell, England ..54 37N 2 18w
22 Middelburg, Netherlds.51 30N 3 40 E
57 Middelburg, S. Africa .31 31s 24 59 E
57 Middelburg, Trans.....25 55s 29 35 E
23 Middelfort, Denmark ..55 30N 9 46 E
57 Middelwit, U. of S. Af. 24 55s 27 0 E
54 Middle Congo, terr.,
　 Fr. Eq. Africa ....2 30s 15 0 E
13 Middleham, England ..54 18N 1 49w
63 Middlesboro, U.S.A. ..36 40N 83 40w
13 Middlesbrough, Eng. ..54 35N 1 14w
15 Middlesex, co., Eng. ..51 34N 0 15w
13 Middleton, Eng. 53 34N 2 13w
13 Middleton in Teesdale,
　 England 54 39N 2 5w
12 Middlewich, England..53 12N 2 27w
12 Midhurst, England....50 59N 0 44w
50 Midhurst, N.Z. ....39 20s 174 18 E
32 Midia, Turkey ....41 39N 28 6 E
19 Midleton, Eire 51 54N 8 11w
17 Midlothian, co., Scot. .55 51N 3 15w
43 Midnapore, India .....22 25N 87 27 E
6 Midway I., Pacific Oc. .28 15N 177 30w
25 Mielec, Poland ....50 15N 21 27 E
64 Mier, Mexico 26 25N 99 23w
35 Mikheli, Finland ......48 55N 5 33 E
28 Milan, Italy ....45 28N 9 12 E
47 Milang, S. Australia ..35 20s 138 57 E
32 Milas, Turkey ....37 17N 27 34 E
29 Milazzo, Sicily ....38 12N 15 13 E
63 Milbank, U.S.A. 45 12N 96 50w
14 Milborne Port, Eng. ..50 58N 2 26w
13 Mildenhall, England...52 21N 0 30 E
47 Mildura, Victoria .....34 11s 142 13 E
32 Milea, Greece ....39 18N 23 10 E
47 Miles, Queensland ....26 35s 150 12 E
62 Miles City, U.S.A. 46 23N 105 49w
14 Milford, Wales 51 43N 5 1w
14 Milford Haven, Wales.51 40N 5 10w
29 Militello, Sicily ....37 18N 14 23 E
21 Millau, France ....44 7N 3 6 E
63 Milledgeville, U.S.A. .33 6N 83 14w
47 Millicent, S. Austl. ...37 35s 140 18 E
12 Millom, England 54 2N 3 17w
17 Millport, Scotland 55 46N 4 45w
19 Millstreet, Eire 52 3N 9 4w
19 Milltown, Eire 53 37N 8 54w
19 Milltown, Eire 52 8N 9 43w
17 Milltown, Scotland ...55 50N 5 57w
19 Milltown Malbay,
　 Eire 52 51N 9 25w
47 Milmerran, Queens....27 55s 151 20 E
12 Milnthorpe, England ..54 14N 2 46w
32 Milos, Greece ....36 42N 24 15 E
48 Milparinka, N.S.W. ..29 40s 141 50 E
15 Milton, England 50 45N 1 39w
15 Milton, England.......51 20N 0 45 E
47 Milton, N.S.W........35 20s 150 15 E
51 Milton, N.Z. ....46 6s 169 59 E
63 Milwaukee, U.S.A. ...43 0N 88 0w
21 Mimizan, France......44 10N 1 15w
51 Mina, New Zealand ..42 46s 173 21 E
41 Minab, Iran ....27 6N 57 5 E
26 Minas de Riotinto, Sp. 37 42N 6 32w
67 Minas Geraes, st., Bra.19 0s 46 0w
67 Minas Novas, Brazil .17 30s 42 30w
64 Minatitlan, Mexico ...18 0N 94 30w
43 Minbu, Burma ....20 10N 94 55 E
16 Minch, The, Scot......58 0N 6 0w
16 Minch, Little, Scot. ..57 32N 6 50w
39 Mindanao I., Philpns. . 7 30N 125 0 E
24 Minden, Germany ....52 56N 8 54 E
39 Mindoro I., Philpns. ..10 3N 121 0 E
14 Minehead, England....51 13N 3 28w
14 Minera, Wales 53 4N 3 5w
47 Minga, S. Australia ...34 45s 140 55 E
58 Mingan, Canada 50 5N 61 30w
46 Mingenew, W. Austl. ..29 12s 115 38 E
26 Minho R., Spain 43 0N 7 40w

Map	Place	Lat.	Long.
54	**Minna**, Nigeria	9 40N	6 30E
63	**Minneapolis**, U.S.A.	45 3N	93 20W
63	**Minnesota, st.**, U.S.A.	47 0N	94 0W
27	**Minorca I.**, Spain	40 0N	4 0E
62	**Minot**, U.S.A.	48 16N	101 15W
37	**Minsk**, U.S.S.R.	53 52N	27 32E
14	**Minsterley**, England	52 38N	2 55W
44	**Minusinsk**, U.S.S.R.	53 42N	91 30E
61	**Miquelon I.**, N. Amer.	47 0N	56 10W
26	**Mira**, Portugal	40 25N	8 46W
67	**Miranda**, Brazil	20 10S	55 50W
26	**Miranda**, Portugal	41 30N	6 19W
21	**Mirande**, France	43 31N	0 24E
26	**Miranda**, Spain	42 41N	3 0W
26	**Mirandella**, Portugal	41 30N	7 13W
41	**Mirbat**, Arabia	17 2N	54 50E
20	**Mirecourt**, France	48 18N	6 8E
31	**Mireny**, Rumania	47 1N	29 1E
67	**Mirim, L.**, S. America	32 30S	53 0W
43	**Mirzapur**, India	25 5N	82 38E
61	**Mishikamau, L.**, Lab.	54 0N	63 50E
67	**Misiones, terr.**, Argen.	27 0S	55 0W
30	**Miskolc**, Hungary	48 7N	20 50E
61	**Missinaibi**, Canada	47 50N	84 10W
63	**Mississippi R.**, U.S.A.	33 30N	91 10W
63	**Mississippi, st.**, U.S.A.	32 0N	90 0W
32	**Missolonghi**, Greece	38 25N	21 26E
62	**Missoula**, U.S.A.	46 50N	113 59W
63	**Missouri R.**, U.S.A.	39 15N	44 0W
63	**Missouri, st.**, U.S.A.	38 0N	93 0W
61	**Mistassini, L.**, Canada	51 0N	73 30W
29	**Mistretta**, Sicily	37 18N	14 21E
35	**Mitau**, Latvia	56 42N	23 43E
47	**Mitchell**, Queensland	26 30S	147 55E
62	**Mitchell**, U.S.A.	43 31N	98 0W
19	**Mitchelstown**, Eire	52 17N	8 15W
45	**Mito**, Japan	36 30N	140 18E
47	**Mittagong**, N.S.W.	34 30S	150 20E
32	**Mitylene**, Greece	39 9N	26 33E
32	**Mitylene I.**, Greece	39 10N	26 15E
45	**Miyasaki**, Japan	31 56N	131 24E
19	**Mizen Hd.**, Eire	51 27N	9 50W
35	**Mjösa, L.**, Norway	60 30N	11 0E
56	**Mkushi**, N. Rhodesia	13 55S	29 20E
25	**Mlava**, Poland	53 8N	20 28E
34	**Mo**, Norway	66 10N	14 0E
47	**Moama**, N.S.W.	36 7S	144 17E
19	**Moate**, Eire	53 24N	7 43W
63	**Moberly**, U.S.A.	39 28N	92 28W
63	**Mobile**, U.S.A.	30 44N	88 7W
63	**Mobile B.**, U.S.A.	30 20N	88 0W
57	**Mochudi**, Bechuanaland	24 27S	26 8E
21	**Modane**, France	45 13N	6 41E
14	**Modbury**, England	50 21N	3 53W
57	**Modder R.**, U. of S. Af.	28 55S	25 30E
28	**Modena**, Italy	44 39N	10 58E
29	**Modica**, Sicily	36 50N	14 43E
23	**Moen I.**, Denmark	54 57N	12 20E
22	**Moerdijk**, Netherlands	51 43N	4 38E
22	**Moere**, Belgium	51 8N	2 55E
17	**Moffat**, Scotland	55 20N	3 26W
53	**Mogadishu**, It. Somal.	2 0N	45 30E
52	**Mogador**, Morocco	31 30N	9 50W
26	**Mogadouro**, Portugal	41 22N	6 47W
37	**Mogilev**, U.S.S.R.	53 54N	39 19E
43	**Mogok**, Burma	22 25N	96 35E
26	**Moguer**, Spain	37 15N	6 52W
30	**Mohács**, Hungary	45 49N	18 40E
57	**Mohalles Hoek**, Basutoland	30 9S	27 28E
18	**Mohill**, Eire	53 56N	7 52W
55	**Mohoro**, Tanganyika	8 7S	39 12E
35	**Moisekul**, Estonia	58 8N	25 6E
21	**Moissac**, France	44 6N	1 6E
27	**Mojácar**, Spain	37 8N	1 54W
45	**Moji**, Japan	33 52N	131 2E
50	**Mokai**, New Zealand	38 38S	175 50E
40	**Mokha**, Arabia	13 23N	43 7E
51	**Mokihinui**, N.Z.	41 32S	171 58E
45	**Mokpo**, Korea	34 50N	126 30E
37	**Mokshan**, U.S.S.R.	53 31N	44 36E
30	**Mokragora**, Yugoslavia	43 45N	19 30E
29	**Mola**, Italy	41 5N	17 7E
32	**Molai**, Greece	36 50N	22 50E
12	**Mold**, Wales	53 10N	3 9W
24	**Moldan, R.**, Cz-slov.	49 40N	12 40E
31	**Moldavia, dist.**, Rum.	46 20N	27 0E
37	**Moldavia**, U.S.S.R.	46 20N	27 0E
34	**Molde**, Norway	62 45N	7 0E
29	**Molfetta**, Italy	41 13N	16 36E
27	**Molina**, Spain	40 51N	1 51W
67	**Mollendo**, Peru	16 40S	72 0W
23	**Mollin**, Germany	53 38N	10 40W
47	**Molong**, N.S.W.	33 4S	148 51E
57	**Molopo, R.**, Africa	26 0S	22 30E
57	**Molopolole**, Bech.	24 30S	25 35E
57	**Molteno**, U. of S. Africa	31 29S	26 27E
39	**Molucca Passage**, Dut. E. Indies	4 0S	124 30E
39	**Moluccas**, E. Indies	1 0S	127 0E
32	**Molyvo**, Greece	39 20N	26 12E
55	**Mombasa**, Kenya	4 4S	39 40E
43	**Momein**, China	25 0N	98 0E
55	**Momias**, Kenya	0 20N	34 30E
66	**Mompos**, Colombia	9 10N	74 30W
65	**Mona I.**, West Indies	18 5N	67 55W
65	**Mona, Passage**, W. Indies	18 5N	67 57W
21	**Monaco**, France	43 43N	7 27E
16	**Monadhliath Mts.**, Scotland	57 6N	4 10W
18	**Monaghan**, Eire	54 15N	6 39W
18	**Monaghan, Co.**, Eire	54 10N	7 0W
19	**Monasterevan**, Eire	53 8N	7 4W
31	**Monastir.** *See* **Bitolj**		
26	**Moncao**, Portugal	42 4N	8 26W
26	**Monchique**, Portugal	37 19N	8 33W
64	**Monclova**, Mexico	26 57N	101 28W
61	**Moncton**, Canada	46 5N	64 10W
26	**Mondego, R.**, Portugal	40 20N	7 50W
26	**Mondonedo**, Spain	42 25N	7 22W
28	**Mondovi**, Italy	44 20N	7 50E
19	**Moneygall**, Eire	52 53N	7 58W
18	**Moneymore**, N. Ireland	54 42N	6 40W
28	**Monfalcone**, Italy	45 49N	13 33E
26	**Monforte**, Spain	42 32N	7 32W
55	**Mongalla**, A.-E. Sud.	5 10N	31 46E
43	**Monghyr**, India	25 18N	86 35E
39	**Mongol Buryat, rep.**, U.S.S.R.	53 30N	111 0E
44	**Mongolia, rep.**, Asia	46 0N	105 0E
17	**Moniaive**, Scotland	55 12N	3 55W
17	**Monifieth**, Scotland	56 29N	2 49W
19	**Monivea**, Eire	53 23N	8 43W
14	**Monmouth**, England	51 49N	2 42W
14	**Monmouth, Co.**, Eng.	51 44N	3 0W
22	**Monnickendam**, Neth.	52 27N	5 4E
29	**Monopoli**, Italy	40 58N	17 19E
27	**Monovar**, Spain	38 28N	0 50W
29	**Monreale**, Sicily	38 6N	13 15E
63	**Monroe**, U.S.A.	32 30N	92 0W
52	**Monrovia**, **Liberia**	6 20N	10 50W
22	**Mons**, Belgium	50 28N	3 57E
35	**Mönsterås**, Sweden	57 5N	16 35E
21	**Mont de Marsan**, Fr.	43 55N	1 28W
65	**Mont Pelée**, Martinique	14 40N	61 0W
20	**Mont St. Michel**, Fr.	48 39N	1 32W
57	**Montagu**, U. of S. Afr.	33 46S	20 10E
27	**Montalban**, Spain	40 49N	0 45W
28	**Montalcino**, Italy	43 2N	11 28E
26	**Montalegre**, Port.	41 49N	7 50W
62	**Montana, St.**, U.S.A.	47 0N	110 0W
20	**Montargis**, France	48 0N	2 43E
21	**Montauban**, France	44 1N	1 22E
20	**Montbéliard**, France	47 31N	6 48E
27	**Montblanch**, Spain	41 23N	1 9E
21	**Montbrison**, France	45 37N	4 4E
21	**Montceau**, France	46 40N	4 23E
20	**Montdidier**, France	49 39N	2 36E
67	**Monte Caseros**, Argen.	30 10S	37 45W
28	**Monte Cristo I.**, Italy	42 10N	10 19E
33	**Monte Rosa**, Switz.	45 57N	7 47E
28	**Monte S. Angelo**, Italy	41 44N	15 59E
47	**Montecollina**, S. Austl.	29 23S	140 0E
26	**Montefrio**, Spain	37 21N	4 1W
65	**Montego**, Jamaica	18 30N	77 38W
29	**Monteleone**, Italy	38 40N	16 5E
21	**Montélimar**, France	44 33N	4 45E
30	**Montenegro**, Y.-slavia	43 0N	19 0E
20	**Montereau**, France	48 23N	2 57E
64	**Monterey**, Mexico	25 39N	100 25W
26	**Monterey**, Spain	41 58N	7 29W
62	**Monterey**, U.S.A.	36 32N	121 58W
67	**Montevideo**, Uruguay	34 40S	56 10W
14	**Montgomery Co.**, Wales	52 34N	3 25W
63	**Montgomery**, U.S.A.	32 22N	86 17W
14	**Montgomery**, Wales	52 34N	3 9W
33	**Monthey**, Switzerland	46 15N	6 52E
26	**Montijo**, Spain	38 53N	6 38W
26	**Montilla**, Spain	37 34N	4 38W
21	**Montluçon**, France	46 21N	2 38E
21	**Montmédy**, France	49 31N	5 22E
21	**Montmirail**, France	48 53N	3 33E
26	**Montoro**, Spain	38 0N	4 25W
63	**Montpelier**, U.S.A.	42 20N	111 24W
63	**Montpelier**, U.S.A.	44 14N	72 40W
21	**Montpellier**, France	43 35N	3 50E
61	**Montreal**, Canada	45 30N	73 36W
21	**Montréjeau**, France	43 6N	0 33E
20	**Montreuil**, France	50 29N	1 48E
33	**Montreux**, Switz.	46 26N	6 55E
17	**Montrose**, Scotland	56 43N	2 28W
62	**Montrose**, U.S.A.	38 30N	107 52W
65	**Montserrat, I.**, W. Ind.	16 42N	62 15W
28	**Monza**, Italy	45 37N	9 18E
42	**Monze, C.**, India	24 50N	66 43E
35	**Moon, I.**, Estonia	58 35N	23 10E
47	**Moonie, R.**, Queensland	27 46S	150 0E
48	**Moonta**, S. Australia	34 3S	137 32E
46	**Moora**, W. Australia	30 38S	116 2E
46	**Moore, L.**, W. Australia	30 0S	117 30E
17	**Moorfoot Hills**, Scotl.	55 45N	3 5W
63	**Moorhead**, U.S.A.	46 52N	96 45W
60	**Moose Jaw**, Canada	50 25N	105 33W
63	**Moosehead, L.**, U.S.A.	45 50N	69 30W
61	**Moosonee**, Canada	50 4N	80 2W
67	**Moquegua**, Peru	16 35S	70 30W
30	**Mór**, Hungary	47 25N	18 12E
27	**Mora**, Spain	41 7N	0 40E
35	**Mora**, Sweden	61 0N	14 25E
42	**Moradabad**, India	28 47N	78 58E
26	**Moral**, Spain	38 48N	3 37W
33	**Morat**, Switzerland	46 56N	7 8E
27	**Moratalla**, Spain	38 13N	1 50W
31	**Morava, R.**, Yugoslavia	44 0N	21 20E
24	**Moravia, prov.**, Cz.slov.	49 20N	17 0E
24	**Moravian Hills**, „ „	49 30N	15 40E
25	**Moravska Ostrava** „	49 47N	18 20E
66	**Morawhanna**, Guiana	8 15N	59 10W
16	**Moray, Co.**, Scotland	57 30N	3 20W
16	**Moray Firth**, Scotland	57 45N	3 40W
20	**Morbihan, dept.**, Fr.	47 33N	2 40W
21	**Morceux**, France	44 2N	0 55W
34	**Möre, co.**, Norway	62 30N	8 0E
32	**Morea, dist.**, Greece	37 45N	22 10E
12	**Morecambe**, England	54 4N	2 53W
12	**Morecambe, B.**, Eng.	54 5N	2 55W
47	**Moree**, N.S.W.	29 29S	149 50E
64	**Morelia**, Mexico	19 42N	101 15W
27	**Morella**, Spain	40 36N	0 3W
64	**Morelos, st.**, Mexico	18 45N	97 15W
60	**Moresby, I.**, Canada	52 50N	132 0W
47	**Moreton, B.**, Queens.	27 15S	153 10E
47	**Moreton, C.**, Queens.	27 1S	153 57E
14	**Moreton Hampstead**, England	50 50N	3 47W
15	**Moreton in the Marsh**, England	51 59N	1 42W
21	**Morez**, France	46 31N	6 3E
48	**Morgan**, S. Australia	34 2S	139 11E
33	**Morges**, Switzerland	46 31N	6 31E
57	**Morija**, Basutoland	29 38S	27 31E
45	**Morioka**, Japan	39 32N	141 3E
34	**Morjärv**, Sweden	66 5N	22 50E
23	**Mörke**, Denmark	56 19N	10 22E
20	**Morlaix**, France	48 34N	3 49W
13	**Morley**, England	53 45N	1 38W
18	**Mornington**, Eire	53 43N	6 17W
47	**Mornington**, Victoria	38 15S	145 5E
52	**Morocco**, Morocco	31 30N	7 50W
62	**Morocco, Fr. Prot.**, Africa	31 30N	7 50W
55	**Morogoro**, Tang.	6 50S	37 45E
65	**Moron**, Cuba	22 1N	78 32W
26	**Morón**, Spain	37 7N	5 28W
53	**Morondava**, Madagas.	20 20S	44 20E
13	**Morpeth**, England	55 10N	1 40W
47	**Morpeth**, N.S.W.	32 47S	151 32E
50	**Morrinsville**, N.Z.	37 40S	175 32E
45	**Morrison, mt.**, Taiwan	23 35N	121 0E
37	**Morshansk**, U.S.S.R.	53 32N	41 33E
23	**Morslet**, Denmark	56 4N	10 8E
20	**Mortagne**, France	48 32N	0 33E
28	**Mortara**, Italy	45 13N	8 45E
21	**Morteau**, France	47 3N	6 46E
14	**Morthoe**, England	51 10N	4 11W
47	**Mortlake**, Victoria	38 2S	142 47E
47	**Moruya**, N.S.W.	35 54S	150 2E
47	**Morven**, Queensland	26 28S	147 7E
17	**Morven**, Scotland	56 37N	5 45W
42	**Morvi**, India	22 49N	70 54E
36	**Moscow**, U.S.S.R.	55 45N	37 36E
20	**Moselle, dept.**, France	49 0N	6 30E
51	**Mosgiel**, N.Z.	45 53S	170 21E
55	**Moshi**, Tanganyika	3 20S	37 22E
34	**Mosjön**, Norway	40 30N	13 20E
36	**Moskva R.**, U.S.S.R.	55 30N	37 30E
64	**Mosquito Coast**, Nic.	13 0N	83 45W
65	**Mosquito G.**, Panama	9 0N	81 0W
35	**Moss**, Norway	59 30N	10 50E
47	**Moss Vale**, N.S.W.	34 35S	150 17E
53	**Mossamedes**, Angola	15 7S	12 15E
51	**Mossburn**, N.Z.	45 50S	168 15E
57	**Mossel B.**, U. of S. Af.	34 10S	22 10E
47	**Mossgiel**, N.S.W.	33 13S	144 31E
30	**Mostar**, Y.-slav.	43 21N	17 50E
25	**Mosti**, Poland	53 25N	24 37E
40	**Mosul**, Iraq	36 13N	43 10E
37	**Mosyr**, U.S.S.R.	52 0N	29 13E
55	**Mota**, Abyssinia	11 0N	37 40E
35	**Motala**, Sweden	58 35N	15 0E
17	**Motherwell**, Scotland	55 47N	3 59W
43	**Motihari**, India	26 45N	85 0E
26	**Motril**, Spain	36 45N	3 32W
51	**Motueka**, N.Z.	41 7S	173 0E
33	**Moudon**, Switzerland	46 41N	6 48E
45	**Moukden**, Manchuria	42 0N	123 0E
47	**Moulamein**, N.S.W.	35 2S	144 1E
21	**Moulins**, France	46 34N	3 22E
43	**Moulmein**, Burma	16 29N	97 40E
57	**Mount aux Sources**, U. of S. Africa	28 45S	29 0E
47	**Mount Barker**, S. Aus.	35 3S	138 48E
18	**Mount Bellew**, Eire	53 28N	8 31W
47	**Mount Cuthbert**, Queensland	19 55S	139 54E
57	**Mount Frere**, U. of S. Africa	30 26S	29 0E
47	**Mount Gambier**, S. Australia	37 50S	140 43E
47	**Mount Garnet**, Queens.	17 40S	145 10E
47	**Mount Hope**, S. Austl.	34 10S	135 10E
47	**Mount Isa**, Queensland	20 47S	139 27E
46	**MountMagnet**, W.Austl.	28 0S	117 58E

MAP
47 **Mount Morgan,** Queensland 23 40 S 150 25 E
46 **Mount Morgans,** W. Australia 28 50 S 121 55 E
14 **Mountain Ash,** Wales 51 40 N 3 24 W
18 **Mountcharles,** Eire *See* **Tantallon**
19 **Mountmellick,** Eire 53 7 N 7 20 W
19 **Mountrath,** Eire 52 59 N 7 29 W
19 **Mountshannon,** Eire 52 35 N 8 27 W
15 **Mountsorrel,** Eng. 52 44 N 1 9 W
66 **Moura,** Brazil 1 40 S 61 40 W
26 **Moura,** Portugal 38 7 N 7 30 W
26 **Mourão,** Portugal 38 40 N 7 25 E
18 **Mourne Mts.,** N. Ire. 54 10 N 6 5 W
18 **Mourne R.,** N. Ireland 54 44 N 7 25 W
33 **Moutier,** Switz. 47 17 N 7 22 E
21 **Moutiers,** France 45 29 N 6 32 E
18 **Moville,** Eire 55 12 N 7 3 W
18 **Moy,** N. Ireland 54 27 N 6 42 W
16 **Moy,** Scotland 57 23 N 4 3 W
18 **Moy, R.,** Eire 54 6 N 8 45 W
57 **Moyena,** Basutoland 30 25 S 27 44 E
18 **Moynalty,** Eire 53 48 N 6 53 W
53 **Mozambique,** Mozam. 15 10 S 41 0 E
53 **Mozambique,** Africa 18 0 S 35 0 E
53 **Mozambique Chan.,** „ 18 0 S 42 0 E
55 **Mpika,** N. Rhodesia 11 50 S 31 35 E
55 **Mpwapwa,** Tanganyika 6 30 S 36 35 E
56 **Mrowi,** Nyasaland 10 45 S 34 12 E
56 **Msoro,** N. Rhodesia 13 38 S 31 56 E
55 **Muata Yamvo,** Bel. Con. 8 20 S 23 0 E
55 **Mubende,** Uganda 0 35 N 31 33 E
32 **Mudania,** Turkey 40 15 N 28 55 E
47 **Mudgee,** N.S.W. 32 38 S 149 32 E
32 **Mudros,** Greece 39 50 N 24 20 E
18 **Muff,** N. Ireland 55 2 N 7 10 W
26 **Muge,** Portugal 39 6 N 8 42 W
32 **Mughla,** Turkey 37 15 N 28 30 E
26 **Mugia,** Spain 43 3 N 9 15 W
24 **Mühlhausen,** Germany 51 15 N 10 26 E
24 **Mühldorf,** Germany 48 18 N 12 30 E
22 **Muiden,** Netherlands 52 20 N 5 4 E
18 **Muilrea, mt.,** Eire 53 38 N 9 49 W
17 **Muirkirk,** Scotland 55 32 N 4 4 W
13 **Muker,** England 54 23 N 1 9 W
27 **Mula,** Spain 38 4 N 1 26 W
26 **Mulhacen, mt.,** Spain 37 5 N 3 18 W
24 **Mülheim,** Germany 50 59 N 7 0 E
20 **Mulhouse,** France 47 45 N 7 12 E
17 **Mull, I.,** Scotland 56 27 N 6 0 W
17 **Mull, Sd of,** Scotland 56 32 N 5 54 W
19 **Mullagh,** Eire 52 48 N 9 25 W
42 **Mullaittivu,** Ceylon 90 15 N 80 53 E
18 **Mullet Pen.,** Eire 54 15 N 10 5 W
46 **Mullewa,** W. Austl. 28 28 S 115 15 E
19 **Mullinahone,** Eire 52 31 N 7 31 W
19 **Mullinavat,** Eire 52 22 N 7 11 W
18 **Mullingar,** Eire 53 32 N 7 21 W
14 **Mullion,** England 50 2 N 5 15 W
42 **Multan,** India 30 14 N 71 38 E
49 **Mulwala,** N.S.W. 36 0 S 146 0 E
25 **Munkačevo,** Cz.-slov. 48 28 N 22 47 E
24 **München.** *See* **Munich**
24 **Münden,** Germany 51 22 N 9 40 E
15 **Mundesley,** England 52 53 N 1 26 E
15 **Mundford,** England 52 30 N 0 40 E
47 **Mungindi,** N.S.W. 28 55 S 148 57 E
24 **Munich,** Germany 48 10 N 11 36 E
24 **Münster,** Germany 51 58 N 7 36 E
19 **Munster, prov.,** Eire 52 18 N 8 45 W
33 **Münster,** Switzerland 46 29 N 8 16 E
34 **Muonio,** Finland 67 55 N 23 55 E
34 **Muonio R.,** Finland 68 20 N 24 20 E
32 **Muradli,** Turkey 41 10 N 27 32 E
21 **Murat,** France 45 6 N 2 52 E
55 **Murchison Falls,** Uganda 2 30 N 31 45 E
51 **Murchison,** N.Z. 41 49 N 172 20 E
47 **Murchison,** Victoria 36 50 S 145 30 E
46 **Murchison R.,** W. Aust. 27 30 S 115 0 E
27 **Murcia,** Spain 38 0 N 1 7 W
27 **Murcia, prov.,** Spain 38 30 N 2 0 W
21 **Muret,** France 43 28 N 1 19 E
47 **Murgon,** Queensland 26 15 S 152 0 E
33 **Muri,** Switzerland 47 17 N 8 18 E
26 **Murias,** Spain 42 52 N 6 17 W
27 **Murillo,** Spain 42 18 N 0 44 W
23 **Müritz,** Germany 54 15 N 12 17 E
47 **Murwillumbah,** N.S.W. 28 19 S 153 20 E
36 **Murmansk,** U.S.S.R. 68 55 N 33 10 E
36 **Murom,** U.S.S.R. 55 36 N 41 53 E
45 **Muroran,** Japan 42 30 N 141 0 E
26 **Muros,** Spain 42 45 N 9 5 W
63 **Murphysboro,** U.S.A. 37 50 N 89 30 W
47 **Murray Br.,** S. Austl. 35 7 S 139 15 E
47 **Murray R.,** Australia 34 0 S 140 45 E
47 **Murrayville,** Victoria 35 15 S 141 15 E
33 **Mürren,** Switzerland 46 33 N 7 52 E
47 **Murrumbidgee R.,** N.S.W. 34 30 S 145 45 E
47 **Murrurundi,** N.S.W. 31 45 S 150 50 E
43 **Murshidabad,** India 24 17 N 88 15 E
47 **Murton,** Victoria 36 38 S 142 30 E
26 **Murtosa,** Portugal 40 45 N 8 38 W

MAP
27 **Murviedro.** *See* **Sagunto**
52 **Murzuk,** Libya 25 50 N 14 0 E
40 **Musa J.,** Egypt 28 10 N 34 0 E
31 **Musalla, mt.,** Bulg. 42 8 N 23 38 E
63 **Muscatine,** U.S.A. 41 23 N 91 5 W
46 **Musgrave Ranges,** S. Australia 26 10 S 131 30 E
40 **Mush,** Turkey 38 41 N 41 17 E
63 **Muskegon,** U.S.A. 43 12 N 86 15 W
63 **Muskogee,** U.S.A. 35 35 N 95 28 W
17 **Musselburgh,** Scot. 55 57 N 3 2 W
21 **Mussidan,** France 45 2 N 0 22 E
31 **Mustafa Pasha,** Bulg. 41 48 N 26 13 E
38 **Mustagh Ata, mt.,** U.S.S.R. 39 0 N 72 30 E
47 **Muswellbrook,** N.S.W. 32 18 S 150 59 E
17 **Muthill,** Scotland 56 20 N 3 49 W
47 **Muttaburra,** Queens. 22 38 S 144 32 E
42 **Muttra,** India 27 25 N 77 47 E
42 **Muzaffarabad,** India 34 25 N 73 31 E
42 **Muzaffarnagar,** India 29 22 N 77 48 E
55 **Mwanza,** Tanganyika 2 31 S 32 54 E
55 **Mweru, L.,** C. Africa 9 0 S 29 0 E
43 **Myingyan,** Burma 21 30 N 95 27 E
43 **Myitkyina,** Burma 25 30 N 97 25 E
32 **Mykonos I.,** Greece 37 27 N 25 25 E
47 **Myrtleford,** Victoria 36 33 S 146 45 E
25 **Myslowice,** Poland 50 15 N 19 12 E
42 **Mysore,** India 12 15 N 76 40 E
42 **Mysore, st.,** India 12 30 N 76 0 E

22 **Naarden,** Netherlands 52 18 N 5 10 E
19 **Naas,** Eire 53 13 N 6 40 W
57 **Naauw Poort, U. of** South Africa 31 5 S 25 0 E
41 **Nablus,** Palestine 32 15 N 35 16 E
25 **Nadwórna,** Poland 48 40 N 24 35 E
45 **Nafa,** Japan 26 15 N 127 40 E
33 **Nafels,** Switzerland 47 7 N 9 3 E
43 **Naga Hills,** India 26 0 N 94 0 E
45 **Nagano,** Japan 36 40 N 138 0 E
45 **Nagasaki,** Japan 32 43 N 129 57 E
37 **Nagorny Karabagh, prov.,** U.S.S.R. 40 0 N 46 0 E
45 **Nagoya,** Japan 35 8 N 137 3 E
42 **Nagpur,** India 21 4 N 79 13 E
31 **Nagybánya,** Rumania 47 40 N 23 35 E
30 **Nagykanizsa,** Hungary 46 30 N 17 1 E
30 **Nagykörös,** Hungary 47 2 N 19 48 E
31 **Nagyszalonta,** Rum. 46 50 N 21 41 E
31 **Nagyszeben.** *See* **Sibiu**
25 **Nagyszollös,** Cz.-slov. 48 10 N 23 5 E
31 **Nagyvarad.** *See* **Oradea**
67 **Nahuel Huapi, L.,** Argentina 41 0 S 71 0 W
14 **Nailsworth,** England 51 42 N 2 13 W
41 **Nain,** Iran 32 54 N 52 50 E
61 **Nain,** Labrador 56 30 N 61 55 W
42 **Naini Tal,** India 29 20 N 79 32 E
16 **Nairn, & Co.,** Scotland 57 35 N 3 52 W
16 **Nairn, R.,** Scotland 57 33 N 3 55 W
55 **Nairobi,** Kenya 1 18 S 36 48 E
55 **Naivasha,** Kenya 0 43 S 36 28 E
25 **Nakel,** Poland 52 35 N 17 36 E
37 **Nakhichevan,** U.S.S.R. 47 30 N 39 45 E
57 **Nakob,** U. of S. Africa 27 55 S 20 0 E
23 **Nakskov,** Denmark 54 52 N 11 8 E
55 **Nakuru,** Kenya 0 15 S 36 8 E
42 **Nalgonda,** India 17 3 N 79 20 E
56 **Nalolo,** N. Rhodesia 15 35 S 23 22 E
55 **Namasagali,** Uganda 1 0 N 33 0 E
44 **Nam-dink,** Fr. Indo-China 20 30 N 106 0 E
56 **Nameta,** N. Rhodesia 16 15 S 23 22 E
25 **Namslau,** Germany 51 8 N 17 42 E
34 **Namsos,** Norway 64 30 N 11 35 E
22 **Namur,** Belgium 50 29 N 4 51 E
22 **Namur, prov.,** Belg. 50 30 N 5 0 E
44 **Namyr,** U.S.S.R. 56 10 N 103 0 E
45 **Nan Hai.** *See* **South China Sea**
43 **Nan,** Siam 18 40 N 100 40 E
44 **Nan-Shan Mts.,** China 25 30 N 110 0 E
60 **Nanaimo,** Canada 49 5 N 123 58 W
49 **Nanango,** Queensland 26 40 S 152 0 E
45 **Nanao,** Japan 37 0 N 137 4 E
45 **Nan-chang,** China 28 25 N 116 0 E
20 **Nancy,** France 48 41 N 6 12 E
42 **Nandair,** India 19 10 N 77 20 E
51 **Nandi, Vanna Levu,** Fiji Islands Inset 17 50 S 177 15 E
45 **Nan-hung,** China 25 15 N 114 0 E
45 **Nan-kang,** China 29 25 N 116 0 E
45 **Nanking,** China 32 10 N 118 50 E
46 **Nannine,** W. Australia 26 48 S 118 26 E
44 **Nanning,** China 23 0 N 108 5 E
58 **Nansen Sd.,** Canada 81 0 N 91 0 W
20 **Nantes,** France 47 14 N 1 34 W
21 **Nantua,** France 46 9 N 5 37 E
14 **Nantwich,** England 53 4 N 2 31 W
45 **Nan-yang,** China 33 10 N 112 35 E
27 **Nao C.,** Spain 38 42 N 0 15 E
50 **Napier,** New Zealand 39 30 S 176 57 E
29 **Naples,** Italy 40 50 N 14 17 E
29 **Naples, B. of,** Italy 40 20 N 14 20 E
66 **Napo, R.,** Ecuador 2 0 S 75 0 W

MAP
47 **Naracoorte,** S. Aust. 36 57 S 140 13 E
54 **Naraguta,** Nigeria 9 58 N 8 55 E
41 **Narazim,** U.S.S.R. 38 45 N 64 5 E
42 **Narbada, R.,** India 22 50 N 78 30 E
14 **Narberth,** Wales 51 47 N 4 44 W
21 **Narbonne,** France 43 11 N 3 1 E
29 **Nardo,** Italy 40 11 N 18 0 E
25 **Narev, R.,** Poland 52 55 N 23 30 E
28 **Narni,** Italy 42 30 N 12 29 E
47 **Narrabri,** N.S.W. 30 17 S 149 47 E
47 **Narrandera,** N.S.W. 34 44 S 146 31 E
46 **Narrogin,** W. Australia 32 59 S 117 15 E
47 **Narromine,** N.S.W. 32 15 S 148 15 E
42 **Narsinghpur,** India 23 0 N 79 20 E
35 **Narva,** Estonia 59 23 N 28 9 E
34 **Narvik,** Norway 68 30 N 17 20 E
44 **Narwanchi,** Mongolia 47 0 N 97 0 E
39 **Narym,** U.S.S.R. 59 0 N 81 40 E
35 **Näs,** Sweden 60 25 N 14 33 E
15 **Naseby,** England 52 25 N 0 59 E
51 **Naseby,** New Zealand 45 3 S 170 9 E
63 **Nashville,** U.S.A. 36 8 N 86 50 W
30 **Našice,** Yugoslavia 45 30 N 18 6 E
42 **Nasik,** India 20 0 N 73 50 E
32 **Nasilli,** Turkey 37 53 N 28 21 E
43 **Nasirabad,** India 26 15 N 74 44 E
42 **Nasirabad,** Iran 31 8 N 61 33 E
40 **Nasiriyeh,** Iraq 31 5 N 46 15 E
65 **Nassau,** Bahama Is. 25 0 N 77 30 W
55 **Nasser,** A.-E. Sudan 8 34 N 33 2 E
35 **Nässjö,** Sweden 57 50 N 14 40 E
31 **Naszod,** Rumania 40 19 N 24 26 E
66 **Natal,** Brazil 6 0 S 35 20 W
57 **Natal, prov.,** U. of S. Afr. 32 0 S 31 0 E
63 **Natchez,** U.S.A. 31 32 N 91 32 W
63 **Natchitoches,** U.S.A. 31 41 N 93 0 W
44 **Nati,** China 24 55 N 107 20 E
47 **Natimuk,** Victoria 36 45 S 141 57 E
66 **Natividade,** Brazil 12 10 S 46 40 W
34 **Nätra,** Sweden 63 10 N 18 42 E
39 **Natuna Is.,** Dut. E. Ind. 4 0 N 108 0 E
24 **Naumburg,** Germany 51 10 N 11 50 E
56 **Naünis,** Bechuanaland 17 56 S 22 55 E
32 **Nauplia,** Greece 37 32 N 22 49 E
7 **Nauru I.,** Pacific Oc. 0 25 S 166 0 E
42 **Naushahra,** India 27 0 N 68 5 E
34 **Naustvik,** Norway 65 25 N 12 40 E
66 **Nauta,** Peru 4 30 S 73 30 E
26 **Nava,** Spain 41 9 N 4 29 W
26 **Navalcarnero,** Spain 40 18 N 4 3 W
26 **Navalmoral,** Spain 39 52 N 5 31 W
18 **Navan,** Eire 53 40 N 6 42 W
32 **Navarino,** Greece 36 56 N 21 42 E
27 **Navarre, prov.,** Spain 42 43 N 1 40 W
65 **Navassa I.,** W. Indies 18 30 N 75 0 W
26 **Návia,** Spain 43 30 N 7 3 W
51 **Navigators Is.** *See* **Samoa Is.**
41 **Nawa,** Syria 32 55 N 36 2 E
56 **Nawalia,** N. Rhodesia 12 40 S 32 5 E
32 **Naxos, Tn. & I.,** Gr. 37 8 N 25 28 E
64 **Nayarit, st.,** Mexico 22 0 N 105 5 W
15 **Nayland,** England 50 58 N 0 53 E
41 **Nazareth,** Palestine 32 42 N 35 20 E
15 **Naze, The,** England 51 53 N 1 17 E
56 **Nchanga,** N. Rhodesia 12 30 S 27 50 E
54 **Ndumba Atembo,** Angola 11 25 S 19 0 E
54 **Ndélé,** Fr. Eq. Africa 8 22 N 20 40 E
18 **Neagh, L.,** N. Ireland 54 35 N 6 25 W
31 **Neamtu,** Rumania 47 14 N 26 23 E
32 **Neapolis,** Greece 36 30 N 23 6 E
14 **Neath,** Wales 51 39 N 3 48 W
63 **Nebraska,** U.S.A. 40 42 N 95 58 W
62 **Nebraska, st.,** U.S.A. 40 0 to 43 0 N 95 15 to 104 0 W
34 **Neder Kalix,** Sweden 65 55 N 23 10 E
40 **Nedjran,** Arabia 17 40 N 45 10 E
15 **Needham Mkt.,** Eng. 52 9 N 1 2 E
15 **Needles, The,** England 50 40 N 1 35 W
22 **Neerpelt,** Belgium 51 15 N 5 26 E
40 **Nefud, Desert,** Arabia 28 30 N 42 0 E
42 **Negapatam,** India 10 45 N 79 50 E
42 **Negombe,** Ceylon 7 15 N 79 55 E
31 **Negotin,** Yugoslavia 41 29 N 22 9 E
43 **Negrais C.,** Burma 15 55 N 94 25 E
26 **Negreira,** Spain 42 52 N 8 46 W
31 **Negresci,** Rumania 46 15 N 27 28 E
67 **Negro, R.,** Argentina 38 50 S 67 0 W
66 **Negro, R.,** Brazil 0 40 S 62 30 W
32 **Negropont.** *See* **Euboea**
39 **Negros I.,** Philippine Is. 10 0 N 123 0 E
41 **Neh,** Iran 31 33 N 60 6 E
34 **Neiden,** Norway 69 35 N 29 20 E
25 **Neidenburg,** Germany 53 22 N 20 26 E
25 **Neisse,** Germany 50 28 N 17 20 E
24 **Neisse, R.,** Germany 50 40 N 17 30 E
66 **Neiva,** Colombia 2 55 N 75 30 W
40 **Nejd, dist.,** Arabia 25 0 N 46 0 E
40 **Nejef,** Iraq 31 58 N 44 25 E
39 **Nelkan,** U.S.S.R. 58 0 N 135 40 E
42 **Nellore,** India 14 27 N 80 0 E
58 **Nelson,** Canada 49 28 N 117 16 W
13 **Nelson,** England 53 52 N 2 14 W
51 **Nelson,** New Zealand 41 16 S 173 20 E
51 **Nelson, prov.,** N. Zeal. 42 20 S 172 20 E

MAP
20 **Nemours**, France 48 16N 2 41E
45 **Nemuro**, Japan 43 29N 145 41E
19 **Nenagh**, Eire 52 52N 8 12W
33 **Nendaz**, Switzerland 46 17N 7 18E
15 **Nene, R.**, England 52 13N 1 0W
43 **Nepal, st.**, Asia 28 0N 84 0E
62 **Nephi**, U.S.A. 39 41N 111 50W
18 **Nephin Beg Mts.**, Eire 54 0N 9 40W
21 **Nérac**, France 44 8N 0 20E
47 **Nerang**, Queensland 28 0S 153 20E
45 **Nerchinsk**, U.S.S.R. 52 0N 116 40E
26 **Nerja**, Spain 36 43N 3 53W
34 **Nesala**, Finland 64 58N 26 50E
16 **Ness, Loch**, Scotland 57 15N 4 30W
33 **Nesslau**, Switzerland 47 13N 9 12E
16 **Neston**, England 53 18N 3 5W
16 **Nethybridge**, Scotland 57 17N 3 39W
15 **Netley**, England 50 54N 1 21W
61 **Nettiling, L.**, Canada 66 40N 72 0W
24 **Neu Brandenburg**, Germany 53 34N 13 18E
23 **Neu Bukow**, Germany 54 2N 11 40E
24 **Neu Ruppin**, Germany 52 55N 12 50E
25 **Neu Sandec**, Poland 49 37N 20 40E
24 **Neuburg**, Germany 48 42N 11 10E
33 **Neuchâtel, L., & Canton**, Switzerland 47 0N 6 45E
25 **Neufahrwasser**, Danz. 54 23N 18 40E
22 **Neufchâteau**, Belgium 40 50N 5 26E
20 **Neufchâtel**, France 48 22N 5 45E
20 **Neufchâtel**, France 49 27N 4 2E
23 **Neuhaus**, Germany 47 48N 8 35E
24 **Neumarkt**, Germany 49 16N 11 30E
25 **Neumarkt**, Poland 49 29N 20 0E
24 **Neumünster**, Germany 54 5N 10 0E
67 **Neuquen**, Argentina 38 55S 68 25W
25 **Neurode**, Germany 50 38N 16 30E
24 **Neusalz**, Germany 51 50N 15 43E
30 **Neusatz.** *See* **Novi Sad**
24 **Neuss**, Germany 51 12N 6 38E
23 **Neustadt**, Germany 49 22N 8 7E
24 **Neustadt**, Germany 50 23N 17 38E
24 **Neustadt**, Germany 47 55N 8 13E
25 **Neustettin**, Germany 53 21N 16 42E
24 **Neustrelitz**, Germany 53 20N 13 0E
24 **Neuulm**, Germany 48 4N 10 0E
24 **Neuweid**, Germany 50 27N 7 26E
63 **Nevada**, U.S.A. 37 50N 94 20W
62 **Nevada, st.**, U.S.A. 37 50N 94 20W
36 **Nevel**, U.S.S.R. 56 8N 29 58E
22 **Nevele**, Belgium 51 3N 3 32E
20 **Nevers**, France 46 59N 3 10E
14 **Nevin**, Wales 52 57N 4 30W
65 **Nevis, I.**, Leeward Is. 17 5N 62 33W
31 **Nevrokop**, Bulgaria 41 33N 23 47E
36 **Nevyanski**, U.S.S.R. 57 34N 60 4E
17 **New Abbey**, Scotland 54 59N 3 38W
63 **New Albany**, U.S.A. 38 20N 85 55W
15 **New Alresford**, Eng. 51 6N 1 10W
66 **New Amsterdam**, Brit. Guiana 6 10N 57 25W
57 **New Amsterdam**, U. of S. Africa 26 42S 30 40E
7 **New Amsterdam, I.**, Indian Oc. 37 0S 77 10E
63 **New Bedford**, U.S.A. 41 40N 71 0W
62 **New Braunfels**, U.S.A. 29 43N 98 9W
12 **New Brighton**, Eng. 53 27N 3 1W
48 **New Britain**, Pac. Oc. 5 30S 151 0E
61 **New Brunswick**, Can. 50 0N 66 30W
15 **New Buckenham**, England 52 28N 1 2E
7 **New Caledonia, I.**, Pacific Oc. 21 0N 152 0E
26 **New Castile, prov.**, Spain 39 0N 4 0W
17 **New Castleton**, Scot. 5 11N 2 48W
17 **New Cumnock**, Scot. 55 24N 4 10W
16 **New Deer**, Scotland 57 31N 2 13W
47 **New England Ra.**, N.S.W. 30 0S 151 45E
15 **New Forest**, England 50 50N 1 38W
17 **New Galloway**, Scot. 55 5N 4 10W
30 **New Gradiska**, Y.-slav. 45 18N 17 21E
7 **New Guinea, I.**, Asia. 5 30S 140 30E
63 **New Hampshire**, U.S.A. 44 0N 61 30W
7 **New Hebrides, Is.**, Pacific Oc. 17 0S 168 0E
13 **New Holland**, England 53 42N 0 21W
48 **New Ireland**, Pac. Oc. 4 0S 153 0E
63 **New Jersey, st.**, U.S.A. 40 15N 75 0W
17 **New Luce**, Scotland 54 57N 4 50W
62 **New Mexico, st.**, U.S.A. 34 0N 105 0W
47 **New Norfolk**, Tas. 42 42S 147 2E
63 **New Orleans**, U.S.A. 30 0N 90 0W
16 **New Pitsligo**, Scotland 57 35N 2 12W
50 **New Plymouth**, N.Z. 39 5S 174 5E
65 **New Providence I.**, Bahama Is. 24 30N 78 15W
14 **New Quay**, Wales 52 13N 4 20W
14 **New Radnor**, Wales 52 15N 3 9W
15 **New Romney**, Eng. 51 0N 0 56E
19 **New Ross.**, Eire 52 24N 6 56W
15 **New Shoreham**, Eng. 50 50N 0 16W
39 **New Siberia I.**, U.S.S.R. 75 0N 145 0E
39 **New Siberian Is.**, U.S.S.R. ....
47 **New South Wales, st.**, Australia 32 30S 147 0E
60 **New Westminster**, Canada 49 17N 122 40W
63 **New York**, U.S.A. 40 20N 74 0W
63 **New York, st.**, U.S.A. 42 45N 76 0W
7 **New Zealand, dom.**, S. Pacific Oc., 34 20 to 47 20S 166 25 to 178 35E
55 **Newala**, Tang. Terr. 11 0S 39 10E
13 **Newark**, England 53 5N 0 49W
63 **Newbern**, U.S.A. 35 5N 77 5W
63 **Newberry**, U.S.A. 34 19N 81 37W
13 **Newbiggin**, England 54 19N 3 23W
19 **Newbridge**, Eire 53 11N 6 48W
16 **Newburgh**, Scotland 57 19N 2 0W
17 **Newburgh**, Scotland 56 21N 3 14W
15 **Newbury**, England 51 24N 1 20W
12 **Newby Bri.**, England 54 16N 2 57W
61 **Newcastle**, Canada 47 2N 65 37W
19 **Newcastle**, Eire 52 27N 9 3W
13 **Newcastle**, England 54 59N 1 36W
47 **Newcastle**, N.S.W. 32 56S 151 42E
51 **Newcastle**, N.Zealand 44 45S 169 30E
18 **Newcastle**, N. Ireland 54 12N 5 53W
57 **Newcastle**, U. of S. Afr. 27 46S 29 55E
62 **Newcastle**, U.S.A. 43 52N 104 16W
14 **Newcastle Emlyn**, Wales 52 2W 4 27W
14 **Newcastle under Lyme**, England 53 1N 2 14W
46 **Newcastle Waters**, N. Territory 17 25S 133 25E
45 **Newchwang**, Manchuria 40 50N 122 5E
14 **Newent**, England 51 56N 2 12W
61 **Newfoundland**, N.Amer. 49 0N 56 0W
15 **Newhaven**, England 50 47N 0 3E
63 **Newhaven**, U.S.A. 41 24N 73 0W
15 **Newlyn**, England. Inset 50 7N 5 40W
19 **Newmarket**, Eire 52 13N 9 0W
19 **Newmarket**, Eire 52 46N 8 55W
15 **Newmarket**, England 52 15N 0 25E
47 **Newnes**, N.S.W. 33 8S 150 15E
14 **Newnham**, England 51 48N 2 25W
63 **Newport, Ark.**, U.S.A. 35 37N 91 19W
18 **Newport**, Eire 53 54N 9 33W
19 **Newport**, Eire 52 43N 8 25W
15 **Newport, Essex**, Eng. 50 43N 1 18W
15 **Newport, I. of W.**, Eng. 50 43N 1 18W
17 **Newport**, Scotland 56 26N 2 56W
14 **Newport, Shrop.**, Eng. 52 46N 2 24W
63 **Newport**, U.S.A. 38 58N 84 30W
14 **Newport**, Wales 52 1N 4 50W
63 **Newport News**, U.S.A. 37 2N 76 25W
15 **Newport Pagnell**, Eng. 52 6N 0 43W
14 **Newquay**, England 50 26N 5 4W
18 **Newry**, N. Ireland 54 11N 6 20W
12 **Newton**, England 53 28N 2 37W
14 **Newton Abbot**, Eng. 50 32N 3 37W
17 **Newton Stewart**, Scot. 54 58N 4 35W
14 **Newtown**, Wales 52 30N 3 19W
18 **Newtownards**, N. Ire. 54 36N 5 41W
19 **Newtownbarry**, Eire 52 39N 6 39W
18 **Newtownbellew**, Eire 53 29N 8 34W
18 **Newtownbutler**, N. Ireland 54 11N 7 23W
18 **Newtownforbes**, Eire 53 46N 7 51W
18 **Newtownhamilton**, N. Ireland 54 12N 6 35W
19 **Newtownmountkennedy**, Eire 53 6N 6 8W
18 **Newtownstewart**, N. Ireland 54 53N 7 23W
23 **Nexelö**, Denmark 55 47N 11 17E
14 **Neyland**, Wales 51 40N 4 57W
51 **Ngaloa**, Fiji Is. Inset 19 0S 178 0E
56 **Ngami, L.**, Bech. 20 30S 22 30E
50 **Ngaruawahia**, N.Z. 37 43S 175 11E
54 **Ngaudere**, Cameroons 7 16N 13 30E
63 **Niagara Falls**, U.S.A. 43 6N 79 6W
44 **Niam-cho**, China 34 30N 96 40E
55 **Niangara**, Belg. Congo 3 25N 28 10E
23 **Nibe**, Denmark 56 59N 9 40E
64 **Nicaragua, L.**, Nic. 11 30N 85 30W
64 **Nicaragua, st.**, Cent. America 13 0N 85 30W
32 **Nicaria, I.**, Greece 37 38N 26 10E
29 **Nicastro**, Italy 39 0N 16 20E
21 **Nice**, France 43 44N 7 14E
66 **Nickerie**, Dut. Guiana 5 55N 57 15W
39 **Nicobar Is.**, India 8 0N 94 0E
65 **Nicolas Chan.**, Cuba 23 30N 80 30W
40 **Nicosia**, Cyprus 35 12N 33 32E
29 **Nicosia**, Sicily 37 48N 14 22E
29 **Nicotera**, Italy 38 36N 15 56E
64 **Nicoya, G. of**, Costa Rica 9 45N 84 50W
67 **Nictheroy**, Brazil 23 0S 43 0W
13 **Nidd, R.**, England 53 59N 1 22W
23 **Niebüll**, Germany 54 56N 8 50E
24 **Nienburg**, Germany 52 40N 9 12E
22 **Nieuwpoort**, Neth. 51 56N 4 52E
22 **Nieuport**, Belgium 51 8N 2 45E
57 **Nieuwveld Ra.**, U. of S. Africa 32 15S 21 30E
64 **Nieves**, Mexico 24 0N 102 58W
20 **Nièvre, dept.**, France 47 7N 3 40E
40 **Nigde**, Turkey 37 50N 34 43E
54 **Niger, Col. of**, Fr. W. Africa 15 3N 6 0E
54 **Nigeria, Col.**, W. Afr. 9 0N 9 0W
16 **Nigg**, Scotland 57 8N 2 6W
51 **Nightcaps**, N.Zealand 45 57S 168 3E
32 **Nigrita**, Greece 40 54N 23 32E
40 **Nihavend**, Iran 34 6N 48 17E
45 **Nügata**, Japan 37 58N 139 2E
27 **Nijar**, Spain 36 22N 2 13W
22 **Nijkerk**, Netherlands 52 12N 5 30E
22 **Nijmegen**, Netherlands 51 50N 5 51W
36 **Nijne Tagilsk**, U.S.S.R. 58 0N 60 0E
36 **Nijni Novgorod.** *See* **Gorki**
54 **Nikki**, Dahomey 9 52N 3 18E
37 **Nikolayev**, U.S.S.R. 46 59N 32 0E
37 **Nikolayevsk**, U.S.S.R. 50 9N 45 35E
45 **Nikolayevsk**, U.S.S.R. 53 0N 141 0E
45 **Nikolsk**, U.S.S.R. 59 33N 45 30E
37 **Nikopol**, U.S.S.R. 47 32N 34 25E
31 **Nikopoli**, Bulgaria 43 40N 24 47E
30 **Niksic**, Yugoslavia 42 48N 18 58E
52 **Nile, R.**, Egypt 27 30N 30 45E
42 **Nilgiri Hills**, India 11 25N 76 45E
23 **Nim**, Denmark 55 57N 9 41E
21 **Nîmes**, France 43 49N 4 20E
55 **Nimule**, A.-E. Sudan 3 50N 32 5E
40 **Nineveh**, Iraq 36 16N 43 14E
44 **Ning-hia**, China 38 10N 106 0E
45 **Ning-kwe**, China 31 0N 118 45E
45 **Ning-po**, China 25 55N 121 40E
44 **Ningshia, prov.**, China 40 0N 103 30E
45 **Ninguta**, Manchuria 44 30N 129 50E
21 **Niort**, France 46 19N 0 28W
32 **Nios**, Greece 36 42N 25 20E
61 **Nipigon**, Canada 49 10N 88 20W
61 **Nipigon, L.**, Canada 49 42N 88 30W
41 **Niriz**, Iran 29 10N 54 16E
31 **Niš**, Yugo-slavia 43 19N 21 53E
41 **Nishapur**, Iran 36 11N 58 44E
39 **Nishni Kolimsk**, U.S.S.R. 68 30N 161 0E
39 **Nishni Udinsk**, U.S.S.R. 54 40N 99 0E
32 **Nisi**, Greece 37 3N 22 1E
40 **Nisibin**, Turkey 37 1N 41 17E
25 **Nisko**, Poland 50 32N 22 8E
17 **Nith, R.**, Scotland 55 6N 3 36W
25 **Nitra**, Czechoslovakia 48 20N 13 7E
22 **Nivelles**, Belgium 50 36N 4 18E
26 **Niza**, Portugal 39 30N 7 42W
25 **Njemenchin**, Poland 54 53N 25 30E
35 **Njurunda**, Sweden 62 10N 17 20E
56 **Nkala**, N. Rhodesia 15 53S 26 4E
55 **Nkata**, Nyasaland 11 32N 34 10E
42 **Noagarh**, India 20 32N 82 15E
47 **Noarlunga**, S. Austl. 35 7S 138 0E
18 **Nobber**, Eire 53 50N 6 46W
47 **Noccundra**, Queens. 27 50S 142 28E
29 **Nocera**, Italy 40 45N 14 39E
23 **Noer**, Germany 54 28N 10 1E
20 **Nogent le Rotrou**, France 49 19N 0 50E
33 **Noirmont**, Switzerland 47 23N 6 52E
20 **Noirmoutier**, France 47 1N 2 14W
54 **Noki**, Angola 6 0S 13 30E
29 **Nola**, Italy 40 59N 14 32N
28 **Noli**, Italy 44 14N 8 25E
36 **Nolinsk**, U.S.S.R. 57 34N 49 57E
58 **Nome**, Alaska 64 30N 165 0W
45 **Nonni, R.**, Manchuria 46 30N 124 0E
35 **Nora**, Sweden 59 35N 15 10E
61 **Noranda**, Canada 48 28N 79 20W
57 **Norap**, U. of S. Africa 30 5S 18 13E
28 **Norcia**, Italy 42 18N 13 5E
20 **Nord, dept.**, France 50 50N 2 31E
34 **Nord Tröndelag, co.**, Norway 64 0N 12 0E
23 **Nordborg**, Denmark 55 4N 9 44E
35 **Norddalen**, Norway 62 10N 7 10E
24 **Norden**, Germany 53 38N 7 12E
24 **Nordenham**, Germany 53 30N 8 30E
24 **Nordhausen**, Germany 51 32N 10 48E
34 **Nordkapp**, Norway 71 10N 25 40E
34 **Nordkyn, C.**, Norway 71 5N 27 40E
34 **Nordland, co.**, Norway 66 30N 14 20E
24 **Nordlingen**, Germany 48 54N 10 30E
34 **Nordmaling**, Sweden 63 35N 19 30E
23 **Nordorf**, Germany .....
35 **Nore**, Norway 60 15N 8 45E
62 **Norfolk**, U.S.A. 41 59N 97 22W
63 **Norfolk**, U.S.A. 36 55N 76 15W
15 **Norfolk, co.**, England 52 42N 0 55E
7 **Norfolk, I.**, Pacific Oc. 28 58S 168 3E
13 **Norham**, England 55 44N 2 10W
60 **Norman**, Canada 65 0N 125 30W
50 **Normanby**, N.Zealand 39 33S 174 17E
20 **Normandy**, France 48 50N 0 30E

MAP

13 Normanton, England..53 42N 1 25W
47 Normanton, Queens... 17 39 s 141 8 E
34 Norrbotton, co., Swed..66 35N 19 20 E
35 Norrköping, Sweden ..58 40N 16 20 E
34 Norrland. See Väs-
terbotten ....63 15N 17 40 E
34 Norrnas, Finland......62 35N 21 20 E
35 Norrtalje, Sweden.....59 45N 18 40 E
46 Norseman, W. Austl...32 12 s 121 15 E
34 Norsjö, Sweden ......64 55N 19 30 E
17 North Berwick, Scot. .55 55N 2 30W
22 North Brabant, prov.,
Netherlands ....51 35N 41 10 E
34 North C., Norway .....71 10N 25 40 E
50 North Cape, N.Zealand 34 35 s 173 2 E
63 North Carolina, st.,
U.S.A. ....34 30N 80 0 E
10 North Chan., Brit. Is. .55 20N 6 0W
62 North Dakota, U.S.A. .47 30N 100 0w
58 North East Foreland,
Greenland 8 2N 11 45W
6 North Graham Land,
Antarctica 67 0s 64 0w
22 North Holland, prov.,
Netherlands ....52 30N 4 50 E
37 North Osetin, rep.,
U.S.S.R. ....43 0N 44 30 E
62 North Platte, U.S.A. .41 8N 100 50w
13 North Riding, England 54 21N 1 20w
16 North Ronaldshay, I.,
Scotland 59 21N 2 27w
58 North Saskatchewan,
R., Canada 54 0N 112 0w
8 North Sea, Europe ...52 30N 3 30 E
13 North Shields, England 55 1N 1 26w
13 North Somercotes,
England ....53 27N 0 8 E
13 N. Sunderland, Eng. ..54 55w 1 22w
50 North Taranaki B.,
New Zealand ....38 50 s 174 45 E
14 North Tawton, Eng. ..50 48N 3 54w
16 North Vist, I., Scotland 57 36N 7 20w
15 North Walsham, Eng. .52 49N 1 23 E
42 North West Frontier,
prov., India ....34 0N 71 30 E
60 N.W. Territories, Can. 72 0N 100 0w
62 North Yakima, U.S.A..46 35N 120 32w
13 Northallerton, England 54 26N 1 26w
46 Northam, W. Australia 31 39 s 116 45 E
15 Northampton, England 52 51N 1 0w
46 Northampton, West
Australia ....28 16 s 114 32 E
15 Northampton, co.,
England 52 15N 0 54w
46 Northcliffe, W. Austl. .34 50 s 116 25 E
24 Northeim, Germany ..51 42N 10 0 E
10 Northern Ireland,
British Isles ....54 30N 6 30 E
56 Northern Rhodesia,
Africa ....13 30N 27 0 E
46 Northern Territory,
st., Australia ....18 0N 133 0 E
15 Northleach, England ..51 50N 1 50w
13 Northumberland, co.,
England 55 13N 2 5w
13 Northwich, England...53 15N 2 31w
13 Norton, England 54 8N 0 47w
62 Norton, U.S.A........39 50N 99 53w
57 Norvals Pont, U. of S.
Africa ....30 39 s 25 27 E
8 Norway, King., Europe 64 0N 10 0 E
68 Norwegian Sea, Arctic
Ocean ....68 0N 2 0 E
15 Norwich, England.....52 38N 1 18 E
55 Nosob, R., Africa ....23 30 s 18 40 E
29 Noto, Sicily ....36 53N 15 10 E
7 Nottingham, & co.,Eng.43 12N 1 0w
7 Noumea, New Cale-
donia I. ....22 7 s 166 30 E
67 Nova Coimbra, Brazil .19 40 s 58 0w
61 Nova Scotia, prov.,
Canada 45 15N 63 0w
31 Nova Zagora, Bulgaria 42 29N 26 0 E
28 Novara, Italy ....45 25N 8 38 E
36 Novaya Zemlya,
U.S.S.R. ....74 0N 60 0 E
54 Nouvelle-Anvers,
Belgian Congo ..... 1 38N 19 9 E
36 Novgorod, U.S.S.R. ..58 32N 31 2 E
37 Novgorod Syeversk,
U.S.S.R. ....52 2N 33 4 E
28 Novi, Italy ....44 47N 8 50 E
30 Novi, Yugoslavia .....45 1N 16 21 E
31 Novi Pazar, Bulgaria ..43 20N 27 14 E
30 Novi Sad, Yugoslavia .45 16N 19 53 E
30 Novi Varosh, Y.-slav. .43 20N 19 47 E
30 Novigrad, Yugo-slavia.43 45N 15 29 E
30 Novipazar, Bulgaria ..43 20N 27 14 E
25 Novo Georgievsk, Pol. 52 26N 20 43 E
25 Novo Radomsk, Pol. .41 4N 19 29 E
54 Novo Redondo, Angola 11 12 s 13 52 E
44 Novo Selenginsk,
U.S.S.R. ....51 5N 106 30 E
31 Novo Selo, Bulgaria ..43 3N 27 21 E
29 Novo Sibirsk, U.S.S.R. 54 50N 83 0 E

MAP

37 Novo Uzensk, U.S.S.R. 50 32N 48 11 E
37 Novocherkask,
U.S.S.R ....47 26N 40 3 E
37 Novorossisk, U.S.S.R. .44 43N 37 32 E
31 Novoselitsi, Rumania ..48 13N 26 16 E
37 Novosybkov, U.S.S.R. .52 32N 31 57 E
25 Novoyelnya, Poland ..53 27N 25 35 E
25 Novy Zámky, Cz.-slov..48 0N 18 12 E
25 Novyeviorka, Poland ..55 0N 25 50 E
25 Nowogródek, Poland ..53 45N 25 48 E
25 Nowogródek, co., Pol..53 30N 26 0 E
49 Nowra, N.S.W. ....34 56 s 150 38 E
26 Noya, Spain 42 45N 8 52w
40 Nubian Desert,
A.-E. Sudan ....21 0N 33 0 E
65 Nuevitas, Cuba 21 30N 77 20w
64 Nuevo Leon, st.,
Mexico............25 30N 100 0w
35 Nuke, Estonia ....59 3N 23 30 E
37 Nukha, U.S.S.R. .....41 12N 47 6 E
60 Nuklukahyet, Alaska .65 20N 152 0w
58 Nulato, Alaska 65 10N 158 0w
46 Nullagine, W. Austl. ..21 43 s 120 8 E
46 Nullarbor Plain,
S. Australia ....30 45 s 130 0 E
27 Numancia, Spain 41 50N 2 30w
13 Nuneaton, England....52 32N 1 28N
58 Nunivak, I., Alaska ...60 0N 166 0w
29 Nuoro, Sardinia ......40 22N 9 11 E
24 Nuremberg, Germany 49 30N 11 5 E
44 Nurinsk, U.S.S.R. ....50 0N 71 30 E
34 Nurmes, Finland......63 40N 29 8 E
24 Nürnberg. See Nuremberg
29 Nurri, Sardinia ....39 42N 9 8 E
42 Nushki, India ....29 35N 66 2 E
34 Ny Karleby. See Uusikaarlepyy
55 Nyangwe, Belg. Congo. 4 20 s 26 20 E
55 Nyasa, L., E. Africa ...12 0 s 34 30 E
56 Nyasaland, prot., Afr. .13 0N 33 30 E
23 Nyborg, Denmark .....55 19N 10 49 E
31 Nyíregyháza, Hungary 48 0N 21 46 E
23 Nykjöbing, Falster,
Denmark...........54 46N 11 52 E
23 Nyköbing, Zealand,
Denmark...........55 56N 11 47 E
23 Nyköbing, Mors, Den. 56 48N 8 47 E
35 Nykoping, Sweden ...58 50N 17 10N
34 Nyland, Sweden ......63 57N 17 40 E
35 Nylstroom, U. of S. Af.24 40 s 28 31 E
47 Nymagee, N.S.W. ....32 5 s 146 18 E
23 Nymindegab, Denmark55 49N 8 14 E
35 Nynäshamn, Sweden .59 40N 18 0 E
47 Nyngan, N.S.W. .....31 31 s 147 15 E
33 Nyon, Switzerland .....46 23N 6 14 E
34 Nyslott. See Savonlinna
35 Nystad. See Uusikaupunki
23 Nysted, Denmark .....54 40N 11 46 E
36 Nyuchotsk, U.S.S.R. .64 1N 36 3 E

49 Oahu I., Hawaii Is.....21 30 s 158 0 E
15 Oakham, England.....52 41N 0 44w
62 Oakland, U.S.A.......37 47N 122 18w
15 Oakley, England 52 11N 0 32w
62 Oakley, U.S.A........42 12N 113 54w
51 Oamaru, New Zealand.45 6 s 171 2 E
68 Oates Land, Antarct..70 0s 160 0 E
42 Oatlands, Tasmania ..42 8 s 147 11 E
64 Oaxaca, & St., Mexico.17 1N 96 49w
36 Ob, R., U.S.S.R. .....60 0N 70 0 E
36 Ob, G. of, U.S.S.R. ..68 0N 73 30 E
17 Oban, New Zealand...46 55 s 168 8 E
17 Oban, Scotland.......56 25N 5 28w
52 Obbia, It. Somaliland.. 6 0N 48 50 E
36 Obdorsk (Salegard) ..66 32N 66 50 E
30 Obeesa, Yugoslavia...45 35N 20 5 E
41 Obeh, Afghanistan....34 25N 63 2 E
24 Ober Drauburg,
Austria-Germany....46 48N 13 0 E
24 Oberammergau, Ger. .47 40N 11 2 E
24 Oberstein, Germany...49 42N 7 19 E
39 Obi Is., Dut. E. Indies. 1 30 s 127 40 E
66 Obidos, Brazil .... 1 50 s 55 40w
26 Obidos, Portugal 39 19N 9 10w
24 Öbisfelde, Germany ..52 28N 11 0 E
25 Obok, French Som. ...11 58N 43 20 E
30 Obrenovatz, Y.-slav. ..44 40N 20 14 E
37 Obshchi Syrt, U.S.S.R. 52 0N 52 0 E
63 Ocala, U.S.A.........29 12N 82 9w
26 Ocaña, Spain 39 55N 3 30w
37 Ochemchiri, U.S.S.R. .42 35N 41 30 E
17 Ochil Hills, Scotland ..56 14N 3 45w
34 Ockelbo, Sweden .....60 50N 16 40 E
31 Ocnele Mari, Rum....45 4N 24 20 E
65 Ocumare, Venezuela ..10 2N 66 52w
45 Odate, Japan ....40 0N 140 33 E
23 Odde, Norway ....60 3N 6 30 E
23 Odder, Denmark .....55 58N 10 10 E
26 Odemira, Portugal ...37 35N 8 38w
32 Odemish, Turkey .....38 12N 27 59 E
30 Odenburg. See Sopron.
23 Odense, Denmark ....55 25N 10 20 E
24 Oder, R., Germany...53 15N 14 20 E
28 Oderzo, Italy ....45 48N 12 32 E
62 Odessa, U.S.A........31 50N 102 20w
37 Odessa, U.S.S.R......46 29N 30 36 E

MAP

31 Odobesti, Rumania....45 47N 27 2 E
45 Odomari. See Korsakovsk.
22 Odoorn, Netherlands ..52 52N 6 52 E
66 Oeiras, Brazil 7 0s 42 50w
26 Oeiras, Portugal 38 40N 9 18w
19 Offaly, Co., Eire 53 0N 7 40w
24 Offenbach, Germany...50 5N 8 46 E
24 Offenburg, Germany ..48 30N 7 59 E
34 Ofoten Fd., Norway ..68 30N 17 0 E
34 Öfver Torneå, Sweden 66 20N 25 20 E
68 Ogden, U.S.A.........41 15N 112 0 E
63 Ogdensburg, U.S.A. ..44 40N 75 25w
54 Ogoja, Nigeria .... 6 40N 8 45 E
30 Ogulin, Yugoslavia ...44 59N 15 18 E
63 Ohio, St., U.S.A. 40 0N 82 0w
63 Ohio R., U.S.A. 39 45N 80 55w
39 Oiratsk A.A., U.S.S.R. 51 0N 86 30 E
22 Oirschot, Netherlands .51 30N 5 20 E
20 Oise, dept., France ...49 28N 2 30 E
20 Oise, R., France......49 34N 3 10 E
45 Oitu, Japan ....33 15N 131 41 E
64 Ojinaga, Mexico 29 30N 104 27w
45 Oka, R., U.S.S.R. ....56 30N 43 0 E
57 Okahanja, S.W. Africa.22 0s 16 55 E
56 Okanahana, S.W.Afr. .18 40 s 15 40 E
51 Okarito, New Zealand .43 15 s 170 8 E
56 Okavango Swamp,
Bechuanaland ......20 0s 22 30 E
45 Okayama, Japan......34 48N 134 2 E
63 Okeechobee, L., U.S.A.27 0N 81 0w
14 Okehampton, England 50 45N 4 1w
39 Okhotsk, U.S.S.R. ....59 0N 143 0 E
39 Okhotsk, S. of,
U.S.S.R. ....55 0N 150 0 E
45 Oki Is., Japan ....36 26N 133 25 E
62 Oklahoma,& St.,U.S.A.35 28N 97 30w
31 Okna, Rumania ......48 38N 25 58 E
35 Oknist, Latvia ....56 10N 25 45 E
31 Oknitsa, Rumania....48 23N 27 25 E
30 Okrid, Yugoslavia ....41 7N 20 49 E
35 Öland, I., Sweden ....56 40N 16 50 E
47 Olary, S. Australia ....32 16 s 140 16 E
67 Olavarria, Argentina ..36 50 s 60 25w
26 Old Castile, old div.,
Spain 41 0N 3 0w
52 Old Dongola,
Anglo-Egyptian Sud. .18 20N 31 0 E
30 Old Gradiska, Y.-slav..45 10N 16 15 E
16 Old Meldrum, Scot...57 20N 2 20w
22 Old Rhine R., Neth...52 9N 4 30 E
18 Oldcastle, Eire 53 45N 7 9w
24 Oldenburg, & St., Ger..53 8N 8 12 E
22 Oldenzaal, Netherlands 52 19N 6 55 E
13 Oldesloe, Germany ...53 49N 10 22 E
13 Oldham, England 53 33N 2 8w
39 Olekminsk, U.S.S.R. ..60 15N 120 5 E
23 Olgod, Denmark .....55 50N 8 38 E
26 Olgopol, Russia ......48 12N 29 28 E
26 Olhao, Portugal 37 4N 7 49w
55 Olifants R., U.S.of Afr..24 0s 30 30 E
35 Olita, Lithuania ......54 24N 24 0 E
27 Oliva, Spain 38 55N 0 9w
26 Oliveira, Brazil ......21 15 s 45 10w
26 Olivenza, Spain 38 40N 7 7w
33 Olivone, Switzerland ..46 32N 8 57 E
67 Ollague, Chile ....21 50 s 68 10w
26 Ollerton, England 53 12N 1 2w
26 Olmedo, Spain 41 18N 4 41w
25 Olmütz. See Olomonc.
15 Olney, England 52 10N 0 42w
25 Olomouc, Cz.-slovakia .49 48N 17 15 E
36 Olonets, U.S.S.R. ....60 59N 33 1 E
21 Oloron, France.......43 11N 0 38 E
26 Olosno, Spain 37 33N 7 9w
27 Olot, Spain ....42 10N 2 30 E
25 Öls, Germany ....51 2N 17 20 E
25 Olshani, Poland ......54 15N 26 1 E
24 Olsnitz, Germany ....50 24N 12 12 E
33 Olten, Switzerland ...47 22N 7 53 E
37 Olti, Turkey ....40 32N 42 1 E
32 Olvera, Spain 36 56N 5 15w
32 Olympia, Greece .....37 40N 21 37 E
62 Olympia, U.S.A.......47 0N 122 53w
32 Olympus, Mt., Greece .40 7N 22 21 E
18 Omagh, N. Ireland ...54 36N 7 19w
62 Omaha, U.S.A........41 15N 96 0w
41 Oman, St., Arabia ....23 30N 57 0 E
41 Oman, G. of, S.W. Asia 24 30N 58 0 E
51 Omarama, N. Zealand.44 30 s 170 0 E
55 Omaruru, S.W.Africa..21 26 s 15 56 E
55 Omdurman, A.-E. Sud.15 40N 32 40 E
49 Omeo, Victoria ....37 7 s 147 38 E
22 Ommen, Netherlands .52 31N 6 26 E
55 Omo, R., Abyssinia .. 6 10N 36 0 E
39 Omsk, U.S.S.R. ......55 0N 73 38 E
39 Omu, U.S.S.R. ....67 40N 146 0 E
30 Omurdza, Rumania ..43 45N 26 58 E
26 Oña, Spain 42 44N 3 25w
26 Onda, Spain 39 55N 0 15w
57 Onderste Doorns,
U. of S. Africa ......30 15 s 20 37 E
32 Öne, Turkey ....38 28N 29 12 E
36 Onega, U.S.S.R. .....64 2N 38 23 E
36 Onega, L., U.S.S.R. ..61 30N 35 30 E
36 Onega, R., U.S.S.R. ..63 0N 39 30 E

MAP
28 Pieve, Italy ....40 26N 12 23 E
64 Pyyiapan, Mexico 15 40N 93 10w
62 Pikes Peak, U.S.A. ..38 47N 105 30w
46 Pilbarra, W. Australia 21 20 s 118 30 E
67 Pilcomao, R., S. Amer. 20 0 s 62 30w
42 Pilibhit, India ....28 35N 79 52 E
25 Pilitsa, Poland .....50 29N 19 45 E
67 Piliar, C., Chile ......52 50 s 75 0w
25 Pillau, Germany .....54 40N 19 56 E
47 Pilliga, N.S.W. .....30 18 s 148 50 E
24 Pilsen, Czechoslovakia .49 45N 13 23 E
19 Piltown, Eire 52 21N 7 20w
65 Pinar del Rio, Cuba ...22 20N 83 45w
25 Pinchov, Poland ...50 33N 20 33 E
32 Pindus, Mts., Greece ..39 40N 21 20 E
63 Pine Bluff, U.S.A. ...34 10N 92 0w
46 Pine Creek, N. Terr. .13 55 s 132 3 E
25 Pinerolo, Italy .....44 54N 7 21 E
57 Pines Village, U. of
    S. Africa ....22 45 s 28 29 E
57 Pinetown, U. of S. Afr. 29 50 s 30 52 E
44 Ping-liang, China ...35 35N 106 25 E
45 Ping-lo, China ....24 25N 110 30 E
46 Pingrup, W. Australia 33 30 s 118 35 E
45 Ping-yang, China ...35 55N 111 30 E
45 Ping-yang, Korea ...39 0N 126 0 E
46 Pinjarra, W. Australia 32 36 s 116 0 E
47 Pinnaroo, S. Australia 35 14 s 140 52 E
23 Pinneberg, Germany ..53 40N 9 49 E
65 Pinos, I. de, Cuba ...21 40N 82 40w
25 Pinsk, Poland ....52 9N 26 7 E
17 Pinwherry, Scotland .55 9N 4 49w
62 Pioche, U.S.A. 37 58N 114 13w
28 Piombino, Italy .....42 58N 10 31 E
50 Pipiriki, New Zealand .39 30 s 175 0 E
57 Piquetburg, U. of S.
    Africa ....32 42 s 18 35 E
32 Piræus, Greece .....37 59N 23 50 E
66 Piranhacúara, Brazil . 4 15 s 53 30w
66 Piranhas, Brazil ... 9 30 s 47 20w
28 Pirano, Italy ......45 33N 13 43 E
67 Pirapora, Brazil ...17 45 s 45 0w
24 Pirmasens, Germany .49 12N 7 36 E
24 Pirna, Germany ...50 58N 13 57 E
31 Pirot, Yugoslavia ...43 9N 22 40 E
28 Pisa, Italy ....43 43N 10 25 E
67 Pisagua, Chile ....19 13 s 70 10w
28 Pisciotta, Italy ....40 7N 15 10 E
66 Pisco, Peru ....13 30 s 76 30w
24 Pisek, Czechoslovakia .49 19N 14 10 E
42 Pishin, dist., India ..30 35N 67 0 E
28 Pisino, Italy ....45 18N 13 54 E
29 Pisticci, Italy .....40 25N 16 35 E
28 Pistoja, Italy ....43 58N 10 58 E
25 Pisuerga, R., Spain .41 50N 4 40w
6 Pitcairn I., Pacific Oc. 25 5 s 130 5w
34 Piteå, Sweden ....65 20N 21 10 E
31 Pitesti, Rumania ...44 52N 25 52 E
20 Pithiviers, France ...48 11N 2 15 E
28 Pitigliano, Italy ....42 38N 11 39 E
17 Pitlochry, Scotland ..56 43N 3 43w
43 Pitsanulok, Siam ...16 50N 100 10 E
15 Pitsea, England .....51 34N 0 30 E
17 Pittenweem, Scotland .56 13N 2 34w
63 Pittsburgh, U.S.A. ...40 30N 79 55w
47 Pittsworth, Queens. ..27 40 s 151 40 E
31 Piua Petri, Rumania ..44 46N 27 52 E
66 Piura, Peru .... 5 20 s 80 50w
29 Pizzo, Italy ....38 42N 16 10 E
61 Placentia, B., Newf. .47 30N 54 10w
61 Placentia, Newf. 47 15N 54 0w
33 Plaffeyen, Switzerland .46 47N 7 18 E
27 Plan, Spain ....42 32N 0 18 E
63 Plant City, U.S.A. ...28 0N 81 45w
26 Plasencia, Spain ...40 2N 6 7w
43 Plassy, India ....28 47N 88 22 E
67 Plata, Rio de la, S.
    America ....35 30 s 57 0w
32 Platamona, Greece ..40 1N 22 36 E
62 Platte, R., U.S.A. ...41 53N 99 0w
24 Plauen, Germany ...50 28N 12 8 E
46 Playford, N. Territory .13 14 s 132 0 E
51 Pleasant Pt., N.Zealand44 19 s 171 10 E
26 Plencia, Spain 43 25N 2 58w
50 Plenty, B.of, N.Zealand37 40 s 177 10 E
25 Pleschen, Poland ...51 53N 17 45 E
36 Plesetskaya, U.S.S.R. .62 45N 40 20 E
57 Plettenbergs B., U. of
    S. Africa ....34 0 s 23 30 E
31 Pleven, Bulgaria ...43 25N 24 35 E
31 Plevna. See Pleven, Bulgaria
20 Ploermel, France 47 56N 2 23w
31 Ploesti, Rumania ...45 54N 26 0 E
20 Plombières, France ..47 58N 6 29 E
23 Plön, Germany ....54 10N 10 24 E
25 Plonsk, Poland ....52 37N 20 29 E
25 Plotsk, Poland .....52 32N 19 40 E
25 Ploudalmezeau, Fr. ..48 32N 4 40w
31 Plovdiv. See Philippopolis
35 Plungyani, Lithuania ..55 56N 21 52 E
14 Plymouth, England ..50 23N 4 8w
63 Plymouth, U.S.A. ...41 54N 70 53w
14 Plymouth Sd., Eng. ..50 20N 24 10w
14 Plympton Earle, Eng. 50 23N 4 2w
14 Plynlimmon, Wales ..52 28N 3 47w

MAP
24 Plzen. See Pilsen
39 Pnom Penh, Fr. Indo-
    China ....11 30N 104 53 E
28 Po, R., Italy ....45 8N 10 50 E
62 Pocatello, U.S.A. 42 52N 112 24w
13 Pocklington, England .53 56N 0 47w
30 Podgorica, Yugoslavia 42 27N 19 20 E
30 Podgorije, Albania ...40 50N 20 52 E
32 Podima, Turkey .....41 24N 28 30 E
37 Podolia, dist., U.S.S.R. 48 45N 28 30 E
23 Poel, I., Germany ....54 0N 11 25 E
65 Pointe à Pitre,
    Guadeloupe I. 16 17N 61 28w
54 Pointe Noire, Fr.
    Equatorial Africa .. 0 56 s 12 0 E
21 Poitiers, France......46 33N 0 20 E
21 Poitou, old prov., Fr. .46 44N 0 30w
43 Pokhra, Nepal ....28 20N 84 0 E
37 Pokrovskaya, U.S.S.R. 51 29N 46 3 E
28 Pola, Italy ....44 53N 13 47 E
9 Poland, rep., Europe 52 0N 22 0 E
35 Polangen, Lithuania ..55 46N 21 3 E
15 Polegate, England....50 50N 0 14 E
25 Polesia, co., Poland ..52 0N 25 45 E
29 Polignano, Italy ......41 0N 17 12 E
32 Poligyros, Greece ...40 22N 23 26 E
27 Pollensa, Majorca I. .39 53N 3 5 E
34 Polmak, Norway ...70 2N 28 1 E
36 Polotsk, U.S.S.R. ...55 29N 28 58 E
37 Poltava, U.S.S.R. ...49 33N 34 29 E
44 Polu, Sinkiang ......36 5N 81 30 E
34 Polvijarvi, Finland ...63 50N 29 20 E
26 Pomarão, Portugal ..37 34N 7 28w
29 Pombal, Portugal 39 55N 8 37w
24 Pomerania, prov., Ger.53 0N 15 0 E
18 Pomeroy, N. Ireland .54 36N 6 56w
16 Pomona, I., Orkney Is. 59 0N 3 10w
25 Pomorze, co., Poland..53 30N 18 30 E
29 Pompeii, Italy ......40 30N 14 23 E
48 Ponape I., Pac. Oc... 7 0N 158 30 E
65 Ponce, Pto. Rico.....18 0N 66 48w
42 Pondicherry, India....12 0N 79 50 E
57 Pondoland, U. of S.Afr. 31 15 s 29 30 E
35 Ponevej, Lithuania ...55 40N 24 28 E
26 Ponferrada, Spain ..42 32N 6 33w
66 Pongo de Manseriche,
    Peru............. 4 20 s 77 20w
57 Pongola, U. of S.Africa 27 25 s 32 0 E
36 Ponoi, U.S.S.R. .....67 0N 41 0 E
21 Pons, France 45 34N 0 33w
21 Pont St.Esprit, France 44 15N 4 40 E
20 Pontarlier, France ...46 54N 6 21 E
26 Ponte de Lima, Port...41 43N 8 36w
26 Ponte de Sôr, Portugal 39 16N 8 4w
28 Pontebba, Italy ......46 30N 13 18 E
29 Pontecorvo, Italy ....41 27N 13 39 E
28 Pontedera, Italy .....43 39N 10 40 E
13 Pontefract, England ..53 42N 1 19w
26 Pontevedra, Spain .. 42 6N 8 38w
55 Ponthierville, Belg.Con. 011s 27 30 E
39 Pontanak, Borneo .... 0 0 109 25 E
28 Pontine Is., Italy .....41 0N 12 55 E
28 Pontine Marshes, Italy 41 20N 13 0 E
20 Pontivy, France ......48 4N 2 58 E
47 Ponto, N.S.W. ....32 25 s 148 50 E
20 Pontoise, France .....49 3N 2 3 E
28 Pontremoli, Italy .....44 21N 9 50 E
33 Pontresina,Switzerland 46 30N 9 57 E
14 Pontrilas, England ...51 57N 2 51w
14 Pontypool, England ..51 42N 3 2w
14 Pontypridd, Wales ...51 35N 3 19w
14 Poole, England.......50 43N 1 59w
14 Poole Harb., England .50 43N 1 58w
16 Poolewe, Scotland ...57 46N 5 36w
42 Poona, India.........18 30N 73 59 E
47 Pooncarie, N.S.W. ...33 20 s 142 33 E
67 Poopo, L., Bolivia ...19 0 s 67 0w
66 Popayan, Colombia .. 2 30N 76 50w
22 Poperinghe, Belgium .50 52N 2 43 E
63 Poplar Bluff, U.S.A. .36 35N 90 24w
64 Popocatepetl, Mt.,
    Mexico............19 10N 98 45w
28 Popoli, Italy ....42 9N 13 52 E
42 Porbandar, India ....21 41N 69 40 E
61 Porcupine, Canada ..48 32N 81 20w
60 Porcupine, R., Alaska .67 0N 143 0w
28 Pordenone, Italy......45 58N 12 40 E
64 Porfirio Diaz, Mexico 28 37N 100 35w
35 Pori, Finland ....61 29N 21 32 E
29 Porlezza, Italy ....46 3N 9 7 E
14 Porlock, England 51 13N 3 35w
20 Pornic, France 47 7N 2 5w
32 Poros, Greece ....37 28N 23 30 E
21 Porquerolles, I., Fr. .43 0N 6 14 E
33 Porrentruy, Switz. ...47 26N 7 3 E
35 Porsgrunn, Norway ..59 10N 9 40 E
47 Port Adelaide, S.
    Australia..........34 48 s 138 30 E
57 Port Alfred, U. of S.
    Africa ....33 35 s 26 58 E
55 Port Amelia, Mozam..13 0 s 40 23 E
65 Port Antonio, Jamaica 18 12N 77 2w
17 Port Appin, Scotland ..56 33N 5 23w
61 Port Arthur, Canada ..48 30N 89 0w
45 Port Arthur. See Lushun.

MAP
47 Port Augusta,S. Austl. 32 28 s 137 46 E
65 Port au Prince, Haiti .18 40N 72 20w
61 Port aux Basques,
    Newfoundland 47 50N 59 0w
43 Port Blair, Andaman Is.11 42N 92 40 E
47 Port Broughton,
    S. Australia........33 33 s 137 58 E
65 Port Castries,
    St. Lucia I. W. Indies..14 0N 60 58w
51 Port Chalmers, N.Z. ..45 47 s 170 38 E
17 Port Charlotte, Scot. ..55 45N 6 22w
47 Port Dalrymple, Tas. .41 2 s 146 45 E
46 Port Darwin, N. Terr. .12 20 s 130 50 E
47 Port Davey, Tasmania .43 15 s 145 55 E
47 Port Denison, Queens. 20 8 s 148 17 E
21 Port de Bouc, France..43 25N 5 0 E
47 Port Douglas, Queens.16 30 s 145 26 E
55 Port Durnford,
    Ital. Somal. .... 1 5 s 41 45 E
57 Port Elizabeth,
    U. of S. Africa.......33 55 s 25 35 E
17 Port Ellen, Scotland...55 37N 6 13w
47 Port Elliot, S. Austl. .35 32 s 138 47 E
12 Port Erin, I. of Man...54 6N 4 12w
60 Port Essington, Can...54 5N 130 0w
46 Port Essington,
    N. Territory........11 5 s 132 7 E
46 Port Eyre, S. Austl. .31 47 s 132 30 E
47 Port Fairy, Victoria ..38 18 s 142 13 E
54 Port Francqui,
    Belg. Congo .... 4 30 s 20 5 E
47 Port Germein,S.Austl.33 0 s 138 0 E
17 Port Glasgow, Scot...55 57N 4 41w
57 Port Grosvenor,
    U. of S. Africa.......31 23 s 29 55 E
54 Port Harcourt, Nig.... 4 46N 7 1 E
46 Port Hedland, W.Austl. 20 18 s 118 43 E
56 Port Herald, Nyasa...16 58 s 35 16 E
47 Port Hunter, N.S.W. ..32 56 s 151 42 E
63 Port Huron, U.S.A. ...42 59N 82 30w
47 Port Jackson, N.S.W. .33 55 s 151 12 E
47 Port Kembla, N.S.W. .34 24 s 150 55 E
47 Port Lincoln, S. Austl. .34 42 s 135 50 E
17 Port Logan, Scotland..54 43N 4 57w
20 Port Louis, France....47 42N 3 21w
47 Port MacDonnell,
    S. Australia.........38 5 s 140 45 E
47 Port Macquarie,
    N.S.W. ....31 29 s 152 51 E
65 Port Maria, Jamaica ..18 22N 76 58w
48 Port Moresby, Papua. 9 15s 147 15 E
60 Port Nelson, Canada..57 0N 93 2w
57 Port Nalloth, U.of S.Afr.29 15 s 16 50 E
16 Port of Ness, Scotland.58 28N 6 13w
65 Port of Spain, Trinidad 10 38N 61 29w
42 Port Okha, India .....22 20N 69 5 E
17 Port Patrick, Scot....54 51N 5 7w
47 Port Phillip, Victoria ..38 10 s 145 20 E
47 Port Pirie, S. Austl. ..33 10 s 138 1 E
65 Port Royal, Jamaica ..18 0N 76 52w
63 Port Royal, U.S.A. ...32 20N 80 45w
40 Port Said, Egypt......31 15N 32 19 E
57 Port St. Johns,
    U. of S. Africa.......31 33 s 29 33 E
12 Port St. Mary, I. of Man54 4N 4 45w
60 Port Simpson, Canada 54 30N 130 52w
47 Port Stephens, N.S.W. 32 44 s 152 0 E
40 Port Sudan, A.-E. Sud.19 10N 37 0 E
63 Port Townsend,U.S.A. 48 8N 122 45w
15 Port Victoria, England 51 26N 0 41 E
47 Port Wakefield,
    S. Australia.........34 11 s 138 12 E
17 Port William, Scot. ...54 46N 4 34w
18 Portadown, N. Ireland .54 25N 6 27w
18 Portaferry, N. Ireland .54 23N 5 33w
60 Portage la Prairie,
    Canada 50 1N 98 28w
26 Portalegre, Portugal ..39 16N 7 29w
19 Portarlington, Eire ...53 10N 7 11w
60 Portendick, Fr. W. Af..18 0N 16 0w
14 Porteynon, Wales 51 32N 4 25w
18 Portglenone, N. Ire...54 53N 6 29w
14 Porthcawl, Wales 51 29N 3 40w
15 Porthcurno, Eng. Inset 50 4N 5 40w
15 Porthleven, Eng. Inset 50 5N 5 19w
14 Porthscatho, England .50 12N 4 57w
14 Portishead, England ..51 28N 2 46w
63 Portland, Maine,U.S.A. 43 40N 70 5w
62 Portland, U.S.A. 45 30N 122 31w
47 Portland, Victoria ....38 18 s 141 33 E
14 Portland, I. & Bill,
    England 50 33N 2 25w
19 Portlaw, Eire 52 18N 7 20w
17 Portlethen, Scotland...57 3N 2 8w
14 Portmadoc, Wales 52 55N 4 7w
16 Portmahomack, Scot..57 56N 3 48w
67 Porto Alegre, Brazil...30 0 s 51 0w
66 Porto Altura, Colom.. 2 25N 73 0w
29 Porto Anzio, Italy ....41 20N 12 40 E
65 Porto Bello, Panama .. 9 32N 79 35w
67 Porto Deseado, Arg. ..47 45 s 66 10w
29 Porto Empedocle, It. .37 19N 13 27 E
67 Porto Madrin, Arg....42 55 s 65 0w
66 Porto Maldonado,
    Peru..............12 30 s 69 0w

MAP
21 Rochefort, France.....45 56N 0 59w
15 Rochester, England ... 5 13N 0 30 E
63 Rochester, New York, U.S.A................43 8N 77 50w
63 Rochester, Minnesota, U.S.A...............44 3N 92 25w
47 Rochester, Victoria...36 20 S 144 40 E
15 Rochford, England ...51 35N 0 42 E
63 Rock Island, U.S.A...41 27N 90 30w
62 Rock Spring, U.S.A..41 31N 109 18w
63 Rockford, U.S.A......42 17N 89 15w
47 Rockhampton, Queens. 23 22 S 150 36 E
47 Rockingham B., Queensland..........32 11 S 115 48 E
66 Rockstone, Br. Guiana. 5 50N 58 40 S
58 Rocky Mts., N. Amer. .30 0N 64 0N
20 Rocroi, France.......49 56N 4 32 E
26 Roda, Spain..........37 12N 4 26w
23 Rodby, Denmark......54 42N 11 24 E
23 Rödding, Denmark...55 24N 9 0w
21 Rodez, France........44 21N 2 36 E
16 Rodil, Scotland......57 44N 6 57w
23 Rodkjærbro, Den......56 22N 9 30 E
30 Rodoni, C., Albania ..41 37N 19 24 E
7 Rodriguez I., Indian Oc.19 48 S 63 10 E
23 Rödvig, Denmark....55 16N 12 24 E
46 Roebuck B., W. Austl..18 5 S 122 13 E
46 Roeburne, W. Austl...20 45 S 117 11 E
22 Roermond, Nether....51 14N 6 0 E
22 Roeulx, Belgium .....50 29N 4 6 E
35 Rogaland, co., Norway 59 0N 6 0 E
16 Rogart, Scotland......58 1N 4 8w
25 Rogasen, Poland......52 43N 17 0 E
57 Roggeveld Mts., U. of S. Africa........32 0 S 20 0 E
21 Rogliano, Corsica ...42 56N 9 28 E
29 Rogliano, Italy.......39 12N 16 12 E
31 Rogotina, Yugoslavia..44 1N 22 18N
21 Rohatyn, Poland......49 25N 24 40 E
42 Rohri, India..........27 43N 68 58 E
21 Rojan, Poland........52 53N 21 27 E
33 Rolle, Switzerland....46 26N 6 18 E
47 Rolleston, Queens. ....24 25 S 148 38 E
47 Roma, Queensland....26 40 S 148 48 E
31 Roman, Rumania .....46 58N 26 58 E
13 Roman Wall, England .55 3N 2 17w
63 Romano C., U.S.A....26 0N 82 57w
21 Romans, France.......45 3N 5 4 E
33 Romanshorn, Switz. ..47 35N 9 23 E
28 Rome, Italy..........41 54N 12 29 E
63 Rome, U.S.A.........34 15N 85 6w
15 Romford, England ....51 35N 0 10 E
20 Romilly, France.......48 31N 3 43 E
15 Romney Marsh, Eng. .51 3N 0 55 E
17 Romny, U.S.S.R......50 40N 33 20 E
23 Römö, Denmark......55 7N 8 32 E
33 Romont, Switzerland ..46 42N 6 53 E
20 Romorantin, France...47 22N 1 44 E
34 Romsdal Fd., Norway 63 50N 6 30 E
15 Romsey, England 51 0N 1 29w
31 Rónaszék, Rum.......47 50N 24 6 E
26 Roncesvalles, Spain ..43 0N 1 17w
26 Ronda, Spain.........36 44N 5 10w
23 Rönne, Bornholm, Denmark.............55 6N 14 44 E
35 Ronneby, Spain ....56 10N 15 20 E
66 Roosevelt, R., Brazil .. 8 0 S 60 5w
21 Roquefort, France....44 5N 3 11w
66 Roraima, mt., Guiana ..5 0N 62 0w
57 Rorkes Drift, U. of S. Africa..............28 20 S 30 30 E
34 Röros, Norway.......62 35N 10 45 E
33 Rorschach, Switz......47 28N 9 29 E
34 Rörstad, Norway.....67 35N 13 30 E
23 Rorvig, Denmark.....55 56N 11 39 E
67 Rosario, Argentina ...33 0 S 61 0w
64 Rosario, Mexico......23 5N 106 2w
27 Rosas, Spain.........42 18N 3 18 E
19 Rosberesn, Eire......52 23N 6 57w
20 Roscoff, France 48 44N 3 59w
18 Roscommon,&co.,Eire53 39N 8 12w
19 Roscrea, Eire.........52 57N 7 49w
65 Roseau, Dominica I. ..15 26N 61 27w
62 Roseburg, U.S.A......43 12N 123 22w
16 Rosedale Abbey, Eng..54 21N 0 51w
16 Rosehearty, Scotland..57 42N 2 8w
55 Roseires, A.-E. Sudan .11 52N 34 25 E
24 Rosenheim, Germany..47 53N 12 5 E
57 Rosenkal, U. of S. Afr. 25 5 S 30 4 E
49 Rosetta, Egypt.......31 30N 30 25 E
47 Roseworthy, S. Austl. .34 35 S 138 50 E
41 Rosh Pinah, Palestine .32 56N 35 35 E
31 Roshiori de Vede, Rumania.............47 7N 25 0 E
23 Roskilde, Denmark....55 40N 21 8 E
37 Roslavl, U.S.S.R......54 0N 32 48 E
23 Roslev, Denmark.....56 43N 8 58 E
29 Rosolini, Sicily.......36 47N 14 58 E
14 Ross, England 51 55N 2 34w
51 Ross, N. Zealand.....42 54 S 170 26 E
16 Ross & Cromarty, co., Scotland 57 6 to 58 8N 3 45 to 5 52w
68 Ross Dependency, Ant.70 0 S 180 0 E
68 Ross, I., Antarctica ..78 0 S 165 0 E
68 Ross Sea, Antarctica ..75 0 S 179 0 E

MAP
18 Rossan, Pt., Eire......54 43N 8 49w
29 Rossano, Italy ....39 35N 16 40 E
19 Rosscarberry, Eire....51 35N 9 2w
35 Rossieny, Lithuania ...55 20N 23 2 E
19 Rosslare, Eire........52 17N 6 24w
24 Rosslau, Germany....51 54N 12 16 E
24 Rostock, Germany....54 4N 12 8 E
36 Rostov, U.S.S.R......57 21N 39 29 E
37 Rostov, U.S.S.R......47 15N 39 32 E
62 Roswell, U.S.A.......33 28N 104 25w
13 Rosyth, Scotland......56 2N 3 25w
13 Rothbury, England...55 19N 1 54w
24 Rothenburg, Germany.49 27N 10 10 E
13 Rotherfield, England ..51 3N 0 13 E
13 Rotherham, England .53 26N 1 21w
16 Rothes, Scotland......57 31N 3 12w
17 Rothesay, Scotland...55 50N 5 2w
14 Rothwell, England ...52 26N 0 47w
21 Rotondo Mte., Corsica 42 15N 9 0 E
50 Roto Rua, L., N.Zeal..38 5 S 176 18 E
50 Rotorua, N. Zealand..38 9 S 176 18 E
22 Rotterdam, Neth......51 55N 4 29 E
24 Rottweil, Germany....48 10N 8 35 E
20 Roubaix, France......50 41N 3 10 E
20 Rouen, France........49 28N 1 4 E
22 Roulers, Belgium.....50 57N 3 7 E
19 Roundstone, Eire.....53 23N 9 57w
21 Roussillon, old prov., France.............42 30N 2 30 E
57 Rouxville, U. S. Afr. 30 25 S 26 53 E
61 Rouyn. See Noranda
34 Rovaniemi, Finland ...68 7N 26 45 E
34 Rovanieri, Finland ...68 10N 26 40 E
33 Roveredo, Switz......46 15N 9 7 E
28 Rovereto, Italy ....45 52N 11 5 E
28 Rovigo, Italy.........45 3N 11 47 E
55 Rovuma, R., E. Africa.11 0 S 39 30 E
25 Rowne, Poland.......50 40N 26 16 E
51 Roxburgh, N. Zealand .45 32 S 169 19 E
17 Roxburgh, & co., Scot. 55 34N 2 29w
21 Royan, France 45 39N 1 3w
15 Royston, England 52 4N 0 2w
22 Rozendaal, Neth. .....51 31N 4 28 E
23 Rožnava, Cz.-slovakia..48 37N 20 32 E
14 Ruabon, Wales.......53 0N 3 4w
55 Ruaha R., Tanganyika . 7 30 S 34 30 E
55 Ruanda, Belgian Congo. 2 0 S 30 0 E
55 Ruapehu, mt., N.Zeal. .39 19 S 175 39 E
14 Ruardean, England ...51 52N 2 34w
55 Ruchugi, Tanganyika.. 5 0 S 30 25 E
55 Ruchuru, Belg. Congo . 1 0 S 29 20 E
41 Rudbar, Afghanistan ..30 9N 62 47 E
14 Ruddington, England..52 54N 1 9w
23 Rudköbing, Denmark..54 57N 10 45 E
17 Rudnitsa, Russia......58 32N 27 52 E
35 Rudnitsa, U.S.S.R....58 32N 27 52 E
44 Rudok, Tibet.........33 30N 79 40 E
55 Rudolf, L., E. Africa ..3 40N 36 0 E
24 Rudolstadt, Germany..50 45N 11 22 E
23 Ruds Vedby, Denmark.55 33N 11 22 E
33 Rue, Switzerland......46 37N 6 50 E
21 Ruffec, France........44 1N 0 11 E
55 Rufiji, R., Tanganyika . 7 56 S 38 0 E
67 Rufino, Argentina ....34 20 S 62 50w
14 Rugby, England.......52 23N 1 17w
14 Rügeley, England 52 45N 1 55w
14 Rügen I., Germany....54 25N 13 40 E
25 Rügenwalde, Germany 54 28N 16 26 E
24 Ruhama, Palestine ....31 28N 34 35 E
24 Ruhr, R., Germany....51 20N 8 0 E
39 Rukhlovo, U.S.S.R....54 0N 124 0 E
55 Rukwa, L., Tang. Terr.. 8 20 S 32 40 E
16 Rum I., Scotland......57 0N 6 20w
16 Rum, Sound of, Scot. .56 57N 6 15w
30 Ruma, Yugoslavia....45 2N 19 51 E
9 Rumania, King., Eur. .46 0N 25 0 E
55 Rumbek, A.-E. Sudan . 6 50N 29 40 E
14 Runcorn, England 53 20N 2 44w
34 Ruona, Finland.......65 55N 26 4 E
32 Rupel, Greece........41 18N 23 25 E
66 Rupert House, Can. ...51 20N 78 40w
66 Rurenabaque, Bol.....14 0 S 67 40w
55 Rusambo, S. Rhod. ...16 35 S 32 0 E
31 Ruschuk, Bulgaria ....43 45N 25 59 E
15 Rush, Fire...........53 31N 6 5w
15 Rushden, England....52 18N 0 35w
15 Ruskington, England..53 2N 0 23w
37 Russell, N. Zealand ...35 15 S 174 9 E
36 Russian S.F.S.,U.S.S.R.55 0N 50 0 E
33 Russuksesse, Bulg. ....42 30N 27 14 E
57 Rustenburg, U. of S. Africa.............25 15 S 27 20 E
26 Rute, Spain..........37 19N 4 25w
25 Ruthenia, prov., Cz.-slovakia.........48 30N 23 0 E
17 Rutherglen, Scotland..55 49N 4 12w
17 Ruthin, Wales........53 7N 3 19w
17 Ruthwell, Scotland ...55 0N 3 23w
14 Rutland, co., England..52 40N 0 35w
29 Ruvo, Italy..........41 8N 16 38 E
55 Ruwe, Belgian Congo .10 38 S 25 32 E
55 Ruwenzori, mt., Afr. ..0 28N 29 55 E
25 Rużomberok, Cz.-slov..49 40N 19 18 E
37 Ryajsk, U.S.S.R......53 40N 40 0 E
17 Ryan, Loch, Scotland..54 46N 5 3w

MAP
37 Ryazan, U.S.S.R......54 41N 39 38 E
36 Rybinsk, U.S.S.R......58 8N 38 58 E
31 Rybnitsa, Russia......47 46N 29 1 E
15 Ryde, England........50 44N 1 11w
28 Rye, Denmark........56 6N 9 47 E
15 Rye, England.........50 57N 0 45 E
13 Rye, R., England 54 12N 0 55w
37 Ryechitsa, U.S.S.R....52 20N 30 22 E
35 Ryejitsa, Latvia......56 30N 27 20 E
37 Rylsk, U.S.S.R.......51 37N 34 34 E
47 Rylstone, N.S.W......33 50 S 149 58 E
23 Ryomgaard, Den......56 23N 10 29 E
25 Rypin, Poland ....53 3N 19 31 E
25 Rzeszów, Poland......50 1N 21 27 E

24 Saalfeld, Germany ....50 40N 11 22 E
20 Saareguemines, Fr....49 8N 7 5 E
35 Saarentaa. See Ösel
33 Saas, Switzerland.....46 8N 7 56 E
27 Sabadell, Spain ......41 32N 2 5 E
66 Sabanilla, Colombia ..11 0N 74 52w
29 Sabaudia, Italy.......41 25N 13 5 E
64 Sabinas, Mexico......26 26N 100 15w
63 Sabine, U.S.A........29 42N 93 55w
33 Sablé, France........47 51N 0 20w
63 Sable, C., U.S.A......25 5N 81 5w
61 Sable, I., Canada.....43 30N 60 0w
26 Sabugal, Portugal....40 21N 7 10w
24 Sachsenburg, Austria, Germany ..46 50N 13 22 E
62 Sacramento, U.S.A...38 31N 121 32w
55 Sadani, Tanganyika .. 6 4 S 38 46 E
47 Saddleworth, S. Austl..34 0 S 138 55 E
43 Sadiya, India........27 55N 95 42 E
15 Sæby, Denmark......57 20N 10 32 E
23 Sædder, Denmark....55 26N 12 8 E
41 Safed, Palestine......33 0N 35 20 E
8 Saffi, Morocco.......32 19N 9 12w
15 Saffron Walden, Eng. .52 2N 0 15 E
43 Saga, Japan.........33 14N 130 29 E
43 Sagaing, Burma......22 0N 95 55 E
43 Sagar, India.........16 30N 76 50 E
63 Saginaw, U.S.A......43 27N 84 0w
26 Sagres, Portugal 37 0N 8 55w
65 Sagua la Grande, Cuba 22 46N 80 5w
27 Sagunto, Spain 39 42N 0 14w
26 Sahagun, Spain 42 57N 5 0w
8 Sahara Desert, N. Afr..20 0N 5 0 E
42 Saharanpur, India....29 58N 77 40 E
34 Saida Guba, U.S.S.R..69 0N 33 20 E
44 Saidapet, India ......13 0N 80 12 E
33 Saignelègier, Switz. ..47 16N 7 0 E
39 Saigon, Fr. Indo-China.10 45N 106 45 E
14 St. Agnes, England...50 19N 5 12w
15 St. Albans, England ..51 45N 0 21w
20 St. Amand, France ...47 31N 3 3 E
51 St. Andrews, N.Zeal..44 32 S 171 11 E
17 St. Andrews, Scotland 56 21N 2 48w
61 St. Anne, Canada 47 2N 71 0w
12 St. Annes, England...53 44N 2 57w
65 St. Anns, Jamaica 18 27N 77 12w
12 St. Asaph, Wales.....53 15N 3 18w
65 St. Augustine, U.S.A. .29 57N 81 20w
14 St. Austell, England ..50 21N 4 48w
65 St. Bartholomew, I., West Indies........17 57N 62 50w
14 St. Blazey, England ..50 23N 4 43w
20 St. Brieue, France ...48 30N 2 50w
21 St. Ceré, France ......44 51N 1 52 E
63 St. Charles, U.S.A....38 52N 90 33w
65 St. Christopher I., Leeward Is., W. Indies 17 15N 62 40w
21 St. Claude, France ...46 23N 5 52 E
14 St. Clears, Wales 51 48N 4 30w
63 St. Cloud, U.S.A......45 35N 94 10w
14 St. Columb Major, England.............50 27N 4 56w
16 St. Combs, Scotland..57 39N 1 55w
14 St. Davids, Wales 51 53N 5 17w
20 St. Denis, France .....48 56N 2 23 E
20 St. Dié, France.......48 18N 6 58 E
20 St. Dizier, France ....48 38N 4 58 E
60 St. Elias, Mt., Alaska..60 10N 140 30w
21 St. Etienne, France...45 27N 4 24 E
65 St. Eustatius, W. Inds. 17 28N 63 0w
16 St. Fergus, Scotland..57 33N 1 51w
17 St. Fillans, Scotland ..56 24N 4 6w
33 St. Gall, & Canton, Switzerland........47 25N 9 23 E
21 St. Gaudens, France .43 7N 0 25 E
14 St. Gennys, England ..50 44N 4 36w
65 St. George, Grenada I..12 0N 61 50w
11 St. George's Chan., British Isles.........52 0N 6 0w
20 St. Germain, France..48 53N 2 4 E
21 St. Girons, France ...42 59N 1 8 E
33 St. Gotthard P., Switz. 46 30N 8 40 E
57 St. Helena B., U. of S. Africa.........32 40 S 18 10 E
6 St. Helena I., At. Oc. .15 30 S 6 40w
12 St. Helens, England ..53 28N 2 45w
20 St. Helier, Channel Is..49 11N 2 6w
20 St. Hippolyte, France..47 18N 6 50 E
66 St. Ignacio, Bolivia ..16 0 S 62 0w
15 St. Ives, England.....52 21N 0 5w

MAP			
15	**St. Ives**, Eng. ...Inset	50 13N	5 28W
21	**St. Jean**, France	45 18N	6 20E
21	**St. Jean de Luz**, Fr.	43 23N	1 39W
21	**St. Jean Pied de Pont**, France	43 9N	1 14W
60	**St. John**, Canada	56 20N	121 25W
61	**St. John**, Canada	45 20N	66 2W
61	**St. Johns**, Newf.	47 20N	52 50W
63	**St. Joseph**, U.S.A.	39 49N	94 52W
21	**St. Juan les Pins**, Fr.	43 34N	7 7E
21	**St. Junien**, France	45 54N	0 25E
15	**St. Just** Eng. ...Inset	50 9N	5 39W
14	**St. Keverne**, England	50 3N	5 5W
65	**St. Kitts, I.**, Leeward Is.	17 15N	62 40W
61	**St. Lawrence, G. of**, Canada	48 0N	62 0W
58	**St. Lawrence I.**, N. America	63 0N	170 0W
61	**St. Lawrence R.**, Can.	44 55N	75 2W
15	**St. Leonards**, England	50 51N	0 34E
21	**St. Louis**, France	43 24N	4 50E
52	**St. Louis**, Fr. W. Afr.	16 0N	16 30W
63	**St. Louis**, U.S.A.	38 39N	90 13W
65	**St.Lucia,I.**,WindwardIs.	14 0N	60 58W
21	**St. Maixent**, France	46 25N	0 12W
20	**St. Malo**, France	49 39N	2 2W
65	**St. Marc**, Haiti	19 0N	73 0W
33	**St. Maria**, Italy	41 4N	16 14E
21	**St. Martin**, France	45 5N	7 15E
65	**St. Martin, I.**, W. Indies	18 2N	63 3W
33	**St. Maurice**, Switz.	46 13N	7 1E
14	**St. Mawes**, England	50 20N	5 2W
58	**St. Michael**, Alaska	63 30N	162 0W
15	**St. Michaels Mt.**, England ...Inset	50 7N	5 28W
20	**St. Mihiel**, France	48 55N	5 33E
33	**St. Moritz**, Switz.	46 30N	9 50E
20	**St. Nazaire**, France	47 17N	2 16W
15	**St. Neots**, England	52 15N	0 17W
33	**St. Nicholas**, Switz.	46 10N	7 47E
22	**St. Nicolas**, Belgium	52 10N	4 8E
20	**St. Omer**, France	50 48N	2 13E
21	**St. Paul**, France	42 50N	2 28E
63	**St. Paul**, U.S.A.	45 0N	92 3W
20	**St. Peter Port**, Ch. Is.	49 27N	2 33W
65	**St. Pierre**, W. Indies	14 45N	61 10W
61	**St. Pierre I.**, Canada	46 40N	56 20W
20	**St. Pol**, France	50 23N	2 20E
24	**St. Pölten**, Austr., Ger.	48 12N	15 40E
20	**St. Quay**, France	48 39N	2 52W
20	**St. Quentin**, France	49 52N	3 18E
20	**St. Servan**, France	48 37N	2 1W
54	**St. Thomas, I.**, W. Afr.	0 20N	6 40E
65	**St. Thomas I.**, W. Ind.	18 25N	65 0W
22	**St. Trond**, Belgium	50 49N	5 11E
20	**St. Valéry-en-Caux**, France	49 52N	0 44E
20	**St. Valéry-sur-Somme**, France	50 11N	1 38E
24	**St. Veit**, Aust., Germ.	46 46N	24 27E
6	**St. Vincent I.**, At. Oc.	17 0N	26 0W
65	**St. Vincent I.**, W. Indies	13 18N	62 12W
22	**St. Vith**, Belgium	50 27N	6 8E
21	**Saintes**, France	45 46N	0 41W
21	**Saintes Maries**, France	43 27N	4 26E
45	**Sakai**, Japan	35 31N	133 13E
45	**Sakata**, Japan	38 52N	139 50E
45	**Sakhalin I.**, U.S.S.R.	50 30N	143 0E
37	**Sakharnaya**, U.S.S.R.	49 38N	52 28E
26	**Salamanca**, Spain	40 57N	5 40W
48	**Salamaua**, N. Guinea	7 25S	147 0E
66	**Salavery**, Peru	8 30N	79 0W
26	**Saldaña**, Spain	42 32N	4 45W
42	**Salem**, India	11 35N	78 12E
62	**Salem**, U.S.A.	42 28N	70 59W
29	**Salerno**, Italy	40 40N	14 47E
13	**Salford**, England	53 30N	2 17W
62	**Salina**, U.S.A.	38 50N	97 40W
64	**Salina Cruz**, Mexico	16 9N	95 19W
67	**Salinas Grandes**, Arg.	29 10S	64 30W
20	**Salins**, France	46 56N	5 52E
15	**Salisbury**, England	51 4N	1 48W
56	**Salisbury**, S. Rhodesia	17 50S	31 7E
14	**Salisbury Plain**, Eng.	51 13N	1 55W
35	**Salmi**, Finland	61 22N	31 48E
35	**Salo**, Finland	60 25N	23 0E
21	**Salon**, France	43 38N	5 6E
32	**Salonika.** *See* **Thessaloniki**		
62	**Salt Lake City**, U.S.A.	40 44N	112 0W
67	**Salta**, Argentina	24 40S	65 30W
14	**Saltash**, England	50 25N	4 13W
13	**Saltburn**, England	54 35N	0 59W
17	**Saltcoats**, Scotland	55 38N	4 48W
14	**Saltcombe**, England	50 20N	3 45W
34	**Saltdal**, Norway	67 1N	15 35E
13	**Saltfleet**, England	53 25N	0 11E
64	**Saltillo**, Mexico	25 29N	101 5W
67	**Salto**, Uruguay	31 20N	57 50W
67	**Salto Grande**, Brazil	22 30S	51 0W
43	**Salur**, India	18 30N	83 15E
28	**Saluzzo**, Italy	44 40N	7 29E
64	**Salvador, st.**, Central America	13 45N	89 0W
26	**Salvaterra**, Portugal	39 52N	7 2W
27	**Salvatierra**, Spain	42 52N	2 23W
39	**Salween, R.**, Burma	22 20N	98 40E
37	**Salyani**, U.S.S.R.	39 30N	48 58E
24	**Salzburg**, Austria, Ger.	47 48N	13 3E
24	**Salzburg, prov.**, Austria, Germany	47 20N	13 0E
30	**Samac**, Yugoslavia	45 5N	18 26E
33	**Samaden**, Switzerland	46 33N	9 43E
31	**Samakov**, Bulgaria	42 19N	23 38E
39	**Samarang**, Java	7 0S	110 20E
41	**Samaria.** *See* **Sebustiye**		
41	**Samaria, dist.**, Pal.	32 20N	35 10E
39	**Samarinda**, Borneo	0 30S	117 0E
41	**Samarkand**, U.S.S.R.	39 40N	66 55E
40	**Samarra**, Iraq	34 8N	43 56E
40	**Samawa**, Iraq	31 12N	45 15E
43	**Sambalpur**, India	21 28N	84 6E
42	**Sambhar**, India	26 54N	75 13E
25	**Sambor**, Poland	49 32N	22 14E
22	**Sambre, R.**, Belgium	50 20N	4 0E
55	**Samburu**, Kenya	3 47S	39 16E
51	**Samoa Is.** ...Inset	13 30S	171 0W
32	**Samos, I.**, Greece	37 45N	27 45E
32	**Samothrace, tn. & I.**, Greece	40 27N	25 40E
45	**Samshui**, China	23 15N	113 20E
23	**Samsö I.**, Denmark	55 50N	10 35E
40	**Samsun**, Turkey	41 13N	36 15E
67	**San Ambrosio I.**, Chile	26 35S	79 30W
29	**San Angelo**, Italy	40 55N	15 10E
62	**San Angelo**, U.S.A.	31 30N	100 30W
62	**San Antonio**, U.S.A.	29 15N	98 30W
66	**San Antonio Falls**, Brazil	8 40S	66 0W
26	**San Bartholomeu**, Portugal	37 15N	8 20W
28	**San Bartolomeo**, Italy	41 35N	14 40E
62	**San Bernardino**, U.S.A.	34 7N	117 19W
64	**San Blas**, Mexico	21 31N	105 22W
64	**San Cristobal**, Mexico	16 42N	92 45W
62	**San Diego**, U.S.A.	32 45N	117 7W
67	**San Felipe**, Chile	32 40S	70 45W
67	**San Felix I.**, Chile	26 30S	80 0W
64	**San Fernando**, Mexico	29 59N	115 15W
26	**San Fernando**, Spain	36 30N	6 12W
65	**San Fernando**, Trinidad	10 17N	61 26W
66	**San Fernando**, Venez.	4 30N	68 0W
67	**San Francisco**, Arg.	32 30S	66 12W
62	**San Francisco**, U.S.A.	37 45N	122 30W
64	**San Gerónimo**, Mexico	16 30N	95 10W
27	**San Gines de la Jara**, Spain	37 35N	0 43W
29	**San Giovanni**, Italy	39 18N	16 40E
64	**San Ignacio**, Mexico	24 2N	106 30W
66	**San Joaquim**, Brazil	0 10S	67 25W
67	**San José**, Brazil	20 30S	49 40W
64	**San José**, Costa Rica	9 59N	84 12W
64	**San José**, Guatemala	14 0N	90 55W
62	**San Jose**, U.S.A.	37 20N	121 28W
66	**San José**, Venezuela	6 0N	63 40W
64	**San Jose del Cabo**, Mexico	23 3N	109 46W
67	**San Juan**, Argentina	31 15S	68 50W
65	**San Juan**, Porto Rico	18 29N	66 2W
64	**San Juan Bautista**, Mexico	18 0N	93 0W
64	**San Juan del Sur**, Nicaragua	11 15N	85 51W
26	**San Lucar**, Spain	37 30N	7 25W
67	**San Luis**, Argentina	33 10S	66 30W
67	**San Luis de Caceres**, Brazil	16 0S	57 35W
62	**San Luis Obispo**, U.S.A.	35 13N	120 40W
64	**San Luis Potosi**, St. & Tn., Mexico	22 2N	101 1W
66	**San Luiz**, Brazil	2 58S	43 59W
28	**San Marco**, Italy	41 45N	15 40E
64	**San Marcos**, Guatem.	14 59N	91 50W
28	**San Marino**, Italy	43 57N	12 30E
27	**San Martin**, Spain	41 25N	2 13E
26	**San Martinho**, Port.	39 40N	9 20W
52	**S. Miguel I.**, Azores	38 30N	0 28W
64	**San Miguel**, Salvador	13 29N	88 12W
67	**San Pedro**, Paraguay	24 0S	58 0W
62	**San Pedro**, U.S.A.	33 41N	118 19W
65	**San Pedro de Macoris**, Dom. Rep.	18 30N	69 17W
67	**San Rafael**, Argentina	34 33S	68 40W
28	**San Remo**, Italy	43 49N	7 42E
26	**San Roque**, Spain	36 15N	5 22W
54	**San Salvador**, Angola	6 15S	14 18E
66	**San Salvador**, Brazil	12 0S	38 30W
64	**San Salvador**, Salvador	13 45N	89 18W
27	**San Sebastian**, Spain	43 29N	1 59W
28	**San Sepolcro**, Italy	43 33N	12 8E
28	**San Severo**, Italy	41 42N	15 23E
32	**San Stefano**, Turkey	40 57N	28 50E
64	**San Vincente**, Mexico	24 20N	00 40W
26	**San Vincente de la Barquera**, Spain	43 40N	4 20W
65	**Sanchez**, DominicanRep.	19 11N	69 41W
39	**Sandakan**, Brit. N. Borneo	5 50N	118 0E
62	**Sanderson**, U.S.A.	30 10N	102 24W
15	**Sandgate**, England	51 5N	1 9E
15	**Sandhurst**, England	51 21N	0 49W
25	**Sandomir**, Poland	50 42N	21 45E
43	**Sandoway**, Burma	18 23N	94 30E
15	**Sandown**, England	50 39N	1 9W
62	**Sandpoint**, U.S.A.	47 50N	117 0W
15	**Sandringham**, Eng.	52 50N	0 31E
46	**Sandstone**, W. Austrl.	28 1S	119 13E
63	**Sandusky**, U.S.A.	41 26N	82 47W
23	**Sandvig, Bornholm**, Denmark	55 17N	14 46E
15	**Sandwich**, England	51 17N	1 20E
15	**Sandy**, England	52 8N	0 17W
24	**Sangerhausen**, Germ.	51 30N	11 18E
26	**Sanlúcar**, Spain	36 43N	6 22W
25	**Sanok**, Poland	49 37N	22 14E
39	**San-po, R.**, Tibet	29 0N	90 0E
17	**Sanquhar**, Scotland	55 23N	3 54W
45	**Sansing**, Manchuria	46 20N	129 40E
64	**Santa Barbara**, Hond.	15 1N	88 15W
62	**Santa Barbara**, U.S.A.	34 29N	119 40W
62	**Santa Barbara Is.**, U.S.A.	34 0N	120 0W
62	**Santa Catalina I.**, U.S.A.	33 20N	118 30W
67	**Santa Catharina I.**, Brazil	27 30S	48 30W
67	**Sta. Catharina, st.**, Brazil	27 0S	51 0W
65	**Santa Clara**, Cuba	22 20N	79 58W
67	**Santa Cruz**, Argentina	50 10S	68 55W
67	**Santa Cruz**, Bolivia	17 25S	63 15W
65	**Santa Cruz**, Cuba	20 40N	78 10W
26	**Santa Cruz**, Spain	38 37N	3 27W
62	**Santa Cruz**, U.S.A.	36 55N	122 0W
65	**Santa Cruz I.**, West Indies	17 30N	64 58W
7	**Santa Cruz Is.**, Pac. O.	10 30S	166 0E
27	**Santa Eulalia**, Spain	38 58N	1 38E
67	**Santa Fé**, Argentina	31 30S	60 59W
62	**Santa Fé**, U.S.A.	35 44N	106 1W
54	**Sta. Isabel**, Fern. Po	3 46N	8 46E
52	**Santa Maria**, Azores	37 30N	25 0W
67	**Santa Maria**, Brazil	29 30S	53 40W
26	**Santa Maria**, Spain	41 5N	4 26W
66	**Santa Marta** Colom.	11 20N	74 13W
67	**Sta. Martha, Sa. de**, Brazil	18 30S	51 30W
32	**Santa Maura**, Greece	38 40N	20 40E
66	**Santa Rosa**, Peru	14 30S	71 0W
62	**Santa Rosa**, U.S.A.	38 26N	122 45W
64	**Sta. Rosalia**, Mexico	27 40N	105 12W
64	**Santander**, Mexico	24 20N	98 0W
26	**Santander**, Spain	43 29N	3 52W
27	**Santañy**, Spain	39 20N	3 10E
66	**Santarém**, Brazil	2 40S	54 40W
26	**Santarem**, Portugal	39 14N	8 40W
67	**Santiago**, Bolivia	18 15S	59 30W
67	**Santiago**, Chile	33 25S	70 30W
65	**Santiago**, Cuba	20 0N	75 50W
65	**Santiago**, Dom. Rep.	19 30N	70 45W
26	**Santiago de Compostela**, Spain	42 53N	8 31W
67	**Santiago del Estero**, Argentina	27 50S	64 30W
65	**Santo Domingo**, Hisp.	18 55N	70 30W
26	**Santo Domingo**, Spain	42 26N	2 58W
29	**Santo Stefano**, Sicily	38 1N	14 20E
26	**Santoña**, Spain	43 28N	3 30W
67	**Santos**, Brazil	24 0S	46 30W
45	**Santuao**, China	26 40N	119 55E
67	**São Borja**, Brazil	28 40S	56 3W
66	**São Francisco, R.**, Brazil	10 0S	42 0W
67	**São Paulo, & st.**, Brazil	23 40S	46 35W
21	**Saône, R.**, France	47 35N	5 50E
21	**Saône et-Loire, dept.**, France	46 37N	4 32E
45	**Sapporo**, Japan	43 0N	142 0E
27	**Saragossa**, Spain	41 40N	0 51W
30	**Sarajevo**, Yugoslavia	43 54N	18 26E
42	**Sarangpur**, India	23 34N	76 31E
36	**Sarapul**, U.S.S.R.	56 10N	53 30E
63	**Saratoga Springs**, U.S.A.	43 5N	73 58W
37	**Saratov**, U.S.S.R.	51 33N	45 59E
39	**Sarawak, st.**, Borneo	2 30N	113 0E
30	**Sárbogárd**, Hungary	46 53N	18 40E
29	**Sardinia, I.**, Italy	40 15N	9 10E
63	**Sardis**, U.S.A.	34 23N	89 55W
31	**Saridza**, Rumania	43 29N	27 46E
20	**Sark, I.**, Channel Is.	49 25N	2 22W
21	**Sariat**, France	44 55N	1 13E
61	**Sarnia**, Canada	42 58N	82 23W
35	**Sarpsborg**, Norway	59 17N	11 7E
20	**Sarthe, dept.**, France	47 52N	0 15E
60	**Saskatchewan R.**, Can.	53 17N	105 0W
60	**Saskatoon**, Canada	52 10N	106 48W
29	**Sassari**, Sardinia	40 47N	8 33E
28	**Sassnitz**, Germany	54 30N	13 38E
28	**Sassuolo**, Italy	44 34N	10 46E
42	**Satara**, India	17 40N	74 3E
31	**Sátoraljaújhely**, Hung.	48 24N	21 40E
42	**Satpura Ra.**, India	21 45N	75 0E

MAP	Place	Lat.	Long.
31	**Satu Mare**, Rumania	47 46N	22 55E
40	**Saudi Arabia, st.**, Asia	25 0N	45 0E
20	**Saulieu**, France	47 16N	4 13E
61	**Sault Ste. Marie**, Can.	46 33N	84 32W
63	**Sault Ste. Marie**, U.S.A.	46 25N	84 25W
20	**Saumur**, France	47 14N	0 5W
51	**Savaii, I.**, Samoa Is. Inset	13 40S	172 20W
65	**Savanna la Mar**, Jamaica	18 10N	78 15W
63	**Savannah Ga.**, U.S.A.	32 2N	81 7W
63	**Savannah, Tenn.**, U.S.A.	35 10N	88 15W
30	**Save, R.**, Yugoslavia	44 40N.	19 55E
20	**Savenay**, France	47 20N	1 55W
21	**Savoie, dept.**, France	45 30N	6 42E
28	**Savona**, Italy	44 16N	8 26E
35	**Sävsjo**, Sweden	57 22N	14 40E
15	**Sawtry**, England	52 28N	0 17W
13	**Saxilby**, England	53 17N	0 20W
15	**Saxmundham**, Eng.	52 14N	1 28E
24	**Saxony, prov.**, Ger.	51 35N	11 50E
54	**Say**, Fr. W. Africa	13 10N	2 22E
12	**Sca Fell**, England	54 28N	3 13W
16	**Scapa Flow**, Ork. Is.	58 54N	3 0W
13	**Scarborough**, England	54 17N	0 25W
33	**Schaffhausen**, Switz.	47 43N	8 37E
22	**Schelde E., R.**, Neth.	51 34N	4 0E
22	**Schelde, W., R.**, Neth.	51 28N	4 0E
63	**Schenectady**, U.S.A.	42 50N	73 55W
22	**Scheveningen**, Neth.	52 7N	4 16W
28	**Schio**, Italy	45 43N	11 12E
33	**Schleitheim**, Switz.	47 47N	8 29E
24	**Schleswig**, Germany	54 32N	9 36E
24	**Schleswig Holstein, prov.**, Germany	54 20N	9 40E
20	**Schlettstadt**, France	48 15N	7 28E
24	**Schlüchtern**, Germany	50 20N	9 32E
24	**Schmalkalden**, Germ.	50 43N	10 28E
25	**Schneidemühl**, Germ.	53 10N	16 46E
25	**Schönberg**, Cz.-slov.	49 58N	16 58E
22	**Schouwen**, Neth.	51 40N	4 0E
19	**Schull**, Eire	51 31N	9 32W
33	**Schuls**, Switzerland	46 48N	10 18E
25	**Schütt Is.**, Cz.-slov.	47 55N	17 40E
23	**Schwartau**, Germany	53 56N	10 41E
33	**Schwarzenburg**, Switz.	46 48N	7 20E
25	**Schweidnitz**, Germany	50 52N	16 30E
24	**Schweinfurt**, Germany	50 3N	10 15E
24	**Schwerin**, Germany	53 38N	11 26E
24	**Schwerin**, Germany	52 36N	15 30E
33	**Schwyz**, Switzerland	47 2N	8 37E
29	**Sciacca**, Sicily	37 31N	13 3E
11	**Scilly Is.**, British Is.	49 56N	6 22W
17	**Scone**, Scotland	56 26N	3 24W
10	**Scotland**, British Is.	57 0N	4 0W
7	**Scott, I.**, Antarctica	67 30S	180 0E
47	**Scottsdale**, Tasmania	41 4S	147 31E
16	**Scrabster**, Scotland	58 37N	3 32W
63	**Scranton**, U.S.A.	41 26N	75 40W
32	**Scripero**, Greece	39 45N	19 50E
13	**Scunthorpe**, England	53 36N	0 35W
30	**Scutari**, Albania	42 5N	19 30E
32	**Scutari**, Turkey	41 0N	29 1E
15	**Seaford**, England	50 47N	0 6E
13	**Seaham Harb.**, Eng.	54 51N	1 20W
13	**Seamer**, England	54 14N	0 26W
12	**Seascale**, England	54 24N	3 30W
14	**Seaton**, England	50 43N	3 4W
62	**Seattle**, U.S.A.	47 31N	122 15W
47	**Seaview Mt.**, N.S.W.	31 20S	152 25E
30	**Sebenik**, Yugoslavia	43 46N	15 52E
41	**Sebustiye**, Palestine	32 18N	35 16E
41	**Sebzewar**, Afghan.	33 30N	62 10E
41	**Sebzewar**, Iran	36 40N	57 50E
42	**Secunderabad**, India	17 27N	78 30E
63	**Sedalia**, U.S.A.	38 45N	93 17W
20	**Sedan**, France	49 42N	4 58E
12	**Sedbergh**, England	54 19N	2 32W
51	**Seddon**, New Zealand	41 40S	174 5E
13	**Sedgefield**, England	54 39N	1 27W
32	**Sedil Bahr**, Turkey	40 1N	26 11E
57	**Seeheim**, S.W. Africa	26 45S	17 37E
41	**Seffurieh**, Palestine	32 46N	35 17E
51	**Sefton Mt.**, N. Zealand	43 45S	170 9E
31	**Segesvar**, Rumania	46 14N	24 50E
35	**Segevold**, Latvia	57 10N	24 52E
27	**Segorbe**, Spain	39 52N	0 28W
26	**Segovia**, Spain	40 56N	4 8W
34	**Seinäjoki**, Finland	62 45N	22 57E
20	**Seine, dept.**, France	48 48N	2 20E
20	**Seine, R.**, France	49 0N	1 50E
20	**Seine-et-Marne, dept.**, France	48 40N	3 2E
20	**Seine et Oise, dept.**, France	48 42N	2 10E
20	**Seine Inférieure, dept.**, France	49 38N	1 13E
41	**Seistan, region**, Iran	31 40N	61 15E
53	**Sekondi**, Gold Coast	4 58N	1 43W
13	**Selby**, England	53 47N	1 4W
17	**Selkirk, co. & tn.**, Scotland	53 50N	2 51W
60	**Selkirk**, Canada	50 8N	97 0W
60	**Selkirk Ra.**, Canada	51 0N	117 30W
15	**Selsey**, England	50 44N	0 48E
56	**Selukwe**, S. Rhodesia	19 30S	30 20E
47	**Selwyn**, Queensland	21 35S	140 30E
30	**Semendria**, Y.-slavia	44 39N	20 52E
44	**Semipalatinsk**, U.S.S.R.	50 30N	8 5E
30	**Semlin.** *See* **Zemun**		
33	**Sempach**, Switzerland	47 8N	8 11E
20	**Semur**, France	47 30N	4 21E
43	**Senbo**, Burma	24 45N	97 0E
45	**Sendai**, Japan	38 9N	140 38E
52	**Senegal, dist.**, Fr. W. Africa	15 0N	15 0W
52	**Senegal, R.**, Fr. W. Africa	16 10N	16 25W
57	**Senekal**, U. of S. Afr.	28 23S	27 42E
20	**Senlis**, France	49 13N	2 37E
55	**Sennar**, A.-E. Sudan	13 30N	33 44E
20	**Sens**, France	48 13N	3 19E
25	**Sensburg**, Germany	53 53N	21 19E
30	**Senta**, Yugoslavia	45 55N	20 4E
42	**Seoni**, India	22 10N	79 35E
45	**Seoul**, Korea	37 26N	126 58E
31	**Sepsiszentgyorgy**, Rumania	45 50N	25 35E
22	**Seraing**, Belgium	50 37N	5 30E
30	**Serbia, dist.**, Y-slavia	45 0N	20 0E
55	**Serenje**, N. Rhodesia	13 13S	30 40E
55	**Serenli**, It. Somaliland	2 30N	42 0E
32	**Seres**, Greece	41 4N	23 36E
31	**Sereth**, Rumania	47 59N	26 4E
44	**Sergiopol**, U.S.S.R.	47 50N	80 10E
66	**Sergipe, st.**, Brazil	11 0S	37 30W
42	**Seringapatam**, India	12 25N	76 42E
57	**Serowe**, Bechuanaland	22 24S	26 45E
21	**Serres**, France	44 25N	5 42E
32	**Servia**, Greece	40 10N	21 59E
47	**Servicetown**, Victoria	36 22N	141 0E
56	**Sesheke**, N. Rhodesia	17 23S	25 10E
29	**Sessa**, Italy	41 14N	13 55E
35	**Sesvegan**, Latvia	56 59N	26 20E
	Sète. *See* **Cette**		
13	**Settle**, England	54 4N	2 16W
57	**Settlers**, U. of S. Africa	25 0S	28 55E
26	**Setubal**, Portugal	38 30N	8 55W
37	**Sevastopol**, U.S.S.R.	44 41N	33 31E
15	**Sevenoaks**, England	51 16N	0 12E
21	**Séverac**, France	44 20N	3 5E
14	**Severn, R.**, England	51 55N	2 12W
26	**Seville**, Spain	37 25N	6 0W
58	**Seward**, Alaska	60 0N	149 30W
7	**Seychelles, Is.**, Indian Ocean	4 30S	55 30E
57	**Seymour**, U. of S. Afr.	32 35S	26 29E
47	**Seymour**, Victoria	37 2S	145 6E
20	**Sézanne**, France	48 44N	3 44E
52	**Sfax**, Tunis	35 0N	10 40E
22	**S'Gravenhage**, Neth.	52 4N	4 18E
56	**Shabani**, S. Rhodesia	20 15S	30 12E
30	**Shabatz**, Yugoslavia	44 46N	19 42E
44	**Sha-chau.** *See* **Saitu**		
14	**Shaftesbury**, England	51 0N	2 10W
40	**Shagra**, Arabia	13 50N	45 30E
42	**Shahabad**, India	27 40N	80 0E
42	**Shahpura**, India	25 37N	75 1E
41	**Shahr-i- Zabul**, Iran	31 8N	61 33E
41	**Shahrud**, Iran	36 30N	55 0E
41	**Shaib**, Palestine	32 52N	35 12E
42	**Shahjahanpur**, India	27 46N	79 58E
41	**Shakra**, Syria	33 13N	35 28E
40	**Shammar, J.**, Arabia	27 0N	42 30E
44	**Shamo Desert.** *See* **Gobi Desert**		
56	**Shamva**, S. Rhodesia	17 34S	31 25E
45	**Shanghai**, China	31 25N	121 30E
15	**Shanklin**, England	50 39N	1 9W
50	**Shannon**, New Zealand	40 32S	175 22E
19	**Shannon, R.**, Eire	52 35N	9 15W
45	**Shansi, prov.**, China	38 0N	112 0E
45	**Shantung, prov.**, China	36 10N	118 0E
45	**Shaochow**, China	24 55N	113 30E
45	**Shaoking**, China	30 0N	120 40E
45	**Shaowu**, China	27 15N	117 40E
12	**Shap**, England	54 32N	2 42W
45	**Shara-muren**, China	44 25N	111 14E
41	**Sharja**, Arabia	25 5N	55 15E
32	**Sharkeui**, Turkey	40 36N	27 7E
62	**Sharon Springs**, U.S.A.	38 53N	101 41W
45	**Shasi**, China	30 27N	112 15E
62	**Shasta, mt.**, U.S.A.	41 25N	122 0W
37	**Shatsk**, U.S.S.R.	53 35N	27 40E
35	**Shavli**, Lithuania	55 50N	23 18E
63	**Shawnee**, U.S.A.	35 20N	97 0W
43	**Shazipur**, India	25 40N	83 30E
63	**Sheboygan**, U.S.A.	43 45N	87 47W
41	**Schechem.** *See* **Nablus**		
15	**Sheerness**, England	51 27N	0 45E
13	**Sheffield**, England	53 23N	1 27W
15	**Shefford**, England	52 3N	0 20W
41	**Sheikh Sagd**, Syria	32 55N	36 5E
61	**Shelburne**, Canada	43 46N	65 20W
15	**Shelford**, England	52 10N	0 7E
46	**Shellborough**, W. Australia	20 5S	119 12E
37	**Shemakha**, U.S.S.R.	40 37N	48 30E
40	**Shendi**, A.-E. Sudan	16 30N	33 40E
44	**Shensi, prov.**, China	34 40N	108 0E
57	**Sheppmansdorf**, S.W. Africa	23 25S	14 30E
47	**Shepparton**, Victoria	37 22S	145 25E
15	**Sheppey, I. of**, Eng.	51 24N	0 50E
15	**Shepshed**, England	52 47N	1 12W
14	**Shepton Mallet**, Eng.	51 10N	2 31W
14	**Sherborne**, England	50 58N	2 30W
13	**Sherburn**, England	53 47N	1 15W
62	**Sheridan**, U.S.A.	44 46N	107 2W
17	**Sheriff Muir**, Scotland	56 12N	3 54W
15	**Sheringham**, England	52 57N	1 12E
63	**Sherman**, U.S.A.	33 34N	96 23W
22	**S'Hertogenbosch**, Netherlands	51 41N	5 19E
8	**Shetland Is.**, British Isles	60 15N	1 30W
45	**Shidzuoka**, Japan	38 40N	141 27E
14	**Shifnal**, England	52 41N	2 23W
39	**Shigansk**, U.S.S.R.	66 10N	121 10E
44	**Shigatze**, Tibet	29 20N	88 40E
42	**Shikarpur**, India	28 0N	68 39E
45	**Shikoku I.**, Japan	33 45N	133 30E
19	**Shillelagh**, Eire	52 45N	6 33W
43	**Shillong**, India	25 30N	91 59E
56	**Shiloh**, S. Rhodesia	19 45S	28 39E
45	**Shimizu**, Japan	35 2N	138 3E
42	**Shimoga**, India	13 55N	75 30E
45	**Shimonoseki**, Japan	34 1N	131 2E
45	**Shinchow**, China	28 0N	110 15E
55	**Shinyanga**, Tanganyika	3 35S	33 20E
31	**Shipka P.**, Bulgaria	42 42N	25 30E
13	**Shipley**, England	53 50N	1 47W
15	**Shipston on Stour**, England	52 4N	1 38W
55	**Shirati**, Tanganyika	1 37S	34 1E
40	**Shiraz**, Iran	29 33N	52 36E
41	**Shirwan**, Iran	37 22N	57 58E
30	**Shkodra.** *See* **Scutari**		
35	**Shlok**, Latvia	56 55N	23 35E
55	**Shoa, prov.**, Abyssinia	9 30N	38 30E
15	**Shoeburyness**, Eng.	51 32N	0 48E
42	**Sholapur**, India	17 40N	75 55E
15	**Shorncliffe Camp**, England	51 7N	1 8E
62	**Shoshona**, U.S.A.	42 59N	114 19W
57	**Shoshong**, Bechuanaland	23 3S	26 46E
13	**Shotton**, England	52 45N	1 22W
63	**Shreveport**, U.S.A.	32 29N	93 52W
14	**Shrewsbury**, England	52 43N	2 45W
14	**Shropshire, co.**, Eng.	52 40N	2 40W
40	**Shugra**, Arabia	13 29N	45 22E
31	**Shumla.** *See* **Choumen**		
45	**Shuning**, China	32 50N	114 0E
44	**Shunking**, China	31 5N	106 5E
44	**Shunning**, China	24 35N	100 0E
40	**Shuster**, Iran	37 7N	48 59E
35	**Shvanenburg**, Latvia	57 10N	26 45E
43	**Shwebo**, Burma	22 23N	95 45E
42	**Sialkot**, India	32 31N	74 30E
39	**Siam, st.**, Asia	15 0N	103 0E
39	**Siam, G. of**, Asia	11 0N	101 0E
44	**Sianfu**, China	34 15N	108 50E
45	**Siangtan**, China	28 0N	112 55E
45	**Siangyang**, China	32 5N	112 0E
32	**Siatista**, Greece	40 15N	21 33E
39	**Siberia. reg**, U.S.S.R.	60 0N	110 0E
42	**Sibi**, India	29 30N	67 55E
31	**Sibiu**, Rumania	45 49N	24 8E
22	**Sibret**, Belgium	49 58N	5 36E
15	**Sibsey**, England	53 3N	0 1E
29	**Sicily, I.**, Italy	39 20N	14 0E
35	**Sideby**, Finland	62 0N	21 20E
14	**Sidmouth**, England	50 42N	3 14W
62	**Sidney**, U.S.A.	42 0N	103 0W
41	**Sidon**, Syria	33 34N	35 28E
24	**Siegen**, Germany	50 52N	8 2E
28	**Siena**, Italy	43 20N	11 19E
26	**Siero**, Spain	43 28N	5 40W
62	**Sierra Blanca**, U.S.A.	31 17N	105 20W
52	**Sierra Leone**, Africa	8 0N	12 0W
64	**Sierra Madre**, Mexico	25 0N	105 30W
65	**Sierra Maestra**, Cuba	20 0N	77 0W
26	**Sierra Morena, mts.**, Spain	38 20N	4 30W
26	**Sierra Nevada, mts.**, Spain	37 10N	3 20W
62	**Sierra Nevada**, U.S.A.	39 0N	120 0W
33	**Sierre**, Switzerland	46 17N	7 33E
31	**Sighet**, Rumania	47 57N	23 52E
31	**Sighisoara.** *See* **Segesvar**		
24	**Sigmaringen**, Germ.	48 6N	9 10E
44	**Sikang, prov.**, China	30 0N	98 0E
34	**Sikeå**, Sweden	64 14N	21 5E
45	**Sikiang, R.**, China	23 0N	110 2E
43	**Sikkim, st.**, India	27 30N	88 25E
43	**Silchar**, India	24 47N	92 55E
25	**Silesia, prov.**, Ger.	50 0N	17 0E
31	**Silistra**, Rumania	44 4N	27 19E
23	**Silkeborg**, Denmark	56 10N	9 30E

MAP	Name	Lat.	Long.
63	**Springfield, Ohio,** U.S.A.	39 53N	83 45W
57	**Springfontein,** U. of S. Africa	30 15S	25 43E
13	**Spurn Hd.,** England	53 35N	0 8E
39	**Spuz,** Yugoslavia	42 30N	19 10E
29	**Squillace,** Italy	38 46N	16 32E
30	**Srebrenica,** Yugoslavia	44 9N	19 18E
42	**Srinagar,** India	34 12N	74 50E
24	**Stade,** Germany	53 35N	9 26E
23	**Stadil,** Denmark	56 13N	8 14E
34	**Stadsbygden,** Norway	63 25N	9 50E
14	**Stafford & Co.,** Eng.	52 43N	2 6W
15	**Staines,** England	51 26N	0 31W
13	**Staithes,** England	54 34N	0 48W
14	**Stalbridge,** England	50 57N	2 21W
33	**Stalden,** Switzerland	46 14N	7 52W
15	**Stalham,** England	52 47N	1 30E
38	**Stalinabad,** U.S.S.R.	38 30N	68 40E
37	**Stalingrad,** U.S.S.R.	48 40N	44 22E
37	**Stalino,** U.S.S.R.	47 59N	37 35E
39	**Stalinsk,** U.S.S.R.	53 50N	87 30E
13	**Stalybridge,** England	53 29N	2 5W
15	**Stamford,** England	52 39N	0 29W
13	**Stamford Bri.,** Eng.	54 0N	0 54W
57	**Standerton,** U. of S. Afr.	27 0S	29 17E
13	**Stanhope,** England	54 45N	2 0W
31	**Stanimaka,** Bulgaria	42 0N	24 53E
25	**Stanislawow & Co.,** Poland	48 51N	24 40E
67	**Stanley,** Falkland Is.	52 0S	58 30W
17	**Stanley,** Scotland	56 30N	3 26W
47	**Stanley,** Tasmania	27 30S	152 45E
55	**Stanley Falls,** Belg. Con.	0 15N	25 32E
54	**Stanley Pool,** Belg. Con.	4 15S	15 35E
55	**Stanleyville,** Belg. Cong.	0 34N	25 15E
39	**Stanovoi Mts.,** U.S.S.R.	60 0N	140 0E
47	**Stansbury,** S. Austl.	35 5S	137 40E
47	**Stanthorpe,** Queens.	28 44N	151 59E
33	**Stanz,** Switzerland	46 57N	8 22E
55	**Star of the Congo,** Belgian Congo	11 30S	27 40E
31	**Stara Zagora,** Bulg.	42 23N	25 40E
36	**Staraya Russa,** U.S.S.R.	57 59N	31 21E
24	**Stargard,** Germany	53 20N	15 2E
37	**Starodub,** U.S.S.R.	52 37N	32 37E
24	**Stassfurt,** Germany	51 52N	11 38E
67	**Staten I.,** Argentina	54 40S	64 0W
35	**Stavanger,** Norway	58 55N	5 40E
13	**Staveley,** England	53 16N	1 20W
22	**Stavelot,** Belgium	50 24N	5 55E
22	**Stavoren,** Netherlands	52 53N	5 23E
37	**Stavropol,** U.S.S.R.	45 8N	41 59E
47	**Stawell,** Victoria	37 6S	142 48E
33	**Steckborn,** Switzerland	47 39N	8 59E
57	**Steelpoort,** U. of S. Afr.	25 10S	29 30E
22	**Steenwijk,** Netherlands	52 48N	6 7E
55	**Stefanie, L.,** Abyssinia	4 30N	37 0E
33	**Steffisburg,** Switz.	46 47N	7 38E
23	**Stege,** Denmark	55 0N	12 17E
33	**Stein,** Switzerland	47 42N	8 52E
35	**Steinkjer,** Norway	63 58N	11 10E
57	**Steinkopfontein,** U. of S. Africa	29 15S	17 40E
57	**Stellenbosch,** U. of S. Africa	33 56S	18 51E
28	**Stelvio, P.,** Italy	46 35N	10 40E
20	**Stenay,** France	49 30N	5 10E
24	**Stendal,** Germany	52 37N	11 50E
23	**Stendrup,** Denmark	55 28N	9 38E
34	**Stensele,** Sweden	65 0N	17 15E
57	**Sterkstroom,** U. of S. Africa	31 35S	26 35E
62	**Sterling,** U.S.A.	40 38N	103 12W
25	**Sternberg,** Cz.-slov.	49 45N	17 15E
23	**Sternberg,** Germany	53 43N	11 51E
24	**Stettin,** Germany	53 26N	14 30E
15	**Stevenage,** England	51 55N	0 12W
22	**Stevensveert,** Neth.	51 8N	5 52E
60	**Stewart,** Canada	55 57N	129 59W
51	**Stewart I.,** N. Zealand	47 0S	167 55E
17	**Stewarton,** Scotland	55 42N	4 30W
18	**Stewartstown,** N. Ire.	44 58N	71 30W
15	**Steyning,** England	50 53N	0 20W
57	**Steynsburg,** U. of S. Africa	31 20S	25 50E
57	**Steynsdorp,** U. of S. Africa	26 10S	31 0E
24	**Steyr,** Austria, Germany	48 3N	14 24E
57	**Steytlerville,** U. of S. Africa	33 20S	24 19E
28	**Stia,** Italy	43 49N	11 42E
63	**Stillwater,** U.S.A.	45 7N	92 48W
17	**Stirling & Co.,** Scot.	44 19N	77 35W
15	**Stockbridge,** England	51 7N	1 29W
24	**Stockerau,** Aust., Ger.	48 23N	16 14E
35	**Stockholm & Co.,** Sweden	59 17N	18 3E
13	**Stockport,** England	53 25N	2 11W
62	**Stockton,** U.S.A.	38 0N	121 20W
13	**Stockton on Tees,** Eng.	54 34N	1 20W
13	**Stockwith,** England	53 28N	0 50W
57	**Stoffberg,** U. of S. Afr.	25 20S	29 45E
25	**Stojanow,** Poland	50 20N	24 40E
51	**Stoke,** New Zealand	41 20S	173 15E
15	**Stoke Ferry,** England	52 34N	0 31E
14	**Stoke Prior,** England	52 19N	2 5W
14	**Stoke on Trent,** Eng.	53 1N	2 11W
13	**Stokesley,** England	54 28N	1 11W
18	**Stokestown,** Eire	52 22N	6 59W
30	**Stolac,** Yugoslavia	43 6N	17 40E
25	**Stolovichi,** Poland	53 16N	26 5E
25	**Stolp,** Germany	54 28N	17 5E
25	**Stolpmünde,** Germany	54 35N	16 55E
14	**Stone,** England	52 53N	2 8W
16	**Stonehaven,** Scotland	56 58N	2 13W
14	**Stonehenge,** England	51 10N	1 50W
15	**Stony Stratford,** Eng.	52 4N	0 51W
34	**Stören,** Norway	63 4N	10 10E
58	**Storm Berge,** U. of S. Africa	31 25S	27 0E
16	**Stornoway,** Scotland	58 13N	6 22W
35	**Storvik,** Sweden	60 35N	16 30E
22	**Stoumont,** Belgium	50 24N	5 48E
14	**Stour, R. (Dor.),** Eng.	50 53N	2 12W
14	**Stourbridge,** England	52 27N	2 8W
14	**Stourport,** England	52 20N	2 15W
23	**Stövring,** Denmark	56 53N	9 51E
15	**Stowmarket,** England	52 12N	1 0E
15	**Stow on the Wold,** England	51 55N	1 43W
18	**Strabane,** N. Ireland	54 49N	7 28W
17	**Strachur,** Scotland	56 11N	5 4W
19	**Stradbally, Leix,** Eire	53 1N	7 9W
19	**Stradbally, Wat.,** Eire	52 8N	7 27W
28	**Stradella,** Italy	45 3N	9 20E
47	**Strahan,** Tasmania	42 7S	145 18E
24	**Stralsund,** Germany	54 18N	13 6E
18	**Strangford & L.,** N. Ireland	54 22N	5 33W
47	**Strangways Springs,** S. Australia	29 10S	136 32E
18	**Stranorlar,** Eire	54 48N	7 46W
17	**Stranraer,** Scotland	55 54N	5 2W
20	**Strasbourg,** France	48 37N	7 42E
25	**Strasburg,** Poland	53 18N	19 28E
31	**Strassburg,** U.S.S.R.	46 48N	30 1E
50	**Stratford,** N. Zealand	39 19S	174 17E
15	**Stratford on Avon,** England	51 32N	1 43W
17	**Strathaven,** Scotland	55 40N	4 20W
18	**Strathdon,** Scotland	57 13N	3 4W
17	**Strathmore,** Scotland	56 35N	3 15W
16	**Strathpeffer,** Scotland	57 35N	4 33W
16	**Strathy,** Scotland	58 33N	4 0W
14	**Stratton,** England	50 50N	4 30W
24	**Straubing,** Germany	48 55N	12 34E
14	**Street,** England	51 7N	2 43W
35	**Strengnas,** Sweden	59 20N	17 1E
13	**Strensall,** England	54 2N	1 2W
45	**Stretensk,** U.S.S.R.	52 0N	117 50E
23	**Strib,** Denmark	55 34N	9 47E
35	**Ström,** Sweden	63 50N	15 40E
29	**Stromboli, I.,** Italy	38 47N	15 13E
16	**Strome Ferry,** Scot.	57 20N	5 33W
16	**Stromness,** Orkney Is.	58 59N	3 20W
35	**Strömstad,** Sweden	58 55N	11 15E
17	**Strontian,** Scotland	56 42N	5 32W
14	**Stroud,** England	51 45N	2 13W
47	**Stroud,** N.S.W.	32 25S	152 0E
23	**Struer,** Denmark	56 29N	8 37E
30	**Struga,** Albania	41 11N	20 41E
31	**Struma, R.,** Bulgaria	41 40N	23 18E
57	**Strydenburg,** U. of S. Africa	29 56S	23 43E
25	**Stryj,** Poland	49 17N	23 50E
47	**Stuarts Cr.,** S. Austl.	29 30S	137 10E
14	**Sturminster, Newton,** England	50 56N	2 17W
57	**Stutterheim,** U. of S. Africa	32 36S	27 30E
24	**Stuttgart,** Germany	48 50N	9 10E
32	**Styra,** Greece	38 10N	24 19E
24	**Styria, prov.,** Austria, Germany	47 0N	15 20E
40	**Suakin,** A.-E. Sudan	19 0N	36 50E
26	**Suánces,** Spain	43 27N	4 5W
28	**Subiaco,** Italy	41 56N	13 6E
30	**Subotica,** Yugoslavia	46 8N	19 41E
44	**Su-chow,** China	39 48N	99 34E
45	**Süchow,** China	34 3N	117 30E
67	**Sucre,** Bolivia	18 50S	65 15W
31	**Suczawa,** Rumania	47 38N	26 20E
61	**Sudbury,** Canada	46 29N	80 55W
15	**Sudbury,** England	52 3N	0 43E
24	**Sudetes, Mts.,** Cz.-slov.	50 30N	16 0E
27	**Sueca,** Spain	39 13N	0 19W
40	**Suez, Can., & G. of,** Egypt	29 59N	32 30E
15	**Suffolk, Co.,** England	52 0N	1 0E
24	**Suhl,** Germany	50 35N	10 42E
45	**Sui-chau,** China	28 15N	115 20E
45	**Suifenho,** Manchuria	44 0N	131 10E
44	**Sui-fu,** China	28 50N	104 40E
45	**Suiting,** China	31 30N	107 30E
45	**Suiyuan, prov.,** China	39 50N	107 0E
34	**Sukajoki,** Finland	64 50N	24 45E
41	**Sukhain,** Palestine	32 52N	35 17E
42	**Sukkur,** India	27 47N	68 53E
42	**Sulaiman Mts.,** Ind.	30 30N	69 45E
35	**Suldal,** Norway	59 29N	6 31E
40	**Suleimanieh,** Iraq	35 31N	45 29E
31	**Sulina,** Rumania	45 9N	29 39E
34	**Sulitelma, mt.,** Sweden	67 15N	17 20E
20	**Sully,** France	47 43N	2 20E
28	**Sulmona,** Italy	42 6N	13 50E
64	**Sultepec,** Mexico	18 49N	99 58W
43	**Sumao,** China	22 47N	101 8E
39	**Sumatra, I.,** Asia	0 0	100 0E
33	**Sumiswald,** Switz.	47 2N	7 44E
49	**Sunbury,** Victoria	37 34S	144 42E
39	**Sunda Is.,** Asia	14 0S	110 0E
43	**Sundarbans,** India	22 0N	89 30E
23	**Sundby, Nörre,** Den.	57 4N	9 55E
13	**Sunderland,** England	54 55N	1 22W
23	**Sunds,** Denmark	56 13N	9 2E
35	**Sundsvall,** Sweden	62 25N	17 20E
45	**Sung-kiang,** China	31 5N	121 5E
34	**Suolahti,** Finland	62 32N	25 51E
34	**Suomussalmi,** Finland	64 50N	29 12E
34	**Suonenjoki,** Finland	62 40N	27 30E
63	**Superior City,** U.S.A.	46 40N	92 5W
60	**Superior Junc.,** Canada	50 1N	90 10W
61	**Superior, L.,** N. Amer.	42 30N	88 0W
39	**Surabaya,** Java	7 25S	112 50E
39	**Surakarta,** Java	7 30S	110 50E
42	**Surat,** India	21 12N	72 55E
31	**Surata,** Rumania	46 1N	29 42E
38	**Surgut,** U.S.S.R.	61 30N	73 0E
15	**Surrey, co.,** England	51 25N	0 45W
33	**Sursee,** Switzerland	47 10N	8 5E
33	**Süs,** Switzerland	46 45N	10 4E
28	**Susa,** Italy	45 7N	7 4E
52	**Susa,** Tunis	35 50N	10 30E
30	**Susak,** Yugoslavia	45 20N	14 23E
15	**Sussex, co.,** England	51 0N	0 0
16	**Sutherland, co.,** Scot.	58 0N	4 0W
57	**Sutherland,** U. of S. Africa	32 25S	20 40E
42	**Sutlej, R.,** India	30 0N	73 0E
15	**Sutton,** England	51 22N	0 12W
13	**Sutton-in-Ashfield,** England	53 6N	1 19W
13	**Sutton-on-Sea,** Eng.	53 20N	0 15E
51	**Suva,** Fiji Is. Inset	18 0S	178 20E
25	**Suvalki,** Poland	54 8N	22 56E
50	**Suwarrow I.** Inset	13 12S	163 15W
68	**Svalbard,** Arctic Oc.	78 0N	17 0E
23	**Svaneke, Bornholm,** Denmark	55 9N	15 9E
35	**Sveaborg,** Finland	60 10N	22 5E
35	**Svealand, dist.,** Swed.	60 8N	15 0E
35	**Sveg,** Sweden	62 5N	14 20E
23	**Svendborg,** Denmark	55 3N	10 38E
36	**Sverdlovsk,** U.S.S.R.	56 52N	60 42E
68	**Svernaya Zemlya,** U.S.S.R.	78 0N	100 0E
23	**Svinöby,** Denmark	55 7N	11 44E
25	**Svir,** Poland	54 52N	2 24E
31	**Svistova,** Bulgaria	43 36N	25 22E
34	**Svolvör,** Norway	68 25N	14 45E
24	**Swabia, dist.,** Germany	48 0N	10 15E
15	**Swadlincote,** England	52 46N	1 33W
15	**Swaffham,** England	52 39N	0 42E
57	**Swakopmund,** S.W. Africa	22 40S	14 30E
13	**Swale, R.,** England	54 9N	1 22W
48	**Swan Hill,** Victoria	35 18S	143 35E
14	**Swanage,** England	50 32N	1 57W
47	**Swansea,** Tasmania	42 6N	148 6E
14	**Swansea,** Wales	51 37N	3 55W
45	**Swatow,** China	23 35N	116 40E
57	**Swaziland,** S. Africa	26 0S	31 45E
8	**Sweden, King.** Europe	63 0N	15 0E
62	**Sweet Water,** U.S.A.	32 10N	100 26W
57	**Swellendam,** S. Africa	34 3S	20 25E
60	**Swift Current,** Canada	50 24N	107 55W
15	**Swindon,** England	51 33N	1 45W
24	**Swinemünde,** Germany	53 54N	14 14E
15	**Swineshead,** England	52 58N	0 9W
18	**Swinford,** Eire	53 57N	8 57W
13	**Swinton,** England	53 29N	1 20W
8	**Switzerland,** Europe	47 0N	8 0E
51	**Switzers,** New Zealand	45 46S	168 50E
18	**Swords,** Eire	53 27N	6 14W
61	**Sydney,** Canada	46 7N	60 14W
47	**Sydney,** N.S.W.	33 55S	151 12E
25	**Syedlets,** Poland	52 11N	22 12E
40	**Syene,** Egypt	24 6N	32 51E
43	**Sylhet,** India	52 11N	22 12E
24	**Sylt, I.,** Germany	54 55N	8 22E
17	**Symington,** Scotland	55 36N	3 36W
38	**Syr Daria, R.,** U.S.S.R.	42 0N	68 10E
25	**Syeradz,** Poland	51 40N	18 40E
63	**Syracuse,** U.S.A.	43 0N	76 10W
35	**Syrenets,** Estonia	59 0N	27 40E
40	**Syria, rep.,** Asia	35 0N	38 0E
40	**Syrian Des.** *See* **El Hamed Des.**		
37	**Syrtinsk,** U.S.S.R.	56 0N	58 25E
37	**Syzran,** U.S.S.R.	53 15N	48 29E
30	**Szabadka.** *See* **Subotica**		
31	**Szamosújvár,** Rum.	47 0N	23 54E
30	**Szarvas,** Hungary	46 50N	20 35E
31	**Szásrégen,** Rumania	46 48N	24 44E

MAP
44 **Szechwan, prov.**, Ch. 30 0N 100 0E
30 **Szeged**, Hungary 46 16N 20 10E
31 **Székelyudvarhely**, Rumania 46 19N 25 20E
30 **Székesfehervar**, Hung. 47 13N 18 25E
30 **Szekszárd**, Hungary 46 22N 18 41E
44 **Szemao**, China 22 32N 101 0E
30 **Szentes**, Hungary 46 40N 20 20E
30 **Szigetvar**, Hungary 46 4N 17 46E
31 **Szilágysomlyó**, Rum. 47 14N 22 44E
30 **Szolnok**, Hungary 47 10N 20 13E
25 **Szolyva**, Czechoslovakia 48 32N 23 2E
30 **Szombathely**, Hungary 47 14N 16 39E
30 **Szongrád**, Hungary 56 45N 20 10E
31 **Szovata**, Rumania 46 35N 25 4E
44 **Szu-ching**, China 24 30N 106 25E
44 **Szu-nan**, China 28 0N 108 25E
44 **Szu-ngen**, China 23 30N 107 55E

40 **Tabah**, Egypt 29 27N 34 55E
64 **Tabasco, St.**, Mexico 18 0N 93 0W
66 **Tabatinga**, Brazil 4 0S 70 0W
57 **Table Bay**, U. of S. Af. 33 55S 18 25E
24 **Tabor**, Czechoslovakia 49 24N 14 29E
41 **Tabor, Mt.**, Palestine 32 38N 35 25E
55 **Tabora**, Tanganyika 5 3S 32 48E
40 **Tabriz**, Iran 37 59N 46 22E
43 **Tachin**, Siam 13 31N 100 12E
67 **Tacna**, Peru 17 50S 70 10W
62 **Tacoma**, U.S.A. 47 14N 122 28W
13 **Tadcaster**, England 53 54N 1 16W
33 **Tafers**, Switzerland 46 49N 7 12E
37 **Taganrog**, U.S.S.R. 47 15N 38 46E
19 **Taghmon**, Eire 52 19N 6 40W
26 **Tagus, R.**, Portugal 39 55N 3 50W
51 **Tahakopa**, N. Zealand 46 38S 169 20E
6 **Tahiti, I.**, Pacific Oc. 17 45S 149 30W
45 **Tai-chow**, China 28 50N 121 5E
40 **Taif**, Arabia 20 50N 40 52E
50 **Taihape**, N. Zealand 39 40S 175 48E
45 **Taihoku**, Taiwan 25 5N 26 35E
16 **Tain**, Scotland 57 49N 4 3W
45 **Tainan**, Japan 23 0N 120 10E
34 **Taipale**, Finland 62 40N 29 20E
44 **Tai-ping**, China 28 30N 121 15E
41 **Tait**, Iran 32 0N 54 10E
45 **Taiwan I.**, Japan 23 30N 121 0E
44 **Taiyuan**, China 38 0N 112 30E
55 **Tajura**, Fr. Somaliland 11 47N 42 54E
51 **Takaka**, N. Zealand 40 50S 172 49E
45 **Takao**, Taiwan 22 45N 120 30E
50 **Takapau**, N. Zealand 40 0S 176 20E
45 **Takasaki**, Japan 36 10N 138 46E
45 **Takata**, Japan 36 51N 137 58E
43 **Takau**, Burma 21 30N 99 10E
53 **Takoradi**, Gold Coast 4 58N 1 43W
45 **Taku**, China 39 0N 117 45E
26 **Talavera**, Spain 39 55N 4 6W
67 **Talca**, Chile 35 20S 71 40W
67 **Talcahuano**, Chile 36 25S 73 0W
14 **Talgarth**, Wales 52 0N 3 14W
62 **Tallahassee**, U.S.A. 30 25N 84 15W
35 **Tallinn.** *See* **Reval**
19 **Tallow**, Eire 52 5N 8 1W
67 **Taltal**, Chile 25 20S 70 30W
34 **Talvik**, Norway 70 0N 23 0E
52 **Tamale**, Gold Coast 9 22N 0 50W
30 **Tamasi**, Hungary 46 40N 18 14E
53 **Tamatave**, Madagascar 18 0S 49 10E
37 **Tambov**, U.S.S.R. 52 46N 41 16E
35 **Tammerfors.** *See* **Tampere**
63 **Tampa**, U.S.A. 28 0N 82 20W
35 **Tampere**, Finland 61 33N 23 33E
64 **Tampico**, Mexico 22 4N 97 59W
45 **Tamsui**, Taiwan 25 10N 121 30E
24 **Tamsweg**, Aust., Ger. 47 6N 13 48E
15 **Tamworth**, England 52 38N 1 42W
49 **Tamworth**, N.S.W. 31 6S 150 55E
53 **Tananarive**, Mad. 19 0S 47 20E
43 **Tanda**, India 26 30N 82 45E
31 **Tandara**, Rumania 44 39N 27 39E
67 **Tandil**, Argentina 37 0S 59 25W
50 **Taneatua**, N. Zealand 38 2S 177 1E
45 **Tane-ga-shima**, Japan 30 30N 131 0E
55 **Tanga**, Tanganyika 5 6S 39 5E
55 **Tanganyika, Terr. & L.**, Africa 8 30S 31 0E
52 **Tangier**, Africa 35 40N 5 50W
43 **Tani**, Siam 6 45N 101 20E
42 **Tanjore**, India 10 45N 79 17E
42 **Tank**, India 32 15N 70 25E
25 **Tannenberg**, Germany 53 25N 20 9E
44 **Tannu Tuva**, Asia 52 30N 95 0E
40 **Tanta**, Egypt 30 46N 30 56E
18 **Tantallon**, Eire 54 30N 8 12W
44 **Taonanfu**, Manchuria 45 29N 22 57E
29 **Taormina**, Sicily 37 52N 15 18E
62 **Taos**, U.S.A. 36 25N 105 38W
35 **Taps**, Estonia 59 15N 26 0E
42 **Tapti R.**, India 21 30N 74 10E
67 **Taquary, R.**, Brazil 19 0S 56 0W
47 **Tara**, Queensland 27 18S 150 30E
50 **Taranaki, Prov.**, N.Z. 39 10S 174 40E
27 **Tarancon**, Spain 40 2N 2 56W
31 **Tarantino**, Rumania 46 9N 29 15E
29 **Taranto**, Italy 40 29N 17 15E
67 **Tarapaca**, Chile 19 45S 69 30W
66 **Tarapaca**, Colombia 3 0S 69 55W
21 **Tarare**, France 45 55N 4 27E
21 **Tarascon**, France 43 49N 4 41E
33 **Tarasp**, Switzerland 46 47N 10 17E
50 **Tarawera**, N. Zealand 38 13S 176 32E
27 **Tarazona**, Spain 41 53N 1 40W
19 **Tarbert**, Eire 52 35N 9 24W
16 **Tarbert**, Scotland 57 54N 6 47W
17 **Tarbert**, Scotland 55 58N 5 49W
21 **Tarbes**, France 43 13N 0 3E
47 **Tarcoola**, S. Australia 30 43S 134 38E
27 **Tardienta**, Spain 42 0N 0 30W
47 **Taree**, N.S.W. 31 53S 152 28E
34 **Tärendö**, Sweden 67 15N 22 30E
31 **Targu Jiu**, Rumania 45 0N 23 20E
31 **Tari Verdi**, Rumania 44 35N 28 37E
64 **Tarifa**, Mexico 16 39N 95 3W
26 **Tarifa**, Spain 36 2N 5 36W
57 **Tarkastad**, U. of S. Africa 32 3S 26 15E
23 **Tarm**, Denmark 55 54N 8 32E
21 **Tarn, dept.**, France 43 43N 2 10E
21 **Tarn-et-Garonne**, dept., France 44 3N 1 7E
25 **Tarnopol**, & co., Pol. 49 34N 25 38E
25 **Tarnów**, Poland 50 1N 21 1E
25 **Tarnowitz**, Poland 50 28N 18 52E
12 **Tarporley**, England 53 10N 2 40W
27 **Tarragona**, Spain 41 6N 1 17E
29 **Tarsi**, Italy 40 15N 16 27E
40 **Tarsus**, Turkey 36 58N 34 50E
36 **Tartar, rep.**, U.S.S.R. 55 0N 49 0E
35 **Tartu.** *See* **Dorpat**
35 **Tarvasjoki**, Finland 60 30N 22 37E
41 **Tashkent**, U.S.S.R. 41 25N 69 15E
51 **Tasman, B.**, N. Zeal. 41 0S 173 20E
7 **Tasman Sea**, Pac. Oc. 41 0S 170 0E
31 **Tatar Bunar**, Rum. 45 50N 29 45E
31 **Tatar Pazarjik**, Bulg. 42 12N 24 18E
56 **Tati**, & dist., Bech'lnd. 21 30S 27 43E
44 **Ta-ting**, China 27 0N 105 50E
42 **Tatta**, India 24 45N 68 0E
13 **Tattershall**, England 53 7N 0 11W
45 **Tatung**, China 31 0N 117 50E
45 **Ta-tung**, China 40 0N 113 15E
00 **Tauern, Mts.**, Austria, Germany 47 10N 13 20E
43 **Taung Ngu**, Burma 19 0N 96 25E
57 **Taungs**, U. of S. Africa 27 30S 24 50E
14 **Taunton**, England 51 1N 3 6W
50 **Taupo**, New Zealand 38 40S 176 5E
50 **Taupo, L.**, New Zealand 38 49S 175 53E
50 **Tauranga**, N. Zealand 37 42S 176 9E
35 **Tauroggen**, Lithuania 55 14N 22 17E
40 **Taurus, Mts.**, Turkey 37 0N 34 0E
24 **Taus**, Czechoslovakia 49 25N 13 0E
27 **Táuste**, Spain 41 57N 1 17W
35 **Tavastehus**, Finland 61 0N 24 25E
33 **Taverne**, Switzerland 46 4N 8 56E
55 **Taveta**, Kenya 3 23S 37 43E
26 **Tavira**, Portugal 37 8N 7 41W
14 **Tavistock**, England 50 33N 4 10W
43 **Tavoy**, Burma 14 3N 98 15E
51 **Tavua**, Fiji Is. Inset 17 20S 177 45E
17 **Tay, Firth of**, Scotland 56 24N 3 10W
62 **Taylor**, U.S.A. 30 30N 97 10W
17 **Tayport**, Scotland 56 27N 2 55W
37 **Tbilisi**, U.S.S.R. 41 45N 44 57E
51 **Te Anau, L.**, N.Zeal. 45 15S 167 46E
50 **Te Aroha**, N. Zealand 37 32S 175 44E
50 **Te Awamutu**, N.Zeal. 38 0S 175 19E
50 **Te Hana**, N. Zealand 36 15S 174 30E
50 **Te Hauke**, N. Zealand 39 45S 176 38E
50 **Te Kuiti**, New Zealand 38 21S 175 12E
29 **Teano**, Italy 41 15N 14 4E
12 **Tebay**, England 54 26N 2 36W
31 **Tecuci**, Rumania 45 51N 27 25E
13 **Tees, R.**, England 54 32N 1 18W
48 **Teetulpa**, S. Australia 32 20S 139 40E
29 **Teggiano**, Italy 40 22N 15 30E
33 **Teglio**, Italy 46 10N 10 4E
64 **Tegucigalpa**, Hond. 14 13N 87 0W
40 **Tehran**, Iran 35 40N 51 27E
64 **Tehuacan**, Mexico 18 25N 97 30W
64 **Tehuantepec, G., & Isth. of**, Mexico 16 10N 95 19W
14 **Teignmouth**, England 50 34N 3 30W
32 **Tekirdag**, Turkey. *See* **Rodosto**
40 **Tekrit**, Iraq 34 38N 43 40E
41 **Tel Aviv**, Palestine 32 3N 34 45E
40 **Tel-el Kebir**, Egypt 30 30N 31 45E
35 **Telemark, co.**, Norway 59 20N 8 10E
31 **Telish**, Bulgaria 43 18N 24 13E
41 **Tell Hum**, Palestine 32 50N 35 35E
42 **Tellicherry**, India 11 45N 75 30E
35 **Teishi**, Lithuania 56 0N 22 18E
57 **Tembu Land**, U.of S.Afr. 31 45S 28 30E
56 **Tembwe**, N. Rhodesia 11 17S 32 40E
14 **Teme, R.**, England 52 19N 2 25W
30 **Temesvar.** *See* **Timisoara**
47 **Temora**, N.S.W. 34 28S 147 32E
29 **Tempio**, Sardinia 40 55N 9 7E
63 **Temple**, U.S.A. 31 3N 97 7W
19 **Templemore**, Eire 52 48N 7 51W
67 **Temuco**, Chile 38 25S 72 40W
51 **Temuka**, New Zealand 44 16S 171 18E
14 **Tenbury**, England 52 18N 2 35W
14 **Tenby**, Wales 51 40N 4 41W
28 **Tenda**, Italy 44 8N 7 30E
52 **Tenduf**, Algeria 27 10N 9 0W
32 **Tenedos I.**, Turkey 39 48N 26 0E
52 **Tenerife I.**, Canary Is. 28 20N 16 30W
45 **Teng-chow**, China 37 50N 120 35E
55 **Tenke**, Belgian Congo 10 30S 26 15E
43 **Tenasserim, & div.**, Burma 11 59N 99 0E
63 **Tennessee, R.**, U.S.A. 36 30N 88 10W
63 **Tennessee, st.**, U.S.A. 35 30N 85 0W
15 **Tenterden**, England 51 4N 0 41E
46 **Tenterden**, W. Austl. 34 20S 117 30E
47 **Tenterfield**, N.S.W. 29 1S 152 0E
64 **Tepic**, Mexico 21 30N 105 0W
30 **Tepisa**, Yugoslavia 43 12N 19 2E
24 **Teplice**, Czechoslovakia 50 39N 13 43E
28 **Teramo**, Italy 42 41N 13 47E
47 **Terang**, Victoria 38 14S 142 54E
31 **Tergul Frumas**, Rum. 47 14N 27 0E
29 **Terlizzi**, Italy 41 9N 16 32E
41 **Termez**, U.S.S.R. 37 30N 67 30E
68 **Termination Barrier**, Antarctica 65 0S 100 0E
29 **Termini**, Sicily 37 59N 13 40E
28 **Termoli**, Italy 42 0N 15 0E
22 **Terneuzen**, Netherlands 51 22N 3 48E
28 **Terni**, Italy 42 36N 12 40E
48 **Terowie**, S. Australia 33 5S 138 57E
29 **Terracina**, Italy 41 19N 13 18E
29 **Terralba**, Sardinia 34 43N 8 38E
29 **Terranova**, Sardinia 40 57N 9 29E
63 **Terre Haute**, U.S.A. 39 30N 87 27W
63 **Terrell**, U.S.A. 32 36N 96 5W
68 **Terror, mt.**, Antarc. 77 30S 166 0E
22 **Terschelling**, Neth. 53 25N 5 22E
27 **Teruel**, Spain 40 22N 1 5W
34 **Tervola**, Finland 64 5N 25 0E
30 **Tešanj**, Yugoslavia 44 39N 18 0E
25 **Teschen**, Poland 49 45N 18 39E
14 **Tetbury**, England 51 38N 2 9W
13 **Tetney**, England 53 30N 0 1W
31 **Tetven**, Bulgaria 42 58N 24 17E
17 **Teviot, R.**, Scotland 55 32N 2 34W
14 **Tewkesbury**, England 52 0N 2 9W
63 **Texarkana**, U.S.A. 33 0N 94 5W
47 **Texas**, Queensland 28 50S 151 5E
62 **Texas, st.**, U.S.A. 32 0N 100 0E
40 **Tez**, Arabia 13 37N 44 4E
43 **Tezpur**, India 26 38N 92 52E
57 **Thaba'nchu**, U.of S.Afr. 29 15S 26 57E
42 **Thal**, India 33 25N 70 35E
47 **Thallon**, Queensland 28 32S 148 50E
33 **Thalwil**, Switzerland 47 17N 8 34E
15 **Thame**, England 51 45N 0 59W
15 **Thames, R.**, England 51 25N 0 30W
50 **Thames**, New Zealand 37 8S 175 33E
42 **Thana**, India 19 15N 73 1E
15 **Thanet, I. of**, England 51 22N 1 20E
42 **Thar Des.**, India 27 30N 71 0E
32 **Thasos, I.**, Greece 40 40N 24 40E
43 **Thaungdut**, Burma 24 45N 94 40E
15 **Thaxted**, England 51 57N 0 20E
43 **Thayet Myo**, Burma 19 15N 95 15E
22 **The Hague**, Neth. 52 5N 4 18E
60 **The Pas**, Canada 53 57N 101 15W
40 **Thebes**, Egypt 25 45N 32 26E
32 **Thebes**, Greece 38 20N 23 22E
47 **Theebine**, Queens. 25 55S 152 30E
30 **Theiss, R.** *See* **Tisza**
37 **Theodosia**, U.S.S.R. 45 2N 35 14E
32 **Therapia**, Turkey 41 5N 29 0E
66 **Therezina**, Brazil 5 50S 42 50W
32 **Thermopylæ**, Greece 38 48N 22 34E
32 **Thessaloniki**, Greece 40 40N 23 0E
32 **Thessaly, dist.**, Greece 39 30N 22 0E
15 **Thetford**, England 52 25N 0 45E
46 **Thevenard**, S. Australia 32 30S 133 30E
22 **Thielt**, Belgium 51 0N 3 20E
21 **Thiers**, France 45 49N 3 34E
32 **Thira**, Greece 36 25N 25 26E
12 **Thirlmere**, England 54 35N 3 4W
13 **Thirsk**, England 54 14N 1 20W
23 **Thisted**, Denmark 56 58N 8 42E
21 **Thiviers**, France 45 25N 0 57E
22 **Tholen**, Netherlands 51 33N 4 13E
26 **Thomar**, Portugal 39 35N 8 25W
19 **Thomastown**, Eire 52 32N 7 8W
63 **Thomasville**, U.S.A. 30 47N 84 0W
22 **Thommen**, Belgium 50 25N 6 8E
21 **Thonon**, France 46 21N 6 30E
25 **Thorn.** *See* **Torun**
13 **Thornaby**, England 54 34N 1 20W
14 **Thornbury**, England 51 37N 2 30W
13 **Thorne**, England 53 38N 0 58W
51 **Thorney**, England 52 39N 0 5W
17 **Thornhill**, Scotland 55 15N 3 46W
12 **Thornton**, England 53 10N 2 50W
23 **Thorso**, Denmark 56 18N 9 49E
20 **Thouars**, France 46 58N 0 16W
22 **Thourout**, Belgium 51 4N 3 6E

MAP
62 **Tucson**, U.S.A. 32 15N 110 52W
67 **Tucuman**, Argentina .. 26 48S 66 2W
27 **Tudela**, Spain 41 35N 4 33W
26 **Tudela**, Spain 42 2N 1 36W
57 **Tugela R.**, U. of S. Africa 29 25S 31 30E
52 **Tugurt**, Algeria 33 20N 5 50E
35 **Tukkum**, Latvia 56 58N 23 8E
55 **Tukuyu**, Tanganyika .. 9 15S 33 40E
37 **Tula**, U.S.S.R. 54 15N 37 32E
62 **Tulare**, U.S.A. 36 16N 119 20W
31 **Tulcea**, Rumania 45 11N 28 44E
57 **Tuli**, S. Rhodesia 21 55S 29 25E
62 **Tulia**, U.S.A. 34 32N 101 45W
41 **Tulkarm**, Palestine 37 15N 35 2E
19 **Tulla**, Eire 52 53N 8 47W
19 **Tullamore**, Eire 53 16N 7 30W
47 **Tullamore**, N.S.W. 32 18S 147 32E
21 **Tulle**, France 45 15N 1 45E
53 **Tullear**, Madagascar ... 23 10S 44 0E
21 **Tullins**, France 45 15N 5 32E
16 **Tulloch**, Scotland 56 53N 4 42W
19 **Tullow**, Eire 52 47N 6 44W
63 **Tulsa**, U.S.A. 36 6N 95 58W
39 **Tulun**, U.S.S.R. 54 20N 100 20E
66 **Tumaco**, Colombia 1 40N 78 45W
47 **Tumbarumba**, N.S.W. 35 46S 148 2E
66 **Tumuc Humac, Mts.**, Guiana 1 50N 54 0W
47 **Tumut**, N.S.W. 35 18S 148 16E
41 **Tun**, Iran 34 2N 58 7E
15 **Tunbridge Wells**, Eng. 51 8N 0 16E
45 **Tungchang**, China 36 50N 116 0E
44 **Tung-chau**, China 34 55N 109 50E
44 **Tung-chuan**, China ... 26 30N 103 20E
45 **Tunghai**. *See* **East China Sea.**
44 **Tung-shin**, China 27 40N 109 0E
45 **Tung-tung hu**, China .. 29 10N 112 30E
52 **Tunis, & Col.**, Africa .. 36 45N 10 15E
67 **Tupiza**, Bolivia 21 20S 65 50W
31 **Turda**, Rumania 46 35N 23 50E
25 **Turek**, Poland 52 1N 18 30E
44 **Turfan**, Sinkiang 43 0N 89 30E
38 **Turgai**, U.S.S.R. 49 40N 63 30E
28 **Turin**, Italy 45 5N 7 38E
38 **Turkestan**, U.S.S.R. ... 41 0N 62 0E
40 **Turkey, st.**, Asia 39 0N 35 0E
65 **Turks Is.**, Jamaica. *See* **Caicos Is.**
35 **Turku**, Finland 60 28N 22 16E
31 **Turlaki**, Rumania 46 14N 30 18E
22 **Turnhout**, Belgium 51 21N 4 57E
31 **Turnu Magurele**, Rum. 43 43N 24 52E
31 **Turnu Severin**, Rum. . 44 38N 22 40E
23 **Turö, Denmark** 55 4N 10 43E
16 **Turrif**, Scotland 57 32N 2 28W
31 **Turtucaia**, Rumania ... 44 0N 26 35E
41 **Turut**, Iran 35 31N 55 7E
31 **Tusara**, Rumania 47 17N 28 20E
63 **Tuscaloosa**, U.S.A. 33 9N 87 31W
28 **Tuscany, dept.**, Italy . 43 20N 11 0E
62 **Tuscarora**, U.S.A. 41 19N 116 10W
63 **Tuskegee**, U.S.A. 32 30N 80 42W
31 **Tusla**, Rumania 44 1N 28 38E
42 **Tuticorin**, India 8 52N 78 10E
24 **Tuttlingen**, Germany .. 47 59N 8 49E
51 **Tutuila I.**, Inset 14 20S 170 40W
40 **Tuwaim**, Arabia 26 45N 46 5E
15 **Tuxford**, England 53 13N 0 54W
64 **Tuxpan**, Mexico 20 58N 97 32W
26 **Tuy**, Spain 42 3N 8 38W
30 **Tuzi**, Yugoslavia 42 21N 19 20E
30 **Tuzla**, Yugoslavia 44 35N 18 41E
35 **Tvedestrand**, Norway . 58 38N 8 56E
23 **Tversted**, Denmark 57 35N 10 13E
17 **Tweed, R.**, Scotland ... 55 35N 1 30W
47 **Tweed Heads**, N.S.W. . 28 12S 153 20E
13 **Tweedmouth**, England 55 46N 2 3W
63 **Two Harbors**, U.S.A. . 47 0N 91 45W
63 **Tyler**, U.S.A. 30 40N 94 30W
45 **Tymovsk**, U.S.S.R. 50 55N 142 30E
17 **Tyndrum**, Scotland ... 56 26N 4 42W
13 **Tyne, R.**, England 54 59N 1 52W
13 **Tynemouth**, England .. 55 1N 1 25W
41 **Tyre**, Syria 33 16N 35 15E
32 **Tyrnavo**, Greece 39 45N 22 20E
24 **Tyrol, Prov.**, Austria, Germany 47 18N 11 10E
18 **Tyrone, co.**, N. Ireland 54 37N 7 10W
29 **Tyrrhenian Sea**, Italy . 40 10N 12 50E
36 **Tyumen**, U.S.S.R. 57 23N 65 32E
31 **Tzari Brod**, Yugoslavia 43 0N 22 47E

54 **Ubangi, R.**, Cent. Afr. . 3 0N 18 40E
54 **Ubangi Shari**, Africa .. 5 20N 23 0E
26 **Ubeda**, Spain 38 2N 3 22W
66 **Ucayali, R.**, Peru 7 30S 75 30E
42 **Uch**, India 29 13N 71 9E
24 **Uckermünde**, Germany 53 43N 14 3E
15 **Uckfield**, England 50 58N 0 6E
42 **Udaipur**, India 24 32N 73 45E
23 **Udby**, Denmark 56 35N 10 19E
35 **Uddevalla**, Sweden 60 10N 12 8E
28 **Udine**, Italy 46 4N 13 15E
36 **Udmurt, rep.**, U.S.S.R. 57 35N 52 35E
55 **Uele R.**, Belgian Congo . 4 0N 25 0E
36 **Ufa**, U.S.S.R. 54 46N 55 47E

MAP
35 **Ugalen**, Latvia 57 17N 21 2W
55 **Uganda Prot.**, E. Afr. . 2 0N 33 0E
26 **Ugijar**, Spain 36 59N 3 8W
57 **Uitenhage**, U. of S. Afr. 33 45S 25 25E
55 **Ujiji**, Tanganyika 4 57S 30 1E
42 **Ujjain**, India 23 16N 75 55E
57 **Ukamas**, S.W. Africa . 27 50N 19 47E
37 **Ukraine, rep.**, U.S.S.R. 49 0N 28 0E
16 **Ulbster**, Scotland 58 21N 3 9W
34 **Uleåborg**, Finland 65 0N 25 32E
37 **Ulianovsk**, U.S.S.R. .. 54 20N 48 25E
34 **Ullånger**, Sweden 63 0N 18 20E
16 **Ullapool**, Scotland 57 54N 5 9W
24 **Ulm**, Germany 48 27N 10 0E
31 **Ulmu**, Rumania 44 57N 27 19E
12 **Ullswater**, England .. 54 35N 2 54W
18 **Ulster, prov.**, N. Ire. .. 54 30N 7 0W
23 **Ulstrup**, Denmark 56 24N 9 46E
57 **Ulundi**, U. of S. Africa 28 15S 31 25E
23 **Ulvborg**, Denmark 56 18N 8 22E
12 **Ulverston**, England .. 54 13N 3 6W
47 **Ulverstone**, Tasmania . 41 7S 146 8E
24 **Ülzen**, Germany 52 58N 10 35E
37 **Uman**, U.S.S.R. 48 43N 30 15E
42 **Umarkot**, India 25 22N 69 46E
28 **Umbertide**, Italy 43 17N 12 20E
62 **Umbria**, U.S.A. 41 20N 114 0W
28 **Umbria, dept.**, Italy .. 42 50N 12 30E
34 **Umeå**, Sweden 63 50N 20 20E
56 **Umjinga**, S. Rhodesia . 16 0S 29 10E
56 **Umtali**, S. Rhodesia .. 18 53S 32 35E
57 **Umtata**, U. of S. Africa 31 35S 28 50E
56 **Umvuma**, S. Rhodesia 19 20S 30 42E
57 **Umzinto**, U. of S. Afr. . 30 35S 30 32E
61 **Ungava B.**, Canada 59 30N 67 30W
25 **Ungvar**, Czechoslovakia 48 36N 22 20E
67 **Uniao da Victoria**, Brazil 26 20S 51 10W
40 **Unieh**, Turkey 41 8N 37 15E
63 **Union**, U.S.A. 34 35N 81 38W
50 **Union Is.** *See* **Tokelau Is.**
53 **Union of S. Africa** 32 0N 25 0E
38 **Union of Soviet Socialist Rep.**, Asia .. 60 0N 80 0E
57 **Uniondale**, U. of S. Afr. 33 38S 23 15E
42 **United Provinces**, Ind. 28 0N 80 0E
59 **United States**, N. Amer. 40 0N 100 0E
33 **Unterwalden, Canton**, Switzerland 46 55N 8 15E
15 **Upavon**, England 51 17N 1 49W
61 **Upernivik**, Greenland .. 72 45N 55 0W
57 **Upington**, U. of S. Afr. 28 30S 21 15E
51 **Upolu, I.** .... Inset 13 50S 171 35W
40 **Upper Egypt**, Egypt .. 26 0N 33 0E
39 **Upper Tunguska, R.**, U.S.S.R. 59 0N 100 0E
15 **Uppingham**, England . 52 36N 0 43W
35 **Uppsala, & Co.**, Swed. . 59 55N 17 30E
14 **Upton on Severn**, Eng. 52 4N 2 12W
38 **Ural Area**, U.S.S.R. ... 60 0N 65 0E
36 **Ural Mts.**, U.S.S.R. ... 60 0N 59 0E
37 **Ural, R.**, U.S.S.R. 48 0N 51 35E
37 **Uralsk**, U.S.S.R. 51 14N 51 17E
45 **Urawa**, Japan 36 0N 139 30E
28 **Urbino**, Italy 43 55N 12 39E
28 **Urchanlar**, Turkey 39 55N 27 35E
37 **Urda**, U.S.S.R. 48 50N 48 57E
13 **Ure, R.**, England 54 6N 1 27W
50 **Urenui**, New Zealand .. 39 0S 174 22E
40 **Urfa**, Turkey 37 10N 38 56E
24 **Urfahr**, Aust., Germ. .. 48 19N 14 20E
44 **Urga**, Mongolia 48 0N 106 50E
33 **Uri, Canton**, Switz. ... 46 48N 8 40E
32 **Urlu**, Greece 41 30N 26 30E
40 **Urmia, & L.**, Iran 37 31N 45 2E
33 **Urnasch**, Switzerland . 47 19N 19 17E
67 **Uruguay, R.**, S. Amer. 27 30S 52 30W
67 **Uruguay, st.**, S. Amer. 32 0S 55 0W
67 **Uruguayana**, Brazil .. 30 0S 57 0W
44 **Urumchi**, Sinkiang ... 43 25N 87 50E
55 **Urundi**, Belg. Congo .. 3 20S 30 0E
31 **Urziseni**, Rumania 44 44N 26 40E
20 **Ushant I.**, France 48 29N 5 4W
14 **Usk**, England 51 42N 2 52W
14 **Usk, R.**, England 51 57N 3 25W
31 **Usküb**. *See* **Skoplje**
32 **Üsküdar**. *See* **Scutari**
37 **Usman**, U.S.S.R. 53 3N 39 47E
36 **Usole**, U.S.S.R. 59 30N 56 20E
21 **Ussel**, France 45 32N 2 20E
39 **Ust Maisk**, U.S.S.R. ... 60 45N 134 30E
41 **Ust Yurt**, U.S.S.R. 43 0N 55 0E
36 **Ust Zylma**, U.S.S.R. .. 65 28N 52 18E
33 **Uster**, Switzerland 47 21N 8 43E
24 **Usti**, Czechoslovakia .. 50 41N 14 5E
45 **Usti Stryelka**, U.S.S.R. 53 20N 121 25E
39 **Ustyansk**, U.S.S.R. 71 0N 136 0E
36 **Ustyushna**, U.S.S.R. .. 58 54N 36 15E
55 **Usumbura**, Belg. Cong. 4 30S 29 10E
41 **Usunada**, U.S.S.R. 39 40N 53 45E
45 **Usuri, R.**, Asia 46 30N 134 0E
42 **Utakamund**, India 11 30N 76 42E
43 **Utaradit**, Siam 17 41N 100 1E
23 **Utersen**, Germany 53 40N 9 40E
63 **Utica**, U.S.A. 43 0N 74 12E

MAP
22 **Utrecht, & prov.**, Neth. 52 5N 5 8W
57 **Utrecht**, U. of S. Africa 27 42S 30 15E
34 **Utsjoki**, Finland 69 55N 27 2E
35 **Utsyani**, Lithuania 55 30N 25 39E
23 **Utterslev**, Denmark ... 54 56N 11 12E
15 **Uttoxeter**, England 52 54N 1 52E
35 **Uusikaupunki**, Finland 60 50N 21 25W
34 **Uusikaarlepyy**, Fin. ... 63 55N 22 30E
30 **Uvatz**, Yugoslavia 33 35N 20 45E
55 **Uvira**, Belgian Congo .. 3 30S 29 0E
15 **Uxbridge**, England ... 51 33N 0 29E
67 **Uyuni**, Bolivia 20 15S 67 10W
21 **Uzerche**, France 45 26N 1 32W
21 **Uzès**, France 44 0N 4 25E
30 **Užice**, Yugoslavia 43 52N 19 51E
25 **Uzok**, Czechoslovakia .. 49 0N 22 50E
32 **Uzunköpri**, Turkey 41 15N 26 47E

57 **Vaal, R.**, U. of S. Afr. .. 26 55S 27 20E
34 **Vaala**, Finland 64 32N 26 45E
22 **Vaals**, Netherlands 50 47N 6 1E
57 **Vaalwater**, U. of S. Afr. 24 12S 28 32E
34 **Vaasa**, Finland 63 8N 21 42E
30 **Vácz**, Hungary 47 47N 19 7E
28 **Vada**, Italy 43 23N 10 28E
39 **Vadomsk**, U.S.S.R. 58 30N 119 0E
34 **Vadsö**, Norway 70 5N 29 45E
35 **Vadstena**, Sweden 58 30N 15 0E
33 **Vaduz**, Liechtenstein ... 47 10N 9 32E
36 **Vaigach**, U.S.S.R. 70 0N 59 0E
33 **Valais, Canton**, Switz. . 46 10N 7 35E
35 **Valamo**, Finland 61 20N 31 0E
36 **Valdai Hills**, U.S.S.R. . 57 30N 32 30E
67 **Valdivia**, Chile 39 50S 72 25W
63 **Valdosta**, U.S.A. 30 53N 83 18W
31 **Valegotsalovo**, Russia . 47 30N 22 59E
21 **Valence**, France 44 56N 4 53E
26 **Valencia**, Spain 39 6N 7 15W
27 **Valencia, & prov.**, Sp. 39 28N 0 21W
66 **Valencia**, Venezuela ... 10 15N 68 20W
20 **Valenciennes**, France .. 50 21N 3 32E
31 **Valeni**, Rumania 45 10N 26 3E
19 **Valentia, I.**, Eire 51 54N 10 30W
28 **Valenza**, Italy 45 2N 8 39E
29 **Valetta**, Malta 35 52N 14 30E
29 **Valguarnera**, Sicily ... 37 30N 14 22E
30 **Valjevo**, Yugoslavia 44 16N 19 55E
35 **Valk**, Estonia 57 47N 26 5E
64 **Valladolid**, Mexico 20 30N 88 20W
26 **Valladolid**, Spain 41 38N 4 41W
35 **Valle**, Norway 59 15N 7 30E
26 **Vallecas**, Spain 40 25N 3 40W
62 **Vallejo**, U.S.A. 38 11N 122 15W
67 **Vallenar**, Chile 28 40S 70 40W
62 **Valley**, U.S.A. 46 58N 97 50W
29 **Vallo**, Italy 40 15N 15 18E
28 **Vallombrosa**, Italy 43 47N 11 35E
33 **Vallorbe**, Switzerland . 46 43N 6 23E
20 **Valognes**, France 49 32N 1 30W
30 **Valona**, Albania 40 30N 19 29E
26 **Valoria**, Spain 41 48N 4 32W
67 **Valparaiso**, Chile 33 0S 71 30W
21 **Valreas**, France 44 25N 4 58E
28 **Valtellina**, Italy 46 10N 10 0E
26 **Valverde**, Spain 37 35N 6 47W
40 **Van, & L.**, Turkey 38 28N 43 15E
60 **Vancouver, & I.**, Can. . 49 7N 122 47W
62 **Vancouver**, U.S.A. 45 35N 122 30W
23 **Vandel**, Denmark 55 43N 9 14E
30 **Vandens**, Albania 42 0N 18 55E
35 **Vanern, L.**, Sweden 58 50N 13 20E
35 **Vänersborg**, Sweden .. 58 25N 12 25E
55 **Vanga**, Kenya 4 36S 39 15E
34 **Vännäs**, Sweden 64 0N 19 45E
20 **Vannes**, France 47 39N 2 47W
51 **Vanua-Levu, I.** Inset 17 0S 179 0W
21 **Var, dept.**, France 43 20N 6 20E
28 **Varallo**, Italy 45 50N 8 12E
34 **Varanger Fd.**, Norway . 70 0N 31 0E
30 **Varazdin**, Yugoslavia . 46 20N 16 21E
35 **Varberg**, Sweden 57 10N 12 30E
31 **Vardar, R.**, Balkans ... 41 45N 22 0E
23 **Varde**, Denmark 55 38N 8 30E
30 **Vardishte**, Yugoslavia . 43 45N 18 26E
34 **Vardö**, Norway 70 20N 31 10E
20 **Varennes**, France 49 15N 5 1E
28 **Varese**, Italy 45 50N 8 50E
30 **Varjas**, Rumania 46 2N 20 58E
35 **Värmland, co.**, Swed. . 60 20N 13 0E
31 **Varna**, Bulgaria 43 12N 27 57E
31 **Vasiliko**, Bulgaria 42 10N 27 50E
25 **Vasilkov**, Poland 53 15N 23 15E
31 **Vaslui**, Rumania 46 37N 27 41E
34 **Väster Norrland, co.**, Sweden 63 0N 17 30E
34 **Västerbotten, co.**, Sweden 65 0N 18 0E
35 **Västervik**, Sweden 57 55N 16 35E
28 **Vasto**, Italy 42 8N 14 42E
32 **Vathy**, Greece 38 15N 27 0E
35 **Vättern, L.**, Sweden .. 58 20N 14 20E
21 **Vaucluse, dept.**, Fr. .. 44 5N 5 20E
33 **Vaud, Canton**, Switz. . 46 30N 6 30E
51 **Vavau, I.** Inset 18 35S 174 0E
35 **Vaxholm**, Sweden 59 24N 18 21E

MAP			
22	**Veendam,** Netherlands	53 8N	6 52E
65	**Vega,** Dominican Rep.	19 18N	70 30W
34	**Vega,** Norway	19 18N	17 30W
35	**Veissenstein,** Estonia	59 10N	25 30E
23	**Vejen,** Denmark	55 25N	9 8E
26	**Vejer de la Frontera,** Spain	36 15N	5 59W
23	**Vejle,** Denmark	55 43N	9 33E
23	**Vejsnæs,** Denmark	54 49N	10 24E
30	**Vel Becherek,** Rum.	45 20N	20 30E
31	**Veles,** Yugoslavia	41 17N	20 37E
32	**Velestino,** Greece	39 22N	22 42E
26	**Velez Malaga,** Spain	36 49N	4 9W
27	**Velez Rubio,** Spain	37 42N	2 5W
23	**Velgast,** Germany	54 17N	12 48E
26	**Velha,** Portugal	40 40N	8 30W
30	**Velika Plana,** Y.-slav.	44 19N	21 6E
36	**Veliki Ustyug,** U.S.S.R.	60 47N	46 3E
36	**Velikiye Luki,** U.S.S.R.	56 23N	30 31E
30	**Veliky Kikinda,** Rum.	45 55N	20 25E
28	**Velletri,** Italy	41 41N	12 46E
23	**Velling,** Denmark	56 4N	8 20E
42	**Vellore,** India	12 55N	79 8E
33	**Veltheim,** Switz.	47 30N	8 40E
26	**Vendas Novas,** Port.	38 48N	8 26W
21	**Vendée, dept.,** France	46 40N	1 13W
35	**Venden,** Latvia	57 19N	25 21E
20	**Vendôme,** France	47 47N	1 4E
28	**Veneto, dept.,** Italy	45 35N	12 0E
28	**Venezia Giulia,** Italy	45 30N	14 0E
28	**Venezia Tridentina, dept.,** Italy	46 20N	11 0E
66	**Venezuela, st.,** S. Amer.	6 0N	66 0E
28	**Venice, & G. of,** Italy	45 23N	12 20E
22	**Venlo,** Netherlands	51 21N	6 10E
57	**Ventersburg,** U. of S. Africa	28 5S	27 15E
57	**Ventersdorp,** U. of S. Africa	26 30S	26 48E
28	**Ventimiglia,** Italy	43 48N	7 38E
15	**Ventnor,** England	50 25N	1 12W
35	**Ventspils.** *See* **Vindau**	57 25N	21 35E
64	**Vera Cruz,** Mexico	19 11N	96 13W
64	**Vera Cruz, st.,** Mexico	20 20N	97 0W
42	**Verawal,** India	20 54N	72 27E
28	**Vercelli,** Italy	45 21N	8 22E
52	**Verde, C.,** Fr. W. Afr.	14 40N	17 30W
24	**Verden,** Germany	52 55N	9 17E
20	**Verdun,** France	49 12N	5 26E
57	**Vereeniging,** U. of S. Africa	26 43S	28 0E
28	**Vergato,** Italy	44 19N	11 10E
44	**Verkhne Udinsk (Ulan Ude),** U.S.S.R.	52 3N	107 35E
36	**Verkhne-Uralsk,** U.S.S.R.	53 57N	59 27E
39	**Verkhni Kolimsk,** U.S.S.R.	65 30N	150 0E
36	**Verkhoturie,** U.S.S.R.	58 48N	60 45E
39	**Verkhoyansk,** U.S.S.R.	67 0N	134 0E
60	**Vermilion,** Canada	53 21N	110 40W
63	**Vermont, st.,** U.S.A.	43 30N	72 10W
28	**Verona,** Italy	45 27N	11 1E
35	**Vernamo,** Sweden	57 10N	14 10E
20	**Versailles,** France	48 48N	2 4E
57	**Verulam,** U. of S. Afr.	29 38S	31 5E
22	**Verviers,** Belgium	50 36N	5 52E
20	**Vervins,** France	40 52N	3 55E
35	**Vesenberg,** Estonia	59 20N	26 20E
20	**Vesoul,** France	47 38N	6 10E
34	**Vest Fd.,** Norway	67 50N	14 0E
35	**Vest-Agder, co.,** Nor.	58 30N	7 0E
34	**Vesterålen Is.,** Norway	69 15N	12 40E
35	**Vesterås,** Sweden	59 40N	16 30E
23	**Vestero,** Denmark	57 15N	10 55E
35	**Vestfold, co.,** Norway	59 20N	10 20E
35	**Vestmanland, co.,** Sweden	59 50N	16 20E
29	**Vesuvius, Mt.,** Italy	40 45N	14 25E
33	**Vevey,** Switzerland	46 27N	6 51E
33	**Vex,** Switzerland	46 12N	7 25E
35	**Vexiö,** Sweden	56 50N	14 45E
22	**Vianden,** Luxemburg	49 57N	6 12E
66	**Vianna,** Brazil	3 0S	44 55W
26	**Vianna,** Portugal	38 20N	7 8W
26	**Vianna do Castello,** Portugal	41 41N	8 50W
28	**Viareggio,** Italy	43 52N	10 12E
23	**Viborg,** Denmark	56 25N	9 20E
35	**Viborg,** *See* **Viipuri**		
21	**Vic, France**	43 24N	0 3E
28	**Vicenza,** Italy	45 34N	11 32E
27	**Vich,** Spain	41 57N	2 17E
21	**Vichy,** France	46 8N	3 28E
28	**Vico,** Italy	41 52N	15 59E
63	**Vicksburg,** U.S.A.	32 16N	90 50W
47	**Victor Harb.,** S. Aust.	35 31S	138 32E
67	**Victoria,** Brazil	20 25S	40 30W
60	**Victoria,** Canada	54 5N	112 20W
60	**Victoria,** Canada	48 20N	123 2W
45	**Victoria,** China	22 20N	113 55E
64	**Victoria,** Mexico	23 43N	99 13W
54	**Victoria,** Nigeria	4 0N	9 10E
63	**Victoria,** U.S.A.	28 50N	96 58W
60	**Victoria I.,** Canada	70 0N	105 0W
55	**Victoria, L.,** Africa	1 0S	33 0E
47	**Victoria, st.,** Austl.	37 0S	145 0E
66	**Victoria da Conquista,** Brazil	15 10S	41 0W
56	**Victoria Falls,** Rhod.	18 0S	25 47E
57	**Victoria West,** U. of S. Africa	31 25S	23 33E
26	**Vidago,** Portugal	41 14N	7 35W
26	**Vidigueira,** Portugal	38 12N	7 51W
31	**Vidin,** Bulgaria	43 49N	22 54E
67	**Viedma,** Argentina	41 0S	63 0W
27	**Viella,** Spain	42 41N	0 46E
24	**Vienna,** Aust., Germany	48 12N	16 23E
21	**Vienne,** France	45 31N	4 52E
21	**Vienne, dept.,** France	46 30N	0 30E
21	**Vienne, R.,** France	47 8N	0 10E
24	**Viersen,** Germany	51 35N	6 22E
20	**Vierzon,** France	47 15N	24 0E
33	**Viesch,** Switzerland	46 24N	8 7E
28	**Viesti,** Italy	41 53N	16 9E
31	**Vietovo,** Bulgaria	43 40N	26 19E
28	**Vigevano,** Italy	45 19N	8 57E
26	**Vigo,** Spain	42 10N	8 40W
35	**Viipuri,** Finland	56 28N	9 26E
42	**Vijapur,** India	23 35N	72 45E
23	**Vikso,** Denmark	55 46N	12 14E
25	**Vileika,** Poland	54 30N	26 55E
34	**Vilhelmina,** Sweden	64 35N	16 45E
35	**Viljandi,** Estonia	58 20N	25 30E
35	**Vilki,** Lithuania	55 4N	23 37E
35	**Vilkomir,** Lithuania	55 15N	24 45E
66	**Villa Bella,** Bolivia	10 30S	65 25W
66	**Villa Bella,** Brazil	10 30S	64 0W
52	**Villa Cisneros,** Africa	24 0N	26 0W
67	**Villa del Pilar,** Paraquay	27 0S	58 10W
26	**Villa do Bispo,** Port.	37 5N	8 55W
67	**Villa Dolores,** Argent.	31 45S	65 20W
67	**Villa Maria,** Argentina	32 12S	63 10W
67	**Villa Mercedes,** Arg.	33 30S	65 30W
26	**Villa Nova de Gaia,** Portugal	41 7N	8 37W
26	**Villa Nova de Portimão,** Portugal	37 8N	8 31W
26	**Villa Real,** Portugal	41 16N	7 39W
67	**Villa Rica,** Paraguay	25 45S	56 30W
26	**Villa Velha,** Portugal	39 38N	7 45W
26	**Villa Viçosa,** Portugal	38 46N	7 27W
26	**Villacañas,** Spain	39 36N	3 20W
26	**Villacarrillo,** Spain	38 6N	3 5W
24	**Villach,** Aust., Germany	46 35N	13 15E
28	**Villafranca,** Italy	45 22N	10 50E
26	**Villafranca,** Spain	42 36N	6 49W
27	**Villafranca,** Spain	41 23N	1 40E
26	**Villagarcia,** Spain	42 35N	8 45W
27	**Villajoyosa,** Spain	38 30N	0 15W
26	**Villalba,** Spain	43 15N	7 44W
26	**Villalba,** Spain	40 38N	3 59W
26	**Villalon,** Spain	42 5N	5 3W
76	**Villalpando,** Spain	41 52N	5 25W
26	**Villanueva,** Spain	39 28N	1 59W
26	**Villanueva de Cordoba,** Spain	38 19N	4 37W
26	**Villanueva de la Serena,** Spain	38 58N	5 46W
29	**Villaputzi,** Sardinia	39 27N	9 30E
26	**Villarcayo,** Spain	42 55N	3 35W
29	**Villarosa,** Sicily	37 39N	14 21E
27	**Villarrobledo,** Spain	39 17N	2 34W
27	**Villarroya,** Spain	41 30N	1 46W
26	**Villarrubia,** Spain	39 14N	3 35W
33	**Villars,** Switzerland	46 17N	7 5E
66	**Villavicencio,** Colombia	4 20N	74 20W
26	**Villaviciosa,** Spain	43 30N	5 26W
21	**Villefranche,** France	45 59N	4 43E
27	**Villena,** Spain	38 36N	0 48W
21	**Villeneuve,** France	48 6N	3 51E
33	**Villeneuve,** Switzerland	46 24N	6 55E
24	**Villingen,** Germany	48 4N	8 24E
22	**Vilvoorden,** Belgium	50 56N	4 24E
63	**Vincennes,** U.S.A.	38 52N	87 35W
35	**Vindau,** Latvia	57 20N	21 20E
23	**Vinderup,** Denmark	56 30N	8 45E
42	**Vindhya Mts.,** India	23 0N	76 0E
44	**Vinh,** Fr. Indo-China	18 55N	105 35E
30	**Vinkovci,** Yugoslavia	45 20N	19 0E
37	**Vinnitsa,** U.S.S.R.	49 13N	28 36E
28	**Vipiteno,** Italy	46 52N	11 30E
34	**Virdois,** Finland	62 15N	23 46E
20	**Vire,** France	48 50N	0 55W
65	**Virgin Is.,** W. Indies	18 30N	64 30W
18	**Virginia,** Eire	53 51N	7 5W
63	**Virginia,** U.S.A.	47 30N	92 40W
63	**Virginia, st.,** U.S.A.	38 30N	80 0W
62	**Virginia City,** U.S.A.	39 17N	119 40W
30	**Virovitica,** Yugoslavia	45 50N	17 10E
30	**Virpazar,** Yugoslavia	42 14N	19 5E
22	**Virton,** Belgium	49 33N	5 31E
35	**Visby,** Sweden	57 38N	18 20E
22	**Visé,** Belgium	50 44N	5 41E
30	**Višegrad,** Yugoslavia	43 47N	19 18E
35	**Vishki,** Latvia	56 5N	26 50E
36	**Vishni Volochek,** U.S.S.R.	57 34N	34 30E
33	**Visp,** Switzerland	46 18N	7 53E
25	**Vistula, R.,** Poland	52 23N	20 20E
36	**Vitebsk,** U.S.S.R.	55 11N	30 12E
28	**Viterbo,** Italy	42 24N	12 7E
51	**Vita Levu, I.,** Inset	17 50S	177 50E
39	**Vitim,** U.S.S.R.	59 30N	112 30E
27	**Vitoria,** Spain	42 50N	2 40W
20	**Vitré,** France	48 8N	1 14W
20	**Vitry le François,** Fr.	48 44N	4 34E
29	**Vittoria,** Sicily	36 59N	14 30E
28	**Vittorio,** Italy	45 58N	12 20E
26	**Vivero,** Spain	43 39N	7 35W
21	**Viviers,** France	44 28N	4 42E
32	**Viza,** Turkey	41 36N	27 47E
43	**Vizagapatam,** India	17 40N	83 23E
31	**Vizakna,** Rumania	45 55N	24 6E
26	**Vizéu,** Portugal	40 40N	7 58W
43	**Vizianagram,** India	18 3N	83 30E
29	**Vizzini,** Sicily	37 11N	14 42E
22	**Vlaardingen,** Neth.	51 54N	4 20E
36	**Vladimir,** U.S.S.R.	56 13N	40 17E
25	**Vladimir Voliniski,** Poland	50 53N	24 20E
37	**Vladimirovka,** U.S.S.R.	48 16N	46 2E
45	**Vladivostok,** U.S.S.R.	43 10N	132 0E
22	**Vlieland,** Netherlands	53 15N	5 0E
22	**Vlissingen.** *See* **Flushing**		
25	**Vlodava,** Poland	51 32N	23 30E
25	**Vlotslavsk,** Poland	52 38N	19 5E
32	**Vodena,** Greece	40 50N	22 5E
28	**Voghera,** Italy	45 0N	9 0E
55	**Voi,** Kenya	4 30S	38 30W
21	**Voiron,** France	45 23N	5 37E
23	**Vojens,** Denmark	55 15N	9 18E
35	**Vökhma,** Estonia	58 25N	25 30E
34	**Volden,** Norway	62 10N	6 0E
37	**Volga, R.,** U.S.S.R.	49 30N	45 30E
25	**Volhynia, co.,** Poland	51 0N	26 30E
31	**Volkoneshti,** Rumania	45 42N	28 27E
25	**Volkovysk,** Poland	53 8N	24 28E
57	**Volksrust,** U. of S. Afr.	27 20S	29 57E
22	**Vollenhove,** Neth.	52 41N	5 57E
35	**Volmar,** Latvia	57 32N	25 30E
32	**Volo,** Greece	39 23N	22 59E
36	**Vologda,** U.S.S.R.	59 20N	39 56E
25	**Volojin,** Poland	54 6N	26 30E
37	**Volsk,** U.S.S.R.	52 0N	47 20E
52	**Volta, R.,** Gold Coast	7 0N	5 0E
28	**Volterra,** Italy	43 24N	10 48E
28	**Voltri,** Italy	44 25N	8 45E
22	**Vonêche,** Belgium	50 5N	4 57E
32	**Vonitza,** Greece	38 53N	20 55E
35	**Voranya,** Estonia	58 32N	27 16E
24	**Vorarlburg,** Germany	47 15N	9 50E
23	**Vordingborg,** Den.	55 2N	11 55E
37	**Voronej,** U.S.S.R.	51 44N	39 5E
25	**Voronovo,** Poland	54 10N	25 20E
39	**Voroshilov,** U.S.S.R.	43 0N	133 0E
37	**Voroshilovsk,** U.S.S.R.	45 8N	41 59E
20	**Vosges, dept.,** France	48 14N	6 30E
20	**Vosges, mts.,** France	48 0N	6 50E
35	**Voss,** Norway	60 45N	6 20E
36	**Votkinski,** U.S.S.R.	57 5N	53 55E
20	**Vouviers,** France	48 24N	4 43E
20	**Voves,** France	48 15N	1 35W
22	**Vracene,** Belgium	51 14N	4 13E
31	**Vranje,** Yugoslavia	42 31N	21 53E
31	**Vratza,** Bulgaria	43 12N	23 32E
57	**Vrede,** U. of S. Africa	27 30S	29 15E
57	**Vredenburg,** U. of S. Africa	32 55S	18 0E
30	**Vreszpreni,** Hungary	47 6N	17 52E
30	**Vrsac,** Yugoslavia	45 10N	21 20E
30	**Vrtace,** Yugoslavia	43 29N	19 10E
57	**Vryheid,** U. of S. Africa	27 45S	30 45E
57	**Vryburg,** U. of S. Afr.	26 58S	24 45E
30	**Vukovar,** Yugoslavia	45 20N	19 0E
32	**Vulgaro,** Greece	40 46N	24 39E
32	**Vurgareli,** Greece	39 20N	21 35E
32	**Vurla,** Turkey	38 20N	26 47E
36	**Vyazma,** U.S.S.R.	55 10N	35 0E
14	**Vyrnwy, L.,** Wales	52 44N	3 13W
22	**Waal, R.,** Netherlands	51 48N	5 10E
63	**Waco,** U.S.A.	31 30N	97 12W
60	**Waddington, mt.,** Can.	51 20N	126 30W
14	**Wadebridge,** England	50 31N	4 49W
55	**Wadelai,** Uganda	2 40N	31 27E
40	**Wadi Halfa,** A.-E. Sud.	21 55N	31 20E
47	**Wagga Wagga,** N.S.W.	35 8S	147 26E
46	**Wagin,** W. Australia	33 18S	117 26E
51	**Waiau,** New Zealand	42 40S	173 1E
50	**Waihi,** New Zealand	37 23S	175 52E
47	**Waikerie,** S. Australia	34 11S	139 58E
50	**Waikohu,** New Zealand	38 20S	177 20E
50	**Waikokopu,** N. Zealand	39 2S	177 52E
51	**Waikouaiti,** N. Zealand	45 38S	170 40E
51	**Waimangaroa,** N.Z.	41 30S	171 49E
50	**Waimarino,** N. Zealand	39 11S	175 25E
51	**Waimate,** New Zealand	44 44S	171 5E
50	**Waioura,** New Zealand	39 30S	175 41E
51	**Waipara,** New Zealand	43 2S	172 42E
50	**Waipawa,** New Zealand	39 53S	176 46E
50	**Waipiro,** New Zealand	38 0S	178 18E
50	**Waipu,** New Zealand	35 57S	174 28E

MAP
50 Waipukurau, N.Zealand 40 0 s 176 33 E
50 Wairoa, New Zealand .39 3 s 177 26 E
50 Waitakere, N.Zealand..36 50 s 174 34 E
50 Waitangi, New Zealand 35 13 s 174 0 E
50 Waitara, New Zealand .39 1 s 174 13 E
50 Waiuku, New Zealand 37 15 s 174 45 E
45 Wakayama, Japan....34 4 N 135 2 E
43 Wake I., Pac. Oc.... 19 30 N 166 40 E
13 Wakefield, England ..53 41 N 1 30 w
45 Wakkanai, Japan ....45 24 N 141 42 E
57 Wakkerstroom, U. of
   S. Africa .... 27 23 s 30 12 E
31 Walachia, dist., Rum. 44 40 N 25 0 E
33 Wald, Switzerland ...47 17 N 8 55 E
24 Waldeck, prov., Germ. 51 20 N 8 50 E
62 Waldenberg, Germany. 50 46 N 16 20 E
33 Waldenburg, Switz. ..47 23 N 7 43 E
14 Wales, British Isles ..52 0 N 3 30 w
47 Walgett, N.S.W. ....30 0 s 148 7 E
62 Walla Walla, U.S.A. ..46 2 N 118 18 w
62 Wallace, U.S.A. .....47 30 N 115 53 w
47 Wallaroo, S. Australia .33 55 s 137 34 E
12 Wallasey, England ...53 25 N 3 5 w
33 Wallenstadt, Switz. ..47 7 N 9 22 E
15 Wallingford, England .51 36 N 1 8 w
15 Wallington, England ..52 40 N 0 25 E
13 Wallsend, England ...54 59 N 1 32 w
15 Walmer, England ....51 12 N 1 23 E
12 Walney, I., England ..54 5 N 3 15 w
15 Walsall, England ....52 34 N 1 58 w
62 Walsenburg, U.S.A. ..37 37 N 104 45 w
15 Walsingham, England 52 55 N 0 53 E
15 Walsoken, England....52 42 N 0 10 E
15 Waltham Abbey, Eng..51 41 N 0 1 w
15 Walthamstow, England 51 38 N 0 1 w
57 Walvis Bay, S. Africa.. 22 40 s 14 25 E
52 Walwal, Abyssinia .... 7 5 N 45 20 E
45 Wan-chow, China ....28 1 N 110 22 E
50 Wanganui, N.Zealand .39 54 N 175 3 E
33 Wangen, Switzerland ..47 14 N 7 38 E
56 Wankie, S. Rhodesia ..18 5 s 27 0 E
15 Wantage, England....51 36 N 1 26 w
47 Waratah, Tasmania ...41 24 s 145 29 E
24 Warburg, Germany...51 30 N 9 10 E
47 Warburton, Victoria..37 43 s 145 41 E
51 Ward, New Zealand ..41 45 s 174 15 E
42 Wardha, India ....20 38 N 78 44 E
33 Wardenberg, Switz. ..47 11 N 9 29 E
15 Ware, England ....51 49 N 0 2 w
14 Wareham, England ...50 41 N 2 6 w
22 Waremme, Belgium ..50 43 N 5 15 E
52 Wargla, Algeria ......31 50 N 5 10 E
15 Warkworth, England .55 4 N 1 8 w
50 Warkworth, N.Zealand 36 23 s 174 42 E
57 Warmbad, S.W. Africa 28 28 s 18 40 E
14 Warminster, England .51 12 N 2 10 w
24 Warnemünde, Germ. ..54 9 N 12 4 E
22 Warneton, Belgium ..50 46 N 2'56 E
18 Warrenpoint, N. Ire. .54 6 N 6 15 w
57 Warrenton, U. of S.
   Africa ....28 8 s 24 51 E
47 Warri Warri, N.S.W. .20 0 s 141 58 E
12 Warrington, England ..53 25 N 2 38 w
47 Warrnambool, Vict. ..38 19 s 142 30 E
25 Warsaw & Co., Poland 52 15 N 21 1 E
15 Warwick, & co., Eng. 52 17 N 1 35 w
47 Warwick, Queensland ..28 10 s 152 3 E
15 Wash, The, England ..53 0 N 0 5 E
63 Washington, U.S.A...39 33 N 77 0 w
49 Washington I., Pac. Oc. 4 50 N 160 3 w
62 Washington, st., U.S.A. 47 0 N 120 0 w
24 Wasserburg, Germany. 48 4 N 12 15 E
20 Wassy, France ....48 30 N 4 59 E
12 Wast Water, England..54 27 N 3 18 w
23 Wastrow, Germany ...54 22 N 12 25 E
14 Watchet, England ...51 11 N 3 19 w
56 Waterberg, S.W. Africa 20 29 s 17 25 E
19 Waterford, & co., Eire 52 15 N 7 7 w
57 Waterford, U. of S. Afr. 33 2 s 24 59 E
22 Waterloo, Belgium ...50 45 N 4 22 E
12 Waterloo, England ...53 29 N 3 3 w
63 Waterloo, U.S.A. ....42 30 N 92 15 w
63 Watertown, N.Y.,
   U.S.A. ....43 55 N 75 59 w
62 Watertown, S.D.,
   U.S.A. ....44 57 N 97 12 w
63 Watertown, Wis.,
   U.S.A. ....43 15 N 88 45 w
19 Waterville, Eire.......51 50 N 10 10 w
15 Watford, England ....51 40 N 0 25 w
13 Wath, England ....53 30 N 1 17 w
61 Watkins, Mts., Green. .69 45 N 29 40 w
15 Watlington, England ..51 39 N 1 0 w
15 Watton, England .....52 34 N 0 50 E
15 Waveney, R., England 52 28 N 1 30 E
50 Waverley, N.Zealand ..42 2 N 76 34 w
22 Wavre, Belgium ......50 43 N 4 36 E
63 Waycross, U.S.A. ....31 17 N 82 25 w
42 Wazirabad, India ....32 27 N 74 8 E
13 Wear, R., England ...54 54 N 1 27 w
12 Weaver, R., England ..53 10 N 2 31 w
63 Webb City, U.S.A. ...37 8 N 94 26 w
68 Weddell Sea, Antarc. .67 0 s 40 0 w
14 Wednesbury, England 52 33 N 2 0 w
57 Weenen, U. of S. Africa 28 55 s 30 6 E

MAP
45 Wei-hai-wei, China ..37 30 N 122 0 E
24 Weilheim, Germany ..49 36 N 8 40 E
24 Weimar, Germany ...51 0 N 11 20 E
33 Weinfelden, Switz. ...47 34 N 9 7 E
24 Weinheim, Germany ..49 36 N 8 40 E
62 Weiser, U.S.A. ....44 13 N 117 0 w
22 Weismes, Belgium ...50 25 N 6 9 E
20 Weissenburg, France .49 2 N 7 58 E
24 Weissenfels, Germany 51 12 N 11 58 E
31 Weisskirchen. See Bela Crkva
15 Welford, England ....52 25 N 1 4 w
15 Welland, R., England .52 30 N 0 40 w
15 Wellingboro', England 52 19 N 0 42 w
14 Wellington, England ..50 58 N 3 14 w
14 Wellington, England ..52 43 N 2 31 w
47 Wellington, N.S.W. ..29 50 s 151 40 E
41 Wellington, & Prov.,
   New Zealand ....41 15 s 174 46 E
47 Wellington, S. Australia 35 20 s 139 25 E
14 Wells, England ......51 12 N 2 37 w
15 Wells, England ......52 57 N 0 51 E
24 Wels, Austria, Germany 48 10 N 14 0 E
14 Welshpool, Wales ....52 40 N 3 9 w
14 Wem, England ....52 52 N 2 43 w
17 Wemyss Bay, Scot. ..55 53 N 4 54 w
45 Wen-chow, China ....28 0 N 120 30 E
15 Wendover, England ..51 45 N 0 45 w
14 Wenlock, England ...52 37 N 2 34 w
13 Wensleydale, England 54 18 N 2 10 w
47 Wentworth, N.S.W. ..34 3 s 141 57 E
14 Weobley, England ...52 9 N 2 51 w
57 Wepener, U. of S. Afr. 29 45 s 27 7 E
24 Wernigerode, Germany 51 50 N 10 45 E
24 Wertheim, Germany ..49 46 N 9 30 E
24 Wesel, Germany......51 40 N 6 36 E
33 Wesen, Switzerland ..47 8 N 9 5 E
24 Weser, R., Germany ..52 40 N 9 8 E
24 Wesermünde, Germany 53 35 N 8 34 E
23 Wesselburen, Germany 54 13 N 8 55 E
25 West Beskids, Mts.,
   Czechoslovakia .....49 45 N 19 40 E
14 West Bromwich, Eng. .52 31 N 2 0 w
17 West Calder, Scotland 55 49 N 3 26 w
22 West Flanders, prov.,
   Belgium ....51 0 N 3 0 E
15 West Ham, England ..51 33 N 0 2 E
13 West Hartlepool, Eng. 54 41 N 1 13 w
12 West Kirby, England ..53 23 N 30 11 w
17 Westhinton, Scotland. .53 45 N 3 34 w
14 West Looe, England ..50 20 N 4 26 w
17 West Lothian, co.,
   Scotland ....55 55 N 3 35 w
56 West Nicholson,
   S. Rhodesia ....21 8 s 29 32 E
13 West Riding, co., Eng. 53 46 N 1 30 w
63 West Virginia, st., U.S.A. 38 N 82 0 w
14 Westbury, England ...45 26 N 71 48 w
15 Westerham, England..51 16 N 0 4 E
46 Western Australia, st. 25 0 N 120 0 E
51 Western Samoa .Inset 12 0 s 174 0 w
15 Westgate, England ...51 23 N 1 22 E
47 Westgate, Queensland .26 37 s 146 11 E
51 Westland, prov., N.Z. .43 30 s 170 0 E
19 Westmeath, co., Eire ..53 30 N 7 30 w
12 Westmorland, co., Eng. 54 29 N 2 40 w
57 Weston, U. of S. Africa 29 15 s 30 3 E
14 Weston super Mare,
   England ....51 21 N 2 59 w
24 Westphalia, prov., Ger. 51 45 N 8 0 E
18 Westport, Eire ......53 48 N 9 32 w
14 Westward Ho, Eng. ...51 2 N 4 15 w
60 Wetaskiwin, Canada..52 49 N 113 15 w
12 Wetheral, England ...54 54 N 2 50 w
13 Wetherby, England ...53 56 N 1 23 w
22 Wetteren, Belgium ...51 0 N 3 53 E
33 Wettingen, Switzerland 47 28 N 8 20 E
24 Wetzlar, Germany.....50 34 N 8 30 E
19 Wexford, co. & harb.,
   Eire ....52 20 N 6 28 w
60 Weyburn, Canada ....49 38 N 103 50 w
15 Wey, R., England....51 19 N 0 30 w
14 Weymouth, England ..50 37 N 2 26 w
50 Whakarewarewa, N.Z. 38 13 s 176 10 E
50 Whakatane, N. Zealand 37 58 s 177 0 E
50 Whangarei, & harb.,
   New Zealand ....35 4 s 174 19 E
50 Whangaroa, N. Zealand 35 4 s 173 47 E
13 Wharfe, R., England..53 52 N 1 13 w
63 Wheeling, U.S.A......40 3 N 80 43 w
13 Whernside, England..54 14 N 2 24 w
13 Whitby, England .....54 29 N 0 37 w
13 Whitchurch, England..51 14 N 1 20 w
14 Whitchurch, England..52 58 N 2 42 w
47 White Cliffs, N.S.W...30 50 s 143 7 E
51 White Cliffs, N.Zeal. ..43 30 s 171 55 E
60 White Horse, Canada .60 45 N 135 10 w
55 White Nile, R.,
   Anglo-Egyptian Sudan. 12 0 N 32 45 E
37 White Russia, rep.,
   U.S.S.R. ....51 30-56 N 27-32 E
36 White Sea, U.S.S.R. ..66 0 N 40 0 E
12 Whitehaven, England. .54 34 N 3 35 w
47 Whitfield, Victoria ...36 50 s 146 30 E
17 Whithorn, Scotland ...54 44 N 4 25 w

MAP
13 Whitley & Cullercoats,
   England ....55 1 N 1 27 w
62 Whitney, Mt., U.S.A. .36 30 N 118 10 w
15 Whitstable, England...51 21 N 1 2 E
13 Whittington, England .53 16 N 1 25 w
13 Whitton, England ....53 44 N 0 39 w
52 Whydah, Fr. W. Africa. 6 22 N 2 27 E
63 Wichita, U.S.A. ......37 42 N 97 15 w
62 Wichita Falls, U.S.A. .33 56 N 98 30 w
16 Wick, Scotland ......58 26 N 3 5 w
15 Wickford, England ...51 37 N 0 31 E
15 Wickham Market, Eng. 52 10 N 1 20 E
19 Wicklow, co., & Mts.,
   Eire ....52 58 N 6 3 w
12 Widnes, England .....53 22 N 2 45 w
25 Wieliczka, Poland ....49 59 N 20 8 E
24 Wien. See Vienna
22 Wieringen, Netherlands 52 55 N 5 0 E
24 Wiesbaden, Germany. .50 6 N 8 15 E
12 Wigan, England......53 33 N 2 38 w
12 Wight, I. of, England..50 33 N 1 15 w
12 Wigtown, England ...54 50 N 3 10 w
12 Wigtown, & co., Scot. 54 52 N 4 26 w
22 Wijk, Netherlands ...50 52 N 5 40 E
24 Wild, Czechoslovakia. .49 59 N 16 24 E
22 Wildervank, Nether...53 4 N 6 52 E
28 Wild Spitze, Mt., Aus. .46 52 N 10 36 E
24 Wilhelmshaven, Germ. 53 30 N 8 8 E
63 Wilkes Barre, U.S.A. .41 15 N 75 55 w
68 Wilkes Land, Antarc. .66 45 s 133 0 E
15 Willesden, England ...51 32 N 0 14 w
65 Willemstad, Curacao I. 12 12 N 69 6 w
22 Willemstad, Nether. ..51 42 N 4 25 E
60 Williams Lake, Can. ..52 0 N 122 0 w
47 Williamstown, Vict. ..37 52 s 144 29 E
13 Willingham, England. .53 22 N 0 40 w
62 Williston, U. of S. Afr. .31 16 s 20 58 E
35 Willmanstrand. See Lappeehsanta
13 Willoughby, England..53 14 N 0 13 E
63 Wilmington, Del.,
   U.S.A. ....39 48 N 75 35 w
63 Wilmington, N.C.,
   U.S.A. ....34 14 N 77 55 w
47 Wilmington, S. Aust. .32 38 s 138 4 E
25 Wilno, & Co., Poland .54 40 N 25 20 E
14 Wilton, England .....51 5 N 1 52 w
22 Wiltz, Luxemburg ....49 37 N 5 53 E
46 Wiluna, W. Australia ..26 30 s 120 30 E
14 Wimborne Minster,
   England ....50 48 N 1 58 w
47 Wimmera, Victoria ...36 15 s 142 0 E
57 Winburg, U. of S. Afr. .28 30 s 27 4 E
14 Wincanton, England...51 4 N 2 23 w
15 Winchcomb, England .51 57 N 1 58 w
15 Winchelsea, England .50 55 N 0 43 E
15 Winchester, England ..51 4 N 1 18 w
12 Windermere, & L.,
   England ....54 24 N 2 55 w
57 Windhoek, S.W.Africa .22 32 s 17 10 E
60 Windsor, Canada ....42 20 N 83 0 w
15 Windsor, England ....51 29 N 0 37 w
47 Windsor, N.S.W. .....33 38 s 150 50 E
65 Windward Is., W. Ind. 13 0 N 61 0 w
60 Winnipeg, & L., Can. .49 57 N 97 17 w
60 Winnipegosis, L., Can. 52 30 N 100 0 w
63 Winona, U.S.A. ......44 0 N 91 42 w
13 Winslow, England....51 56 N 0 53 w
62 Winslow, U.S.A. .....34 59 N 110 40 w
13 Winster, England ....53 8 N 1 37 w
63 Winston-Salem, U.S.A. 36 5 N 80 22 w
57 Winterhoek, Gt., Mt.,
   U. of S. Africa .....33 35 s 25 0 E
22 Winterswyk, Neth.....51 58 N 6 43 E
33 Winterthur, Switz. ...47 30 N 8 43 E
13 Winterton, England ..52 43 N 1 42 E
51 Winton, New Zealand .46 7 s 168 20 E
47 Winton, Queensland ..22 20 s 143 1 E
13 Wirksworth, England ..53 5 N 1 35 w
12 Wirral, Dist., England. 53 18 N 3 3 w
15 Wisbech, England ....52 41 N 0 10 E
63 Wisconsin, st., U.S.A. 44 30 N 90 0 w
17 Wishaw, Scotland ....55 47 N 3 59 w
66 Wismar, Brit. Guiana. 6 0 N 56 30 w
24 Wismar, Germany....53 54 N 11 25 E
15 Witham R., England ..53 3 N 0 7 w
13 Withernsea, England. .53 44 N 0 3 E
15 Witney, England .....51 48 N 1 29 w
24 Wittenburg, Germany .51 55 N 12 40 E
24 Wittenberge, Germany 53 0 N 11 44 E
23 Wittenburg, Germany .53 32 N 11 3 E
24 Wittstock, Germany ..53 8 N 12 30 E
55 Witu, Kenya .... 2 20 s 40 30 E
57 Witwatersrand,
   U. of S. Africa......26 0 s 27 0 E
14 Wiveliscombe, England 51 2 N 3 17 w
15 Wivenhoe, England ...51 51 N 0 58 E
15 Woburn, England ....52 0 N 0 37 w
25 Wohlau, Germany ....51 20 N 16 33 E
15 Woking, England .....51 18 N 0 33 w
15 Wokingham, England .51 25 N 0 50 w
24 Wolfenbüttel, Germany 52 10 N 10 35 E
24 Wolfsberg, Aus., Germ. 46 52 N 14 50 E
24 Wolgast, Germany ...54 5 N 13 22 E
24 Wollin, Germany .....53 52 N 14 35 E
47 Wollongong, N.S.W. ..34 26 s 150 54 E